ROBERT KENNEDY AND HIS TIMES

Volume I

Books by Arthur M. Schlesinger, Jr.

Orestes A. Brownson: A Pilgrim's Progress

The Age of Jackson

The Vital Center

The General and the President
(*with Richard H. Rovere*)

The Age of Roosevelt
I. *The Crisis of the Old Order, 1919–1933*
II. *The Coming of the New Deal*
III. *The Politics of Upheaval*

The Politics of Hope

A Thousand Days: John F. Kennedy in
the White House

The Bitter Heritage: Vietnam and
American Democracy, 1941–1966

The Crisis of Confidence: Ideas, Power and
Violence in America

The Imperial Presidency

Robert Kennedy and His Times

Arthur M. Schlesinger, Jr.

ROBERT KENNEDY AND HIS TIMES

Illustrated with Photographs

Volume I

HOUGHTON MIFFLIN COMPANY   BOSTON

A portion of this book has appeared in *Esquire*.

Copyright © 1978 by Arthur M. Schlesinger, Jr.

All rights reserved. No part of this work may be reproduced or transmitted in any form by any means, electronic or mechanical, including photocopying and recording, or by any information storage or retrieval system, without permission in writing from the publisher.

Printed in the United States of America

For Ethel, Jean and Steve

Great men, great nations, have not been boasters and buffoons, but perceivers of the terror of life, and have manned themselves to face it.

—EMERSON

Contents

Volume I

	Illustrations	xi
	Foreword	xiii
	Acknowledgments	xvii
	Prologue: 1968	1
1.	The Family	3
2.	The Father	22
3.	The War	43
4.	The Third Son	66
5.	The Brothers: I	94
6.	The First Investigating Committee: Joe McCarthy	103
7.	Interlude: William O. Douglas and Adlai Stevenson	126
8.	The Second Investigating Committee: Jimmy Hoffa	143
9.	The Second Investigating Committee: Walter Reuther	177
10.	1960	201
11.	To the Department of Justice	232
12.	The Pursuit of Justice: J. Edgar Hoover	256
13.	The Pursuit of Justice: The Mob	272
14.	The Pursuit of Justice: Civil Rights	298
15.	The Pursuit of Justice: Ross Barnett and George Wallace	330

16. The Pursuit of Justice: Martin Luther King	357
17. The Politics of Justice	383
18. Justice and Poverty	408
19. The Kennedys and the Cold War	435
20. The CIA and Counterinsurgency	462
21. The Cuban Connection: I	488
22. Robert Kennedy and the Missile Crisis	521

Illustrations

Surrounded by their family at the house in Bronxville: Joseph P. Kennedy, Kathleen, John, Jean, Eunice, Robert, Patricia, Edward, Rosemary, Joseph Jr., and Rose Kennedy. (Portrait by Bachrach)

Seaman Robert Kennedy describes equipment on the *Joseph P. Kennedy Jr.* to Joseph P. Kennedy, Sr., and an accompanying officer.

The Harvard Football Team, 1947.

In Jerusalem, 1948, as an accredited correspondent of the *Boston Post*.

Ethel Skakel dancing with her future husband.

The young parents flanking the head of the family behind their first three children, Kathleen, Joseph III, Robert Jr.

The counsel to the Senate Labor Rackets Committee during a hearing in Washington, March 1957. With him are Senators Joseph P. McCarthy and Karl Mundt. (United Press International)

The chief counsel in a rare exchange with James R. Hoffa, president of the Teamsters Union. (AP Wirephoto)

The brothers map strategy during John F. Kennedy's campaign for the Democratic presidential nomination in 1960. (AP Wirephoto)

The Attorney General reports on his 1962 round-the-world tour. At the White House were Secretary of State Dean Rusk, Vice President Lyndon Johnson, Robert Kennedy and the President. (United Press International)

Riding before breakfast, the Attorney General follows his children Kathleen, Joseph, and Robert.

Shooting the rapids.

Ethel and Robert Kennedy enjoying a day of skiing. (Norm Betts, Associated Press)

Robert Kennedy talks in his office at the Department of Justice with James Meredith, the first black man admitted to the University of Mississippi. (AP Wirephoto)

Chatting with employees at a Fuji Electric Company plant in Japan.

At a White House reception, the First Lady and President Kennedy greeting Ethel Kennedy and the Attorney General.

Robert, Jacqueline and Edward Kennedy lead the cortège following the coffin of John F. Kennedy to Arlington National Cemetery.

A distant handshake before Lyndon Johnson's first address as President to a joint session of Congress. Adlai Stevenson stands behind them. (AP Wirephoto)

The Attorney General with his wife and Averell Harriman at the Democratic convention in 1964. (AP Wirephoto)

The senatorial candidate speaking to a crowd in Watertown, New York. (United Press International)

The family lines up across the lawn at Hickory Hill. (Elizabeth Kuhner, Westport, Connecticut)

The crowd reaches out—California, 1968.

Thanking the crowd that gathered in Los Angeles to celebrate his victory in the California presidential primary, just before he stepped into a nearby room and was shot. (United Press International)

Senator Edward Kennedy delivers a tribute to his slain brother at St. Patrick's Cathedral in New York. (United Press International)

The grave at Arlington.

The prints for all of the pictures, unless otherwise credited, were provided through the courtesy of the John F. Kennedy Library.

Foreword

ROBERT KENNEDY died on June 6, 1968, at the age of forty-two—a decade ago as I write today. He lived through a time of unusual turbulence in American history; and he responded to that turbulence more directly and sensitively than any other political leader of the era. He was equipped with certitudes of family and faith—certitudes that sustained him till his death. But they were the premises, not the conclusions, of his life. For he possessed to an exceptional degree what T. S. Eliot called an "experiencing nature." History changed him, and, had time permitted, he might have changed history. His relationship to his age makes him, I believe, a "representative man" in Emerson's phrase—one who embodies the consciousness of an epoch, who perceives things in fresh lights and new connections, who exhibits unsuspected possibilities of purpose and action to his contemporaries.

He never had the chance to fulfill his own possibilities, which is why his memory haunts so many of us now. Because he wanted to get things done, because he was often impatient and combative, because he felt simply and cared deeply, he made his share of mistakes, and enemies. He was a romantic and an idealist, and he was also prudent, expedient, demanding and ambitious. Yet the insights he brought to politics—insights earned in a labor of self-education that only death could stop—led him to see power not as an end in itself but as the means of redeeming the powerless.

Any historian who has written about the 1930s as well as the 1960s must recognize a terrible monotony in our national problems. The conditions of misery and inequity that troubled Franklin Roosevelt and the New Dealers troubled the Kennedys twenty years later—after an interval during which, while misery and inequity persisted, people in power were untroubled. We appear to be in another such interval today. Robert Kennedy's message of commitment to the desolate and the disinherited is rarely sounded in the 1970s. But the problems about which he cared so much remain. The time will surely come again when the richest nation on earth will overcome its indifference to the degradation of its citizens. When that time returns, Robert Kennedy's journey will, I believe, be seen to have exemplary value.

Any book about Robert Kennedy is inextricably bound up with John Kennedy and his Presidency. Here I have tried to avoid retelling familiar stories. This work treats the Kennedy administration primarily as Robert Kennedy took part in events or as his papers cast particular light on them. On occasion I have added information that I did not know when I wrote *A Thousand Days* or that seemed inappropriate for publication in 1965. I have also taken the opportunity for a new look at some of the more controversial issues of the Kennedy years. The passage of time, the knowledge of consequences, the illumination of hindsight, the rise of new preoccupations—all give problems of the past new form and perplexity. While there would be little point, for example, in going through once again the day-by-day development of the Cuban missile crisis, there would appear considerable point in assessing latter-day interpretations of that crisis—or of the Indochina War, the civil rights struggle, the Central Intelligence Agency, the Federal Bureau of Investigation. In this sense, *Robert Kennedy and His Times* is a sort of sequel to *A Thousand Days*—though the earlier work was a personal memoir and this one is a biography.

It draws heavily on the personal papers of Robert Kennedy, made available to me through the generosity of Ethel Skakel Kennedy and of the Kennedy family. The Robert Kennedy Papers include diaries, kept for brief intervals at various times in his life, letters, *aides-mémoires* and oral history interviews. Robert Kennedy was a direct and candid man, often brusque in manner and opinion. He hated circumlocution. He distrusted what he considered high-flown or self-serving expression. His instinct was to cloak idealism in throwaway phrases and laconic jokes. His deflationary, self-mocking, sometimes grim wit was employed often as a means of relieving tension in the midst of crisis. Some of the remarks in the Robert Kennedy Papers, wrenched from context, will no doubt be used against him. This is a risk that must be run. The serious reader will be able to set Robert Kennedy's words in the totality of his life. I am sure that he would have been entirely content to stand on the record. I must add that the

Foreword

Kennedy family made no attempt to influence my use of the papers and that the interpretations and judgments are exclusively my own.

Some readers may wonder about the extensive use made in these pages of oral history—i.e., of transcribed interviews conducted with participants after the fact. We all know that interviews can be no better than a person's memory and that little is more treacherous than that. Yet historians have rarely hesitated to draw on written reminiscences, which are no less self-promoting; nor have they hesitated, in order to impart immediacy to narrative, to quote conversations as recalled in diaries, letters and memoirs, when the content of the conversation is plausibly supported by context or other evidence. I have extended this tolerance to oral history and employed the literary convention with the same critical caution, I hope, illustrious predecessors have applied to written documents. It remains a convention. The recollected material cannot pretend to the exactitude of, say, the White House tapes of the Nixon years.

It is necessary to declare an interest. I was a great admirer and devoted friend of Robert Kennedy's. Association with him over the last decade of his life was one of the joys of my own life. It was not only that he deepened one's understanding of America, of its problems and possibilities, but that he was the occasion of such good and happy times. No one could be more fun than Robert Kennedy; no one more appealing, with those impulses of irony, bravado, gentleness and vulnerability so curiously intermingled in his vivid personality; no one in our politics, as I deeply believed, held out more promise for the future. I thought him the most creative man in American public life when he was killed. I am well aware that not everyone did. Some saw him as cold, vengeful, fanatical, "ruthless." But to adopt a phrase A. J. P. Taylor used in his life of Lord Beaverbrook, if it is necessary for a biographer of Robert Kennedy to regard him as evil, then I am not qualified to be his biographer.

Still, sympathy may illumine as well as distort. In any case, the story of his life tells a great deal about the American ordeal in the middle decades of the twentieth century. I have tried to tell that story as accurately as I can, strengthened by the conviction that the last thing Robert Kennedy would have wished was hagiography. He was not a hard man, but he was a tough man. He valued bluntness, precision and truth. I have not hesitated to portray him in his frailty as well as in his valor. I can imagine no better way to serve his memory. What he had in the way of weakness was an essential part of his strength. For he was truly a perceiver of the terror of life, and he manned himself nobly to face it.

Acknowledgments

I AM DEEPLY GRATEFUL to Jean Kennedy Smith and John Douglas for their careful reading of the manuscript. Though I did not adopt all their suggestions, their contribution to a clearer and more accurate text has been indispensable. I equally thank and absolve other friends who took time from overcrowded lives to read, correct and improve portions of the book—George W. Ball, Richard Boone, William Bundy, William B. Cannon, Ramsey Clark, Archibald C. Cox, Frederick W. Flott, Michael V. Forrestal, Richard Goodwin, David Hackett, Barbara Wendell Kerr, Mieczyslaw Maneli, Burke Marshall, Clark Mollenhoff, Lloyd Ohlin, Joseph L. Rauh, Jr., Pierre Salinger, Stephen C. Schlesinger, Frederick A. O. Schwarz, Jr., John Seigenthaler, Stephen E. Smith.

Obviously the book could not have been written had it not been for the great generosity of Ethel Kennedy in permitting me unrestricted access to the papers of Robert F. Kennedy. I am also greatly indebted to the Kennedy family for letting me see the collection of family papers herein designated as the Hyannis Port Papers as well as the papers of Joseph P. Kennedy and Stephen Smith in New York. All these collections will go in due course to the Kennedy Library in Boston. Like all students of the recent political history of the United States, I have benefited immeasurably from the ready and expert cooperation of the directors and staffs of the presidential libraries —especially of Dan H. Fenn, Jr., John F. Stewart, William W. Moss, Joan-Ellen Marci and so many others at the Kennedy Library, which houses the papers of John F. Kennedy, Frank Mankiewicz, Burke Marshall, Theodore C. Sorensen and William vanden Heuvel as well as the transcripts produced in the John F. Kennedy and Robert F. Kennedy Oral History Programs; and also of archivists at the Lyndon B. Johnson Library in Austin, Texas, and the Herbert Hoover

Library in West Branch, Iowa. Selections from Robert Kennedy's FBI files, made available to me under the Freedom of Information Act, are designated in the notes as 'RFK/FBI/FOIA release.' I thank Jules Feiffer, Mary Bailey Gimbel, Richard Goodwin, David Hackett, Thomas Johnston, Patricia Kennedy Lawford, Allard Lowenstein, William Manchester, Mieczyslaw Maneli, John Bartlow Martin, Barrett Prettyman, Jr., Abba Schwartz, James Stevenson, William C. Sullivan, Felicia Warburg, James Wechsler and Theodore H. White for their kindness in making personal papers available to me; A. J. P. Taylor and the Beaverbrook Foundation for sending me copies of the correspondence between Joseph P. Kennedy and Lord Beaverbrook from the Beaverbrook Papers; the late Herman Kahn and the Yale University Library for facilitating my consultation of the papers of Walter Lippmann and Chester Bowles; and John C. Broderick and the Manuscript Division of the Library of Congress for the papers of James M. Landis and Hugo Black.

I stand in particular debt to the oral history interviewers who have done so much to enrich and amplify the record of the time: Anthony Lewis, William Manchester, John Bartlow Martin and John Stewart for their interviews with Robert Kennedy; the host of volunteers who conducted interviews for the Kennedy Library after the death of John F. Kennedy; and the expert corps of Kennedy Library professionals who have interviewed close associates of both John and Robert Kennedy—notably Roberta Greene and L. J. Hackman, who between them conducted more than sixty interviews, and to many others. Jean Stein generously allowed me to see the oral history interviews she undertook for her invaluable book, edited in collaboration with George Plimpton, *American Journey* (New York, 1970). I thank especially the innumerable interviewees who kindly permitted me to quote from their transcripts as well as many other persons, cited in the notes, who allowed me to interview them directly.

At Houghton Mifflin, Richard McAdoo watched the book stretch out in time and length with exemplary patience, and Helena Bentz Dorrance prepared the manuscript for the printer with exemplary thoroughness. I must also thank Luise Erdmann for reading the proofs and Julia Stair for an excellent index.

Once again I rejoice to express my unlimited gratitude to Gretchen Stewart and to Mary Chiffriller for the devoted and meticulous care they expended on typing several drafts of the manuscript, collating texts, checking references, getting the manuscript to the publisher and meanwhile keeping a busy office in a semblance of order. President

Acknowledgments

Harold Proshansky and the Graduate School of the City University of New York, especially the efficient librarians, were helpful at all times. Above all, I thank Alexandra Emmet Schlesinger, who not only read the manuscript with fastidious and unerring eye but suffered and sustained the author during the throes of composition; and I thank our children still at home, Robert Emmet Kennedy Schlesinger and Peter Cushing Allan, for putting up with it all.

ARTHUR M. SCHLESINGER, JR.

Prologue: 1968

THE TRAIN LEFT New York City at one o'clock on a sweltering June afternoon. In the last of twenty-two cars lay a coffin, covered by an American flag. A diversity of people filled the cars ahead—politicians and writers, government officials and entertainers, diplomats and trade unionists, astronauts and agitators, social workers and athletes, society figures and stenographers. They talked in somber tones, they rejoiced in the happier past, they despaired of the future, they stared out of the window.

Along the tracks people waited in the blazing sun. "For eight agonizing hours, as the train passed," said a senator, "I looked into their faces. I saw sorrow . . . bewilderment. I saw fury and I saw fright."[1] Some stood at rigid attention, hand over heart. Some waved. Some buried their faces in their hands. Some knelt. Some held up handprinted signs—REST IN PEACE, ROBERT, or, ominously, WHO WILL BE THE NEXT ONE? or, desperately, WE HAVE LOST OUR LAST HOPE, or, starkly, PRAY FOR US, BOBBY. Many cried. Some threw roses at the last car. Some as if in a daze followed the train down the roadbed. As the train crossed rivers on its journey south, boats, clustered by the bridges, sounded their whistles. On a river before Newark, New Jersey, three men on a fireboat saluted; the boat bore the name *John F. Kennedy*.

The train slowed to a crawl with thousands—perhaps a million in all—crowding the way.[2] At Elizabeth, New Jersey, a northbound express, rounding a curve at high speed, plowed into mourners overflowing onto the tracks, killing a man and a woman. The bell of the funeral train rang incessantly. The whistle blew in long, piercing, melancholy blasts. As the train moved south through the Pennsylvania countryside, one occasionally saw a man or woman, far from any visible town, standing gravely and alone, enveloped in private grief. In Baltimore a great silent mass of people, mostly black, had waited for hours. When the train pulled in, they joined hands and sang "The Battle Hymn of the Republic." So, 103 years before, a crowd had sung in Baltimore as another funeral train had passed. The sun set, a baleful orange ball in the west. Shortly after nine o'clock the train reached Washington in the glimmering dark.

(1)

The Family

ROBERT FRANCIS KENNEDY was born in Brookline, Massachusetts, on November 20, 1925, the seventh child of Rose Fitzgerald and Joseph Patrick Kennedy. His great-grandparents had come from Ireland some three quarters of a century before. The legacy they brought to Boston was but mildly diluted in the next two generations. The nineteenth-century Irish saw themselves as the victims of history. Memories of dispossession and defeat filled their souls. They had lost their national independence, their personal dignity, their land, even their language, to intruders from across the sea. Joyce defined the Irish view: "History, Stephen said, is a nightmare from which I am trying to awake."[1]

I

They had kept trying to awake. Pessimism mingled with pride and romantic defiance. They countered fate by talk, incessant and extravagant; by irony and self-mockery; by fantasy and by drink. They evaded fate, as oppressed people do, by donning masks to deceive the oppressors. Some came to believe the blarney act they put on to bemuse the English. Others used it as a cloak for resistance. They fought fate, according to temperament, by terror or by politics. The struggle for Catholic emancipation had initiated the Irish in the arts of political organization well before they began to leave for the United States. Irish politics incorporated the code of the family. It was a tribal politics, dominated by expectations of unswerving loyalty and vindictive against what was often too eagerly seen as defection or betrayal.

Most important in securing life, along with the family, was the church. Life in Ireland was hard, and so was religion. Jansenism pervaded the Irish church, encouraging clerical tendencies toward censoriousness and bigotry. But the priests remained with the people, and faith was the ultimate consolation in a hopeless world. Catholicism absorbed and vindicated the Irish experience—the suffering, the bloodshed, the fatalism. It explained that man was weak and life more than a little absurd, unless redeemed by the grace of God mediated through the church.

The culture Robert Kennedy's great-grandparents transported to Boston was filled with this conviction of the bloodiness of life. The sense of disorder, tragedy and evil was not unlike that of the Puritans, three centuries earlier. But what the Puritans had placed on the isolated soul in the quest for salvation the Irish assigned to the family and the church. By the time the Fitzgeralds and Kennedys arrived, the descendants of the Puritans were turning away from Calvin and Jonathan Edwards to embrace the inevitability of progress and the perfectibility of man. In short, they were being Americanized. The Irish newcomers were set apart by their awareness of historic failure and human sinfulness and by their faith in the redemptive magic of family and church. They were set apart by their addiction to the scathing comedy that relieved the gloom of life. They were set apart by their lack of power, money, education and self-esteem—and by the complacent contempt in which the Yankees held them.

Separation preserved their legacy. But the Irish were being Americanized too. Robert Kennedy's grandfathers—Patrick Joseph Kennedy, born in Boston in 1858; John Francis Fitzgerald in 1863—prospered in the new land. Kennedy was a quiet man, a saloonkeeper and ward boss, wielding influence softly, indifferent to publicity and to noise. Fitzgerald was an Irish talker, interested in everything and forever putting on a show ("Honey Fitz can talk you blind/On any subject you can find").[2] The two men were together in the state senate in the early 1890s and did not like each other then or later.

Rose, the oldest of Honey Fitz's six children, was born on July 22, 1890. She grew up in a great Dorchester house, with mansard roof and stained-glass windows. Her father took her on vacations to Old Orchard Beach in Maine and to Palm Beach in Florida and in 1911 gave her a spectacular coming-out party. By this time rich Irish Catholics were creating a social world of their own, paralleling the rich Yankee Protestant society that excluded them. Rose Fitzgerald, a bright and pretty girl, found life in this world enjoyable and fulfilling. For a moment, it is true, she had wanted to go to Wellesley College; but, as she said in later life, "in those days you didn't argue with your father."³ Instead she was packed off to convents in Boston, New York and the Netherlands. She learned French and German in Europe and spoke them fluently for the rest of her life.

P. J. Kennedy's only son, Joseph Patrick, was born on September 6, 1888. Where the Fitzgeralds believed in duplicating the institutions of Yankee society, the Kennedys believed in infiltrating them. Young Kennedy went with the Yankee boys to the Boston Latin School and then on to Harvard College. Here he made a moderate mark—a rather considerable mark for an Irish Catholic—and graduated in 1912. In the meantime, Rose Fitzgerald and Joseph Kennedy had fallen in love. John F. Fitzgerald thought it a most unsuitable match and tried through domestic admonition and foreign travel to steer his daughter in other directions. The courtship was pursued clandestinely. In the end, Honey Fitz surrendered. Cardinal O'Connell married the young couple in October 1914.

A fortnight later Joseph Kennedy moved his bride into a house in Yankee Brookline. He had already begun his assault on Anglo-Saxon society. Instead of becoming a contractor in the Irish style, he chose banking, a Protestant preserve. Soon he went into utilities, forcing his way onto the board of the Massachusetts Electric Company; he explained to a friend, "Do you know a better way to meet people like the Saltonstalls?"[4] During the First World War he was assistant general manager of the Bethlehem Shipyards at Fore River, south of Boston. Here he met Franklin D. Roosevelt, then assistant secretary of the Navy. "Roosevelt was the hardest trader I'd ever run up against," Kennedy told Ernest K. Lindley twenty years later.[5] They ended on terms of mutual esteem. After the war, Kennedy joined the Yankee investment banking house of Hayden, Stone & Company and began his bold career in the stock market.

II

Kennedy was a loner who operated with a small staff and an astute instinct. He used to say, "Only a fool holds out for the top dollar"—a piece of wisdom that enabled him to escape the Wall Street crash relatively unscathed.[6] He played the game brilliantly. He also played it cynically. The game did not consume his life or even command his respect. It was a means to an end. By 1926, he was a millionaire and far more successful than his Yankee contemporaries. Still they denied him the acceptance he sought for himself and his family.

He resented exclusion. "They wouldn't have asked my daughters to join their debutante clubs," he told Joe McCarthy (the writer, not the senator) thirty years later.[7] In 1926 Joseph Kennedy abandoned Boston, taking his family by private railroad car to a house in Riverdale, an affluent New York suburb. Returning a decade later for the St. Patrick's Day dinner of the Clover Club, Kennedy observed that the Boston Irish "suffered under the handicap of not possessing family tradition adequate to win the respect and confidence of the Puritan neighbors. This Yankee pride of ancestry developed a boastfulness and a snobbishness which, though difficult to understand, explains many of the strange idiosyncrasies of Boston." He did not think that the dual society could last. "The influence of the Irish culture in this country," he told the Clover Club, "must be recognized as on the wane. Nor is it likely that anything or any person can change this process of cultural absorption."* If cultural absorption was inevitable, he was determined that his children—certainly his sons—should improve his own record.

When Robert Kennedy discussed apartheid in South Africa in 1966, he said that his father had left Boston because of the signs NO IRISH NEED APPLY. "Maybe," a skeptic named Michael Mooney wrote him. "But I can't help thinking of . . . the Irishman who left Boston (and all those signs) in his own Railway car." Mooney added, "It has always been a distinct right of all the Irish to invent for themselves mythological backgrounds—little lies that amuse their audience and serve their tellers well in diplomacy and love and politics."[8] Robert Kennedy replied, "Yes but—It was symbolic. The business establishment, the clubs, the golf course—at least that was what I was told at a very young age. . . . Undoubtedly lack of opportunity which had nothing to do with racial or religious background but were just Boston had something to do with it—But both my parents felt very strongly about the discrimination so you'll have to take the matter up with them. Excuse the scrawl—I'm in a plane. . . . [P.S.] Actually I don't write any better anywhere."[9]

No doubt there was an element of genuine hurt in Kennedy's atti-

* J. P. Kennedy, Clover Club speech (typescript), March 13, 1937, 2, 3, JPK Papers. His papers contain a garbled quotation from the autobiography of Charles Francis Adams, in which the tough old Yankee offered a view of Boston that the tough young Irish American obviously found sympathetic. "I can say little that is pleasant," Adams wrote, ". . . I have tried Boston socially on all sides: I have summered it and wintered it, tried it drunk and tried it sober; and, drunk or sober, there's nothing in it—save Boston!" The sheet with the garbled quotation is dated November 16, 1944. The exact quotation, used here, can be found in C. F. Adams, *An Autobiography* (Boston, 1916), 39.

tude toward Boston. But he would very likely have left in 1926 even if he had been elected president of the Somerset Club. His Harvard classmate Ralph Lowell, a Boston banker, told R. J. Whalen, "This city was a small, clear puddle. New York was a big, muddy one, and that's what Joe wanted." "If you want to make money," Joe Kennedy himself liked to say, "go where the money is."[10]

III

Joseph Kennedy was not quite thirty-eight when he left Boston, a tall, slender, reddish-haired man with heavy horn-rimmed glasses over penetrating blue eyes. The intensity of his personality made an immediate impression. He could be endlessly charming when he wished but could also be—and often was—blunt and brusque to the point of rudeness. In fact, he did not give a damn about most people. Perhaps, with his commitment to the Americanization of the Irish, he reacted against the stage-Irishman stereotype, all gregariousness and blarney, as embodied, for example, in his irrepressible father-in-law; at any rate, he had no trouble being as frosty as the frostiest Yankee. Other businessmen thought him rough and remorseless. "There are no big shots" was a Kennedy aphorism—a proposition deeply offensive to all who saw themselves as big shots. He had little regard for businessmen per se and few close friends in the business world, beyond a circle of cronies who stayed with him through the years.

When he gave affection, he was bountiful. But he expected fidelity in return. "His friendship," wrote Arthur Krock, the political pundit of the *New York Times* and for years a Kennedy intimate, ". . . is a mixture—of lavish generosity, fierce loyalty, excessive gratitude, harshly-articulated candor and sudden termination—that is without parallel in my experience."[11] He had a hot temper, but some considered it more admonitory than uncontrollable. "When he got mad," said his friend Morton Downey, the Irish American tenor, "I always suspected it was an act."[12]

He was a faithful Catholic, but described himself to his children as anticlerical. His daughter Eunice said, "He always trusted experience as the greatest creator of character. (My mother believed religion was.)"* He was personally abstemious—perhaps another reaction against the stereotype—smoked and drank little and did his best to in-

---

* Edward M. Kennedy wrote in *The Fruitful Bough*, 207, "Although he said he was anti-clerical, two of his closest friends were churchmen." Eunice Kennedy Shriver's observation is on 218.

duce his children to follow his example. His hobby was classical music—a taste formed at Harvard. One summer in Washington, while his family was in Hyannis Port, Kennedy played symphonies so incessantly that the cronies with whom he was sharing his house complained. "You dumb bastards don't appreciate culture," Kennedy said, putting on another symphony.[13] His children did not inherit his love of serious music any more than they inherited their mother's aptitude for foreign languages.

Making money was never enough. He had, said his perceptive friend Morton Downey, "a strange, almost turbulent interest in more seemingly unrelated topics and things than any man I ever knew."[14] Turbulent—a significant choice of word, suggesting the restlessness of personality that drove him from job to job and challenge to challenge. The ranging concern extended inescapably, for P. J. Kennedy's son, to politics. This was, in any case—far more than money—the Irish American road to power.

IV

In 1928, Kennedy had been too deeply engaged in business to do more than vote for the first Irish Catholic to run for the Presidency as the candidate of a major party. A year later the Great Depression began. "I am not ashamed to record," Kennedy recalled in 1936, "that in those days I felt and said I would be willing to part with half of what I had if I could be sure of keeping, under law and order, the other half. Then it seemed that I should be able to hold nothing for the protection of my family."[15]

An outsider in Wall Street as well as in the Back Bay, he had no deep allegiance to the old order. By this time his acquaintance from shipbuilding days in the First World War was the progressive governor of New York. Henry Morgenthau, Franklin D. Roosevelt's conservation commissioner, brought the two men together again.[16] Kennedy decided to back Roosevelt for the Democratic nomination. Why Roosevelt rather than Smith? Kennedy hardly knew Smith personally, but may have felt he knew Smith's Irish American generation too well. Very likely he was put off by the vociferous support Smith had in 1932 from unreconstructed Boston Irishmen like his father-in-law. "I knew that big drastic changes had to be made in our economic system," Kennedy told Joe McCarthy a quarter century later, "and I felt that Roosevelt was the one who could make these changes. I wanted him in the White House for my own security, and for the security of our kids, and I was ready to do anything to help elect him."[17]

Kennedy was an early and generous contributor to Roosevelt's campaign and served as a Roosevelt emissary to William Randolph Hearst, the newspaper publisher. Victory brought disappointment. Kennedy hoped to be Secretary of the Treasury. For whatever reason —partly because Louis Howe, Roosevelt's possessive and populist-minded adviser, disliked Wall Street speculators in general and Kennedy in particular—the post went to William H. Woodin, and, when Woodin retired in a few months because of ill health, to Morgenthau. Roosevelt remained amiable but evasive. Kennedy was privately upset. "If I were to send you a short summary of the whole situation in the country," he wrote Felix Frankfurter at Oxford in December 1933, "I would just say 'confusion.'"[18] Raymond Moley, a close Roosevelt adviser, noted after a holiday with Kennedy in Florida, "There must have been hundreds of dollars in telephone calls to provide an exchange of abuse of Roosevelt between Kennedy and W. R. Hearst."[19]

It must be supposed that Kennedy expected Frankfurter and Moley to report his discontent to the White House. But Roosevelt had an exact sense both of Kennedy's ability and of his intractability. Kennedy in the Treasury, for example, would have been a constant problem for a President with a penchant for experiment. Roosevelt proposed that Kennedy head a commission to negotiate reciprocal trade agreements in South America or that he become minister to Ireland. "I told him," Kennedy wrote his oldest son, "that I did not desire a position with the Government unless it really meant some prestige to my family."[20]

Later in 1934 Congress created the Securities and Exchange Commission (SEC) to oversee the stock market. Roosevelt decided to make Kennedy chairman. The appointment would inspire confidence in the financial community. At the same time, Kennedy knew all the tricks of the trade and was evidently ambitious to establish himself as a public servant. But word that a notorious speculator was scheduled to police Wall Street provoked a minor New Deal revolt. Roy Howard ran an editorial in the Scripps-Howard papers calling the proposal "a slap in the face" to Roosevelt's most loyal supporters.[21]

Unperturbed, FDR offered Kennedy the job. Kennedy said, "I don't think you ought to do this. I think it will bring down injurious criticism." Moley, who was present, asked whether there was anything in Kennedy's business career that could hurt the President.

"With a burst of profanity," Moley recalled, "[Kennedy] defied anyone to question his devotion to the public interest. . . . What was more, he would give his critics—and here again the profanity flowed freely—an administration of the SEC that would be a credit to the country, the President, himself, and his family—clear down to the ninth child."[22]

The invocation of the family made an impression. It should have; it was Kennedy's profoundest commitment. Harold Ickes, the Secretary of the Interior, sourly recounted the meeting in which Roosevelt told the cabinet. "Apparently he is going on the assumption that Kennedy ["a former stockmarket plunger"] would now like to make a name for himself for the sake of his family, but I have never known many of these cases to work out as expected."[23] This case did work out. The SEC was a complex and demanding assignment, requiring enormous knowledge, toughness and skill. Kennedy was an indefatigable worker. Over the next fifteen months he did a first-class job in establishing a vigilant and effective regulatory agency. In September 1935 Kennedy, having restored the capital market and secured the adoption of new trading rules, resigned. Later that month the Kennedys embarked for Europe.

v

In England Winston Churchill invited them to luncheon at Chartwell, his country house in Kent. Rose Kennedy thought that Churchill, "with his puckish face . . . looked more like a country squire than an English statesman." Unlike Lord Beaverbrook, who had asked countless questions two nights earlier, volunteering little on his own, Churchill "talked expansively, narrating, explaining and trying to convince us of the wisdom of his points." England and the United States, he said, should build a navy strong enough to police the world; this was the way to counter Nazism. But he acknowledged that this would be a hard idea to sell in America; there were too many isolationists, "too many Irish haters of England, too many people that would prefer to remain outside England's sphere." Mrs. Churchill asked whether Eleanor Roosevelt was an exhibitionist using her husband's high office to court publicity for herself. "I tried to convince her that I thought Mrs. Roosevelt was sincere," noted Rose Kennedy, and that "gradually people would become accustomed to her unconventional approaches."[24]

Later Churchill wrote Kennedy, "I have invited a distinguished company to meet you on the 28th and have already a great many acceptances." But Kennedy's second son, John, who had just entered the London School of Economics, was seriously ill with hepatitis. "I am deeply grieved at your anxiety about your son," Churchill continued, "and earnestly trust it will soon be relieved. Of course you must not think of being at all hampered by this engagement. On the whole however I think it would be well to carry on."[25] Kennedy nevertheless replied, "After a week of great concern and anxiety, I have sent my boy back to America this morning. I propose following him on Wednesday."[26]

Kennedy gave Roosevelt a gloomy report on conditions in Europe and then busied himself profitably as a consultant on corporate problems. As the 1936 election approached, he prepared to help in the campaign. In July, a newspaperman remarked at a presidential press conference, "Joe Kennedy is writing a book on what is going to happen to children under Roosevelt." FDR replied, "Very good; he has nine children and should qualify."[27] The newspaperman was only slightly off the mark. The first chapter of *I'm for Roosevelt,* published in August, was titled: "In Which the Father of Nine Children Explains What He Thinks This Election Means to Them."

The book, written with the help of Arthur Krock,[28] opened with a somewhat disingenuous disclaimer: "I have no political ambitions for myself or my children."* Kennedy's argument was that Roosevelt had saved capitalism from the capitalists. Disclosures of business malpractice, he wrote, had "completely shattered . . . the belief that those in control of the corporate life of America were motivated by honesty and the ideals of honorable conduct." Yet the New Deal was founded on "a basic belief in the efficacy of the capitalistic system." Roosevelt had been "at pains to protect the invested wealth of the nation." Business hatred of Roosevelt was therefore "the strangest hatred in history, because the most articulate and venomous among the opposition are those very persons whose fortunes have been repaired through Presidential activities since March, 1933." Kennedy found the business attack on government planning especially mindless. "An organized functioning society requires a planned economy. The more complex the society the greater the demand for planning."

* A quarter century later, William Manchester asked him what he meant. Joseph Kennedy replied: "I wasn't thinking of the Presidency then. I just wanted them to be useful civic servants. If they'd become sheriffs or selectmen, that would've been OK with me." Manchester's comment is apt: "Sequiturwise, this was non." William Manchester, *Portrait of a President* (Boston, 1962), 173.

Mass unemployment was "the Achilles heel of freedom . . . the root of all the ills and ailments of subjugated people in Europe. . . . Planned action is imperative, or else capitalism and the American scheme of life will be in serious jeopardy."[29]

Businessmen were bitter in 1936. Marquis Childs of the *St. Louis Post-Dispatch* described the mood in his book *They Hate Roosevelt*. Kennedy was a rare and valued exception. To the idea, expounded by his old friend Hearst, that the New Deal was a communist plot, Kennedy replied contemptuously, "There has been scarcely a liberal piece of legislation during the last sixty years that has not been opposed as Communistic."[30] In a radio speech in October he praised the New Deal for having done away with the popular myth that business success was a guarantee of civic virtue. This was why, he surmised, "men of wealth" hated Roosevelt. The businessman's "material position" had not been harmed,

> but his *moral* prestige is gone. . . . He is being judged by new standards which are quite unfamiliar to him. He feels exposed. He has been shaken in his own faith in himself. He is made to doubt secretly that he represents the American system in its most perfect expression. All this is unconscious and all the more frightful. Being unable—and certainly unwilling—to analyze with coolness the cause of his anxiety, he seeks relief in vituperation and hatred.[31]

VI

Kennedy had his forty-eighth birthday two months before the 1936 election. This proud, profane, imperious, frank, indiscreet, scheming, relentless, sensitive, vital man had had spectacular success in business and government. He owned houses in Bronxville, Hyannis Port and, after 1934, in Palm Beach. He was known in Europe as well as in the United States. He had left far in his wake the Yankees who had patronized him at Harvard and on State Street. Still he had not quite achieved the goal he had long since set himself. When a Boston newspaper described him as an Irishman, he exclaimed, "I was born here. My parents were born here. What the hell do I have to do to be called an American?"[32]

His complaint did not imply repudiation of his origins. He did not resent being Irish but the condescending Yankee theory of what being Irish involved. We must, he wrote Joseph I. Breen of the Association of Motion Picture Producers, "see if we can't add a little more lustre to the Irish reputation."[33] Most of his close friends were of Irish descent. His character was formed by his Irish cultural inheritance—the pessimism, the romantic defiance, the political instinct, the irony, the sexual chauvinism, the Catholicism, the sense that the world was a mess and not likely to improve very much—though he fused these traits with a strictly American passion for competition, achievement and victory. Still, powerful as this passion was, it was conditioned by the Irish tradition; above all by his supreme belief in the family—in *his* family.

"The measure of a man's success in life," Kennedy often said, "is not the money he's made. It's the kind of family he has raised." One day on the golf course at Palm Beach, Bernard Gimbel asked, "What are you doing these days, Joe?" Kennedy replied, "My work is my boys."[34] In the 1920s, when he had been away for long periods in New York and later in Hollywood ("I did not think it was vital," his wife wrote in her memoirs, "for my husband to be on hand for the birth of the babies"),[35] the care of the young fell to Mrs. Kennedy. As the children grew older, their father spent more time with them. LeMoyne Billings, John Kennedy's Choate roommate and an intimate of the household after 1934, could not remember visiting the Kennedys when Mr. Kennedy was not there.[36] The balance of authority shifted. "When he was there," recalled Eunice, "it was his personality that dominated. Our mother . . . let him sort of take over."[37]

Joe Jr. was the child in whom the parents invested their deepest hope. He was twenty-one years old in 1936, a sophomore at Harvard after spending 1933–34 with Harold Laski at the London School of Economics. He had charm, confidence and gusto. His brother John recalled his "amazing intensity. . . . Even when still, there was always a sense of motion forcibly restrained."[38] Laski remembered abler students but not many with "either his eager zest for life or his gift of winning one's affection. . . . He has often sat in my study and submitted with that smile that was pure magic to relentless teasing about his determination to be nothing less than President of the United States."[39]

John, nineteen, was preparing to enter Harvard in the fall. He had spent much of his childhood sick in bed, surrounded by books. "Jack is far from being a well boy," his father had written as recently as the preceding November.[40] A family joke, evidently made up by his younger brother Robert: "If a mosquito bit Jack Kennedy, the mosquito would die."[41] There were occasional troubles between the older brothers. Joe was purposeful and methodical. Jack was casual, untidy and absent-minded. Joe was robust and, for all his gentleness with the younger children, hot-tempered. Jack was frail but quick-witted and provocative. Their mother described their childhood relationship as one of "friendly enmity."[42] Jack won the arguments, Joe the fights. When James MacGregor Burns asked Jack whether anything had really bothered him as a child, he could think only of his big brother. "He had a pugnacious personality," he replied laconically. "Later on it smoothed out but it was a problem in my boyhood." Burns added, "Bobby Kennedy to this day remembers cowering with his sisters upstairs while his older brothers fought furiously on the first floor."[43]

After the two brothers came four girls: Rosemary, 18 in 1936, who her parents now realized was mentally retarded; Kathleen, 16, gay and pretty; Eunice, 15, and Patricia, 12, still tomboys. There followed Robert, 11, Jean, 8, and Edward, the baby, who was 4. The family was the center of Joseph Kennedy's existence. Everything else took second place. His houses were designed not to impress his guests but to cherish his children. In Hyannis Port the Kennedys had an open, rambling, white Cape Cod house separated by eel grass from a fringe of beach along Nantucket Sound. The Palm Beach house was a white stucco 1920s villa overlooking the ocean. The Bronxville house, to which they had moved from Riverdale in 1929, was a large brick Georgian mansion on six acres of ground. All were notable for their large, comfortable rooms, their space and sunlight and flowers, their ample lawns easily converted into touch football fields and staging areas for pets.

Joseph Kennedy expended all the power, conscious and unconscious, of a demanding personality on pressing his children, especially the boys, to develop their potentialities to the full, on driving them beyond themselves. "He wanted a son to be something," said Kenneth O'Donnell, the long-time friend of John and Robert. ". . . Maybe it was to prove something for himself."[44] His insistence on competition and success became in time legendary—perhaps because it represented so quintessential a version of a basic American legend.

"We don't want any losers around here," he told the children. "In this family we want winners. . . . Don't come in second or third—that doesn't count—but win."[45] He subjected defeat to rigorous analysis and, if the postmortem revealed that the loser had not tried hard enough, registered severe paternal disapproval. "He tolerated a mistake once," his youngest son later testified, "but never a second time."[46] Losers had to keep their sorrows to themselves. "I don't

The Family

want any sourpusses around here," he would say. ". . . We don't want any crying in this house"—a proposition his children came to render, somewhat sardonically, as "Kennedys never cry."[47]

The win-win-win compulsion dominated the household. Still it was not so bad as it sounded. The point was less to win than to do one's best to win. "We were to try harder than anyone else," Robert Kennedy wrote. "We might not be the best, and none of us were, but we were to make the effort to be the best. 'After you have done the best you can,' he used to say, 'the hell with it.' "[48] Failing to do your best was the mortal sin, not losing.

VII

The athletic code was accompanied by equally incessant pressure for intellectual development. Everyone knows about mealtime at the Kennedys, where Joseph Kennedy liked to preside over a family seminar. Among the children the two older boys did most of the talking. Their father sometimes took the other side in order to sharpen the discussion. "There was no frivolity," Lem Billings said of the family meals, "but they were always exhilarating and fun."[49]

The forbidden topic was business. "I have never discussed money with my wife and family," Kennedy once said, "and I never will."[50] The subject ultimately bored him. He did not wish to inflict it on his children. "He had made enough money not to need to make any more," Lem Billings commented; "he saw no reason for them to do what he had done."[51] The boys grew up cheerfully indifferent to business. "Listening to them talk about money," said Charles Spalding, another close friend of the brothers, "was like listening to nuns talk about sex."[52]

In any event, Joseph Kennedy thought, the reign of money per se was finished. "The boys might as well work for the government," he told his wife, "because politics will control the business of the country in the future."[53] Public affairs ruled the dinner table. "I can hardly remember a mealtime," Robert Kennedy later wrote, "when the conversation was not dominated by what Franklin D. Roosevelt was doing or what was happening in the world."[54] "Any of the children," recalled one of John's Choate friends, "could ask him questions and [he replied] in the greatest detail, no matter how simple or how stupid the questions might seem. . . . However, if an outsider, such as myself would ask the Ambassador a question . . . he would just answer it curtly as though he didn't want to be bothered with your questions. He was only concerned about educating his own children."[55]

His concern pursued the children everywhere. Excerpts from letters to John convey the flavor:

> I strongly urge you to pay a little more attention to penmanship. Mine has always been pretty bad, so I am not a very good authority to speak about it, but yours is disgraceful and should get some attention.
>
> I don't want to give the impression that I am a nagger, for goodness knows I think that is the worst thing any parent can be, and I also feel that you know if I didn't really feel you had the goods I would be most charitable in my attitude toward your failings. . . . Aren't you foolish not to get all there is out of what God has given you and what you can do with it yourself. . . . It is very difficult to make up fundamentals that you have neglected when you were very young and that is why I am always urging you to do the best you can.
>
> Don't let me lose confidence in you again, because it will be pretty nearly an impossible task to restore it—I am sure it will be a loss to you and a distinct loss to me. The mere trying to do a good job is not enough—real honest-to-goodness effort is what I expect. Get yourself into shape so that a man can't write a halfway report on you. . . . You have the goods; why not try to show it?[56]

"I grew up in a very strict house," John Kennedy said in 1960, "and one where . . . there were no free riders, and everyone was expected to do, give their best to what they did. . . . There was a constant drive for us for self-improvement."[57] Discipline was enforced, on the father's part, by moral rather than physical means. "I'm sure Mr. Kennedy never slapped a child in his life," said Lem Billings. "But his eyes would just take you right out of the window."[58] That cold, appraising, steely glance over the top of his glasses was known in the family as "Daddy's look."[59] The children's greatest anguish came when Daddy was disappointed in them; their greatest happiness lay in his approval. His commanding presence awed their young friends, most of whom their father ignored but a few of whom, like Billings and Spalding, were received into the bosom of the family and became auxiliary brothers. Even they thought Mr. Kennedy remote, a little humorless and infinitely intimidating. Billings found him "a most emotional man—but also a man of complete self-control."[60] He was, said Spalding, "the first unbridled force I ever encountered."[61]

VIII

Rose Kennedy was her husband's staunch ally. She was a remarkably handsome, controlled, organized, and impervious woman. She was also a cultivated woman, better read and in some ways more worldly than her husband. Her father had instilled in her an enthusiasm for history; she kept up her languages; all her life she remained a student, dedicated to self-improvement. She adored balls and trips to Paris, while Joseph Kennedy, as she later said, considered parties a waste of time, where he would either be solicited for tips on the stock market or be required to argue about the New Deal. Pressed to go out, he would say, "We eat better at home."[62] Nor did he much like entertaining non-Kennedys even at home, except for the children's friends.

Her husband's conventional religious faith paled next to her serene and inexhaustible piety. This led to one of their few express disagreements. "I wanted all of the children to have at least a few years in good Catholic schools," Rose Kennedy later wrote, "where . . . they would receive thorough instruction in the doctrines of their religion and intelligent answers to any doubts."[63] Joseph Kennedy told her that children ought to learn their religion at home and at church; his deeper view was that they should not be deflected from the mainstream of American life.

The result was predictable in a family culturally bound to regard girls as less important than boys. The boys went in the main to secular institutions; the girls first to convents and then to Catholic colleges. Joe Jr. was a loyal Catholic in the style of his father. John took religion, like everything else, with detachment. One day, passing a church, he said to his friend Charles Spalding, "How do you come out on all this?" Spalding, who had been born a Catholic, replied that he had never had time to work it all out; if he did, he supposed he would end by saying, "I don't know." John Kennedy observed that was about where he stood too.[64] Yet he said his prayers and remained generally faithful in religious observance. Robert, always the overachiever, was the most religious among the sons. As a small child in Bronxville, he aspired to be an altar boy and could be heard practicing his Latin in his room.[65] His devotion never, however, contrary to later suggestions, carried him to the point of contemplating the priesthood.[66]

No child could hope to escape father by appealing to mother. She was as articulate as he on the virtues of winning, as given to didactic questions at the dinner table, though hers went more to history and theology than to current affairs, as stern in her discipline, as unrelenting in her determination to make the children meet high standards. Letters suggest her maternal style:

> I do hope you are working harder, dearest Teddy. As I said before, the Kennedy boys worked hard and were usually at the top of their classes in Boston, and I am sure the first question most people ask about you is, "Are you smart like your father?"—not to mention that I graduated from good old Dorchester High School with honors myself—so please get on your horse.[67]

(To a daughter-in-law)

> I think in the future it might be well to review history and current events with him [a grandson] so that he may remember facts in that way. You might ask him questions like who the President of France is; what holidays are national holidays or church holidays, or both; the name of the Queen of England, etc.
>
> The reason I am sometimes reluctant about extra goodies for the children is that I read once that youngsters should get used to a few disappointments or jolts when they are young. They thus build up an immunity against them, so that when they encounter life's vicissitudes when they are older, they are not too shocked and they can take them with a smile.[68]

Her daughter Eunice later said, "It was this terrific drive, she wanted everyone to do their best. There was quite a little pressure around."[69]

IX

Everyone who has written about the Kennedys has discussed this pressure, the parental insistence, unceasing and unsparing, on competition, achievement, victory. The psychic burden must have been considerable. The desire to please parents forces children to some degree into roles set for them from above. Such a process can create doubts about worth and identity and lead to overcompensation or to despair. American life is littered with the wrecks of men and women who cared too much about pleasing their parents.

The mystery is why the parental demands did not crush the Kennedy children.* It would be hard to demonstrate that their upbringing disabled their capacity for affection, self-reliance and happiness. Rather the contrary: Charles Spalding, visiting Hyannis Port for the

---

* Some writers think they were crushed. See, for example, Nancy G. Clinch, *The Kennedy Neurosis* (New York, 1973), especially 8–9, 15, 60–61, 108. This book is a splendid specimen of the heads-I-win-tails-you-lose school of psychohistory. Whatever the Kennedys did—one thing or its opposite—was grist to the analytical mill. If a Kennedy went up in a balloon, he would be an exhibitionist; if he refused to go up, he would be a coward.

first time in 1940, registered a general impression when he described a family "moving in every direction and vitally involved and interested in what was going on. I had never seen . . . any family like that. . . . I thought to myself, 'Well, this is really the best possible way to approach life.' "[70] Winston Churchill and Franklin D. Roosevelt were incomparably greater public men than Joseph P. Kennedy. Yet Randolph Churchill and Franklin D. Roosevelt, Jr., youths of ability and ambition, never fulfilled their potentialities. The Kennedy sons, for whatever reason, pursued their capacities to the uttermost limits. Had the parents no part in this result?

I put this question to John Kennedy one evening at the White House. He said, "It was due to my father. He wasn't around as much as some fathers; but . . . he made his children feel that they were the most important things in the world to him."[71] When someone asked Franklin D. Roosevelt, Jr., what Joseph Kennedy was like as a father, he replied, no doubt out of some indecipherable mixture of memories, "From everything I saw he was a great father. He didn't leave a stone unturned to encourage his boys. . . . He loved doing things with his boys."[72]

In the spring of 1961, John Kennedy stopped off in Hyannis Port before leaving for Europe to see Khrushchev. A heavy fog was sweeping across the compound. He was walking to his father's house for dinner when Caroline, his daughter, came off the porch crying to him. As he started to comfort her, the kitchen door opened, and someone said, "Mr. President, they want you on the White House phone—they said it's important." Kennedy said, "Caroline, I'll be back in just a moment. Let me go take this phone call." When dinner began, there was an edgy silence. Finally Mr. Kennedy said, "Jack, I saw what happened outside. Caroline was in tears and came out. You had a call from the White House. I know there are a lot of things on your mind about your meeting with Khrushchev. . . . But let me tell you something: Nothing that will happen during your Presidency will be as important as how Caroline turns out. And don't forget it."[73] Joseph Kennedy had never forgotten it. But then he had never been President.

If pressure created problems for the children, love gave the children strength to meet those problems. "Mr. Kennedy was somehow able," LeMoyne Billings later said, "not to spoil his kids and yet not frighten them with his aggressive desires. . . . He did it with love, and yet with strictness."[74] It was a love that put "Daddy's look" and his eternal emphasis on competition in context. Still love by itself was not the answer to the mystery. Parental love is often suffocating. Joseph Kennedy's evidently was not.

His whole effort, in one aspect, was to make his children independent of him. "At an early age," Robert recalled, "we were sent on trips. . . . We were given tasks of responsibility. We embarked on study programs under teachers or political leaders who held views quite different from his."[75] A highly opinionated man, Joseph Kennedy did not require his children to adopt his opinions. What mattered was that they should be able to defend their own. "He always encouraged his children to argue with him," said Lem Billings, veteran of so many Kennedy dinner tables. ". . . He *never* wanted them to agree with him."[76]

The Laski connection was characteristic. Kennedy regarded Laski as "a nut and a crank. I disagreed with everything he wrote. We were black and white. But I never taught the boys to disapprove of someone just because I didn't accept his ideas. They heard enough from me, and I decided they should be exposed to someone of intelligence and vitality on the other side."[77] When Laski proposed taking young Joe to the Soviet Union, his father was delighted. "I think it would be wise for you to go with Laski," he wrote, "particularly because it would give you a very favorable viewpoint in consideration of things here."[78] Young Joe came back, "exultant," his mother later said, "in his enthusiasm" and engaged in vigorous debate with his father over capitalism and communism.[79] John Kennedy observed from the sidelines, "Joe seems to understand the situation a little better than Dad."[80] (Young Joe's enthusiasm infected Rose, and in 1936 she took Kathleen on a visit to the Soviet Union, concluding tolerantly that "many of its aims, if not many of the methods, were worthy of respect and discussion and study.")[81] Mr. Kennedy remained unperturbed. "If I were their age," he told his wife, "I probably would believe what they believe, but I am of a different background. . . . I don't care what the boys think about my ideas. I can always look out for myself. The important thing is that they should stick together."[82]

He was willing to take his chances. In the 1920s he had consulted his friend Hearst about setting up a trust fund for each child. Hearst warned him not to make them independent; when they got older they would leave him and go off with their money. Kennedy's comment was, "If that's the only way to hold them, I've been a lousy father."[83] He set up the trusts, fixing it, as he said, "so that any of my children, financially speaking, could look me in the eye and tell me to go to

The Family

hell."[84] "If they want to be slobs," he told Frank Waldrop of the *Washington Times-Herald,* "they can, and I can't do anything about it."[85] It was family, not money, that would keep them together. "My father used his money," said Robert Kennedy, "to free us—not to hold us."[86]

"The generation that follows me," Joseph Kennedy once said, "may have to stand for everything that I stood against—and I realize that includes even my own sons. I made my choice among the philosophies offered when I was young. Each of them will have to make his or her choice."[87] He remained an Irish pessimist; but when his sons "were more optimistic about the future of life on this planet," Robert Kennedy remembered, "then in a more mellow mood he would say, 'If I were your age I would hold those views also.' "[88] Ideas were not the ultimate reality. The ultimate reality was family.

Joseph Kennedy's "fierce sense of family" (Morton Downey's phrase) was perhaps the key to the mystery.[89] It gave his children the ability to withstand his own pressure. And the family provided a protection against inordinate parental demands in part, it may be surmised, because it was an Irish Catholic family. In a Protestant family, where salvation was an individual responsibility, competition threw each child back on himself and parental demands could become an individual burden. In an Irish Catholic family, where salvation was culturally mediated through institutions, the destructive effect of competition, the suffocating effect of love, could be tempered by corporate solidity and mutual reinforcement. "The Kennedys," Joseph Alsop used to say, "are all in love with each other."[90] The Irish legacy had not faded away in the third American generation.

Of course, lest one appear to endorse theories of parental determinism, it is necessary to add that the character of the children themselves—their spirit, vitality, toughness, irreverence—had something to do with their capacity to survive. There was something very Irish about those traits too.

(2)

The Father

BY THE TIME of the seventh child, Rose Kennedy said, "Even the most enthusiastic parent may feel less excitement about 'another baby.' "[1] Robert Kennedy must have perceived that his older brothers and sisters enjoyed more parental attention. Apprehensions of inferiority were no doubt intensified when it became apparent that he would be a good deal shorter than his tall older brothers; even, in time, than his petted younger brother. His father, in addition, was away much of his early childhood. When at home, Joseph Kennedy was on occasion impatient and rough with him. His mother, compensating, protected and consoled him. Problems with his father increased a sense of inadequacy. They also inspired him to strive to the utmost to win his father's approval and love.

I

From all accounts, he was an extremely sweet child. "I loved Bobby from the day I set eyes on him," said Lem Billings, who saw him first when he was eight years old. "He was the nicest little boy I ever met." Once Billings commented to Joseph Kennedy on Bobby's exceptional generosity with possessions. Bobby's father grunted, "I don't know where he got that."[2] Luella Hennessey, who joined the household as the children's nurse when Bobby was twelve, called him "the most thoughtful and considerate of all the Kennedy children."[3]

A couple of letters written when he was nine are revealing:

Dear Daddy,
    I went to the circus Saturday. Dave, Frank, and Tommie went with me and we liked it very much. I wish you were with me. [Clyde] Beatty the lion trainer wasn't there this year. I liked the horses jumping over the fire the best.

I will probably see you this week. I hope so.

Love,
Bobby[4]

Dear Mr. President,

I liked the stamps you sent me very much and the little book is very useful. I am just starting my collection and it would be great fun to see yours which mother says you have had for a long time.

I am going to frame your letter and I am going to keep it always in my room.

Daddy, mother, and all my brothers and sisters want to be remembered to you.

Bobby Kennedy[5]

The school administrator at the Bronxville public school, where he attended his third, fourth and fifth grades, remembered him thirty years later as a "nice little freckle-faced kid. . . . He needed no special handling."[6] And a report from Camp Winona in Maine where he went when he was eleven:

> *Unit Director's Comment:* His progress has been fair. He shines in swimming and sailing. He is a boy who needs plenty of encouragement which he is now getting. . . .
>
> *Tent Counselor's Comment:* Bob is erratic. At times he is as good as any boy in the tent group, but at other times he is quite diffident. Always obedient, he has a tendency to do only what he thinks is expected of him. . . .[7]

He was the gentlest and shyest in the roaring family, the least articulate orally and the least coordinated physically, the most conscientious and the most dutiful. "While they all knew what was expected of them," his mother recalled, "Bobby really worked at it."[8] Punctuality was much emphasized by the elder Kennedys. Once when Bobby was four, rushing to be on time for dinner, he careened into a heavy glass door and gashed his head. Something like this was always happening. Joseph Kennedy to Joe Jr. in 1937:

> A boy threw some hot tar at Bobby and struck him in the eye. Through the grace of God, he has not lost the sight of his eye and will probably come out of it all right but it was a very narrow escape.[9]

"What I remember most vividly about growing up," Robert Kennedy told Jack Newfield in later years, "was going to a lot of different schools, always having to make new friends, and that I was very awkward. I dropped things and fell down all the time. I had to go to the hospital a few times for stitches in my head and my leg. And I was pretty quiet most of the time. And I didn't mind being alone."[10]

He kept rushing. He always had to prove himself. Nothing was easy for him. Slow in swimming, he threw himself off a yawl into Nantucket Sound as if determined to learn all at once or to drown. His brother Joe pulled him out. "It showed," John Kennedy observed, "either a lot of guts or no sense at all, depending on how you looked at it."[11] "I was," Robert said, "the seventh of nine children, and when you come from that far down you have to struggle to survive."[12] Struggle was the answer to the fear of inadequacy—struggle to fight his way, through sheer drive and nerve, into his father's attention and respect.

II

Early in 1937, Joseph Kennedy returned to Washington as chairman of the Maritime Commission. Roosevelt had other reasons, besides his desire for a strong executive in a tough job, to want Kennedy in the administration. The New Deal desperately needed friends in the business community. Kennedy was ready to tell businessmen at the New York Economic Club to "stop bellyaching." He faithfully backed Roosevelt's plan to enlarge the Supreme Court.[13]

Knowing how cordially most Harvard graduates detested Franklin D. Roosevelt, '04, the President must particularly have appreciated Kennedy's loyalty in telling Harvard '12, at the twenty-fifth class reunion in 1937, that big government "is not *foisted* on us by politicians. It has *grown* upon us because certain things have to be done which no one but government can do." If businessmen were disturbed by sit-down strikes and "bloody warfare at the factory gates," Kennedy said they should realize they were "reaping the whirlwind of a quarter century mishandling of labor relations. We complain about the lack of responsibility of labor and for years we did our best to render labor organizations impotent." Kennedy concluded by telling the anti-New Deal conclave that he could frankly see "nothing which justifies the hate and the despair which are all around."[14] Kennedy's classmates booed and jeered him.[15] He never went to a class reunion again. Still he remained, in an administration under mounting business attack, a precious symbol.

As Kennedy was a Roosevelt ambassador to the business community, so he was a Roosevelt ambassador to the Catholic Church. In the early thirties he had tried to keep Father Coughlin, the radio priest from Detroit, on the New Deal reservation. When Cardinal Pacelli (later Pope Pius XII) visited the United States in 1936, Kennedy arranged a luncheon for him with Roosevelt at Hyde Park and later had him to a family tea at Bronxville.[16] All this was quite nontheological. Kennedy did mention Leo XIII's encyclical "The Condition of the Working Classes" in *I'm for Roosevelt*. But he had no particular contact with those Catholic New Dealers, like Father John A. Ryan, who labored in the spirit of *De Rerum Novarum*.[17] Nor was a man who cheerfully sent his wife and a couple of children to godless Russia hewing to the Vatican's political line.

Roosevelt liked Kennedy, liked Rose Kennedy even more and was touched by Kennedy's preoccupation with his family. James A. Farley, it is true, claimed that Roosevelt "never liked" Kennedy.[18] But Farley, who felt snubbed by the Roosevelts, may have concluded that Roosevelt was socially opposed to all Irish Catholics. In fact, the Kennedys, unlike the Farleys, came often to the White House, and, what was more unusual, Roosevelt went on occasion to Kennedy's house along the Potomac, which he would never have done had he not counted on a good time. Morgenthau and Harold Ickes also noted with satisfaction Roosevelt's complaints that he always had to hold Joe Kennedy's hand.[19] But Roosevelt spent a great deal of time holding Morgenthau's and Ickes's hands too. His remark about Kennedy was among other things a warning, evidently too subtle, to them.

"I always think of the Roosevelts with great affection, as they all were very gracious to us as a family," Rose Kennedy wrote in a personal memorandum circa 1940. "The President had more charm than any man I ever met." A family that had no tolerance for self-pity could not but admire FDR's refusal to admit pain.

> There must have been times when the braces seemed insupportable, and his limbs ached, but still he would keep smiling. The only indication of suffering was in the stronger determination of that jaw. I recall the Review of the Fleet. We went to the house in New York to meet the President, and went to the pier where we were to board the President's yacht. . . . Amidst horns blowing and special police, we arrived at the pier which he slowly traversed amidst shouting applauding audiences still smiling and beaming. He again crossed a ramp onto the yacht and went above deck. Then, for a fleeting second, I caught a glimpse of him sinking exhausted into a chair saying, "For God's sake let's take off these darn braces."[20]

III

The Maritime Commission was a demanding job. But Kennedy found time to keep his eye on other matters. At the Securities and Exchange Commission he had struck up unexpected friendships with two young

New Deal lawyers—James M. Landis of the Harvard Law School, who was a fellow commissioner, and William O. Douglas of the Yale Law School, whom he had brought down to head a study of corporate reorganization. After getting Roosevelt to appoint Landis his successor as chairman in 1935, Kennedy had got him to appoint Douglas to the SEC in 1936. Now his New Deal protégés had fallen out. Landis, scheduled to return to Cambridge in September 1937 as dean of the Harvard Law School, resolved to stay in the job long enough to keep the more radical Douglas, who had been named dean of the Yale Law School, from becoming the next chairman. Since Yale opened earlier than Harvard, Douglas thought he had lost. Two hours before the last train to New Haven, Kennedy told Douglas to expect a call from the White House; he had just left FDR, Kennedy said, and everything was back on the track. In a moment the President was on the phone to Douglas: "Unpack your bag—you are the new chairman." "If I had gone back to Yale," Douglas later wrote, "I . . . would not have been appointed to the [Supreme] Court."[21]

The episode illustrates something of Kennedy's complexity. He deeply liked both Landis and Douglas. They were outsiders too—one a missionary's son, born in Japan; the other, a kid from the wrong side of the tracks in Yakima, Washington. Both were men of impressive ability and fidelity. On the issues that now divided them, Douglas's position was probably, on the merits, less acceptable to Kennedy. Yet, as Kennedy had been loyal to Landis in 1935, so he was determined to be loyal to Douglas in 1937. He remained close to the able and taciturn Landis, but something especially delighted him about Douglas, with whom he shared a bluntness of speech, a skepticism about motives and an expansive scorn for the eastern establishment. Douglas had been five years old when his father died; and Kennedy, though only ten years his senior, filled a vacancy in his life. "Our friendship grew," Douglas later wrote, "until . . . we were almost father and son."[22]

As his work on the Maritime Commission drew to an end, Kennedy could well expect a higher and better assignment. He still wanted the Treasury. This was impossible. Morgenthau had tried to carry out New Deal policies in every respect, Roosevelt told Farley in 1938, while "Joe would want to run the Treasury in his own way, contrary to my plans and views." Declaring himself "thoroughly dissatisfied" with Daniel C. Roper, the Secretary of Commerce, Roosevelt said that this was the spot for Kennedy.[23] But Robert W. Bingham, the ambassador to England, was in poor health, and the

Kennedys, Rose too, set their hearts on London. This ambition, Arthur Krock said, "was made known emphatically to the President."[24] FDR admired Kennedy's administrative ability, knew he could afford the post and was doubtless diverted by the idea of sending a Massachusetts Irishman to the Court of St. James's.

"The most thrilling, exciting, and interesting years of my life," Rose Kennedy wrote later, "were the ones I spent in London when Joe was Ambassador."[25] The mother and five children embarked on the *Manhattan* in March 1938. "The most tender parting," the Associated Press reported, "was that of Bobby and his Bronxville pal, Francis Deignan. They discussed schemes for raising $300 to get Francis to London and told each other solemnly, 'I'll write to you.'" As the ship prepared to sail, Robert launched a handmade parachute through the porthole in his stateroom.[26]

The family was soon established in the ambassadorial residence in Prince's Gate near Kensington Gardens. Felix Frankfurter wrote the new ambassador that his Massachusetts predecessors at the Court of St. James's, John Adams and Charles Francis Adams, had used their sons as personal assistants.[27] Encouraged by such weighty Yankee precedent, Joseph Kennedy put Joe Jr. on the embassy staff; John too, when he was in London on holiday. As always, the father was pushing his sons to move out on their own. Joe went to Czechoslovakia during the Munich crisis and to Spain in the last months of the Civil War, John to Czechoslovakia at the time of the German invasion in March 1939. "We were furious," George Kennan recalls, when the Prague embassy received word of John Kennedy's arrival on a fact-finding mission. "Joe Kennedy was not exactly known as a friend of the career service. . . . His son had no official status and was, in our eyes, obviously an upstart and an ignoramus. . . . That busy people should have their time taken up arranging his tour struck us as outrageous."[28]

Kathleen helped her mother deal with London society. Her younger sisters were distributed among local convents. The smaller boys went to Gibbs, a day school where Robert, now thirteen, did well in mathematics, poorly in Latin, which he finally dropped, and the best he could in cricket and rugby.[29] He also discharged occasional diplomatic tasks, such as laying a foundation stone at a newsboys' club. Here he delivered "a piece of oratory" that the clergyman who ran the club described improbably as "magnificent in its diction and delivery."[30]

Everyone adored the Kennedys in 1938, from the ambassador

down. "His language," wrote the columnists Joseph Alsop and Robert Kintner that year, "is a cheerful torrent of profanity and picturesque expression. No one is better, or more ebullient company. Because he is rich, because he plays at being a rough diamond, because he is clever and because his brood of nine handsome children fascinate and astonish the British . . . he has been a vast success."[31] Harold Caccia of the Foreign Office noted that Kennedy had proved "he possesses every quality necessary for the success of his mission."[32]

Over Christmas, with her husband back in America, Rose took the children to St. Moritz. "Everybody had a wonderful time," Eddie Moore wrote back to the United States. The Kennedys had a special notion of a wonderful time. ". . . Fortunately [young] Joe's accident didn't amount to much, but it was necessary to have six stitches taken in his elbow, but while it kept him off the skis for three days, he skated in the meantime. Bobby didn't have any accident, but Teddy wrenched his knee."[33]

"Rose, this is a helluva long way from East Boston," the ambassador had said in the spring when they were spending a weekend with the royal family at Windsor Castle.[34] Indeed it was. "The children and I saw the Old Year out here at St. Moritz," Rose Kennedy wrote Franklin Roosevelt, "and we thought of all the interesting and stimulating experiences which we had enjoyed during 1938 . . . made possible through the honor which you had conferred upon Joe. And so we want to thank you again for 1938, and we want you to know that we are hoping and praying that you may enjoy every happiness in the New Year of 1939."[35]

IV

Nineteen thirty-nine did not turn out to be a year of much happiness for anyone. When he appointed Kennedy, Roosevelt seems not to have talked to him at length about Hitler. The President doubtless supposed that Kennedy would give the same generally loyal support in foreign policy he had given the New Deal at home. He was sure that Kennedy, as a good Irishman, would be ethnically immune to the blandishments of the Chamberlain government. And it was probably the case that Kennedy himself had no clear ideas about foreign affairs when he set forth for London.

The new ambassador had, however, one profound emotion—a dread of war. As a businessman, he believed that prosperity required a peaceful world. As a capitalist, he feared that war would lead to socialism; "a return even to our modified capitalism of today will hardly be feasible."[36] Above all, as a father, he could not bear the thought of his own sons going to war. When Hitler intensified his pressure on Czechoslovakia in the summer of 1938, Kennedy proposed saying in a speech, "I should like to ask you all if you know of any dispute or controversy existing in the world which is worth the life of your son, or of anyone else's son." Secretary of State Cordell Hull vetoed the thought.[37]

Kennedy found himself in chronic contention with the State Department. And, contrary to Roosevelt's expectations, Kennedy and Neville Chamberlain hit it off famously. "I can talk Chamberlain's language," Kennedy bragged to Hull.[38] (Rose Kennedy liked the Prime Minister too; he charmed her by remarking that he had married his wife "because she had made good treacle.")[39] Soon Walter Lippmann was warning Kennedy that he was showing "some of the same symptoms which have appeared in every American ambassador [to London] I have known since Walter Hines Page, namely the tendency . . . to be taken into camp by the government and the governing class."[40] "Who would have thought that the English could take into camp a red-headed Irishman?" Roosevelt said to Morgenthau. "Joe has been taken in by the British government people and the royal family," he told Farley.[41] This reading did Kennedy an injustice. His dread of war was leading him to a general view of America's role in the world—a view he advocated honestly and stubbornly at the cost of his political career and held for the rest of his life.

On Trafalgar Day in October 1938, a month after Chamberlain returned from Munich, Kennedy spoke again, this time eluding Hull's blue pencil by presenting his view as only "a pet theory of my own," not a policy of his government. "It has long been a theory of mine," he said,

> that it is unproductive for both the democratic and dictator countries to widen the division now existing between them by emphasizing their differences, which are now self-apparent. . . . There is simply no sense, common or otherwise, in letting these differences grow into unrelenting antagonisms. After all, we have to live together in the same world, whether we like it or not.[42]

In the nuclear age these propositions would be considered defensible if not inevitable. In the age of Hitler they aroused alarm and outrage. "It must be," wrote the columnist Heywood Broun, "that the

British have some secret drug which they slip into the tea of visiting celebrities. And in the case of our Ambassadors they give them double dosage." After all, Broun continued, Kennedy had come "from a ward where the kids are taught to twist the lion's tail even before they learn to roll their hoops." But he "has drunk the draught which makes the eagle cease to flap and induces it to lie down with the lion. Even his extensive and charming family has proved insufficient bodyguard."[43] Roosevelt tacitly disclaimed Kennedy's Trafalgar Day speech by saying a week later in a speech of his own that "peace by fear" had "no higher or more enduring quality than peace by the sword. . . . There can be no peace if national policy adopts as a deliberate instrument the threat of war."[44]

Kennedy's pessimism grew in 1939. If war came, he was sure that England and France would lose. At times, he was also sure that America would ultimately be dragged in.[45] At other times he thought it "nonsense to say that an Axis victory spells ruin for us"; America depended very little on foreign markets and could survive as "an intelligent self-contained national economy."[46] At still other times, he feared that an Axis victory would leave America "alone in a jealous and hostile world" where the "cost of maintaining 'splendid isolation' would be such as to bring about the destruction of all those values which the isolation policy had been designed to preserve."[47] His vacillations disabled him from developing a clear line of his own and prevented his differences with Washington from becoming impassable.

New Deal interventionists, however, became increasingly unhappy. Harold Ickes fed Roosevelt gossip about Kennedy's association with the Cliveden set, his disloyalty to the President, his own presidential ambitions. But Roosevelt, who was receiving ardently pro-allied messages from Bullitt in Paris, evidently saw value in hearing something different from London. In late August 1939, Ickes noted disappointedly in his diary, "The President said that Kennedy was as good as anyone in reporting carefully what was transpiring in England and in diplomatic circles and he gave no indication that he had an intention of removing him."[48]

The Soviet-Nazi Pact was announced on August 23. On September 1 Hitler invaded Poland. Telephoning the President to describe Chamberlain's speech declaring war on Germany, a distraught Kennedy cried, "It's the end of the world, the end of everything."[49]

V

"My family gets smaller and smaller," Kennedy wrote his wife in September 1939. Joe Jr. had sailed on the *Mauretania;* John was about to fly on the Clipper. Their father's letter showed his confusion of emotion:

> I think just as strong as ever that if England has a chance to make an honorable peace she had better do it. . . .
> If by any chance USA doesn't change present neutrality law then the position of the French and of British I think will be nothing short of disastrous. . . .
> I talk to Bullitt occasionally. He is more rattle brained than ever. His judgment is pathetic and I am afraid of his influence on F.D.R. because they think alike on many things.

He concluded that, with all the family safe in America, "I have no worries. I will miss you terribly but . . . with the state of the world I doubt if I could be happy in business. . . . This position at the minute is probably the most interesting and exciting in the world."[50]

Back in the United States, the children dispersed to boarding schools and convents. It appeared time for Robert, now almost fourteen, to go away. Exercising his paternal preference for secular education, Joseph Kennedy had enrolled him at St. Paul's in Concord, New Hampshire. But St. Paul's turned out not to be all that secular; and its unremitting Episcopalianism was too much for Rose. "The Protestant Bible was read at different times in the school," she later explained. "It was for this reason that I withdrew Bobby."[51] The ambassador cabled from London, BY ALL MEANS PUT BOBBY IN RIVERDALE IF YOU ARE MORE COMFORTABLE.[52] However, Rose Kennedy took advantage of her husband's absence to send Robert to Portsmouth Priory, a sound Benedictine school near Newport, Rhode Island, with morning and evening prayers, mass three times a week and high mass on Sundays.

The Priory more than made up for St. Paul's. "I just got out of about 3 hours of praying in Chapel," Robert wrote his parents at one point, "and so feel like a saint. Our retreat starts Thursday so I'm certainly going to be doing a lot of praying this week."[53] He became acquainted too with the liabilities of the faith. "I got another one of those post cards," he wrote his mother, "telling me like the last one how awful we Catholics are."[54] There were extracurricular excitements. He had hardly arrived at the school when a Boston newspaper reported: "Robert Kennedy, 13 year old son of Ambassador Joseph P. Kennedy, shared hero honors with a girl telephone operator, as fire destroyed the gymnasium at Portsmouth Priory."[55]

He did not distinguish himself in the classroom. "I guess it was because I wasn't studying as hard as I should have that I got such bad marks,"[56] he wrote his parents manfully. By February 1941 mathematics was his best subject. His worst grades were in history (60) and Christian doctrine (64).[57] Where his father had bombarded Joe and John with counsel and reprimand, he was now across the Atlantic and, perhaps, less interested. The letters of admonition came from Rose Kennedy, who was particularly concerned that Robert read more books. His replies provided exculpatory lists:

> I've read the following books
>   Finished "The Crisis"
>   Read "The Hurricane"
>   Reading "Men Against the Sea." . . .
> I'm reading "Berlin Diary" now . . . really a neat book.[58]

In the spring of 1940, the associate headmaster, thanking the ambassador for his contribution to the fund for a new gymnasium, added that Bobby was getting along better. "He is doing fairly well in his studies, and this Term has been playing on the Junior Basketball Squad. He seems to have settled down and appears happy."[59] A year later: "Bob's habit of not being neat is receiving considerable attention from all of his masters."[60]

Sports were his consuming interest. He tried his awkward hardest in school competitions:

> I haven't got a chance for the [football] team but I'll try and stay on the squad.[61]

> I don't play hockey very well but I've gotten much better since I started this year. There was one cut in the squad but I was lucky enough to stay on.[62]

He finally did succeed in becoming manager of the hockey team "which ought to be a lot of fun though I have to type all the letters I write to different schools because my writing is so bad."[63] His triumph was in sailing where he became vice commodore of the yacht club, in charge of racing.

His mother hoped for social graces and wanted to send him to dancing school in Providence. "Mother," Robert wrote back, "I don't think it would be worth going way up to Providence for dancing as it is quite far away and I wouldn't be able to play hockey and on most of the days I would probably miss study."[64] He won that one. In May 1941, Teddy was deposited at the Priory, though he was much younger than most of the students. He remembers complaining to his older brother that the bigger boys were picking on him. "You'll just have to look out for yourself," Bobby said crossly.[65] So three years passed without Robert Kennedy's making much impression on the school or the school on him.

VI

The first year of the European war was a lonely time for Joseph Kennedy—lonely and bitter. Returning to America for a visit in December 1939, he told a group in Boston, "This is not our fight."[66] The only victor, he predicted to a meeting of Army and Navy officers in Washington, would be communism.[67] He was appalled by the war, tired of being ambassador, homesick for his family. He spilled over to Robert Murphy, the counselor of the Paris embassy, about "his bad health, his discontent over returning to London, his belief that everything he could do there could just as well be done by a $50-a-month clerk, that he wanted to quit but didn't see how he gracefully could before the elections. He said the United States would be crazy to go into the war."[68]

As Kennedy talked in his indiscreet way, knowledge of his views spread around London. His popularity crumbled away. Harold Nicolson, in a blast relayed by Edward R. Murrow to the United States over CBS, wrote that Kennedy's return from his American visit was welcomed mainly by "the friends of Herr von Ribbentrop, the Nürembergers, the Munichois and the *disjecta membra* of former pro-Nazi organizations."[69] Most American newspapermen in London were pro-British and now had little use for their ambassador. His own military attaché, General Raymond E. Lee, wrote in his journal about his boss's "suave, toothy and inane grin" and found him "crude, blatant, and ignorant in everything he did or said."[70]

Sir Robert Vansittart, permanent head of the Foreign Office, had come to detest him. "Mr. Kennedy is a very foul specimen of double crosser and defeatist," he told the Foreign Secretary. "He thinks of nothing but his own pocket. I hope that this war will at least see the elimination of this type."[71] The head of the American desk pronounced him "malevolent and pigeon-livered."[72] The Foreign Office described Kennedy's "defeatist attitude" to Lord Lothian, the British ambassador in Washington, "in case it should later become necessary to ask you to drop a hint in the proper quarter." The British may even have considered declaring Kennedy persona non grata. In any event the Foreign Office resolved to minimize contact with him. When Churchill took over as Prime Minister in May, both governments felt that the American embassy in London had become an "undesirable channel."[73]

"You would be surprised how much anti-American [the English] have become," Kennedy had written his wife in March. ". . . I feel it strongly against me. . . . If the war gets worse which I am still convinced it will . . . I am sure they will all hate us more."[74] "Joe dear," Rose Kennedy wrote back with sublime tact, "I have a definite idea that it would be a wonderful feat if you could put over the idea that altho you are against America's entering the war—still you are encouraging help to England in some way. [Most Americans would be sympathetic,] and it would endear you to the hearts of the British."[75] "It is easy enough to say we should do something," Kennedy replied, "but the real difficulty is—what? My sympathies are completely with the Allies, but they must not run away with my judgment of what can happen to the United States. We may have to fight Hitler at some later date over South America, but we had better do it in our own backyard where we will be effective and not weaken ourselves by trying to carry on a fight over here." And a scrawled postscript: "Its Hell to be here without all of you. . . . I get news that you are more beautiful than ever. Maybe you do better away from me. All my love."[76]

He used the better-fight-in-our-own-backyard argument in cables to Washington. "The President and I were asking each other the same question," Cordell Hull later observed, "but we reached a different conclusion. . . . It seemed to us we should do better to keep the fighting away from our own back yard."[77] Kennedy's compulsive gloom was isolating him from Washington almost as much as it had already isolated him in London. "When real world forces come into conflict," Roosevelt wrote him in early May, trying to cheer him up, "the final result is never as dark as we mortals guess it in very difficult days."[78] It was to no avail.

VII

In May 1940 the Nazi armies swept into the Low Countries and France. On May 20 Kennedy sent his wife an urgent hand-written letter:

Rose darling,

> . . . The situation is terrible . . . I think the jig is up. The situation is more than critical. It means a terrible finish for the Allies. . . . The English will fight to the end but I just don't think they can stand up to the bombing indefinitely. What will happen then is probably a dictated peace with Hitler probably getting the British Navy, and we will find ourselves in a terrible mess.
>
> My God how right I've been in my predictions. I wish I'd been wrong. Well darling its certainly been a great adventure. . . . I'll probably be home sooner than we thought.[79]

The only hope, he believed, was a negotiated peace. The English, he told Hull, "have not demonstrated one thing that would justify us in assuming any kind of partnership with them."[80]

Rose tried to divert him with news of the children. John Kennedy's book *Why England Slept* was out:

> Jack has certainly had the most astounding success. . . . Bobby is a different mold. He does not seem to be interested particularly in reading or sailing or his stamps. He does a little work in all three, but no special enthusiasm. He does follow the war news with interest and is reading "The Failure of a Mission." [Summer 1940]

> I am trying to get Bob to do some reading. He doesn't seem to care for sailing as much as the other boys. Of course he doesn't want to go to any of the dances. [July 11]

> Bobby has had a few boils and so it has held up his swimming a little. It is funny that he should have them this time of year, the same as Joe. We once thought it was from eating corn, but these days we do not have any corn. [August 9][81]

She made a family recording for her husband's fifty-second birthday. "I have played it at least twenty times already," Kennedy wrote. "I can't say that any of my children's voices have improved in tone quality . . . but there is still plenty of pep in the sound."[82]

Not even the children distracted him for long. "I wonder," he said in the same letter, "what satisfaction any living person can be getting out of believing that this war will accomplish any of the things they thought it would accomplish. The so-called fight for Democracy and for liberty will enslave every nation in the world, and leave them nothing of either Democracy or Liberty. . . . I get sick to my stomach when I listen to all the drivel that is being poured out to the American public."[83]

The sourness of these days roused Kennedy's concern about Jewish pressure to keep the war going. It was a concern he shared with Neville Chamberlain. After the British guarantee to Poland, so Kennedy told Herbert Hoover in later years, Chamberlain had said to him that "he hoped the Americans and the Jews would now be satisfied but that he (Chamberlain) felt that he had signed the doom of civilization."[84] Kennedy later wrote in a draft autobiography that "a number of Jewish publishers and writers" assailed him after the Trafalgar Day speech. They wanted war, he thought. "They should not be condemned for such an objective. After all, the lives and fortunes of their compatriots were being destroyed by Hitler. Compromise could hardly cure that situation; only the destruction of Nazism could do so. . . . [But] they did not hesitate to resort to slander and falsehood to achieve their aims. . . . I was hardly prepared . . . for the full viciousness of this onslaught."[85]

On the other hand, he attacked religious persecution in the fascist states. He called the anti-Semitic outrages of November 1938 "the most terrible things I have ever heard of." He busied himself with schemes for the rescue of Jewish refugees to an extent that led the Arab National League of Boston to call him a "Zionist Charlie McCarthy."[86] Nor was he at all anti-Jewish in individual relations. In Palm Beach he played golf at a predominantly Jewish country club. "One of his most constant riding companions and closest collaborators in the Embassy," noted D. W. Brogan, who knew more about America than any other Briton, "was a Jew whose career in the Department was not helped by this part of his record."[87] Still, the ambassador's fear of war now moved him for a moment to speak of Jews collectively as a menacing influence.

By the autumn of 1940, Kennedy wanted to come home. Angry at being left out when Roosevelt and Churchill negotiated the exchange of overage American destroyers for British bases in the Western Hemisphere, Kennedy wired Hull that he did not enjoy being a dummy and threatened resignation. Roosevelt, handholding again, replied, "You are not only not a dummy but are essential to all of us both in the Government and in the Nation."[88]

The question arises why Roosevelt wished to keep so disaffected an ambassador in London. The answer lay in domestic politics. Nineteen forty was an election year. Knowing Kennedy's influence among businessmen and Catholics and the weight his London experience would give his criticisms of the administration's foreign policy, Roosevelt reckoned he would cause less trouble in England than in America.* Unless, that is, he came back as part of the campaign; but

* See Alsop and Kintner in the *Boston Globe*, October 7, 1940: "The President regards Kennedy as likely to do less harm in London than in New York. . . . The President has repeatedly urged him to remain in London in order to keep him quiet."

The Father

when FDR, at the suggestion of James F. Byrnes, offered Kennedy the national chairmanship after the resignation of James A. Farley (for whom Joseph P. Kennedy, Jr., had cast his delegate's vote at the Democratic convention), Kennedy declined.[89]

Kennedy—"primed," said General Lee, "for a vindictive and vigorous assault upon Roosevelt"—was determined to get back before the election.[90] The State Department put him off. In October, Kennedy (or so he later told his friend Krock) phoned Sumner Welles, the under secretary, to complain that he had been ignored for three months. He had sent a full account of his treatment to his office in New York, he continued, with instructions to release the story if he were not back in the United States by a specified date. The administration capitulated but took protective action. Roosevelt invited the Kennedys to spend the night at the White House, and Rose Kennedy met her husband at the airport to escort him to Washington. "The President sent you, a Roman Catholic, as Ambassador to London, which probably no other President would have done," she told him. ". . . You would write yourself down an ingrate in the view of many people if you resign now."[91]

When they arrived at the White House, they found the President at his desk, "shaking a cocktail shaker," Rose Kennedy recorded, "and reaching over for a few lumps of ice with his powerful hands." Senator Byrnes and his wife were there along with Marguerite LeHand, the President's secretary. After dinner, "Joe did most of the talking. The President looked rather pale, rather ashen, and I always noticed the nervous habit he had of nervously snapping his eyes."[92] FDR might well have been nervous. Joe Kennedy, as Byrnes noted, was "a forceful talker, and in his vocabulary are many words not found in dictionaries." He used them that night to denounce the humiliations inflicted on him by the State Department. Roosevelt was sympathetic, obliged by denouncing the Department himself and by the end of the evening had talked Kennedy around to making a radio speech advocating his reelection.[93] For all Kennedy's inner misgivings about its theme, his speech was accounted one of the most effective in the campaign. The day after Roosevelt won his third term Kennedy called at the White House and submitted his resignation.

VIII

A few days later in Boston, in an impassioned rush of words before a couple of newspapermen, Kennedy said, "I'm willing to spend all I've got to keep us out of the war." Democracy was "finished in England.

It may be here." For the moment, "aid England as far as we can; that's our game. As long as she can hold out, give her what it takes . . . and don't expect anything back." But stay out of the war: "I know more about the European situation than anybody else, and it's up to me to see that the country gets it."[94] He carried his campaign to the west coast; returning to New York later in the month, he called on Herbert Hoover, whom he had opposed so energetically in 1932. Now a common fear of war brought them together. He told the former President, as Hoover later recorded it, "that if we went into the war, we would have a National Socialist state—he could see no return to democratic forms."* Kennedy also saw Charles A. Lindbergh, whose terrifying estimates of German air power had impressed him during the Munich crisis, and told him that the "best possible thing" for the British "would be a negotiated peace."[95]

Lindbergh was emerging as a leading spokesman for the passionately isolationist America First Committee; and attempts were made to enlist Kennedy. Kennedy kept away. Lindbergh's wartime journals report no further meeting. Kennedy was unwilling to take an irrevocable anti-Roosevelt, anti-Britain line. "I hope to God England wins," he summed up his position to a friend, "but I'm not willing to sacrifice everything we have left here to see it done, and that is what war would do to us."[96] He therefore continued both to support military aid and to oppose military intervention.

This complicated his life when the lend-lease bill came up early in 1941. In a radio speech he simultaneously disclaimed the bill and advocated further aid to England. Robert Kennedy telegraphed his father from Portsmouth Priory, "Your speech was absolutely marvelous."[97] He wrote his mother, "I think it was the best speech that he ever made. I thought he really cleared himself from what people have been calling him and what he said about the President's bill will certainly change a lot of people's minds."[98] The columnist Dorothy Thompson, less sympathetic, said that Joseph Kennedy had out-

* As for England, Kennedy said he had warned Roosevelt that aid to Britain was "a bet on a losing horse." The previous September, Kennedy told Hoover, Hitler had offered England peace through Sweden, guaranteeing the empire and the fleet. "Why didn't the British accept?" asked Hoover. "Nothing but Churchill's bullheadedness," said Kennedy; Churchill was "an entirely bellicose character" (Herbert Hoover, memorandum, November 22, 1940, Hoover Papers). Kennedy was probably referring to an approach through the president of the High Court of Sweden to the British minister in Stockholm at the request of Ludwig Weissauer, a Berlin lawyer who claimed to be an emissary of Hitler's.

The Father

Hamleted Hamlet: Instead of "to be or not to be," it was "to be *and* not to be."[99]

There was more of Hamlet when he testified on lend-lease before the House Foreign Affairs Committee. He criticized the bill "in its present form" on constitutional grounds because it involved the surrender of too much power by Congress to the Presidency, but went on to insist that he trusted this President, hated Nazism, supported aid to Great Britain short of war, was not an isolationist and even would favor the bill if Congress passed it.[100] Years later Robert claimed that his father "tipped the balance in favor of Lend-Lease" within the committee. "The America Firsters thereafter called him worse names than any the liberals have ever had for him."[101] This was an overstatement, but Kennedy's testimony did the bill no harm and honestly represented his own mixture of feelings.

What was consistent was his pessimism. "The death and destruction of everything we stand for is inevitable," he told the editors of *Collier's* in a characteristic outburst. "We'll get hell for saying this but that's what is going to happen to us. I have seen many a fellow in the stock market lose his fortune because he was right too soon, but it is true. . . . I think our way of life is finished—it is merely a question of what we can save for ourselves."[102] Disaster was coming, it appeared, whether England won or lost the war, whether America went in or stayed out; but it would be most certain and lasting if America went in.

By the spring of 1941 he had decided to give up the Bronxville house and settle in Palm Beach, maintaining his summer (and voting) residence in Hyannis Port. "I've been in New York for about eleven years," he explained, "and I haven't averaged two months a year there. In addition to that I think the day is gone when a man can maintain three houses. . . . With the economic and financial outlook as I visualize it a man will have all he can do to have one house."[103] He even had doubts about Palm Beach. Frank Waldrop, editor of the isolationist *Washington Times-Herald,* recalls Kennedy pointing at breaks in the sea wall and saying he wasn't going to fix the goddamn thing. Let it go. The whole world was falling apart, so why should he bother with a goddamn house in Palm Beach.[104] "I'm so terribly pessimistic about the outlook for us," he wrote a Boston friend in April 1941, "and yet realize that there's no constructive suggestion that I could make that would have the slightest chance of being accepted in Washington, that I just think I'd better keep my mouth shut."[105]

He did open his mouth the next month in a commencement address at Oglethorpe University. Here he reaffirmed his support of the policy "the overwhelming majority of our people have approved . . . to rearm as swiftly as possible, to give every possible aid to Great Britain, but to stay out of war." He condemned Nazism as the "new paganism" but scoffed at the idea that America was in danger of attack or that an Axis victory "spells ruin for us." Nothing could spell more ruin than war. He demanded on the part of the American government "the freest debate" and "the fullest disclosure." To all this he added a new theme—an attack on the idea of a military crusade for democracy.

> Democracy cannot be imposed by force or otherwise. It would not last even if we were able to present [other nations] with the most up-to-date constitutional system. In our very attempt at this colossal crusade we would end in failure and disgrace abroad, in disillusionment and bankruptcy at home.

The United States must not overestimate its power to decide the destiny of other nations.

> We cannot, my fellow Americans, divert the tides of the mighty revolution now sweeping Asia and Europe. They were not of our making and they will not be subject to our control, no matter how courageously or exhaustingly we strive to subject them.

Let us forswear ringing phrases, Kennedy said, and concentrate on the struggle for justice in our own society. "When the history of these times has been written, I hope and pray it will show that the American lads of 1941 did not pave the way for a radical change by fostering class antagonism . . . and that they realized and took vigorous steps to spread the gospel of equality."[106]

Interventionists bitterly criticized the speech. Three days later Roosevelt proclaimed a state of national emergency. In another few days at Notre Dame, Kennedy, observing darkly that "there is much in our Western civilization that does not deserve to survive" (he specified monopolistic capitalism and racketeering unionism), went on to say that the presidential proclamation deserved the "unlimited loyalty" of all Americans.[107] After the Nazi invasion of Russia on June 22, Hoover asked Kennedy to join with him, Alfred M. Landon, Robert M. Hutchins and others in a new manifesto against intervention. The western decision to aid Russia, the proposed statement began, made it "abundantly clear that this war is not a world conflict between tyranny and freedom." American entry into the war was "far more likely to destroy democracy in this country" than to establish democracy in Europe and Asia. Kennedy replied evasively. Hoover kept pressing him. Kennedy finally wired bluntly: I MUCH PREFER TO GO MY WAY ALONE. I CAN THEN TAKE MY POSITION ON ANY SUBJECT AND AT ANY TIME AS THE OCCASION DEMANDS WITHOUT CONSULTATION WITH ANYONE.[108]

IX

His older sons, each in his own style, adopted their father's position on the war. Joe Jr. now at Harvard Law School, was the activist. "As a member of the Harvard Committee against Marital [sic] Intervention," he wrote in January 1941 to John T. Flynn, a leading America Firster, "I want to extend an invitation to you. . . ."[109] A few weeks later he took the platform himself as a member of College Men for Defense First in a meeting in Washington; Senator Robert A. Taft was the main speaker.[110]

John Kennedy as usual remained detached. He intended to go to law school, his father wrote James Landis from London, "although he thought he would go to Yale, principally because he feels it would be better not to be constantly in direct competition with his brother, and I rather sympathize with him in that point of view. However, Jack has been having trouble for a number of years with his stomach and I now hear that the doctors advise him to take a year off."[111] *Why England Slept* was a singularly dispassionate statement to be flung into America's most passionate foreign policy debate of the century—so dispassionate, indeed, that it was impossible to conclude from the text whether the author was an interventionist or an isolationist. "I of course don't want to take sides too much," he had told his father.[112] "If Britain is defeated," he wrote in the book, ". . . we shall be at a definite disadvantage" in a world of dictatorships; but "we may be able to survive." If Britain wins, "we must be prepared to take our part in setting up a world order that will prevent the rise of a militaristic dictatorship."[113] The second brother was already finding a distinctive voice. The bit about setting up a world order was hardly in the paternal line. But his father cared less what his son had written in his book than that he had written a book at all, and a successful one at that.* On balance John Kennedy leaned toward the isolationist side in the great debate.

---

* After reading the honors essay submitted to the Harvard government department, Joseph Kennedy relayed to his son the report that "one or two of those who have

Still, whatever their hope that America could avoid involvement, the Kennedys were strong advocates of preparedness. Early in 1941 Joe Jr. decided to enlist. "I think," he wrote his father, "in that Jack is not doing anything, and with your stand on the war, that people will wonder what the devil I am doing back at school with everyone else working for national defense." Jack was not to be left behind. His father sought the assistance of Captain Alan Kirk, who had been his naval attaché in London and was now director of the Office of Naval Intelligence; and Kirk somehow contrived to spirit John Kennedy past the Navy's stringent physical standards.[114] When the Japanese struck on December 7, the oldest Kennedy sons were both in naval training.

---

read it complain that you have gone too far in absolving the leaders of the National Government from responsibility for the state in which England found herself at Munich" (JPK to JFK, May 20, 1940, JFK Papers). John Kennedy adopted a number of his father's suggestions when he turned the paper into a book. Joseph Kennedy subsequently wrote Landis: "He has done a fine job on the book, I understand. I saw the original manuscript, but I know he has made a great many changes since then. I have always told him that to write a book at the age of 23 that commanded respect would be of great service to him in time to come" (JPK to Landis, August 6, 1940, Landis Papers).

(3)

The War

PEARL HARBOR found Robert Kennedy, just turned sixteen, in his third year at Portsmouth Priory. The school, only a few miles from the naval base at Newport, responded quickly to the tremors of war. The headmaster decreed a blackout. "We all had to go sit in the basement for 20 minutes."[1] When the aircraft carrier *Ranger* steamed into Narragansett Bay, the boys watched planes practicing dive-bombing in the hazy distance.[2] A fortnight after the Japanese attack, Robert went to Palm Beach for Christmas. He was "just the same," Rose Kennedy reported. "He plays a very good golf game and shot a 95 the other day with me. He also astonished me by his prowess at bridge the other night. . . . But he is very unsociable. . . . He absolutely refused to go to the Bath and Tennis [Club] and when he has gone out he doesn't seem to like any of the boys here."[3] After the holiday, Robert wrote from the Priory, "I've read about 8 books since I've been back at the school, and I'm now reading 'Botany Bay' which is very good."[4] His mother passed on the word that Robert "seems to have improved very much in his desire for reading," though in her letter she cut his estimate of books read to "five or six." She added, perhaps in gentle admonition to the others, "He also sent us two or three recommendations about serving Mass."[5]

I

Robert's marks arrived. "I was so disappointed in your report," his mother wrote him with appropriate sternness.

> . . . The mark in Christian Doctrine was very low. . . . Certainly in a Catholic school you should be taught that above everything else and you should apply yourself to that subject. . . . Please get on your toes. . . . You have a good head and certainly you ought to use it. You owe it to

yourself as well as to me to make the most of your advantages. Remember, too, that it is a reflection on my brains as the boys in the family are supposed to get their intellect from their mother, and certainly I do not expect my own little pet to let me down.[6]

The Priory was not accounted a great success. Joseph Kennedy, worried that his third son was not learning enough to get into Harvard, decided to shift Robert in the autumn of 1942 to Milton Academy in Massachusetts. A new boy entering an upper form of a boarding school does not have an easy time at best. For a shy Irish Catholic boy, who had already attended six schools in ten years and was now plunged into what a Milton friend described with precision as "a consummate WASP school,"[7] it could have been an ordeal.

Robert lived in Forbes House, never complained and worked doggedly on his studies. His grades were undistinguished. His father reminded him that his mother had received honors in school. "I don't know where I got my brains," Bobby wrote back ruefully, "but its [sic] quite evident that I received them from neither my father nor my mother."[8] Mathematics was now a particular trouble. "On our last day of school," he told his father, "the math teacher made a small speech to the class in which he said that two great things had happened to him; one that Rommel was surrounded in Egypt and 2nd that Kennedy had passed a math test."[9]

When it came to public affairs, the Kennedy mealtime seminars stood him in good stead. One classmate, Samuel Adams, said later he had never met anyone his own age so well informed on international politics.[10] "We had Time's Current Events test here," Robert wrote his parents, ". . . and though I wasn't too sharp I didn't do badly, except for the questions on business and finance which I got almost entirely wrong."[11] In spite, or perhaps in consequence, of his deficiency, he insisted on finding a job in the summer of 1943. Let Clem Norton, a famous Boston character—Charlie Hennessey in Edwin O'Connor's *The Last Hurrah*—tell the story:

> At first, he wanted to go out and work on a fishing vessel. To really rough it. Asked me to have him signed on so that nobody would know who he was and would have to work just as hard as any fisherman. His ma objected and had her way saying, "Two of our boys are at the front now. This boy will have to go soon, so I want him as long as I can have him now." So young Bobby is working as a clerk at the East Boston bank where his dad started. . . . He is very punctual and very neat in the way he keeps his clothes about the room. He doesn't object to riding on the Elevated railway with common people, rather likes it.[12]

The bank job was as close to business as he ever got.

The War

His letters home were sometimes assertions in a small way of his own identity. After the Cocoanut Grove fire killed nearly five hundred people in Boston on a Saturday night in November 1942, Robert noted that if Boston College had beaten Holy Cross in football in the afternoon, the B.C. team would have celebrated at the nightclub on the fatal evening. "Losing that game," he wrote his father, "really saved their lives."[13] An unconscious protest against the eternal emphasis on winning? But he still wanted to win. Football was his chosen medium. "I am alternating first string now, but I hit my shoulder during blocking practice so I'm not sure whether I'll be able to scrimmage."[14] Football presented itself as some sort of moral test. "Bobby ran every practice play," Sam Adams said, "and tackled and blocked dummies as if he were in a hard fought game. To another sixteen-year-old kid this Gung-ho attitude seemed a little weird. But, gradually, I became aware of the characteristic of Bobby's which I admired most—his ability to ridicule himself and his efforts and still go all out."[15] He watched his own performance with dispassion. "I played in the football game against St. Marks," he wrote his father, "but I was quite nervous and so did not do very well."[16]

His contemporaries remembered particularly his shyness, his determination and his self-mocking humor. Milton had a girls' school; and, while there was no coeducation, there was social contact. "He used to walk with his head way down, buried in his neck, like a bird in a storm," recalled Mary (Piedy) Bailey, a contemporary at the girls' school. "Everything was buried, including the bones of his face. He was moon-faced then; there was no hint of the angular frame that eventually came out. . . . He mostly stood on one foot with the other toe resting on top, his hands way down in his pockets." In his second year he used to take Piedy Bailey home after chapel on Sunday night, "walking four feet behind, his head down, looking out from underneath his forelock." This was a gain. The year before he had had a consuming crush on Ann Appleton but had never dared speak to her at all. Bobby, said Piedy Bailey, "was appealing, funny, larky, separate and a little bit solitary."[17]

Sam Adams, noting the disadvantage of coming in for two years when most of the class had been there at least four, said:

> Bobby certainly tried hard. He showed absolute determination; he decided to do something, he just gave it everything he had. He wasn't staging it; he was just doing it his way. He didn't care whether people noticed he was doing it, or kidded him because he was doing it. He wasn't trying for any particular reaction from people. He just did it because that's the way he

was. He really did go absolutely all-out. Not exactly so at studies. The things he was interested in, he did go all-out.

He joined in bull sessions, but "he didn't participate too much when the conversation involved dirty jokes and that sort of thing. He was really bored to tears by that . . . also angered, although he usually didn't say much; he just sort of crawled into his shell and ignored it." He disliked the adolescent sport of ganging up on one particular boy. "He wasn't one of those guys that stood there and said in some dramatic way: 'Don't lay a hand on this kid,' but he would make his feelings known and would walk away from it and say 'that was a horrible way to behave.' "[18]

He used to invite Adams to go to mass with him, and Adams concluded that his "absolute faith in God . . . gave him faith in himself and appeared to make him oblivious of his lack of popularity among many of his classmates."[19] Bobby evidently hoped they might come to see the light. "Am now leading an underground movement to convert the school," he wrote his mother, "and am taking a lot of the boys to church on Sunday. Most of them like it very much, but I'm sorry to say I think the Protestant Ministers, who visit here are better speakers than the Priests at church."[20] This improved. "A Jesuit, Father Ford, is coming to speak to the school," he wrote,

> . . . about the beliefs of the Catholic Church which should be very good. Eunice suggested that I have Father Keller come and speak . . . so I am working on that.*

There were secular speakers too. Wendell Willkie addressed the school, and Robert persuaded his father to follow. "Dad made a great speech," Robert told his mother. ". . . Everybody was crazy about him."[21] His father wrote Kathleen that Bobby seemed "perfectly satisfied; in fact he said he thought it was better than Willkie's, believing that he was paying me a great compliment. I told him that if it weren't better than Willkie's I would have expected him to hiss me off the platform."[22]

II

He was not the most popular boy in the school. But in these years he formed his first strong friendship outside the family. David Hackett, a

---

* RFK to his mother, n.d. [January 1944], Hyannis Port Papers. The Reverend George B. Ford was a notable figure at Columbia University. The Reverend James Keller was founder of the Christophers.

class behind him, had been at Milton since he was a small boy and had long since become, in Piedy Bailey's words, "the hero of our school and the star of everything." He was, said Sam Adams, "one of the greatest athletes that Milton ever had in that decade or other decades." "Hackett had such glamour [Piedy Bailey again] that the littlest kids from the lower school would just trail around as though they were tin cans tied to him every place he went. . . . He'd never push you around or anything or be arrogant. He just had this incredible way about him so that people would stop and their jaws would hang open."[23] A portrait of Hackett is preserved in John Knowles's memorable novel about Exeter, where Hackett, an indifferent student, had gone one year to summer school. He was Phineas at Devon Academy in *A Separate Peace,* "the best athlete in the school," who "possessed an extra vigor, a heightened confidence in himself, a serene capacity for affection which saved him. Nothing as he was growing up at home, nothing at Devon, nothing even about the war had broken his harmonious and natural unity."[24]

Like Phineas, David Hackett was a boy with an uncommon gift for sympathy. "Maybe my first impression of him," Hackett said later of Robert Kennedy, "was that we were both, in a way, misfits."[25] It is not evident why Hackett considered himself a misfit—perhaps because he was a day boy from Dedham, more modestly circumstanced than the boarders at Milton, perhaps because, lacking the grade-getting knack, he underestimated his own perceptive intelligence. But it was evident why Robert Kennedy seemed a misfit. "He was," Hackett said later, "neither a natural athlete nor a natural student nor a natural success with girls and had no natural gift for popularity. Nothing came easily for him. What he had was a set of handicaps and a fantastic determination to overcome them. The handicaps made him redouble his effort." Because he had problems of his own, because he was "an underdog in sports, with studies and girls and as a Catholic," he was sensitive to the problems of others and went directly to their assistance however personally inconvenient it might be to himself or those with him. If a Sunday mass was short an altar boy, for example, he volunteered at once, though older and larger than the rest. Hackett admired Kennedy's readiness to do the things one knew one should do oneself but flinched from doing because they violated the iron conventions of adolescence. "From the moment I met him," Hackett said, "I knew that he would embarrass his friends"—and he loved him for it.[26]

They met on the football field, took to each other at once and soon grew inseparable. "They spent a lot of time wrestling," said Sam Adams, "and going in each other's room and throwing things out the window and wearing each other's clothes and generally horseplaying around."[27] Robert Kennedy was identified in the school as Hackett's friend, his best friend. This gave him status among his classmates. It also no doubt gave him new and needed reassurance about himself.

So Robert Kennedy's years at Milton passed tranquilly, at least as tranquilly as could be with the violent sounds of war in the background, V-mail letters from brothers overseas, a burning desire to get into uniform oneself. His housemaster was Albert Norris, who, as an earlier Miltonian, Cleveland Amory, put it, taught "Latin and Public Speaking and Tennis and Sarcasm" and could bring the class to order "with one fiercesome glower."[28] On the eve of Robert's own departure for the armed services, the fiercesome Norris summed up his Milton career to his mother:

> You have great reason to be proud of Bobby's record here. His studies have been an uphill battle all the way but he now (despite the D which I gave him myself in November!) has his scholastic feet well under him. If he were to be here until June, I believe that he would be on the Honor List. . . .
> Bobby also deserves a good pat on the back for the way he has adapted himself generally. Entering a group which has been together for several years is not easy, but Bobby has done it successfully, participating generously in school activities and winning himself warm friends.[29]

Looking back thirty years later, Norris recalled Robert Kennedy's particular qualities as "seriousness of purpose, hard work, and a refusal to be discouraged." He also recalled his sense of humor, "delightful" if sometimes "pretty caustic," his concern for "those who were less fortunate than he was" and his piety.[30] "I think he has been happy here," Arthur B. Perry, the principal, wrote Joseph Kennedy, "and I am very glad you decided to send him to Milton."[31] Joseph Kennedy was evidently glad too, for, when the time came, he sent his youngest son to Milton.

III

Joseph Kennedy had few enough things to be glad about in these years. The war he dreaded now enveloped his own country. When he offered the President his services immediately after Pearl Harbor (IN THIS GREAT CRISIS ALL AMERICANS ARE WITH YOU. NAME THE BATTLE POST. I'M YOURS TO COMMAND), Roosevelt did not reply. In March

1942, after trying in vain to reach the President by phone, Kennedy sent a stiff letter—"I feel that our relationship in the past certainly justifies my writing to you"—enclosing a copy of his Pearl Harbor telegram and concluding that, while he did not want to appear "in the role of a man looking for a job for the sake of getting an appointment, . . . Joe and Jack are in the service and I feel that my experience in these critical times might be worth something in some position."[32]

He met with Roosevelt. It is not altogether clear why the President, who brought so many inveterate opponents into the defense establishment, did not use a man of Kennedy's tested administrative ability. "When I saw Mr. Roosevelt," Kennedy wrote his faithful English friend Max Beaverbrook, "I was of the opinion that he intended to use me in the shipping situation, but the radicals and certain elements in the New Deal hollared [sic] so loud that I was not even considered."[33] This was only part of the story. Very likely, as James Roosevelt later surmised, Roosevelt himself had lost confidence in Kennedy's judgment during the London experience.[34] "I don't suppose it ever enters the head of a Joe Kennedy," said his one-time friend Felix Frankfurter, "that one who was so hostile to the whole war effort as he was all over the lot, and so outspoken in his foul-mouthed hostility to the President himself, barred his own way to a responsible share in the conduct of the war."[35]

When the matter came up at a meeting with congressional leaders toward the end of 1942, FDR, as Vice President Henry Wallace noted in his diary, "said something about how he always liked Joe Kennedy but how he especially liked Mrs. Kennedy." The President added that unfortunately Joe Kennedy told everything he knew to Arthur Krock and Frank Kent, both columnists notoriously unsympathetic to the administration. Wallace observed dryly that other high officials leaked to Krock and Kent, and Senator Lister Hill of Alabama suggested that Kennedy be put in charge of the problems of small business.[36] Soon James F. Byrnes, now director of Economic Stabilization, did indeed ask Kennedy to become head of the Office of Civilian Supply. "But," Kennedy wrote Frank Kent (as FDR had predicted), "I told him to stick it, because I feel that, in the first place, if I were of any use at all from an executive point of view, I was entitled to something I could really get my teeth into, and if it was merely an excuse for putting me under cover, I resented that equally, so . . . I am still in the leper colony."[37]

His disaffection grew. "Dissatisfaction is rife and lack of confidence in the leaders and in Congress is definitely high," he wrote Beaverbrook in August 1942, "and there is a great undercurrent of dissatisfaction with the appointment of so many Jews in high places in Washington. . . . If you want everybody yelling for our team, Mr. Roosevelt is certainly not attaining that end."* Kennedy rejoiced to Beaverbrook that the August primaries had thus far "returned, with one or two exceptions, men who were accused of being isolationists previous to Pearl Harbor." He mentioned the fight that James A. Farley was organizing in New York on behalf of the conservative Democrat John Bennett against the New Deal senator James Mead for the gubernatorial nomination. He added casually, "I am taking a slight interest in the politics of Massachusetts and that is giving me something to work on."[38]

The issue in the Massachusetts primary was the senatorial nomination. The administration was backing a debonair liberal congressman from Clinton named Joseph E. Casey, a personal favorite of FDR's whom William V. Shannon has accurately described as "the brightest of the young Irish New Dealers in the House."[39] Where the incumbent Republican senator, Henry Cabot Lodge, Jr.,† in the tradition of the Lodges, had taken an anti-English position from 1939 to 1941, Casey, against the tradition of the Massachusetts Irish, had vigorously supported aid to Britain.

Kennedy wanted to vindicate pre-Pearl Harbor isolationism. He wanted to warn Roosevelt not to disregard the conservative Democrats. In addition—or so Casey came to believe—Kennedy had a precautionary eye on the future. Once elected to the Senate, an Irish Democrat with Casey's ability and broad appeal would very likely stay there indefinitely. Since in those days the Yankees had a lien on the other Senate seat, this would place a considerable impediment in

---

* JPK to Beaverbrook, August 12, 1942, Beaverbrook Papers. Kennedy gently deflected an evident attempt by Beaverbrook to enlist him in the campaign for a second front in Europe. They had become stout friends and, as outsiders who had made it against the establishment, they had much in common. In a later letter (October 23, 1944) Kennedy spoke of "the natural cynicism that I know you and I share about a great many things." Kennedy, it is true, could in a moment of exasperation call Beaverbrook a "treacherous little bastard" (as reported in *The London Journal of Raymond E. Lee, 1940–1941*, ed. James Leutze [Boston, 1971], 92). But then all of Beaverbrook's best friends thought this about him at one time or another.

† So he somewhat inaccurately styled himself. His father was the poet George Cabot Lodge, about whom Henry Adams wrote a moving memoir. The original Henry Cabot Lodge was his grandfather; but Henry Cabot Lodge II doubtless seemed an impractical name for practical politics.

the political future of Joseph P. Kennedy, Jr.[40] The elder Kennedy even found a candidate within the family. John F. Fitzgerald, who had nearly beaten Cabot Lodge's grandfather for the Senate a quarter century before, was only seventy-nine and delighted at the prospect of a last hurrah.

"In Washington," wrote William E. Mullins of the *Boston Herald,* "this contest is regarded as a fight between Joseph P. Kennedy and the Roosevelt administration."[41] Of Fitzgerald's reported expenditures, contributions from Joseph P. Kennedy, Joseph P. Kennedy, Jr., and John F. Kennedy covered more than half.* The elder Kennedy took an active role in the campaign. Once, submitted an especially nasty anti-Casey cartoon for his approval, Kennedy rejected it summarily: "I have two boys now in the war. Should they go into public life, their heritage must be high—if they come back." As Edward B. Hanify, later a prominent Boston lawyer, remembered the scene:

> With those words, "if they come back," he turned away, his head bowed. The summer day seemed suddenly dark and cold. The crumpled cartoon lay at his feet like a withered leaf blown by a wintry wind.[42]

Kennedy was surely under no illusion that his father-in-law could beat Casey. But no doubt the thought passed through his mind that Honey Fitz's more fervent supporters might move on to Lodge in the general election. Casey took the primary comfortably by 30,000 votes, carrying eighteen out of twenty-two wards in Boston itself. In November, Lodge, who used recordings of Fitzgerald's radio attacks on Casey in his own campaign, won 53 percent of the vote. There may have been more specific assistance too. According to Arthur Krock, Lodge was "substantially aided by Joe Kennedy."[43] Casey, his political career at an end, went on to a lucrative law practice. One of his first important clients was Aristotle Onassis.

IV

"I am so damn well fed up with everything," Joe Kennedy wrote in March 1943, "and so disgusted at sitting on my fanny at Cape Cod and Palm Beach when I really believe I could do something in this war effort that it is better I don't see anybody."[44] As his older chil-

---

* Fitzgerald filed his financial report, claiming a total expenditure of $5575, with the Secretary of the Commonwealth in December (*New York Herald Tribune,* December 8, 1942).

dren began to go to the war fronts, he was haunted by a mixture of emotions—pride in his sons, fear for them, fear for the world.

He was proud that Joe Jr. and John had enlisted before Pearl Harbor. "I often smile to myself when I think of the many groups that suggested America should go to war. . . . Too many of them are storekeepers, in the intelligence service or other types of work belying their former firm determination to fight, but that is life and it is amusing at times."* Not so amusing perhaps. John was the first to go overseas. By March 1943 he was commanding his own PT boat in the South Pacific. His parents waited eagerly for his letters, duplicated them and sent them on to the other children.

> Going out every other night for patrol. On good nights it's beautiful—the water is amazingly phosphorescent—flying fishes which shine like lights are zooming around and you usually get two or three porpoises who lodge right under the bow and no matter how fast the boat goes keep just about six inches ahead. . . .
>
> I was interested in what you said about MacArthur's popularity. Here he has none—is, in fact, very, very unpopular. His nickname is "Doug-Out-Doug." . . . There is no doubt that as men start to come back that "Doug-Out-Doug" will spread—and I think would probably kill him off. No one out here has the slightest interest in politics—they just want to get home—morning, noon and night. . . . I didn't mean to use "They"—I meant "WE." . . .
>
> As far as Joe wanting to get out here, I know it is futile to say so, but if I were he I would take as much time about it as I could. . . . As regards Bobby, he ought to do what he wants. You can't estimate risks, some cooks are in more danger out here than a lot of flyers.[45]

In August, the Japanese destroyer rammed John Kennedy's PT-109 in Blackett Strait west of New Georgia, plunging Kennedy and his crew into the waters of Ferguson Passage, now suddenly aflame with burning gasoline. With calm bravery he led most of the crew to refuge on a tiny island, towing one man through the water by gripping the end of the life jacket belt in his teeth. "We have just come back from a fairly trying time," he wrote a friend. "They believed us lost for a week—but luckily thank God—they did not send the telegrams—but unfortunately some telegrams will have to be sent."[46]

He wrote his parents:

> On the bright side of an otherwise completely black time was the way that everyone stood up to it. Previous to that I had become somewhat cynical

---

* JPK to John Griffin, August 24, 1943, JPK Papers. As a pre-Pearl Harbor interventionist who ended in the intelligence service, I fully accept the justice of Mr. Kennedy's strictures.

The War

> about the American as a fighting man. I had seen too much bellyaching and laying off. But with the chips down—that all faded away. I can now believe—which I never would have before—the stories of Bataan and Wake. For an American it's got to be awfully easy or awfully tough. When it's in the middle, then there's trouble.
>
> It was a terrible thing though, losing those two men. One had ridden with me for as long as I had been out here. He had been somewhat shocked by a bomb that had landed near the boat about two weeks before. He never really got over it; he always seemed to have the feeling that something was going to happen to him. He never said anything about being put ashore—he didn't want to go—but the next time we came down the line I was going to let him work on the base force. When a fellow gets the feeling that he's in for it, the only thing to do is to let him get off the boat because strangely enough, they always seem to be the ones that do get it. . . . He had a wife and three kids. The other fellow had just come aboard. He was only a kid himself. . . .

John Kennedy was an old man of twenty-six.

> When I read that we will fight the Japs for years if necessary and will sacrifice hundreds of thousands if we must—I always like to check from where he is talking—it's seldom out here. People get too used to talking about billions of dollars and millions of soldiers that thousands of dead sounds like a drop in the bucket. But if those thousands want to live as much as the ten I saw—they should measure their words with great, great care.[47]

In November 1943 he wrote that he would not be home by Christmas. "Am now the Executive Officer of our squadron. . . . I only hope I don't stay here long enough to make the next step—Supreme Commander—or I'll never get out."[48] In fact, however, the ramming of PT-109 had revived his old back injury, and he was invalided home in December 1943.

In the meantime, Kathleen Kennedy, now twenty-three, had gone to London in June to work in a Red Cross canteen. She was witty and enchanting, "Full of charm and love of life and uncertainty," Susan Mary Patten wrote, and, as an English friend put it, with the transcendent quality of making life gay when things were desperate.[49] Kick, as everyone called her, resumed her English friendships with zest and entertained the family with lively accounts of wartime London. Joseph Jr. had been chafing in the United States while his younger brother was becoming a hero in the Pacific. It was "the first time," their mother wrote, "Jack had won such an 'advantage' by such a clear margin. . . . It cheered Jack and must have rankled Joe Jr."[50] In September, Joe finally received overseas orders, going to England in the first naval squadron to fly B-24s with British Coastal

Command. Here he distinguished himself in dangerous winter missions over the Bay of Biscay.

v

Robert Kennedy had been chafing too, and for some time. "He is begging and pleading to be permitted to enlist," his father wrote a friend in October 1942, "so that he can get into the Navy Aviation."[51] BOTH UNCLE SAM AND I EXPRESS OUR HEARTIEST CONGRATULATIONS TO YOU ON THE OCCASION OF YOUR BIRTHDAY, his brother John wired when he turned seventeen in November 1942, AS DOES GENERAL HERSHEY.[52] Robert importuned his older brothers for news about life in the Navy. "Thanks for your letter[s]," John replied early in 1943. "What makes them so particularly interesting is that you can't read them. . . . I got my orders yesterday, and am on my way to war. Am taking my boat to Florida. . . . For a guy who never could find Gardiners Rock, Florida seems like a hell of a distance. Am typing this as we b^o$_u$n$_c$e along."[53] In the spring his father went to Washington to see about getting Robert into Navy V-12 training. "He still wants to follow in yours and Joe's footsteps," he wrote John, now on his PT boat in the Pacific.[54]

For a moment, PT boats seized Robert's imagination. His brother disapproved and wrote their father:

> In regard to Bobby, he said something about wanting to get in the boats. I don't think he should. By the time he's ready to get out here the usefulness of the boats will be done, I think. I think he should go into that V-12 and stay there for a good long time. He's too young to be out here for a while. When he has at least a year of college he'll be more effective and he will be better able to handle a job. The war will last long enough for him. . . . To try to come steaming out here at 18 is no good. . . .
> It's just that the fun goes out of war in a fairly short time and I don't think Bobby is ready yet to come out.[55]

In October 1943, six weeks before his eighteenth birthday, Robert enlisted in the Naval Reserve as apprentice seaman, released from active duty until the following March when (after some behind-the-scenes intervention by his father) he was scheduled to enter the V-12 training unit at Harvard.* Meanwhile he returned to Milton. His photograph appeared in the newspapers—"Kennedy's Third Son in Navy"

---

* "I was more than happy to be of service to you in accomplishing a change in the college assignment of Bobby to permit him to go to Harvard" (Captain J. B. Lynch to JPK, April 28, 1944, JPK Papers).

The War

—with Robert a pensive and exceedingly youthful seventeen and his proud father standing by his side.[56] The picture provoked much merriment in the family. "He certainly didn't look too enthusiastic," Joe Jr. wrote his parents.[57] John Kennedy wrote his younger brother:

> The folks sent me a clipping of you taking the oath. The sight of you up there, just as a boy, was really moving particularly as a close examination showed that you had my checked London coat on. I'd like to know what the hell I'm doing out here while you go stroking around in my drape coat, but I suppose that [is] what we are out here for. . . .
> In that picture you looked as if you were going to step outside the room, grab your gun, and knock off several of the houseboys before lunch. After reading Dad's letter, I gathered that the cold vicious look in your eyes was due to the thought of that big blocking back from Groton.[58]

There would be more about that "cold vicious look" in years to come.

In March 1944 Robert reported for active duty at the V-12 headquarters at Harvard. He was assigned to a room and roommate in Eliot House. "His name is Hans Anguelmueller so you can see he is not very Irish."[59] He sent his course of studies to his father, who responded with sage paternal counsel:

> I think you have developed a maturity in the last year that is surprisingly good. Previous to that time I don't think any real strides had been made. I don't think I'd be thinking too much about what's going to happen three, four, five, or six months from today. The important thing is to do a good job now and every day. After all, you've got your life ahead of you and heaven knows it's going to require all the brains anyone has to work out a satisfactory existence, and the only way to do that is to be well prepared, so stick in there and work as hard as you possibly can.[60]

Robert wrote Joe Jr. in England that "at this point you are about the only one of us many that has the good graces of the head of the family but I give you about four days after your arrival in this country before you'll join the rest of us. I am constantly hacking things but the hope still remains in the family that the Navy will make a man of me." He added, "We haven't really had too much action here in Harvard Square but we're on the alert at every moment for an attack and I'm sure when that time comes we will conduct ourselves according to Navy standards."[61]

It was one more unsettling shift in a highly unsettled education. To his parents: "I'm certainly not hitting the honors like my older brothers."[62] "I am now sitting in my room by myself with no friends," he wrote David Hackett, who was still at Milton, "wishing I were back at Milton where although I might not have had any friends

I had a radio I could listen to and had pictures of my family I could look at, neither of which I have here at present but c'est la guerre."[63] The tone was mock self-pity, but vulnerability showed. "I don't like this place," he soon wrote, "and I'm homesick and need someone to cheer me up. I also feel sorry for myself. . . . I wish I could be throwing furniture out of windows or having a fight with you or making you a hero with some superb blocking."[64] In time his spirits revived. "Say hello to all the Irish Catholics for me, and tell em that next to John F. Fitzgerald and J. P. Kennedy I'm the toughest Irishman that lives which makes me the toughest man that lives."[65]

VI

The spring of 1944 brought a new threat to the integrity of the family. Chief among the prewar friends whom Kathleen saw again in London was William John Robert Hartington, the eldest son of the Duke of Devonshire, a descendant of Cavendishes and Cecils, now an officer in the Coldstream Guards. They fell in love. But the Devonshires were as ineradicably Anglican as the Kennedys were invincibly Catholic. History as well as religion argued against the match. The Duke of Devonshire was a leading Freemason, and the Cavendish family had played a notorious role, at least in the Irish view, as British viceroys in Ireland. When Honey Fitz had taken his daughter Rose to Dublin long ago, he had shown her the spot in Dublin where Irish revolutionaries had assassinated Billy Hartington's granduncle.[66]

It all looked hopeless. "Of course I know he would never give in about the religion," Kathleen wrote her brother John in the summer of 1943, "and he knows I never would. . . . It's really too bad because I would be a most efficient Duchess of Devonshire in the postwar world."[67] As time went on, and with the knowledge that Hartington would go into combat when the second front was opened in France, the lovers grew increasingly determined to circumvent the obstacles. There were complicated negotiations. The apostolic delegate in London was brought in, Cardinal Spellman, even the Vatican. But the rules were firm. Kathleen could be married within the church to a non-Catholic only if Hartington agreed to have the children raised as Catholics, and this the son of the Duke of Devonshire could not do.

In this troubling time Joe Jr. became Kathleen's closest confidant.

The War

"I went to see the Bishop who was a nice fellow," he wrote his father in April 1944.

> His attitude seemed to be that if they loved each other a lot, then marry outside the church. He didn't seem to be disturbed about its creating a bad example. He of course said there would be a danger of her drifting away from the church, as she would not be able to receive the sacraments.
>
> I told her that she would have to decide whether she thought her life would really be broken up if she didn't marry him.... If this is the love of her life, and she will not be happy with anyone else, then she will probably be unhappy the rest of her life for not having done it.
>
> I think that Billy should make some kind of concession on the girls, for it wouldn't affect his family line. He on the other hand thinks it would be difficult to have half the family one thing, and the rest the other. It is a hell of a problem, and I certainly sympathize with her....
>
> She was quite worried as to what Mother would think of the whole business.[68]

Kathleen was right to worry. Her mother was much distressed by the prospect of her daughter marrying outside the church.

Her father was at his best. He cabled her: I FEEL TERRIBLY UNHAPPY YOU HAVE TO FACE YOUR BIGGEST CRISIS WITHOUT MOTHER OR ME. YOUR CONFIDENTIAL MEMORANDUM WORTHY OF CHESTERTON MAGNIFICENT. WITH YOUR FAITH IN GOD YOU CAN'T MAKE A MISTAKE. REMEMBER YOU ARE STILL AND ALWAYS WILL BE TOPS WITH ME. LOVE DAD.[69] A long letter of reassurance followed.

> I want you to know that I feel for you very deeply. It is very difficult for a person to get a true perspective three thousand miles away from the source of action. I can remember when I was in the picture business that when I was in New York and sent wires to California every time I arrived in California and read the wires I sent I was sure that I was crazy and so I would send wires back to New York outlining a plan of action and when I got back to New York and read them I know that nobody lived crazier than I, so unless you are on the ground you can't understand what goes on in people's minds....
>
> You will be interested to know that as Mother and I walked down the street last Saturday she said that of all the children, and she made no exceptions whatsoever, she felt that basically your judgment was the soundest.
>
> Now none of this means that I am attempting to tell you how you should handle your life. You are the one that has to live it and it is a long one and also quite a difficult one, but as I have said to you before you are "tops" with me and you always will be.

He added a budget of family gossip. "Jack, much to my amazement because I am not particularly impressed with the depth of his Catholic faith, feels that some kind of concession should be made on the part of Billy." Bobby was playing rugby at Harvard. "He now weighs

165 and is easily the strongest of all the boys." Cardinal O'Connell had died, and they had been having masses, processions and parades. "I think it is a disgraceful exhibition but it seems to be what they want up there. I, of course, will have to go up and be an honorary pallbearer because he married Mother and me."[70]

On May 6, 1944, Kathleen Kennedy and William Hartington were married at the Chelsea Registry Office in London. Joe Jr. gave his sister away. "Never did anyone have such a pillar of strength," she wrote later, "as I had in Joe in those difficult days before my marriage. . . . He constantly reassured me and gave me renewed confidence in my own decision."[71] In Washington, Franklin Roosevelt, hearing the news, "laughed and laughed. . . . The President said he had known the Duke of Devonshire for a long time and that his family were rabid Protestants."[72] In Boston, Rose Kennedy, ill in the hospital, asked nuns to offer special prayers. Jean Kennedy was in a convent; and her father, concerned that the nuns would upset her by condemning Kathleen's decision, came to see her, explaining that this was her sister's conscientious choice and that the main thing was to keep on loving her.[73] "I see now that I've lost one of my daughters to England," Joseph Kennedy wrote Beaverbrook later. "She was the apple of my eye and I feel the loss because I won't have her near me all the time, but I'm sure she's going to be wonderfully happy and I can assure you that England is getting a great girl."[74]

He added that young Joe had just volunteered for an extra month's duty, which would give him forty missions. "Although he's had a large number of casualties in his squadron, I'm still hoping and praying we'll see him around the first of July." But when the first of July came, young Joe, his second tour safely over, volunteered to fly an experimental Navy plane designed to strike German flying bomb sites on the French coast. On August 12, 1944, his plane exploded in midair over England.* His body was never recovered.[75]

It was the most terrible moment of his father's life, the annihilation of the hope and dream of nearly thirty years. John Kennedy defined the impact: young Joe's "success was so assured and inevitable that his death seems to have cut into the natural order of things."[76] Desolate and inconsolable, Joseph Kennedy withdrew in silent anguish, spending long hours sitting alone and listening to his beloved symphonies.[77] "He was the oldest boy," Joseph Kennedy wrote Grace

---

* Among the witnesses of the midair explosion was Colonel Elliott Roosevelt, accompanying the mission in a Mosquito; the lives of the two families were curiously intertwined.

The War

Tully, FDR's secretary, "and I have spent a great deal of time making what I thought were plans for his future. I have learned, however, that God takes quite a hand in the lives of His souls on earth."[78]

The pain was inextinguishable. A few weeks later, Harry S. Truman, the Democratic candidate for Vice President, came to Boston. Kennedy, still in agony, said to him, "Harry, what the hell are you doing campaigning for that crippled son of a bitch that killed my son Joe?"* The wound never healed. When the reporter Bob Considine mentioned young Joe thirteen years later, Joseph Kennedy "suddenly and terribly burst into tears at the lunch table and for five full minutes was racked with grief that cannot be described."[79]

Then, a month after the Kennedys had received word of Joe's death, they heard in early September that Lord Hartington had been killed leading an infantry patrol in Belgium.

"For a fellow who didn't want this war to touch your country or mine," Joseph Kennedy wrote Max Beaverbrook in October, "I have had rather a bad dose—Joe dead, Billy Hartington dead, my son Jack in the Naval Hospital. I have had brought home to me very personally what I saw for all the mothers and fathers of the world."[80]

VII

It was a black time for the Kennedys. With one brother killed and another nearly killed, with one sister married outside the faith and the country and then her husband killed, the global war had ravaged the family itself. In the meantime, another sister retired from the family; it had become sadly clear that Rosemary, falling farther and farther behind, would live more tranquilly with the nuns in a Wisconsin convent. Robert Kennedy in his nineteenth year was receiving abrupt instruction in the incertitudes of life.

During the summer of 1944 he was still in V-12 training at Harvard. It has been written that he objected to Kathleen's marriage;[81] but this finds no corroboration in evidence or memory. More probably he followed the lead of his father and oldest brother. He was at Hyannis Port when word came of Joe's death. His father, summoning the children, told them they must be brave; that was what their

---

* Or so Truman recalled over a quarter century later in a not very reliable set of conversations with Merle Miller. Truman claimed to have told Kennedy, "If you say another word about Roosevelt, I'm going to throw you out the window." He nonetheless accepted a sizable campaign contribution. He added to Miller, "Old Joe Kennedy is as big a crook as we've got anywhere in the country" (Merle Miller, ed., *Plain Speaking* [New York: Berkley reprint, 1974], 199).

brother would want from them. He even insisted they go ahead with their plans to race that day. Robert was probably among those who "obediently" did so. Only "Jack could not. Instead he walked for a long time on the beach in front of our house."[82]

No one knows how Robert Kennedy, in his solitary life, dealt with the inner turmoil incited by these events. He paid a visit to Milton and reported to David Hackett, who was now with the paratroops: "School was kind of queer and I certainly wouldn't want to go out there too much. It all seems so inconsequential changing to blue suits and being on time for Chapel and all that sort of thing. I am very glad I am finished with it although we did have such good fun the last year."[83] He got to Hyannis Port over Labor Day. Kathleen, husband at the front, was home for a visit. John had invited PT boat friends from the South Pacific. A rollicking lot, they bridled under the ambassador's strict one-cocktail-before-dinner rule and took to foraging in the kitchen liquor closet after the cooks had departed. One of their wives recalled Robert, "a scrawny little guy in a white sailor suit . . . very upset that we were sneaking booze in the kitchen. He was afraid his father might catch us and he knew his father's wrath. But Kathleen handled him. She told him to get lost."[84]

In November Robert was scheduled to move on to the V-12 unit at Bates College in Lewiston, Maine. "Due to the fact that I'm off to Maine for the winter and after that off to beat the Japs, and you're off to the paratroopers and after that?" Robert wrote Hackett, "then we might as well let the fair sex see more of *me* and you."* His particular girl was Betty Blackburn of Pittsburgh, whom he had met in summers on the Cape and who was now at Sarah Lawrence.

Lewiston turned out to be far away—from family, from friends, from the war, even from the faith; for the local church held mass for its French Canadian constituency in French, a language that continued to elude him. Finally he located an English-speaking church; he wrote his parents that by the end of the week his soul should be "as white as snow. Hope everyone is impressed."[85]

He wrote endlessly. "Bobby is the best letter writer in the family," Kathleen, who had gone back to live in London, told her family in February. "Practically every week a little billet doux arrives from him reporting on the latest activities in the Maine woods."[86] He bragged to Hackett about his skiing prowess: "but you know how I am in

---

* RFK to Hackett, postmarked October 4, 1944, Hackett Papers. He added a postscript: "Just read this letter over and can't understand any of it. I should join the Code Department of the Navy."

sports, natural athlete and everything."[87] He described himself as "my usual moody self. I get very sad at times. . . . Did you know that Barry Turner has gone overseas. If I don't get the hell out of here soon I'll die."[88] Going overseas was an obsessive motif. "Still can't get over Tom Clark [?] saying he'll be fighting before me and the possibility makes me feel more & more like a Draft Dodger or something. But I suppose somebody has to be in V-12 but the attitudes of some of these guys really makes me mad especially after Joe being killed."[89]

The big thing was to get overseas before the war ended. His family regarded this idea with limited enthusiasm. The decision was that he should go to officers' training school. "I wish to hell," he wrote Hackett, ". . . people would have let me alone to do as I wished, but I suppose I simply must be an officer. . . . I guess the rest of this war is going to be won by you and your brothers for I think the Kennedys have all about shot their bolt."[90] His marks, he told Hackett, were pretty good, and he had been appointed platoon leader. "Something I've learned from the first year in my country's service is that you certainly have to be more independent and you have to depend much more on yourself than before." He kept trying to wriggle out of officers' training. "I talked to Papa about it and told him I didn't feature the R.O.T.C. and would try to get back in aviation right away. . . . I am not sure, between you and me, just how much I go for flying but I guess that's the best thing to do."[91] In May he reported, doubtless with some inner relief: "Am not going to fly as I found out yesterday I failed a test in Flight aptitude. This, of course, hurts me, but everything bad that happens now people say it's God's will so I guess I will chalk that up to it also."[92] At the end of June he was transferred back to Harvard to complete his officers' training.

His father was more than ever in these years the dominating figure in Robert's life; the struggle to command his respect more than ever the dominating theme. "I congratulate you on your marks," his father had written him in January 1945. ". . . By the look of some of those subjects of yours, I know that I would never be able to get even an E." He concluded: "Let me know if there is anything I can do for you."[93] Robert responded at once. "I wish, Dad," he wrote from Maine, "that you would write me a letter as you used to Joe & Jack about what you think about the different political events and the war as I'd like to understand what's going on better than I now do."[94] Joseph Kennedy sent back a two-page, single-spaced letter expatiating upon FDR, military developments in Europe and in the Far East,

Henry Wallace and his new book *Sixty Million Jobs*. "There will be great confusion finding jobs for everybody. There will be a cry that the only way to solve all these problems is to let the Government do it, and that will be the beginning of some form of socialism in this country. Now, it sounds like a terrific prophecy to make, but I can't see anything except the Government mixing itself more and more into everybody's lives." His father concluded: "This is a quick summary of the conditions as I see them, and I will write you about it all the time if this is what you want. Just tell me what problems seem to be sticking in your mind."[95] "Thanks very much for your letter Dad," Robert replied, "which is just what I wanted."[96] Joseph Kennedy's letters continued through the winter and spring:

> I was very much interested in your letter about the Morgenthau Plan. I don't think anybody really had an idea of what the plan was because it was never fully explained. Of course, it was never his plan—he wouldn't know enough to have a plan. It was conceived by a Jew named Bernstein, who is now Assistant Secretary of the Treasury.
>
> This morning I read of the discussion about three votes for Russia [in the United Nations], and one can begin to see plenty of disputes for the future.
>
> [enclosing a document] This is about as good an outline of the OPA situation as you can find.[97]

His pessimism about the war so sadly verified, Joseph Kennedy looked on the postwar world with unremitting apprehension. "I see that the problems of living standards, economics, stability, and national pride," he wrote Beaverbrook, "are still standing on shaky ground." He could not share Beaverbrook's hope about postwar collaboration with the Soviet Union; the Russians would play the game, Kennedy thought, only so long as it was going their way.[98] Roosevelt's death in April 1945 found him in a bitter mood. There was "real sorrow" for two or three days, he wrote Kathleen, "but there is also no doubt that it was a great thing for the country." Roosevelt had stirred up so much hatred that "no matter whether he proposed anything good or bad, half the country would be against it." As for Truman, "I know him very well"; his great attributes were his common sense, his choice of advisers and "his advocating Americanism as the Mid West knows it and not as the elements in New York want it. . . . I'm seriously considering . . . whether I might not say to him that I'd like to help any way I can; but if he's going to give me a job, I'd rather have him give it to Jack and maybe make him minister

The War

to some country or Assistant Secretary of State or Assistant Secretary of the Navy."[99]

VIII

In the autumn of 1945 the Navy commissioned a new destroyer and named it the *Joseph P. Kennedy, Jr.* Without telling his family, Robert went to Washington and asked the Secretary of the Navy, James V. Forrestal, to release him from officers' training and assign him to the ship as a seaman.[100] On February 1, 1946, Robert Francis Kennedy, Apprentice Seaman, Class V-12, U.S. Naval Reserve, having passed satisfactorily courses in elementary and advanced seamanship, damage control and engineering, piloting and celestial navigation, left the Naval Reserve Officers' Training Corps program to join the new boat on its shakedown cruise. "During his stay in the NROTC unit," the executive officer wrote, "his conduct was without question, and his loyalty and cooperation were above average. He is leaving . . . at his own request so that he may acquire sea experience. It is recommended that when possible he be given a Quartermaster rating because of his intense interest in navigation. We are sorry that the above-mentioned man is leaving this Unit."[101]

The *Joseph P. Kennedy, Jr.*, was under orders for Guantanamo, the American base in Cuba. The voyage down, Bobby told his parents, was uneventful after the first day, which "was rather rough & it was a very sea sick crew, but your No. 7 passed the test in true Kennedy fashion & held on to his stomach."[102] He wrote Lem Billings, "It's not much better than a bum's life particularly for a seaman." Most of the crew was from the south and had spent even less time in the Navy than he had. "I get along with them very well," he told Billings, "for they have a lot of something, a lot of those guys at Harvard lacked."[103] He wrote his parents, "I certainly am meeting people with a different outlook & interests in life. . . . P.S. The Franklin Delano Roosevelt just moved into the bay so we're all together once more."[104]

After six weeks he was transferred—"from the lowest grade of chippers, painters & scrubbers, the 2nd Division, up into one of the highest grades of chippers, painters & scrubbers, the I division. . . . The fact that I stands for Intelligence must make you all realize instantaneously without further discussion that I am in exactly the right place for me. I am sure if the fact that Robert Kennedy was in the Intelligence Division of one of the U.S. Navy's fighting ships was made known to the public women & children would sleep more comfortably in their beds." He noted that international news, as summarized in the ship's newspaper, often gave "the wrong idea & to us all it seemed that we would all certainly be at war by the end of the month." (This was the time of Stalin's hard speech of February 9, which William O. Douglas privately described as "the Declaration of World War III," and of Churchill's Iron Curtain rejoinder a month later at Fulton, Missouri.)[105] "If they are going to have a war again," Robert wrote his parents, "I can tell you they are going to have a very tough time getting this group of men to fight it."[106] In the spring he was back in the United States. On May 30, 1946, he received his honorable discharge.

The war had hardly brushed him, but it had altered things nevertheless. With young Joe dead and John confirmed by war in attitudes of detachment and independence, Joseph Kennedy was paying more attention than ever before to his third son. Robert responded with alacrity. The transformations and griefs of war intensified a process of change that had begun much earlier. The sweetness and defenselessness of the small boy had gone underground. The code of the Kennedys discouraged undue emotion, unless disguised as humor. "You didn't express your emotions," said Charles Spalding, "in front of anybody."[107] Robert Kennedy was, in effect, remaking his personality, or at least his *persona,* in his determination to overcome doubts of his own worth and to win the love of the most important person in his life. Unlike John, who imperturbably went his casual and cool way, Bobby felt an overpowering need to please his father; to demonstrate his sense of family, always more sustained than John's; to demonstrate that, like his father, he was not soft but tough.

Emotionalism remained, both as concern and as vulnerability, expressed in moodiness, taciturnity or a certain brusque harshness, expressed too in persisting sympathy for other underdogs. But a protective covering formed over it. He was learning not to expose himself too much, not to seem to care too much. "His idea of a man," said Joseph Dolan, a close associate in later years, "was that you never asked for any quarter."[108] He became in these years the scrappy adolescent, the relentless kidder, the ferocious competitor, the combative mick. Only those who knew him very well perceived the gentleness within.

There was perhaps something very Irish about it all—the loyalty to family, the irony and self-mockery, the mingling of romantic defiance with a deep sadness; something very Irish American too, for the Irish legacy in its Kennedy form had to accommodate itself to the puritan ethic, the belief in discipline, work and achievement. Being an Irish American, Henry James might have said, was a complex fate.

(4)

The Third Son

ROBERT KENNEDY came out of the Navy just in time for a new family undertaking: the election of his brother John to the House of Representatives from Massachusetts. Apart from summers on the Cape and four winters at Harvard, John Kennedy had not lived in the state for nearly twenty years. Though a Massachusetts voter, he was in effect a carpetbagger. His residence during the campaign was Boston's famous political hotel, the Bellevue, across the street from Bulfinch's State House. But the Eleventh District, which wandered from East Boston and the North End into Charlestown, Somerville and Cambridge, was rich in Fitzgerald and Kennedy memories. The young candidate worked the neighborhoods diligently. Robert spent a day during a naval leave accompanying John on his rounds. They met, he wrote their mother, "quite a divergent group of people from Irish bartenders to Negro members of the V.F.W. [Veterans of Foreign Wars]. Everyone seems to agree he is doing very well."[1]

I

Once discharged, Robert offered to join up full-time. "It's damn nice of Bobby wanting to help," John Kennedy told Paul Fay, a Navy friend who had crossed the continent from San Francisco, "but I can't see that sober, silent face breathing new vigor into the ranks. The best plan is to make it known to the press. One picture of the two brothers together will show that we're all in this for Jack. Then you take Bobby out to [the] movies." When Robert arrived, Fay knew he was present, he later wrote, "only because I could see him. Words came out of his mouth as if each one spoken depleted an already severely limited supply." Off they went to the movies, Fay trying to make conversation, Robert Kennedy responding with a terse yes or no. When the stage show began, a comedian reduced Fay to helpless laughter. "I looked over to make sure he was enjoying this as much as I was. From his expression he might have been paying his last respects to his closest friend."[2]

Robert was eventually turned over to LeMoyne Billings, who was in charge of Cambridge, and Billings assigned him three Italian wards in East Cambridge. There was already a generational split in the campaign. Joseph Kennedy had set up headquarters at the Ritz Hotel, where he telephoned politicians of his own age, briefed the press and dispensed campaign funds. Honey Fitz, a still sprightly eighty-three, and other venerable politicos crowded John Kennedy's rooms at the Bellevue, filling the air with cigar smoke and ancient tales about forgotten elections. The campaign, however, went off in another direction. John Kennedy summoned his contemporaries—schoolmates like Billings, Navy pals like Fay, young Irish veterans like his campaign manager Mark Dalton. His dashing sisters enlisted friends of their own. Jean Kennedy brought along her Manhattanville roommate, a spirited girl from Greenwich, Connecticut, named Ethel Skakel.

Robert Kennedy observed the tug of generations. Grandpa, he said, "felt very strongly about [the campaign], and he felt very close to my brother. But I think that his effectiveness, in some of these areas, was not overwhelming. He had some important introductions and contacts which were significant. But the appeal that John Kennedy had was to an entirely different group. It was to young people and it was to people who had not been involved in politics and a lot of servicemen."[3]

In East Cambridge Robert himself set grimly to work, not bothering to hide his disgust with the old pols sitting around the Bellevue. East Cambridge was home territory for his brother's leading opponent. "I was in a tough area," Robert recalled, "so there was a good deal of antagonism toward . . . me and the operation."[4] He disarmed at least the young by playing softball in a park across the street from his headquarters. "All that propaganda that the Kennedys were the high-hat kind," said a Cambridge politician, "was dissipated in my area by Bobby playing with those kids."[5] Robert lost his wards on primary day, but the margin was smaller than anticipated. John Kennedy easily carried the district. The primary result in June determined the election in the fall.

For both brothers it was an initiation into politics; also, in a sense, into their Irish legacy. Though traditional Boston politicians left them skeptical (in John's case) or exasperated (in Robert's), the young Kennedys relished the stories and characters of the past. David Powers, whose friendship with John Kennedy began in this campaign, said, "It took Jack three months before he found out that Mother Galvin wasn't a woman"—Mother Galvin so called because of the maternal solicitude he displayed for the interests of his constituents. They were enchanted by the discovery that Jim Curley's henchman Up-Up Kelly received his name by running into political meetings shouting, "Up! up! Everybody up for Governor Curley!"[6] The baroque politics of Boston was not their style. John Kennedy benefited indeed from the contrast. But it remained part of their inheritance.

With the primary out of the way, Robert joined Lem Billings on a trip to Latin America. It was Robert's first long journey away from the family. They began at Rio de Janeiro, where Robert appalled his friend by insisting on plunging into the treacherous surf of Copacabana Beach in the pitch dark of midnight. They went on to Montevideo and Buenos Aires, to Chile and Peru, ending in Panama and Mexico. Apart from Robert's athletic excesses, it was, somewhat to Billings's dismay, an exceedingly seemly trip. Robert was determined to win the $2000 prize offered by Joseph Kennedy to all his children who did not drink or smoke till their twenty-first birthday. When they went to bars, he ordered Coca-Colas and demanded to move on as speedily as possible to dinner.[7] The travelers were occasionally asked what they had done in the war. "Bobby didn't have anything to say," Billings remembered later. "I used to kid him about it. He didn't think it especially funny."[8] In September 1946 Robert was back at Cambridge and Harvard.

II

Harvard after the war was a confusion of ages. Graying veterans of Anzio and Okinawa mingled with boys fresh from secondary school. Robert Kennedy was chronologically in between. He had received academic credit for his work in V-12 and, now almost twenty-one, was entering his junior year. His marks had been mediocre, except for a B in International Law in the winter term of 1945–46. They did not improve now. He was promptly put on probation, from which he was relieved in the spring of 1947.[9]

His field of academic concentration was government. This was nominal. He attended the classes of eminent scholars and popular lecturers—C. H. McIlwain, Roscoe Pound, Payson S. Wild, William

Yandell Elliott, Rupert Emerson, Bruce Hopper. No one can remember a professor who particularly interested him; no professor can particularly remember him. Wild, who had known his brothers well, had no impression of Robert at all.[10] "I didn't go to class very much," Robert said later.[11] His grades attested to that. A string of C's was broken only by D's in Anglo-American Law and in the Principles of Economics.

Like his older brothers, he was elected to the Spee Club, but he got mad when another Irish Catholic was blackballed, and never went to the club again. Or so at least he pretended: "I think he just used it for an excuse," said Sam Adams, his Milton friend and now his fellow clubman. "He just wasn't particularly happy around those guys; he was rather uncomfortable."[12] He was rather uncomfortable with most of his college contemporaries, including some who later became good friends. George Plimpton remembers seeing him once at the house of K. K. Hannon, a beauty of the day. "It always struck me; there was a party going on. There was this one fellow working on a paper or something [on a table] in the kitchen."[13] John Knowles—not the novelist but the physician and later head of the Rockefeller Foundation—found himself next to Kennedy in classes where seating was arranged in alphabetical order. "Intellectually I think he was very bright. . . . I found him very serious in the classes I was in with him . . . nor did I in any way find him so rigid or dogmatic. He was tough on himself and tough on the people around. . . . He was tougher than hell. He stood up for what the hell he believed and kept going at it." Knowles added that he was looked on as "kind of a nasty, brutal, humorless little fellow when he got going"; and that was no doubt how many classmates regarded him.[14] Thus Anthony Lewis, later of the *New York Times:* "Hardly knew him and didn't like him and thought he was callow and tough. . . . He was a remote figure . . . sort of a football player."[15]

For a while he went with other Catholic students to the St. Benedict Center where Father Leonard Feeney inveighed against the infidel. Feeney expounded a rigid version of the doctrine *extra ecclesiam nulla salus*—no salvation outside the church—and anathematized Harvard as "a pest-hole" of atheists and Jews. All this vastly irritated Robert Kennedy, who put up an argument, angrily abandoned the center and shocked his mother by denouncing Father Feeney at the Kennedy dinner table. Feeney's suspension by Cardinal Cushing in 1949 and his excommunication by the Vatican in 1953 no doubt gave Rose Kennedy retrospective comfort.[16]

He was still diffident about girls, though his sisters did their best to encourage flirtations. Over the Christmas holiday of 1945–46 Jean had brought Ethel Skakel along on a skiing expedition at Mont Tremblant in Canada. Robert liked Ethel and, after the 1946 congressional campaign, invited her occasionally to Cambridge. But he took out her older sister Patricia rather more. In his senior year, when Robert invited Pat Skakel to Palm Beach, Ethel managed an invitation for herself from Jean. Ethel attracted him by her high spirits and her proficiency in sports. But all this was on the margin of his life.

His real field of concentration at Harvard was football. Perhaps this seemed the most direct way to prove to his family, and to himself, that he was approaching paternal standards of toughness. An early football friend was Kenneth O'Donnell of Worcester, Massachusetts, whose father was football coach at Holy Cross and whose older brother was captain of the 1946 Harvard team. Ken O'Donnell himself was to be captain later. "I can't think of anyone," he said afterward, "who had less right to make the varsity squad than Bobby." Veterans from across the country were flocking to Harvard under the GI bill. When Robert Kennedy, 5' 10", 155 pounds, reported for practice as an end in 1946, he was faced "with the biggest and most talented group of ends that the University had ever gathered." Kennedy was relegated to the lowest squad. He would not give up. He arrived on the field an hour early every afternoon and stayed an hour late. In scrimmage "he'd come in from his end like a wild Indian. If you were blocking Bobby, you'd knock him down, but he'd be up again going after the play. He never let up," O'Donnell said. ". . . He just *made* himself better."[17] "His intensity about football," said a classmate and fellow fanatic, William J. Brady, Jr., of Philadelphia, "was really an all-consuming feeling. . . . I don't think he gave a darn about anything else."[18]

In 1947, his senior year, he started the first game as varsity end and scored the only touchdown of his college career. A few days later he broke his leg in practice but characteristically told no one and kept on trying to play till he collapsed on the field, showing once again, as his brother John had said, either a lot of guts or no sense at all, depending on how you looked at it. The injury knocked him out for the rest of the season. But the sympathetic coach sent him in for his letter during the closing moments of the game with Yale. His leg was still in an enormous cast, and he somehow got mixed up in the final scrimmage but emerged unscathed. It was a small triumph. His

The Third Son

father had won a Harvard letter (in baseball), but neither of his older brothers had done so.

It was among athletes that Robert Kennedy felt truly comfortable. They were not traditional Harvard types. Most would not have been at Cambridge except for the GI bill. "They were," said Kenneth O'Donnell,

> a very irreverent, disinterested group of fellows just out of the service . . . and weren't very much interested in who the hell Bob Kennedy was. . . . They were all two, three, four, sometimes five years older than he was. At first they didn't like him very much. They didn't want to pay any attention to him; they didn't think he was that good a football player, and they thought he was just a rich kid who was hanging around.[19]

Most of them, O'Donnell said, "couldn't scrape twenty-five cents together."[20] Bob exasperated them especially by his negligence about money. "We'd go on trips," said Bill Brady, "and he never had any money and whatever it was I'd pay. . . . It always amazed me that he literally never had any money."[21] But they forgave him for it. "After about six months, he became one of the group," remembers O'Donnell.[22] "He was rather lonely when he was young," observed Eunice, ". . . so I think he picked friends who were sort of different. They weren't in the usual social stream at all; they were tough and rough . . . all big and bulky and very unsophisticated"; very different, Eunice thought, from John's friends, so smooth and assured and adept with girls and parties. "My father was always very immaculate and well dressed. . . . Bobby thought it was rather amusing to bring home people that were neither."[23]

His Harvard life was the football field, the training table, the Varsity Club. But, if his college years were spent with athletes, they were not altogether consumed by athletics. "I used to talk and argue a lot, mostly about sports and politics," he said later. "I began thinking about issues about the time I went to college." Sometimes football itself posed the issue. In 1947 Harvard had a black tackle; and the team was scheduled to meet the University of Virginia at Charlottesville. No Negro had ever played against a white university in the south. When word came of southern objection, it was, said O'Donnell, "a shock to everybody on the team. . . . Everybody agreed that if he couldn't stay in the same hotel with us, we wouldn't play."[24] Robert Kennedy shared the general outrage, and Harvard made its point.

Politics, as one of the water boys recalled twenty years later, was "the favorite topic of conversation outside of football shop talk."[25]

The veterans had wide experience, strong opinions and little respect for authority. "We were," said O'Donnell, "the dozen most know-it-alls in the history of the world."[26] The talk Robert Kennedy heard at the training table could very well have been better than the talk he missed at the Spee Club.

III

Robert Kennedy's opinions were still substantially his father's. Joseph Kennedy in the years after the war lived according to quiet routine at the Cape or in Palm Beach, plugged into the world of affairs by the omnipresent telephone. "I really began to make money," he told James M. Landis, who had remained a Kennedy intimate and became, after he left government in 1948, a Kennedy lawyer, "when I came down here to sit on my butt and think."[27] He seemed to drop out of politics, although, according to recurrent rumors (which Felix Frankfurter regularly passed on to his brethren on the Supreme Court), Kennedy was "actively promoting" William O. Douglas for the presidential or vice presidential nomination.[28] While there is no evidence of great activity, that was certainly his preference. Arthur Krock wrote in 1952 that Douglas was always Kennedy's first choice for the Presidency.[29] Douglas remembers Kennedy saying to him at Palm Beach in the late 1940s, "I must be nuts. The two men in public life that I love most are Jack and you. And I disagree with you guys more than anyone else. What's wrong with me?"[30]

His consuming public concern was as it had been before the war: that the United States might be deluded into mounting a world crusade for democracy. He was perfectly consistent. He saw communism in the forties as he had seen Nazism in the thirties—as a detestable system but not as a mortal threat to American security. "Russia does not want a major war now or in the near future," he wrote in *Life* in March 1946. The Soviet Union no doubt had an ideological hope for the worldwide victory of communism, but in practice, he said, Communist ambitions would be subordinate to Russian national interests.

The United States, as Joseph Kennedy saw it, had the choice of two foreign policies. The idea of "pressing steadily and persistently to establish liberal democracy throughout the world" attracted supporters who were "ardent, sincere, active and optimistic. It appeals to the best in the best of men and the best of nations." But it had, Kennedy thought, signal defects. By its very nature it involved the United States "in a program of minding other people's business on a global scale." He warned against "the war-breeding risks of worldwide meddling under the guise of benign interest. . . . *The basic world policy for the U.S. should be to prevent World War III.*"[31]

The Truman Doctrine of 1947 brought the elder Kennedy into open opposition to the Cold War. "If it could be demonstrated that giving dollars to stop the spread of Communism in the Balkans could accomplish that objective," he wrote in an article for the Hearst newspapers, "I would make no comment. . . . But it is obvious to anyone with even limited experience in world politics that a few hundred million dollars is but a beginning." As for aid to Greece or Turkey, "I suspect that the Russian people resent that as our people would resent Russian aid to a Mexican Pancho Villa or a Communist adventurer in Cuba." What was the panic about? Kennedy's recommendation was to "permit Communism to have its trial outside the Soviet Union if that shall be the fate or will of certain people. In most of these countries a few years will demonstrate the inability of Communism to achieve its promises, while through this period the disillusioned experimenters will be observing the benefits of the American way of life, and most of them will emulate it. . . . The dangers at home are far more real to me"—budget deficits, high taxes, inflation, depression, socialism.* "I insist that, when public officials advocate the policy of underwriting the salvation of the rest of the world from Communism, they are morally bound to show the American people just where the money can come from—OUT OF THE POCKET OF THE AMERICAN TAXPAYER."[32]

As the Cold War deepened, Kennedy insisted more and more on parallels between 1938 and 1948. After the policy of "cooperation" failed, he wrote, Britain had shifted in 1939 "to a policy that parallels the one we have been pursuing under the so-called Truman doctrine." As the British course had rashly committed British prestige to

* Interview with Arthur Krock, *New York Times*, March 21, 1947. I am bound to quote my own response to that interview at the time: "Even in America, the capitalist fatherland, the death wish of the business community appears to go beyond the normal limits of political incompetence. . . . The foreign policy of the business community is characteristically one of cowardice rationalized in terms of high morality. The great refusal to take on the Russians today is perfectly typical. That *doyen* of American capitalists, Joseph P. Kennedy, recently argued that the United States should not seek to resist the spread of Communism . . ." (*Partisan Review*, May–June 1947). In retrospect, I believe there was more force in Kennedy's position than I understood in 1947. On the other hand, I still think he gravely overestimated the freedom that "disillusioned experimenters" would have to abandon totalitarian experiments. Given the economic chaos and political confusion in western Europe in the year before the Marshall Plan, the Kennedy prescription still seems to me unduly complacent, if my response to it seems unduly shrill.

the defense of vulnerable European states, so "the Truman doctrine has committed us in situations all over the world. . . . It assumes that our nation of 145 million people will control the destiny of Europe's 245 million, not to speak of Asia's hundreds of millions." He added that we were now told that the Marshall Plan—"the grandiose subsidization of the world"—would bring about European recovery in a few years and thereby halt the rising tide of communism. "In my judgment it will do neither."[33]

Kennedy was willing to send $5 billion to Europe for humanitarian purposes. But Europe's real difficulties, he said, were not physical but moral—especially the historic selfishness of European capitalism in declining to share its gains with the workers. "The seeds that make for communism in Europe are too deep to be reached by a recovery plan." Nor could he see that the United States had any great stake in the balance of power in Europe.

> We cannot base our foreign policy on the thesis that the United States cannot tolerate the attainment by any nation of a predominant position in Europe. If we do this, we shall either have to fill the vacuum ourselves or fight war after war to prevent some other nation from achieving that paramount position. This, however, is what we are asked to do when we are urged to make defensive and offensive alliances with the sixteen or more nations to whom we contemplate extending aid.

As for the larger design for which the Marshall Plan might be only the prelude: "No matter what we try to do, 145 million people cannot reform, police and feed the globe. Russia cannot do it either. No nation that has sought to assume that burden has been able to stand the strain. And the atom bomb will not alter that basic fact, for wars as such solve nothing."[34]

In supposing that a nation, once it had tried communism, could readily overthrow a police state, Kennedy was unwontedly optimistic. And in disclaiming the idea that the United States had no stake in the European balance, he was rejecting an ancient theme in American foreign policy. "It cannot be to our interest," Jefferson had written in 1814, "that all Europe should be reduced to a single monarchy"; it would be better to fight "than see the whole force of Europe wielded by a single hand."[35] If the European balance was deemed essential to the safety of the United States in the age of the frigate, it would conceivably seem even more essential in the age of the bomber.

For Kennedy the answer lay in hemisphere solidarity. "We cannot dominate the world. But we can make ourselves too expensive to conquer. This is not a plea for isolation, but it is a plea against impe-

The Third Son

rialism." He visualized "the Western Hemisphere as a self-sufficient economic unit" under North American protection. The pursuit of hemisphere self-sufficiency, he believed, would be far less costly than the world war to which global meddling would eventually lead. "War, at any time, would be hideous. At present or in the foreseeable future war would wreck our present civilization."[36]

"People are talking war," he wrote Beaverbrook early in 1948. ". . . I shudder to think what the end of the next one would be. There are so many more places now where war could break out, as compared with the last World War, that I haven't much confidence in the situation." If Henry Wallace stayed in the presidential contest, Joseph Kennedy added, "any Republican can beat Truman. . . . Wallace is surprisingly strong because he is advocating peace."[37]

IV

His views were sharply at odds with the orthodoxies of the day. They did not prevail even in his own family. Congressman John F. Kennedy strongly backed both the Truman Doctrine and the Marshall Plan. The disagreement between his father and his brother may have been one explanation of Robert Kennedy's remark that he began thinking about issues when he went to college. These were certainly among the questions vigorously debated when the know-it-alls gathered in the evening at the Varsity Club.

Of the Varsity Club group O'Donnell had the most lively interest in politics. He was an all-out New Deal Democrat. Nothing impressed him less than the discovery that his new friend was the son of the celebrated Ambassador Kennedy. "I didn't really care very much who Ambassador Kennedy was," O'Donnell said later, "and I don't know anybody in the city of Worcester that cared. . . . The Kennedys were famous people. They were not famous people in Massachusetts." Moreover, O'Donnell had never thought much of the ambassador; "he was an isolationist and I was not . . . I had been very pro-Roosevelt and he was not."[38]

"Bobby espoused, naturally, his father's views," O'Donnell recalled. ". . . I had just spent three years in Europe and I saw it totally differently." The football players sat around and listened to O'Donnell and Kennedy argue; "we had a nightly dissertation on politics in which there'd be twenty or thirty members of the squad and those who came over to listen just for the fun. . . . We were the acknowledged leading debaters in that segment of the University."[39]

Robert used to bring O'Donnell to Hyannis Port on weekends, perhaps in order to expose him to his father, perhaps in order to expose his father to him, perhaps out of sheer mischief. On an early visit, Robert outlined an argument and provoked his father into vehement rejoinder. "I didn't say anything," O'Donnell remembered, "because I was a guest in the house and wasn't that rude as yet." After the ambassador finished, Robert said, "Dad, now that you're all done, I want you to know that Kenny absolutely, totally disagrees with you, don't you, Kenny?" O'Donnell laughed nervously, "and the old man laughed like hell. We had our confrontations, but he was always a gentleman."[40] O'Donnell said later, "I totally disagreed with Ambassador Kennedy throughout our whole association, and he never cared too much for me. . . . His ideas and mine were very, very contrary."[41] What bothered the ambassador, however, was not contrariety in ideas but moral delinquency. Once the two boys joked at dinner about finishing last in a sailing race. Mr. Kennedy listened with mounting disgust. "What kind of guys are you to think that's funny?" he said and left the table.[42]

V

In March 1948 Robert Kennedy received his A.B. degree. His father regarded him with increasing hope but still evidently with a certain dubiety. "He is just starting off," he wrote Beaverbrook shortly after Robert's graduation, "and he has the difficulty of trying to follow two brilliant brothers, Joe and Jack. That in itself is quite a handicap, and he is making a good battle against it."[43]

The next step in the battle was a trip abroad. As usual, Joseph Kennedy had everything in hand. He arranged for the *Boston Post* to accredit his son as a correspondent and for Cardinal Spellman and James M. Landis to supply letters of introduction. Armed also with a financial letter from the National City Bank of New York and certification from the Cambridge police department that he had no criminal record, Robert set forth on the *Queen Mary* on March 5, accompanied by a college friend, George Terrien.[44] When his father discovered that Beaverbrook was crossing on the same boat, he enjoined Robert to go and speak to him. This perhaps was one of the last things Robert, diffident as ever, wished to do; but, as his mother said later, he knew that his father would be disappointed if he didn't do it, so he did it.[45]

The Third Son

They dined together on the second night out. Robert wrote in his diary:

> We discussed the differences in his and Dad's pre-war views. Beaverbrook believed that war was not inevitable. Turn Germany toward East. To hell with Czech[s]. Attacked Chamberlain's policies not [for] the reason Churchill did but because they did not go far enough. Dad believed War between Germany and Russia would bring on a Universal War.[46]

They saw the evening movie and then went to the lounge where Beaverbrook ruminated at length.

> Beaverbrook believes we are living in potentially the most happy of times, because it is the most exciting of times. Happiness comes only from the facing and the attempting of answers for problems. The Victorian age could not achieve happiness except thru the pursuit of women.

Robert remarked that he was going to the Middle East. Beaverbrook said that the United States was a "subjugated nation to a Jewish minority." As for Britain, it had become "a satellite to the United States." He said he did not like the British (he was, of course, a Canadian), but he gave them full credit for "the two great attributes of tolerance and bravery." Roman Catholicism, Beaverbrook added, was "the great hope of mankind because of its organizational ability and its great leaders . . . Spellman and Griffiths [he probably meant Cardinal Bernard Griffin] for example." Arriving in London, Beaverbrook wrote Joseph Kennedy: "He is a remarkable boy. He is clever, has good character, energy, a clear understanding, and fine philosophy. You are sure to hear a great deal of him if you live long enough."[47] At least Robert Kennedy was a good listener.

After a few days in London, Robert and his companion went on to Cairo. The fervor of Egyptian nationalism impressed him. "Everyone hates the British . . . who, they believed, kept them subjugated without advance in order to keep their own prominence." The poverty impressed him too. "No middle class at all. The lower class are absolute peons. . . . Poor children have a terrible existence with flies crawling in eyes & nose & it seems to bother them not one iota. They know no better. . . . Beggars everywhere & all want American Dollars. Will not take English hard currency. . . . Honking of horns incessant. . . . Men go around holding hands like mad."

He met a young Jew from Tel Aviv who gave him letters to leaders of Haganah, the Jewish defense organization, and then a representative of the Arab League who "became most vehement & said he doubted very much if the people to whom I have the letters would still be alive when I arrived. 'We will cut them out by the roots.' "[48] The RKO Radio Pictures representative in Cairo, to whom Joseph Kennedy had entrusted the boys, told them they should not go on to so agitated a land.[49]

This had the usual effect. On March 26, Good Friday, they flew to Lydda airport and traveled to Tel Aviv by armored car, with Haganah escort, along roads menaced by Arab guerrillas. In Tel Aviv, soldiers took them to Haganah headquarters for an examination of their credentials. After release, "went for a walk, but picked up by the police & as large crowd gathered were blindfolded & put in car & again taken to headquarters to be interrogated by Security Police. Advised us to stay off streets unless with someone." They wanted to push on to Jerusalem but it was difficult until a British major who had heard of Ambassador Kennedy offered them a ride in an armored car. "Very fortunate we arrived as we did, as the next Jewish convoy that left Tel Aviv if reports are correct is being cut to ribbons in its attempt to get through."

Remembering his assignment for the *Boston Post,* Robert talked to everyone he could find—to Haganah soldiers who held the British responsible for everything; to a British soldier who had been there for two years and was sympathetic toward the Jews. "Admitted British had been responsible for much of terrorism but said officers had tough time controling [sic] men who had seen some of their buddies blown to hell." He talked to members of Irgun, the resistance organization that had recently dynamited a British train and the King David Hotel. "They'll fight any soldiers no matter what uniform they are wearing if they attempt to administer their homeland." He talked to a girl in the propaganda service.

> Very nice & only 23 years old. I never saw anyone so tired. . . . It was through her that I really began to see the imense [sic] tragedy & horribleness of it all. She was 6th generation & has four brothers in the Haganah starting at 13 years of age. Before the youngest was finally taken her mother used to make him behave by threatening him [that] the Haganah wouldn't take him unless he behaved. Told one story of a girl who carried on with the British police until finally the Stern Gang caught up with her and shaved her head. When her brother returned from the front and saw her, he shot and killed her. We had a very good time as she laughed a great deal but—

He visited a kibbutz through the kindness of a Jew who, forty years before, had made speeches in Boston for Honey Fitz. "It was self supporting & very impressive but several things I did not like, i.e., taking children away from their parents at age of one year so Mother and Father can concentrate whole of their time on work of farm & not be bothered with children the whole day. Children & parents see each other at night when both are at their best & in much more love & respect supposedly." He talked to a former major in the Russian army who believed that the Russian leaders and people "as a whole are more anti-Semitic than the Germans." Nor did he find much enthusiasm about Americans. "We are certainly not the good little saints," he noted, "we imagine ourselves in the eyes of these people." He summed up Jerusalem: "Firing is going on at all times. Still impressed by vehemence of all parties. More & more horrible stories pouring in. . . . Correspondents all very jumpy. As much shooting is going on things very nervous."

They went on to Lebanon. A letter arrived in Beirut from his mother bringing news of Ethel Skakel's prowess on the tennis court. Rose Kennedy concluded: "If anyone does a lot for you, such as luncheon at the Embassy, you might send the lady flowers afterward. At any rate, try to write a note. As you are young, it need not be a big gesture."[50] He wrote his parents about Palestine early in April: "the only way to describe the situation is 'very very horrible.' That and a universal hatred for the British seems to be the only points agreed on by all." He was considerably impressed by the Jews. "They are different from any Jews I have ever know[n] or seen." As for the Arabs, "I just wish they didn't have that oil."[51]

On May 14 the British mandate came to an end. A Jewish provisional government proclaimed the republic of Israel, and the Arab League soon launched an attack on the new state. The *Boston Post* ran four articles from its "Special Writer" in the Middle East on June 3–6. The first bore a headline guaranteed to sell papers in Boston: BRITISH HATED BY BOTH SIDES. The author, after commenting on the ambiguity of the Balfour Declaration, gave objective statements of the Arab and Jewish viewpoints. "It is an unfortunate fact that because there are such well-founded arguments on either side each grows more bitter toward the other."

His second piece revealed his own commitment. The Jews in Palestine, he wrote, "have become an immensely proud and determined people. It is already a truly great modern example of the birth of a nation with the primary ingredients of dignity and self-respect." His original draft added at this point: "Many of the leading Jewish spokesmen for the Zionist cause in the United States are doing immeasurable harm for that cause because they have not spent any or sufficient time with their people to absorb the spirit." On reflection he deleted this thought and simply praised the Jews in Palestine as "hardy and tough," their "spirit and determination" created not only by their desire for a homeland but by "the remembrance of the brutal inhuman treatment received by the Jews in the countries of Europe." He gave a lyrical account of his kibbutz visit, omitting the reservations expressed in his diary. The Jews, he said, had "an undying spirit" the Arabs could never have. "They will fight and they will fight with unparalleled courage."

The third piece was sharply critical of British policy for its "bitterness toward the Jews." As for the United States, he noticed himself becoming more and more conscious, as he traveled abroad, "of the great heritage and birthright to which we as United States citizens are heirs and which we have the duty to preserve." A prime motive in writing his dispatches, he said, "is that I believe we have failed in this duty or are in great jeopardy of doing so." We had failed because we had been taken in by the British.

> Our government first decided that justice was on the Jewish side in their desire for a homeland, and then it reversed its decision temporarily. Because of this action I believe we have burdened ourselves with a great responsibility in our own eyes and in the eyes of the world. We fail to live up to that responsibility if we knowingly support the British government who behind the skirts of their official position attempt to crush a cause with which they are not in accord. If the American people knew the facts, I am certain a more honest and forthright policy would be substituted for the benefit of all.

The final piece dismissed the notion, then prevalent, that a Jewish state might go Communist. "That communism could exist in Palestine," Robert Kennedy said, "is fantastically absurd. Communism thrives on static discontent as sin thrives on idleness. With the type of issues and people involved, that state of affairs is nonexistent. I am as certain of that as of my name." He recalled how Robert Emmet met the accusation that he was in league with Napoleon by saying he had not fought one foreign oppressor in order to replace him by another.

His original draft concluded: "I think the word 'hate' sums up the situation in Palestine better than anything I can think of. There will be a bloody war because there must be a bloody war. There is no other alternative." He was marginally more hopeful in the *Post*. He had seen Jews and Arabs working side by side in the fields and orange groves outside Tel Aviv; perhaps these would make a greater contribution than those who carried guns. If a Jewish state were formed, it might be the "only stabilizing factor" in the Middle East. "The United States and Great Britain before too long a time might well be looking to a Jewish state to preserve a toehold in that part of the world." In any case, peace-loving nations could not stand by and watch people kill each other. "The United States through the United Nations must take the lead in bringing about peace in the Holy Land."

His father, with his dread of American meddling, conceivably winced a little at this last proposition. Not too much, probably: he cared less what his sons said than whether they said it persuasively. On these grounds he must have admired Robert's series. The pieces showed a maturity, cogency and, from time to time, literary finish creditable for a football player of twenty-two hardly out of college.

VI

From the Middle East the wayfarers went on to Istanbul, Athens and Rome, where they arrived on April 15, three days before the election of 1948. They rushed to hear Togliatti, the Communist leader, denounce the United States before a crowd of 200,000 (or so Robert estimated it). "The fellow who was translating for us was very frightened by the crowd & the fact he had to speak English. He was very anti-Commie but took to clapping when the crowd did so as not to be noticeable." The crowd, Robert reported, sang "The Internationale" again and again but the speech did not appear to arouse uncontrollable enthusiasm. Christian Democratic planes, no doubt subsidized by the CIA, circled overhead dropping leaflets.

With the Christian Democrats returned by a safe majority on April 18, Kennedy and Terrien headed south, meditating—two young men who had missed the war—over the smashed monastery at Monte Cassino; then to Naples and afterward the breathtaking Amalfi road—the "most beautiful drive that I have ever seen." Suddenly tragic news: Kathleen Hartington had flown from London in a private plane for a weekend in the south of France; the plane crashed in fog near Lyons; the ravishing girl was dead. It was one more appalling blow for the Kennedy family, already sorely tried by the hand of God. Joseph Kennedy, who was in Paris, brought his beloved daughter's body back to England. "I can still see the stricken face of old Joe Kennedy," Alastair Forbes recalled nearly thirty years later, "as he stood alone, unloved and despised, behind the coffin of his eldest daughter amid the hundreds of British friends who had adored her and now mourned her." She was, Forbes said, "the best and brightest-eyed of all Kennedys . . . upon whose gravestone at Chatsworth is most truthfully written 'Joy she gave.' "[52]

Robert Kennedy, unable because of jaundice to attend Kathleen's funeral, went to London immediately thereafter. "I never saw Dad here in England," he wrote his sister Patricia, "but everyone said he looked terrible. I talked to him on the phone & he was no laughs to use an old expression. All these people loved Kick so much it's really impressive." He added: "Between you & me except for a few individuals you can have the bunch."[53]

The fun had gone out of the grand tour. They pressed on to Belgium.

> Went to Billy's grave. People around the area where war has passed through so many times take it all rather objectively which is hard for me to understand. They went thru all the motions of how Billy was killed & how he fell etc. which was a little much for me. The farm house he was killed attacking & into which he threw his grenade now houses a couple of little children & parents with the man having difficulty keeping his pants up. The people all tell their stories of the war as if they just came out of a wild western movie.

In Holland they encountered widespread criticism of the English. "Came to the conclusion today that if I were an Englishman I would be very proud of so being." They entered Germany by way of Aachen, not far from the convent that Rose Kennedy had attended forty years before. Aachen "was far worse than anything I imagined. Streets not cleared of the rubble which at places reached heights of 10 feet or more. . . . Passed blocks and blocks where only the shells of houses were left standing. It was even more eerie than Cassino." They went to Cologne, where tourists were forbidden to go into the cathedral, "but as I looked like a workman dressed as I was I went through inside. Very sad. Statues with missing heads or limbs, rubble all over floor, piled up high on sides."

They went to Heidelberg and to Frankfurt. "The people in all these cities," he wrote his parents, "walk around in dazed silence. . . . If one blows one's horn, they jump wildly as if you woke them out of a dream, but that's the only reaction for they don't give you more than a fleeting glance." He reported it as "the universal opinion that the majority of the Germans don't feel the least sorry for their 'sins.' " He asked a German veteran where he thought Hitler was. The answer was "in Heaven." He was also critical of the American occupation.

17 & 18 year olds & bitter displaced nationals & Jews because they could speak German were placed in prominent positions where justice was anything but imparted. If you were in a concentration camp you automatically received without investigation an administrative post with the result that people who had been placed in the camps because they were sex perverts or such became mayors.

Many people, he added, "expect war by July tenth. . . . Nobody believes the Russians want it but as the backing down by either side would be a great loss of face almost anything could happen."[54] He was soon writing from Vienna, where he plunged into the atmosphere of *The Third Man*. "The intrigues, plots, and counterplots make even a visitor feel that he is part of something unreal. It is Alfred Hitchcock at his best. The city is a primary focal point in the struggles of the so-called East and West." There was more worrying talk about the future:

> Everybody in Embassy wants to go to war with their comprehension of results built not on history but on own rather idealistic beliefs. I'm afraid they might sweep us right into war. The same may well apply for military.
> Many here believe we want war now as we have A Bomb and Russia is not yet back on her feet. Many also evidently believe we are imperialistic ranging from the extreme that we actually want to take over the territory till that we want to impose such business ties on the countries that we are supposedly helping that they will virtually be our colony. Many think we are using Marshall Plan because we have to have an export market. Military Men & Civs always shooting mouths off that US is best in everything alienates them, particularly when they refuse to take criticism on own country. Belief infused by the fact we are supporting these countries & have a right to say what we wish. Of course ideally we should be just the opposite.

In Vienna as in Frankfurt he heard much complaint from the American military about the wartime and postwar agreements with the Soviet Union. In early July, he decided to see eastern Europe for himself. They crossed the Russian zone of Austria into Czechoslovakia. "Were kept for an hour at border while the authorities went minutely thru our bags reading as best they could *all* our letters." Czechoslovakia—this was four months after the death of Jan Masaryk and a month after the resignation of President Beneš—was depressing. "All mumble now—What can we do? My question is what are we all going to do?"

He failed to get into Hungary. He had applied for a visa in London; but, after being assured there would be no problem, he was stalled, and no visa ever arrived. Someone told him later that the Hungarians feared he might be carrying secret messages from Cardinal Spellman to Cardinal Mindszenty. Instead the travelers went back to London and then back again to West Germany, where the great airlift, by which the western allies hoped to circumvent the Soviet blockade of ground traffic into West Berlin, was now, in mid-July, two and a half weeks old. Planes were taking off and landing every three or four minutes at the Frankfurt airport. "It is a very moving and disturbing sight to see plane after plane take off amidst a torrent of rain, particularly when I was aboard one."

West Berlin was filled with gloom. "Everybody seems to agree the blockade can't possibly hold out & we will have to ignominiously pack up or attempt to run in with armed force." The airlift "can't possibly" provide sufficient coal, he was told, and, "as coal gets shorter, unemployment will increase & although Germans strongly behind us new resentment is bound to grow & we will not have right to subject them to such increased hardships."

The travelers journeyed on to meet a couple of Kennedy sisters in Copenhagen. "In their thirst for culture they included George and I [the Kennedys could never get this right] so every morning bright and early we hustled off to a different museum to study Denmark's art. I never even knew there was any."[55] Then to Stockholm and to Dublin and the horse show. The summer was drawing to an end. "Would you please make the necessary reservations for George & I to return to the US," Robert wrote his father's office. "We would like to go tourist if possible."[56]

His diary notes for the six months abroad showed sharp and generally dispassionate observation, relentless curiosity, laconic courage, wry humor and a certain sobriety of judgment. He did not evidently share his father's view that the United States should stop minding other people's business. On the other hand, he was appalled at the talk of war and was not, at least in the field, an ideological crusader. This changed somewhat when he got home. At the end of the year the Hungarian government arrested Mindszenty and put him on trial. Robert Kennedy wrote an emotional article in the *Boston Advertiser:*

> We can look back over the last four or five years and see the colossal mistakes that we have made. Every day we hear someone groaning about it. Every day someone is heard to say, "How could anyone be so stupid as to act like that." Yalta, Potsdam, how ignominious!
>
> Here is a great opportunity for forceful action. . . . All eyes will now be turned our way to see if [Mindszenty] will be betrayed, or if resistance to evil can expect support. This is our second chance. Let us not now once again grovel in uncertainty.

For if we fail, the fault as with Julius Caesar's Romans will be "not in our stars but in ourselves."
LET US NOT FAIL![57]

VII

"I just didn't know anything when I got out of college," he said later. "I wanted to do graduate work, but I didn't know whether to go to law school or business school. I had no attraction to business, so I entered law school."[58] His marks were not good enough for Harvard or Yale. The University of Virginia told him that "in view of your record at Harvard College, you are unlikely to be admitted to this Law School, unless you do well on the [Law] Aptitude Test."[59] As a fallback, Robert applied to the Harvard Business School. "They let football players in with very little trouble," he informed his father's office.[60] He wrote his sister Patricia:

> I suppose you have heard it rumored about that there is a small question of what college is going to have my services for the next couple of years. Virginia law school has rather insulted me as well as my whole family [of] which when I looked around you were a member by saying that I had a "far from outstanding record at Harvard." We must stick together on this sort of thing. . . .
>
> There has been some mention of business school . . . I think the idea of me at business school has more comical than serious aspects. The result I'm afraid is that we should all suck around Dr. Cloney [the family dentist] & get old Bobby into Georgetown Dental School.[61]

But Charlottesville finally decided to admit him, adding that "unless he does better work than he did at Harvard, he is most unlikely to succeed in this Law School."[62]

He returned on the *Queen Mary* in August and arrived at Charlottesville in September. As usual, nothing came easy, but, as usual, will was hardened by difficulty. He did not talk much in the classroom but listened carefully and applied himself diligently. "It was like everything he had done," said Charles Spalding; "it was like trying to make the football team at Harvard all over again."[63]

For Professor Charles O. Gregory's noted seminar on labor relations he wrote a paper (submitted with a handwritten note: "Here it is—what you have been waiting for these many weeks!") analyzing the application of seniority rules to layoffs and finding in each case for the union.[64] His great effort in constitutional law was a discourse entitled "The Reserve Powers of the Constitution." This was an encomium on the Ninth and Tenth amendments, which had been designed, he wrote, "to prevent the [national] government from entering into fields which have not been specifically covered by the rest of the Constitution and in that way claiming the prerogative by default." The republic had started to go wrong, he suggested, when John Marshall, "the leading proponent of an all powerful government," took the supremacy clause "as his bible." Fortunately, from Marshall's death to 1936, the power of the states had been "comparatively well protected." In recent years, however, the Supreme Court had been looking at the Constitution "with a magnifying glass and if it could discover there any express or implied power for the federal government to act, then that act was constitutional, the 10th Amendment ineffective." His peroration, no doubt pleasing to his father, called for "effective control of the great leviathan, the federal government."[65]

His major success—at least in the eyes of the Law School, which deposited the paper in the Law Library's Treasure Trove—was an essay on Yalta, written in his last year, for Hardy Dillard's seminar on international law and relations. The Korean War had begun; the Cold War was growing colder; and Robert Kennedy shared enthusiastically in the conservative revulsion of the time against the diplomacy of Franklin Roosevelt. "By Feb. 11, 1945," he declared in his paper, "it can be said that the peace of the world was lost." If the United States had gone to Yalta knowing the real problems and "the correct philosophy," it would not have been too late to rectify earlier errors. But "we were there seeking solutions to the wrong problems and we were there with a bankrupt philosophy. By Feb. 11 we had taken the final step from which there was no salvation."*

The Far Eastern agreement at Yalta, he argued, was the "most amoral of acts whose potential disaster has long since become for us present-day catastrophe"—a reference to Chinese intervention in Korea. It had not been in our interest, he wrote, to beg for Russia's entry into the Pacific war. "For this mistake we are paying in blood." As for the agreement on liberated Europe, this was

> a clear violation of the basic tenets of International Law. With a stroke of the pen we made forever farcial [sic] the principles for which we had repeatedly told the world we were fighting. England violated her guarantee of Poland of March 1939. . . . The U.S. and G.B. violated the Atlantic Charter.

* He added in a footnote: "I do not believe that because we have lost the peace, that war is inevitable. We have lost the peace but it does not follow that we have lost also the opportunity to prevent a war. That fortunately lies before us" (Robert F. Kennedy, "A Critical Analysis of the Conference at Yalta, February 4–11, 1945," 33, University of Virginia Law Library).

The Third Son

He drew a fancy conclusion: "Human history has demonstrated too dramatically that terms such as these only give birth to new conflicts. The God Mars smiled and rubbed his hands."

Why these monumental errors? "President Roosevelt felt that the way to beat the Common Enemy as well as to have future peace was to stay friendly with Russia. . . . This was the philosophy that he and his lieutenants, Hopkins, Harriman, Winant, etc. kept as their guiding star throughout the entire war—a philosophy that reached its epitomy [sic] at Yalta, and a philosophy that spelled death and disaster for the world."* The United States had failed to place itself on the right side morally, "and it will be to our everlasting dishonor. One lesson we can learn from all this is that the Bible concept of 'It is better to give than to receive' does not always apply."[66]

The paper was a forceful statement of the right-wing case against Roosevelt's Russian policy. It was written, of course, long before later fashions in revisionism condemned Roosevelt as an imperialist who ignored legitimate Soviet security concerns and proposed to dominate eastern Europe in the interests of expanding American capitalism. It was revealing for the arguments it did not make. Though written after Alger Hiss's conviction for perjury and after Senator Joseph McCarthy's discovery that Communists had been running United States foreign policy, it attributed the errors of Yalta to bad judgment, not to sinister intent. Hiss, for example, had been at Yalta. Kennedy did not mention his name. In this regard it differed from the right-wing boilerplate of the day.

VIII

Robert Kennedy came into his own at Charlottesville in the extracurricular life—especially when in his last year he became president of the somewhat moribund Student Legal Forum, an institution set up to bring outside speakers to the Law School. Drawing on his father's stock of friends, he produced in rapid succession James M. Landis, William O. Douglas, Arthur Krock and Joe McCarthy. Thurman Arnold and Ralph Bunche came too, as well as Congressman John F. Kennedy and, on December 12, 1950, Joseph P. Kennedy himself.

---

* In a draft he said, "In criticizing the Yalta Agreement, I recognize that Franklin Roosevelt and his advisors were faced with immensely complicated problems, and that they were dealing with a dictator who did not share their sincere and generous hopes for the future. But even though this may be true, I believe that mistakes were made and that the American people can only plan for the future by knowing these mistakes."

The elder Kennedy spoke six months after the Truman administration had brought the United States into the Korean War and three weeks after MacArthur's insistence on invading North Korea had provoked massive Chinese intervention. It was a melancholy December. In Kennedy's view the Korean debacle vindicated every apprehension he had felt about postwar American policy. "From the start I had no patience with a policy—what has become known as the 'Truman Doctrine'—that, without due regard to our resources—human and material—would make commitments abroad that we could not fulfill." Beginning with our intervention in the Italian elections and our aid to Greece and Turkey, "we have expanded our political and financial programs on an almost unbelievably wide scale." To what end? "What business is it of ours to support French colonial policy in Indo-China or to achieve Mr. Syngman Rhee's concepts of democracy in Korea?" The interventionist policy, Kennedy said, was "suicidal." It won no dependable friends; it scattered military power over the globe; it thrust us into battlefields impossibly removed from our sources of supply. Far from containing communism, "it has solidified Communism, where otherwise Communism might have bred within itself internal dissensions."

The only hope was "to wash up this policy" and return to fundamentals. The first step, Kennedy said, "is to get out of Korea—indeed, to get out of every point in Asia which we do not plan realistically to hold in our own defense." The second step was to apply the same principle to Europe. "What have we gained by staying in Berlin?" The Russians could, he believed, push us out whenever they chose.

> It may be that Europe for a decade or a generation or more will turn Communistic. But in doing so, it may break of itself as a unified force. Communism still has to prove itself to its people as a government that will achieve for them a better way of living. The more people that it will have to govern, the more necessary it becomes for those who govern to justify themselves to those being governed. The more people that are under its yoke, the greater are the possibilities of revolt.
>
> Moreover, it seems certain that Communism spread over Europe will not rest content with being governed by a handful of men in the Kremlin. French or Italian Communists will soon develop splinter organizations that will destroy the singleness that today characterizes Russian Communism. Tito in Yugoslavia is already demonstrating this fact.

He added, with impressive foresight, "Mao in China is not likely to take his orders too long from Stalin, especially when the only non-Asiatics left upon Asiatic soil to fight are the Russians." His policy,

Kennedy said, would be denounced as appeasement. But was it appeasement to withdraw from unwise commitments, arm yourself to the teeth and make clear for what you will fight? He would gladly, he said, choose a Munich to escape a Dunkirk.[67]

It was in retrospect a tantalizing mixture of prescience and perversity. *Pravda* happily reprinted the full text. Congressman John Rankin of Mississippi, the most rabid reactionary in Congress, inserted it with high praise into the *Congressional Record*. Walter Lippmann saw merit in it.[68] Joseph and Stewart Alsop saw none, writing that ten years before Kennedy had advocated giving the world to Nazi Germany; now he "has just crawled out of his richly upholstered burrow to advocate giving the world to the Soviet Union." He might not put it quite that way, they conceded, but his program "insures total triumph for Stalin."[69]

Kennedy's Charlottesville speech, followed by a speech on similar lines from Herbert Hoover a week later, opened the so-called Great Debate of 1951. The debate, however, was speedily derailed, once Senator Robert A. Taft entered it, into an argument, with merit of its own, over the President's constitutional power to commit troops abroad. Kennedy's substantive propositions—especially his opposition to American armies on the Asian mainland and his conviction that communism would not be a monolith to the end of time—were ignored. His contention that the United States should not commit itself to the defense of untenable positions also deserved more attentive hearing. Unfortunately he defined tenable as penuriously as the globalists defined it extravagantly. Western Europe, even South Korea, were not in fact beyond the reach of American military power. Kennedy's perversity in the end defeated his prescience. His critics, fixing on the excesses in his argument, found it easy to dismiss him as an incorrigible appeaser repeating in 1950 his folly of 1940.

If Joseph Kennedy at the Student Legal Forum was a national event, Ralph Bunche caused considerably more excitement locally. Remembering Charlottesville's agitation over the black tackle on the Harvard football team, Robert Kennedy must have anticipated trouble. When he proposed Bunche, there was, he later recalled, "tremendous opposition." Opposition mounted when a courteous letter arrived from Bunche: "May I ask whether the seating of the audience will be on a strictly unsegregated and unseparated basis? . . . As a matter of firm principle, I never appear before a segregated audience."[70]

Virginia law, however, forbade the mingling of blacks and whites in meeting halls. Kennedy decided to ask the student government to call for an integrated audience. A classmate, Endicott Peabody Davison, described ensuing developments:

> There was a meeting with about ten people from all the classes. Bobby said we must adopt a resolution. Everyone agreed until he asked them to sign it. Then the Southern boys began to say, "I've got to go home to Alabama later—I can't sign it. I'm for it, but I can't put my name to it." Bobby blew his stack. He was so mad he could hardly talk. He had a lack of understanding of the problems these people faced; to him it seemed illogical to support something but be unwilling to sign for it. It's his black-and-white view of things. The resolution failed.

It may have failed there, but the Student Legal Forum adopted it, and a ringing statement went to the university president under Kennedy's signature. "We would like to register the strong conviction," the statement said, "reenforced by our belief in the issues presented by the last war in which most of us fought, and by our belief in the principles to which this country is committed in the Bill of Rights and the United Nations Charter, that action which would result in the cancellation of Dr. Bunche's lecture appears to us morally indefensible."[71]

In the past, the university had evaded the state law by posting one section of the hall for blacks and then letting people sit where they pleased. When Dillard proposed this as the way out, Kennedy rejected the compromise; he felt the principle was bad and had to be confronted. He carried the case to the Law School's governing body, the Board of Visitors, where, according to Davison, "the madder he got, the worse he got at talking. Very little came out." Finally, Professors Gregory and Dillard, impressed by his concern, accompanied the Law School dean to see the university president, Colgate Darden. Darden, who came from an old Virginia family and had been governor of the state, was personally opposed to this form of segregation. When the Law School professors noted that the Supreme Court in the recent case of *Sweatt* v. *Painter* had required the University of Texas Law School to admit a Negro, Darden seized the point, defined the Bunche lecture as an educational meeting and declared that it would be unsegregated.

Bunche found an integrated audience, one third black, and was visibly affected. In his talk, three months after Joseph Kennedy, he vigorously condemned the new isolationism that, he said, had "come out of hiding and has even become respectable again."[72] The Bunche episode may well have given Robert Kennedy second thoughts about

The Third Son

the virtue of concentrating governmental power on the state level. In any case he had struck a blow for decency and, after some instruction in the limitations of rage, had learned the efficacy of law.

He graduated in June 1951, fifty-sixth in a class of 124. His best course was Constitutional Law, where he was marked 3.5 out of 4.00, followed by Labor Law (3.0); his average for all courses was 2.54. The impression among the faculty was that he had not worked hard academically because native ability enabled him to do sufficiently well with a minimum of effort.[73] If he had not distinguished himself, he had shown that he could handle the material. He was now the first Kennedy of his generation to have a profession.

IX

He was seeing Ethel Skakel with increasing frequency. He called on her at Manhattanville College; she visited him at Charlottesville; and by 1949 they were enthusiastically in love.[74]

Ethel, born in Chicago on April 11, 1928, was two and a half years younger. The Skakel and Kennedy families had superficial resemblances. George Skakel, a self-made millionaire, had built a small company into the Great Lakes Carbon Corporation and now sold his petroleum coke around the world. He was a quiet man, withdrawn from the family hurly-burly. A Dutch Protestant, he had married Ann Brannack, an Irish Catholic, fat, warm-hearted, eccentric and fervently religious. They had seven children; Ethel was next to last. The Skakels moved east in the mid-thirties, into a stupendous brick mansion in the midst of a large estate outside Greenwich, Connecticut. The Skakel family, like the Kennedy family, was athletic, boisterous, competitive and filled with the will to win.

There were differences. The Kennedys had absorbed enough of the Boston ethos to have a certain reserve, discipline and frugality as well as a large measure of civic and intellectual aspiration. The Skakels, more in the style of Chicago and Fairfield County, did not conceal their wealth or restrain their children. The two oldest boys were always swinging from trees, shooting air rifles from bedroom windows, driving cars into the pond. Ethel's friends often found them scary. The Skakels, in so far as they cared about public affairs, were conservative Republicans. George Skakel wrote Joseph Kennedy after his Charlottesville speech, "It was a fine, constructive and courageous thing for you to do."[75]

Ethel was a sparkling girl, bubbling over with jokes and charm.

The Manhattanville yearbook caught her rather well: "An excited hoarse voice, a shriek, a peal of screaming laughter, the flash of shirttails, a tousled brown head—Ethel! Her face is at one moment a picture of utter guilelessness and at the next alive with mischief."[76] An excellent athlete, she hated losing as much as any Kennedy. She was bright and responsive, not, at this point, much of a reader but indefatigably curious. Her gregariousness, teasing humor and endless vitality made her the jolliest of companions. Existence around her was an unceasing swirl of activity. Her ideas of life were simple and passionate. Her sympathy was inexhaustible, which gave her the capacity to grow. Her spirit was indomitable. Her piety rivaled Rose Kennedy's. She loved Robert Kennedy with all her heart.

An obstacle arose: Ethel's sudden conviction that instead of marrying she should become a nun. Robert, walking along the beach at Hyannis Port, said disconsolately to his sister Jean, "How can I fight God?"[77] This passed. They decided to marry with Robert still in law school. "I had misgivings about that," said Rose Kennedy, though none about Ethel.[78] "My financee [sic] followed me down here," Robert wrote his sister Pat from Charlottesville in the spring of 1950, "and wouldn't let me alone for a minute—kept running her toes through my hair & things like that. You know how engaged couples are."[79]

The Greenwich wedding in June was preceded by a memorable bachelors' dinner at the Harvard Club in New York, where the redoubtable Skakel brothers encountered Robert's rowdy football friends. The Harvard Club later sent the Kennedys a bill for the wreckage. Most of his ushers were football players, so big that they could hardly get down the aisle side by side. Mrs. Skakel, said Kenneth O'Donnell, "couldn't understand where Bobby got these characters that were around him, who all weighed 250 pounds and were Greeks, Armenians, Italians."[80] Someone dropped a few coins when the wedding procession was forming, and, as Lem Billings, an usher, politely bent to help pick them up, George Skakel, Jr., kicked him hard in the pants; they had not yet been introduced.[81]

The seventh child thus produced the second marriage. Most of the Kennedys married late. "That family," said Lem Billings, "stayed home longer than any family in history."[82] Except for Kathleen, Robert was the only one of the children to marry before their late twenties, and, with Kathleen dead, he was the only married child until Eunice married R. Sargent Shriver, Jr., three years later. Perhaps he felt a particular need for a family of his own.

The Third Son

The young couple—Robert was twenty-four, Ethel, twenty-two—escaped to Hawaii for their honeymoon and settled, in the autumn, in Charlottesville for Robert's last year at law school. Ethel had technical defects as a wife. She was a flop at cooking and sewing, detested cleaning and spent money carelessly. In the circumstances the sins were venial. They could afford cooks, maids and extravagance. In fundamental ways she was a superb wife, at least in the old sense of being her husband's helpmate. For Ethel Kennedy, reared as she was and believing as she did, ministering to her husband was not self-sacrifice or self-betrayal but self-fulfillment. It did not result in any manifest repression of an irrepressible personality.

For Robert Kennedy it was the best thing that could have happened. Her enthusiasm and spontaneity delighted him. Her jokes diverted him. Her social gifts offset his abiding shyness. Her inextinguishable gaiety lightened his times of moodiness and pessimism. Her passion moved him. Her devotion offered him reassurance and security. Robert, his sister Eunice said, was more dependent emotionally than his brothers, "more anxious for affection and approval and love, and therefore when he got a lot of that, which I think he did when he married Ethel, he blossomed." She awakened his sympathy and his humor and brought him out emotionally.[83] He never had to prove himself to her. Ethel gave him unquestioning confidence, unquenchable admiration, unstinted love.

(5)
The Brothers: I

THIRTEEN MONTHS after the wedding Robert Kennedy became the father of the first Kennedy grandchild. They named her Kathleen Hartington. In another year Joseph Patrick Kennedy III was born; early in 1954 Robert Francis Kennedy, Jr.; in 1955 David Anthony Kennedy; in 1956 Mary Courtney Kennedy.[1] In the meantime, after rejecting the idea of running for Congress from Connecticut, Robert took a job with the Internal Security Division of the Department of Justice at $4200 a year. Ethel found a house at 3214 S Street in Georgetown.

I

In September 1951, before he went to work, the *Boston Post* sent him to cover the conference in San Francisco where fifty nations had gathered to conclude a peace treaty with Japan. What impressed him most was the strength of Asian nationalism. "It is a new Asia with which we are dealing," he wrote in his final piece. By tradition Americans should be "in complete sympathy with the revolutionary aspirations." But, with "communism rampant throughout the world," the United States had to act warily. If revolutionary forces were "subservient to Russia," then should not the United States intervene against them? Still,

> if we adopt the policy of intervention, a strong temptation is presented to those in power to picture all opposition forces as communistic in order to gain American aid, remain in control and incidentally save their own lives. The United States if it wishes to keep its friends in Asia cannot afford to be duped.[2]

This was an early formulation of the problem that harassed American policy for the next generation. "Bobbie is really growing up and thinking hard in this last article of his," James Landis wrote his father.[3]

He learned more about Asian nationalism when Congressman John F. Kennedy invited him and their sister Patricia to come along on a trip from Israel to Japan in early October. In Israel an old friend, Congressman Franklin D. Roosevelt, Jr., received all the attention. "I have finally solved the problem," Robert wrote home, "as to why the Jews did not accept Jesus Christ. F.D.R., Jr. is what they have been waiting for."[4] He added in his diary, "He has been very nice to us, though his statements sometimes irritate me." One Arab with whom they talked

> suggested U.S. join itself with the liberal elements of the countries of Asia & prepare for the nationalistic revolutions that are sweeping over the land. FDR, Jr. & rest of State Dept. that was present said this impossible to do as U.S. not that kind of nation.[5]

"He summed up his feeling to an Arab leader," Robert wrote his father, "by saying, 'Don't you people realize the important question is the struggle between U.S. and Russia. Why do you get so upset about these smaller things?' I almost got sick." FDR, Jr., he thought, had "simply completely missed the whole point of the nationalist revolution that is sweeping Asia." As for the State Department, Robert would get rid of the whole crowd "and replace these 'diplomats' with W. O. Douglas and James Landis. Then we might have a chance."[6]

In another week they were in India. Nehru had them to dinner but gazed, bored, at the ceiling as if he did not know why he was thus wasting his time. Only their pretty sister roused him from languid condescension. "He hardly spoke during dinner," Robert noted in his journal, "except *to Pat*." Afterward John asked Nehru about Vietnam. It was, Nehru said, a classic example of colonialism fighting a doomed battle; "said twice 'poor French' in patronizing way." The west, he added, was "pouring money & arms down a bottomless hole." As for communism, it thrived on discontent. "Might beat communists in a war but will create a situation which will give birth to other communism by destroying all sources of human wealth." (Writing this in his journal, Robert penciled on the margin: "Same as *Taft!*") Communism, Nehru told the boys, was "something to die for. Must give the same aura to democracy.... We only have status quo to offer these people. Commies can offer a change." Robert appended a family note: "Dad would have a hayday [sic] here. Nehru's posit. on India is same as his on U.S."

On October 19 they were in Saigon, where the French were fighting Ho Chi Minh and his Viet Minh. "Cannot go outside city because of guerrillas," Robert observed. "Could hear shooting as evening wore on." General de Lattre de Tassigny assured them the French army could not be beaten, adding that, if the west lost the Mekong Delta, it would lose Asia. They met Bao Dai, the former emperor of Annam whom the French had installed as token chief of state. John Kennedy noted that he seemed "in [S. J.] Perelman's words—'fried in Crisco.'" Robert thought that, if a plebiscite were held, 70 percent of the people throughout Vietnam would vote for Ho Chi Minh.

The French, Robert wrote his father, were "greatly hated." Our aid had made us also "quite unpopular." He wondered how to persuade the "masses that we are not back of the French in keeping control of this country." Had the Voice of America made enough of the fact that the United States had freed the Philippines? "Also do we stress fact that we do not care what kind of Gov [sic] a country has as long as that Govt [sic] is not controlled by a foreign nation i.e. Russia?" He told his father: "Our mistake has been not to insist on definite political reforms by the French toward the natives as prerequisites to any aid. As it stands now we are becoming more & more involved in the war to a point where we can't back out." He concluded: "It doesn't seem to be a picture with a very bright future."[7]

II

The trip in a real sense introduced Robert Kennedy to his older brother. Eight years had been a large gap. "The first time I remember meeting Bobby," Jack once said, "was when he was three and a half, one summer on the Cape."[8] Soon John left home, for school, for college, for war. Afterward Robert was away at college and law school. Apart from family gatherings they had seen little of each other. Seven weeks of arduous travel made them closer than ever before.

They had flown 25,000 miles, "eastward, always eastward," John Kennedy said in a radio speech after their return, over lands "in which the fires of nationalism so long dormant have been kindled and are now ablaze . . . an area of revolution." If there was one thing the trip had taught, he continued, it was that "Communism cannot be met effectively by merely the force of arms." The United States appeared "too ready to buttress an inequitable status quo." Vietnam produced a severe paragraph:

> We have allied ourselves to the desperate effort of a French regime to hang on to the remnants of empire. . . . To check the southern drive of Communism makes sense but not only through reliance on the force of arms. The task is rather to build strong native non-Communist sentiment within these areas and rely on that as a spearhead of defense rather than upon the legions of General de Lattre, brilliant though he may be, and to do this apart from and in defiance of innately nationalistic aims spells foredoomed failure.

He was severe too on American diplomats. "One finds too many of our representatives toadying to the shorter aims of other Western nations, with no eagerness to understand the real hopes and desires of the people to whom they are accredited, too often aligning themselves too definitely with the 'haves' and regarding the action of the 'have-nots' as not merely the effort to cure injustice but as something sinister and subversive."[9] These sons of American capitalism displayed no interest in integrating the underdeveloped world into the American economic system. In their view, the more a nation did for its have-nots the better, so long as its foreign policy was not made in Moscow.

The trip, Robert Kennedy said later, made a great impression on his brother, "a very very major impression . . . these countries from the Mediterranean to the South China Sea all . . . searching for a future; what their relationship was going to be to the United States; what we were going to do in our relationship to them; the importance of the right kind of representation; the importance of associating ourselves with the people rather than just the governments, which might be transitional, transitory; the mistake of the war in Indochina; the mistake of the French policy; the failure of the United States to back the people."[10]

A month after John Kennedy's radio report, his father addressed the same subject on the same network but to very different effect. By contracting unnecessary alliances, the ambassador warned, "we have delegated to others the power to determine our own fate. . . . Perhaps our next effort will be to ally to ourselves the Eskimos of the North Pole and the Penguins of the Antarctic." The great need was, not to assume new burdens, but "to disentangle ourselves from the far-flung commitments . . . recently made." Nehru was right to question American policy in the Cold War: "were I of his race, I could easily join in his hesitation."[11]

"I couldn't possibly have a worse argument with anyone about foreign policy than I have had with my son," Joseph Kennedy said the next year.[12] At the end of the decade John Kennedy said, "We don't even discuss [foreign policy] any more because we're just so far apart, there's just no point in it. I've given up arguing with him."[13]

III

At the end of 1951, Robert Kennedy began work for the Department of Justice. The Internal Security Division was engaged in investigations of Soviet agents, real and fancied. After a short time Kennedy transferred to the Criminal Division, where his first important assignment was to help present before a Brooklyn grand jury a case against two former Truman officials charged with corruption. The work absorbed him—so much so that when his older brother decided to run for the Senate in Massachusetts, Robert, Kenneth O'Donnell later said, was really "out of touch with Jack and unaware of Jack's problems."[14]

He was sufficiently aware to ask O'Donnell to join his brother's campaign. Challenging the popular Republican senator Henry Cabot Lodge, Jr., was hardly a project without risk. As in 1946 the ambassador moved to take personal charge. But the generational problems had intensified. Joseph Kennedy, O'Donnell complained, associated with "elder statesmen who knew nothing about the politics in this day and age, and he assumed, despite the fact that he had not been in Massachusetts for twenty years, that it was the same thing . . . and he's such a strong personality that nobody could—nobody *dared*—fight back."[15] The campaign, O'Donnell thought, was headed toward "absolute catastrophic disaster."[16] He pleaded with Robert Kennedy in New York to come up and take over. Robert was "very angry," O'Donnell remembered. He loved what he was doing in the Department of Justice. He did not look forward to a summer arguing with his father. In any case, he knew nothing about Massachusetts politics: "I'll screw it up and . . . I just don't want to come." O'Donnell said, "Unless you come, I don't think it's going to get done."[17]

He came and took over. "Bobby could handle the father," said O'Donnell, "and no one else could have."[18] The Kennedys spent money freely, setting up committees in a multitude of ethnic and professional categories. "We couldn't win relying on the Democratic political machine," Robert said later, "so we had to build our own machine."[19] Polly Fitzgerald, a cousin, and Helen Keyes, daughter of the Kennedy dentist in Brookline days, organized the famous teas for the candidate's mother and sisters. Franklin D. Roosevelt, Jr., campaigned in Jewish areas where John Kennedy, because of his father's reputation, was supposed to be weak. Robert worked eighteen hours a day, losing a dozen pounds in the process. "I didn't become involved in what words should go in a speech, what should be said on a poster or bill-board, what should be done in television. . . . I was so busy with my part of it that I didn't see any of that."[20]

His part of it—organization—was in its nature an affront to the old-line politics of the state; and Robert himself, twenty-six years old, cocky, unknown except as a millionaire's son, pressing, always pressing, was an affront to old-line politicians. Nor did he do much to assuage wounded feelings. Perhaps, in addition, he felt that a tough exterior was the only means by which a novice could hope to keep the campaign under control. Perhaps, too, he was proving things to his father, and to himself.

The "ruthless Bobby" idea seems to have been born in 1952. One day when a leading labor figure sat chatting in the headquarters, as Massachusetts politicians were wont to do, Robert brusquely ushered him out: "If you're not going to work, don't hang around here."[21] A local pol, celebrated for singing "Danny Boy" from a sound truck, was incredulous to discover that Robert Kennedy had never heard of him. "And you call this a political headquarters?" he said with a burst of profanity, thereby inciting Kennedy, who disapproved of swearing in the presence of women, to throw him out.[22] "Politicians do nothing but hold meetings," he said later, reflecting on the 1952 campaign. ". . . You can't get any work out of a politician." The interviewer noted that he spat out the word "politician" as if it were something "unclean and unwanted."[23]

As Paul Dever, the veteran Democratic governor running for reelection, saw himself slipping behind, he proposed to John Kennedy that they merge organizations and run in tandem. The ambassador thought a joint campaign a fine idea. The candidate disagreed. "Don't give in to them," John told Robert, "but don't get me involved in it."[24] The younger Kennedy broke the bad news to Dever in a stormy meeting. "He got furious at me and almost broke off any kind of relationship with us, except it was patched up really by my father, who [sic] he liked. It was rather a big debacle." Dever sent word to keep that "young kid" out of his office, saying that hereafter he would deal only with the ambassador. "In any case," Robert reflected afterward, "we ran our own campaign, which is all that I wanted."[25] The ambassador accepted it philosophically. "He had confidence in any Kennedy, whether they're right, wrong or indifferent," said O'Donnell. "They really couldn't do anything wrong."[26]

The elder Kennedy was meanwhile cheered by national developments. Eisenhower, he concluded (prematurely) in September, was "the most complete dud we have had for a candidate in my fifty years of presidential elections." As for the Democratic nominee, Adlai Stevenson of Illinois, "he has made a sensational start," Kennedy wrote Beaverbrook. ". . . the hottest thing we have in America on television, [in his speeches] he runs Churchill an even race." Unless the newspapers succeeded in sticking a leftist tag on him, "I would think that he would murder Eisenhower—and I don't think it would even be close. . . . Unquestionably he would be a great man for the United States." Best of all: "He is a great friend of mine and of the family."*

Eisenhower carried Massachusetts by 200,000 votes. Dever lost by 15,000. Kennedy won by 70,000. It was a triumph for Robert as well. But it cannot be said that he enjoyed politics, Massachusetts style. "I never heard Bob Kennedy ask anyone 'How's the family?'" said Lawrence O'Brien, a master organizer from Springfield who played a key role in the victory. "The entire hand-shaking, small-talking side of politics was repugnant to him; he often said to me, 'Larry, I don't know how you stand it.'"[27] Robert had a job to do for his brother, and he meant to do it. He did not care whether or not people liked him along the way.

IV

His brother was considerably impressed by the job Robert had done. "I don't think [Jack] was aware," Lem Billings said, "that Bobby had all this tremendous ability." John understood, too, the supreme importance in politics of a partner on whom he could count absolutely, for loyalty and for results. Their intimacy grew in the senatorial campaign. It was still, for a time, limited to politics. Along with the difference in age there remained differences in temperament and outlook. "All this business about Jack and Bobby being blood brothers has been exaggerated," their sister Eunice once said. ". . . They had different tastes in men, different tastes in women. They didn't really become close until 1952, and it was politics that brought them together."[28] "Bobby and Jack," said Lem Billings, who loved

---

* JPK to Beaverbrook, September 6, 1952, Beaverbrook Papers. As a member of Governor Stevenson's campaign staff that autumn, I can attest to Mr. Kennedy's eager interest in Stevenson. He knew me as a friend of his older son's and called me from time to time in Springfield to pass on his ideas about the tactics and strategy of the campaign.

them both, "had very different personalities and really different interests outside of politics. . . . Their closeness was really based on their political work."[29]

John Kennedy was the more secure, the freer, of the two—freer of his father, of his family, of his faith, of the entire Irish American predicament. "Jack tended to be a little bit fey, a little offhand around his father," Stephen Smith, whom Jean married in 1956, later said.[30] Robert Kennedy, on the other hand, accepted the tradition. Seeking the paternal approval for which he had longed as a small boy, he somberly took on the obligations from which his older brother had casually disengaged himself. His father appreciated that. "It was Bobby with whom he would discuss family matters," said O'Donnell.[31] "Bobby's a tough one," Joseph Kennedy himself told Bob Considine, the reporter, in 1957; "he'll keep the Kennedys together, you can bet."[32]

The two brothers had moved in different directions in adolescence and young manhood, John establishing his intellectuality, Robert his toughness, John his independence, Robert his commitment to the family. John had got along better with his father, Robert with his mother; and the result was not unexpectedly paradoxical. "Bobby was more like his father," said William O. Douglas, who saw both brothers a good deal in the 1950s, "and Jack was more like his mother. . . . Bobby was more direct, dynamic, energizing; Jack was more thoughtful, more scholarly, more reflective."[33] They emerged as contrasting figures. "Jack Kennedy," said Paul Dever after the campaign, "is the first Irish Brahmin. Bobby is the last Irish Puritan."[34] But intimacy had begun and would increase.

The head of the family was equally impressed by Robert's work in the campaign. It was, Lem Billings later said, as if "the father suddenly found he had another able son, which I don't think he realized."[35] In 1948 he had told Beaverbrook that Robert was making a good battle against his handicaps. In 1952 the battle was largely won. Robert was proving himself at last. He persuaded his father that he was truly his father's son.

His father was supposed to have said in later years that Robert was more like him than any of the other children because "he hates like me." In 1960 he denied to John Seigenthaler of the *Nashville Tennessean* that he had ever said this. But he did call Robert "the most determined person" he had ever known.[36] To another reporter he said proudly, "Bobby's as hard as nails."[37] Chatting with Charles Spalding, he remarked of John Kennedy, then well on his way to the

Presidency, "I don't understand it. He's not like me at all. I never could have done it. But Bobby is like me."[38]

In part it was an imposture. The Irish were always good role players. The gentle self was never extinguished, and the tension between Robert Kennedy's soul and his *persona* took the form of dialectic rather than war. Friendships—Hackett, O'Donnell, Billings—nourished the self; marriage nourished it even more. The inner tension, instead of stultifying, eventually enlarged and enhanced sensibility and character. It did not destroy the ultimate unity of personality. Arthur Krock described Robert Kennedy at fifteen: "bullied by his elder brothers but still managing to keep a kind of savage individuality."[39] That individuality became confused for a season, out of admiration and adoration of his father. It was never crushed.

It took long years, a family of his own, experience with life, experience with death, to reintegrate the elements of personality loosened by the shock, in so many respects the salutary shock, of his upbringing. But it happened—in spite of his father, because of his father. Robert Kennedy was indeed a most determined person. His father made him what he appeared to be. Yet Jacqueline Kennedy, who adored both Robert and his father, once said that, of the brothers, he was "least like his father."[40]

(6)

The First Investigating Committee: Joe McCarthy

VICTORY brought euphoria. Robert and Ethel, with Kenneth O'Donnell and Lawrence O'Brien and their wives, joined the new senator in Hyannis Port for the family celebration. John Kennedy was the only Democrat running statewide in Massachusetts to have survived the Eisenhower sweep. His brother had managed the campaign. The younger generation was feeling proud of itself. But Joseph Kennedy, as usual, represented the reality principle. Late one November afternoon he said to Robert, "What are you going to do now?" Robert said, "What do you mean?" "You haven't been elected to anything," his father replied. "Are you going to sit on your tail end and do nothing now for the rest of your life? You'd better go out and get a *job*."[1]

I

Early in December 1952 Joseph Kennedy telephoned to Senator Joseph McCarthy, Republican, of Wisconsin, whom Eisenhower's victory had made chairman of the Permanent Subcommittee on Investigations of the Senate Government Operations Committee. Joe McCarthy was a recent Kennedy acquaintance. He claimed to have met John Kennedy fleetingly in the Solomon Islands in 1943;[2] and in the late 1940s, after he slipped into the Washington scene as senator in 1947, he had come to know other members of the family. He took Pat and Jean out amiably in the evening and spoke for Robert's forum in Charlottesville. Eunice liked him, as did Sargent Shriver, who was the ambassador's staff assistant and whom Eunice married in May 1953. Joseph Kennedy liked him most of all and invited him from time to time to Hyannis Port.

He was a black Irishman, lowbrow and roughneck, with a certain animal vitality, coarse charm, broad humor and amusing impudence.

Something about him, perhaps his instinctive insolence toward the establishment, may have reminded Joseph Kennedy agreeably of his own youth. In the 1940s he was a man of marked personality without known political principles. Writing in 1947 about "The Senate's Remarkable Upstart," in the *Saturday Evening Post,* Jack Alexander noted that McCarthy was studying Russian. "His friends insist that he has hopes ultimately of . . . charming Stalin in his own language."[3] In the late fall of 1949, suddenly discovering the threat of communism, he forswore this earlier ambition.[4] The crusade against Communists, which he launched inadvertently at Wheeling, West Virginia, in February 1950, quickly became the vehicle for his free-floating destructiveness. The Korean War began four months after Wheeling. Growing casualty lists gave him an ever more attentive audience. If Reds were killing American boys in Korea, why should they be free to walk the streets of America? McCarthy explored the frustrations of limited war with cunning and skill. A natural demagogue, he had rare ability to implant suspicions, to confuse issues and, when challenged, to change subjects. He had a bully's tactile instinct for weakness or fear. No politician of the age, wrote Richard Rovere, had "surer, swifter access to the dark places of the American mind."[5]

All this was amply evident when Joseph Kennedy called him in December 1952. None of it worried the ambassador, even though on occasion he himself criticized the practice of smearing all leftists as Communists. "There is a strong liberal feeling throughout Europe that is a valuable asset in the fight against communism," he said in an interview in 1951, fifteen months after McCarthy had begun his jihad. "By terming this as a communistic movement we are only convincing the people over there that we are driving them into a war."[6] Nevertheless he was fond of McCarthy and now asked him to appoint Robert Kennedy chief counsel of the Permanent Subcommittee on Investigations.[7]

His older son was not enthusiastic. McCarthy's vulgarity was hardly to John Kennedy's Brahmin taste. He understood perfectly that the adoration McCarthy aroused in one section of his constituents was matched by the loathing of another section, less numerous but more influential and one whose approval meant a good deal to him. He told his bright new senatorial assistant Theodore Sorensen that he hoped Bobby would not take the job. "His reasons," Sorensen wrote later, "were political, not ideological."[8]

Joseph Kennedy's request was embarrassing for McCarthy too. He had already decided to name as chief counsel a twenty-five-year-old

New York lawyer, notable for anti-Communist zeal, named Roy Cohn. According to Cohn, McCarthy feared that Robert Kennedy's appointment might be taken as a payoff for his father's help in McCarthy's campaigns. One day Cohn found McCarthy sitting irritably in his office listening to Joseph Kennedy's voice crackling over the telephone. After a time McCarthy laid the receiver on his desk, the ambassador's voice still sounding away, scribbled a note and passed it to Cohn: "Remind me to check the size of his campaign contribution. I'm not sure it's worth it."[9]

He named young Kennedy an assistant counsel. McCarthy and Cohn set noisily to work to unearth subversives in the State Department and the Voice of America. Kennedy, assisted by LaVern Duffy, a young investigator, undertook a more prosaic inquiry into the trade carried on by American allies with Communist China. Duffy later recalled his first sight of Robert Kennedy—sleeves rolled past the elbows, collar open, necktie pulled loose, and, "most remarkable" of all, his white, woolen athletic sweat socks. These last, Duffy said, he invariably wore until Ethel or someone persuaded him that they did not go with business suits.[10]

Kennedy and Duffy pored over the Lloyds of London shipping index, British parliamentary debates and reports from the Maritime Commission and the Central Intelligence Agency. In a couple of months they were able to demonstrate that, since the outbreak of the Korean War, 75 percent of all ships carrying goods to mainland China had sailed under western flags—most of this while Chinese troops were shooting at Americans in Korea. Kennedy also discovered that some of the shippers were simultaneously collecting large sums from the United States government for delivering defense materials to western Europe. The British role in the China trade appeared particularly reprehensible. "Great Britain's rubber shipments went up sixty per cent last year over the previous year," Kennedy told one newspaperman. "Natural rubber is needed for the tires of jet planes." He said, typically, that he could not "appreciate" the English position.[11] Joe McCarthy appreciated the English position even less. One day he wrathfully showed the Senate a copy of Beaverbrook's *Sunday Express* with the headline BIG BOOST IN OUR TRADE TO CHINA. "We should perhaps keep in mind," said McCarthy,

> the American boys and the few British boys, too, who had their hands wired behind their backs and their faces shot off with machine guns—Communist machine guns, Mr. President, if you please—supplied by those flag vessels of our allies. . . . Let us sink every accursed ship carrying mate-

rials to the enemy and resulting in the death of American boys, regardless of what flag those ships may fly. . . . We can go it alone.

He finished with compliments to "Comrade Attlee," the British Prime Minister, and offered the Senate a photograph of Attlee reviewing the International Brigade in Madrid, his hand raised, McCarthy asserted, in the Communist salute.[12]

Kennedy's statistics also showed a large Greek role in the China trade. McCarthy and the staff opened negotiations with Greek ship owners. As a result the owners of 327 vessels promised to stop carrying to Communist China. This infuriated the State Department, which in more circumspect fashion had been trying to persuade allied carriers to abandon the China trade and regarded McCarthy's action as a flagrant violation of the separation of powers. Harold Stassen, the director for Mutual Security, told McCarthy that his intervention "undermines the effort we are carrying on."[13] McCarthy was now the infuriated party. Fearing a brawl, Vice President Richard M. Nixon arranged a summit meeting between McCarthy and John Foster Dulles, the Secretary of State. Dulles cut the ground out from under Stassen, endorsing McCarthy's action as "in the national interest."

II

Robert Kennedy was at McCarthy's side when he announced the Greek arrangement. The *Boston Post* reported him "alarmed and shocked at the manner in which the McCarthy haters hopped all over the deal. . . . 'I don't know,' said Kennedy. 'I really don't. I had supposed that it just didn't make sense to anybody in this country that our major allies, whom we're aiding financially, should trade with the communists who are killing GIs.'" The *Post* added, "Kennedy, contrary to general belief, apparently, has not taken part in any of the McCarthy committee's probes into subversives in the State Department, the Voice of America, and other government agencies. What he has done is work on ways to shut off strategic materials of war to countries in the Russian zone, including North Korea. He'll continue to do so."[14] His work pleased the committee. On April 2 his salary was increased from $4952.20 to $5334.57. "This raise," Flanagan informed him, "is given in recognition of the very excellent job you have been doing in connection with our investigation into East-West trade. You are to be commended on the energy, judgment and imagination which you have exercised in the conduct of this inquiry."[15]

In May, Robert Kennedy, with Ethel and a sister or two looking on, laid out the damning statistics in a public hearing. It was his debut. LaVern Duffy noticed his trembling hands and general nervousness.[16] The issue was not perhaps so simple as the assistant counsel supposed. John Leddy, the acting deputy assistant secretary of state for economic affairs, set forth the complexities. England had interests in Hong Kong and Malaya that would be damaged by a cutoff of trade with mainland China. Japan had been shipping seaweed to China and receiving iron ore in return. "It would be very hard to come to a conclusion that this exchange aids Red China." American efforts to force allies to stop trading with China might use up diplomatic bargaining power needed for more vital purposes. In any case, Leddy said, the effects of blacklisting allied ships engaged in the China trade would be "negligible." There would be "some slight reshuffling of ships' availability, but the overall effect on the 8,000 or 10,000 tramp steamers available in the world would be barely visible." In answer to a direct question, Leddy forthrightly told McCarthy, "We are not seeking at this time the discontinuation of all trade . . . with Red China."[17]

McCarthy shut off Leddy in a pretense of anger and stalked from the room. "No diplomatic subtleties can excuse this condition to the American people," said the *New York Journal-American* irately. "We may be thankful to the McCarthy committee and to its hard-digging assistant counsel Kennedy (brother of Sen. John F. Kennedy, D.-Mass.) for bringing it to light."[18] A few days later McCarthy harangued the Senate. He expressed his appreciation to the ranking Democratic member of the committee "for consenting to lend me, for the day, the very able minority counsel, Mr. Kennedy . . . so that he can furnish me facts and figures." With Kennedy sitting at his desk, McCarthy restated his thesis:

> Of 81 million tons of shipping available to the entire world, non-Communist nations control 78 million tons. If we deny that shipping to the Communists, it will be a death blow to their war-making power. . . . We can do it by simply telling our allies that they will not get one American dollar while any of their flag ships are plying this immoral, dishonest, indecent trade.[19]

The next day, when testimony made it clear that the Defense Department tended to agree with McCarthy, Senator Stuart Symington of Missouri, a Democratic member of the committee, proposed that the chairman ask Eisenhower what the American policy was.[20] Robert Kennedy drafted the letter. It inquired whether State or Defense was speaking for the President, whether the White House thought it a breach of security to disclose the volume of strategic materials shipped to China and whether the government would refuse contracts to allied shipping firms trading with Communist China.

McCarthy had retired for a moment to the Bethesda Naval Hospital, where the letter went for his signature. Robert Kennedy then carried it to the White House. The document was respectful in tone, and Congress had every claim to the information sought. But the request exasperated a White House staff already sorely tried by McCarthy. As so often, the executive branch began talking about national security and the need to protect secret information. This was reaching rather far. The information was no secret from the Chinese Communists, who were after all the recipients of the strategic materials. Still it was deemed important to keep it from the American Congress. Sherman Adams, Eisenhower's chief of staff, noted that, if Eisenhower pronounced on allied trade with China, "he could avoid neither antagonizing the British nor stirring up criticism from anti-Communist groups at home. . . . Like most of the calamities built up by McCarthy, whatever was done about it seemed likely only to worsen the situation."[21] Nixon once again got them out of it. He persuaded McCarthy that he had fallen into a Democratic trap. McCarthy thereupon withdrew the letter. When a newspaperman asked Kennedy about his White House visit, "he appeared flustered and asked, 'Did somebody see me go in there?' "[22]

In the meantime, Kennedy worked on an interim report, filed with the Senate on July 1. The report rested on two unexamined premises: that the United States could compel its allies to conduct their trade in ways contrary to their sense of their own interests; and that total cessation of trade with mainland China would make a substantial difference to the Korean War. The animating tone was moral outrage. "This shocking policy of fighting the enemy on the one hand and trading with him on the other," the report said, "cannot be condoned." Even if official action had little practical effect, the subcommittee believed "that on moral grounds these shipping firms should be made to choose."[23]

Within the limits of its assumptions it was an able job, its facts well marshaled, its argument well organized, its tone cool. At no point did the report hint, in the McCarthy manner, that traitors were making American policy. Arthur Krock praised it as "congressional investigation at its highest level with documentation given for each statement represented as a fact and with conclusions and opinions expressed dispassionately."[24] The tart liberal columnist Doris Fleeson called it "that rara avis" in McCarthy's stormy history—"a documented and sober story. It was thoroughly prepared by Robert Kennedy.... It received much more credence, therefore, than normal for anything to which Senator McCarthy's name is attached."[25] Kennedy's salary was raised to $7342.[26]

III

This did not offset his growing dissatisfaction with the committee. While he had been tediously analyzing commercial statistics, McCarthy and Roy Cohn had been loudly hunting Communists in the American government. McCarthy's interest in foreign policy was at best fitful. Though he paused now and again to bellow about the "blood trade" with China, he had juicier fish to fry at home. Kennedy's shipping report differed from the characteristic McCarthy investigation in two particulars: no one questioned Kennedy's facts, and Kennedy did not question the loyalty of those under investigation. Roy Cohn's investigatory style was directly opposite: nearly everyone questioned his facts, and he questioned nearly everyone's loyalty. McCarthy had been right in making him chief counsel, since this was McCarthy's style too.

The twenty-seven-year-old Kennedy was no doubt irritated from the start by the fact that he had been passed over in favor of a man eighteen months younger. As Cohn proceeded to cater to McCarthy's hit-and-run inquisitorial instincts, personal dislike was compounded by genuine concern. Cohn attached to the committee staff as "chief consultant" a young man named G. David Schine who had qualified himself as an expert by writing a hair-brained tract called "Definition of Communism," copies of which had been placed next to the Gideon Bible in hotels owned by Schine's father. After pursuing subversives in the Voice of America in February and March 1953, Cohn and Schine left for a magical mystery tour of western Europe, where they careened through embassy libraries, plucked offending books from the shelves and terrorized hapless employees.

Kennedy considered it all madness. He told McCarthy that he "disagreed with the way that the Committee was being run," and that "the way they were proceeding I thought it was headed for disaster.... I told him I thought he was out of his mind and was going to destroy himself." Later he commented, "Cohn and Schine took him up the mountain and showed him all those wonderful things. He destroyed himself for that—for publicity. He had to get his name in the paper. . . . He was on a toboggan. It was so exciting and exhilarating as he went downhill that it didn't matter to him if he hit a tree at the bottom." As he summed up the McCarthy committee after he had run a major investigation of his own:

> With two exceptions no real research was ever done. Most of the investigations were instituted on the basis of some preconceived notion by the chief counsel or his staff members and not on the basis of any information that had been developed. Cohn and Schine claimed they knew from the outset what was wrong; and they were not going to allow the facts to interfere. Therefore no real spade work that might have destroyed some of their pet theories was ever undertaken. I thought Senator McCarthy made a mistake in allowing the Committee to operate in such a fashion, told him so and resigned.[27]

Thus ended, after six months, Robert Kennedy's partnership with Joe McCarthy. By May 1953 he had sufficiently distanced himself so that McCarthy introduced him to the Senate as the minority counsel; and in July, after he completed the only solid report ever issued by the committee, he got out. In later years he bore criticism over the McCarthy relationship stoically. He rarely tried to explain, partly because this was not his way, but also because he had initially shared McCarthy's concern. A decade later the writer Peter Maas said to him, "I just cannot understand how you could ever have had anything to do with Joe McCarthy." Kennedy replied, "Well, at that time, I thought there was a serious internal security threat to the United States; I felt at that time that Joe McCarthy seemed to be the only one who was doing anything about it." After a moment, he said, "I was wrong."[28]

Most of all, he retained a fondness for McCarthy. McCarthy was an affable fellow who put on a tremendous show of beastliness and somehow did not expect his victims to take it personally. "He was no kind of fanatic," wrote Richard Rovere in the most perceptive book about him; he was "as incapable of true rancor, spite, and animosity as a eunuch is of marriage. He just did not have the equipment for it. He faked it all and could not understand anyone who didn't."[29] The record is filled with anecdotes of McCarthy's astonishment when people he vilified in the hearings cut him in the corridors. "He was a very complicated character," Robert Kennedy said a few years later. "His whole method of operation was complicated because he would get a guilty feeling and get hurt after he had blasted somebody. He wanted so desperately to be liked. . . . He was sensitive and yet insensitive. He didn't anticipate the results of what he was doing. He was very thoughtful of his friends, and yet he could be so cruel to others."[30]

Kenneth O'Donnell, who described himself as "one of the few Irish Democrats that were violently anti-McCarthy in the state of Massachusetts," used to call Robert Kennedy and fulminate about McCarthy. "There'd be silence. . . . After a while he'd say, 'He isn't that bad, but I agree, you know—but . . .' And he kept defending his pasha. Bobby had the greatest capacity for the underdog."[31] He spent much time defending his pasha. Once, at a Kennedy dinner, someone asked William McCormick Blair, Jr., Adlai Stevenson's personal aide in 1952 and now his law partner, his view of McCarthy. Blair said exactly what he thought. Robert was loud in disagreement. "Mr. Kennedy, Sr., of all people," Blair later recalled, "had to come over and tell us to quiet down."[32]

Given this personal feeling, resignation from McCarthy's staff could not have been easy. There is no record of his father's reaction. When Robert Lovett, the former Secretary of Defense, had observed to Robert's father, "That's pretty tough company he's travelling with," the ambassador replied, "Put your mind to rest about that. Bobby is just as tough as a bootheel."[33] One assumes that he respected the toughness of his son's decision. For Robert the experience was another step in education. He was learning in particular that patriotic declarations did not make due process of law superfluous and that he owed a debt to his own inner standards.

"With the filing in the Senate of the Subcommittee report on Trade With the Soviet Bloc," Kennedy wrote McCarthy formally, "the task to which I have devoted my time since coming with the Subcommittee has been completed. I am submitting my resignation at this time as it is my intention to enter the private practice of law." The liberal Democrats on the committee, Stuart Symington and Henry Jackson, sent glowing letters:

> Your investigation into the details of shipping to communist China during the war in Korea, along with your subsequent testimony before the Committee and your work on the final report, in my opinion, is one of the two outstanding jobs I have seen done in committee work during the some eight years I have been in Washington. (Symington)

> I was particularly impressed with the thorough, impartial and fair way in which you handled all matters coming to your attention. I noted that in all your investigations you were most diligent in adhering to the facts in order to obtain the best judicial determination in each instance. (Jackson)[34]

IV

One finds no indication that Robert Kennedy seriously intended to enter private practice. His bent more than ever was toward public service. His father, who had been a member of the Commission on Reorganization of the Executive Branch, headed by Herbert Hoover in 1947–49, was now a member of a second Hoover commission appointed by Eisenhower. In August 1953 young Kennedy joined the staff as his father's assistant.

In the twenty years since he had opposed Hoover's reelection, Joseph Kennedy had come to have inordinate admiration for the old man.[35] Robert Kennedy, in principle, shared that admiration. Hoover, who had his eightieth birthday the month young Kennedy came aboard, presided over the commission in a fairly arbitrary way. Thus when Clarence Brown, a conservative Republican congressman from Ohio, proposed a task force on military procurement, Hoover flatly turned the proposal down. Brown took Robert Kennedy aside to complain.

"He says," Robert reported to his father, "that he told Hoover he was dissatisfied, that the people who had opposed this Commission originally, Arthur Flemming and [Nelson] Rockefeller, are now Hoover's big pals, while he is shunted aside, but that he did not intend to be shunted aside any more. . . . He told Hoover that all Hoover thought of him was an irascible old man with no judgment or sense, but he would show him that he had been around a long time too and knew what he wanted." Hoover had replied by telling Brown that, if these disputes continued, he might resign. "Brown said that in view of the circumstances and the way he had been treated, he was not at all sure that it was a bad idea."[36] "My impression of the whole thing," Robert wrote after three months, "was that Hoover was very impatient with those who disagreed with him, and felt that setting up these task forces with eighty-five men was a major accomplishment and that he shouldn't be criticized on some of these smaller matters."[37]

Robert was soon exasperated by the squabbling among the septuagenarians. His own job seemed inconsequential. Probably it was difficult (or so Lem Billings thought) "to be working under the old man who still considered him a child." Most of all, the uncertainty of his own future oppressed him. "He had decided to dedicate himself to the government," Billings said later, ". . . and felt he was accom-

The First Investigating Committee: Joe McCarthy

plishing nothing and getting nowhere. He just didn't see any future."[38]

This was a low time in his life—a time, as Billings said, of "bad doldrums." Lawrence O'Brien recalled Kennedy touch football one afternoon in a Georgetown park. Georgetown University students playing baseball nearby kept hitting flies into the middle of the game. Ted Kennedy shouted to them to stop. They persisted. Finally Ted squared off for a fight with one of the larger among the enemy. Robert, though he gave away about thirty pounds, pushed his younger brother aside. "It was an uneven match," said O'Brien, "which was no doubt what Bob wanted." No one tried to stop it. "It became a bloody brawl, with each man determined to score a knockout. . . . Finally the fight stopped when they simply couldn't raise their arms any longer." That night they all had dinner at John Kennedy's house. Ethel, looking at her husband's bruised face, said, "That must have been a rough game of touch." "Yeah," Robert mumbled and went on eating.[39]

When they went out, evenings often ended in embarrassing argument. Robert was a "really very cross, unhappy, angry young man," Billings remembered, always telling people off and getting into fights.[40] My own first brush with him came in these months. In February 1954 he sent a letter to the *New York Times* condemning the Yalta agreement.* I dispatched a testy reply, describing his letter as "an astonishing mixture of distortion and error."[41] The exchange amused John Kennedy who told me, "My sisters are very mad at you because of the letter you wrote about Bobby." Bobby was mad too and dashed off a second letter to the *Times,* concluding that he did not "wish to appear critical of Mr. Schlesinger's scholarship for his polemics cover such a wide variety of subjects that he is not always able to read all of the documents he so vigorously discusses." This letter, he wrote me crisply, ought to "clarify the record sufficiently for you to make the necessary public apology."[42] I replied in like spirit.

Many people formed their first impression of him in this period. He was, thought Theodore Sorensen, "militant, aggressive, intolerant, opinionated, somewhat shallow in his convictions . . . more like his father than his brother."[43] The view was widely shared.

---

* *New York Times,* February 3, 1954. He was commenting on a *Times* editorial of January 26 attacking the Bricker Amendment. Without endorsing the amendment, Kennedy argued that "the United States Senate, if this matter had been put up to them, would have done a more thorough job" than Roosevelt, with Averell Harriman and Harry Hopkins as his "sole advisers," had done at Yalta.

V

In July 1953 the three Democratic members of the Investigations subcommittee—Symington, Jackson and John L. McClellan of Arkansas—had walked out when the Republican majority voted to give McCarthy sole control over the hiring and firing of committee staff. Then in January 1954, having forced McCarthy to relinquish control over appointments, the Democrats ended their boycott. As part of the settlement, they received the authority to appoint a minority counsel. The job was promptly offered to Kennedy, who as promptly accepted. In a kindly response to his letter of resignation from the Hoover commission, Herbert Hoover said he realized that "a restless soul like you wants to work."[44] In February, McCarthy requested an FBI investigation of Kennedy, but none was made since Kennedy had already been appointed.[45]

McCarthy made these concessions only because his budget was coming before the Senate. A few days later J. William Fulbright of Arkansas was the single senator to vote against his hectoring demand for a larger appropriation than ever. The Wisconsin senator seemed at his zenith. This was illusory. The Korean War had made McCarthyism possible. But that war was coming to an end. The fears and frustrations it had generated were subsiding. Not only was McCarthyism losing its emotional base, but McCarthy himself, in his increasingly erratic course, had become embroiled with a formidable antagonist, the United States Army. In the fall of 1953 he had launched a sensational, if unproductive, search for Communists and spies in a Signal Corps installation at Fort Monmouth, New Jersey. In the meantime, G. David Schine had been threatened by the draft; and Roy Cohn showed quite singular zeal, first in demanding an Army commission or a soft job in the CIA for his sidekick, and then, after Schine was drafted, in getting him treatment and privileges never before accorded buck privates. An Army document later recorded forty-four specific instances of improper pressure. A Republican member of the committee, Senator Charles E. Potter of Michigan, observed of Cohn, "His campaign over David Schine bordered on lunacy."[46]

Enraged by the Army's callousness, Cohn urged McCarthy on to battle. McCarthy, who lived by headlines, needed no encouragement. "The key," he soon announced, "to the deliberate Communist infiltration of our armed forces" lay in the mysterious promotion of a

The First Investigating Committee: Joe McCarthy 115

fellow-traveling dentist named Irving Peress from captain to major.[47] The "Who Promoted Peress" inquisition absorbed him for several pleasurable weeks. In a high point he told one much decorated general he was not fit to wear his uniform. The Army, at last tormented beyond endurance, retaliated in March 1954 by releasing a chronological record of Cohn's interventions on behalf of Schine. Feelings were running high within the committee. "I think I shall enjoy my new job," Kennedy wrote Herbert Hoover. "However every night when I come home from work I feel my neck to see if my head is still attached."[48]

One day McCarthy summoned a hapless black woman named Annie Lee Moss, a teletype operator in the Signal Corps, as a further example of the way the Army coddled Communists. Mrs. Moss timidly but firmly denied Communist connections. Her demeanor impressed the Democrats on the committee. McCarthy, seeing things were going badly, excused himself, leaving the questioning to Cohn.[49] Cohn proceeded to harry Mrs. Moss about her statement that a black man named Robert Hall had left a copy of the *Daily Worker* in her house, insinuating that Hall was a Communist organizer. A newspaperman informed Robert Kennedy that the Communist Hall was white. Kennedy tried to pass on the point to Cohn. Cohn ignored him and persisted in harsh interrogation. A sharp exchange ensued:

SENATOR JACKSON. Mr. Kennedy has something. . . .
MR. KENNEDY. Was Mr. Hall a colored gentleman, or—
MRS. MOSS. Yes, sir.
MR. KENNEDY. There is some confusion about it, is there not, Mr. Cohn? Is the Rob Hall we are talking about, the union organizer, was he a white man or colored man?
MR. COHN. I never inquired into his race. I am not sure. We can check that, though.
MR. KENNEDY. I thought I just spoke to you about it.
MR. COHN. My assumption has been that he is a white man, but we can check that.
SENATOR SYMINGTON. Let us ask this: The Bob Hall that you knew, was he a white man?
MRS. MOSS. He was colored, the one I knew of.
SENATOR SYMINGTON. Let's decide which Robert Hall we want to talk about.
MR. KENNEDY. When you spoke about the union organizer, you spoke about Rob Hall and I think we all felt that was the colored gentleman?
MR. COHN. I was not talking about a union organizer, Bob. I was talking about a Communist organizer who at that time, according to the public record, was in charge of subscriptions for the Daily Worker in the District of Columbia area.

MR. KENNEDY. Evidently it is a different Rob Hall.
MR. COHN. I don't know that it is. Our information is that it was the same Rob Hall.
SENATOR MCCLELLAN. If one is black and the other is white, there is a difference.

Cohn, retreating, said that perhaps this was something the committee should "get some more exact information on." "I think so too," said Kennedy.[50]

Symington asked Mrs. Moss whether she had heard of Karl Marx. "Who is that?" she replied. At the end of her testimony, he told her he thought she was telling the truth ("I certainly am," Mrs. Moss said), and added that if the Signal Corps did not take her back, he would get her a job himself.[51] Later Cohn told Symington that he was making a mistake; "our information is totally accurate." Symington said he would check with the Federal Bureau of Investigation. He then sent Kennedy to see whether the Bureau had anything. According to Cohn, not an unbiased source, Kennedy "stormed in and demanded" the Moss dossier. The assistant to the director, Louis Nichols, told him that no outsider could see FBI files. Kennedy then asked for a decision from J. Edgar Hoover personally. "The attitude of Kennedy in this matter," Hoover noted, "clearly shows need for absolute circumspection in any conversation with him."[52] Roy Cohn later wrote, "Kennedy was not one of the Director's favorites. He regarded him as an arrogant whipper-snapper, who pushed around his family's money and power." Hoover, on the other hand, was fond of McCarthy, with whom he used to dine, and fond enough of Cohn to offer the ultimate accolade in 1954 and insist that Cohn call him "Edgar."* Kennedy recalled the incident later as "a rather major dispute [with the FBI] because they lied to me about some documents that they made available to the Committee. . . . So I had a fight with them, and that was really my first."[53]

Early in April the once loyal *Boston Post* ran an article from its Washington correspondent saying that "no chairman of a communist-hunting Congressional committee has ever escaped smearing" and

---

* Roy Cohn, "Could He Walk on Water?" *Esquire*, November 1972. In 1958 the Subversive Activities Control Board claimed that, according to Communist party records, Mrs. Moss had been a party member in the mid-1940s. Her listing on the rolls, if true, is hardly conclusive, given what we know now about the disposition both of CPUSA organizers and of FBI informants to pad membership lists in order to increase their prestige. Nothing specifically has come to light indicating that Mrs. Moss was anything but the bewildered and harmless woman that Symington and Kennedy supposed her to be.

that it was now McCarthy's turn. A chief villain, it appeared, was the minority counsel, who "represents the subcommittee members who have been vigorously hostile to McCarthy." It was "no longer even an open secret that Robert F. Kennedy . . . has no use for Roy Cohn." But "McCarthy, of course, will stand by his chief counsel to the bitter end. . . . He is not expected to attempt to rebuke Kennedy even though the younger brother of the Massachusetts Senator has made comments to at least one person that were considered to be highly out of order."[54]

VI

The accumulation of charges and countercharges involving McCarthy, Cohn and the Department of the Army produced a general cry for an investigation. The Army-McCarthy hearings began on April 22, 1954. Joseph Welch, a soft-spoken and elaborately ironic Boston lawyer, represented the Army. His assistant was another Boston lawyer named James St. Clair. Ray Jenkins of Tennessee was counsel for the subcommittee majority. A fascinated television audience, amounting at times to 20 million people, watched the hearings.

If they looked hard, they could see Robert Kennedy, sitting quietly behind the Democratic senators and passing them occasional notes as the witnesses testified. His role was inconspicuous. There was one exception. On June 11, Jackson was interrogating McCarthy about an anti-Communist plan proposed by G. David Schine. Let us begin with Roy Cohn's account.

> Bobby Kennedy's job was to write out pertinent questions for the Democratic senators to ask at the hearing. In this Schine plan he saw an opportunity to gibe at us. He fed his questions to Senator Jackson, who used them to fire a barrage of ridicule. . . . They picked at point after point in Dave's plan, finding something hilarious in each. And every time Kennedy handed him something, Senator Jackson would go into fits of laughter. I became angrier and angrier.[55]

The hearing recessed. Cohn had sent out for a file marked "Jackson's record." One reporter wrote, "Carrying it like a weapon he headed for the committee table."[56] There he found Kennedy. "I want you to tell Jackson," Cohn said furiously, "that we are going to get to him on Monday." Cohn threatened, Kennedy told reporters later, to accuse Jackson of having "written something favorably inclined toward Communists." "His blue eyes snapping" (according to the *New York Daily News*), Kennedy said, "You can't get away with it,

Cohn." Cohn told reporters he had accused Kennedy of "having a personal hatred" for the McCarthy side. Kennedy said, "I told him he had a ——— nerve threatening me. I told him he had been threatening all the Democrats and threatening the Army and not to try it on me." When he said to Cohn, "Don't you make any warnings to us about Democratic senators," Cohn replied, "I'll make any warnings to you that I want to—any time, anywhere." Then: "Do you want to fight right here?" He started to swing at Kennedy. Two men separated them, and Kennedy, with a small, contemptuous smile, turned away. The banner headline in the *Daily News* the next day was: COHN, KENNEDY NEAR BLOWS IN 'HATE' CLASH.[57]

Walking out with LaVern Duffy, Kennedy said, "I lost my temper." "It isn't like you," Duffy said. "You shouldn't have done it." In visible distress Kennedy went to the Capitol in search of his brother, finally finding him in the Senate cloakroom. For a few moments they had a serious and evidently consoling talk.[58]

The hearings ended a week later. The Republican majority roundly supported McCarthy. The Democratic minority, in a report written by Kennedy, concluded that for "inexcusable actions" in the Schine case "Senator McCarthy and Mr. Cohn merit severe criticism," that McCarthy deserved further criticism for his conduct "throughout the hearings" in "attacking the character and impugning the loyalty of individuals who were in no way associated with or involved in the proceedings" and that McCarthy's "countercharges against Secretary Stevens [of the Department of the Army] and Mr. Adams [general counsel of the Department of the Army] which impugned their patriotism and loyalty, were totally unsubstantiated and unfounded."[59] In a section of the draft the minority did not adopt, Kennedy had written of McCarthy, "The Senator cannot escape responsibility for the misconduct of Cohn. Nor can he excuse the irresponsibility attaching to too many of his charges. The Senate should take action to correct this situation."[60]

The minority report registered popular sentiment. The national audience, well trained by TV westerns to distinguish between white hats and black hats, had little trouble deciding to which category McCarthy belonged. After thirty-five days of the grating voice, the sarcastic condescension, the weird giggle, the irrelevant interruption ("point of order, Mr. Chairman, point of order") and the unsupported accusation, McCarthy had wrought his own downfall. On July 30, Ralph Flanders of Vermont submitted a resolution of censure against McCarthy. At the end of August a committee under the

The First Investigating Committee: Joe McCarthy 119

chairmanship of Arthur Watkins of Utah, and including such respected conservatives as John Stennis of Mississippi and Sam Ervin of North Carolina, began hearings. On September 27 the Watkins committee recommended censure. On December 2 the full Senate voted censure.

The Kennedys viewed all this with mixed feelings. John Kennedy prepared a speech in support of censure, but he made his case on exceedingly narrow grounds. He declined to base his vote on "long-past misconduct of Senator McCarthy to which I registered no public objection at the time." His judgment, he said, involved "purely a question of the dignity of the United States Senate"—a dignity impeached by Cohn, acting with McCarthy's full support.[61] Robert Kennedy, much closer to McCarthy, evidently saw his downfall as a mixture of public necessity and personal tragedy. Three years later, after a member of Symington's staff asserted that Kennedy's friendship with McCarthy had prejudiced his conduct in the hearings, Kennedy wrote Symington: "As you know, I always liked Senator McCarthy. However, after the very close relationship that I enjoyed with you during the Army-McCarthy hearings, I am sure that you would not feel that the statement that I allowed my likes and dislikes to interfere with my work was justified."[62] No one thought him opposed to censure. Two weeks after the vote, John Stennis—who had said in the debate that McCarthy had poured "slush and slime" on the Senate and that if censure failed "something big and fine will have gone out of this chamber"—wrote Kennedy: "One of the best parts of my year has been my work and association with you and I look forward to our work together in 1955."[63]

Still his Irish conception of loyalty turned him against some he felt had treated McCarthy unfairly. In March 1954, Edward R. Murrow of CBS had castigated McCarthy in a brilliant television "documentary." The show had great impact, though even anti-McCarthy commentators, like Gilbert Seldes in the *Saturday Review* and John Cogley in *Commonweal,* criticized the technique of offering as a "report" what was in fact a superbly calculated attack. In January 1955, Murrow spoke at the banquet honoring those, Kennedy among them, who had been selected by the Junior Chamber of Commerce as the Ten Outstanding Young Men of 1954. Kennedy grimly walked out.*

On the other hand, Joseph Welch, who far more than Murrow—far more than anyone, indeed, except for McCarthy and Cohn—had

---

* The resentment was transient: two and a half years later Murrow visited the Kennedys at home to do an installment of his popular program *Person to Person.*

brought about McCarthy's ruin, congratulated Kennedy on the Chamber of Commerce award. Kennedy replied with utmost cordiality. "You were very kind to think of me," he wrote,

> and I greatly appreciate it. I hope you will give my best wishes to Jim St. Clair. I saw him briefly at a football game last fall and he looked so relaxed I hardly recognized him. I hope the same thing has happened to you. I don't get to Boston very often, but I hope on one of my visits there we can get together for a few minutes anyway.

Welch as promptly responded:

> What you say about being in Boston makes me say that it would be a delight to see you and that I shall be sad indeed if you come this way and don't come in.[64]

Other reactions to the award were less enthusiastic. "Things have come to a pretty pass," one woman wrote Robert Kennedy, "when a man is commended for doing everything he can to stop a fellow countryman from fighting the worst enemy this country has ever known. . . . You know that God and communism do not go together. I have chosen God." Kennedy wrote back, "I am sorry that I have already turned out to be such a disappointment to you."[65]

VII

The midterm elections in 1954 produced a Democratic majority in the Senate. John McClellan became chairman of the Investigations Subcommittee, and Robert Kennedy chief counsel. The committee, Theodore Sorensen advised Robert Kennedy in December 1954, ought now to revise its rules to show that it was "off to a fresh and thoughtful beginning, and intended to safeguard the rights of individuals." This was done, and the *Louisville Courier-Journal* reported in January, when Kennedy arrived for the Junior Chamber of Commerce dinner, that he was "rather proud of the new set of rules."[66]

"Hardly anyone recognized boyish Robert F. Kennedy," the *Courier-Journal* added, "when he strode bare-headed and casual into the Kentucky Hotel last night, carrying a couple of books under his arm." His reading habits were beginning to improve. He said that he thought the Investigations Subcommittee would gradually return to its old function—looking into waste, fraud, corruption and mismanagement in government. But that did not mean, he continued, that it was "a whit less interested in rooting Communists out of government than it was when Senator McCarthy ran the show."[67] Recommending subjects for investigation, Kennedy wrote McClellan that it seemed only fair to all concerned to answer the unanswered questions in the Peress case. "If there is a rotten situation in the Army it should be exposed; if there is not, the bogeyman should be put to rest."[68]

The committee held a new series of Peress hearings in March 1955 and rendered its report in July. The question was whether "the original appointment of Peress, his subsequent change of orders, and his promotion had been, in fact, inspired by subversive interests." The committee found nothing to substantiate McCarthy's insinuations. The report went on to criticize the Army for forty-eight errors "of more than minor importance" and concluded that Peress's promotion and honorable discharge resulted from "individual errors in judgment, lack of proper coordination, ineffective administrative procedures, inconsistent application of existing regulations, and excessive delays, not from treason."[69] Though this conclusion put McCarthy's bogeyman to rest, he extracted what solace he could and blandly commended the committee staff.

Kennedy also reviewed McCarthy's files on Communist infiltration into defense plants. "The derogatory information," he informed McClellan, ". . . is not extensive, ranging anywhere from a couple of sentences to a page or so. The charges vary from allegations that an individual was seen reading the Daily Worker, to the charge that the individual is an active member of the Communist Party." Most of the persons accused did not work at plants handling classified material; those who worked at such plants mostly did not do classified work. "I mention these facts so there will be some understanding of this investigation and to place it in correct perspective. However, there is no intention of minimizing its importance for it is recognized that even if one security risk is removed from a strategically important spot, a distinct service has been performed."[70]

Kennedy was in fact more involved in Communist investigations than he had ever been when McCarthy was chairman, no doubt because the Democrats now in charge did not wish to seem less zealous in saving the Republic than their Republican predecessors. His approach to the professional witnesses, however, was skeptical. "Being anti-Communist," as he observed of Roy Cohn in January 1955, "does not automatically excuse a lack of integrity in every other facet of life."[71] Instead of seeking out voluble and imaginative informers like J. B. Matthews and Louis Budenz as his experts, he turned to scholars like Professor Philip Mosely of Columbia.[72] He even went to see Earl Browder, who had been till 1945 the leader of the American

Communist Party. "I appreciate your kindness in talking to me last Saturday morning," he subsequently wrote Browder. "It was of tremendous interest to me to receive your ideas and thoughts on the history of the Communist Party in this country. It is only with an understanding of the past that we can proceed to map out our future with confidence."[73] Browder found Kennedy "pleasant and eager" and was impressed that anyone from a congressional committee should try to learn what communism was all about.[74]

More and more, however, as Kennedy had forecast in Louisville, the committee was returning to its old functions. It now concentrated on such subjects as fraud in the government purchase of military uniforms (an inquiry that resulted in six convictions); contracts let by the Foreign Operations Administration for the erection of grain storage elevators in Pakistan; inefficiencies in the Department of Agriculture's grain storage bin program; and similar issues of waste or graft in federal operations. Kennedy proposed other areas, such as wiretapping in Washington. This prospect agitated the FBI. "Kennedy's attitude," it was reported within the Bureau, "was such that impression could be gained he might not be friendly disposed toward the FBI."[75] The counsel for the Republican minority protested, and the investigation stopped.[76] His relations with the Bureau remained prickly. When he began an investigation into the manufacture of military uniforms, Hoover noted acidly, "Kennedy was completely uncooperative until after he had squeezed all the publicity out of the matter he could."[77]

The committee dropped out of the headlines. One 1956 investigation did, however, attract attention. Harold Talbott, Eisenhower's Secretary of the Air Force, had retained half-ownership in Paul B. Mulligan & Company, a firm of so-called efficiency engineers. Early in 1955 John Kennedy's friend Charles Bartlett heard that Talbott was hustling business for the firm out of his Pentagon office. Bartlett thereupon proposed a joint inquiry to Robert Kennedy, an alliance of the newspaperman and the Senate investigator, each tapping his own sources and pooling the results.

Talbott was a genial fellow. His vivacious wife was even more popular. They were Palm Beach acquaintances of the elder Kennedys and had many friends in the Senate. But Bartlett soon published letters by Talbott, on Air Force stationery, soliciting contracts for Mulligan from firms doing business with the Pentagon. Called before the committee, Talbott denied wrongdoing. Committee members responded admiringly. Joe McCarthy said virtuously that he deemed it "extremely important . . . to make sure that by innuendo, or otherwise, that the Secretary does not get an unfair deal and a smear." "None of the members of McClellan's committee," Bartlett wrote later, "would give Kennedy any support, and the young counsel had to pursue the case in a hearing in which he was the only one asking any questions."

Kennedy, aged thirty, began a tough cross-examination. He asked Talbott, aged sixty-seven, whether he had ever instructed anyone in the Air Force to make representations to RCA for not renewing a Mulligan contract. Talbott: "Absolutely not." Kennedy broke down his story. Talbott, wrote Arthur Krock, was not a crook but rather a man whose "excessive egotism" led him to suppose that no one could question his motives. Eisenhower requested Talbott's resignation. Bartlett won a Pulitzer Prize. Kennedy confirmed a reputation as a relentless prosecutor.[78]

VIII

These were good years for the young Kennedys. Robert, after the bad doldrums of the Hoover Commission, was working hard and cared deeply about what he was doing. Ethel was raising children—five by 1956—and rushing to cheer Bobby on in hearing rooms at the Capitol. They lived unpretentiously on S Street, simple in their tastes, unsophisticated in their ways. For a time, there was neither alcohol nor even ashtrays in the house. David Ormsby-Gore* stayed with them for a week in 1955. "No doors were ever shut," he recalled, "and everybody wandered through every room all the time. . . . It was great fun but it was quite unlike living in any other house I'd ever lived in before." These were the days when, as Ormsby-Gore later said, the dogs still outnumbered the children. "It was the happiest time," said David Hackett, who had moved to Montreal but visited Robert and Ethel whenever he could. "There was not yet a world to solve."[79]

Robert remained private, intense, with an exacting sense of individual responsibility. Once he picked up Charles Spalding at the airport. As they drove back, a dog raced in front of the car. There was no way of stopping, and the dog was killed. "It upset him so," Spalding said later. ". . . We must have spent three hours going up and down the road. . . . We went into every single house for ten miles, I suppose, until we finally found . . . the owner. And Bobby explained what had happened and said how terribly sorry he was and asked

* Later, Lord Harlech.

about the dog—could he replace it or was there anything possible that could be done."[80] When Ethel's father and mother were killed in a plane crash in October 1955, Robert, not unused to sudden death, drew on deep wells of sympathy and strength for Ethel.

He was still a prickly figure. "He was just always very sensitive," said Eunice, "and he got hurt easily. . . . He just either would look mad or he'd be a little sarcastic and talk back to you." His friends understood this and knew it did not last. As Eunice said, "Bobby never sulked."[81] Acquaintances did not understand it, misconceived his laconic humor, and sometimes found him curt and contentious. He did not like to be put on the defensive and avoided this, in the family style, by asking his own questions before others could question him first. This was partly, too, the result of his incessant curiosity. But, where John Kennedy asked questions impersonally, Bobby asked them with curious intensity. This added to his reputation as an inquisitor.

Politically he was accounted a conservative Democrat, his father's son, though more interested in investigations than in politics. Arthur Krock, seconding his nomination in 1955 for that most respectable of institutions, the Metropolitan Club of Washington, called him in some respects "the number one member of that remarkable tribe . . . distinguished for both scholarship and athletic ability, in the military service for courage . . . of unsurpassed integrity," etc.[82] No doubt the "number one member" crack was induced by Krock's apprehensions about John Kennedy, whose politics had begun to display what he doubtless saw as wayward tendencies.

Nineteen fifty-four was the year when Secretary of State Dulles and Vice President Nixon advocated American military intervention in Vietnam. "In Dienbienphu the French are fighting heroically the battle of the free," as the *New York Times* resoundingly said. The world's biggest democracy could not "stand idly by" while communism swallowed small countries and toppled the dominoes of Asia.[83] John Kennedy opposed intervention. "No amount of American military assistance in Indochina," he told the Senate, "can conquer an enemy which is everywhere and at the same time nowhere, 'an enemy of the people' which has the sympathy and covert support of the people."[84] Later he condemned the administration's refusal to share information and decisions in foreign affairs. Documents were withheld "whose publication could do no more harm than the release of the Secretary of State's laundry ticket." The makers of foreign policy looked with "condescending disdain on those who challenge their omniscience," supposing the layman unable to comprehend the "mystic intricacies" of diplomacy. They would have to "give up the luxury of their exclusive control over our role in world affairs."[85]

Robert Kennedy doubtless agreed. But his interests lay elsewhere. His brother, though now a member of the Government Operations Committee, was not on the Investigations Subcommittee. They saw each other mainly in the evenings. John Kennedy was taking out the exquisite Jacqueline Bouvier. The courtship was on occasion conducted at the younger Kennedys' house in Georgetown, where the four often met at the end of the day for dinner and a movie. At one big Kennedy weekend at Hyannis Port, the boys were playing touch football on the lawn while Jacqueline read on the veranda. John caught a pass and called to her: "Did you see that?" She answered indifferently. In a few moments Robert came over and said that he could well understand why she might think football barbaric, but it did mean a lot to Jack. He said it with such sweet concern that, Jacqueline said later, "I felt at once that I had a friend who would always explain things to me."[86]

John and Jacqueline were married in September 1953 at Newport. The Kennedys gathered in advance at Hyannis Port. Spirits were high; and Bobby and Teddy, completing their assignment in a scavenger hunt, stole a policeman's hat. The policeman complained in person the next morning. An outraged father called the family together and delivered a polemic on the enormity of this offense; it would get into the columns and make the family look ridiculous. When Bobby tried to explain, the ambassador fixed him with a baleful eye and said, "No. You keep quiet and listen to me. This is childish behavior, and I don't want anything more like it."[87]

After the John Kennedys came back to Washington, they moved from Georgetown into an ante-bellum mansion in McLean, Virginia, called Hickory Hill. John was increasingly drawn toward foreign policy, Robert increasingly to the exposure of corruption. For a season the two brothers, their fondness undiminished, had separate preoccupations.

(7)

Interlude: William O. Douglas and Adlai Stevenson

THE TALBOTT investigation ended at 1:30 P.M. on July 28, 1955. Two hours later, Robert Kennedy, in the same rumpled, drip-dry seersucker suit he had worn at the last hearing, was on a transatlantic plane. He was in bad humor. His mother, who flew with him to Paris, gathered that making the trip was about the last thing he wanted to do.[1] But it was his father's project, and the simplest thing was to accept his fate. After a long midnight wait at Orly, he boarded another plane. At 7:30 the next morning, dead tired and harassed, he arrived in Teheran. Here he met his father's friend William O. Douglas. The two now set off on a long-meditated tour of Soviet central Asia.

I

Joseph Kennedy was the only man in the country who could preserve simultaneous friendships with Senator McCarthy, the deadly enemy of the Bill of Rights, and Justice Douglas, its devoted champion. Off the bench, Douglas was an incorrigible traveler. He preferred high mountains, primitive lands and places where few men had traveled before. He had already traversed non-Soviet central Asia and in 1950 conceived the plan of visiting the contiguous Soviet republics to find out whether communism had made a difference.

Joseph Kennedy, never neglecting a chance to widen a son's experience, asked Douglas to take Robert along. Douglas recalled only the "very much subdued" little boy he had seen years before; but he liked the young law student he soon encountered when he spoke at the Charlottesville Forum.[2] The two made their first visa applications in February 1951. These were the last paranoid years of Stalin. The Soviet press had unmasked Douglas as an American spy when he climbed Mt. Ararat in Turkey on an earlier trip. The applications were turned down then and in succeeding years. Robert Kennedy went to work for McCarthy. Mercedes Douglas asked her husband why he still wanted to take this rigid and hostile young man to Russia. Douglas replied, "I have to do it. Joe wants me to do it. Joe thinks it would do him some good."[3]

In 1955 they applied for a fifth time. Stalin was dead, the line had changed, and the Kremlin was preparing for a conference with Eisenhower at Geneva. They received visas within a week.[4] Kennedy also received indignant letters. "I am sorry that you so heartily disapprove," he replied to one Irish American critic. "However, I would like to call your attention to the fact that up until the past several weeks, there has been an American Catholic priest in Russia since 1933."[5]

The American embassy in Teheran had assigned a young Foreign Service officer named Frederick W. Flott to Douglas. When Kennedy arrived, Flott's impression was of a high-strung, take-charge young man. Douglas had suggested that Flott come along as interpreter. Kennedy told Flott loftily, "I haven't decided whether or not you are going." Douglas had also wangled a miscellany of equipment from the Army. The bush jackets came in three sizes and were distributed according to seniority. Douglas took 'large' and Kennedy 'medium,' leaving 'small' to Flott. 'Small' turned out far too small, so Flott ruefully gave his bush jacket to a girl in Teheran.[6]

After an audience with the Shah, they crossed the Elburz Mountains by automobile and drove along the steaming Caspian Sea to Pahlevi. "Pahlevi and the hotel we stayed [in] smelled," Kennedy wrote. "It was terribly, terribly hot and I was never so glad to leave any place in my life."[7] Kennedy and Douglas embarked for Baku the next morning, carrying their Army gear and a supply of ball-point pens with which to edify the natives. Flott, who had not yet received his Soviet visa, parted company with them at Pahlevi.

"The boat is very nice and clean, newly painted," Kennedy reported. "Nobody speaks English but we are treated in the highest style. The cabins are very good and the food never stops coming. . . . They put this terrific spread before us of soup, all kinds of fruit, watermelon, honeydew, apples, cherries, chicken, etc. We both agreed that we would give in easily. I slept on the deck all afternoon sunning myself." They smelled the oil of Baku fifteen miles away. As they disembarked, Douglas pressed a ball-point pen on the captain, who at first declined, till, as Kennedy wrote, "the crew raised a storm and he finally took it."

The Intourist agent in Baku told them no interpreters were available. Douglas said that the Soviet embassy in Washington had promised them one. The Intourist man was "singularly unimpressed." They went to the hotel, holding on the way a whispered conversation on strategy. Once in their rooms, Douglas said loudly to the concealed microphones that he would call Khrushchev and tell him of their wretched treatment. Within an hour an interpreter arrived.

They liked the bustle of the city. At a music festival, "the dancers showed boundless energy and the music for the most part was very catchy." At a collective farm near Baku, they were served a twenty-one-course meal. Their hosts "were disappointed in me that I did not eat more. Douglas made a valiant effort." Someone toasted Douglas and his family and then Ethel and the four children. "One of our hosts said it was very proper that they should drink to us as we had already fulfilled the plan."

From Baku they flew on to Ashkhabad, the capital of Turkmenistan, where Kennedy, an ardent photographer, was arrested for taking snapshots. The Intourist guide got him off. In Bokhara, once the holy city of central Asia, it was 145 degrees in the sun. They inspected the notorious Bug Pit, where, a century before, the Emir Nasullah had consigned two adventurous Englishmen for refusing to acknowledge Mohammedanism as the true faith; after two months among reptiles and vermin, they were beheaded. The American travelers, Kennedy wrote later, "were fortunately received somewhat more warmly by the local officials."[8]

In Samarkand they saw the tomb of Tamerlane, the great blue-domed mosque of Shir Dar, the graceful square of the Registan. Kennedy wrote his children from Stalinabad, the capital of Tadzhikistan: "Say your prayers and get to bed on time and you won't grow up to be a juvenile delinquent like your mother." They watched Tadzhik dancing—"everyone by himself—jumping up and down—moving in rhythm, swaying and moving heads back and forth. Sensuous, weird and interesting." Cultural notes alternated in Kennedy's diary with data about wages, prices, working conditions, housing, child care, courts, factories, and rather especially churches.

Douglas and Kennedy disagreed on the tactics of information gathering. Douglas, the judge, was all suavity. His technique was to appear interested and accommodating, drawing out the people with whom he talked until, having won their confidence, he could hit them with a factual issue and hope for a frank response. Kennedy, the investigator, was exasperated and hostile, as if determined to find nothing good. Fred Flott, who finally got his visa, followed their trail through central Asia. At each airport, he heard much the same story: "We liked Justice Douglas. We can see he is a wise man. But [great sigh, looking at the ground] with him there is Mr. Kennedy. He seems always to be saying bad things about our country." Kennedy carried mistrust to inordinate extremes. The Intourist guide brought along a footlocker filled with caviar. Douglas could not eat caviar because of a liver complaint. Kennedy announced that Russian food was dirty and refused the caviar. The fortunate Flott therefore had three jars of caviar every meal. Throughout the trip Kennedy ate very little and drank nothing, subsisting mainly on watermelon and nervous energy.

II

Kennedy's automatic contentiousness irritated Douglas. He explained to Flott that he hardly knew the boy; his father, to whom he owed his Supreme Court seat, had said that Bobby had never gone on a he-man trip and asked that he be taken along. "You can never argue with these fellows," Douglas finally told Kennedy, "so why don't we just forget about it, and spend an evening doing something else rather than wasting it trying to convert some guy who will never be converted." This worked. "We never had any problems then."[9]

Even Douglas could not always avoid argument. At the University of Tashkent Kennedy asked an English-speaking professor why no one ever criticized the Soviet government. Douglas joined the discussion, pointing out, Kennedy wrote in his journal, "that we in the United States had been brought up on the fundamental [right] we possessed to find fault with government where we found things going wrong. The professor said that in U.S. people criticized just to criticize and that was because Democrats always wanted to criticize Republicans and vice-versa so that they could be elected." Douglas brought up academic freedom, suggesting that the professors would be in trouble if they criticized communism in their classrooms. This was not well received.

The travelers here and elsewhere inquired especially about the indigenous peoples of central Asia, whose high cheekbones and dark complexions, language, schools and customs set them so sharply apart from their Russian overlords. They were as different, the travelers thought, as the Moroccan from the Frenchman or the Malay from the Englishman, and quite as subject to imperial rule. When

Douglas mentioned that one third of the Kazakh population had apparently been liquidated during the collectivization of the farms, the professor dismissed the figure as the invention of British intelligence. Douglas and Kennedy pointed out that Soviet census statistics showed a decline of almost one million Kazakhs between 1926 and 1939. The professor was displeased and, as Kennedy noted, "became rather vehement."

"I hope," Kennedy wrote the children from Tashkent in mid-August, "you are all . . . doing what your mother and Ena [the nanny] tell you to do. (I admit that this gets a little difficult when they tell you to do opposite things but play along with them.)" It was now a rather jolly party. Cables of congratulation to Kennedy over the Talbott affair pursued them; and his companions took pleasure in introducing him as the People's Prosecutor, the American Vyshinsky. Kennedy was forever sending postcards, when he could find any—a portrait of Lenin, for example, to Cardinal Spellman with a cryptic message scratched on the back.

They went to the opera at Tashkent. "Beautiful opera house," Kennedy noted. "Tremendously large chandelier. Kirghese design of white figures on gold background. One of the prettiest I have ever seen. . . . Live horses on the stage. . . . A few good looking girls in the chorus and the heroine looked like a Metropolitan Opera star." They visited a Baptist church with a congregation of more than a thousand. "Douglas made a speech which was good and caused some of them to cry." At a Tashkent park, Douglas got into a discussion with a crowd. Someone asked about the Sacco-Vanzetti case. "Douglas told them that a worker's payroll had been stolen. I borrowed a fellow's bike and had myself a ride around town."

They visited a collective farm near Frunze in Kirgizia. Coming back, Kennedy fell off his seat when the jeep went over a bump. "The two or three Russians, who were riding with me, grabbed hold of me for every bump afterwards. It did not speak very well for the strength and resilience of American youth." In Alma Ata, to the east, they visited more collective farms and were served more gargantuan meals. At one "there were two young things who kept staring at Douglas and vice versa." At another, there were "many toasts, the host got looped, spilled champagne over Douglas. We sang the Whiffenpoof Song, Home on the Range, which didn't go over, and America the Beautiful."

Kennedy's natural curiosity was overcoming his initial hostility. "He worked hard on the trip," Douglas said later, "and came back

Interlude: William O. Douglas and Adlai Stevenson 131

with some considerable insight."[10] "People have no idea how our system of government works," Kennedy wrote in his diary. ". . . We, I think, are equally ignorant of their system." In the university at Alma Ata, the rector, a biochemist, observed that, while Soviet scientists read American scientific journals, American scientists, judging from the absence of citation, did not read Soviet scientific journals. Was this because of a lack of interest? "Douglas explained he was sure it was not and he was surprised to hear about it. I am afraid it is a result of the McCarran Act"—the Internal Security Act, passed over Truman's veto in 1951.

Douglas insisted that the travelers stop for a breather in the Tien Shan range. "We'd get up to ten, eleven thousand feet I think," Douglas recalled. "I wouldn't call it real mountain climbing." He was struck by the wholehearted way Kennedy threw himself into mountaineering. "Bobby was an all-out. . . . If he was climbing a peak or hiking a trail there was nothing else in the world to do but that."[11] The Siberian weather was already turning cold. On August 29 they flew west from Novosobirsk to Omsk. Kennedy developed a chill. By the time they arrived in Omsk, "I was shaking all over and was freezing cold except for my head which felt hot." Douglas decided to summon a doctor: "No communist is going to doctor me," Kennedy said. "I promised your daddy I would take care of you," said Douglas. "I'm going to call a doctor." It took three hours for a large, heavy-boned woman physician to appear. Robert's temperature was now well over 100 and rising steadily. There were signs of delirium. He was shot full of penicillin and rushed to bed, while the others went on, as scheduled, by train.

"Slept most of the next day," Kennedy recorded in his diary. ". . . Doctor stayed with me all yesterday and two nights. Mayor came to see me yesterday." In this laconic fashion he glided over both an intense illness and the devotion of the Soviet doctor. Perhaps he was disinclined to yield too much credit either to his own weakness or to Communist medical care. In another twenty-four hours he had recovered sufficiently to take the plane west. On September 2, Ethel Kennedy, accompanied by Jean and Pat, met the party in Moscow. Looking at Bobby, pale and thin, Ethel cried to Douglas, "What have you done to my husband?"[12]

Charles E. Bohlen, the American ambassador, had them to dinner. They saw *Swan Lake* at the ballet. Then the Kennedys left Moscow to inspect the beauties of Leningrad. A few hours later, a hotel maid knocked at the door of Fred Flott's room and handed him, with a note from Robert Kennedy, an Army bush jacket, 'medium,' freshly laundered.

III

In the aftermath of the Geneva summit, the travelers encountered a confusion of moods in the Soviet Union. Douglas offered the more optimistic reading. While doubting that the Kremlin had changed its objectives, he thought the Russian people "in the mood for friendship with the American. . . . They want peace so that they can enjoy the dividends of the society they have created."[13] As for Kennedy, his views, he wrote David Lawrence, editor of *U.S. News & World Report,* differed "from the reports of some of the other people who visited Russia in that I was far more distrustful of Russia's intentions."[14] "We all want peace," he told an interviewer in Paris on his way home, "but are apt to be blinded by the bear's smile."[15] "My feeling," he said on arrival in New York, "is that before we make a great number of concessions we have to have something more concrete from the Russians, such as the dissolution of the Comintern and a workable disarmament plan."[16]

He developed this theme in October at Georgetown University. He had called Angie Novello, the most efficient stenographer on the Investigations Subcommittee staff, to Hyannis Port where he dictated a text. Slides selected from the more than a thousand photographs he had taken on the trip illustrated the lecture.[17] They were magnificent. But Angie, sitting in the middle of the auditorium, could hardly hear the speaker. "His voice was very high-pitched and he'd slur his words and go down to nothing." Afterward Kennedy asked, "How did you think it went?" She said, "The pictures were great, but I think you could have spoken better than that." Ethel Kennedy said quickly, "I thought he was very good!"[18] Lem Billings agreed with Angie Novello. He said later, "Bobby was the worst speaker that I ever . . . It was just horrifying to hear him."[19]

His primary point, after a meticulous survey of life and labor in the Soviet Union, was that history had shown it to be "suicidal for the United States or its allies to make major concessions to the Soviet Union without a quid pro quo." He had a ringing Cold War peroration:

> All I ask is that before we take any more drastic steps that we receive something from the Soviet Union other than a smile and a promise—a smile that could be as crooked and a promise that could be as empty as

they have been in the past. We must have peaceful coexistence with Russia but if we and our allies are weak, there will be no peace—there will be no coexistence.[20]

There was a subsidiary theme which grew in the next months until he transmuted it into a forceful article for the *New York Times Magazine*. This was the question that so exercised Douglas of the Russian treatment of ethnic nationalities in central Asia. Kennedy gave the Soviet government full credit for economic development. "Every time I have spoken on my trip through Central Asia," he wrote the director of the United States Information Agency, "I have said that I felt that the standard of living of the people had improved." But he also insisted on the price the native peoples had to pay. "Western Colonialism hasn't been made acceptable by arguing that material gains have been made in Colonial areas. Why then should Soviet Colonialism?"[21] In fact, Kennedy argued, the Russian record itself reproduced "all the evils of colonialism in its crudest form"—denial of self-government, segregation of Western masters from native subjects, mass executions of local peoples in order to preserve imperial rule.[22] By every standard used to judge Western colonialism, he told the Virginia State Bar Association, the Soviet performance "qualifies as colonialism of a peculiarly harsh and intractable kind."[23]

His anticolonialism was severely consistent. Unlike more obdurate Cold Warriors, he did not see western empire as a bulwark against communism nor suppose that anticolonialism in Asia and Africa was organized in Moscow. It was difficult for Americans to understand the power of anticolonialism in the underdeveloped world, he explained to one correspondent, "because we think that the uppermost thought in all people's minds is Communism."[24] He wrote in the *New York Times Magazine,* "We are still too often doing too little too late to recognize and assist the irresistible movements for independence that are sweeping one dependent territory after another."[25] "The fatal error" in United States foreign policy, he told a communion breakfast at Fordham University, was its commitment to colonialism. "If we are going to win the present conflict with the Soviet Union, we can no longer support the exploitation of native people by Western nations. We supported the French in Indochina far too long."[26]

In the short run, the journey confirmed Kennedy's mistrust of the Soviet government, which was reasonable enough, and his mistrust of negotiations and contracts, which he carried a little far. The ultimate impact was more complicated. The regime was detestable, and he detested it; but he came back with a considerably more differentiated sense of the Soviet Union. His notes include a paper entitled "Good Things":

> More school construction work.
> Great deal of hustle—people seem generally better off than people in comparable areas of Middle East.
> If you agree with principal [sic] of nurseries certainly the ones we saw were well managed.
> Rent very little though housing is admittedly a problem.
> Government loosening up
> 1) people allowed in Kremlin
> 2) Amnesty for criminals
> 3) Sentences being reviewed
> 4) MVD power cut
> 5) Farmers allowed more freedom
> 6) Visitors allowed in country
>
> People enthusiastic about their work
> Music good—Azerbaijan music group in Baku as good as anything we have seen—music catchy and dancers excellent.[27]

Before the trip he saw Russians as soulless fanatics. Afterward he saw them, Douglas said later, as human beings and achievers, "people with problems."[28] When Kennedy displayed his Russian photographs one evening, David Ormsby-Gore noticed that "he'd developed very much of a sympathy with the Russian people irrespective of the regime."[29] In *U.S. News* Kennedy questioned the efficacy of Communist propaganda, "because, if they had been told for 9 or 10 years that we were really their enemies and believed it, I don't think they could turn that off and have people as genuinely friendly as they were."[30] The Russian experience took time to penetrate, but Douglas and his wife later thought that it meant for Kennedy "the final undoing of McCarthyism."[31]

IV

Back in Washington, Kennedy returned to the Investigations Subcommittee and his old concern that east-west trade might build the military power of Communist nations. The ensuing investigation led to a prolonged wrangle in which the administration claimed the right to deny information about trade policy to Congress—both classified information, on the ground that it was a breach of national security; and "working-level papers," on the ground that exposing the internal policy process was contrary to the public interest.[32] The term "executive privilege" had not yet been coined to give such denial specious constitutional status. But the idea had emerged in full force and with the support of right-minded people during the Army-McCarthy hearings. It was now adorned with sweeping historical assertions and buttressed by an irrelevant anthology of judicial decisions (none bearing on the question of the executive power to withhold information from the Congress).

The administration, half persuaded it was defending some lofty constitutional principle, righteously declined to answer questions about items removed from the embargo list in 1954, even though, as Kennedy said, "some of our allies have published the lists of strategic materials which can be shipped to the Communists, and certainly the Soviet Union knows what it has bought and can buy."[33] The administration declined, in addition, to explain the reasons behind American policy on east-west trade. One Department of Commerce official said he only wished he could tell the committee why the executive branch had removed petroleum from the embargo: "I think it makes at least a reasonable record."[34]

This attitude infuriated the committee. "It is not national security," said Jackson, ". . . it is just sort of a national coverup." "Can you tell me," said Sam Ervin, "anything in the world that a witness is privileged . . . to tell this committee about what this committee is investigating?" "The real crux of this thing, as I see it," said McClellan, "is whether the Congress is entitled to know what is going on."[35] "I am afraid if the Senate does not wholeheartedly support Senator McClellan," Robert Kennedy wrote William Loeb, the publisher of the *Manchester Union-Leader,* "we will all be in difficulty in the years to come."* "If the position of the executive department were to prevail," the committee concluded, "it would mean that they would have an absolute right to deny to Congress or the public any information from the executive departments except in such matters as are required to be public by statute."[36]

As Robert Kennedy took leave from the committee to go as a Massachusetts delegate to the Democratic convention in Chicago, Wayne Morse, the old incorruptible from Oregon, wrote him, "In your unwavering dedication to the principle that the facts must speak for themselves . . . you have earned for yourself a very fine reputation among the members of the Senate."[37]

* RFK to William Loeb, April 4, 1956, RFK Papers. A prescient remark—though by the time, fifteen or so years later, the difficulty threatened the Republic itself, Loeb was on the other side.

V

John Kennedy had endorsed Adlai Stevenson the previous October. "My brother . . . admired him a good deal," Robert said later; there had never been a question of John's not supporting him for renomination.* As for Robert himself, "In 1952 I had been crazy about him. I was excited in 1956."[38]

Their father, however, had soured on Stevenson and looked with extreme disapproval on John's determination to depose the anti-Stevenson leadership of the Democratic state committee in Massachusetts. Staying out of local fights, Robert recalled, was a lesson his father had taught them "when we were very, very young." Local politics was "an endless morass from which it is very difficult to extricate oneself." As Robert summed it up, "You're either going to get into the problems of Algeria or you're going to get into the problems of Worcester."[39] Nevertheless John Kennedy and his Massachusetts agents, O'Donnell and O'Brien, went ahead and won their battle.

The ambassador was equally disapproving of his older son's growing interest in the vice presidential nomination. "If you are chosen," he wrote John in May, quoting Clare Boothe Luce with approval, "it will be because you are a Catholic and not because you are big enough to do a good job. She feels that a defeat would be a devastating blow to your prestige."[40] By August the ambassador must have thought the idea had passed, for he went off to the Riviera. But Theodore Sorensen was busy lining up support for Kennedy as Vice President. As for Kennedy himself: "I think," Robert Kennedy said later, "he just wanted to . . . put his foot in the water and see how cold it was, but he hadn't made up his mind to swim."[41]

The convention, Robert Kennedy's first, began on August 13. He had brought O'Donnell along. Peter Lawford, the actor, who had married Patricia Kennedy in 1954, offered them the penthouse suite he rented by the year in the Ambassador East. Robert's puritanism was offended by the idea of keeping so expensive an apartment and

---

* RFK, in recorded interview by John Stewart, July 20, 1967, 36; August 1, 1967, 51, JFK Oral History Program. In 1971 Lyndon Johnson described a phone call from Joseph Kennedy in October 1955 saying that he and John wanted to support Johnson for President in 1956; if he was not interested, they would go for Stevenson. Johnson said he was not interested (Lyndon B. Johnson, *The Vantage Point*, New York, 1971, 3). This incident reflected the father. The son came out for Stevenson that same month.

using it so rarely. To O'Donnell's dismay, he insisted that they move to a double room several floors below.[42]

Stevenson was nominated on August 16. He now faced the conundrum of the Vice Presidency. His preferences were unclear. On July 26 he had recounted to me his discussions with Harry Truman, James A. Farley, Sam Rayburn and other party elders about the contenders—Kennedy, Estes Kefauver of Tennessee and Hubert Humphrey of Minnesota:

> HST thinks Humphrey "too radical"; dismisses Kennedy as a Catholic; has no use for Kefauver. Mentions [Albert] Gore [of Tennessee] and [George] Leader [of Pennsylvania].
> Farley told AES, "America is not ready for a Catholic yet."
> Rayburn: "Well, if we have to have a Catholic, I hope we don't have to take that little piss-ant Kennedy. How about John McCormack?"[43]

A few days later Stevenson gave me the impression that he was "strongly for Humphrey on the merits, and also as a slam-bang campaigner."[44] But he liked Kennedy and had obligations to Kefauver, who, after contending with him in the primaries, had assured his nomination by declaring for him before the convention. In the end, Stevenson made his decision, or nondecision, to throw the vice presidential nomination to the convention.

John Kennedy, who had been testing the water, decided to swim. "Call Dad," he said to Robert, "and tell him I'm going for it." He then intelligently departed while Robert put the call through to Cap d'Antibes. "The Ambassador's blue language flashed all over the room," said O'Donnell, who remained. "The connection was broken before he was finished denouncing Jack as an idiot who was ruining his political career. Bobby quickly hung up. . . . 'Whew!' Bobby said. 'Is he mad!' "[45]

Twelve hours of frenzy followed. Abe Ribicoff of Connecticut nominated Kennedy. John McCormack, "literally propelled toward the platform at the last minute by Bob Kennedy," as Sorensen described it, seconded the nomination.[46] "Bobby and I ran around the floor like a couple of nuts," said O'Donnell. ". . . We didn't know two people in the place." Bobby did know Senator McClellan; but McClellan told him, "Just get one thing through your head. . . . Senators have no votes; I'm lucky to be a delegate; Orval Faubus is the governor of Arkansas, and that's it; and where he goes the Arkansas delegation goes."[47] In the end, Faubus went for Kennedy. So did much of the south in Confederate resentment over Kefauver's courage on civil rights.[48] Pat Lynch, whom John Kennedy had made

Massachusetts state chairman, told James A. Farley that he had "one hell of a nerve" opposing Jack Kennedy after young Joe Kennedy had stuck with him in 1940.[49] Sorensen asked Hubert Humphrey's campaign manager, Congressman Eugene McCarthy, whether, if Humphrey dropped out, Minnesota would go for Kennedy. McCarthy replied concisely, "All we have are Protestants and farmers," later complaining that Kennedy had sent a boy to talk to him. Lyndon Johnson announced that his state was switching to Kennedy: "Texas proudly casts its votes for the fighting sailor who wears the scars of battle." Then Tennessee shifted from Albert Gore to Kefauver, and the fight was over.[50]

Kennedy in a graceful speech asked that Kefauver be named by acclamation. Privately he was depressed. No Kennedy liked losing. Robert said to him, "You're better off than you ever were in your life, and you made a great fight, and they're not going to win and you're going to be the candidate the next time."[51] "This morning all of you were telling me to get into this thing," John Kennedy said, "and now you're telling me I should feel happy because I lost it."[52] In a day or two his natural equanimity reasserted itself.

Bobby was angry longer. "He was bitter," said the Massachusetts delegate who sat next to him on the plane back to Boston. "He said they should have won and somebody had pulled something fishy and he wanted to know who did it."[53] But he was learning: the importance of communications at a convention; the importance of an accurate delegate count; the importance of the rules ("If we had known parliamentary procedures, we could have stopped things after Tennessee switched");[54] the importance of friendship ("Kefauver had visited people and sent out cards and this is what paid off");[55] the unimportance of celebrated senators; the importance of uncelebrated party professionals—all points filed away in that retentive mind.

John Kennedy went off to Europe to rest up from the convention. Jacqueline, now pregnant (when she told Robert and Ethel she wanted a baby, they had said they would pray for her every morning), was with her mother in Newport. Suddenly she was taken sick and rushed to the hospital. When she recovered consciousness around two in the morning, her baby lost, the first person she saw, sitting by her bed, was Robert. Her mother had phoned him, and he had driven over at once from the Cape. Many years later Jacqueline learned that Robert had arranged for the burial of the dead child. "You knew that, if you were in trouble, he'd always be there."[56]

VI

Robert Kennedy's education in national politics was only beginning. Stevenson now asked him to join the campaign party. From the Stevenson viewpoint, Robert Kennedy's presence would signal Catholics, conservatives and friends of his father that all was not lost. From the Kennedy viewpoint, here was a chance to find out how to run, or not to run, a presidential campaign. From my own viewpoint on Stevenson's staff, Robert Kennedy seemed an alien presence, sullen and rather ominous, saying little, looking grim and exuding an atmosphere of bleak disapproval.

My reaction was colored by recollections of our altercation two years before. William McCormick Blair, Jr., back again as Stevenson's aide, said later, "I know he felt that we made lots of mistakes, and, of course, we did, but he was always nice about it and never critical." He was, Blair said, "very helpful and did a lot of things on his own initiative." Blair may have had in mind the whistle stop in Lewiston, Pennsylvania, when a group of children made so much noise that Stevenson could not begin his speech. After a moment of confusion, Kennedy climbed down from the train, shouted, "I can beat anyone from here to the lamppost," and took off with the children in hot pursuit.[57]

Blair was a family friend and therefore all right. Robert Kennedy seemed uncomfortable with the rest of us. One's memory was of Bobby making notes, always making notes, whether huddled by the window in the rear of the bus or plane or even sitting on a railroad track while the candidate spoke from the rear of the train. Occasionally he revealed himself, but in a rather solitary way. When we came into Springfield, Illinois, Kennedy said to Newton N. Minow, Stevenson's law partner, "I have heard the Governor speak before, but I have never been in Springfield before. Do you know where the Lincoln house is?" They skipped the speech, and Minow took him to the Lincoln house. Kennedy grew even more silent than usual, and Minow saw that he was deeply moved. "For the first time," Minow said later, "I understood there were depths of feeling in him I had never suspected."[58]

One afternoon in October the campaign party found itself in Morgantown, West Virginia. Stevenson was scheduled to speak that evening in New York City. Fog and rain set in, and a single plane was available to fly the candidate out of Morgantown. Eventually buses arrived to take the rest of us to Pittsburgh. Under pelting rain we scrambled aboard, groping for seats in the gathering darkness. I turned to look at my seatmate and found—I am sure to our mutual dismay—Robert Kennedy. For the next several hours we rode through the storm to Pittsburgh. Having no alternative, we fell into reluctant conversation. To my astonishment he was altogether pleasant, reasonable and amusing. We became friends at once and remained so for the rest of his life. I could never take seriously thereafter the picture of Robert Kennedy as a bearer of grudges, vindictive and unforgiving.

As for Stevenson, the candidate "sparkles," Kennedy wrote, ". . . in small groups discussing matters in which he is interested." When Kennedy took him to see the bishop of Denver, he talked about the Middle East "and really handled himself very well." Kennedy also liked Stevenson's humor. In Arizona they coincided with a parade for the Feast of St. Anthony. Back on the plane, Mrs. Ernest Ives, Stevenson's sister, asked Kennedy, "Isn't St. Anthony the one who keeps travelers safe?" Kennedy said, "Mrs. Ives, St. Christopher keeps travelers safe—St. Anthony finds things." At this moment Stevenson, passing by, said, "I hope he can find me some votes."[59] For the rest, the campaign was a deeply disillusioning experience. He considered it, he told O'Donnell, "the most disastrous operation" he had ever seen.[60]

Harrison Salisbury of the *New York Times* recalled Kennedy, sitting as so often on a railroad track during a whistle stop, talking about what a candidate should do in a campaign, "and he should do practically all the things that Stevenson didn't do."[61] Stevenson, it is true, spent too little time cultivating politicians and too much embellishing speeches. Kennedy also correctly objected, in a memorandum written after the campaign, to Stevenson's practice of reading prepared texts even on whistle stops:

> Because of his looks and his accent and his known background, this gave an appearance of insincerity. He was talking about the price of goods and the fact that big business was controlling the U.S. and I am sure the people felt that if he really believed all of this, that he could give it off the cuff and from the heart and would not have to read it. . . . He could never get it clear that it was not so much what he said but how he said it. I spoke again and again to people around him to try to get him to change his technique but he never would do it.[62]

He also spoke to Stevenson himself. On the way to Boston: "I said again that I felt his speeches should be extemporaneous and that he

Interlude: *William O. Douglas and Adlai Stevenson* 141

should concentrate on the women there to win or lose the election. He seemed interested." As for his Boston speech, an attack on big business, Kennedy pronounced it "incredibly bad."

> I told him I didn't think it would go over in Boston but Schlesinger and Galbraith were of a different opinion although a compromise was ultimately worked out. I told him that I felt he should talk about something he was interested in so he would appear sincere and that necessarily would be foreign policy. I told him I thought it was a great mistake to talk about matters he was obviously not interested in because he did not make an impression on television.[63]

Kennedy was even more distressed by the candidate's disorganization. He joined us one Sunday at Stevenson's house in Libertyville for an exasperating session on campaign planning in general and on Stevenson's controversial proposal for a ban on nuclear testing in particular. "It was probably the most enlightening discussion I ever had with him," Kennedy noted later,

> and it was a real eye-opener for me. It was a conference that really disturbed me as far as thinking that he should be president of the United States. He spent all day long discussing matters that should have taken, at the most, a half hour. For instance, for four hours, with 8 or 12 people there, we discussed who should go on his television program—Senator Anderson, Senator Jackson or Senator Symington. For another couple of hours we discussed whether the hydrogen bomb was fission or fusion and whether it was safe to say hydrogen bomb tests should be stopped at one mega-ton.
> At the first discussion, I thought one of his clerks could have made that decision and contacted Anderson, Jackson or Symington and made the arrangements. On the second question, I didn't think it made much sense for 8 or 12 men to discuss scientific matters about which no one knew anything.
> Stevenson just did not seem to be able to make any kind of decision. . . . The ostensible purpose of the meeting was to plan how the campaign for the last three weeks would be handled and that was hardly discussed at all. The subject of Nixon came up and I was strongly against making the campaign built around an attack on him. . . . People who didn't like Nixon were with Stevenson and they were not going to convince anybody by making any statements about him. . . .
> These matters were discussed rather pleadingly, and again no decisions were made. Stevenson was just not a man of action at all.[64]

In the end, Robert Kennedy found his candidate a profound disappointment. "People around Stevenson lost confidence in him. There was no sort of enthusiasm about Stevenson personally. In fact, to the contrary, many of the people around him were openly critical, which amazed me."[65] "It was a terrible shock," Kennedy said later. ". . . I came out of our first conversation with a very high opinion of him. . . . Then I spent six weeks with him on the campaign and he destroyed it all." On election day Kennedy quietly marked his ballot for Eisenhower.[66]

Stevenson wrote him afterward, "It was good to have you along and I have seldom heard sounder, more sensible and thoughtful remarks stated with better verbal conservation. I hope we'll see more of each other as time goes on, even if my public role is sharply diminished. And my affectionate regards to your charming wife."[67]

The campaign was another stage in education. "What struck me about him at that time, in spite of his great youth and seeming detachment from what was going on," said Harrison Salisbury, "was his great analytical ability . . . I had the feeling after the Stevenson campaign that Bobby knew every single thing there was to know about a campaign. He just squeezed all that absolutely dry."[68]

(8)

The Second Investigating Committee: Jimmy Hoffa

EIGHT DAYS after the 1956 election, Robert Kennedy, back as counsel for the Senate Permanent Subcommittee on Investigations, arrived in Los Angeles. He had embarked on a new inquiry. An investigation earlier in the year into government procurement of uniforms had turned the committee's attention to a fresh subject—labor racketeering. Hoodlums and mobsters, attracted by the spectacular growth of trade-union welfare and pension funds, attracted also by the convenience of unions as a cover for exercises in bribery and shakedown, were, it appeared, engaged in a systematic invasion of the American labor movement.

I

The labor movement itself was in a time of stagnation. The idealism generated in the great organizing battles of the 1930s was largely spent, except in the United Automobile Workers and a few other unions. The American Federation of Labor and the Congress of Industrial Organizations, mending their historic split in 1955, had chosen George Meany of the AFL Plumbers as president. But the new federation was doing little to police its own ranks. Nor, for that matter, did state or federal law provide effective standards for the management of the burgeoning welfare and pension funds.[1]

Congress had looked into the misuse of the funds, but its investigation was diffident, its glance quickly averted. In the meantime, newspapermen across the country—Edwin Guthman in Seattle, John Seigenthaler in Nashville, William Lambert and Wallace Turner in Portland, Pierre Salinger in San Francisco, Clark Mollenhoff in Washington—dug into the problem. They found the International Brotherhood of Teamsters an especially rewarding field. Mollenhoff, a lawyer as well as a newspaperman, was a hectoring and fearless reporter in the fashion of the old muckrakers. Early in 1956 he began to importune Kennedy about setting the Investigations Subcommittee on the trail of labor racketeers.

Kennedy was skeptical. He doubted whether the Government Operations Committee had jurisdiction; trade union affairs belonged to the labor committees. Mollenhoff replied that the labor committees were afraid of labor's political power. If unions were misusing tax-exempt funds and rendering dishonest financial reports to the Labor Department, this involved government operations. "Occasionally, I taunted him by questioning his courage to take on such an investigation."[2] Kennedy talked to people involved in earlier congressional inquiries. In August he got Senator McClellan to authorize a preliminary check into labor racketeering.

Kennedy remembered something about labor law from Charlottesville, but he knew little about the labor movement and was especially innocent about the Teamsters. This was understandable. The Teamsters were still in good repute in lay circles. Daniel J. Tobin, president for nearly half a century, had been everybody's friend, especially Franklin Roosevelt's. It was to the Teamsters that FDR had given the famous speech in the 1944 campaign about his little dog Fala. David Beck, Tobin's successor in 1952, was vain and pompous, but he had diligently used modern management methods to build the Western Conference of Teamsters. "I run this place just like a business," he said, "—just like the Standard Oil Company. . . . Our business is selling labor."[3] Beck, Murray Kempton of the *New York Post* wrote, was "the first national labor leader who unashamedly talks the language of a Chamber of Commerce secretary."[4] With his Rotary Club orations and his entrée to the Eisenhower White House, Beck was saluted in business circles as the labor statesman of his generation. In a welcome to the convention that anointed Beck, Governor Earl Warren of California declared his own "increasing admiration" for the Teamsters and pronounced the union as "not only something great of itself, but splendidly representative of the entire labor movement."[5]

Through his new friend, the rising young criminal lawyer Edward Bennett Williams,* Kennedy met a Williams associate, Edward

---

* Kennedy had met Williams as Joe McCarthy's counsel during the censure proceedings. Williams had become McCarthy's lawyer a year earlier, when Drew Pearson, the columnist, sued McCarthy after a brawl at the Sulgrave Club; McCarthy's Washington lawyer, a stalwart Italian American named John J. Sirica, decided he had

Cheyfitz; and Cheyfitz invited him early in 1956 to visit the Teamsters' new building in Washington, erected by Beck as a monument to himself and popularly known as the "marble palace." Beck was not there, but Kennedy met other Teamster grandees. Over lunch in the Teamsters' cafeteria, Cheyfitz, an ex-Communist, confided to Kennedy that he had seen Walter and Victor Reuther in Russia in 1933 and was still not sure the Reuther brothers had ever broken with communism. At Cheyfitz's suggestion, Robert asked his brother John to send Beck an inscribed copy of his new book, *Profiles in Courage*. "I don't know if he ever did," Robert said later. "I have never dared inquire."[6]

II

The Teamsters had begun in 1903 as an organization of city delivery crafts—essentially drivers of coal, milk, ice and bread trucks. In 1933 the union membership was only about 75,000, hardly three times what it had been when Dan Tobin became president in 1907.[7] Tobin, a craft unionist of the old school, had no use for the mass unionism of the 1930s. "We do not want," he liked to say, "to charter the riffraff."[8]

Younger leaders, however, embraced the new gospel of industrial organization. In Minneapolis a group of Trotskyites, led by Farrell Dobbs and the Dunne brothers, controlled the Teamster locals. They were all for chartering the riffraff. Farrell Dobbs's particular goal was to bring in the "over-the-road" drivers—the long-haul interstate truckers—whom the old leadership had disdained. He also wanted to shift from citywide to regional bargaining. His instrumentality was the new Central States Drivers Council. One of his ardent disciples was a young organizer from Detroit named James Riddle Hoffa. "I was studying," Jimmy Hoffa said many years later, "at the knee of a master."[9]

In 1939 Dobbs decided to concentrate on the Socialist Workers party, whose presidential candidate he later became. Hoffa, who moved to the fore after Dobbs's departure, disavowed his mentor's Trotskyism. But he never disavowed his admiration for Dobbs as an organizer and later offered large salaries to lure him back to the union.[10] Even Dobbs's Trotskyism may have had more influence than Hoffa admitted. Dobbs, Hoffa told the writer John Bartlow Martin,

---

a conflict of interests and passed McCarthy on to Williams (Edward Bennett Williams, in interview by author, January 23, 1976).

"was a very far-seeing man. He used to talk by the hour about what was going to happen in the country, and we'd listen."[11] Ralph and Estelle James, after long conversations with Hoffa in the 1960s, concluded that Dobbs's ruminations had left a deep imprint. Hoffa, they wrote, was "in the incongruous position of one who likes the present system, but does not believe it can work."[12] He plainly regarded capitalism as a racket that the strong manipulated to their own advantage —a system in which everyone was on the take, morality was bullshit and no holds were barred.

In any case Hoffa had come out of a hard school. The thirties was a savage decade for labor. Hoffa was designed for fighting—five feet, five and a half inches tall, with broad shoulders, big hands, thick legs; built, as John Bartlow Martin observed, like one of his own trucks.[13] He had an incisive intelligence, an unparalleled knowledge of the trucking industry, a stinging tongue, unlimited energy and, for his followers, unlimited charm. Unlike Beck, Hoffa could not care less about respectability. The rank and file saw in him their own aggressiveness, primitive prejudice and profane disrespect writ large. His achievements in raising wages, reducing hours and improving working conditions for the drivers were beyond dispute. Even the trucking associations were soon grateful to him for stabilizing labor relations in an industry notoriously vulnerable to unexpected work stoppages. He was also devious and perverse, had a raging temper, a bullying and sadistic disposition, a total absence of scruple and an impressive capacity for hatred. Paul Jacobs, an ex-Trotskyite himself and far from unsympathetic to Hoffa, wrote, "When Hoffa becomes really angry, his gray-green eyes get incredibly cold and menacing. It's then that his ruthlessness, his obvious belief in physical violence as an instrument of power, shows through as an important element in his personality."[14]

The Dobbs-Hoffa campaign to build a mass union in the middle west paralleled Beck's drive on the Pacific coast. By 1956 the Teamsters, with a million and a third members and welfare and pension funds rising toward a quarter of a billion dollars, were the largest and richest union in the country.

There was one other exception to the prevailing labor stagnation— the United Auto Workers. The two unions had a symbiotic relationship: the Auto Workers built the machines the Teamsters drove. If the Teamsters owed their vitality in great part to the organizing energy of Jimmy Hoffa, the Auto Workers owed theirs to the intellectual drive of another Detroit trade unionist, Walter Reuther. Like

Hoffa, Reuther was a veteran of the bloody thirties. Both men had been baptized in political radicalism: Reuther by the Socialists as Hoffa by the Trotskyites. Both lived in Detroit. On one occasion, when John L. Lewis conducted a raid against the Detroit Teamsters, Reuther opposed Lewis and saved Hoffa.[15] "We knew each other in the rough and tumble days," Hoffa once said to John Bartlow Martin. "For some reason, it's kind of inexplicable, we drifted apart. There's no reason today we should have any arguments. He depends on us and we depend on him. . . . If Walter would have stayed in the labor movement rather than getting into politics, we'd never had any trouble. We still see each other. He's all right. What the hell, he's got his problems, I got mine. At least he knows what the union business is all about. George Meany don't."[16]

Despite this nostalgia for the old days, Reuther and Hoffa stood by 1956 at opposite poles. Reuther, with his commitment to union democracy, his modest salary, his personal frugality, his activity in the Democratic party, his spacious liberalism on every question of domestic and foreign policy, represented the afterglow of the labor idealism of the thirties. Hoffa, with his dictatorial control, his high salary, his expensive suits, his Cadillacs, his manifold deals on the side, his sweetheart relations with employers, his sympathy for the Republican party, was the epitome of business unionism. As he told Paul Jacobs, "I don't want to change the world."[17]

III

The west coast trip was Robert Kennedy's initiation into labor racketeering. An accountant named Carmine Bellino accompanied him. Bellino, who had run the accounting unit in the FBI before becoming a consultant to congressional committees, was an artist in his profession. With ledgers and canceled checks spread out before him, he could reconstruct the most carefully disguised financial transactions. He had watched earlier congressional investigations into labor racketeering come to nothing. "Unless you are prepared to go all the way," Bellino had told Kennedy, "don't start it." "We're going all the way," Kennedy replied.[18]

In Los Angeles they learned of collusive arrangements between the Teamsters Union and trucker associations. They heard reports of extortion and beatings. They met a Los Angeles union organizer who, as Kennedy wrote later, "had traveled to San Diego to organize jukebox operators. He was told to stay out of San Diego or he would be killed. But he returned to San Diego. He was knocked unconscious. When he regained consciousness the next morning he was covered with blood and had terrible pains in his stomach. The pains were so intense that he was unable to drive back to his home in Los Angeles and stopped at a hospital. There was an emergency operation. The doctors removed from his backside a large cucumber. Later he was told that if he ever returned to San Diego it would be a watermelon. He never went back."[19]

Kennedy flew north to Portland. There William Lambert and Wallace Turner of the *Oregonian* explained to him the complex local relations among politicians, Teamster officials and the underworld. His next stop was Seattle, Dave Beck's home town. Clark Mollenhoff had phoned Edwin Guthman of the *Seattle Times*, a Beck specialist, to say that Kennedy was coming. Guthman had won the Pulitzer Prize for national reporting in 1950. He had never heard of Kennedy and told Mollenhoff he had no interest in being used by the Senate committee and then left high and dry. "Can you trust him?" he asked. Mollenhoff vouched for Kennedy. Guthman, still dubious, met Kennedy at the airport. When Kennedy assured him that the committee was serious and that informants would be protected, Guthman decided to cooperate.[20]

He put Kennedy in touch with a group of dissident Teamsters. "I noticed almost immediately," Guthman wrote later, "that . . . he began to identify with the rank and file members of the union."[21] Kennedy soon uncovered information about Beck's raids into the union treasury. He learned, for example, that Beck, who had sold his lakefront Seattle house to the union for $163,000 two years before while receiving rent-free tax-free occupancy, had actually used union funds to build the house in the first place. Kennedy's informant also told him that Nathan W. Shefferman, head of a Chicago labor relations (i.e., as it later developed, union-busting) firm, held the key to Beck's financial operations.

Two weeks later Kennedy and Bellino were back in Seattle. This time they saw the waggish Frank Brewster, head of the Western Conference of Teamsters, who owned racehorses and used union funds to transport his jockey and trainer and maintain a box at the track. Then they went to Chicago a few days before Christmas to interview Shefferman, who had been making purchases for Beck and receiving payment from union funds. Shefferman yielded up his records, and they carried them back through a blizzard to the hotel for examination. "In an hour," Kennedy wrote later, "we had come to the startling but inescapable conclusion that Dave Beck, the president of America's largest and most powerful labor union, the Teamsters, was a crook."[22]

He went back to Hyannis Port for Christmas in a state of exhilaration. The atmosphere was unsympathetic. His father thought the inquiry into labor racketeering a terrible idea. An investigation, he said, would not produce reform; it would only turn the labor movement against the Kennedys. He was deeply, emotionally opposed, and father and son had an unprecedentedly furious argument.[23] The ambassador, who did not give up easily, asked Justice Douglas to intervene. Douglas told his wife that his mission to Robert had failed: "He feels it is too great an opportunity."[24]

The top labor leadership did not want an investigation. Then Kennedy, as George Meany's biographer put it, "jolted" the AFL-CIO president by telling him that Beck was a crook. "It's going to be rough, Mr. Meany," Kennedy said. "The evidence is here, and there's no way Beck can answer it." CIO leaders like Reuther meanwhile reminded Meany that they had dealt with their Communists; now the AFL leaders had to deal with their criminals. Moreover, the new AFL-CIO constitution, breaking with hallowed traditions of union autonomy, authorized the executive council to suspend or expel unions involved in corrupt practices. Late in January 1957 Meany got the executive council, over Beck's bellowing opposition, to pledge full cooperation with a congressional investigating committee.[25]

But which committee? Meany thought John McClellan "an antilabor nut" and objected to the Investigations Subcommittee.[26] McClellan objected to what he called the "traditionally gentle" Labor Committee.[27] The Senate compromised by establishing a select committee with four members drawn from Investigations and four from Labor. This led to much soul-searching and maneuver among the senators. McClellan told Kennedy he deserved the chairmanship; "he had taken a lot of bad jobs from the Senate . . . and if they were going to deprive him of this one, he was going to be very upset."[28] Neither Symington nor Jackson, the Democrats next in seniority on Investigations, wanted to go on the select committee. Jackson, declining the assignment, explained to Kennedy that Beck had "a great deal of power [in the state of Washington] and . . . could make things most difficult" in 1958 when he was up for reelection.[29] After some vacillation Symington, who had presidential ambitions, followed Jackson's example. This made Sam Ervin, a conservative on labor issues, the second Democrat from Investigations on the select committee.

Senator Patrick McNamara of Michigan, a former trade unionist, agreed to be one of the two Democrats from the Labor Committee. John Kennedy was next in seniority. He felt at first that one Kennedy investigating the labor movement was quite enough. Joseph Kennedy undoubtedly agreed. Lyndon Johnson, the majority leader, told Kennedy it was madness for him to think he could take on labor and survive as a serious contender in 1960.[30] Still, if Kennedy refused, his place would go to Strom Thurmond of South Carolina, a Democrat in 1957 and noted then, as later, for regressive views on all questions. "Bobby wanted me on that committee," John Kennedy subsequently said, "in order to keep it more balanced. He asked me to come and give him some support or the committee would be too conservative and would have seemed anti-labor. You see, McClellan and Ervin went on, and if I hadn't, then Thurmond would have, and you can imagine what would have happened with Thurmond thrown in with McClellan and Ervin."[31]

The Republican members were Joe McCarthy and Karl Mundt from Investigations; Irving Ives of New York, a liberal, and Barry Goldwater of Arizona, a conservative, from Labor. On January 30, 1957, the Senate unanimously approved the Select Committee on Improper Activities in the Labor or Management Field with an appropriation of $350,000 and McClellan as chairman.

IV

Kennedy set up headquarters in room 101 of the old Senate Office Building. The office, cluttered with documents stacked in piles, had, John Bartlow Martin thought, the air of a secondhand bookshop.[32] Kennedy asked the tireless and cheerful Angie Novello, who happened also to be Carmine Bellino's sister-in-law, to be his secretary. When she said she would think about it, he said, "You're not going to think about it. I'm telling you. You are going to be my secretary." She said with a laugh, "Oh, yes, sir," saluted and clicked her heels.[33] He drafted his old friend Kenneth O'Donnell as his administrative assistant. "If the investigation flops," Robert Kennedy told him, "it will hurt Jack in 1958 and in 1960, too. . . . A lot of people think he's the Kennedy running the investigation, not me. As far as the public is concerned, one Kennedy is the same as another Kennedy." Assuming that the job had been cleared with John Kennedy, O'Donnell came to Washington. When the senator heard about it, he had words with his brother and later told O'Donnell irritably, "I need you up in Massachusetts. Nobody tells me anything."[34] O'Donnell became the point of coordination for the investigations as well as the guardian of the door to Robert Kennedy's inner office. Within, while they discussed investigatory strategy, they used to pass a football back and forth as if they were still at Harvard.[35]

Carmine Bellino was of course a necessity. Kennedy took the reliable LaVern Duffy from the Investigations Subcommittee. In February he broke from the usual committee pattern by hiring a portly, cigar-smoking newspaperman, Pierre Salinger. The previous summer, *Collier's* had asked John Bartlow Martin to do an exposé of the Teamsters. When Martin joined the Stevenson campaign, the assignment fell to Salinger, an experienced reporter in San Francisco. In the autumn, Salinger heard about the Senate investigation. He thereupon arranged an interview with Kennedy. "In five minutes," Salinger wrote later, "the roles were reversed. I was not interviewing him; he was interviewing me. . . . I was surprised at the information I gave him." In December, as the Salinger series was awaiting publication, *Collier's* expired as a magazine. In the gloomy aftermath Salinger received two phone calls. Einar Mohn, a Teamsters vice president whom Salinger knew from California, asked him to be public relations director for the Teamsters. Robert Kennedy asked him for his Teamsters research. Salinger, who suspected the Teamster offer as a device to insure his silence, turned his material over to Kennedy. The job followed.

McClellan, who disapproved of newspapermen, was not enthusiastic. Glaring at Salinger across his desk, he said, "If I ever hear of you talking to the press, I will deal with you in the harshest manner possible." On Salinger's first day in the office Kennedy directed him to serve a subpoena; it turned out to be for Einar Mohn. Salinger walked over to Mohn's office in the marble palace and said, "Einar, you know you offered me a job as public relations director for the Teamsters. I want you to know I was also offered another job at the same time and that was investigator for the Senate Labor Rackets Committee. I'm here to tell which job I've accepted. Here," and handed him the subpoena. That evening Kennedy took him home for dinner. When they reached the main course, Ethel asked, "What would like like to drink?" Salinger said, "I'd like a glass of red wine." Ethel said, "You know, we've never had any wine in this house." Salinger said, "Well, Mrs. Kennedy, don't worry about it. I happen to have a bottle in my suitcase."[36]

The next morning Salinger was on his way to Seattle. He spent most of the next year on the road. Kennedy later wrote that he "could grasp the importance of a document better than almost anyone on the staff."[37] He was also a man of courage, spirit and irrepressible wit and soon became a Kennedy intimate. Kennedy kidded him about his cigars, devised contests to bring down his weight, without much success, and took the Salingers along on Christmas skiing expeditions.[38]

In April another investigator joined the staff, a lawyer and former FBI agent named Walter Sheridan. Kennedy, rushing to a hearing, hired Sheridan going up the stairs from his office. "It was so typical," Sheridan said later, "because most of my conversations with him since then were walking up steps or riding in cars or up and down elevators or going to airplanes because he was always on the move and the only time he had to talk was while he was getting there." Later they discovered they were both born on the same day in the same year. Soon after Sheridan was taken on, Kennedy ordered him to Chicago to join Salinger on the investigation of Nathan Shefferman. Sheridan made a reservation on the noon plane. The next morning, coming upon Sheridan going through the files in the office, Kennedy "gave me this soft look and said, 'I never go any place at noon.' So, after that, I never went any place at noon."[39]

Leaving at noon wasted a day. They all worked, Sheridan said, "at an unbelievable pace." No one worked harder than Kennedy, jacket off, shirtsleeves rolled up, necktie pulled loose under his button-down collar, horn-rimmed glasses pushed to the top of his head, sitting under photographs (improbably) of Franklin Roosevelt and Douglas MacArthur.[40] For all his intensity, Kennedy, as John Bartlow Martin observed him, "infused his office and staff with a certain youthful light-hearted atmosphere."[41] The staff, numbering more than a hundred by 1958, was devoted to him, and he to them.

The investigators, Kennedy liked to say, "are the backbone of the hearings, and without their work we'd have nothing. I think we have the best investigators and staff of any congressional committee."[42] He was demanding but fair. "I'd worked in the FBI," said Sheridan, "and if an agent makes a mistake in the FBI, as Bob Kennedy would say, 'It's his ass.' But with him, you always knew that if you made an honest mistake, he was going to be behind you and he always was. . . . He was aggressive and he was direct and he was terribly honest in his approach to people and to life."[43] Years later, LaVern Duffy, reflecting after nearly a quarter century on the Government Operations Committee, said, "I've seen a lot of counsels here. There

The Second Investigating Committee: Jimmy Hoffa 153

was no one like him. He had an uncanny ability to get people to do more than they thought they could do. He didn't do this by bringing pressure on them. It was because they wanted to please him. He gave people a sense of personal interest in themselves, their work, their families. This was his secret. He never got mad except when someone lied to him. He couldn't stand that."[44]

As the committee got under way, letters flowed into the office, a thousand a week. People wrote about union officials who declined to call union meetings or to audit union books. They wrote about rigged elections and theft of union funds, about racial discrimination, goons, intimidation, extortion, about beatings, acid throwing, murder. "I have been a union member for 25 years," someone wrote from Akron, "and until lately, have never been ashamed." "Please come in and restore our union rights and privileges to us. If we can get this exposé going we can kick them all out, with open elections" (Philadelphia). Letters ended: "I regret that I do not feel secure enough to sign my name, but my children also play in the streets"; or, "Please do not use my name—please—I'll be a gone goose if you do"; or simply, "I cannot sign my name."[45] About a third contained information that warranted at least preliminary investigation.[46] "There's something very curious I've learned," Kennedy mused to Murray Kempton one day. "If you get a letter typed on stationery, seven paragraphs in length, and signed by somebody, you can be absolutely sure it's a lie. But if you get a letter which says, 'I saw Jimmy Hoffa take $300 from somebody in a bar in 1947,' signed 'A Workingman,' it's always true."[47]

He kept in close touch with newspapermen. He was "under the illusion," Kempton said, "that journalists knew something about crime." Even the sardonic Kempton was impressed by his "way of asking direct, pertinent questions . . . just cutting to the heart of it."[48] In return Kennedy leveled with the press. "As a reporter," Edwin Guthman said, "I had never encountered a person in public life who answered my questions as candidly and completely as he did."[49] "Most reporters who covered Mr. Kennedy during this period liked him," wrote Joseph A. Loftus, the labor reporter for the *New York Times*. ". . . He was both available and truthful; there is no more effective way to disarm a reporter who by training and experience is a skeptic."[50]

John Seigenthaler of the *Nashville Tennessean* was not disarmed. Distressed by Teamster corruption and violence in Tennessee, Seigenthaler tried to give the story to Kennedy but caught him on a busy day in New York, was sent summarily to the assistant chief counsel, the able Jerome Adlerman, and told to put it all in a memorandum. A second attempt in Washington produced the same result; so did a third approach through Senator McClellan. As Seigenthaler later liked to tell it, Kennedy "kept saying, 'See Mr. Adlerman,' and . . . Mr. Adlerman kept saying, 'Send me a memo on it.'" Seigenthaler decided that Kennedy was a rich snob and a phony.

Around eleven o'clock at night some weeks later, Kennedy called Scigenthaler in Nashville and said he was sending down two investigators. The investigation led eventually to the impeachment and conviction of a judge, the dismissal of a district attorney, the defeat of a sheriff and the conviction of a number of police officials. Kennedy himself went down to testify against the judge. There were two planes back to Washington at the end of the afternoon, two hours apart, and, as Seigenthaler was driving Kennedy to the earlier flight, Kennedy said, "You know, I've never seen the Hermitage. . . . I'm a great admirer of Jackson and I'd like to go out there." They went to the Hermitage, where Robert called Ethel to say where he was and spent so much time that he nearly missed the second plane.[51]

V

The countdown on Dave Beck had begun even before the formation of the select committee. Early in January 1957 Kennedy met the Teamster president in New York. Beck began with a forceful denunciation of racketeering. "His face," Kennedy wrote later, "grew red and florid and his voice began to climb to a higher pitch until he was almost shouting." It was as if he felt "he could yell us into believing in the righteousness" of his cause.

Kennedy listened politely and then began to ask questions, derived from the Shefferman papers, about Beck's financial life. Beck said that, though he had nothing to hide, he could not indulge in a discussion of private matters. Kennedy asked about his house in Seattle. Beck said it was a private matter. Watching Beck, Kennedy was struck by his eyes—at first appearing lost in his large, moonlike face, but "soon you realized it was Dave Beck's eyes more than anything else that attracted your attention. They seemed like tiny pinpoints of light that were constantly moving back and forth."[52]

The investigation went forward. Many of Beck's vital files had been destroyed. But the committee staff, drawing on independent records and ancillary witnesses, was able, with the accounting wizardry of Carmine Bellino, to reconstruct much of the story—$370,000 taken by Beck from the Western Conference of Teamsters; $85,000 turned over to Shefferman to pay for personal purchases; loans from trucking companies; even thefts from a trust fund set up for a friend's widow. When Beck appeared before the committee in the Senate caucus room in March 1957, Kennedy felt momentarily sorry at the spectacle of a man who had grossly betrayed his union brothers, stolen their money and was now "about to be utterly and completely destroyed before our eyes."[53]

But Beck, exuding confidence, dominated the early hours of the hearing. Mundt and Goldwater fed him general questions to which he returned the pontifical answers of a certified labor statesman. Toward the end of the day, McClellan called on Kennedy. The chief counsel asked about Beck's use of union funds. Faltering before the onslaught of detail, Beck retreated to the Fifth Amendment, invoking it sixty-five times before the hearing was over. "The closing half hour on Wednesday," Edwin A. Lahey, the seasoned correspondent of the *Chicago Daily News,* wrote Kennedy, "was about the finest job I've ever seen done on Capitol Hill. If ever Providential justice was ladled out in the Caucus room, you did it that day."[54]

In subsequent appearances Beck's story, confidence and reputation steadily disintegrated. "This is the case," Meany soon observed, "of a very, very wealthy individual spending every waking moment, if you can credit the testimony, to find some way to use his union as an instrumentality for his own personal profit."[55] In due course Beck was convicted and imprisoned for larceny and income tax evasion. (In May 1975 he received a full pardon from President Gerald Ford.) The abrupt downfall of one of the most powerful and respected labor leaders in the country made the Rackets Committee overnight a national phenomenon.

The spotlight played particularly on the chief counsel. "Even with a couple of veteran inquisitors" like McClellan and Mundt on hand, wrote Harry Taylor in the *Cleveland Press,* "it is plain that this is Bob Kennedy's show so far."[56] Not all television viewers liked what they saw. An assistant professor of political science at Berkeley wrote Kennedy, declaring himself

sickened by the radio and television accounts of your activities, . . . your humiliating, badgering questioning of the witnesses. . . . Perhaps another Kennedy will contribute . . . *Profiles in Bullying.* . . .

To those of us who see your brother, John Kennedy, as probably the most dramatic liberal personality on the national scene today, the unfortunate possibility that he might be a victim of "guilt by association" and suffer from your current juvenile antics is depressing.[57]

Another correspondent complained to John Kennedy:

> Being wholeheartedly in sympathy with your committee, I was therefore greatly disturbed to observe in the televised segments that the chief interrogator . . . engaged in brow-beating, badgering and attempts to bulldoze the witnesses. . . . It was this same insolent and overbearing manner which was the downfall of Senator McCarthy.[58]

From Chicago, Sargent Shriver relayed to Joseph Kennedy (who promptly attended the hearings to see for himself) the observations of Richard Walsh, the executive editor of Hearst's *Chicago American*. "Words used to describe Bobby's manner," Walsh said, "ranged all the way from 'overeagerness' or 'intolerance' to 'viciousness.'" Even his collaborator in the Talbott case, Charles Bartlett, spoke of "the solemn moral tone with which he is wont to suggest the evil of a witness's ways."[59] He lacked, wrote Paul Healy of the *New York Daily News*, "the cool inward poise of his brother."[60]

Some reviews were more favorable. The *New York Herald Tribune* thought him "calm and polite, never baiting witnesses, but his questions are so penetrating that a witness is often caught off base."[61] The *Toledo Blade* remarked on his "innocent-looking blue eyes" and his habit of twisting a paper clip as he questioned bull-necked men about payoffs and call girls; "you expect him to blush any moment."[62] John R. Cauley of the *Kansas City Star* found him "stern in his interrogation of witnesses, but never abusive and seldom sarcastic"; all in all, "a remarkable personality even for Washington," who had "by his own intelligence, initiative and courage established himself as a real 'comer' and at only 31."[63] Robert Kennedy, Robert Riggs wrote in the *Louisville Courier-Journal*, was winning "a reputation as one of the most competent investigators any Congressional committee ever had."[64]

"My biggest problem as counsel," Robert Kennedy himself conceded, "is to keep my temper. I think we all feel that when a witness comes before the United States Senate he has an obligation to speak frankly and tell the truth. To see people sit in front of us and lie and evade makes me boil inside. But you can't lose your temper—if you do, the witness has gotten the best of you."[65]

VI

For all the exasperations in the caucus room, this was the most fulfilling time Robert Kennedy had ever known. He was committed to something that mattered; he was convinced of the rectitude of his cause; and he knew he was doing a good job. "He wasn't frustrated during that period," Lem Billings recalled. "This is when he blossomed.... He wasn't the angry man any more and he was much more pleasant to be around because he hadn't this terrible feeling that he wasn't contributing."[66]

In October 1957, when the Soviet Union beat the United States into space, Lyndon Johnson said that "a successful investigation of Sputnik could only take place if [it] had someone like young Kennedy handling it." Recording this remark, Kennedy added: "Am very pleased with myself."[67] He must have been even more pleased by a Christmas letter from Clark Mollenhoff. "You have carried a candle," Mollenhoff wrote, "that has been a beacon to hundreds of reporters and editors, thousands of politicians and labor leaders, and literally millions of the rank-and-file labor union members and their families.... You may go ahead to higher office than committee counsel, but it is doubtful if anything you do will have greater force for good government and clean labor than what you have done this year."[68]

The job was hard on family life. Early in 1957 he bought from his brother John—for the same price, $125,000, that John had paid three years earlier—the fine old manor in McLean, Virginia, known as Hickory Hill, once the Civil War headquarters of General George B. McClellan, latterly owned by Justice Robert H. Jackson of the Supreme Court. After Jacqueline's miscarriage in 1956, the great house, complete with its new nursery, was too sad and echoing for the senator and his wife. It was ideal for Bobby and Ethel, whose five lively children were overflowing their small house in Georgetown. More children came along: Michael LeMoyne on February 27, 1958, Mary Kerry on September 8, 1959. A handsome white quasi-Georgian mansion, rich in historical association, with high ceilings, white woodwork and crystal chandeliers, surrounded by five and a half acres of rolling green land, Hickory Hill happily absorbed the Kennedys, their children and assorted dogs, horses, rabbits, chickens, goats and pigs. The Civil War association did not, however, excite the new owner. "McClellan," he would say sharply, "didn't press!"[69]

Robert Kennedy pressed. Often he did not get out to Hickory Hill till nine or ten at night. "It's nice Ethel has a big appetite," he once observed, "because she eats with the children at 6:30 and then with me again when I come home." ("I get reacquainted with the youngsters," he added, "every weekend.")[70] No doubt Ethel needed two dinners after a day of driving children back and forth to school and, in between, rushing to the Capitol to lend support at the hearings. But nothing discouraged her, and it took a good deal to rein in her high spirits. On an August night in 1957 one of her Skakel sisters-in-law gave a party in Stamford, Connecticut, at which Ethel was photographed standing cheerfully next to a couple identified by the hostess as Mr. and Mrs. Dave Beck, Jr. The local newspaper reported that Dave Beck himself had been at the party too. "Although our politics differ," he was quoted as saying, "socially we get along famously." After this bulletin got on the wires and attracted a certain attention, the "Becks" turned out to be New York friends of the young Skakels. The editor of the *Stamford Advocate,* taken in by the hoax, sourly informed his readers, "If you have any thoughts on adult delinquency, I wish you'd drop me a note." Nor did Robert Kennedy, who had missed the party, think it very funny.[71]

There were other irritations. Eddie Cheyfitz, he heard, was saying "that he had already established information that I had homosexual tendencies and that while in college, I ran across the campus in a girl's dress."[72] Some problems were more worrying. "Mr. Kennedy exposed himself and his family," wrote Joseph Loftus of the *Times* in 1960, "to terrible danger for three years."* In 1959 the *New York Herald Tribune* reported that Kennedy had received anonymous phone calls warning that acid would be thrown in the eyes of his children. He told newspapermen, "I don't care to discuss it."[73] He declined to take special precautions. "Asked by newspaperman if I had 4 bodyguards," he noted at one point. "His paper had that report & that they had been hired by my father to protect me. I replied that the Kennedys have been taking care of themselves for years & bodyguards unnecessary."[74] Fame, however, was incomplete. "Taxicab driver in N.Y.C. said he recognized me," Robert wrote in one of his scribbled memoranda. ". . . 'I know who you are. You're Roy Cohn.' "[75]

VII

Among those who watched the downfall of Dave Beck with equanimity was Jimmy Hoffa. Walter Sheridan's conclusion was that

---

* Joseph A. Loftus, review of *The Enemy Within,* in New York Times Book Review, February 28, 1960. This statement enraged Hoffa, who, Loftus said, "accosted me with great fury. . . . I just sneered at him, and he walked away. . . . The tone that he used at me was a threatening kind of tone. Knowing his background and his ability to get even, why, I was somewhat concerned" (Joseph A. Loftus, in recorded interview by Jean Stein, March 26, 1970, 8, Stein Papers).

Hoffa had "decided to try to use Kennedy to eliminate Beck."[76] Certainly Eddie Cheyfitz, a Hoffa ally, gave Kennedy leads about Beck while trying at the same time, as Kennedy said, "to implant the thought that after a wild and reckless youth during which he had perhaps committed some evil deeds, Hoffa had reformed."[77] In due course Cheyfitz, suggesting that Hoffa could be a force for good, urged Kennedy to sit down with him. "More out of curiosity than anything else," Kennedy agreed to dine with Hoffa at Cheyfitz's house.[78]

A week before the dinner, a lawyer named John Cye Cheasty told Kennedy he had information that would make Kennedy's hair stand on end. "In those days there were few people I talked with who did not claim to have information that would make my hair stand on end, and I tried to see them all."[79] Cheasty's information turned out to be adequately hair-raising. Hoffa had hired him, he said, as a spy, charged with penetrating the McClellan committee and reporting back on the progress of the Teamsters investigation.

Cheasty, an Irish Catholic, had served in the Navy, Secret Service and Internal Revenue Service. "He was the kind of fellow," Kenneth O'Donnell said, "[who] thinks Reuther is a Communist and thought Joe McCarthy was great."[80] As a Catholic, he later told Kennedy, "I believe in right and wrong and that I must answer to God for my conduct. All my life I have regarded good as something to work for, and evil as something to be fought."[81] He produced bribe money, ticket stubs and other evidence to corroborate his story. Kennedy took him to McClellan. Cheasty agreed to work with the FBI as a double agent. He was already handing selected information to Hoffa when Kennedy went to Cheyfitz's house on the snowy evening of February 19, 1957.

Hoffa's enthusiasm about the meeting had been even less than Kennedy's. "I got nothing to talk to him about," he told Cheyfitz crossly, but finally acquiesced.[82] Kennedy was impressed by Hoffa's "strong, firm" handshake. Hoffa was less impressed by Kennedy's handshake: "I can tell by how he shakes hands what kind of fellow I got. I said to myself, 'Here's a fella thinks he's doing me a favor by talking to me.' "[83] Cheyfitz offered his guests a drink. Hoffa "made rather a point of the fact that he did not drink," Kennedy noted in a memorandum two days later.[84] Kennedy, who rarely drank, declined also. Cheyfitz reluctantly followed suit.

They talked for a while about the labor movement. Kennedy, as was his custom, asked direct and personal questions: how Hoffa had got into the union, how much a labor leader earned and so on. He meant nothing by it; he was genuinely curious. Hoffa thought the questions condescending. "It was as though he was asking, with my limited education what right did I have to run a union like this?" He answered them in his own way. He told of battles against employers and cops. He said people were always trying to destroy him and therefore he had to destroy them. Kennedy tried to joke about Hoffa's toughness—"maybe I should have worn my bullet proof vest" —but "it seemed to go over his head." Hoffa kept repeating how tough he was; Kennedy remembered this as "the theme of all his conversation." ("I thought to myself that anyone who kept talking about how tough they are is not really tough.") "I do to others what they do to me," Hoffa said to him, "only worse."

During dinner Cheyfitz rambled on about how Dave Beck had ruined his son by choosing his friends, ordering his meals and turning him into a "jellyfish." Kennedy agreed; of all Beck's sins, he later wrote, "his attitude toward his son was his worst." After dinner, Cheyfitz said something about getting down to business. "If you don't ask a few of the embarrassing questions," he said to Kennedy, "then I will." Cheyfitz proceeded to bring up the "paper locals" in New York City. Paper locals are locals that exist only on paper: locals with charters and officers but no members. In an effort to get control of the New York Joint Council of Teamsters, Hoffa had arranged for the chartering of seven such locals just before the council election in 1956. Many officers in these paper organizations were hoodlums who had worked with Johnny Dio (Dioguardi), Tony (Ducks) Corrallo and other eminent racketeers. Hoffa freely admitted organizing the phony locals but claimed it was done to circumvent the no-raiding pact scheduled to go into effect after the AFL-CIO merger.

Around half-past nine the phone rang: it was Ethel Kennedy. Bobby said, "I'm still alive, dear. If you hear a big explosion, I probably won't be." Ethel said that a driver, skidding on the icy road, had banged into a tree at Hickory Hill and was now sitting, hysterical, in their living room. Kennedy made apologies and prepared to go. Hoffa said, "Tell your wife I'm not as bad as everyone thinks I am."

Kennedy, perhaps parodying Hoffa's own line about doing to others what they did to him, but worse, noted later, "Personally, I thought he was, but worse." Hoffa was equally unadmiring. After Kennedy left he told Cheyfitz, "He's a damn spoiled jerk." Cheyfitz said, "You gotta get to know him." Hoffa said, "You know 'um, I don't wanta know 'um." It was a foredoomed encounter. Each represented what the other detested most. Hoffa saw Kennedy as the arrogant rich kid for whom everything in life had been easy. Kennedy saw Hoffa as the cynic who betrayed honest workingmen and had no object in life beyond money and power for himself.

VIII

Their next meeting took place at midnight three weeks later in the federal courthouse. John Cye Cheasty had continued to supply Hoffa with material, especially Carmine Bellino's analyses of Beck's financial sprees. "If that's the kind of stuff they have on Beck," Hoffa told Cheasty, "it looks as though his goose is cooked." The government decided to spring its trap on the evening of March 13. Cheasty handed Hoffa a large manila envelope on Dupont Circle. Hoffa, shaking hands with him, stuffed a wadded two thousand dollars in his palm. As Hoffa entered the Dupont Plaza Hotel, the FBI arrested him on charges of bribery and conspiracy.

At the courthouse an hour later, Hoffa and Kennedy sat in uneasy silence. "He stared at me for three minutes," Kennedy wrote, "with complete hatred in his eyes." After an interval they fell into an almost friendly conversation about who could do the more pushups. Kennedy claimed the higher figure. Then or later Hoffa said that no doubt Kennedy could do more pushups; "what the hell weight does it take to lift a feather?" Hoffa remembered saying at the time, "Listen, Bobby, you run your business and I'll run mine. You go on home and go to bed, I'll take care of things. Let's don't have no problems." He told John Bartlow Martin afterward, "He was very unhappy because I called him Bobby."[85]

It looked now as though it were Hoffa's goose that was to be cooked. When a reporter asked what he would do if Hoffa were acquitted, Kennedy said lightheartedly, "I'll jump off the Capitol." The trial began at the end of June. Hoffa's lawyer was Kennedy's friend Edward Bennett Williams. Kennedy was a prosecution witness. Hoffa, in his usual style, baited Williams: "Kennedy is a friend of yours so you will go easy on him." Williams, overcompensating, was therefore especially tough.[86] Kennedy lacked "courtroom experience," Clark Mollenhoff wrote, "and Williams tried to take advantage of this fact with a needling cross-examination. Kennedy had a momentary unsteadiness, but then became amazingly firm."[87] Hoffa, to the surprise of the prosecution, took the stand in his own defense.

Employing all his persuasiveness, he contended that he had hired Cheasty as a lawyer and as a matter of course accepted any documents his lawyer gave him. The federal attorney, caught off guard by Hoffa's appearance, was feeble in cross-examination.[88]

The jury was two-thirds black; and the sight one day of Joe Louis embracing Hoffa in the courtroom no doubt had its effect. The *Washington Afro-American* published what was in effect a pro-Hoffa issue, in which columns and advertisements portrayed the defendant as a lifetime friend of the Negro people—he had indeed opposed segregation in the Teamsters—and denounced the judge, Cheasty and Senator McClellan as enemies of civil rights. This had obviously been done, said Edward Bennett Williams, who had not known about it, "in an effort to influence the jury in Hoffa's favor."[89]

Williams's summation was masterly; the prosecutor's was not. The verdict was returned on July 19. Cheasty called Angie Novello: "Angie, you won't believe this, but Hoffa was acquitted." Angie went to the hearing room, where Kennedy was interrogating a witness, and passed him a note. He gasped and looked, Clark Mollenhoff reported, "deathly sick." Mollenhoff himself rushed over to the courthouse in time to hear Williams remind the press of Kennedy's remark about jumping off the Capitol and add, "I'm going to send Bobby Kennedy a parachute." Mollenhoff said to Hoffa, "Jimmy, you are a lucky bastard." "I just live right," Hoffa replied with a wink.[90]

Kennedy, still shaken, returned to his office. Observing downcast faces, he suppressed his own disappointment. "Come on now," he said. ". . . We have a lot of work to do."[91]

IX

A fortnight after Hoffa's acquittal, Kennedy announced a new series of hearings. Racketeers and hoodlums were bad enough anywhere in the labor movement, he said, but worst of all in the Teamsters, for there was "no organization, union or business, that has a greater effect on the community life in this country."[92]

A few days later Pierre Salinger slipped into Detroit. He arrived, it need hardly be said, on an early morning plane, and by midafternoon he had served subpoenas on officials in five Teamster locals. When he returned to his office in the federal building, the phone rang. It was Frank Fitzsimmons from Hoffa's own local. He said, "Jimmy wants to see you." The next morning Salinger, reinforced by Carmine Bellino, went to Teamster headquarters.

The Second Investigating Committee: Jimmy Hoffa

After more than an hour's wait, they were ushered into Hoffa's office and seated in low chairs in front of his desk. Hoffa, his own chair placed, like Mussolini's, on a slightly raised platform, stared down at them. Five union officials, clutching subpoenas, stood uncomfortably in a semicircle behind. In an apparent rage, Hoffa rose, grabbed the subpoenas from their hands and waved them furiously at the men from the Rackets Committee: "You can tell Bobby Kennedy for me that he's not going to make his brother President over Hoffa's dead body." Salinger and Bellino persisted. Hoffa's mood suddenly changed. He became affable and agreed to let them into his records. Given the subpoenas, he had no choice. The great Hoffa investigation had begun.[93]

The records were in poor shape, with names torn off checks and hotel bills. Potential witnesses fell silent or left town. When the hearings began on August 20, 1957, Hoffa appeared confident. "We'd rehearse [with the lawyers] what Kennedy would do," he told John Bartlow Martin. "He isn't the brightest fella in the world. And he's got to investigate for weeks and weeks to find out what we already know. . . . I know what I done wrong and what I didn't. I know what they'll uncover and what they won't. And that's two-thirds of the worrying. All my life I been under investigation."[94]

Hoffa began strong, exchanging deep thoughts about the labor movement with the senators, patronizing the counsel, whom he called "Bob," and responding aggressively to the occasional questions Kennedy got in about his private business dealings. The senatorial meanderings were largely surplusage:

SENATOR MUNDT. Basically, do you believe in socialism?
MR. HOFFA. I positively do not.
SENATOR MUNDT. Do you believe in our private-enterprise system?
MR. HOFFA. I certainly do.
SENATOR MUNDT. Is there some difference in political philosophy between you and some other prominent labor leaders in this country?
MR. HOFFA. Well, there certainly is, and it is going to remain so. . . . I believe that management and labor very definitely must at all times have something in common because one without the other cannot survive.
SENATOR MUNDT. I agree with you on that statement 100 per cent.[95]

Finally Kennedy was able to control the questioning. "Mr. Hoffa," he asked, "do you know Johnny Dio?"[96] Dio, a great chum of Hoffa's, was a particularly unsavory figure. The committee in its 1958 interim report described him as a "three-time convicted labor racketeer and suspected instigator of the blinding of Columnist Victor Riesel."* As Kennedy now dug methodically into Hoffa's relations with mobsters, Hoffa's cockiness began to wilt. Determined not to plead the Fifth Amendment, he chose instead to plead the imperfections of memory. Kennedy pursued him relentlessly, playing tapes of phone conversations recorded—legally in those days—by Frank Hogan, the district attorney of New York County. Under the pressure, the newspapers reported, Hoffa's eyes narrowed, his lips tightened, his facial muscles twitched.[97] At times he lapsed almost into gibberish. In answer to one question:

> MR. HOFFA. To the best of my recollection, I must recall on my memory, I cannot remember.
> MR. KENNEDY. "To the best of my recollection I must recall on my memory that I cannot remember," is that your answer?
> . . . .
> MR. HOFFA. I cannot recall the substance of this telephone call, nor place the facts together concerning what it pertains to.
> THE CHAIRMAN. But if these things [the tapes] do not refresh your memory, it would take the power of God to do it. The instrumentalities of mankind, obviously, are not adequate. . . .
> MR. KENNEDY. You have had the worst case of amnesia in the last 2 days I have ever heard of.[98]

John Bartlow Martin later asked Hoffa why he had performed so poorly. "Maybe I did look silly," Hoffa said mysteriously, "but there was a reason for it." He did not say what the reason was. Kennedy thought that the kind of proof made the difference. "He can say very forcefully someone's a liar—that's easy. But here we had his own voice on the tapes. He couldn't deny it."[99] "Talked with Hoffa after hearing," Kennedy noted.

> Told him I did not want him to talk to our investigators as he had been doing. Told him if he wanted to hate anyone to hate me. He agreed.— His eyes were bloodshot. The last two days of hearing he was a beaten man compared to the beginning. His tone was subdued & no longer did he give the hate looks that he enjoyed so much at the beginning.[100]

A little later Kennedy wrote that things were much more relaxed after the Hoffa hearings; the committee, he thought, might be able to finish its job in another year. "Talked to Tommy Corcoran re doing legislative work. Said he had left Roosevelt Administration voluntarily—only one in Washington that did—Fight with Hopkins—Mistrusted Dad & him because 'We were too Irish to trust the English &

---

* Riesel, a labor reporter, had been exposing underworld penetration of the labor movement. Senate Select Committee, *Investigation of Improper Activities in the Labor or Management Field: Interim Report*, 85 Cong., 2 Sess. (March 24, 1958), 253.

The Second Investigating Committee: Jimmy Hoffa

too Catholic to trust the ?' "[101] The question mark was Kennedy's; he could not remember Corcoran's word, which must have been "Russians." Communism was a remote issue now.

For a moment Hoffa seemed to be on the run. The AFL-CIO Ethical Practices Committee reported that he used union funds for personal enrichment, that he worked with racketeers and that his union was "dominated or substantially influenced by corrupt influences."[102] He had already been indicted in New York on charges of illegal wiretapping. Now came another New York indictment, this time for perjury before a grand jury. But he was a hard man to keep down. The Teamsters rallied behind him, electing him their new president in September by a vast majority and defiantly voting Beck an annual pension of $50,000. At a highly emotional AFL-CIO convention in December, Meany succeeded in expelling the Teamsters. Hoffa remained unrepentant. In the same month his trial on the wiretapping charge ended in a hung jury—11-1 for conviction. Soon the perjury indictment was dismissed.

The wiretapping case was retried in the spring of 1958. One day Kennedy and Hoffa ran into each other in the elevator in the federal courthouse in New York: "Hello, Jimmy"—"Hello, Bobby"—then silence until Kennedy asked how the trial was going. "You never can tell with a jury," Hoffa said. "Like shooting fish in a barrel."[103] As Hoffa remembered the encounter, "I said, 'Hello, Bob, how you getting along?' He'd give me that silly smile and go on about his business."[104] Hoffa was again acquitted; evidently fish could be shot in a barrel. He traveled around the country in triumph, proclaiming new organizing drives and haranguing the faithful.

X

Meany told Kennedy in April 1958 that "he expected great problems and trouble from the Teamsters and that Jimmy Hoffa was a genuinely evil man and that if we did not take care of him by investigation nothing would be done to deal with him."[105] Salinger, Bellino, Sheridan and others sought out witnesses and pored through files. In July a new set of hearings began. After a parade of mobsters marched across the stand, Hoffa himself returned grimly to the Senate caucus room.

The fun had gone out of the hearings. "Kennedy no longer seemed light-hearted," John Bartlow Martin wrote, "Hoffa no longer bantering."[106] The committee had tantalizing leads, but nothing conclusive, like the tapes of the year before. Hoffa maintained an effective defense of evasion and denial. Sometimes, for an hour or so, he appeared, Kennedy wrote in his journal, morose and discouraged. But he had "great stamina and he would bounce back again as forceful as ever." It went on, day after day. The strain told on both men. At the end of one grueling afternoon McClellan proposed a night session. "I was bushed," Kennedy recalled. "I looked at [McClellan] and smiled wearily." Hoffa, standing across the table, snickered, "Look at him, look at him! He's too tired. He just doesn't want to go on."[107] Kennedy himself noted in mid-September:

> I am mentally fatigued—more than during any other hearing. We have been going on for a long time without a break & I have about had it. I shall be happy when Hoffa is finished next week. McClellan also very tired. This year seems to have been tougher than last. Plodding grind. . . . I feel like we're in a major fight. We have to keep going, keep the pressure on or we'll go under.[108]

When Martin asked what Kennedy pinned his hopes on, Kennedy said, "I felt a little like 1864, when Grant took the Union Army to go back into the Wilderness—to go back slugging it out. I didn't pin my hopes on any one thing. Just all these things."[109] On the last day, Martin observed, Hoffa was "confident, almost flip. He seemed to know he was winning." Just before lunch, Kennedy accused him of threatening to kill Sol Lippmann, the general counsel of the Retail Clerks Union. "If I did it," Hoffa had said to Lippmann (or so a frightened Lippmann had told Kennedy the same day), "no jury would ever convict me. I have a special way with juries." Hoffa, denying the story, said menacingly, "Bring Lippmann around here."

During the luncheon recess, Kennedy slumped at his desk before a sandwich and a glass of milk while Pierre Salinger called Lippmann. Taking the phone, Kennedy said, "Sol, can I get you to come over here and testify? It would make a real difference." There was a long silence. Then: "Are you going to let him stand up here and kick everybody around. Just because you can make a deal with him for six months or a year? . . . The fact he threatened you and made these statements to a leading union official like you—everybody would know you're telling the truth. Hell, I talked to you within 20 minutes of the time and I knew it was the truth." Finally: "O.K., Sol," and he slammed the phone down. He turned to Salinger and said, "He said, 'The Retail Clerks depend on the Teamsters in many ways. We have to get along with them.' . . . Shit." He drank his milk somberly.[110] Ethel Kennedy said, "This was the committee's worst day."[111] Hoffa,

Kennedy wrote in his journal, had been alternately "arrogant, angry, pleasant, antagonistic. Tuesday of last week he looked awful. Thursday morning he did well for himself. He is difficult to figure out unless he's slightly mad which I think he might very well be." After the hearings Hoffa was more cocky than ever. "The noble traditions of Congress," he wrote in the *International Teamster,* "will continue to be abused as Senator McClellan of Arkansas and his millionaire counsel, Robert Kennedy, bend to their anti-labor bias and lend fuel to the raging fire of class hatred. . . . America is not the exclusive domain of the wealthy or the privileged. It belongs to all of us."[112]

In December Kennedy noted, "Jimmy has announced that he is going to organize Police & Firemen. This has thrown everyone into a tizzy. . . . His tactics are evidentally [sic] like those of Joe McCarthy—always take the offensive."[113] Then Hoffa called for an alliance of the Teamsters with Joe Ryan's International Longshoremen's Association, expelled from the AFL-CIO because its leaders were corrupt, and Harry Bridges's International Longshoremen's and Warehousemen's Union, expelled as Communist-dominated. This threw even Kennedy into a tizzy. He called it "an unholy alliance that could dominate the United States within three to five years . . . a subversive force of unequaled power in this country."*

Impregnable in his union, a victor thus far in the courts, Hoffa gleefully reminded Clark Mollenhoff that the Rackets Committee would not be around forever. "They'll be going for another nine months, and Bob Kennedy will be running off to try to elect his brother President."[114] "If it is a question, as Kennedy has said, that he will break Hoffa," Hoffa told a cheering audience of Teamsters, "then I say to him, he should live so long."[115]

XI

For all the impassable differences in values and objectives, the two men were not without superficial similarities. Both were blunt, candid and commanding. Both drove themselves and their staffs relentlessly. Both, in separate ways, had an instinct for the underdog; both had the instinct of underdogs themselves. Both had devoted friends and

---

* Robert F. Kennedy, "Hoffa's Unholy Alliance," *Look,* September 2, 1958. Hoffa described Beck's longtime Pacific coast campaign against Bridges as "the worst mistake ever made by the Teamsters." Bridges, appearing at the Teamsters convention in 1961, called Hoffa "one of the greatest, outspoken, and fighting labor leaders of this country" and the Teamsters "one of the greatest hopes of our country." Romer, *Teamsters,* 138.

deadly enemies. Both had strong veins of sardonic humor. Both prided themselves on physical fitness. Neither smoked. Kennedy drank sparingly; Hoffa never. Neither wore hats. Both loved their wives. Both were risk-takers: "Hoffa," said Edward Bennett Williams, "is the kind of man who will jump out of a sixth floor window one day. If he survives, he will jump out of an eighth floor window the next day."[116] There was that aspect to Kennedy.

The same image recurred when journalists wrote about them: "the coiled spring of a man constitutionally unrelaxed . . . like the impatient discipline of the hungry fighter, completely confident but truly relaxed only in the action he craves."[117] This was Hal Clancy of Boston writing about Kennedy; but John Bartlow Martin, writing about Hoffa, said, "It is as though the core of Hoffa's personality were all a tightly-wound steel spring. . . . He is always stripped for a fight, for action."[118] Martin summarized the resemblances in the *Saturday Evening Post* in 1959. They were both, he wrote, "aggressive, competitive, hard-driving, authoritarian, suspicious, temperate, at times congenial and at others curt."[119] Nothing bothered Kennedy more in Martin's manuscript than this passage. "He was amazed and simply could not understand; it had never occurred to him; he had thought of himself as good and Hoffa as evil." Martin retained the passage; his relations with Kennedy were not impaired.[120]

It was an intensely personal duel. Going home, Kennedy had to drive past the Teamsters' marble palace. One night, smiling wryly, he said to Martin, "My first love is Jimmy Hoffa."[121] Another night Kennedy and Salinger left the office at one in the morning. As they drove along, Kennedy noticed a light burning in Hoffa's office. "If he's still at work, we ought to be," Kennedy said, and they went back for two more hours.[122] Hoffa often did indeed work late, but he also, according to Williams, heard of Kennedy's reaction and thereafter, when his day's work was done, took special pleasure in leaving his office lights blazing away.[123]

Hoffa knew what respectable people thought of him and did not care. "I'm no damn angel," he told John Martin. ". . . I don't apologize. You take any industry and look at the problems they ran into while they were building up—how they did it, who they associated with, how they cut corners. The best example is Kennedy's old man."[124] As for the son, "Hell, I hated the bastard," said Hoffa at the end of his life. ". . . He was a vicious bastard and he had developed a psychotic mania to 'get' me at any cost."[125]

During the hearings Hoffa used to fix Kennedy with, as Kennedy perceived it, "a deep, strange, penetrating expression of intense hatred . . . the look of a man obsessed by his enmity, and it came particularly from his eyes. There were times when his face seemed competely transfixed with this stare of absolute evilness." The look sometimes went on for five minutes or so, as if he thought that by staring long and hard enough he could destroy his adversary. "Now and then, after a protracted, particularly evil glower, he did a most peculiar thing: he would wink at me."[126] Hoffa told Victor Lasky years later, "I used to love to bug the little bastard. Whenever Bobby would get tangled up in one of his involved questions, I would wink at him. That invariably got him." Hoffa laughed and laughed.[127]

Kennedy vacillated between thinking Hoffa evil and thinking him mad. It was widely supposed he hated Hoffa; but some who worked most closely with him did not think so. Angie Novello said later, "Deep down he had great respect for Hoffa." Carmine Bellino and LaVern Duffy both said that he "liked" Hoffa.[128] In some obscure personal sense he did, though liking was far overborne by moral disapproval. In later times, when his self-awareness and sense of the complexity of life increased, Kennedy might have seen Hoffa in another context, appreciated his vitality, his impudence, his struggle and the material benefits he had won for the Teamsters. But, just as Hoffa never forgave Kennedy for having been born rich and for believing in the possibility of justice under capitalism, so Kennedy could never forgive Hoffa for his vindictiveness toward dissenting members of his own union, for his ties with the underworld, for his conviction that American society was irremediably corrupt. "We were like flint and steel," said Hoffa. "Every time we came to grips the sparks flew."[129] Hoffa thought that Kennedy "got his jollies playing God."[130] Kennedy, Murray Kempton said, perceived "the devil" in Hoffa, "something absolutely insatiable and wildly vindictive. . . . He recognized in Hoffa a general fanaticism for evil that could be thought of as the opposite side of his own fanaticism for good."[131]

Fanaticism for good was better than fanaticism for evil, but it contained dangers of its own. Nor was Kennedy unaware of the perils of obsession. On January 15, 1959, he scribbled a note after a conversation with Eddie Cheyfitz: "Chafitz [sic] said that I was too e[n]meshed with Hoffa—that it was like Nixon on Alger Hiss."[132]

XII

The testimony before the committee had convinced Robert Kennedy that Jimmy Hoffa had stifled democratic procedures within the union, had ordered the beating and very possibly the murder of union rebels, had misused union funds to the amount of at least $9.5 million, had taken money and other favors from employers to promote personal business deals,* had brought in gangsters to consolidate his control and had tampered with the judicial process in order to escape prosecution.[133]

Kennedy's critics were quick to reduce his pursuit of Hoffa to base motives: frustration over the failure to jail him; exasperation over his success at the hearings; vengefulness and vindictiveness. A great deal more was involved. Kennedy's exposure to the labor movement had given him impassioned sympathy for those in the Teamsters who, at tremendous personal risk to themselves, opposed the Hoffa dictatorship. He came to identify himself with workers who were expelled, beaten, murdered. Hoffa, as Kennedy saw it, had corrupted a movement of the oppressed. He was running not a bona fide trade union but "a conspiracy of evil," a conspiracy that had seized control of "the most powerful institution in this country—aside from the United States Government itself." As he concluded his case,

> Between birth and burial, the Teamsters drive the trucks that clothe and feed us and provide the vital necessities of life. They control the pickup and deliveries of milk, frozen meat, fresh fruit, department store merchandise, newspapers, railroad express, air freight, and of cargo to and from the sea docks. Quite literally your life—the life of every person in the United States—is in the hands of Hoffa and his Teamsters.[134]

He exaggerated Hoffa's importance. The Teamsters no doubt occupied a strategic position in the economy; but their power to bring the nation to a stop was theoretical. It depended on their failure to exercise it. Indeed, the Teamsters were traditionally cautious about calling strikes. It was true also, as Paul Jacobs insisted, that many of Hoffa's sins were practiced by his brethren in the labor movement. But even Jacobs conceded that "Hoffa's underworld ties do mark him off from many other union leaders with whom he otherwise has much more in common than is generally admitted."[135] Dave Beck, for example, had nothing to do with organized crime. It was the mob that roused Kennedy's deepest concern. "We are always going to have stealing and payoffs," he told John Martin. "As long as we have bank tellers we'll have that. And strike violence we'll always have. But this is far more sinister."[136]

There was a Damon Runyon aspect to it—Barney Baker, for example, six feet four inches tall, over three hundred pounds, a Hoffa or-

---

* Asked by Jerry Stanecki in a 1975 interview whether he was a millionaire, Hoffa replied, "I would say" (*Playboy*, December 1975).

The Second Investigating Committee: Jimmy Hoffa 171

ganizer who had been a "collector" for a New York gang, had palled around with Bugsy Siegel, Meyer Lansky, Joe Adonis and other edifying figures and had served two terms in prison before becoming a Teamster official. In his testimony Baker mentioned "a Mr. Dunn."

MR. KENNEDY. Cockeyed Dunn?
MR. BAKER. I don't know him as Cockeyed Dunn. I knew him as John Dunn.
MR. KENNEDY. Where is he now?
MR. BAKER. He has met his Maker.
MR. KENNEDY. How did he do that?
MR. BAKER. I believe through electrocution in the city of New York. . . .
MR. KENNEDY. What about Squint Sheridan? Did you know him?
MR. BAKER. Andrew Sheridan, sir?
MR. KENNEDY. Yes.
MR. BAKER. He has also met his Maker.
MR. KENNEDY. How did he die?
MR. BAKER. With Mr. John Dunn.[137]

There was Joey Gallo, who ran an "enforcer" union in New York and appeared one day in Kennedy's outer office, "dressed like a Hollywood Grade B gangster (black shirt, black pants, black coat, long curls down the back of the neck)," knelt down, felt the rug and said, "It would be nice for a crap game." Someone entered the office on an errand of his own. Gallo pounced on him, frisked him and explained to the bemused Kennedy staff, "No one is going to see Mr. Kennedy with a gun on him. If Kennedy gets killed now everybody will say I did it. And I am not going to take that rap." The visitor fled in consternation. On the stand, Gallo took the Fifth on all questions. Afterward he told Kennedy, "I'll line up my people for your brother in 1960." It was not really very funny. Joey Gallo had been a suspect in a murder case where the victim had been shot so many times in the face that identification was impossible. Kennedy asked him about this and received a giggle and shrug in reply.[138]

There was Joey Glimco, a Chicago hood who gained control of Teamsters Local 777 by strong-arm methods and thereafter enriched himself by misappropriating union funds and shaking down lesser Teamster officials, taxicab drivers and poultry dealers.[139] There was Paul (Red) Dorfman who took over the Waste Handlers local union in Chicago when the president was murdered in 1939. (Among those the police picked up for questioning after the murder was the local's secretary, Jack Rubenstein, who later changed his name to Jack Ruby and moved to Dallas, where in November 1963 he was in frequent touch with Red Dorfman and Barney Baker.)[140] Dorfman served as middleman between Hoffa and the Chicago mob, gaining in exchange the insurance for the Teamsters' Central States Welfare Fund for his stepson. Young Allen Dorfman, who did not even have an insurance brokerage license at the start, became a rich man in short order and a convict in the longer run.[141]

There was Momo Salvatore (Sam) Giancana, whom Kennedy described in the hearings as "chief gunman for the group that succeeded the Capone mob"[142] and other sources identified as don of the Chicago *consiglio* (i.e., boss of organized crime in Chicago).[143] Giancana, who had spent seven years of his youth in penitentiaries, used the Brotherhood of Electrical Workers (AFL) to take over the jukebox, coin-machine and cigarette-vending field in Chicago. He evaded a committee subpoena until investigators finally tracked him down in Las Vegas. "They couldn't catch me for a year," he boasted to the *Chicago Tribune*. "I was in Chicago all the time. . . . It was fun." He added: "What's wrong with the syndicate? Two or three of us get together on a deal and everybody says it is a bad thing. Businessmen do it all the time and nobody squawks." Called before the committee, he took the Fifth Amendment thirty-three times while Pierre Salinger set forth the more colorful features of his record. Finally:

MR. KENNEDY. Would you tell us if you have opposition from anybody that you dispose of them by having them stuffed in a trunk? Is that what you do, Mr. Giancana?
MR. GIANCANA. I decline to answer because I honestly believe my answer might tend to incriminate me.
MR. KENNEDY. Would you tell us anything about any of your operations or will you just giggle every time I ask you a question?
MR. GIANCANA. I decline to answer because I honestly believe my answer might tend to incriminate me.
MR. KENNEDY. I thought only little girls giggled, Mr. Giancana.[144]

Giancana was flashier than most. He was, as sociologists put it, upwardly mobile. One son-in-law ended up on the payroll of an Illinois congressman; the congressman promptly emerged as a doughty defender of Jimmy Hoffa.[145] A dapper fifty in 1958, Giancana liked to hang around show people and attracted show people who liked to hang around gangsters. The singer Frank Sinatra became his buddy;[146] another singer, Phyllis McGuire, his mistress. After a time Giancana's party life disturbed his associates. In 1966, the *Chicago Tribune* reported that he had been haled before a syndicate tribunal in order to "defend himself against charges of having permitted his international playboy activities to interfere with more serious, day-today business of running the underworld organization.[147] Giancana's activities were far more international than anyone could have supposed. Fifteen months after he giggled before the Rackets Committee, a fellow hood named John Rosselli approached him on behalf of the Central Intelligence Agency to solicit his help in a plot to murder Fidel Castro. The syndicates were penetrating corridors of power that not even McClellan or Kennedy in their worst imaginings would have suspected.

Then there was Tony Provenzano of New Jersey, who controlled Local 360 of the Teamsters, had close relations with the mob—New Jersey law enforcement officials listed him as a "capo" in the Vito Genovese "family"—and spent his spare time shaking down businessmen. Before the Rackets Committee he took the Fifth forty-four times. In 1963 he was convicted of extortion and sentenced to seven years in prison. In the meantime, he rose to an international vice presidency in the Teamsters. In 1976 he was indicted for the kidnap-murder of a union opponent. His longtime alliance with Hoffa came to a bitter end in the early 1970s. It was Tony Pro with whom Jimmy Hoffa may have thought he had a rendezvous when he himself disappeared on July 30, 1975.[148]

XIII

With his quasi-Trotskyite views of capitalism, Hoffa probably considered gangsters no more immoral than businessmen or politicians. "Twenty years ago," he told an interviewer, "the employers had all the hoodlums working for them as strike-breakers. Now we've got a few and everybody's screaming."[149] He believed, Ralph and Estelle James reported, "that underworld forces lie just beneath the surface in most American cities, uncontrolled by the ineffective and/or cooperative police. He is fond of stating that a professional killer can be hired 'just like that' (with snap of fingers) for a mere $2000."[150] When Kennedy asked whether Barney Baker's lurid record disturbed him, Hoffa cracked back, "It doesn't disturb me one iota."[151]

It disturbed Kennedy a great deal. He loathed the labor racketeers. "They are sleek," he wrote, "often bilious and fat, or lean and cold and hard. They have the smooth faces and cruel eyes of gangsters; they wear the same rich clothes, the diamond ring, the jeweled watch, the strong, sickly-sweet-smelling perfume."[152] They preyed particularly on decentralized industries where employers were small and weak—trucking, coin machines, garbage removal, laundry and dry cleaning, newspaper distribution. The hearings documented in grim detail the brutality with which they punished those who would not go along.

As Kennedy saw it, Hoffa had begun by hiring hoods as business agents in Detroit because he needed strong-arm men. Once in, he allowed them to exploit workers and employers. Then they told colleagues in other cities that Hoffa was a "right guy" and they should let him in. "Hoffa wants ex-convicts, I think," Kennedy told Martin,

> because, first, he does a favor for them and they'll stick by him; second, by hiring an ex-convict he's doing a favor for another gangster, so then the gangster will do Hoffa a favor; and third, he uses them to move in on a city. To get into Chicago he needed the okay of Joey Glimco and Paul Dorfman, and he gave Dorfman the Teamsters' insurance business. To get into Philadelphia he used Shorty Feldman. . . . To get into New York he was using Johnny Dio.[153]

He was becoming a vital link between the underworld and respectable society. Kennedy was learning from testimony what Hoffa had learned from life—that organized crime was a great unseen power. The Eighteenth Amendment, by driving the liquor business underground, had first changed gangsters into businessmen. The word *racket* appeared in the 1920s to describe the passage of crime from the free enterprise stage into the era of cartels and syndicates. The Twenty-first Amendment ended prohibition but not the criminal organizations prohibition had spawned. The "gangster-outlaw," like John Dillinger and Pretty Boy Floyd, gave way to the "gangster-businessman,"[154] whose specialty was not simple and reckless deeds, like robbing banks, stealing automobiles, kidnapping, but the provision of services. "The criminal as such," Walter Lippmann wrote in 1931, "is wholly predatory, whereas the underworld offers something in return to the respectable members of society. Thus, for example, burglars are lawbreakers who, if they could be abolished miraculously, would not be missed; but bootleggers, panderers, fixers and many racketeers have a social function . . . for which there is some kind of public demand."[155]

The nature of these criminal organizations remained a mystery. In 1950–51 a Senate committee headed by Estes Kefauver, after communing with a number of racketeers of Italian extraction, suggested that "a loose-knit organization" called the Mafia provided the connection among the major criminal syndicates in the United States.[156] The Federal Narcotics Bureau, which was having troubles of its own in stopping the smuggling of heroin, welcomed the alibi of an international criminal cartel. The theory of the Mafia, moreover, plucked chords of romantic memory going back not only to the ancient secret society in Sicily but to the Camorra and Black Hand of America at the turn of the century. It hardly did credit, however, to the notable contributions that Irish and Jewish gangsters had made to the rise of organized crime. Nor did it find sustenance in the experience of the thirties. Thomas E. Dewey conducted his campaign against organized crime, including Lucky Luciano, without ever mentioning the Mafia. After breaking up Murder, Inc., Burton Turkus wrote in 1951, "As a factor of power in national crime, the Mafia has been virtually extinct for two decades."[157]

The theory of the Mafia gained new currency when high chiefs of the mob held a conclave at Apalachin in upstate New York in November 1957. A sergeant of the state police, his curiosity piqued by the influx of black limousines, frightened the gangsters into ignominious flight into the surrounding forests. Fifty-eight conferees, including Vito Genovese himself, were picked up; twenty-two of these were involved in labor or labor-management relations.[158] Sam Giancana made it into the underbrush. "There exists in America today," McClellan said, "what appears to be a close-knit, clandestine, criminal syndicate. This group has made fortunes in the illegal liquor traffic during prohibition, and later in narcotics, vice, and gambling. These illicit profits present the syndicate with a financial problem, which they solve through investment in legitimate business. These legitimate businesses also provide convenient cover for their continued illegal activities."[159]

What had seemed in 1951 a loose-knit organization was beginning to appear as something far more menacing: a monolithic, formally organized, ethnically homogeneous, strictly disciplined secret society, based on esoteric rituals, commanding the absolute obedience of its members and controlling all organized crime—in short, an invisible government of the underworld. The existence of the Mafia in this sense has never been demonstrated.[160] No one could doubt, however, the existence of interstate criminal cartels, sometimes working together, sometimes waging savage war against each other. The word *Mafia* did not appear in Robert Kennedy's book about the Rackets Committee, *The Enemy Within*. But he took from the hearings an appalled sense, defined more carefully than McClellan had done, that "the gangsters of today work in a highly organized fashion and are far more powerful now than at any time in the history of the country. They control political figures and threaten whole communities. They have stretched their tentacles of corruption and fear into industries both large and small. They grow stronger every day."[161]

The Kennedys doubted whether existing methods were adequate against organized crime. After Apalachin, Robert Kennedy had asked for the FBI files on the conventioneers. "The FBI didn't know anything, really, about these people who were the major gangsters in the United States," he said later. ". . . That was rather a shock to me. . . . I sent the same request to the Bureau of Narcotics, and they had something on every one of them."[162] The Kennedys now called for the establishment of a national crime commission as a clearing-house for criminal intelligence. The FBI, Robert Kennedy said, "won't keep these fellows under surveillance. They do it for suspected spies, but they won't do it for gangsters and racketeers."[163]

He was growing disillusioned about the FBI. Angie Novello recalls that he generally mistrusted and sometimes disliked investigators who had once worked for the Bureau; Bellino and Sheridan were exceptions.[164] The Bureau seemed suspiciously wary of unpromising cases. "They want the publicity from their press releases," Kennedy noted in May 1958, "but where they have a natural opportunity to get into these things, particularly where it affects us, they are very reluctant to do so."[165] Kenneth O'Donnell expressed Kennedy's views bluntly in 1959: "The FBI has never been aggressive on big crime. It went after Communists and stayed there." O'Donnell did not spare the then sacrosanct J. Edgar Hoover. "The FBI chief is afraid to step on the toes of local officials—afraid he will lose some popularity and get involved in local politics. But local authorities can't handle nation-wide syndicates."[166]

"If we do not on a national scale attack organized criminals with weapons and techniques as effective as their own," Robert Kennedy concluded, "they will destroy us."[167] They might even destroy Hoffa: asked in 1958 whether Hoffa could clean up his union if he wanted to, Kennedy replied, "He can't say, 'You're out.' He wouldn't live."[168] In the end, Kennedy was indisputably right. By 1975 Hoffa must surely have agreed with him.

(9)

The Second Investigating Committee: Walter Reuther

NOT ALL THE RACKETS COMMITTEE was enthusiastic about the pursuit of Jimmy Hoffa. Senators Goldwater and Mundt did not condone Hoffa's excesses. But they declined to see him as the primary threat. He was, after all, a supporter of Republican candidates, a model of cozy relations with employers, a declared believer in private enterprise. His purpose, he explained to the committee, was to get a better deal for his Teamsters, not to transform the system. "Mr. Hoffa," Goldwater observed, "we have labor leaders in this country today, labor leaders who are not particularly friendly to you, labor leaders . . . who do not think like that." Seizing the cue, Hoffa obligingly condemned the use of union power to bring about political and economic change. "We both recognize," Goldwater said, "that in the writing in the clouds today there is an individual who would like to see that happen in this country. . . . For the good of the union movement I am very hopeful that your philosophy prevails."[1]

I

There was no mystery about the individual whom Goldwater saw in the clouds and whose philosophy he hoped Hoffa would defeat. Walter Reuther had become the supreme bogeyman for American conservatives. Hoffa, for all his sentimental memories of Reuther, craftily nourished this fear. He called Reuther "the leader of Soviet America," insinuated Reuther was protecting organized gambling in the auto plants and hinted that Robert Kennedy was going easy on him in order to get the United Auto Workers behind his brother in 1960. He bragged to Clark Mollenhoff that he had passed this "information" to the Republicans on the Rackets Committee.[2]

The Republicans hardly needed prompting. "Mr. Reuther and the

UAW," said Goldwater, "have done more damage and violence to freedom than was accomplished by all the peculiar financial transactions of Mr. Dave Beck."[3] Joe McCarthy promised that, if and when the committee got around to Reuther, the activities uncovered would leave Beck smelling like a rose. Asked about this on *Meet the Press*, Kennedy said, "We have no information at the present time showing that Mr. Walter Reuther personally misused any union funds. There have been certain complaints about . . . the Kohler strike."[4] The Kohler strike, which the UAW had been conducting in Sheboygan, Wisconsin, since April 1954, had excited national attention because of its bitterness and violence. The Republicans now set up a cry for an investigation of the strike, the UAW and Reuther.

At this point, they had to confront the rather private way Senator McClellan and Robert Kennedy ran the committee. When asked in July whether the committee as a whole decided what to investigate, the counsel said candidly, "No, I pretty well decide it and I have consultations with the Chairman . . . and he is aware of where we're sending investigators and what we're looking for."[5] McClellan was exactly twice Kennedy's age, but after several years together on the committee a surprising fondness had developed between the dour Baptist from the public schools of Sheridan, Arkansas, and the Irish Catholic from the Ivy League. "His practice of treading where McClellan feared to walk," wrote Charles Bartlett, "earned him the senator's deep devotion, broad license, and increasing support. It is almost certain that no hired official of the Senate has ever wielded more committee authority or operated with so free a hand."[6] Kennedy for his part always deferred to McClellan, teased him, LaVern Duffy said, "with respect"[7] and admired him as "the most devastating cross-examiner I ever heard."

Kennedy was also fond of Sam Ervin. He was exasperated by Pat McNamara, who had both Hoffa and Reuther among his constituents and, an old trade unionist himself, regarded the investigation of unions with extreme discomfort. When McNamara resigned from the committee in 1958, Frank Church of Idaho took his place. "He was absolutely fearless," Kennedy wrote later of Church, "asking some of the most astute and penetrating questions that I heard put. I envied his articulateness." Kennedy also liked Irving Ives, a former dean of the New York State School of Industrial and Labor Relations, and valued his special knowledge of labor problems. Despite their disagreements, he liked Goldwater. "He could cut you to ribbons, slit your throat, but always in such a pleasant manner that you would have to like him."[8]

But he considered Karl Mundt a sanctimonious hypocrite who played up to Hoffa and Reuther when they were on the stand and "attacked them viciously when they were not present to defend themselves."[9] Mundt's leaks to the press were a perennial irritation. Once Kennedy and Salinger, in order to verify their suspicions, sent the eight senators a draft report in which the key page was written in eight different ways. The version that promptly appeared in the newspapers was the one sent to Mundt.[10]

II

In the spring of 1957 the Rackets Committee underwent its first change in membership. Joe McCarthy was in marked decline, a specter haunting the scenes where he had so recently swaggered. There were still flashes of the old brutality. Walking past Arthur Watkins's seat in the Senate, he liked to lean over and whisper, "How is the little coward from Utah?"[11] But something had broken within him. Because he was a sensationalist rather than a true believer—his was the glory drive, Edward Bennett Williams used to say, not the power drive—he had no core of inner certitude to sustain him in adversity. By the time of the Rackets Committee, he was a wreck. "He would come into the Caucus Room late," wrote Richard Rovere, "interrupt a line of questioning with questions of his own, some of which were incoherent, and after twenty minutes or so wander out in an almost trance-like state."[12] "He has been drunk the last three times he has been to the hearing," Robert Kennedy noted on March 5, 1957.[13]

One day McCarthy demanded that Kennedy fire an investigator named McGillicuddy on the ground that he was anti-Catholic and had been indicted. After some talk Kennedy ascertained that McCarthy was talking about a man named Robert Greene.

> I told him the Bob Greene indictment had been dismissed and denounced as a political indictment because of the work Greene was doing investigating Mayor Kenny in Jersey City, and furthermore, that he was an Irish Catholic and could not be considered anti-Catholic. The next thing I heard was that he made a speech on the Senate Floor stating that the Committee had hired an investigator who had been indicted. . . . I told the press that afternoon that I had great confidence in Greene and also told the facts surrounding his indictment back in 1951.

McCarthy persisted, explaining to the committee that anyone who wallowed with hogs—Greene had worked for the anti-McCarthy Long Island paper *Newsday*—must be a hog himself. Finally Senators Mundt and McNamara were designated to look into the matter and promptly cleared Greene.[14]

Kennedy watched McCarthy's disintegration with sadness. "I felt sorry for him," he said later, "particularly in the last year, when he was such a beaten, destroyed person particularly since many of his so-called friends, realizing he was finished, ran away from him and left him with virtually no one."[15] The incorruptible Edwin Guthman of Seattle, though impressed by Kennedy's exposure of Beck, still felt, he later said, that "I had to get to the bottom of the Kennedy-McCarthy relationship before I could fully trust Bob." They discussed McCarthy. Guthman decided that Kennedy's chief feeling about McCarthy was pity: "Pity for an acquaintance who could be a pleasant companion but who had made a ruin of his career; pity for the men and women and their families whom McCarthy had forced needlessly and unfairly to live under a cloud."[16] Once Kennedy took Lem Billings over to McCarthy's house. Mrs. McCarthy did most of the talking. McCarthy sat by in a stupor. Billings, somewhat mystified by the occasion, said later, "It was typical of Bobby to go in and see somebody who was in trouble."[17] "Joe has been looking so terribly," Kennedy himself noted. ". . . Couldn't stand straight & often appeared in a trance. His conversation was not intelligible."[18] At the end of April McCarthy entered the Bethesda Naval Hospital. There he died on May 2, 1957.

"Very upsetting for me," Robert Kennedy wrote in his intermittent journal.

> I am only happy that I had a friendly conversation with him last week. . . . Fred Perkins of Scripps Howard after the Bob Green [sic] incident had evidently [sic] gone to Joe & told him I had called him an S.O.B.— Evidentally a Wisconsin newspaperman had heard the same thing because latter told me he was going to print it. . . . I am sure that Joe McCarthy knew of this & I felt a little strain about him. I am glad that we talked in the manner we did before he died.
>
> I dismissed the office for the day. It was all very difficult for me as I feel that I have lost an important part of my life—even though it is in the past.[19]

"The death of so young a Senator of such strong convictions," said Senator Jacob K. Javits of New York, "is truly sad. It should be our hope and aim that in the national interest the warnings of Communist

The Second Investigating Committee: Walter Reuther

subtlety and duplicity uttered by Senator McCarthy will long survive the controversy about his methods of investigation."[20] There was—for the first time since the death of William E. Borah—a state funeral in the Senate chamber. Robert Kennedy also attended the ultimate funeral in Appleton, Wisconsin.

Senator Carl Curtis of Nebraska replaced McCarthy on the committee. The Republicans, except for Irving Ives, were now more deeply conservative than ever. Kennedy detested Curtis, as he later did Homer Capehart of Indiana, who replaced Ives in 1959.

III

As the Rackets Committee set out after Hoffa, the Republicans increased their demand that Reuther and the Kohler strike receive equal time. The National Labor Relations Board had recently concluded two years of hearings on Kohler. Kennedy doubted that the committee would turn up anything new. Newspaper stories quoted unidentified Republican senators as saying that the Kennedys were covering up for Reuther. Kennedy believed Mundt to be the source.[21] In fact, John Kennedy hardly knew Reuther, and Robert had never met him. As for Reuther, he had supported Kefauver against John Kennedy during the vice presidential contest in 1956 and distrusted Robert because of the McCarthy committee.

In July *Newsweek* cited Republican complaints that Robert Kennedy had "ignored continual demands for an investigation of Reuther" and had concentrated instead on the harassment of the union leaders "who had stood in the way of Reuther's domination of American labor." They complained too that Kennedy never told them what he was doing.[22] At the next meeting of the committee, John Kennedy, flourishing *Newsweek,* said that, if this were the way Republican senators felt, let them speak up.

Mundt proposed a reorganization designed to reduce Robert Kennedy's control of the investigations.[23] This was rejected, but the counsel agreed to give the committee a full briefing on investigative developments every Monday morning. As for the Reuther problem, Robert Kennedy suggested that Jack McGovern, a Republican hired at Goldwater's request ("the only appointment made to the staff," Kennedy said later, "because of political considerations"), be assigned to the UAW-Kohler investigation.[24] Goldwater said he was "as happy as a squirrel in a little cage." Mundt said he was "as happy as a South Dakota pheasant in a South Dakota cornfield." Curtis, Kennedy wrote later, "made no comparison between himself and animals or birds" but expressed general happiness. McClellan said ironically, "We shall now adjourn this love feast."[25]

In the next months Kennedy heard nothing from Jack McGovern. The Republican senators, however, received regular reports, and in October McGovern sent a long memorandum to McClellan. While purporting to be the product of McGovern's own investigation, this document, Kennedy noted, was mostly "copied from NLRB files with none of the derogatory info on the company—if he was not a political appointee I would fire him."[26] Kennedy told Goldwater that the full NLRB report seemed essentially correct "and that therefore a new investigation was unlikely to accomplish what he wanted and expected, namely to destroy Walter Reuther."[27]

Goldwater persisted. In January 1958 he called Reuther and the UAW "a more dangerous menace than the Sputnik or anything Soviet Russia might do to America."[28] (When Reuther objected, Mundt disarmingly defended his colleague: "That would not make you very dangerous. Sputniks are not dangerous. They are weather beeping things going around.")[29] "Corruption, misappropriation of funds, bribery, extortion and collusion with the underworld," according to the Republican argument, existed in the UAW "as in the Teamsters." Reuther was an enemy of the capitalist system who used violence and intimidation as "essential parts" of his "formula for power."[30]

The UAW decided to take the offensive. Reuther placed his administrative assistant, Jack Conway, in charge of the operation. Conway, an Irish ex-Catholic with a degree from the University of Chicago, dumped on Kennedy's desk a huge stack of documents covering, he said, everything the UAW knew about the Kohler strike. "I made it very clear that we were going to be open and above board and direct and that if he was the same way that we'd have no trouble but if he wasn't we'd have trouble." Kennedy questioned the UAW charges against Kohler: things couldn't be that bad in Sheboygan. Conway said, "If you believe that, why don't you go out and take a look yourself?"[31] Kennedy said, "I will," and, to the astonishment of Conway, who thought he might go in a month or so, flew to Wisconsin the same night.[32]

He found Sheboygan infinitely depressing. The effects of the long strike "still hung over it like a shroud, touching everything, affecting everyone." It reminded him of the Middle East. "The hatred [between Jew and Arab] I had felt on that visit to Palestine was just as livid here. Unless you can see and feel for yourself the agony that has shattered this Wisconsin community, it is difficult to believe that such a concentration of hatred can exist in this country. . . . It was difficult to believe that this was America 1958."³³

The strike was nearing the end of its third year. Kohler, a family-owned corporation operating a company town, was the second largest manufacturer of plumbing ware in the United States. It had a history of labor violence. In 1934 it had brought in armed guards to break a strike, killing two strikers and wounding nearly fifty more. In 1950 the company union, feeling that band concerts and similar feudal benefits were inadequate substitutes for low wages, sought affiliation with the UAW.*³⁴ In 1952 Kohler reluctantly signed a contract. In 1954, with the contract up for renewal, the company rejected the union demands. The union struck. It engaged in illegal mass picketing. There were violence and vandalism, condoned if not encouraged by UAW officials. Kohler fought back and soon resumed full operation. After a time the union was ready to concede every point except for a small wage increase. The company declined to bargain in good faith. It was evidently seeking—so the NLRB trial examiner reported in October 1957—not an agreement with the union but "the reduction of the union to impotency as an effective bargaining representative of their employees."³⁵

Kennedy went first to the Kohler plant. He saw the enamel shop, where the heat of the ovens brought the temperature well above a hundred degrees and workers took off face shields for a moment to gobble lunch; the UAW had been asking for a thirty-minute luncheon break. He talked to Lyman Conger, the company attorney, who "made no secret of his deep and abiding hate for the union. It was an all-consuming hate—a thing unpleasant to see." He went to the union office, which had the defeated look of "the campaign headquarters of some lesser political candidate who knew he couldn't whip city hall." The contrast between the UAW organizers and the Teamsters struck him. "They wore simple clothes, not silk suits and handpainted ties; sported no great globs of jewelry on their fingers or their shirts; there was no smell of the heavy perfume frequently wafted by the men around Hoffa." They explained the ordeal the town had been through since 1954. "These men felt hatred, too. But it was hatred born of anger and frustration—not the insatiable hatred Conger seemed to feel."³⁶

Kennedy had started with "no strong convictions . . . one way or another" about the strike.³⁷ Sheboygan changed that. On his return to

---

* Kohler had an engine plant department, which made UAW involvement less incongruous.

Washington he joined members of the committee at a dinner with Meany and other labor leaders. After dinner ("the ice cream was good"), Meany sat on a couch with Ives on one hand and McClellan on the other. "The couch was too small for the three of them," Kennedy noted, "and they made a rather peculiar looking group—Ives looking sickly and Meany looking very fat with his cigar; McClellan on the other side looking like he did not want to get too close to a labor leader." Meany, though no fan of Reuther's, observed that the UAW investigation was "a political investigation because we knew as well as he did that there wasn't anything to look for. He said a lot of people disagreed with Walter Reuther politically but that otherwise it was generally known and understood that he was honest."[38]

IV

The time had come for the committee to consider the counsel's draft of a report on its first year. "Mundt, Curtis and Ives," Kennedy wrote in his journal, "were all anxious to defend management—to [delete] references we had to businesses. In my estimation it was a sickening spectacle."[39] When the expurgated report was released, labor spokesmen found it sickening too. It provoked McNamara's resignation. Meany said it raised "grave doubts as to the [committee's] impartiality, objectivity and integrity."[40] Persuaded that the UAW had a case on the merits, Kennedy recommended that the committee hold hearings on the Kohler strike.

This might offer a chance of recovering labor confidence. Nor did Kennedy and O'Donnell neglect the political possibilities in the UAW connection. "Their curiosity about detail and how we worked in different states and areas of the country was more than the usual," Jack Conway recalled. "I was personally convinced that what they were attempting to do was to feel out a potential alliance." One night, at dinner with John Kennedy, Robert Kennedy said bluntly that, if they went into the 1960 convention, they did not want to get caught in the situation of 1956. "We don't want you on the opposite side from us."[41]

The Republicans were counting heavily on a letter Walter Reuther and his brother Victor had written from the Soviet Union in 1934, ending in the spirit of the early depression: "Let us know definitely what is happening to the YPSL [Young People's Socialist League], also if the Social Problems Club at City College is still functioning and what it is doing. Carry on the fight. Vic and Wal." Through the years enemies of the Reuthers had improved this peroration, amending it to read in some versions: "Carry on the fight for a Soviet America." At least five different texts of the letter were in circulation by 1958. The recipient of the letter, Melvin Bishop, had long since turned against the Reuthers. Kennedy brought Bishop to Washington. Bishop said that he had given the original to a schoolteacher in 1935 and had not seen a copy since. Carmine Bellino tracked down the schoolteacher; she said she had never heard of the letter. McClellan spoke contemptuously of Bishop's "established unreliability" and dismissed the whole thing.[42] No one—not even Mundt—brought it up in the hearings.

The Republicans, repenting their enthusiasm for hearings, urged postponement. The Kennedys, knowing they would be blamed for protecting Reuther, insisted that the committee go ahead. The Republicans then concentrated on defeating Robert Kennedy's recommendation that Reuther should be the first witness for the UAW. He would steal the show, Ives said, and everything else would be anticlimactic. "I said," Kennedy wrote in his journal, "that I felt he was the best witness and should have the right to appear." McClellan said grumpily that he could not understand what the Republicans had to fear from letting Reuther lead off. (Kennedy and McClellan lunched together after the meeting. "He didn't speak for 20 minutes," Kennedy noted. "I imagine he is mad because of the fact that he seems to be appearing on the side of the UAW which, of course, kills him.") McClellan, Ervin and John Kennedy argued through four more executive sessions for the early calling of Reuther. "Goldwater, Mundt and Curtis were all very bitter and bitter-looking during these conferences," wrote Robert Kennedy. "Their faces were distorted to what was almost hate." Eventually McClellan yielded. "The proceedings that will be followed here," he said carefully when the hearing opened, "are not the proceedings in keeping with the Chair's views as to how this matter should be presented."[43]

Reuther himself observed that most people hired lawyers in order to stay away from the Rackets Committee; he was hiring a lawyer in order to appear. He had wanted Arthur Goldberg, the special counsel of the AFL-CIO, to represent the UAW. But Jack Conway favored the Washington civil liberties lawyer Joseph L. Rauh, Jr. "Goldberg," Conway said later, "is a broker and Joe Rauh is a battler." Goldberg himself, when approached, felt that his own first obligation was to the Steelworkers, of which he was counsel, and also recommended Rauh.[44] Rauh was indeed a battler. So was Goldwater. The result was a series of long, acrimonious sessions.

Goldwater, for example, defending the arsenal of guns, shells and tear gas built up by the Kohler management, observed that CIO strikes up to 1954 had caused thirty-seven deaths; "this is an example of what this union has been doing in violence ever since its inception."[45] "He did not mention at all," Robert Kennedy wrote angrily in his notes, "that all these people [killed] were strikers."[46] When Goldwater called it "strange" that violence originally associated with the Communist party was now associated with the UAW, John Kennedy observed, "Mr. Chairman, my brother's name is Joe and Stalin's name is Joe. The coincidence may be strange but I don't draw any inference from it."[47]

Lyman Conger was as intransigent in Washington as he had been in Sheboygan. Robert Kennedy pressed him about lunch in the enamel shop.

> MR. KENNEDY. You say that the men can put the [enamel] equipment in the oven, then they can step back and eat their lunch during that period of time. How much time is there then before they have to do some more work?
> MR. CONGER. From 2 to 5 minutes, depending on the piece.
> MR. KENNEDY. So you feel they can step back from the oven and take off their mask and have their lunch in 2 to 5 minutes?
> MR. CONGER. Mr. Kennedy, they have been doing it for 36 years.[48]

This exchange "made me furious," Kennedy later wrote, "madder really than when witnesses took the Fifth Amendment. . . . To hear a reputable American businessman, in 1958, matter-of-factly advocate a two- to five-minute luncheon period—well, until then I had believed that that kind of thinking had long since disappeared from the American scene."[49]

Kennedy regretted in retrospect "that I did not question Conger more. There were those who felt, and I felt at the time, he looked so bad there might be some sympathy created for him. But there were so many things I felt we could have gotten into and established more clearly about the Kohler Company that I should have done it more than I did." However, he had found no support on the committee for bringing out this material, "other than Jack and of course, he and I were both suspect. Neither McClellan, Sam Ervin nor McNamara asked any critical questions of Conger or [Herbert V.] Kohler. I asked all the critical questions of Conger and Jack did all of Kohler."[50]

The Second Investigating Committee: Walter Reuther

"Bobby must have had some form of communication with his brother Jack," Joseph Rauh observed later, "or there really is a thing called extrasensory perception. Every time we were getting into trouble, Jack would enter the Hearing Room, take his seat on the Committee dais and help us out. It got to be a joke inside our crowd as Jack walked down the aisle each time Mundt, Goldwater or Curtis was scoring points against us."[51]

Points were occasionally scored. The UAW official in charge of the Kohler strike was the secretary-treasurer, Emil Mazey, a truculent and emotional man who, as Robert Kennedy accurately said, "shouted first and thought later."[52] Mazey had not been a force for restraint in the early months of the strike; nor was he now at the hearings. After one session he called Conger "a despicable ———," as Kennedy primly reported the scene in his notes,

> and the following day Conger raised a big stink about it. Joe Rauh then got into a shouting match with McClellan in which Mundt joined in. The whole thing was most unpleasant. Rauh went in to see McClellan at the noon hour and apologized.[53]

In the afternoon Mazey lost his temper again and raged against the Catholic priests of Sheboygan for signing a pro-Kohler statement. Later in the day Rauh, who stopped by Kennedy's office each afternoon to check the next day's schedule, found Kennedy and O'Donnell passing the inevitable football back and forth. Kennedy, seeing Rauh's woebegone expression, said, "Don't feel so bad, Joe, the Pope hasn't called yet."[54]

Toward the end of March, Goldwater, after his months of righteous complaint about the Reuther cover-up, astounded the committee by announcing that he saw no reason to call Reuther as a witness. "I thought," Kennedy wrote in his journal, "Senator McClellan was going to faint."[55] The chairman, when he recovered, said he would not be a party to denying Reuther an opportunity to testify. Reuther sent along his opening statement which, Kennedy thought, "wasted time on flowery language . . . democracy, God and mankind, etc."[56] That was, of course, Reuther's style. Once on the stand, with his inexhaustible intelligence, confidence and fluency, he dominated the hearing. He freely admitted past UAW error—mass picketing, violence—and then went on the offensive. When he concluded, Goldwater looked, Kennedy thought, "like a man who had taken a very bad beating." "You were right," he told Kennedy. "We never should have gotten into this."[57] McClellan, who had been saying privately that the senators were all making fools of themselves,[58] publicly disclaimed responsibility for the hearings* and brought them to a close. ("I have to say about that old son of a gun," Jack Conway remarked later, ". . . that he did treat us with fairness.")[59] In September 1960 the NLRB found the Kohler Company guilty of unfair labor practices and of failure to bargain in good faith. The long, cruel strike came to an end, with most strikers given their old jobs and the largest back payment award in American history.

V

As for Goldwater, who had wished the philosophy of Hoffa to prevail over the philosophy of Reuther, he found himself trapped in a paradox. "If we want our trade union organizations to be sympathetic to our private enterprise business system," as Professor John Dunlop of Harvard stated the dilemma in 1957, ". . . we should not be surprised that business unionism by and large adopted business morality. It is inconsistent to expect at the same time business unionism and the morality of the ascetic."[60] The Hoffas, who supported the business system, were, alas, crooked. The Reuthers, who criticized it, were, alas, honest.

Certainly the example provided by businessmen was not always edifying. The Rackets Committee was presumably required by its title to inquire into improper activities in management as well as in labor. Here labor leaders charged an absence of zeal. Kennedy's response was that, because of limited jurisdiction, the committee could not go into improper business activities unless there was some direct connection with labor. Certain investigations, however, like Kohler, did involve what Kennedy later called "the respectables."[61]

The trail of Nathan Shefferman thus led not only to Dave Beck but also to the venerated American house of Sears, Roebuck. Shefferman specialized in wrecking union organization drives in the name of labor relations. After a quarter century diddling labor for Sears, Roebuck, he established a firm that, Walter Sheridan said, was a Sears, Roebuck "creation" and engaged in union-busting activities on behalf of Sears, its subsidiaries and suppliers.[62] When Salinger and Sheridan first asked about Shefferman, the Sears vice president "outright, flatly lied" to them for several hours and, indeed, weeks. Sears officials

---

* "I did not organize these hearings. I did not arrange for the presentation of them, as I have others" (Senate Select Committee on Improper Activities in the Labor or Management Field, *Hearings*, 85 Cong., 2 Sess. [March 29, 1958], 10172).

came to Washington to meet with Kennedy. "If you're going to lie to me," he said, "you might as well go back to Chicago." Kennedy persevered; hearings were held; and, faced with the gloomy necessity of testifying under oath, Wallace Tudor of Sears, Roebuck admitted what had been previously denied, called Shefferman's actions "inexcusable, unnecessary and disgraceful" and promised that the company would not permit a repetition of "these mistakes."[63]

This was rather typical of the committee's experience with the respectables. Nothing took place in the hearings to alter Robert Kennedy's bleak view of business. "Little or no accurate information," he wrote, "came to us from the business community. . . . No investigation was touched off by any voluntary help we received from management." And where the labor movement at least took action against corrupt union leaders, "not one management group or association has made a single move to rid itself of members who were found to be involved in collusive deals." Not one firm had fired a vice president for wrongdoing. "These corrupt businessmen are still sitting down to luncheon and dinner meetings with business groups across the country," Kennedy observed, "and they are getting encouragement and admiration—not censure."[64]

As for the unions themselves: "We thought we knew a few things about trade-union corruption," Meany said in 1957, "but we didn't know the half of it, one tenth of it, or the one-hundredth part of it."[65] A. J. Hayes of the Machinists, chairman of the AFL-CIO Ethical Practices Committee, added that only the subpoena power of government could ferret corruption out.[66] Kennedy's investigations led to the exposure and overthrow of James Cross as president of the Bakers, William E. Maloney as president of the Operating Engineers, Anthony Valente as president of the United Textile Workers. The committee released reports on dismal situations in other unions—the Meat Cutters, the Carpenters, the Hotel and Restaurant Workers, the Sheet Metal Workers. At the same time, the Kohler investigation proved that the committee could distinguish between honest and crooked unions. Among thoughtful labor leaders the committee soon lost its initial antilabor reputation. Arthur Goldberg wrote Robert Kennedy in 1960:

> At our first meeting you told me in straight-forward terms that in your capacity as counsel for the committee you intended to carry on the committee's work in a fair and impartial manner and without any bias, fear or favor. I think it appropriate to say that throughout the entire course of the conduct of the committee's activities, you never departed from this state-

ment of your objectives. . . . You have every reason to be proud of your outstanding work . . . and of the contribution that you have made to decent honest democratic American trade unionism.[67]

VI

Nineteen fifty-nine found Robert Kennedy in a mood of discouragement. In March he told McClellan that he planned to leave the committee in August.[68] The shocking disclosures over two years had had singularly little effect. "Candor compels me to say," he wrote in June, "that in the months since the committee began to work, conditions in the labor and management fields have actually grown worse." Hoffa seemed more secure than ever. Communities infected by corruption had given "the merest lip-service" to clean-up efforts. The National Association of Manufacturers and the U.S. Chamber of Commerce had taken no action whatever against businessmen engaged in questionable activities. Bar associations had done nothing to discipline lawyers engaged in unethical practices. "There is appalling public apathy. . . . Members of Congress receive virtually no mail on the subject."[69]

Most disappointing of all, the Department of Justice had obtained convictions of only three persons—and one was a witness who had helped the committee. "McClellan has written several letters to Justice criticizing their tardiness in moving on some of the cases," Kennedy had noted in 1958. ". . . Their reply which evidently [sic] was handled by [Attorney General William] Rogers himself was bitter & factually in error."[70] William G. Hundley, chief of the Organized Crime Section, explained to the newspapers that the committee's cases required further investigation to produce evidence admissible in courts and that many involved deeds which, however reprehensible morally, were not violations of federal law.[71] Privately Hundley shared the prejudice of Department of Justice lawyers against congressional committees and simply did not think that Kennedy's cases were solid, at least as they came from the Hill. "We'd refer them out to the FBI or the Internal Revenue Service for investigation," he said later, "and I don't think at that time the FBI or the Internal Revenue Service were breaking their back trying to make cases for Bobby Kennedy." Once Kennedy told Hundley, "When you admit to me that there's obvious wrongdoing here and you tell me on top of that that you can't make a case out of it, it makes me sick to my stomach." Hundley said, "I can't be responsible for your gastric juices."

Kennedy hung up on him. Twenty minutes later he called back and said he was sorry. Hundley said he was sorry too.[72]

There remained the possibility of new federal law. "What people expect now, in my estimation," Kennedy wrote a friend, "is not more investigation but laws to deal with the problems that we have uncovered."[73] In early 1958, John Kennedy had begun, with the assistance of professor Archibald Cox of the Harvard Law School, to prepare a bill. He talked with George Meany, who indicated (Robert Kennedy reported) "that possibly matters dealing with finances would be accepted but that the statements about internal democracy were absolutely out of the question." A. J. Hayes told him, "If you start regulating internal union affairs that is the beginning of the destruction of the free union movement."[74] The Kennedys found Walter Reuther "far more liberal" in his approach; "control of union funds, democracy within the unions, limitation on trusteeships, and the rest— he supported all of these in principle."[75]

In due course Kennedy enlisted the support of Irving Ives. The Kennedy-Ives bill required union officials to guarantee regular elections with secret ballots, to file financial reports with the Labor Department and to disclose financial transactions that might involve conflicts of interest. The AFL-CIO endorsed the bill. It passed the Senate 88-1 in June 1958. Two months later a strange coalition of business, the Teamsters and the Eisenhower administration killed the bill in the House.

Kennedy reintroduced the bill in 1959. Again, after amendment, it passed the Senate. Only Goldwater voted against it. In the meantime, the House was considering a far more severe bill proposed by Robert Griffin of Michigan and Philip Landrum of Georgia. The Landrum-Griffin restrictions, Robert Kennedy wrote Congressman Chester Bowles of Connecticut, went "beyond the scope of the McClellan Committee's findings to affect the economic balance at the bargaining table by honest and legitimate unions and employers."[76]

Public apathy still appeared to prevail. Robert Kennedy now launched a personal campaign in support of his brother's bill. He gave speeches, wrote articles, went on television. "Bob's done a terrific job," said the ranking Republican on the House Education and Labor Committee. "I've never had so many letters . . . as I received in response to his TV appearances."[77] Alas, the letters failed to discriminate between the Kennedy-Ervin and Landrum-Griffin bills; and the House, responding to a personal appeal by President Eisenhower, passed Landrum-Griffin. Only heroic effort by John

Kennedy in conference achieved a tolerable compromise between the House and Senate bills. Though labor leaders harshly denounced the new law, the machinery it established for honest and supervised elections made a vital contribution in later years to union democracy in the United Mine Workers, the Steelworkers and other unions.

"With the passage of effective labor legislation by the Congress—the purpose to which we have pointed two years of effort—" Robert Kennedy wrote McClellan on September 10, 1959, "I submit my resignation."[78] These had been extraordinarily busy years—nearly 300 days of public hearings, more than 1500 witnesses, 20,432 pages of testimony in the printed record, 2.5 million miles traveled in pursuit of evidence.[79] Few congressional investigations in American history had lasted so long, spread so wide a net, raised such difficult questions—from the rights of a worker in a union to the rights of a witness before a congressional committee—or drawn so much attention to the committee counsel. When John Bartlow Martin's absorbing *Saturday Evening Post* series "The Struggle to Get Hoffa" came out in the summer of 1959, even McClellan seemed a little annoyed, afraid perhaps that Robert Kennedy was getting all the glory.[80] No longer merely his father's son or his brother's brother, Kennedy was emerging as a national figure in his own right.

Goldwater made the point after his resignation. Still on the trail of Reuther, Goldwater had snapped out a statement accusing Kennedy of running out on the UAW investigation. Kennedy, indignant, asked if there was anything further Goldwater thought he ought to do. "No, no," said Goldwater. "I want to get back to Arizona now. I don't want any more hearings." "Then why did you say it?" asked Kennedy. "That's politics," Goldwater said. Kennedy said he did not consider himself in politics; it was a bipartisan committee, and he had tried to run the investigation on nonpolitical lines. Goldwater said crisply, "You're in politics, Bob, whether you like it or not."[81]

VII

As a national figure, Kennedy continued to receive mixed notices. Some observers rejoiced to see a fearless young crusader exposing wickedness. Others saw more than ever a merciless prosecutor, battering witnesses and overriding constitutional rights.

An assessment of Kennedy's performance requires an understanding of the congressional investigative power. In defending congressional inquiries into the Harding scandals thirty years before,

Felix Frankfurter had rejected the analogy between a trial in the courtroom and a hearing before a congressional committee. The first, he said, placed a man's liberty in jeopardy and therefore called for stringent rules of evidence and procedure; the second was an "exercise of the informing function of Congress" and had different standards. Frankfurter condemned the idea of trying to introduce the "technical limitations" of a trial "into a field where they have never been resorted to and where they are wholly out of place."[82] Three years later, the Supreme Court in *McGrain* v. *Daugherty*[83] rejected the theory that a Senate committee, by inquiring into the affairs of Harding's Attorney General, was exercising a judicial function. Anything the committee reasonably claimed as necessary to the exercise of a valid legislative function, the Court concluded, was permissible. "Unlike a criminal trial where the prosecution has the burden of proving its essential facts by proof beyond a reasonable doubt," Professor Philip B. Kurland has written, "a congressional investigation may arrive at a judgment that is based on the preponderance of the evidence."[84]

In discharging the informing function, Congress often encountered resistance. When Senator Hugo Black conducted his investigation of the public utility holding company lobby in 1935, he wrote, "There is no power on earth that can tear away the veil behind which powerful and audacious and unscrupulous groups operate save the sovereign legislative power armed with the right of subpoena and search." Newspapers might complain about the "bullying and badgering" of witnesses; but Black, reprinting passages of disingenuous and evasive testimony, observed that, after an investigator

> has tried every technique, politeness, kindness, blandishments, . . . he is sometimes driven in the presence of a witness who is deliberately concealing the facts to attempt to shake it out of him with a more drastic attack.[85]

This was Robert Kennedy's view. He quoted his friend Justice Douglas:

> The right to ask a question and the right to demand an answer are essential to the democratic process. . . . That is why the embarrassing question from the Senator or Congressman sitting at the end of the table serves a high function. His right to demand an answer spells in a crucial way the difference between the totalitarian and the democratic regime.[86]

Still the McCarthy experience, as Kennedy knew at first hand, had aroused justified concern about collisions between the investigative power and the Bill of Rights. In 1954 a former Communist named John T. Watkins told the House Committee on Un-American Activities that he would answer questions about himself or about persons he believed still to be members of the Communist party but not about people who had left the Communist movement. This refusal led to his conviction for contempt. Joseph Rauh argued the Watkins case before the Supreme Court. In overturning the conviction in 1957, the Court vigorously reaffirmed the right of Congress to conduct inquiries in furtherance of law-making tasks. But there was "no congressional power to expose for the sake of exposure. . . . Investigations conducted solely for the personal aggrandizement of the investigators or to 'punish' those investigated are indefensible." Moreover, the Court ruled, the investigative power was subject to the restraints of the Bill of Rights.[87]

VIII

In spite of the multitude of investigators—"the largest investigative team," Kennedy said, "ever to operate from Capitol Hill"[88]—and the service of more than eight thousand subpoenas for witnesses and documents, the Rackets Committee, unlike Black's committee twenty years before, was not charged with abusing the subpoena power. Kennedy, Pierre Salinger said, talked "to every investigator before he went on the road about the proper use of the subpoena—the fact that these were not to be used for fishing expeditions. You had to have some legitimate reason to believe that what you were going after was there."[89] Nor, Kennedy said most explicitly, did the committee ever wiretap.[90] Carmine Bellino developed a technique by which, through close analysis of long distance telephone toll tickets, he could find out to whom anyone talked on a given day. The staff indexed thousands of toll tickets and plotted the calls on worksheets.[91] "This is why they always thought we were wiretapping," said Walter Sheridan, "but we weren't."[92]

The chief criticism was directed not at the investigations but at the hearings. The committee rules were in fact designed to avoid the excesses of the McCarthy era. Witnesses were assured the right to counsel and the right to submit questions for cross-examination. One-senator hearings, a device beloved by McCarthy, were banned. When the committee anticipated derogatory testimony about a person not present, Kennedy notified him in advance and offered the opportunity for instant denial.

Remembering the slovenliness of the McCarthy investigations, Kennedy prided himself on the care with which his own hearings were prepared. He checked and rechecked testimony before he put witnesses on the stand; and he rarely asked a question in public hearings to which he did not know the answer. "For every witness who was called before the Committee," he said, "we interviewed at least thirty-five. For every hour a witness testified on the stand before the Committee, he was interviewed on an average of five hours. For every document that was introduced, five thousand were studied. For every hearing held, there were approximately eight months of intensive investigation."[93]

All this was very well. But Kennedy's style as cross-examiner caused serious controversy. There was, it should be said, testimony in his favor. "I did not think he was 'persecuting' Hoffa or infringing his civil liberties," John Bartlow Martin said. "As a crime reporter, I had seen far far worse prosecutions. Indeed, I thought he treated Hoffa fairly, on the whole."[94] Paul Porter of the New Deal law firm of Arnold, Fortas & Porter wrote Kennedy that the 1957 Hoffa hearings were "an outstanding example of preparation, presentation and fairness. . . . I was impressed with the Chairman's observance of the *Watkins* case criteria and am convinced that your magnificent architecture of this proceeding demonstrates that *Watkins* constitutes no serious limitation on proper congressional investigations."[95] Joseph Rauh, the *Watkins* winner, did not think that Kennedy violated the guidelines. "He was trying to be a fair investigator," Rauh said later, "and any abuses were not due to 'vindictiveness,' but to his lack of experience. If it sometimes led to abuse of witnesses, it sometimes led to witnesses like Hoffa getting away with murder. . . . Far from browbeating Hoffa, it was more of a case of Hoffa browbeating him."[96]

Goldwater agreed with Rauh on this if on nothing else. Kennedy, he later told Victor Lasky, often became flustered before labor hoods or their lawyers. "When the going would get rough," according to Goldwater, "John McClellan was likely to take over the questioning, thus saving Bobby from embarrassment."[97] Nor, for that matter, did Hoffa think for a moment that he had been persecuted. He considered Kennedy's questioning "painfully amateurish" and said it was "ridiculously simple to get him to lose his temper. It was equally easy to get him to wander from the subject he was pursuing and to tie him up in knots of verbiage and dialectics."[98]

On the other hand, Professor Alexander Bickel of the Yale Law

School summed up a widespread impression in a severe article in the *New Republic*. Where Rauh, Frankfurter's first law clerk, viewed congressional investigations in the spirit of Professor Frankfurter, Bickel, the twentieth clerk, viewed them in the spirit of Justice Frankfurter, a more conservative figure. Accusing Kennedy of conducting "purely punitive expeditions," Bickel cited two Fifth Amendment cases—Dave Beck and the Chicago hood Joey Glimco—where Kennedy had persisted in questioning witnesses whom he knew had debarred themselves (by declining on self-incrimination grounds to answer a single question) from answering related questions. In such cases, Bickel argued, Kennedy was not discharging the informing function but rather trying to punish by publicity. "No one since the late Joseph R. McCarthy," wrote Bickel, "has done more than Mr. Kennedy to foster the impression that the plea of self-incrimination is tantamount to a confession of guilt"; under his direction the Rackets Committee "often—though not always—held hearings for the sole purpose of accusing, judging and condemning people."[99]

Part of Bickel's case rested on the fallacy rejected by Frankfurter and by the Supreme Court—that a congressional hearing was the equivalent of a trial, and that a witness had "the right to an impartial judge who is not at the same time also the prosecutor."[100] The theory that the Rackets Committee had abused judicial functions was never taken seriously enough for anyone—even Glimco or Beck—to invoke it as a basis for an appeal to the courts. The committee was plainly dealing with questions on which legislation could be (and was) had; and it is hard to see that Bickel's horrid examples were greatly different from things that Hugo Black and other sorely tried congressional investigators had done in the past.

Nonetheless, he raised a troubling point about the Fifth Amendment—a point to which Kennedy himself was sporadically sensitive. In 1957 Edward Bennett Williams, speaking at the University of Virginia's Student Legal Forum, accused the committee of calling witnesses into executive session, ascertaining that they would take the Fifth and then asking them questions in open session. Edward Kennedy, now at the Virginia Law School, challenged Williams's assertion.[101] He also reported Williams's charge to his brother, who wrote angrily in his journal, "As of yet we have not had a witness in Executive [session] who has taken 5th & whom we have had in open. Old McCarthy trick & it irritates me that he now an officer of American Civil Liberties Union [Williams was on the ACLU national committee] should relate it to us."[102]

Nearly one fifth of the witnesses who appeared before the committee—343 out of 1526—refused questions on grounds of self-incrimination.[103] Kennedy stoutly defended the Fifth Amendment and called it one of the distinguishing marks between democracy and dictatorship. "I would not have it changed." On the other hand, he clearly used it as a polemical weapon, and did so, as he admitted, because, "although the Fifth Amendment is for the innocent as well as the guilty, I can think of very few witnesses who availed themselves of it who in my estimation were free of wrongdoing." Practically, in such cases as Beck and Glimco, he may well have been right. But his attitude weakened what he himself called "one of the rights that a free people possess against the potential abuses of government."

Moreover, this approach encouraged further abuse. It was one thing if the interrogator pursued witnesses, as Kennedy declared he had done, "only on matters I would have asked about if he were answering questions." But he admitted he did not always have "positive proof" on such matters; and he instanced a case where Senator Curtis asked a Fifth Amendment witness a question on which the committee had no information at all and thereby put a wholly fanciful innuendo into circulation.[104] All this suggests that the Fifth Amendment presents problems that Kennedy, and no doubt Bickel too, failed satisfactorily to solve.

But there lay indistinctly behind Bickel's not always forceful contentions a genuinely forceful apprehension—that Kennedy in these matters had displayed an excess of zeal; that he was a man driven by a conviction of righteousness, a fanaticism of virtue, a certitude about guilt that vaulted over gaps in evidence. "Mr. Kennedy knows," Bickel wrote, "and when he knows he is very sure that he knows." The courts might acquit Hoffa, and Kennedy might say he accepted that as "a citizen or a lawyer," but still in some deeper sense, Bickel felt, he *knew* Hoffa to be guilty. "He sees the public interest in terms of ends," Bickel wrote, "with little appreciation of the significance of means."[105]

IX

After resigning as chief counsel, Kennedy set to work on a book about the committee. He asked John Seigenthaler, who was completing a year as a Nieman Fellow at Harvard, to come to Hickory Hill and help on the manuscript. Kennedy wrote the first draft. Seigenthaler cut and edited. When Seigenthaler went off to bed at night, Kennedy would be "sitting on the edge of the bed writing in long hand," and when Seigenthaler got up in the morning, "he'd be up already writing again." In the afternoon they took walks. "During those walks I got to know Bob Kennedy . . . better than I got to know anybody during my whole life. He was completely candid with me about everything."[106]

The Enemy Within, as he called the book, was written in brisk journalistic prose interspersed with personal passages of a curious eloquence. "It is a detective story which can be put on the same shelf as the best thriller fiction of the day," the master journalist Lord Beaverbrook told him. "I feel rather like one who has been sent an account of the Crusade written by Richard the Lionheart himself."[107] The book was briefly a best seller, the royalties going to the care of retarded children.

Most books and articles in America in the 1950s with titles like *The Enemy Within* had a single subject—communism. But the enemy within, as Robert Kennedy saw it, was organized corruption, spreading from the underworld into labor, business and politics, expressing, he asserted, the moral sickness of a greedy society. American history left no doubt, he had told the students at Notre Dame in 1958, "that the great events of which we are proud were forged by men who put their country above self-interest—their ideals above self-profit."[108] Dangerous changes were taking place in the moral fiber of American life. "It seems to me imperative that we reinstill in ourselves the toughness and idealism that guided the nation in the past."[109]

The Rackets Committee was a significant chapter in his education. For the first time he had been forced to confront the power structures of organized labor, of organized business, of organized crime and of law enforcement. It also had unexpected emotional impact. The wracking experience of these years deeply affected him. He saw men lie, cry, run terrible risks, display great cowardice and great courage. He learned, as in the case of the jolly rogue Frank Brewster, that he could quite like people of whom he morally disapproved. "He had an immense sense of humor about sinners," Murray Kempton said, "which I had really not expected."[110] He was also, Kempton thought, surprisingly perceptive. "Let two thugs with identical records on paper come before the committee and he could tell you how they differed as human beings."[111] He unlocked resources of sympathy within himself about ordinary people—as when, after attending mass (in Lithuanian) in Sheboygan, he wrote with unwonted feeling about "the strong, stern faces of people who have worked hard and who have suffered."[112] Emotion, long dammed by the requirement of toughness, was beginning to flow again. The experience helped strengthen the instinct of sympathy within him—that instinct more or less repressed since childhood—and gave it for the first time social direction.

Moreover, he understood more than ever that toughness and concern were not necessarily enemies. "What impressed Bobby Kennedy about the UAW," Walter Reuther said later, "is that we shared the sense of human compassion. . . . Too often, I think he felt that liberals articulated this sense of compassion, but never did anything about it. . . . I think this is the thing that finally rang the bell with Bobby Kennedy. And Jack said to me, 'You know, you fellows are educating Bobby.' And we said, 'Well, we're doing what comes naturally.' "[113] Other things brought the Reuthers and the Kennedys together: both, for example, were teams of brothers. Walter Reuther, Victor said later, actually felt more rapport with Robert than with John Kennedy: Bobby was less detached, more committed, more activist.[114] John Kennedy himself said later of his younger brother, "He might once have been intolerant of liberals as such because his early experience was with that high-minded, high-speaking kind who never got anything done. That all changed the moment he met a liberal like Walter Reuther."[115]

Many liberals still could not understand him. His concern with organized crime, for example, did not fit into their categories; such a preoccupation appeared unseemly and irrelevant. They found him hard to understand because he was a Catholic. Not many liberals believed in original sin. Expressing confidence in 1957 in the future of the trade union movement, Kennedy had said that "the brightest spot" was the work of the Association of Catholic Trade Unionists.[116] Kempton was almost alone in seeing the clue. Catholic politicians fascinated Kempton. "The only non-Catholic interesting politician I know," he once said, "is President Kennedy."[117] He early perceived the Catholic essence in Robert Kennedy.

Kennedy had proceeded into the jungle of labor racketeering, Kempton wrote in 1960, without guide or experience. "But there are persons so constituted that they can go nowhere without some piece of faith to serve for light. Robert Kennedy is a Catholic; and naturally he sought his faith there. It is the difference between his brother, the Senator, and himself, the difference between those who are only properly oriented and those who are truly involved." Robert Kennedy, Kempton wrote, looked upon labor racketeers as men who had betrayed a priesthood. He had become for this journey "a Catholic radical." In the cynicism of American politics, he represented "the survival of the spirit."[118]

(10)

1960

EXCEPT FOR THE JAUNT with Stevenson in 1956, Robert Kennedy had stayed away from politics after 1952. Party grandees exasperated him. Party rituals bored him. When John Kennedy came up for reelection in 1958, Robert's main contribution was to fly to Boston and hear the returns. Nonetheless, as John prepared to run for President in 1960, his younger brother remained, in Theodore Sorensen's words, his "first and only choice for campaign manager." Robert Kennedy, as Sorensen said, could be "trusted more implicitly, say 'no' more emphatically and speak for the candidate more authoritatively than any professional politician."[1]

I

Preoccupied with the Rackets Committee and then with *The Enemy Within,* Robert did not enter the campaign full-time until the end of 1959. Sorensen had run things in the early stages. Later Stephen Smith, who had married Jean Kennedy in 1956, took charge in an inconspicuous Washington office. He was thirty-one years old, had received his political initiation in John Kennedy's 1958 campaign, was soft-spoken, sharp and funny. "He made a major difference to the campaign," Robert Kennedy said later, "when he started back in 1959."[2] O'Donnell and O'Brien worked with Smith.

In the course of the year Robert added David Hackett, the great friend of his youth. Hackett, who had attended McGill University after the war and was now editing a Montreal magazine, was so content in Canada that he was contemplating a change in citizenship. Then his old chum told him over the phone that, since he had done so well in English at Milton, he would be ideal to handle Senator Kennedy's political correspondence. Hackett came to Washington.[3]

Robert also recruited Pierre Salinger to set up the press operation. John Kennedy, Salinger recalled, made it very clear "he was hiring me strictly because Bobby had asked him to." Soon Robert directed him to put out a statement. The next day John asked Salinger with some asperity who had authorized it. "Check those things with me," John Kennedy said. "You're working for me, not for Bob now."[4]

"All right, Jack," Robert said in December at Palm Beach, "what has been done about the campaign? . . . A day lost now can't be picked up on the other end. It's ridiculous that more work hasn't been done."[5] This speech defined his role. Inside the campaign he was the tireless invigorator and goad, responsible for everything except the speeches. Outside he became the man to do the harsh jobs, saying no, telling people off, whipping the reluctant and the recalcitrant into line.

When reporters began in due course to write about the "well-oiled Kennedy machine," the myth arose that the Kennedys were master political planners. This was a misconception. They were not systematic calculators but brilliant improvisers. Their reactions, observed Fred Dutton of California, one of the shrewd political minds of the period, "jump[ed] all over the place—just an incisive thing here, incisive thing there, and you've got it. . . . More was almost communicated in their silences or things they skipped over than in their questions."[6] Robert Kennedy's genius as manager lay in his capacity to address a specific situation, to assemble an able staff, to inspire and flog them into exceptional deeds and to prevail through sheer force of momentum. "When their things worked," said Harris Wofford, the campaign's civil rights coordinator, "it was not because of a great machine but because they released energy in a lot of directions and sort of trusted that . . . the general goal was right."[7]

"If you win," Robert Kennedy told me during his senatorial campaign in 1964,

> the reporters will always write about well-oiled machines and superplanning. If you lose, they will always write about hopeless incompetence. I have a simple theory: that campaigns come to an absolute end within a given time; that you can recruit good people and ask them to do a lot of things in that brief period; that some things will work and some won't; that, if something is not working, change it, and be prepared to change it again; and that out of all the activity a momentum will develop which will carry you through.

This guaranteed organizational confusion. "And yet," as the lawyer Barrett Prettyman, Jr., noted, "the very frenzy of it somehow brings more out of people than if the whole thing was just calculated to the *n*th degree."⁸

This was the Robert Kennedy the campaign staff saw and generally adored. As an emissary to Democrats, he was less adorable. Governor Michael DiSalle of Ohio, a jovial veteran of Truman days, aspired to be his state's favorite son. Kennedy offered DiSalle this distinction if DiSalle would agree to endorse him forthwith for President. DiSalle knew that Kennedy could probably beat him in the primary but had no desire to be the first governor to come out for Kennedy—among other reasons, perhaps, because Truman was so hostile to the Kennedys. He therefore sought to delay his announcement. Robert Kennedy and John Bailey met DiSalle to put on additional pressure. It was an unpleasant session. Bailey had been in politics a long time and, as Kenneth O'Donnell said, did not shock easily, but, he told O'Donnell later, he was "startled by the going-over that Bobby had given DiSalle."⁹ Bailey was still talking about it in March when I encountered him at the Democratic Midwest Conference. According to my journal, "I had a series of drinks with John Bailey, who was most charming and amusing and regaled me with stories about the Kennedy campaign (e.g., Bobby Kennedy's talking to Mike DiSalle in a way which almost led Mike to cancel the Ohio deal)."¹⁰ Still the deal survived. Early in January DiSalle pledged the Ohio delegation to Kennedy.

This left the Kennedys free to concentrate on their first critical test —Wisconsin. "Senator Humphrey is our big rival now," Robert Kennedy said as they prepared in February to run the gantlet of the primaries. He added: "But over the long run I expect Senator Johnson to be the principal opposition."¹¹

II

Hubert Humphrey was one of the brightest and most likable men in the Democratic party. Though he and John Kennedy were in broad agreement on issues, their lives could hardly have been more different. Nearly forty-nine, six years older than Kennedy, Humphrey had come of age during the depression, growing up a druggist's son amidst the dust storms of South Dakota. He worked his way through college, taught, entered politics and flashed into national attention as the fiery champion of civil rights in the Democratic convention of 1948. He was a man of swift intelligence, immense sympathy and great gusto, a stem-winding orator in the style of midwestern populism, sentimental, vulnerable, accommodating, a generous and open man but easily hurt and not always easily forgiving.

His implacably loyal wife, Muriel, joined him in Wisconsin, as did a group of devoted supporters from Minnesota, especially Orville Freeman, the able governor, and the witty and somewhat cynical congressman Eugene McCarthy. "I should be the candidate for President," McCarthy was supposed to have said. "I'm twice as liberal as Humphrey, twice as smart as Symington and twice as Catholic as Kennedy." (Joseph Alsop told John Kennedy that he had encountered McCarthy on the plane to Wisconsin, reading an enormous missal all the way to Milwaukee. Kennedy said, "Well, Joe, there's this old saying in Boston politics, never trust a Catholic politician who reads his missal in the trolley car.")[12]

Humphrey's Minnesotans worked hard. But the Kennedys seemed to be everywhere. "They're all over the state," Humphrey said, "and they look alike and sound alike. Teddy or Eunice talks to a crowd, wearing a raccoon coat and a stocking cap, and people think they're listening to Jack. I get reports that Jack is appearing in three or four different places at the same time."[13] He felt, Humphrey said, like an independent merchant competing against a chain store.[14] It was not only the quantity of Kennedys; it was even more their money, their assurance, their beautiful people, their personal pollsters, their private Convair, the *Caroline,* as against Humphrey's limited funds, plain midwestern folk and rented campaign bus. Hearing a plane overhead one night as he jolted along trying to sleep in his bus, Humphrey shouted, "Come down here, Jack, and play fair."[15]

Robert spoke as often as the rest. Patrick Lucey, the state chairman, told him he should decide whether to be manager or campaigner. "But he insisted on doing both and did both quite well. It was amazing to me how he could find the amount of energy that he was able to put into the thing."[16] He was still not fluent on his feet, but he was gaining confidence. A slight figure—he lost a pound a week in Wisconsin—bare headed, his collar turned up against the icy March winds, he drove from town to town along roads piled high with snow, stopping at high schools, Rotary clubs and political rallies to explain why his brother should be President.

He made new friends in Wisconsin. One was an Italian American named Jerry Bruno, whom John Kennedy had persuaded the summer before to leave his job on the staff of Senator William Proxmire and organize Kennedy clubs around the state. Bruno had dropped out of school in the ninth grade; but, as he later wrote, "John and Robert

Kennedy sized you up very quickly. If there was something about you they thought O.K., then your background and education and all the rest didn't matter." Bruno displayed uncommon talent in an obscure but indispensable political specialty: "advancing" appearances by the candidate. It was a risky job. If the meeting was a success, credit went to the candidate; if a failure, everyone blamed the advance man. (Later in Ohio, when Kennedy and DiSalle found themselves hopelessly mired in a traffic jam and far behind schedule, Kennedy said, "I wonder how Hannibal ever made it across the Alps?" "It was easy," DiSalle said, looking at Bruno. "He didn't have an advance man.")[17]

Another new friend who became, even more than Bruno, a fixture in Robert Kennedy's political operations was a raffish, entertaining and outrageous rogue named Paul Corbin. Forty-six years old, of Canadian birth, at one period very close to the Communist party, at another a devotee of Joe McCarthy, he had lived by his wits on the fringes of the labor movement and the Democratic party. With gravelly voice, authoritative manner and unlimited effrontery, he was a natural-born con man. He took cheerful delight in causing trouble and in reorganizing the truth. When Helen Keyes of Boston came to help in Wisconsin, Robert Kennedy committed her to Corbin's doubtful protection. Corbin paraded her up and down the streets of small Wisconsin towns; and, if anyone opposed John Kennedy on religious grounds, Corbin would point to Helen Keyes, a devout Catholic, and say, "Well, this lady's a Baptist from Boston, and *she's* for Kennedy." Helen Keyes said later, "I kept expecting to be struck by lightning for denying my faith."[18]

Paul Corbin fell in love with Robert Kennedy. He was prepared thereafter to do anything he conceived to be in Kennedy's interests, whether or not Kennedy, if he had known what Corbin intended, would have approved. In time Corbin even became a Catholic himself in order to have Robert and Ethel as godparents. "You need Paul Corbin in the Catholic Church like you need leprosy," Helen Keyes protested. ". . . He wants to be a Catholic because *you're* a Catholic." Kennedy said, "Well, who cares? If he gets something out of it, and he's been through all the instruction. . . ."[19]

Something about Corbin appealed to Robert Kennedy. His impudence perhaps touched some Irish folk memory; Corbin could have been a character out of Ed O'Connor's Boston. His entirely cynical view of people's motives was joined to wondrous investigative skills. As Joseph Dolan of Colorado put it, "He could find out who was cutting the ticket pretty fast, when he went into a town." And Corbin was unquestionably effective. "If you have a job and you want to get it done," Helen Keyes summed it up, "and you don't care how it's done, send Paul Corbin out to do it—but just understand you can never send him back to the same district."[20]

Stephen Smith and John Seigenthaler liked Corbin. Dolan and O'Donnell detested him. Robert Kennedy himself was defensive about him and on occasion exasperated by him. In later years, Robert McNamara, hearing of some Corbin mischief, suggested that he be given a lie detector test. "A lie detector test?" said Robert Kennedy. "Why he'd break the machine!" Many were mystified by the attachment. But the attachment remained.

Humphrey saw in the Kennedy campaign "an element of ruthlessness and toughness that I had trouble either accepting or forgetting."[21] He blamed Robert Kennedy for a rumor that the Teamsters were helping him (which it would not have been surprising for the Teamsters to do, not out of love for Humphrey but out of hatred for the Kennedys). And, though he was not sure that the Kennedys were responsible, he was enraged by the anonymous mailing of anti-Catholic tracts to Catholic households across the state. Others blamed this on Paul Corbin.[22] John Kennedy himself was determined to play down the religious issue. But the issue was irrepressible. The Pope did not have many fans among Wisconsin Lutherans. Nor could the press leave religion alone. Whenever Kennedy shook hands with a nun, the picture appeared in the papers. Corbin, inviting a group of seminarians to a Kennedy rally, begged them to wear sport shirts.

The contest grew acrimonious. Two days before the vote, Humphrey told a Jewish audience in Milwaukee, "They say the Humphrey campaign is disorganized—but I want you to know that the most organized thing that ever happened almost destroyed civilization." "Those cutting remarks," his campaign coordinator observed, "were not lost on a meeting in the Jewish Community Center."[23] Kennedy hoped to win decisively enough to drive Humphrey from the race. He won. But, after a harrowing night, it was evident that the margin was too small to be conclusive. Commentators diminished it further by attributing it to the crossover of Catholic Republicans. John Kennedy was disappointed; Robert Kennedy was exhausted and angry. O'Brien noted the "terrible sense of gloom" in Kennedy headquarters.[24] In an election-night interview Walter Cronkite of CBS asked John Kennedy about the Catholic vote. Kennedy answered frigidly. As soon as the interview was over, as Cronkite later recalled it, "Bobby stormed through the studio saying, 'You violated an agreement! We had an agreement that no question be asked about Catholicism and the Catholic vote. . . . I'm going to see that you never get another interview.' "[25] This was the mood of the evening. In fact, the agreement had not been communicated to Cronkite, and he was to have many more interviews with both Kennedys.

An exultant Humphrey claimed a moral victory. A depressed Robert Kennedy took the *Caroline* to West Virginia.

III

"What I would like," Robert Kennedy told the Kennedy organizers, "is to have a cold-blooded appraisal from each one of you on whether we can win the State of West Virginia; whether . . . these ministers will start telling people that they can't vote for a Catholic because the Pope is coming over. . . . I want to go over, county by county, as to what chances we have."[26]

They told him. A man shouted, "There's only one problem. He's a Catholic. That's our God-damned problem." What had happened to a December poll showing Kennedy ahead, seventy to thirty? In December, the reply came, no one had known that Kennedy was a Catholic. A Catholic could not be elected dogcatcher in West Virginia. The room was in a tumult. "I looked at Bobby," O'Donnell later wrote. "He seemed to be in a state of shock. His face was as pale as ashes."[27] He rallied to lay out the campaign strategy. "If we try to meet the religion issue head on—deal with it frankly," he finally said,

> I think we are feasible. . . . Once that is done and in Jack's speeches he gives answers to rational questions, then he must go on to show that there is something more important to those people than anything to do with religion. Got to have something like the feeling they had for FDR. . . . In Mingo County there are six thousand unemployed. They don't care if he is Catholic—if he can get to them that "I care for you." . . .
>
> It is simply food, family and flag in southern West Virginia.[28]

There was a month to go. John Kennedy addressed the religious issue—"Nobody asked me if I was a Catholic when I joined the United States Navy"[29]—and a state filled with kindly and patriotic people responded to the appeal for tolerance. Having dealt with flag, he proceeded to food and family. This was not difficult. He was genuinely appalled by what he saw as he traveled across the verdant countryside—hungry, hollow-eyed children, dispirited families living on cornmeal and surplus lard, gray, dismal towns, despair about the future. He had never expected to find anything like this in the United States. "West Virginia," Pierre Salinger said later, "brought a real transformation of John F. Kennedy as a person."[30] It upset Robert Kennedy quite as much. Arriving at the tipple of coal mines as the shifts were changing, he would speak to the miners—"My name is Bob Kennedy. My brother is running for President. I want your help" —shake their hands and then drive on, his own hands now black with coal dust, his face grim.[31]

The objective, Robert Kennedy had said, was to rouse among West Virginians "something like the feeling they had for FDR." Joseph Kennedy decided to do this in the most direct possible way. Shortly after Wisconsin he asked Franklin D. Roosevelt, Jr., to meet with his sons in Palm Beach. "You know, Franklin," the ambassador greeted Roosevelt, "if it hadn't been for that guinea [Carmine de Sapio, who had swung the Democratic gubernatorial nomination in New York from Roosevelt to Averell Harriman in 1954], you would have been elected governor, and now we would all be working for you."[32] This was still the season of gloom. The father refused to be downcast. "He was always confident," said Charles Spalding, who was also at Palm Beach, "and always willing to believe it could be done and it would be done and it was just a question of going and doing it."[33] Joseph Kennedy was operating on his familiar principle that, when his children made a decision, no matter how mistaken their father might have thought it, it became at once the best decision in the world. The support he unstintingly gave sometimes helped make it so.

So in July 1957 John Kennedy had made his speech in the Senate calling for the independence of Algeria. The speech shocked the foreign policy establishment. Dean Acheson assailed him with characteristic scorn. Even Adlai Stevenson, whom I saw in Paris a few days after the speech, was appalled: Kennedy was criticizing an ally, imperiling the unity of NATO and so on. Joseph Kennedy privately told James Landis the speech was bad policy and bad politics. But when John Kennedy, disturbed by the criticism, called his father, Mr. Kennedy said, "You lucky mush. You don't know it and neither does anyone else, but within a few months everyone is going to know just how right you were on Algeria."[34] In December 1959, alone with Paul Fay, the ambassador had expressed pessimism about 1960. "Jack is going to have a rough time. . . . I hate to see him and Bobby working so hard if the timing is all wrong." When John entered the room a moment later, his father said emphatically that he would bet a million dollars in Las Vegas on winning the nomination and the election. "He had made," Fay wrote later, "a 180-degree change of position in less than sixty seconds."[35] "The great thing about Dad," John Kennedy said in 1960, "is his optimism and his enthusiasm and how he's always for you. He might not always agree . . . but as soon as I do anything, there's Dad saying: 'Smartest move you ever made. . . . We really got them on the run now.'"[36] "My father would be for me," Kennedy told Dorothy Schiff of the *New York Post*, "if I were running as head of the Communist Party."[37]

Roosevelt, as confident as the ambassador about West Virginia, spoke so eloquently about the prospects that Rose Kennedy thought to herself, "I am glad Franklin's helping Jack and not running against him."[38] Finally Robert said, "There's no question because of the attitude of the people there toward both your mother and your father that you can have a big influence in that state." Would Roosevelt campaign in West Virginia? Roosevelt agreed at once. ("A lot of his kids were there," Roosevelt recalled about Robert Kennedy. "I remember being impressed with the amount of time and attention he devoted to them, and how devoted they were to him.")[39]

IV

Roosevelt's look, his voice, his charm evoked his father; and, with his entry and John Kennedy's head-on attack on the religious issue, the campaign began to turn around. Still West Virginia was tricky terrain. National politics mattered considerably less than local politics. The problem was to acquire the strongest slate in each county. "Bobby was the one," Roosevelt later said, "who had to decide which local county slate we should get Jack on. . . . He would go into a county, analyze it, talk to everybody he could talk to, going directly to the point; and his judgment turned out to be exactly right."[40]

But there was always a quid pro quo. Slating provided a quasi-legal cover under which money flowed to local politicians in the guise of campaign expenses. This was a cherished West Virginia tradition. O'Brien negotiated the payments for the Kennedy organization. "Neither Jack nor Bob Kennedy knew what agreements I made—that was my responsibility."[41] There was no escape from the local folkways. "Our campaign," Humphrey wrote, "had, in fact, already given in to the system. . . . Hoping to get consideration from the party, it had raised money and given it to the party for slating in various counties. . . . Obviously, our highest possible contribution was peanuts compared to what they had received from the Kennedy organization."[42]

"I must tell you," Walter Lippmann had written John Kennedy in January, "that I do not look forward with any pleasure to the contest between Humphrey and you. You both will be doing and saying things that as President you would wish you hadn't had to say and do."[43] "I can't afford to run through this state with a little black bag and a checkbook," Humphrey cried as the tide began to turn. ". . . I can't buy an election. . . . Kennedy is the spoiled candidate and he and that young, emotional, juvenile Bobby are spending with wild abandon. . . . Anyone who gets in the way of . . . papa's pet is going to be destroyed."[44]

For their part the Kennedy people regarded Humphrey as a spoiler, incapable, after losing Wisconsin, of winning the nomination for himself, yet determined to knock out Kennedy and no doubt financed in this ambition by those who could ultimately benefit—Symington, Stevenson, Lyndon Johnson.* An anonymous Minnesotan sent Lawrence O'Brien material representing Humphrey as a draft dodger in the Second World War. "We decided to do nothing with this for the time being, but we agreed that if Humphrey hit us with some extremely low blow, we might use the material to retaliate." They also decided that the retaliation should come, not directly from the Kennedys, but from Franklin Roosevelt, to whom they passed on the material.[45] What happened thereafter is beyond the capacity of history to reconstruct. Roosevelt's memory is that, as Humphrey became more intemperate, he was under insistent pressure, especially from Robert Kennedy, to bring up Humphrey's war record. According to O'Brien, Roosevelt, exasperated by Humphrey's demagoguery, brought it up on his own.[46] In any case, Roosevelt finally told an audience, "There's another candidate in your primary. He's a good Democrat, but I don't know where he was in World War II."[47] The outcry was immediate and vivid. Humphrey had in fact been turned down by both services during the war because of physical disabilities.

---

* Humphrey wrote later, "We began to listen to offers of help from other candidates . . . but when the chips should have been down, Johnson's people refused money absolutely and Symington's were to come up with only a little" (Humphrey, *Education of a Public Man* [Garden City, N.Y., 1976], 213). Humphrey said nothing about Stevenson money, of which he may have received a certain amount.

He later wrote that his organization "made repeated contacts with the Kennedys demonstrating the untruth of the allegations. They believed me, but never shut F.D.R., Jr. up, as they easily could have."[48] John Kennedy heard about it after a highly successful afternoon of campaigning. "Something always happens at the end of a good day," he said angrily to Theodore White, the campaign historian. "I didn't want that."[49] He promptly disowned the issue. But he praised Roosevelt's contribution to the campaign, which indeed had been great, and kept him on as a campaigner. Roosevelt felt he had been used, blaming it on what he saw as Robert Kennedy's determination to win at any cost; "I don't think that Jack really had anything to do with deciding whether to insist on my going ahead with asking the question."*

The contest concluded in bitterness. Robert Kennedy and O'Donnell did not think their gains had sufficed to overcome the anti-Catholic prejudice. "We felt," O'Donnell recalled, "that our Presidential campaign was over." "Damn that Hubert Humphrey," Robert Kennedy said. That day West Virginia gave Kennedy a stunning victory. As the votes came in, Robert Kennedy said, "God, this must be awful for poor Hubert, ending up this way after working so hard."[50]

In Humphrey's hotel suite his advisers debated what to do next. Joseph Rauh and James Loeb, who had founded Americans for Democratic Action and was now a newspaper publisher in Saranac Lake, New York, argued that Humphrey should endorse Kennedy. Others urged Humphrey to keep his delegates together till the convention. Rauh said this would only prove that Humphrey was part of a stop-Kennedy movement. Loeb typed out a statement of withdrawal without endorsement. Humphrey approved it, "and I called Bobby Kennedy," Rauh said later, "and read it to him. Then a strange incident occurred." Let Rauh tell it:

> A few minutes after I called Bobby Kennedy and read him Humphrey's generous withdrawal, the telephone rang in the outer room of Hubert's suite. . . . Someone picked up the telephone from downstairs and said, "Mr. Kennedy is on the way up." Of course, we thought it was Senator Kennedy coming over to thank Hubert. Then we looked at the television, and there Senator Kennedy was, live on television. . . . I said to myself, "Oh my God, it's Bobby, and he is the devil as far as this camp is con-

* It was, Roosevelt said later, "the biggest political mistake" of his career. The next year he went to Humphrey's office to apologize. Fifteen years later Humphrey declared himself still "unforgiving." Roosevelt, in recorded interview by Jean Stein, December 9, 1969, 6–8; Humphrey, *Education of a Public Man*, 475.

cerned." He was the one to whom the enmity went. He was the one whom all our people were so bitter about. . . .

The door opened. Bobby walks in. It was like the Red Sea opening for Moses. Everybody walked backwards, and there was a path from the door to the other side of the room where Hubert and Muriel were standing. I'll never forget that walk if I live to be a hundred. Bobby walked slowly, deliberately, over to the Humphreys. He leaned in and kissed Muriel. I've always wondered whether she had on her mind at that moment that she was going to poke him because she was really not very happy about the outcome. Anyway, he was very nice and very gracious, and it was the right thing for him to have done. But at the moment, it was sure something.*

V

Humphrey's withdrawal left Lyndon Johnson, as Robert Kennedy had predicted in February, the principal opposition. A week after West Virginia I received a call from John Kennedy. He was lunching on the road in Maryland. His talk was punctuated by bites and swallows. He calculated that he needed between eighty and a hundred delegates. Adlai Stevenson, he felt, could provide them. "He is the essential ingredient in my combination. I don't want to go hat in hand to all those southerners. But I'll have to do that if I can't get votes from the north."[51] But Stevenson, though an avowed noncandidate, wanted the nomination himself. His friends were organizing on his behalf. The shooting down of a CIA U-2 over the Soviet Union and the consequent cancellation of the Paris conference between Khrushchev and Eisenhower now galvanized his candidacy. If foreign affairs were crucial, Stevenson appeared the most qualified Democrat. It seemed to some of us that he might develop enough strength to stop Kennedy without developing enough to nominate himself. The beneficiary would be Johnson.

In mid-May, Johnson, trying to block a rush of delegates to Kennedy, told Stevenson, "If I don't get it, it will be you."[52] A few days later Kennedy called on Stevenson in Libertyville. "I told him," Kennedy told me afterward, "that Lyndon was a chronic liar; that he had been making all sorts of assurances to me for years and has lived up to none of them."[53] (Stevenson later told me the mention of Johnson

* Joseph Rauh, in recorded interview by Charles Morrissey, December 23, 1965, 70–72, JFK Oral History Program. Humphrey writes that for the first time in his political career he saw his wife angry about an election. "She did not want to see any Kennedy, much less be touched by one. When Bob arrived in our room, he moved quickly to her and kissed her on the cheek. Muriel stiffened, stared, and turned in silent hostility, walking away from him, fighting tears and angry words" (Humphrey, *Education of a Public Man*, 221).

had provoked the only flash of temper on Kennedy's part. Recalling how fiercely Johnson had spoken against Kennedy, he added, "Obviously the feeling between the two of them is savage."[54] This was not, I think, altogether so. Early in June at Hyannis Port, Kennedy talked about Johnson with a mixture of admiration and despair. "He went into an historical excursus," I noted, "comparing J. to Peel and others who were omnipotent in Parliament but had no popularity in the country. He was quite amusing on J.'s personality, describing him as a 'riverboat gambler.' ")[55]

It was a difficult time, especially for those of us who loved Adlai Stevenson and had labored for him in two campaigns. Early in June I joined a group of liberals—Rauh, John Kenneth Galbraith, Henry Steele Commager, Arthur Goldberg, James MacGregor Burns and half a dozen others—in a statement endorsing Kennedy. Stevenson enthusiasts denounced us for not insisting on the best. I noted in my journal:

> This, I suppose, is the real irony. I have come, I think, to the private conclusion that I would rather have K as President than S. S is a much richer, more thoughtful, more creative person; but he has been away from power too long; he gives me an odd sense of unreality. . . . I find it hard to define this feeling—a certain frivolity, distractedness, overinterest in words and phrases? I don't know; but in contrast K gives a sense of cool, measured, intelligent concern with action and power. I feel that his administration would be less encumbered than S's with commitments to past ideas or sentimentalities; that he would be more radical; and, though he is less creative personally, he might be more so politically. But I cannot mention this feeling to anyone.[56]

My wife, Marian Cannon, announced that she was standing by Stevenson. A few days later I received a letter on another matter from Robert Kennedy. He scrawled in a postscript: "Can't you control your own wife—or are you like me?"[57]

VI

Kenneth O'Donnell and Lawrence O'Brien have written in their books (1972 and 1974) that they went to Los Angeles quietly confident about the outcome. I do not remember all this quiet confidence at the time. Theodore Sorensen wrote in 1971 that "privately, Kennedy was nervous."[58] Robert Kennedy told me in 1965, "We had to win on the first ballot. We only won by 15 votes. Well, North Dakota, they had the unit system . . . we won it by half a vote. California was falling apart. . . . Carmine de Sapio came to me and said what we'd like to do is make a deal—30 [New York] votes will go to Lyndon Johnson and then you'll get them all back on the second ballot. I said to hell with that; we're going to win it on the first ballot. So, you know, it was all that kind of business. There wasn't any place that was stable."[59] That was certainly the way it seemed at the time.

If Kennedy did not win at once, there might have been, as O'Donnell later contended, some strength held in reserve, but there were also delegates, as in Pennsylvania, who would have left him after the first ballot. The main threat, the Kennedys had no doubt, was Johnson. Stevenson aroused far more emotion among the people who flocked around the sports arena. But the operation organized on his behalf consisted not just of true believers, like Eleanor Roosevelt, Herbert Lehman, Thomas Finletter, James Doyle, George Ball; but of surprising newcomers, like Hubert Humphrey and Eugene McCarthy, who were thought to be for Johnson but had unexpectedly declared for Stevenson after they arrived in Los Angeles. The Stevenson drive at the convention therefore struck many of us, from Reuther and Rauh to Robert Kennedy, as a Johnson front, organized to prevent a Kennedy nomination on the first ballot. If it succeeded, Johnson, with his southern delegates and his potential support among northern bosses, appeared far more likely to benefit than Stevenson, a two-time loser with few delegates.

The atmosphere in Los Angeles was ill tempered. John Connally of Texas announced in a press conference that Kennedy had Addison's disease and was physically unfit for the Presidency. Johnson himself was even uglier in private. He described Kennedy to Peter Lisagor of the *Chicago Daily News* as a "little scrawny fellow with rickets." "Have you ever seen his ankles?" he asked. "They're about so round," and he traced a minute circle with his finger. Lisagor passed this on to Robert Kennedy.[60] In public Johnson attacked Joseph Kennedy as an appeaser and, by implication, pro-Nazi, bellowing: "I was never any Chamberlain umbrella policy man. I never thought Hitler was right."[61] When Johnson challenged Kennedy to a debate before the Texas delegation early in convention week, the ambassador, who was ensconced in Marion Davies's estate, told John Seigenthaler as they sat around the swimming pool that Jack would be "a damned fool if he goes near him." Jean Kennedy Smith said, "I know, Daddy, but he's challenged him to a debate"; and to Seigenthaler, "You'll see. That's the way they are. He'll debate him." In a few moments the flash came by radio that Kennedy had accepted the challenge. The ambassador did not look back for a minute; "he will absolutely take this fellow apart."[62]

Everyone who attended the Kennedy staff meetings at room 8315 in the Biltmore remembers the electric impression made by Robert Kennedy, a slight and boyish figure, jacket off, tie loose, climbing on a chair to call his troops to order, stating the tasks of the day with a singular combination of authority, incisiveness, humor and charm. Keeping track of delegates was an arduous job. On Tuesday, when Kennedy announced that the group would meet at eight the next morning, one member mildly suggested making it later; "I didn't get back to my hotel until five, and it's the third night in a row." Kennedy, who probably had not slept at all, fixed him with a cold eye and said, "Look, nobody asked you here. You're not getting paid anything. If this is too tough for you, let us know and we'll get somebody else." Yet, when Joseph Tydings of Maryland misjudged the situation in Delaware and, by agreeing to a unit rule, lost the state to Johnson, he went at once to the Biltmore to tell Robert Kennedy he had blown Delaware. Kennedy said, "The important thing is that you told me right away so that we knew it, so that we're not counting on them. Next time you'll be a little bit wiser."[63]

On Wednesday, the critical day, "he ran through the states," I noted in my journal, "in order to get the rockbottom Kennedy tally. Once again, I was impressed with the sharpness of his direction of the campaign. He insisted practically on the name, address and telephone number of every half-vote. 'I don't want generalities or guesses,' he would say. 'There's no point in our fooling ourselves. I want the cold facts. I want to hear only the votes we are guaranteed to get on the first ballot.'" The count showed 740—21 short of a majority. He concluded crisply: "We can't miss a trick in the next twelve hours. If we don't win tonight, we're dead."[64]

VII

They won that night. The next problem was the Vice Presidency. There has been much speculation as to why and how John Kennedy chose Lyndon Johnson. Early in 1965 Robert Kennedy read my account in the first draft of *A Thousand Days*—an account I had based in part on a memorandum written shortly after the event by Philip L. Graham. In 1960 Graham, the publisher of the *Washington Post* and one of the most brilliant and attractive men of my generation, had served as an intermediary between Johnson and Kennedy, both of whom he knew intimately.[65] Bobby shook his head and said that the Graham memorandum was a reasonable version of things as Graham saw them but that Phil didn't know the real story. "If the indication in the Graham memorandum is what I interpreted from it, that the President had the thought of Lyndon Johnson as Vice President prior to his own nomination other than just passing through his mind, that's not true."[66]

John Kennedy's first thought after his own nomination, his brother told me, was "how terrible it was that he only had twenty-four hours to select a Vice President. He really hadn't thought about it at all. He said what a mistake it was when it was such an important position that you only had twenty-four hours to think about it." I asked why it had not been thought about earlier. "Because we didn't know, you know—we wanted to just try and get the nomination. . . . To keep everybody happy and to keep in contact with everybody, as you remember, it was just a hell of an operation, so we weren't even thinking about [the Vice Presidency]."

"Keeping everybody happy," I take it, was a term of art. Presidential candidates always prefer to keep the vice presidential situation fluid until their own nomination is assured. Key political figures who are led to think they might be under consideration for the Vice Presidency can be helpful in tight spots. Beyond such time-honored tactics, however, John Kennedy unquestionably had given serious, if fragmentary, thought to the second place in the weeks before the convention. He had asked Walter Reuther and Jack Conway to talk to Humphrey about going on the ticket,[67] and he told Galbraith and me at Hyannis Port on June 12 that he was for Humphrey.[68] After Humphrey repeatedly declined to meet with Reuther, Kennedy told Clark Clifford toward the end of June that Symington was his first choice and repeated this to Clifford in Los Angeles.[69] John Seigenthaler, who saw a good deal of Robert Kennedy during the convention, had the "distinct impression" that Robert was also for Symington and wrote for the *Nashville Tennessean* that Symington was the probable choice.[70] Early in the convention labor decided to back Symington.[71]

Actually Robert had reservations about Symington. Edwin Guthman, who came down from Seattle to cover the convention, asked about his own senator, Henry Jackson, another veteran of the Investigations Subcommittee. "He's my choice," Kennedy said, "and Jack likes him. I'd say he and Symington have the strongest chance. Orville Freeman is another possibility. It depends on how things develop." He added that Jackson would have to convince leaders like Mayor Daley of Chicago, Governor Lawrence of Pennsylvania and John Bailey that he could help the ticket the most. "We've told him that, and he understands it. I hope he can do it."[72] As for Freeman, Bobby told me in 1965 that John Kennedy had liked and respected him but did not think he would help the ticket.

Humphrey finally eliminated himself on Tuesday when he went back on the understanding that he would endorse Kennedy.* This left Symington, Jackson, Freeman—all men sufficiently acceptable to the liberals and labor. The one name that no one ever mentioned was Lyndon Johnson. Quite the contrary: the Kennedy people told everyone as categorically as possible that he was not in the picture. "The labor people had warned me repeatedly that they did not want Johnson on the Kennedy ticket," O'Donnell has written. "I had promised them that there was no chance of such a choice. We had given the same assurance, with Kennedy's knowledge, to wavering liberal delegates during the movement earlier in the week to draft Stevenson."[73] This expressed the understanding in the Kennedy headquarters. "There was *never* any talk in the office," wrote Evelyn Lincoln, Kennedy's secretary, "that Mr. Johnson was to be the running-mate."[74]

On Monday, Philip Graham and Joseph Alsop had put the case for Johnson to Kennedy. Kennedy seemed to agree—"so immediately," Graham wrote, "as to leave me doubting the easy triumph." When Graham passed the word on to James Rowe of Johnson's staff, Rowe dismissed it as a traditional and transparent attempt to coax a rival out of the race—a view taken by Johnson himself, who said impatiently that he supposed the same message was going out to all the candidates.[75] Graham in the meantime encouraged the *Post* to report that Kennedy would probably offer the Vice Presidency to Johnson. When the *Post* containing this word was delivered to the District of Columbia delegation, Joseph Rauh, who had been laboring prodigiously to keep black delegates in line for Kennedy, went in some agitation to see Robert Kennedy. Kennedy assured him, as he had before, that it would definitely not be Johnson.

On Wednesday evening, after the presidential nomination, John Kennedy told his brother "that he was going to go offer [the Vice Presidency] to Lyndon Johnson the first thing in the morning." He made clear that this was entirely *pro forma*. "The idea that he'd go

---

* The day before, I had sent Kennedy a memorandum, now for some reason in Theodore H. White's possession, arguing that Humphrey's nomination would be the surest way of enlisting the Stevensonians in the campaign.

down to offer him the nomination in hopes that he'd take the nomination is not true," Robert Kennedy told me in 1965. "The reason he went down and offered him the nomination is because he thought that he should offer him the nomination; because there were enough indications from others that he wanted to be offered the nomination, . . . *but he never dreamt that there was a chance in the world that he would accept it.*"

On Thursday morning John Kennedy made the offer. "I was up in his room when he came back," Robert Kennedy continued, "and he said, 'You just won't believe it.' I said, 'What?' and he said, 'He wants it,' and I said, 'Oh, my God!' He said, 'Now what do we do?' . . . We both promised each other that we'd never tell what happened—but we spent the rest of the day alternating between thinking it was good and thinking that it wasn't good that he'd offered him the Vice Presidency, and how could he get out of it."

The offer caused consternation in Kennedy's immediate circle. When O'Donnell heard the news, "I was so furious that I could hardly talk. I thought of the promises we had made to the labor leaders and the civil rights groups. . . . I felt that we had been doublecrossed." He told Robert Kennedy that it was a "disaster" and John Kennedy that it was "the worst mistake" he ever made; "in your first move after you get the nomination, you go against all the people who supported you." Pierre Salinger joined the protest. John Kennedy became pale with anger, so evidently wounded that it took a moment before he could collect himself. He said that the nomination had been offered but not yet accepted. He added: "If we win, it will be by a small margin and I won't be able to live with Lyndon Johnson as the leader of a small majority in the Senate. Did it occur to you that if Lyndon becomes the Vice President, I'll have Mike Mansfield as the leader in the Senate, somebody I can trust and depend on?"[76] This was the rationalization that, Robert Kennedy later told me, the Kennedys found most persuasive—the thought that Johnson "would be so mean as Majority Leader—that it was much better having him as Vice President where you could control him."

At eleven o'clock a labor group—Reuther, Arthur Goldberg, Jack Conway, Alex Rose—came to see Kennedy. "When we went in," Conway said later, "Bob was there, and he obviously was very distressed. Ken O'Donnell looked like a ghost. Jack Kennedy was very nervous. It was obvious that they were going to convey some information to us that we weren't going to like." John Kennedy made the argument he had made to O'Donnell, adding that all he had done was to make Johnson an offer: "I don't see any reason in the world why he would want it." Conway said to Robert Kennedy, "We've come a long way. If you do this, you're going to fuck everything up."[77]

VIII

It was, Robert told John Bartlow Martin in 1964, "the most indecisive time we ever had.... We changed our minds eight times during the course of it."[78] "Finally," he told me, "we decided by about two o'clock that we'd try to get him out of there and not have him because Jack thought he would be unpleasant with him, associated with him, and if he could get him to withdraw and still be happy, that would be fine."

Robert Kennedy thereupon saw Johnson twice—first to feel him out; then, after further consultation, to ask him to withdraw. Subsequently he described their talk to me:

> There were just the two of us. He was seated on the couch and I was seated on his right. I remember the whole conversation.... This was the famous conversation in which Phil Graham says I went down by myself and on my own.... Obviously with the close relationship between my brother and I, I wasn't going down to see if he would withdraw just as a lark on my own—"my brother's asleep so I'll go see if I can get rid of his Vice President"—you know, that's what flabbergasted me about Phil Graham's memorandum.... So I said, "There's going to be a lot of opposition"—this was what we worked out, that I'd tell him there was going to be a lot of opposition, that it was going to be unpleasant, that it was going to focus attention, and we were going to have trouble with the liberals... and the President didn't think that he wanted to go through that kind of an unpleasant fight.

Instead Robert Kennedy proposed that Johnson become chairman of the national committee.

> The President wanted him to play an important role and he could run the party—the idea being that to run the party he could get a lot of his own people in; and then if he wanted to be President after eight years or something, he could have the machinery where he could run for President or do whatever he wanted. I mean that was sort of the idea at the time. We didn't really know whether he'd want to go through with it, and, in any case, the President wanted to get rid of him.

As Kennedy spoke his lines, Johnson, he said,

> burst into tears. I mean, it was my feeling at that time, although I've seen

him afterwards look so sad I don't know whether it was just an act.* . . . He is one of the greatest sad-looking people in the world—you know, he can turn that on. . . . But he just shook and tears came into his eyes, and he said, "I want to be Vice President, and, if the President will have me, I'll join with him in making a fight for it." So it was that kind of a conversation. I said, "Well, then that's fine. He wants you to be Vice President if you want to be Vice President."

Here the Graham and Kennedy recollections diverge. Graham remembered his calling John Kennedy, Kennedy's reassuring Graham ("Bobby's been out of touch and doesn't know what's been happening"), reassuring Johnson, then speaking to his brother. Robert remembered returning to his brother's room. John Kennedy told him, "'I just got a call from Clark Clifford or somebody saying that "this is disastrous. You've got to take him." I'm going to make an announcement in five minutes.' . . . But during that whole three or four hours, we just vacillated back and forth as to whether we wanted him or not . . . and one time we wanted him and one time we didn't want him and finally we decided not to have him, and we came upon this idea of trying to get rid of him, and it didn't work." "The only people who were involved in the discussion," he told John Bartlow Martin, ". . . were Jack and myself. Nobody else was involved in it."[79]

It was a hard day. According to Bobby Baker, secretary of the Senate and Johnson's *homme de confiance,* the new vice presidential candidate, "as soon as his performance was over . . . spoke of Robert Kennedy in terms of 'that little shitass' and worse." Robert Kennedy said to James Rowe, "My God, this wouldn't have happened except that we were all too tired last night. Don't you think this is a terrible mistake? Don't you think Stuart Symington should be the candidate?"[80] Bobby's old friend Charles Spalding said, "That was a real surprise." "Charlie, we really weren't at our best this time," Robert Kennedy replied. "We were all too tired."[81] "Yesterday was the best day of my life," he said to Charles Bartlett, "and today was the worst day." A year later he said enigmatically to Seigenthaler, "We were right at eight, ten and two and wrong at four."[82]

That evening they dined with their father. The sun was setting, and Robert Kennedy's children were splashing in a fountain in front of

---

* Robert Kennedy's surmise was doubtless correct. Carl Rowan, who served in the Kennedy and Johnson administrations, remembers Johnson crying in his presence as he told a story. "He looked me in the eyes and said, 'You know, a man ain't worth a damn if he can't cry at the right time'" (Carl Rowan, "Accenting the Positive," *New York Post,* June 16, 1976).

Marion Davies's house. Mr. Kennedy, in a velvet smoking jacket, stood grandly in the doorway, his hands clasped behind his back, as John Kennedy drove up. He had had nothing to do with the Johnson decision, despite later stories to the contrary, nor is it easy to imagine why he should have intervened in favor of Johnson on Thursday after having been called pro-Nazi by Johnson on Tuesday. But, as usual, he exuded confidence in his sons. "Don't worry, Jack," he said. "Within two weeks they'll be saying it's the smartest thing you ever did."[83]

IX

Robert Kennedy had no patience with the theory expounded by Richard Nixon, the Republican candidate, of "peaks" and "rhythms" in a campaign. His formula was simple: "run and fight and scramble for ten weeks all the way." Once, when Theodore White was chatting with a couple of Kennedy aides in the Washington headquarters, the manager, tieless and in shirtsleeves, burst into the cramped office. "What are you doing?" he cried. "What are we all doing? Let's get on the road. Let's get on the road tomorrow! I want us all on the road tomorrow!" He slammed the door and disappeared without waiting for an answer.[84]

Action was one principle of his politics. Another was what Seigenthaler, who became his assistant, called "the Kennedy theory . . . embrace your enemies and broaden your base of support."[85] This theory was in my experience rather more characteristic of the Kennedy *modus operandi* than the usual notion that they were a clan of Irish haters. The offer to Johnson was a spectacular example. The morning after Kennedy's nomination, I began urging the importance of bringing the Stevenson people into the campaign. Robert Kennedy listened patiently, then put his hand on my knee and said, "Arthur, human nature requires that you allow us forty-eight hours. Adlai has given us a rough time over the last three days. In forty-eight hours I will do anything you want, but right now I don't want to hear about the Stevensonians. You have to allow for human nature."[86] In a short while he had James Doyle, who ran the Stevenson campaign, Eugene McCarthy and me carrying the message to the Stevenson loyalists of southern California. Eventually most of the Stevenson leaders and even Johnson's John Connally received jobs in the Kennedy administration.

Robert's tactics were flexible. Where the state organization seemed strong, he worked with it. Where it was weak, he worked through the Citizens for Kennedy Committee, headed by Byron White of Colorado. White, an all-American football player, PT-boat veteran and Rhodes Scholar, represented a combination of accomplishments irresistible to the Kennedys. Robert even wanted to make him chairman of the national committee. ("Bobby Kennedy displayed a naiveté at times that was downright astonishing," O'Donnell commented with disapproval.)[87] Henry Jackson, disappointed in his hope for the Vice Presidency, got the job.

New York, still in 1960 the most populous state, was vital. Robert harshly told the New York Reform Democrats, in the presence of such properly revered figures as Herbert Lehman and Thomas K. Finletter, to drop their feuds and get together with the regulars: "Gentlemen, I don't give a damn if the state and county organizations survive after November, and I don't give a damn if *you* survive. I want to elect John F. Kennedy."[88] The tone was offensive but effective. He sent William Walton, urbane and shrewd, to pull the Kennedy operation together in the city. He sent Paul Corbin to get things moving upstate. Professor Richard Wade, the Kennedy coordinator in the Rochester area, told Corbin he had to stop promising the embassy in Ecuador; he had already offered it to three people; there were nineteen republics down there, and he could at least spread his offers around.[89]

Kennedy traveled from state to state lashing local Democrats into activity. Ralph (Rip) Horton, the Kennedy coordinator in Nebraska, had gone to Choate with John Kennedy (whom he had joined in inventing an underground society called the Muckers) and had known Robert as a little boy. Now Robert was appalled by the scantiness of the Nebraska crowds. "Bobby gave me an extremely hard time as a result of it," Horton later recalled. "I stood at the foot of his bed as he lay and relaxed one evening before dinner and he said, 'Rip, can you possibly explain what goes on here to me?' I had no explanation and I felt like I did when I was a Mucker and they were throwing me out of Choate."[90]

Joseph Tydings, the Florida coordinator, saw Robert Kennedy castigate the mayor of Jacksonville, telling him in effect "that we knew he was cutting us, and by God we didn't like it, and that we were going to hold him accountable if we lost Duval County and not for him one minute to think that he was getting away with anything. . . . That shook the hell out of him." Kennedy, said Tydings, was "absolutely strong, steel-willed, didn't mind telling a mayor of a city or governor or anyone else what he thought if he stepped out of line. He just was blunt and hard and tough and was of course a magnificent campaign manager." Tydings added that Kennedy only got rough at the top; "he was never unkind or inconsiderate of anybody who was down in the lower echelon"; he was "fantastic" with volunteers, particularly with women and with the young.[91]

California was, as ever, chaos. The fight between the regulars, organized by the forceful professional Jesse Unruh, and the liberals, led by Thomas Braden, then a newspaper publisher in Oceanside, was more than usually embittered. Joan Braden thought Kennedy "the most terrific man to work for that I've ever known. His decisions were made [clap] like that. You went in and you said, 'I would like to do boom, boom, boom, boom.' And he'd say, 'Do this, do this. Don't do this. And do this.' Over. . . . If he said 'No' and you wanted to do it, he would listen; and he might change, but he didn't want you to stay in there an hour and go over and over it."[92]

His campaign role crystallized the impression of Robert Kennedy many had taken from Rackets Committee days—hard, unforgiving, "ruthless." "Little Brother is Watching You," aggrieved Democrats warned each other. "He has all the patience of a vulture," a Washington journalist said, "without any of the dripping sentimentality."[93] Norman Mailer was reminded of those unreconstructed Irishmen from Kirkland House he had faced in Harvard intramural football games. You said hello as you lined up for scrimmage after kickoff, "and his type would nod and look away, one rock glint of recognition your due for living across the hall from one another all through your Freshman year, and then bang, as the ball was passed back, you'd get a bony king-hell knee in the crotch."[94]

Bobby didn't care. "I'm not running a popularity contest," he told Hugh Sidey of *Time*. "It doesn't matter if they like me or not. Jack can be nice to them. . . . Somebody has to be able to say no. If people are not getting off their behinds and working enough, how do you say that nicely? Every time you make a decision in this business you make somebody mad."[95]

His brother watched all this carefully and admiringly. Once he sent Robert to call on Harry Truman. The former President gave the young campaign manager a genial scolding. "You should learn to moderate your attitude in your dealings with people. I've heard some stories about how you react." Everybody, Truman said, thought Robert Kennedy a son of a bitch. "I understand that," Truman added, "because everybody thinks I'm a son of a bitch." He counseled Kennedy to stop doing things that made people angry. Kennedy protested that the stories were exaggerated; he was not such a monster.[96] But he did not relent. (Nor did he convince Truman, who said the next year: "I just don't like that boy, and I never will. He worked for old Joe McCarthy, you know, and when old Joe was tearing up the Constitution and the country, that boy couldn't say enough for him.")[97]

John Kennedy recognized that a campaign required a son of a bitch—and that it could not be the candidate. Robert was prepared to do what the candidate should not have done. Stewart Alsop called it a "sweet-and-sour brother act, Jack uses his charm and waves the carrot and then Bobby wades in with the big stick."[98] "Every politician in Massachusetts," John Kennedy said, "was mad at Bobby after 1952 but we had the best organization in history."[99]

X

The most celebrated incident in the campaign, next to the debates with Nixon and the discussion of church and state before the Houston Ministerial Association, was Kennedy's phone call to Martin Luther King, Jr.

The initial Kennedy interest in Negro affairs was political. The brothers had been entirely devoid of racial prejudice but only intermittently sensitive to racial injustice. The debate over the Civil Rights Act of 1957 had begun John Kennedy's education. Robert Kennedy was busy elsewhere. His own response to discrimination had always been in individual terms: the black football player at Harvard; Ralph Bunche at Charlottesville; a young witness before the Rackets Committee. "If he was a white fellow," Robert had noted in his journal, "and had a chance for an education he would do extremely well. McClellan, for some reason, got furious with him and threw the various union cards in his face. Poor old Sonie's eyes filled up with tears and sweat appeared on his forehead and his voice got lower and lower. I felt very sorry for him."[100] But Robert Kennedy had not generalized the few cases that had come his way into an encompassing national problem.

In 1959 John Kennedy was ready to welcome what white southern support he could get. When Robert Kennedy made a trip into the Confederacy, his brother charged him to recall that, on two crucial civil rights roll calls in 1957 where "the friends and foes of the South split," Kennedy had voted with Lyndon Johnson while Humphrey and Symington had voted for the north.[101] At the same time, the

Kennedys fully intended to stand for civil rights in the north, and believed they could do so without undue harm to their southern prospects. "Obviously they are going to make a fight on the civil rights problem," Robert Kennedy noted after talks with white leaders in Georgia and Virginia in November 1959, "but I think that they have pretty much decided they will stay with the Democratic Party."[102]

The primaries began to alter John Kennedy's attitude, though politics was still the dominant note. He told me in May that he had learned a lot in West Virginia. He had carried the black vote, he said, simply because Senator Robert Byrd, an ex-Klansman, had backed Humphrey. "This proved to me that it's absolutely fatal to have southern support. I want to be nominated by the liberals. I don't want to go screwing around with all those southern bastards."[103] Soon Robert Kennedy, alarmed by what he deemed an excessively antisouthern tone in one of his brother's public statements, sent him an admonitory memorandum: "I think it should be clarified that what you said was that you feel that you will be nominated without Southern votes—not that you are not interested in having votes in the South. Otherwise, this is going to look like a gratuitous insult to the Southern political leaders who have been interested in you. . . . This should be straightened out today if possible."[104]

Southern concern was not dispelled. In May the candidate had asked Sargent Shriver to organize a civil rights section in the campaign. Shriver brought in Harris Wofford, an ardent young law professor, recommended by Chester Bowles and Father Theodore Hesburgh, as civil rights coordinator. "We really don't know much about this whole thing," Robert Kennedy told Wofford. ". . . I haven't known many Negroes in my life. . . . It's up to you. Tell us where we are and go to it."[105] Shriver and Wofford went to it, and so in due course did Robert Kennedy. Discussing civil rights with southern delegates in Los Angeles, the campaign manager finally said, "My, you've got a lot of cantankerous politicians in the south, haven't you?" A southern voice from the back of the room: "What the hell do you think you Boston Irish are?"[106]

At the convention, Bowles, as chairman of the resolutions committee, drafted with Wofford a "maximum" civil rights plank designed to be used for negotiating purposes. In one of those morning meetings at the Biltmore, Robert told the Kennedy organizers that this was "the best civil rights plank the Democratic party has ever had" and directed them to carry the word that the Kennedy forces were "unequivocally" for it. "Those of you who are dealing with southern delegations make it absolutely clear how we stand on civil rights. Don't fuzz it up. Tell the southern states that we hope they will see other reasons why we are united as Democrats and why they should support Kennedy, but don't let there be doubt anywhere as to how the Kennedy people stand on this." Wofford, astonished, felt like crying out to Kennedy that the plank was beyond where they really wanted to go; they had written it expecting it to be cut down. "When I finally got to Bowles to tell him that the Kennedy word was out to support his *maximum* plank, he couldn't believe it."[107] The southern Democratic seigneurs communed gloomily with each other. "Dick Russell [of Georgia] told me today," Harry F. Byrd of Virginia wrote James F. Byrnes of South Carolina a month after the convention, "that Kennedy will implement the Democratic platform and advocate Civil Rights legislation beyond what is contained in the platform."[108]

XI

On October 19, 1960, Dr. Martin Luther King, Jr., the Baptist preacher who had emerged as the most eloquent southern leader in the battle for racial justice, was arrested in Atlanta for sitting in in a department store. Six months before he had received a suspended sentence and probation for a minor traffic transgression in DeKalb County, Georgia. Though the Atlanta authorities released him, the DeKalb County judge seized the opportunity to sentence him to four months of hard labor for violating probation.

The sentence was frightening to all who knew what hard labor in Georgia might mean, especially for uppity blacks. "The death of Martin King in the state public works camp," wrote the black novelist John A. Williams, "was imminent."[109] Nor was lynching, the traditional Georgia remedy, beyond possibility. King's wife, who was five months pregnant, was wild with concern—all the more so when King was brusquely awakened at four-thirty one morning, put in handcuffs and leg chains, removed from the county jail, transported along dark country roads and deposited in a penetentiary deep in rural Georgia.

Wofford drafted a statement of protest for Kennedy. Then Governor Ernest Vandiver of Georgia begged the candidate not to issue it; it would be politically disastrous in the south, and he would get King out himself. But nothing happened. Mrs. King called Wofford in despair; she was, Wofford said, "terribly hysterical." Wofford thought it might be a good idea for John Kennedy to speak to her. Louis Martin, the wise black newspaperman from Chicago, also working in the civil rights section, agreed. At first they could not reach Kennedy. Wofford meanwhile told the story to Bowles. "I'll call her," Bowles said, "and as a matter of fact I'll have Adlai call her. He's here for dinner." Mrs. King phoned Wofford the next morning to say how wonderful Bowles was to call. She did not mention Stevenson. Bowles later told Wofford, "I tried my best to get Adlai to talk to her but he said he just couldn't possibly, he'd never been introduced to her."

Wofford finally reached Shriver, who tracked down Kennedy in a motel in the Chicago airport. As has often been told, Shriver waited for everyone else to leave the room, fearing that general discussion would kill the idea. Kennedy at once asked Shriver to get Mrs. King on the phone. Later in the day, as the party was arriving in Detroit, he said casually to Salinger, "By the way, I talked to Mrs. King this morning."

Robert Kennedy's initial reaction was very different. He called in Wofford and Martin and gave them hell. "You bombthrowers probably lost the election," he said. Three southern governors had told him that, if his brother were to say a good word for Jimmy Hoffa, N. S. Khrushchev or Martin Luther King, it would end Kennedy hopes in the south. "You've probably lost three states and . . . the civil rights section isn't going to do another damn thing in this campaign."

At the same time he was personally angered by the judge's refusal to grant bail to Dr. King. He wondered whether he ought not call the judge and protest. Might this not, he asked John Seigenthaler of Nashville, now his campaign assistant, draw some of the fire from his brother? Seigenthaler, who had been hearing all day from southern leaders about John Kennedy's phone call, thought it a poor idea. One more Kennedy shock might be too much for the south. Robert was scheduled to speak in New York that afternoon. Seigenthaler drove him to the airport, confident that he had been dissuaded from calling the judge.

Later in the day the wire services began querying the headquarters about a story that a brother of the senator had called the judge and asked for King's release. Edward Kennedy was far away on the west coast. Everyone knew how Robert felt. Seigenthaler told Roger Tubby of the press section to deny the story. Later Robert phoned in. "Guess what that crazy judge says in Georgia?" Seigenthaler said. "He says you called him about King not getting bail." Kennedy (long pause): "Did he say that?" Seigenthaler: "Yes, but don't worry, I had Tubby put out a denial." Kennedy: "Well, you better get him to retract it." Seigenthaler said, "I can't believe it." Kennedy said, "Yes, it just burned me all the way up here on the plane. It grilled me. The more I thought about the injustice of it, the more I thought what a son of a bitch that judge was. I made it clear to him that it was not a political call; that I am a lawyer, one who believes in the right of all defendants to make bond and one who had seen the rights of defendants misused in various ways . . . and I wanted to make it clear that I opposed this. I felt it was disgraceful." The conversation, Kennedy added, was restrained and calm; he had not been angry nor the judge hostile. The next day King was released.[110]

The brothers, in making their phone calls, had acted independently of each other. "The finest strategies," John Kennedy observed to John Kenneth Galbraith in this connection, "are usually the result of accidents."[111] King himself remarked when liberated, "There are moments when the politically expedient is the morally wise," and declined to endorse Kennedy.[112] His father, however, said, "I'll take a Catholic or the Devil himself if he'll wipe the tears from my daughter-in-law's eyes. I've got a suitcase full of votes—my whole church—for . . . Senator Kennedy."[113] (Kennedy remarked later of Daddy King, "He said he was going to vote against me because I was a Catholic, but that since I called his daughter-in-law he will vote for me. . . . That was a hell of a bigoted statement, wasn't it? Imagine Martin Luther King having a bigot for a father." Then he smiled and said lightly, "Well, we all have fathers, don't we.")[114]

After the election, which John Kennedy may well have won because of the black vote, Murray Kempton asked Robert Kennedy whether he was glad he had called King's judge. "Sure I'm glad," Robert Kennedy said, "but I would hope I'm not glad for the reason you think I'm glad."[115]

XII

"Bobby Kennedy holds his head down and looks up through his eyebrows like a coon peering out of a henhouse," wrote Eugene Patterson in the *Atlanta Constitution*. ". . . Throw an arm around those shoulders and the big white teeth might snap at you. . . . A Southerner is a warm-blooded soul who likes his potlikker and his politics hot. The Kennedys are chill dishes indeed. But you feel that they know what to do in a hot fight."[116]

He drove himself relentlessly. George McGovern, running for the Senate in South Dakota, called to say that he was falling behind;

could the national committee send someone out to help. Robert Kennedy knew that McGovern was in trouble because of his staunch support of John Kennedy in an anti-Catholic state. To McGovern's astonishment he flew out to South Dakota himself on the Friday before the election. "South Dakota had four electoral votes; it was obvious they wouldn't go to John Kennedy; and it was obvious that I was behind—probably a losing candidate; and yet . . . yet he came out." After a series of speeches, they sent him back to Chicago on a bitterly cold, windy night, in a lightweight plane with an inexperienced pilot, a local doctor. "He didn't complain."[117]

He never complained, never relaxed, rarely slept. "We can rest in November," he said. By October he was thin, weary, deep gray circles under his eyes, his shoulders slumped with fatigue. "He's living on nerves," John Kennedy said. "Jack works as hard as any mortal man can," said their father. "Bobby goes a little further."[118] Once the two brothers ran into each other at a windswept airport. "Hi, Johnny," said Robert Kennedy. "How are you?" "Man, I'm tired," said the candidate. "What the hell are you tired for?" said the campaign manager. "I'm doing all the work."[119] "I don't have to think about organization," John Kennedy said later. "I just show up. . . . He's the hardest worker. He's the greatest organizer. . . . Bobby's easily the best man I've ever seen."[120]

XIII

"We need someone," Henry Kissinger had told me just before Labor Day, "who will take a big jump—not just improve on existing trends but produce a new frame of mind, a new national atmosphere. If Kennedy debates with Nixon on who can best manage the status quo, he is lost. The issue is not one technical program or another. The issue is a new epoch. If we get a new epoch and a new spirit, the technical programs will take care of themselves."[121]

This, as we saw it, was the issue in 1960. Election night found the Kennedys back in Hyannis Port. The evening began cheerfully enough. Then it sank into an endless strain of uncertainty. By midnight people were wandering restlessly, almost grimly, around the communications center in Robert Kennedy's house. Around three in the morning the atmosphere lightened. Pennsylvania and Michigan looked fairly definite. At three-fifteen Robert Kennedy told his brother to go to bed and sleep well: they had won. But there was no word from Nixon. John Kennedy strolled with Cornelius Ryan across the dark lawn between the houses in the compound. Ryan thought he heard Kennedy say, "I'm angry," and supposed that the awful wait had finally snapped the imperturbable composure. Later, when Theodore White put the story in the manuscript of his book, Kennedy told White, "That isn't what I said in the dark. What I said was, 'I'm hungry.'"[122]

After breakfast the Kennedys met informally with some of the staff at the ambassador's house. More than a third of the states were going one way or another by 2 percent of the vote or less. They expected that Nixon would challenge the results. John Kennedy was calm. If he won by a single electoral vote, it would be enough, and he proposed to go forward on the assumption that he had been elected President of the United States.* Finally they heard that Nixon had scheduled a press conference in Los Angeles. Herbert Klein emerged on Nixon's behalf and read a curt concession. Someone at Hyannis Port observed that Nixon might at least have had the decency to appear

---

* Pierre Salinger, in recorded interview by Theodore H. White, July 19, 1965, 101–104, JFK Oral History Program. Out of nearly 69 million votes cast, Kennedy had a plurality of 120,000, but he had a lead of 84 votes in the electoral college. A legend subsequently arose that Mayor Daley of Chicago put Kennedy over by stealing the election in Illinois. The margin in Illinois was less than 9000, and the Cook County machine was unquestionably skilled in producing Democratic votes out of vacant lots and graveyards. So were the Republicans downstate. One can assume that in Illinois one party stole as many votes as the other. When the Illinois count was challenged, the state electoral board, which was 4–1 Republican, voted unanimously to certify the Kennedy electors (see the AP story by Don McLeod, "Did the Democrats Steal It in 1960?" *New York Post*, July 12, 1973).

Even if Illinois had gone to Nixon, Kennedy would still have won by 276 to 246 in the electoral college. Nixon would have had to carry Texas as well to get a majority. While there were probably irregularities in Texas, Kennedy's margin of 47,000 votes was too great to be reasonably attributed to fraud or acceptably reversed by a recount.

The more difficult question, applying, however, only to the popular vote, was raised by Alabama. The Republican ticket elector slate received 238,000 votes. The Democratic slate consisted of six unpledged and five Kennedy-pledged electors. The unpledged electors voted for Harry F. Byrd in the electoral college. It is impossible to determine what Kennedy's popular vote in Alabama was. If the Kennedy electors were credited with 5/11 of the popular vote, the remaining 6/11 being allocated to a national unpledged elector vote, then the state totals would read: Nixon, 238,000; unpledged, 177,000; Kennedy, 147,000—and Nixon would have won the popular vote by 58,000. (For calculations, see *Congressional Quarterly*, February 17, 1961, and Neal R. Pierce, *The People's President* [New York, 1968], 102–104.) Kennedy would still have won in the electoral college. The possibility of the popular-vote winner losing in the electoral college argues for a reform of the present (1978) system, though not, in my judgment, for a shift to direct popular election. For a proposed change retaining a reformed electoral system while attaining the objectives of direct popular election, see the Twentieth Century Fund task force report "Reform of the Presidential Election Process" (New York, 1978).

himself and thank the people who had voted for him. John Kennedy said, "He went out the way he came in—no class."[123]

Victory was accompanied no doubt by apprehension. Earlier in the autumn Walter Reuther and Jack Conway had come to Hyannis Port. Kennedy suggested they take a swim. It was a crisp fall day, but the sun was warm, and the labor men sat pleasantly on the beach talking with Jacqueline Kennedy. "She really was obsessed," Conway said later, "with this whole idea of the change in her life, the change in Kennedy's life, and how do you protect against assassinations." Gunmen had tried to kill Walter Reuther in 1948 and Victor Reuther in 1949. Jacqueline wondered what security precautions did to family life. Don't let the precautions run your life, Reuther said; you can't stop living.[124]

Such thoughts were now set aside. In the afternoon the President-elect played touch football. He went down for a pass, and someone ran into him, and he fell to the ground. "That's my brother," said Robert Kennedy, who had called the play, "all guts, no brains."[125] A cable arrived from England: ON THE OCCASION OF YOUR ELECTION TO YOUR GREAT OFFICE, it read, I SALUTE YOU. THE THOUGHTS AND SUPPORT OF THE FREE WORLD WILL BE WITH YOU IN THE CHALLENGING TASKS THAT LIE AHEAD. It was signed, WINSTON S. CHURCHILL.[126]

(11)

To the Department of Justice

"WE CAME into this administration without a political obligation," Robert Kennedy recalled in 1964. ". . . I don't mean that people didn't do favors for us and that we wanted to do favors for them. [But] there weren't any promises made to anyone that they would get a job. . . . There were certainly no cabinet positions promised. . . . It was really a fresh slate."[1]

I

On February 9, 1961, he dictated a hasty memorandum about the process of choosing a cabinet. "The toughest decision for all and probably and undoubtedly the most important," he said, "was the selection for Secretary of State."

The President-elect had a clear view, derived from the Roosevelt model, about what he sought in the State Department. "It is the President alone," John Kennedy had said imperially in January 1960 in a speech on the Presidency at the National Press Club, "who must make the major decisions of our foreign policy."[2] He did not want, he now told Robert Lovett, a Secretary of State who would operate a "one-man show" in the style of John Foster Dulles.[3] He was looking for someone who would be wise in counsel, persuasive on the Hill and effective in modernizing what he regarded as an unduly passive and conservative Foreign Service.

> Jack always wanted William Fulbright [Robert Kennedy wrote]. He had worked with Fulbright, knew him better, was very impressed with the way he ran the Senate committee. Prior to the time he was appointed to the Foreign Relations Committee, he thought Fulbright to be rather pompous, opinionated, and didn't like him too much. But after he went on the committee he gained a great respect for him. He didn't know any of the others

that were being considered. . . . It finally came down, the last week, to David Bruce and Dean Rusk and William Fulbright.

I was very strongly against Fulbright. I felt . . . that any time we took a position against any of the nations of Africa, or any time that we would take a position that was unpopular, that the Russians and the others would be able to say, "Well, this is all done because we have a Secretary of State who feels that the white man is superior to the Negro." I said in the last analysis Jack was going to be the Secretary of State; this was a position in which he would be making his own decisions. All he needed was advice and ideas by an expert but the decisions would be made by him and that we'd be unnecessarily burdened by having a man in that job who had this terrible impediment of having signed the Southern Manifesto.*

We had a final discussion about it at the hospital during the christening of young John Kennedy. Charlie Bartlett was there and took the position that Jack could appoint Fulbright. I was extremely strong against it and ultimately prevailed. On the Friday before the selection, Jack was ready to take David Bruce. Arthur Krock was for David Bruce, [as were] Maggie [Marguerite] Higgins [of the *New York Herald Tribune*] and others. Maggie Higgins was for him because she said he was tough with the Russians and would be able to stand up. Nobody knew Dean Rusk particularly. I received word by noon that Robert Lovett was for Dean Rusk so I called up Jack just before he left for Florida and suggested that he call Robert Lovett. It was the conversation with Lovett that convinced him that Dean Rusk should be the selection. The following day he called Dean Rusk and asked him to come down. He came to Florida and the announcement was made the following Sunday afternoon.[4]

Rusk had served in Truman's State Department and was now head of the Rockefeller Foundation. Acheson as well as Lovett backed him. Chester Bowles had recommended him to Kennedy as under secretary. Rusk considered his first meeting with Kennedy a failure—"Kennedy and I could not communicate," he told Bowles immediately afterward[5]—but Kennedy thought him lucid, competent and self-effacing and offered him the job.

In later years Robert Kennedy repented his fight against Fulbright. He also mused over the curious fact that he and his brother had not considered the man who in retrospect would have made the best Secretary of State of all—Averell Harriman. But the Kennedys hardly knew Harriman in 1960. His defeat two years before for reelection as governor of New York was supposed to have ended his career. He was now sixty-nine years old, deaf in one ear, his tall figure a little

---

* The Southern Manifesto of 1956 had attacked the Supreme Court decision calling for school desegregation as a "clear abuse of judicial power" exploited by "outside agitators" and had demanded "a reversal of this decision which is contrary to the Constitution." One hundred one legislators from the old Confederacy had signed it, Fulbright among them. The southern senators who refused were Estes Kefauver and Albert Gore of Tennessee and Lyndon Johnson.

stooped, his mien, now that he was out of power, tinged with melancholy. He was twice Robert Kennedy's age, and even John Kennedy saw him as a figure from the remote Rooseveltian past. Nor was Harriman greatly admired by those of the Roosevelt generation the younger Kennedys knew best. I suppose that Joseph Kennedy thought as little of Harriman (whom Roosevelt had sent to London a few months after Kennedy had departed) as Harriman thought of him. Max Beaverbrook, who had had memorable rows with Harriman during their Moscow mission in 1941,[6] often made cracks about him in subsequent years. After an evening with Beaverbrook in 1958, Robert Kennedy recorded the master's comment on Harriman: "Never has anyone gone so far with so little."*

For such reasons the Kennedys simply did not think of Harriman as a possible Secretary of State. When I mentioned him to John Kennedy on December 1, the President-elect dismissed him as "old hat."[7] A fortnight later I urged him on Robert, who said more sympathetically, "Are you sure that giving Averell a job wouldn't be just an act of sentiment?"[8] Eventually Kennedy made him roving ambassador, considering it a mainly decorative appointment. Both Kennedys changed their minds rapidly, of course, as the old crocodile got his teeth into things. I have often thought that the nation would have escaped much trouble in the 1960s if John Kennedy had chosen Averell Harriman as his Secretary of State.

II

Sargent Shriver [Robert Kennedy wrote in his 1961 memorandum] was responsible for the selection of . . . Robert McNamara.

We were not sure whether we wanted McNamara in the Treasury Department or going in as Secretary of Defense. It was originally thought that maybe [Thomas S.] Gates could stay on as Secretary and possibly I would go in as Under-Secretary. McNamara knew that he had a choice but he wanted to consider it over the weekend. When he came in the following Monday he indicated that he wanted to be Secretary of Defense. By that time Jack had made up his mind that one of the problems in keeping Gates was the fact that the political leaders including David Lawrence of Pennsylvania was concerned that Gates would come and run for Governor in the State of Pennsylvania and so they asked specifically that he not be retained.

The first conversation that Jack had with McNamara, he spoke to him

---

* RFK, handwritten note, 1958, RFK Papers. Beaverbrook must have been laying all about him that night. He said of John Hay Whitney, then American ambassador to London, "There are rumors of his demise but as of this time I understand he has refused to lie down."

about the possibility of hiring Franklin Roosevelt, Jr. McNamara objected saying that the reports he had received on Franklin Roosevelt, Jr., were not very complimentary. Jack said that at least he'd like to have him considered. When McNamara came down on Monday Jack and I both met him. He had a letter with him which he presented to Jack, which set forth that McNamara had complete control over the collection [selection] of those in the Department of Defense. Jack readily agreed as he had agreed verbally before. I put in a plug for Franklin Roosevelt, Jr., but it seemed to go on relatively blank ears.[9]

McNamara preserved his control over Defense appointments with a single exception; "but that wasn't the President's doing," Roswell Gilpatric, the under secretary of defense, said later; "it was Bob Kennedy's doing." Robert Kennedy asked them to find a place for John Kennedy's old PT-boat friend Paul Fay in the Navy Department; and, having turned down Roosevelt for the secretaryship, McNamara decided to accept Fay for the under secretaryship.[10]

As far as the Secretary of the Treasury was concerned [Robert Kennedy recalled in 1961], everybody was considered. I don't think there is any question that the head of the Morgan bank—his name slips me right at the moment [Henry C. Alexander]—would have received the job if during the course of the campaign he hadn't come out as a political supporter of Richard Nixon just after Jack had gone to see him and had spent more than an hour with him. Jack felt that this was a personal insult.

Joe Alsop was a tremendous booster of Douglas Dillon. In view of all the favors that Alsop had done I don't think there's any question that this was a factor. However, obviously if Dillon hadn't shaped up and hadn't impressed Jack the decision would have been quite different.

"My father was opposed," he added in 1964. ". . . He felt he didn't know enough about finances. That's what slowed the President down selecting Dillon."[11]

"There is no question," Robert Kennedy dictated in the 1961 memorandum, "that there was a good deal of pressure on Dillon by Nixon and others—there is no question that they were very angry that he took the job. Politically, it was extremely helpful, because taking Dillon, a Republican, a man of considerable responsibility, . . . buried the idea that the Kennedy Administration was going to pay no attention to their responsibility in the economic field."[12]

III

Stewart Udall [as Secretary of the Interior] was the first position agreed upon. I was a great booster of him as was Teddy. I was a booster despite the introduction Stewart Udall gave me when I spoke in Arizona. There were some rumors around at the time his appointment was being considered that [Senator] Clinton Anderson [of New Mexico, who had been Truman's Secretary of Agriculture] himself was personally interested. Jack called Clinton Anderson after it was virtually agreed that Stewart Udall would be the appointee and Clinton Anderson indicated that he was in fact interested. We were in rather an embarrassing position. We talked it over and the dangers of Clinton Anderson getting in there and putting in cronies and associates, a number of whom we had seen during the course of the campaign who were rather unsavory, unquestionably, and certainly of different viewpoints, different generation, ideas and thoughts as we have. Finally, Jack called him and told him that he just thought that he had to go with Stewart Udall, that he didn't want to make Clinton Anderson give up his Senate position in seniority—it would be too dangerous. Clinton Anderson bought it without any problem or difficulty so Stewart Udall was the first one agreed upon.[13]

Agriculture proved troublesome. The Kennedys were urban types for whom agricultural policy was a mystery. ("I don't want to hear about agricultural policy from any one except you," John Kennedy once said to John Kenneth Galbraith, who had started out as a farm economist, "and I don't want to hear about it from you.") Hubert Humphrey and Stuart Symington pushed a Missouri farm leader named Fred V. Heinkel.

Jack asked me to go in and interview him for a few moments to try to size him up. I asked him if he thought there was any solution to the problem in agriculture and he said that he thought there was, then mentioned as one of the major solutions to sell our surpluses abroad. I then asked what was the answer to the criticism of that made by those who said that it would "glut" the market and then therefore destroy the markets of countries such as the Argentine and Canada who were trying to sell wheat or meat to the same areas. He thought for a moment and said, "Well, that is a problem but I expect there are experts in the Department of Agriculture who had thought about that." . . . He was singularly unimpressive.

We had always considered as the second choice George McGovern but there was a good deal of opposition to him by the members of Congress on the Agricultural Committee. They felt that he did not have the seniority which would warrant such an appointment. This was his biggest problem and then the idea of appointing somebody who had just been defeated as a Congressional candidate was also a problem.

Finally . . . we came back to Orville Freeman because of how impressed everybody was out in Los Angeles with him, his integrity and his vigor. An impossible job. I believe from what I heard that originally he was interested in being Attorney General. I believe that afterwards he felt that somebody had gotten to that position first. . . .

As far as George McGovern is concerned he was disappointed but I had told him right at the beginning that if he didn't get this position he could be head of the Food for Peace [the agency distributing food surpluses abroad under Public Law 480]. I also told him I thought that if he was

To the Department of Justice

interested in ever running for political life again that the Food for Peace was a far better job. He thought the prestige, however, going with the Department of Agriculture would greatly help him in South Dakota. I said that I thought the problems of the Department of Agriculture were insoluble or virtually insoluble and it was rather an unpopular job. . . . He told me afterwards that it finally ended up that he was happy to be over as head of the Food for Peace.[14]

Health, Education and Welfare went to Abe Ribicoff of Connecticut, to whom John Kennedy had originally offered Justice. "Ribicoff didn't want to be Attorney General because he felt that it wouldn't be proper for a Catholic and a Jew to try to put Negroes in white schools in the South. I think also he wants to be Justice of the Supreme Court and he felt that by being Attorney General of the United States that he would incur the wrath of the Southerners who would have to vote on it."[15]

Robert Kennedy's 1961 memorandum did not go into Arthur Goldberg's appointment as Secretary of Labor. Working with Goldberg during the Rackets Committee had given both Kennedys confidence in his intelligence, resourcefulness and friendship. But Goldberg's name oddly was not on the list of candidates submitted by George Meany on behalf of the AFL-CIO, and Goldberg himself had reservations about accepting the job. John Kennedy said to him, "Okay, you can act like Adlai Stevenson if that's what you want, and you can say you haven't decided whether or not you will accept. . . . I am going to tell George Meany I'm appointing you."[16] Robert Kennedy told me in 1965, "Arthur Goldberg wanted to be a judge, and so he wanted to be assured that if he took this he could be perhaps appointed as a Circuit Court judge out in Illinois. . . . I said I couldn't promise him. I wanted him to decide about the position. The building trades were all against him. . . . We had a lot of opposition from the labor movement."[17] In the end Meany received Goldberg's appointment affably and was present at the announcement.

Edward Day was selected [as Postmaster General] in a rather peculiar manner. Jack wanted to finish the selection of the Cabinet at an early date because it had been delayed so much. Somebody suggested Edward Day as a businessman and without a great deal of thought, without really clearing it through any political figures, Jack called him on the phone and asked him to be Postmaster General and he accepted. It probably would have been better politically to have chosen somebody else but I was sure, at least based on the first month or so, that Edward Day would turn out well. We always thought, looking back on it though, that this was a decision that was made with too much alacrity and that perhaps somebody else would have been more deserving. Edward Day had not been active in the campaign and had been difficult to contact when we needed his help.[18]

Robert was also concerned about the White House. This was much on his mind when I lunched with him in Washington on December 15. Effective as the Senate and campaign staffs had been, he said, the President needed some new people around him. Moreover, the two staffs—the Sorensen group and the O'Donnell group—did not get along too well. Bobby planned to introduce a neutral figure to ease the tension. Fred Dutton had accepted this tricky assignment. He asked me how I proposed to serve my country. I said that two weeks earlier his brother had asked whether I would be interested in an ambassadorship. (I had said that I didn't think so. John Kennedy said, "I think an ambassadorship would be a great job. I'd like to be one myself. Are you sure you wouldn't want one?" I repeated that I didn't think so.)[19] Robert now asked whether I would be interested in becoming a special assistant to the President. I said I would. He turned to other matters.

I heard nothing more and really supposed that this had been a passing courtesy. On January 9, John Kennedy came to Massachusetts to address the legislature. He set up headquarters in my house in Cambridge. In between a succession of visitors, he said casually that Bobby had spoken to him; was I ready to come to the White House? I said, "I am not sure what I would be doing as special assistant, but, if you think I can help, I would like very much to come." He said that he didn't know what he would be doing as President either but guessed there would be enough to keep us both busy.[20]

IV

In 1965 I asked Robert Kennedy whether he had given any thought to working in the White House himself. His response was a candid definition of the fraternal relationship. "I didn't want to do that," he said,

> because if I was going to do anything, I wasn't going to work directly for him—the President. I mean, that would be impossible. I had to do something on my own, or have my own area of responsibility; and it would be impossible with the two of us sitting around an office looking at each other all day. You know, it was like the campaign. He had his role in the campaign and I had my role in the campaign and we would meet and discuss when there was a crisis that came up like the Houston ministers. . . . But he never involved himself in what I was doing—the running of the campaign—and I was not directly associated with what he was doing. . . . So

for brothers—or at least for the two of us—we had to have our own areas. I had to be apart from what he was doing so I wasn't working directly for him and getting orders from him as to what I should do that day. That wouldn't be possible. So I never considered working over at the White House.[21]

In fact, he was extremely perplexed about his future. In June 1960 John Kennedy had said to me, "If I'd been knocked out of the presidential thing, I would have put Bobby into the Massachusetts picture to run for governor. It takes someone with Bobby's nerve and investigative experience to clean up the mess in the Legislature and the Governor's Council."[22] Robert himself wrote in his 1961 memorandum, "I thought I'd enjoy going back to Massachusetts in 1962 and running for Governor."[23] There was also now the possibility of appointment to John Kennedy's vacant Senate seat; but Robert said, "I won't take that. The only way I'll go to the Senate is to run for it."[24]

He had a long luncheon with Justice Douglas to discuss his future —the federal government? would this help or hurt his brother? Massachusetts? a college presidency? head of a foundation? Douglas, Kennedy recalled, "suggested very strongly that I go back to Massachusetts" and that "I should make a name on my own, not just work for my brother."[25] "The things that came out most clearly," Douglas said later, "were that he didn't want to practice law. . . . The first choice would be public service; second choice as an interim thing, would be a college presidency maybe. That's the way his mind was going."[26]

John and Robert Kennedy had talked in Hyannis Port immediately after the election. "He asked me if I wanted to be Attorney General. I said I didn't want to be Attorney General. . . . In the first place, I thought nepotism was a problem. Secondly, I had been chasing bad men for three years and I didn't want to spend the rest of my life doing that."[27] Others reinforced his doubts. "You would make a whale of a good Attorney General," the columnist Drew Pearson wrote him. ". . . But in the same breath, I don't believe that you ought to take this job. You would do such a good job, and you would handle so many controversial questions with such vigor that your brother in the White House would be in hot water all the time."[28] Robert agreed it

> would be a very bad mistake. I was very struck with the fact that when Bill Rogers [Eisenhower's last Attorney General; later Nixon's first Secretary of State] went with Nixon to South Carolina [during the campaign] he hid on the plane. . . . He arrived there and never got off. He hid on the

plane so they wouldn't know he was on the plane. And [Governor] Fritz Hollings found out he was on the plane and it was a big issue in South Carolina. . . . I thought with the name the same, and brothers, I would be creating so many problems in civil rights. It would be the "Kennedy brothers" by the time a year was up, and the President would be blamed for everything we had to do in civil rights; and it was an unnecessary burden to undertake. . . .

So then we talked about going as Under Secretary of Defense. They were going to keep Gates on . . . and then Gates would retire and I would become Secretary. [But the acquisition of McNamara eliminated that possibility.] Then I thought about being Assistant Secretary or something for Latin America. My father kept saying that in the first place the President is going to have a lot of problems; and second, considering the relationship that is going to exist between the two of you, you can't be working for somebody else because it is going to make it so difficult for the somebody else . . . so you've got to be cabinet.[29]

By "cabinet" Joseph Kennedy meant Attorney General. This had been a subject of family badinage. At Christmas time in 1959 Eunice Shriver, joking about the future, said, "Bobby we'll make Attorney General so he can throw all the people Dad doesn't like into jail. That means we'll have to build more jails."[30] A year later, the President-elect told Clark Clifford, who was helping to manage the transition, that his father was "absolutely determined" that Bobby become Attorney General. John Kennedy, Clifford recalled, had "very serious reservations."[31]

If so, the reservations concerned the public reaction, not his brother's ability to do the job. Having been turned down by Ribicoff, Kennedy decided to test the water. On November 19, William Lawrence of the *New York Times,* after golfing with the President-elect, reported from Palm Beach that Robert Kennedy was under serious consideration for Justice. The *Times* promptly denounced the idea editorially: "It is simply not good enough to name a bright young political manager, no matter how bright or how young or how personally loyal, to a major post in government that by rights (if not by precedent) ought to be kept completely out of the political arena."[32] Precedent, as the *Times* tacitly conceded, did not oppose the appointment. Homer Cummings, Franklin Roosevelt's first Attorney General, had once been chairman of the Democratic National Committee. So had J. Howard McGrath, whom Truman made Attorney General. Eisenhower had given the job to Herbert Brownell, his campaign manager. Still, the *Times* had an argument. And there were other obvious objections: nepotism; youth; inexperience; Robert's own deep reluctance, reiterated on his return from Mexico after Thanksgiving.

When I talked with John Kennedy on December 1, he still seemed undecided. I mentioned Orville Freeman. Kennedy did not think him quite right by temperament or interest; besides Freeman had been beaten for reelection as governor of Minnesota; "he'd be too vulnerable politically." Then he startled me: "I'd like Stevenson for Attorney General and Paul Freund [of Harvard] for Solicitor General." But when he sounded out William Blair that evening, the word returned that Stevenson preferred foreign affairs.[33]

v

So it came back to his brother. Obviously his father had a point: John Kennedy needed someone in the cabinet whom he knew intimately and trusted utterly. The reaction to the trial balloon suggested that criticism would be sharp but transient and, if Robert did as well as his brother expected, quickly forgotten. Robert remained resistant. "We just vacillated back and forth," he said in 1965, "almost like we did on the Vice President."[34]

He made a round of consultations. J. Edgar Hoover told him he should become Attorney General. (Hoover said afterward to William C. Sullivan of the FBI's Domestic Intelligence Division, "I didn't like to tell him that, but what could I say?"[35] Kennedy said afterward to John Seigenthaler that he really didn't think Hoover meant it.)[36] William Rogers, Kennedy noted in the 1961 memorandum, "said there really wasn't much of a challenge because there wasn't a great deal to be done." James McInerney, his first boss at Justice a decade earlier, said he shouldn't do it. David Ormsby-Gore, in Washington for a night, thought it a poor idea. Justice Douglas said that Kennedy would serve with distinction and that the voices of his critics would be drowned out by his achievements. "The question for him and Ethel, I ventured to say, was whether that office at that time fitted the pattern of the professional career he had for himself."[37]

It was a trying time. "I don't know what's wrong with him," his father said. "Jack needs all the good men he can get around him down there. There's none better than Bobby. You know for six years he hasn't told me what he wants to do."[38] Finally in mid-December, after discussing the question a last time with Ethel and John Seigenthaler over dinner at Hickory Hill, Robert made up his mind to say no. As he picked up the telephone to call his brother, he observed wryly, "This will kill my father."³⁹ "So I called Jack up," he said later, "and said that I'd decided . . . and I'd go back to Massachusetts or do something else."⁴⁰

"Don't tell me now," John Kennedy said. "I want to have breakfast with you in the morning." Taking Seigenthaler with him, Robert set out the next morning for his brother's house in Georgetown. It was very early and very cold. Snow lay deep on the ground. They chatted over bacon and eggs about the formation of the cabinet. Finally Robert said, "Now, Johnny, can we talk about my situation?" John Kennedy replied at length and with emphasis, addressing his remarks as if to Seigenthaler. "In this cabinet," Seigenthaler later remembered his saying, "there really is no person with whom I have been intimately connected over the years. I need to know that when problems arise I'm going to have somebody who's going to tell me the unvarnished truth, no matter what . . . and Bobby will do that." He described his cabinet. "I believe McNamara will make a great contribution, but I don't know him. And Dean Rusk is going to be my Secretary of State. The truth of the matter is, I [have] had no contact with him. . . . Most of these people I have had some cursory contact with. None of them have I had a long-standing close relationship with." He spoke about civil rights: "I don't want somebody who is going to be fainthearted. I want somebody who is going to be strong; who will join with me in taking whatever risks . . . and who would deal with the problem honestly."

Suddenly he was talking to his brother: "If I can ask Dean Rusk to give up a career; if I can ask Adlai Stevenson to make a sacrifice he does not want to make; if I can ask Bob McNamara to give up a job as head of that company—these men I don't even know . . . certainly I can expect my own brother to give me the same sort of contribution. And I need you in this government." With that, he pushed back his chair, got up and went into the kitchen, as if for more coffee. Seigenthaler said, "Let's go, Bob." Robert Kennedy said, "No, wait. I've got some points I want to make." Seigenthaler said, "There's no point to make." John Kennedy walked back and said, "So that's it. General, let's go."⁴¹

"I told him," John Kennedy subsequently remarked to Peter Maas, "I had made up my mind and didn't want to talk about it any more. I also reminded him that every danger is an opportunity."⁴² Robert Kennedy laconically summed up the conversation in his 1961 memorandum: "He said he thought it would be important to him and that he needed some people around that he could talk to so I decided to accept it."[43] "I did it," he said later, "not so much to become Attorney General as to be around during that time."[44]

He had tried for a moment to escape his brother and confirm an independent identity. But, if his brother wanted him, he would not say no—a sacrifice of himself to which John and Jacqueline Kennedy responded in their separate styles. For Christmas they gave him a copy of *The Enemy Within* handsomely rebound in red leather by a London bookbinder, title and author inscribed in gold. Inside John Kennedy wrote in his *en famille* vein: "For Bobby—The Brother Within—who made the easy difficult. Jack, Christmas 1960." Above Jacqueline had written: "To Bobby—who made the impossible possible and changed all our lives."

VI

I lunched with him the day he had agreed to become Attorney General. He seemed both rueful and fatalistic. He wrote in the 1961 memorandum, "Once I had made up my mind . . . I was glad it was all behind. Arthur Goldberg was a great support as were some of the labor people generally. Alex Rose and David Dubinsky were very enthusiastic. . . . On the other hand the building trades [unions] met in Washington and sent an emissary to Jack telling him that he shouldn't appoint me as they would consider it with disfavor. This was one of the motivating forces in my taking the job."[45]

Disfavor was not confined to the building trades, as John Kennedy perfectly understood. When Benjamin Bradlee of *Newsweek* asked how he planned to announce the appointment, the President-elect said, "Well, I think I'll open the front door of the Georgetown house some morning about 2:00 A.M., look up and down the street, and, if there's no one there, I'll whisper, 'It's Bobby.'" Robert Kennedy himself recorded the great moment. "He told me to go upstairs and comb my hair to which I said it was the first time the President had ever told the Attorney General to comb his hair before they made an announcement. And then when we were outside he said, 'Don't smile too much or they'll think we're happy about the appointment.'"[46]

Others were decidedly unhappy. "If Robert Kennedy," the *New York Times* noted sarcastically, "was one of the outstanding lawyers of the country, a preeminent legal philosopher, a noted prosecutor or legal officer at Federal or State level, the situation would have been different. But his experience . . . is surely insufficient to warrant his present appointment."* Robert Novak wrote in the *Wall Street Journal* that Robert Kennedy could turn out to be an "unqualified disaster."[47] Alexander M. Bickel summed up the opposition case magisterially in the *New Republic*. More than any executive officer, Bickel wrote, the Attorney General is required to regard means as above ends, process above results. "In his brief but highly visible professional career, Mr. Kennedy has demonstrated specific grounds of disqualification. . . . On the record, Robert F. Kennedy is not fit for the office."[48]

Press comment was not wholly adverse, and senators were generally indulgent. There were, however, rumbles of opposition on the Judiciary Committee. James O. Eastland, the committee chairman, was a combination of Mississippi demogogue and Washington cynic. Lyndon Johnson once said of him, "Jim Eastland could be standing right in the middle of the worst Mississippi flood ever known, and he'd say the niggers caused it, helped out by the Communists—but, he'd say, we gotta have help from Washington."[49] Most northerners found Eastland grouchy and obscurantist, a planter rich on federal cotton subsidies, given to peevish talk about big government and the "mongrelization of races" and devoid of any socially redeeming quality, like the courtly manners of his Mississippi colleague John Stennis.[50] Robert Kennedy, with his Irish weakness for rogues, liked Eastland, however, and Eastland evidently liked him too.

When Kennedy called on him before the hearings, Eastland leaned back in his chair, his face wreathed in cigar smoke, and ruminated about the Department of Justice. He had got along with Attorney General Rogers, he said, but added: "You can't have the same confidence in him, of course, as you could in [Lawrence E.] Walsh [the deputy attorney general]. . . . Did you know that he never brought a civil rights case in the state of Mississippi?" With that Eastland winked broadly at Kennedy. Kennedy interpreted the wink as meaning (he put it later) "that Bill Rogers hadn't met his responsibility and done his duty in Mississippi, and Jim Eastland felt a certain amount of contempt for him."[51]

* *New York Times*, December 29, 1960. Implicit in the *Times*'s attacks on Robert Kennedy's appointment was the notion that nepotism was a wicked thing. Robert Kennedy took sardonic pleasure in observing the retirement of Arthur Hays Sulzberger as publisher of the *Times* and his replacement by his son-in-law Orville Dryfoos, with Arthur Ochs (Punch) Sulzberger standing next in line. When Punch Sulzberger eventually took over his father's job, Kennedy said, "Well, Punch and I both worked our way to the top through diligence and merit." There were many such jokes. RFK, introducing Adlai E. Stevenson III of Illinois, c. 1966: "If there's one thing I can't stand, it's a fellow running on his family name."

Surrounded by their family at the house in Bronxville; *from left,* Joseph P. Kennedy, Kathleen, John, Jean, Eunice, Robert, Patricia, Edward, Rosemary, Joseph Jr., and Rose Kennedy.

Seaman Robert Kennedy describes equipment on the *Joseph P. Kennedy Jr.* to Joseph P. Kennedy, Sr., and an officer.

The Harvard Football Team, 1947. Robert Kennedy is at far right of front row; Kenneth O'Donnell, second from left in back row.

In Jerusalem, 1948, as an accredited correspondent of the *Boston Post,* when the British mandate was coming to an end.

Ethel Skakel dancing with her future husband.

The young parents flanking the head of the family behind their first three children, Kathleen, Joseph III, Robert Jr., on a Washington sidewalk. Robert Kennedy was then counsel to the Senate Investigations Subcommittee.

The counsel to the Senate Labor Rackets Committee uses a chart during a hearing in Washington, March 1957. In the foreground are Senators Joseph P. McCarthy, *left*, and Karl Mundt.

The chief counsel of the Rackets Committee with a chief target, James R. Hoffa, president of the Teamsters Union.

The brothers map strategy in Los Angeles during John F. Kennedy's campaign for the Democratic presidential nomination in 1960.

The Attorney General reports on his 1962 round-the-world tour. At the White House were Secretary of State Dean Rusk, Vice President Lyndon Johnson, Robert Kennedy and the President.

Riding in Virginia before breakfast, the Attorney General follows his children Kathleen, Joseph, and Robert.

Not all the southerners were so equable. "Dick Russell," Lyndon Johnson told Bobby Baker, "is absolutely shittin' a squealin' worm. He thinks it's a disgrace for a kid who's never practiced law to be appointed. . . . I agree with him. . . . But I don't think Jack Kennedy's gonna let a little fart like Bobby lead him around by the nose." Deciding it was his role to disarm southern opposition, Johnson told Baker: "I want you to lead all our Southern friends in here by their ying-yangs. . . . I'm gonna put it on the line and tell 'em it's a matter of my personal survival."[52] "Russell, and I believe [Herman] Talmadge [of Georgia], were against me," Kennedy himself wrote in his 1961 memorandum, "and [Allen] Ellender [of Louisiana] had suggested to Eastland that he ask me some tough questions on Civil Rights. Actually, they wouldn't have been tough questions because there wasn't much I was prepared to say. Russell was against me . . . because he felt that [it] caused him a problem and difficulty in the South to vote for any Attorney General."[53]

As usual, he prepared carefully for the hearings. "I conferred with Clark Clifford," he noted in 1961, "and then went over and saw Ben Cohen. He is a great gentleman and had some good ideas."[54] James M. Landis helped. On the morning of January 13, 1961, Robert Kennedy rather nervously entered the gleaming marble and walnut-paneled hearing room of the Judiciary Committee. Eastland read into the record messages of support from Whitney North Seymour, president of the American Bar Association, and from J. Edgar Hoover. Everett Dirksen of Illinois, the Republican leader, began the questioning. He saluted Kennedy's "impeccable character" but pointed out that the Attorney General-designate had never practiced law in any state or federal court. Senator Roman Hruska of Nebraska pursued the inexperience point with dogged fervor. Kennedy's old friends from the Rackets Committee, John McClellan and Sam Ervin, intervened from time to time, defending his experience under them. Pressed by Hruska, Kennedy himself finally responded with feeling. "I decided at quite a young age," he told the committee, "that I would . . . work for the Government. . . . I have been working for the Government. In my estimation I think that I have had invaluable experience." He recalled Oliver Wendell Holmes's remark that private practice had hardly prepared him for the broad reach of public law he confronted on the bench. "I would not have given up one year of experience that I have had over the period since I graduated from law school," Kennedy said, ". . . for experience in practicing law in Boston." Hruska persisted: "You have, as I understand it, never negotiated a settlement, for example, of a litigated civil case for damages or the breach of a contract or tort case." Kennedy: "I doubt if I am going to be doing that as Attorney General."[55]

For the rest, it was clear sailing. Asked about his financial holdings, Kennedy said, "I disposed of everything that I could possibly dispose of. . . . The result is now that I do not have any interest in anything other than Government or municipal bonds."[56] Asked about civil rights, he said he would execute the policies laid down by the President. Asked about a national crime commission, he said that he had already worked out an arrangement with the FBI, the Bureau of Narcotics and the Internal Revenue Service for the pooling of intelligence; he planned to give this a try first. Asked about the withholding of information from Congress on the plea of executive privilege, he said, "I feel very strongly about that," and affirmed that Congress, and the public too, had "a right to know many of these matters."[57]

Senator Kenneth Keating, a New York Republican, describing himself as "a longtime personal friend of the nominee and his gracious wife and all the members of his family,"[58] commended the appointment. Except for Hruska, the committee was complaisant. Kennedy had come, James Reston wrote, "expecting to do battle with Jack Dempsey, and instead found himself confronted, most agreeably, by Shirley Temple."[59] The committee, Hruska included, reported the nomination out unanimously. A week later, with only one senator speaking in opposition—Gordon Allott, a conservative Republican from Colorado—the Senate confirmed Robert Kennedy as Attorney General of the United States.

VII

Robert Kennedy turned thirty-five two months before he was sworn in as Attorney General. Only two of his sixty-three predecessors had been younger—Caesar Augustus Rodney, thirty-five by a bare two weeks when Jefferson made him Attorney General in 1807, and Richard Rush, thirty-three when appointed by Madison in 1814. In the days of Rodney and Rush, however, Attorneys General were private lawyers on presidential retainer. They kept up their own law business on the side and did not even live in Washington. It was not until 1853 that an Attorney General—Caleb Cushing—took up full-time residence in the capital, nor until 1870 that the Department of Justice was established. It grew rapidly thereafter. By 1961 it had more than thirty thousand employees. Its annual budget was more than $300 million. The Attorney General, as the government's chief legal officer, had a wide mandate throughout the executive branch. That mandate had been historically construed, in the main, as procedural and protective: to enforce federal law and to assure and defend the legality of executive actions. The Department of Justice was by tradition as well as by function a citadel of the status quo—or at least of *stare decisis*. It had only intermittently been an agency of innovation and reform.

Despite the hostile comment, Robert Kennedy was not wholly unqualified. In one field of importance to law enforcement—organized crime—he knew considerably more than his critics. As for the argument that he lacked courtroom experience, John Kennedy thought this quite missed the point. "The basic requirement for the job," he told an interviewer, "is not that at all. It is the ability to administer a great department."[60] So lightly did the President-elect take the professional complaint that, to Robert's discomfort, he made public jokes about his brother's inadequate preparation. "I can't see that it's wrong," he was soon explaining to the annual banquet of the Alfalfa Club, "to give him a little legal experience before he goes out to practice law." (When Robert objected that this was not very funny, his brother said he had better get used to kidding himself; people liked it. "Yes, but you weren't kidding yourself," Robert said. "You were kidding *me*.")[61]

In picking his associates, the new Attorney General sought men who would make up for his own deficiencies, especially too little law and too much politics. He wanted first-class lawyers who would be strong, nonpolitical and young. "It's ridiculous to wait until a man is 40 to give him a responsible job," he had said in 1957. "By that age he may have lost most of his zeal."[62] The key appointment was deputy attorney general. After the election, Robert, on his brother's instruction, had offered their admired Colorado friend Byron White a choice of jobs: Secretary of the Army, Secretary of the Air Force, deputy attorney general.[63] White, who had not gone to Yale Law School or clerked for a Chief Justice for nothing, decided for Justice. He was a man of stern and circumspect intelligence, realistic judgment, dry humor and solid legal proficiency. He also was well acquainted among the lawyers of his generation, especially where the writ of the Yale Law School ran, and he now recruited some of the best for his new Department.

White's contribution to the roll of assistant attorneys general included Nicholas Katzenbach (Exeter, U.S. Air Force, Yale Law

School, Balliol, Chicago Law School faculty; now Office of Legal Counsel); Burke Marshall (Exeter, U.S. Army, Yale Law School, Covington and Burling; now Civil Rights Division); Louis Oberdorfer (Dartmouth, U.S. Army, Yale Law School, clerk to Justice Black; now Tax Division); William Orrick (Yale, California Law School, U.S. Army; now Civil Division). Later Katzenbach brought in Norbert Schlei (U.S. Navy, Yale Law School, clerk to Justice Harlan; succeeding Katzenbach in the Office of Legal Counsel) and John Douglas (son of Senator Paul Douglas, U.S. Navy, Yale Law School, Oxford, clerk to Justice Burton, Covington and Burling; succeeding Orrick in the Civil Division).

Their overlapping experience—the Ivy League, the war, the *Yale Law Journal*, Rhodes scholarships, Supreme Court clerkships, established law firms—stamped these men with a common moral outlook. They cared deeply and professionally about the law. Military service had trained them to assume responsibilities. They were all Democrats who saw themselves as heirs of the great legal generation of the New Deal, but they were without partisan inclination. Only White had taken an active part in the campaign. Their qualities—integrity, judgment, drive, understatement, personal reserve—commended them to Kennedy. There was logic too in the Yale connection. Kennedy was temperamentally more attuned to the result-oriented jurisprudence propagated in New Haven than to the process-oriented jurisprudence of Cambridge; to William O. Douglas, say, than to Felix Frankfurter. (Alexander Bickel, the most formidable critic of his nomination, was a Harvard outrider in the Yale wilderness.) The appointment of Professor Archibald Cox of the Harvard Law School to the post of solicitor general, the third-ranking job in the Department, broke the Yale monopoly. This was John Kennedy's doing. Cox had worked with the President-elect on labor legislation and had headed his research staff in the 1960 campaign. He was already celebrated, at least in the law school world, for his patrician bearing, direct and lucid mind, crisp style, crew-cut hair and bow ties, the last abandoned when he dressed himself magnificently in swallow-tailed coat to argue before the Supreme Court.

Other places were filled from outside the Ivy League. William O. Douglas and Sam Rayburn urged the appointment of the youngest of the assistant attorneys general, Ramsey Clark of Texas, thirty-three years old, to head the Lands Division. Clark's father had been Attorney General under Truman and was now on the Supreme Court, and Clark himself had met Professor Katzenbach at the Chicago Law

School. For Antitrust, Sargent Shriver and Hubert Humphrey recommended Lee Loevinger of Minnesota, forty-eight years old and the oldest of the new appointees. The head of the Criminal Divison, Herbert J. Miller, Jr., was a Republican whom Kennedy had known as a member of the Board of Monitors appointed by the courts in a vain effort to clean up the Teamsters. Kennedy originally intended to abolish the Internal Security Division.[64] But this threatened complications; so he left it in a separate building under an accommodating Republican holdover, J. Walter Yeagley, who was content to phase out prosecutive action and, as a former FBI agent, able to do so without unduly estranging J. Edgar Hoover.

For his personal staff Kennedy drew on newspaper friends from Rackets Committee days. John Seigenthaler became his administrative assistant, Edwin Guthman his press man. Angie Novello remained his secretary. Byron White brought from Denver as his deputy Joseph Dolan, who had worked for John Kennedy on Senate committees and had served in the Colorado legislature. Seigenthaler, Guthman and Dolan helped segregate the rest of the cast from the importunings of politics.

It was an outstanding group. Even the skeptical Bickel was impelled to second thoughts. "One began to hear of it in a month or so before he took office," Bickel said later. ". . . It was the most brilliantly staffed department we had seen in a long, long time, and that was very impressive. One immediately had the sense of a fellow who wasn't afraid of having able people around him and indeed of a fellow who had a vision of public service that would have done anyone proud."[65]

VIII

The center of action was the Attorney General's office, a vast, somber, walnut-paneled chamber, with arched roof, indirect lighting, red carpet, stately fireplace and, in the past, a general air of solemnity. Over the next years Kennedy filled it with sofas, tables, lamps, children's photographs, a varnished sailfish over the mantelpiece, an old blunderbuss on the wall, a model of a Chinese junk on a table, a stuffed tiger standing near the fireplace. (The Attorney General carefully explained to a foreign newspaperman that he had not shot the tiger himself. If he had shot it himself, the newspaperman reflected, he would not have said anything.)[66] Affixed to the panels by Scotch tape was an ever-changing montage of children's drawings. "There were fish," recalled the astonished Roy Wilkins of the National Association for the Advancement of Colored People, "that only they would describe as fish. There were chimneys sticking up at wrong angles and roads that were going everywhere and airplanes that were flying through what they said was the air. But they were wild, beautiful colors, the kind of thing that would jump out of a child's imagination and fantasy. Robert Kennedy never offered any apology for these pictures, nor did he offer any explanation of them."[67]

The Attorney General leaned casually back in his leather armchair in the midst of genial clutter, foot propped on an open drawer, jacket off, tie yanked aside, trousers rumpled, hair uncombed. "You'd never confuse him with Dean Acheson," said Ethel.[68] Often, in defiance of government regulations, he brought with him his menacing dog Brumus, a large and ill-tempered Labrador to whom Robert and Ethel were devoted, perhaps because most people, even veteran dog-lovers, detested him. On weekends he might import an assortment of children.

A new informality pervaded the staid old Department. Kennedy wandered the corridors, put his head into offices to find out what was going on, talked to people who had worked in the Department for years without ever speaking to an Attorney General. Patricia Collins, a lawyer who had first come to Justice when Robert Kennedy was nine years old and had served fourteen Attorneys General, said, "We never had an Attorney General who had [that] close personal relationship with the staff. He always said he'd been here himself, he'd been an attorney down in the Criminal Division, and nobody had ever paid any darn attention to him, and he was going to fix that."[69] But there was no sacrifice of authority. Early on, calling in the Department's lawyers in a series of informal meetings, he sat on his desk, one of them recalled, "legs crouched beneath him Indian fashion, necktie open, shirtsleeves rolled up, hair askew. . . . Strangely enough, in that posture of utter informality, almost humility, Robert Kennedy lent an air of dignity to the assembly. I felt at one with him and was aware that that was the mood of the entire group."[70] He was a superb question-asker, an excellent listener and an excellent rememberer.

He carried the personal touch to the outlying parts of his domain —federal attorneys through the country, FBI offices, immigration and naturalization offices, prisons. Before he took a trip, he would pass the word to his assistant attorneys general in Washington: "Aren't there some areas I can help you in?"[71] Armed with detail, he prodded regional offices into new effort by his display of knowledge and concern. "He took a very special interest," said Robert Morgenthau, whom he made federal attorney for the Southern District of New York, "in the work being done by young lawyers. . . . This was one of his great gifts: to make people feel that they were part of the team."[72]

As an administrator, he matched his taste in selecting associates by his readiness to leave them alone. He relied on Byron White for day-to-day management of the Department. He expected the assistant attorneys general to keep him informed about anything they were doing that might have public implications, but did not interfere unless they requested his counsel or support. "He really did not second-guess people to whom he gave responsibility," said Louis Oberdorfer.[73] He interrogated them carefully about their legal recommendations, "but I don't believe," said Seigenthaler, "I ever saw him override one."[74] "He never questioned anybody's legal judgment," said Katzenbach; his style was to say, "Everybody here knows more law about this than I do, but I'm the Attorney General and it's my responsibility, so you've got to make it clear to me so that I can make a decision."[75] "Sometimes he would be a little skeptical," said Norbert Schlei, "as to whether the law required some result that seemed to him harsh or foolish or wrong in some way, but basically he would accept the legal assertion that he was confronted with and make his contribution on the level of the policy question."[76]

Archibald Cox summed up the personal characteristics that he felt made Kennedy "a first-rate Attorney General": his "willingness to listen and reconsider his initial reactions"; "his capability to go to the heart of the problem"; his "ability to delegate while reserving his time for what it was most important for him to do"; and, supremely important for his associates, "when a conference in his office ended, one knew what decision had been taken. The decision might be, 'Do what you think best.' In that event he supported you and shared the blame even if what you did turned out to be a mistake. Or the decision might lay down a line of action."[77]

He used his assistant attorneys general not simply as specialists in their own jurisdictions but as problem-tacklers across the board. He never hesitated to put the heads of the Tax, Lands, Legal Counsel and Civil offices (Oberdorfer, Clark, Katzenbach, Douglas) into civil rights, or his civil rights and lands men (Marshall, Clark) into antitrust.[78] "One of the hallmarks of the Kennedys," said William Orrick, "was that they expected you to do everything."[79] But this was done without violation of comradeship. "We never felt we were competing with each other," said Louis Oberdorfer. "There was no feeling that people were being displaced because someone else was called in to help. . . . One always knew where one stood. . . . He had that quality of leadership that made all of us play above our heads."[80]

Above all, said John Douglas, "he treated people decently. . . . He didn't duck or try to shift blame. He didn't say one thing in private and another in public. He never let his subordinates down. He stood up for them, followed their careers and interests, tried to help them, looked for the best in them, and usually found it. . . . He was the most fastidious man in public life I ever met in his personal relationships."[81] He had the quality, said Katzenbach, "of bringing out the very best in everyone who worked for him."[82] "He was as good at delegating power as anybody I ever saw," said Ramsey Clark. ". . . All he really required in return was performance."[83] His staff repaid confidence not only by performance but by protective devotion. They dispatched word about his virtues to the bar associations and the law schools. They took care always to call him Bob, rightly supposing that his detractors used the diminutive in order to emphasize youth and imply unfitness for a serious job. (Nothing, however, could cure his family of calling him Bobby.) They saw themselves, in the romantic title of Edwin Guthman's memoir of the period, as a band of brothers.

IX

Below the top staff, he exerted control, according to mood and need, through humor, through brusqueness, through solicitude. Addressing Justice employees, he sought to inspire them by the example of his own dazzling rise from the ranks: "I started in the Department as a young lawyer in 1950. The salary was only $4000 a year, but I worked hard. (Pause.) I was ambitious. (Pause.) I studied. (Pause.) I applied myself. . . . And then my brother was elected President of the United States."[84] Rueful jocularity, ordinarily at his own expense, was more than ever a conditioned reflex. When Angie Novello admonished him in a plaintive memorandum that "it would be *extremely* helpful if the Attorney General of the United States . . . would notify his immediate staff of his whereabouts at all times," Kennedy returned it with a handwritten scrawl, "What if I'm lost. Love."[85]

He was still on occasion preoccupied, moody and unpredictable.

"He has a horror of wasting time," observed one reporter, "and although he can make a monumental effort to restrain his impatience with long-winded argument, the struggle is sometimes dramatic in the extreme. . . . He clasps his hands as if in prayer and regards his clenched knuckles with a cataleptic stare. If the ordeal continues he comes slowly upright again, pats the arms of his chair in slow and feverish rhythm and looks off into the beyond with . . . muted despair."[86] "Sometimes I wondered," said John Douglas, "if he regarded a display of congeniality or ease with someone he didn't respect as a reflection on his own integrity."[87] "He had," said Robert Morgenthau, "an unusual gift of sensing whether people knew what they were talking about . . . or whether they were just trying to string him along."[88] When he encountered what he took to be indolence or evasiveness, disgust was unconcealed. "His most obvious fault," wrote Patrick Anderson, information officer for the Department's Committee on Juvenile Delinquency, "is his rudeness. His face, when it lacks that boyish, photogenic grin, is not a pleasant sight. It has a certain bony harshness and those ice-blue eyes are not the smiling ones that Irishmen sing songs about. At best, he recalls Fitzgerald's description of Gatsby: 'an elegant young roughneck.' "[89] There were, however, few explosions. Joseph Dolan, who worked closely with him for eight years, thought him exceptionally self-contained. "You used to think you could tell when he was angry. . . . The color reflects in his face, and he'd say, 'Well, really, we can do better, can't we?' You would assume that he was furious, but you couldn't say [so] under oath. . . . You could [only] say, 'Well, you know, he was red, and he was speaking in a kind of different tone than he usually did.' "[90]

He could be tough all the same. He also at times struck people as spoiled in the way the rich, powerful and charming are spoiled: in the sense of entitlement to service. Victor Navasky in his able book *Kennedy Justice* quotes a career attorney: "Bob had the failings of a prince. It might be you who had to schlep Brumus out of the office. If you worked for him he regarded you as working for *all* of him. So if Ethel lost her bags, you might have to track them down through the airport." But he was also unusually considerate. The same witness added: "You knew he would listen, so if you got his attention—it was rewarding."[91]

He genuinely cared about the people who worked for him. Over the resistance of career officials he had a gymnasium built on the roof of the Department. Ethel arranged for a snack bar with tables and umbrellas in the courtyard. When secretaries fell sick, the Attorney General sent them handwritten notes: thus, "I have just learned that you have gone to the hospital. I want you to come back here quickly. The Department of Justice is falling apart without you."[92] When attorneys won difficult cases, they received a telephone call or a letter. He sent periodic circulars to the assistant attorneys general: "Again I would like to ask that you bring to my attention the names of employees in your Division who have been doing outstanding work. Some assistant attorneys general have been doing this. . . . Others I have not yet heard from."[93] A year later: "Once again I want to remind all of you of my continued interest in knowing who in your Division has done so well that I may call or write a note. I have been forced to the conclusion that everyone is doing only mediocre work as I hardly ever hear from you regarding oustanding contributions."[94]

He imbued the Department with his rage for quality. "Robert Kennedy," his discriminating critic Navasky has written, "operated on the simple theory that standards were contagious, that excellence was catching and within the reach of the Justice Department. He expected it at every level and looked for it everywhere."[95] He imbued it too with his conviction of urgency. "I've known the Department of Justice an awfully long time," said Ramsey Clark in 1969. "I used to walk the halls as a kid—preteenage, because my father had joined the Department as a lawyer when I was nine years old—and I'd come to sense the atmosphere and the mood of the place. It was a quiet and sleepy place until January of '61. . . . Then it came *alive*."[96] The premium was always on action. "Don't tell me what I can't do," Kennedy would say to cautious lawyers, "tell me what I can do."[97] He was determined to transform the Department from a citadel of *stare decisis* into an agency of reform.

He was confronted by massive forces of institutional resistance. "We have about as much chance of changing that place," Byron White observed to Ramsey Clark one day as they were walking up to the Department, "as you and I do of . . . putting our shoulders against the building and moving it."[98] And there was so little time. When William Orrick had to decide between job offers at Justice and the Pentagon, Kennedy told him, "Take all the time you want but could you let me know by tomorrow morning?"[99] Clark, going to his first interview with Kennedy, found White gulping down a cup of ice cream. "He just all of a sudden said, 'Come on.' He just went dashing out and leaping up the steps about three steps at a time. I thought,

'My God, I can't carry on like this.'"[100] In two months White was down with a duodenal ulcer.

But they all did carry on like this. It was part of the postinaugural euphoria. "Those were the days," Robert Kennedy later said, "when we thought we were succeeding because of all the stories on how hard everybody was working."[101] He was no fool.

(12)

The Pursuit of Justice: J. Edgar Hoover

THE CENTER of institutional resistance was the Federal Bureau of Investigation. The FBI, the largest single unit within Justice, disposed of nearly 50 percent of the Department's thirty thousand employees and over 40 percent of its budget. Its director, technically a subordinate official, had far more power and fame than his nominal chiefs. Attorneys General came and went. J. Edgar Hoover was there, it seemed, forever. "Mr. Hoover became the Director of the Bureau in 1924, the year before the Attorney General was born," the FBI tour guides used to say in 1961, until Robert Kennedy heard about it.[1] No one could remember the Bureau before Hoover. No one could imagine it after Hoover. Rarely had any institution been so totally the lengthened shadow of a single man.

I

Hoover was a professional bureaucrat of remarkable gifts. Appointed director by Attorney General Harlan Stone in 1924 to clean up a corrupt operation, he rapidly won Stone's unaffected admiration as a man "of exceptional intelligence, alertness, and executive ability."[2] Stone, sensitive to the possibility that "a secret police may become a menace to free government," laid down careful specifications for the Bureau of Investigation. It must not, he said, concern itself "with political or other opinions of individuals" but only with *conduct* forbidden by the laws of the United States. "When a police system passes beyond these limits, it is dangerous to the proper administration of justice and to human liberty."[3] In Stone's view Hoover met those standards. In 1933, when Stone, now on the Supreme Court, heard that the newly elected Franklin Roosevelt might replace Hoover, he sent Felix Frankfurter a powerful letter urging the director's retention.*

The Bureau of Investigation (Hoover added Federal to the title in 1935) soon gained a quiet reputation, largely deserved, as an effective, technologically advanced and law-abiding organization manned by fearless and incorruptible agents. The director proved himself adept at modernizing his methods, at dominating his subordinates and at propitiating his superiors. To first-class administrative capacity he joined unexpected talent for showmanship. Perhaps the rumors of 1933 stimulated him to consolidate his position. Beginning in 1934, articles, books and movies began to pour out celebrating the G-men and their victories over crime. The torrent of publicity about the Bureau dismayed Stone, who observed in 1937, "I only hope that the ultimate effect will not be to break down its morale."[4] But publicity served the director's purpose. It brought national support to the FBI. It won increasing appropriations from Congress. It gave Hoover himself a cloak of infallibility and invincibility.

His investigations and files multiplied. By 1940 Westbrook Pegler, the cranky columnist, could describe the FBI as "the greatest deposit of personal dirt ever amassed."[5] International crisis meanwhile enlarged the Bureau's mandate. Roosevelt, confident of his ability to control Hoover, charged him with investigations of Nazi and Communist activities in the United States. National security was now propelling Hoover across Stone's line between conduct and opinion. When war broke out in Europe, Hoover was forty-four years old; he had been director since he was twenty-nine. Pearl Harbor increased his conviction that he alone knew how to protect the nation from subversive forces. He established a catchall "Security Index" listing people the FBI thought should be locked up in time of national emergency. In 1943 Attorney General Francis Biddle ordered him to destroy the list. Hoover simply disobeyed. He instructed his agents to change the label on the files, to "continue to prepare and maintain security index cards" and, above all, not to mention it to anyone outside the Bureau.[6] All this—the enemies list, the covert defiance of his superior, the secrecy—set a pattern for the future.

The Cold War gave the Bureau new power and the director new glory. Hoover's dossiers grew. So did his command of Congress, his

---

* A. T. Mason, *Harlan Fiske Stone: Pillar of the Law* (New York, 1956), 152. Frankfurter passed the letter on to Roosevelt, who sent a reassuring message back to Stone via Frankfurter (Max Freedman, ed., *Roosevelt and Frankfurter: Their Correspondence, 1928–1945* [Boston, 1967], 129).

manipulation and intimidation of the press, his stature in the country. When Truman wanted the Civil Service Commission to run loyalty-security investigations of government employees, Hoover insisted that this was a job for the FBI. Truman told his staff: "J. Edgar will in all probability get this backward looking Congress to give him what he wants. It's dangerous."⁷ Truman was right on both counts.

Truman's comment suggested the widening gap between the inside perception of the director and the popular myth. Those who dealt closely with the great patriot came to know his authoritarian instincts, his profoundly right-wing prejudices, his egomania and his vindictiveness. They knew his agitation over "bleeding hearts," "professional do-gooders" and other malefactors. "Swaydo-liberals," as he called them, was a favorite term of denunciation. This implied no affection for true liberals; all liberals (except for the New York lawyer Morris Ernst) were evidently pseudoliberals. "He refused," said George Allen—self-appointed chum of notables, author of the faintly amusing book *Presidents Who Have Known Me,* the director's closest friend outside the FBI—"to read either the *Washington Post* or the *New York Times* . . . and he was suspicious even of the *Wall Street Journal.*"⁸

The insiders knew too that Joe McCarthy could not have sustained his rambling crusade without help from Hoover. George Allen: "Hoover was crazy about McCarthy."⁹ "You had us preparing material for him regularly, kept furnishing it to him," William C. Sullivan, who rose to number three man in the Bureau, wrote Hoover in later years, "while you denied publicly that we were helping him."* They knew above all that the FBI had long since forgotten Harlan Stone's

---

* Sullivan to Hoover, October 6, 1971, Sullivan Papers. Sullivan told me on July 26, 1976, that the FBI aid program for McCarthy began very shortly after McCarthy's Wheeling speech in 1950 when McCarthy called Hoover in search of support. Ralph de Toledano confirms this in his fervently pro-Hoover biography: "Hoover spent many hours with Joe McCarthy talking 'business'—lecturing him on Communist strategy and tactics, giving him leads and insights into the Communist apparatus in the United States, and pointing him in the direction of suspect individuals. It is also undoubtedly a fact that though Hoover never gave McCarthy access to FBI files, he did allow him to see reports written to various high-ranking government officials on Communist infiltration" (Ralph de Toledano, *J. Edgar Hoover: The Man in His Time* [New York: Manor Books reprint, 1974], 280). Note also the testimony of William W. Turner, then an FBI agent: "It is very doubtful whether Senator Joseph McCarthy would have long survived in his reckless smearing campaign without the ammunition provided him by Hoover. FBI agents put in long hours poring over Bureau security files and abstracting them for Roy Kohn" (W. W. Turner, *Hoover's FBI* [New York: Dell reprint, 1971], 176). Only the egregious Cohn persists in denying that Hoover gave information to McCarthy (Roy Cohn, "Could He Walk on Water?" *Esquire,* November 1972).

stipulation that it should concern itself only with conduct and not with opinion. They felt that Hoover had too much power and too little accountability.

The FBI was far from a contemptible organization. Its standards compared favorably to those of most police forces at home and abroad. A decade before the *Miranda* decision, Hoover had instructed FBI agents to advise persons in custody of their rights to silence and a lawyer. Agents did not use the third degree. They were under instructions to fire only in self-defense or the defense of others; there was no shooting down of people in flight. Esprit de corps was high; discipline unremitting. This had bad as well as good aspects. "We were sealed off from the outside world and the experiences and thinking of others from the very beginning," said William Sullivan, "and we . . . steadily became inbred for thirty years."[10] Still the impression eventually arose even among agents that their director was a rather eccentric man.

Hoover was a bachelor who had lived for years with his mother. After her death his cherished companion was an FBI associate, Clyde Tolson. He had a brother and sister, but George Allen could not recollect his ever mentioning them.[11] His extracurricular passion was to go to the races with Tolson and Allen. He was obsessed by what he saw as a decline in sexual morality and was exercised even over the personal appearance of FBI agents. He detested long hair and beards. Jackets were to be worn. Suits were to be dark, shirts white, ties conservative. Red ties were evidence of insincerity. He penalized agents who were overweight or who had moist palms.[12] He feared germs, hated flies and could not abide people, especially agents, stepping on his shadow. Subordinates who displeased him were exiled to remote places like Butte, Montana.

"In the FBI under Mr. Hoover," wrote one special agent after twenty-three years, "you had to work on the premise that the Director was infallible. If you did not really believe this—and of course most employees certainly did not—you nevertheless had to pay lip service to it to survive. . . . If you were ambitious and desired to rise in the organization, you had to pay a still higher toll in the form of exaggerated sycophantic respect and adulation for him." In time Hoover's Bureau began to take on the internal lineaments of the Communist party he so fervently hated. "You just listen to what our Leader says about Commonist [pronounced in the Hoover style] Party discipline," one agent remarked to another, "and see if it reminds you of any other organization." Survivors developed great skill in sending Hoover worshipful letters and collecting funds to give him elaborate presents on Christmas and his birthday. As the director grew older, no flattery became too gross for him to swallow.[13]

He regularly misused Bureau employees, equipment and funds for entirely personal purposes. Subordinates rushed to do whatever he told them, zany as his orders might sometimes sound. "You claim you do not want 'yes men,'" William Sullivan protested, "but you become furious at any employee who says 'no' to you."[14] When his limousine had an accident making a left turn, Hoover magnificently forbade his chauffeur to make left turns in the future. After inspection of a new agent training class, Hoover told the instructor, "One of them is a pinhead. Get rid of him!" The instructor dared ask no more but surreptitiously looked at the class. Alas, no head was conspicuously smaller than the rest. Finally he examined hats. Three members of the class wore smaller hats than the others. Taking no chances, the instructor fired all three.[15] Hoover liked to scribble comments on the borders of memoranda; once, when an agent neglected to leave enough space, Hoover wrote irritably, "Watch the borders." For days thereafter special agents patrolled the Canadian and Mexican borders looking for they knew not what.[16] "Most agents," one FBI veteran wrote, "have ambivalent feelings toward the FBI. They are dedicated to the concept of the organization . . . but at the same time they seethe in frustration."[17] Even the worshipful Roy Cohn reported: "A popular joke with Bureau agents was: 'Did you hear what Tolson said to Hoover on Miami Beach? He said, "Nobody's looking now, John, you can take your walk on the water."'"[18]

"We did all possible to build up your legend," Sullivan told Hoover toward the end. ". . . No government Bureau should spend the vast sums of money on public relations as we have done and still do." Sullivan's staff wrote books for Hoover's signature—*Masters of Deceit* (1958), *A Study in Communism* (1962). FBI field offices promoted the books. "We even wrote reviews here at the Headquarters which were sent to the field to have printed by different papers." Since the work was done on government time, Sullivan recommended that the royalties go to charity. Only recently, he told Hoover in 1971, "did I learn that you put some thousands of dollars in your own pocket and Tolson likewise got a share."[19] The propaganda was a huge success. Support for the FBI became a patriotic duty, Hoover himself a national idol. "He was," said Sullivan, "one of the greatest con men the country ever produced."[20]

The Hoover personality cult constrained those who knew better to silence. There were additional inducements: for agents, apprehension about their FBI careers or, should they resign, about blacklisting in private industry; for Presidents, Hoover's assiduity as a courtier; for legislators and journalists, the ominous sweep of his ever-expanding files, crammed with information about the sexual vagaries of public figures. Hoover, William Sullivan said in 1973, was

> a master blackmailer. . . . The moment he would get something on a Senator, he would . . . advise the Senator that "We're in the course of an investigation and by chance happened to come upon this data on your daughter. But . . . don't have any concern—no one will ever learn about it." Well, Jesus, what does that tell the Senator? From that time on the Senator's right in his pocket.[21]

Hoover was nowhere regarded with more veneration, or fear, than in Congress. The House Appropriations Committee always gave him all the money he requested and, on occasion, more. The Senate Appropriations Committee hardly ever asked him to appear at all.[22] In Congress criticism of Hoover was a form of lèse majesté—a fact forgotten in later years by congressional committees when they piously condemned executive officials for reluctantly yielding the FBI a latitude that every Congress for a generation had demanded that they accord him enthusiastically and reverently.

Nor was the press much better. A few, very few, intrepid newspapermen defied the personality cult—James Wechsler of the *New York Post*, I. F. Stone in his *Weekly*, Fred Cook in the *Nation*. But one would search the *New York Times* and *Washington Post*, *Time* and *Newsweek*, of the 1950s in vain for the exposure and disapproval such journals lavished on Hoover twenty years later when it at last became safe to take on the FBI. Roosevelt might have contemplated getting rid of Hoover, but there is no compelling evidence even of that. None of his successors seriously considered taking so drastic a step—a step that would have enraged Congress and the country.

The FBI, as Dean Rusk, a cautious man, said in 1974, had "developed into an extraordinarily independent agency within our Government. It is hard to exaggerate that. Mr. Hoover, in effect, took orders only from himself, sometimes from an Attorney General, usually from a President, and that was it. He had created a kind of kingdom . . . almost unparalleled in the administrative branch of our Government, a combination of professional performance on the job, some element of fear, very astute relations with the Congress, and very effective public relations."[23] By 1961 the FBI was a runaway agency, and its director sacrosanct and untouchable.

II

Through the years, the FBI had depended on a variety of investigative methods. Most important, from the viewpoint of obtaining convictions, were "informants"—members of or infiltrators into groups under suspicion. The advantage of informants was that their testimony could be used in court. Other techniques were employed to gain "strategic" intelligence rather than to build legal cases. There was "electronic surveillance." This had two legally and technologically distinct forms: "wiretapping"—the physical tapping into telephone wires in order to record calls; and "bugging"—the planting of concealed microphones near the person under surveillance. Bugging required "trespass" if the bug was planted inside a person's room; nontrespassory bugs were also possible. Then there was "surreptitious entry" or "black bag" jobs—breaking into an office or dwelling in order to copy papers or for other purposes, such as, very often, the installation of a bug. And there was "mail opening"—intercepting and photographing personal letters.

Some of these methods violated federal law. But anything was all right so long as the director approved. Clarence M. Kelley, an FBI agent for twenty years and later one of Hoover's successors as director, remarked in 1976 that some agents still clung "to the idea that you can do anything you want so long as you follow certain ideas that were embedded in them throughout the many years of the leadership of Mr. Hoover. . . . It was an authoritarian type of leadership."[24] It was indeed. Hoover took care to keep his superiors in ignorance about his methods. "We do not obtain authorization," William Sullivan noted in an internal FBI memorandum in 1966, "for 'black bag' jobs from outside the Bureau."[25] Sullivan later told me, "We never, never told any Attorney General about surreptitious entry or about the opening of mail."[26] FBI intelligence reports, even when distributed to the Attorney General, methodically camouflaged the sources. "T-1, a confidential informant of known reliability" might mean a tap, a bug, a burglary, a mail intercept or even a confidential informant of known reliability. Hoover actually invented a "Do Not File" procedure designed to hide what the Bureau was doing.[27] Since some of the things it was doing were patently illegal means to allegedly patriotic ends, it was not the habit of Attorneys General to inquire too closely.

Of the FBI methods, only one—wiretapping (as distinct from bugging)—required the Attorney General's specific authorization. This was for particular historical reasons. When Harlan Stone reorganized the Bureau of Investigation in 1924, he had banned wiretapping. The Treasury Department's Prohibition Bureau, however, tapped freely. A Seattle bootlegger named Olmstead, protested that wiretapping was a form of unreasonable search and therefore forbidden by the Fourth Amendment. In 1928 the Supreme Court ruled in the *Olmstead* case that wiretapping did not breach the Constitution. It was a 5-4 decision. Justice Brandeis in dissent warned that "the progress of science in furnishing the government with means of espionage is not likely to stop with wiretapping." Justice Holmes contemptuously described wiretapping as "dirty business" and said: "I think it is a less evil that some criminals should escape than that the government should play an ignoble part."[28]

In 1930 the Prohibition Bureau was transferred to Justice. Faced with the anomaly that one of his bureaus was tapping while another was forbidden to do so, Herbert Hoover's Attorney General removed Stone's ban on tapping by the Bureau of Investigation. Congress responded by including in the Communications Act of 1934 a section making it a crime for any person not authorized by the sender to "intercept any communication and divulge or publish the . . . contents." Though J. Edgar Hoover expressed public doubts about tapping till 1939, FBI agents tapped nonetheless while Section 605 was awaiting clarification by the judiciary. The Supreme Court soon ruled that wiretap evidence and evidence derived from wiretap leads were inadmissible in federal courts.[29] In 1940 Attorney General Robert H. Jackson reinstituted Stone's ban. He added his hope that Congress would authorize tapping under safeguards.

Something should be said about the atmosphere of the time. Wiretapping was not the black-and-white issue it became in later years. Ardent New Dealers like Henry Morgenthau, Jr., Harold Ickes and Fiorello La Guardia favored tapping for their own presumably benign purposes. Moreover, the rise of Hitler and fears of his Fifth Column argued for vigilance. "In general," said Franklin D. Roosevelt, "my own personal point of view is close to that of Justice Holmes in his famous dissent in the *Olmstead Case*."[30] But, with Nazi armies poised to overrun western Europe, FDR was willing to make exceptions.

Three months after Jackson's order and under pressure from Morgenthau,[31] Roosevelt gave Justice qualified permission to wiretap "persons suspected of subversive activities against the United States." He directed the Attorney General "to limit these investigations so conducted to a minimum and to limit them insofar as possible to aliens." He added that "under ordinary and normal circumstances wiretapping by Government officials should not be carried on for the excellent reason that it is almost bound to lead to abuse of civil rights."[32] He would also require, he added in 1941, that "the Attorney General be acquainted with the necessity for wire tapping in every single case and that he himself sign a certificate indicating such necessity."[33]

Jackson, worried about reconciling Roosevelt's directive with the Federal Communications Act, resolved the problem by construing Section 605 to require *both* interception and divulgence to become operative and by construing divulgence as disclosure *outside* the executive branch.[34] This strained construction licensed the FBI to tap wires and disseminate the results within the government. Jackson, who regarded the whole business with distaste, thereafter left the problem to Hoover without himself passing on each case. Francis Biddle, his successor in 1941, established the practice of case-by-case authorization by the Attorney General, sometimes turning down Hoover's requests.[35]

Roosevelt saw wiretapping primarily as a wartime measure of counterespionage. After his death and the war's end the FBI continued to tap. The Cold War offered new justification. In 1946 Attorney General Tom Clark, transmitting a draft prepared in the Bureau, asked Truman to renew Roosevelt's 1940 authorization.[36] The FBI version of the directive, however, broadened it spectacularly, omitting Roosevelt's instruction to confine tapping to aliens, espionage and sabotage. After Truman approved the Hoover-Clark draft, George Elsey of his White House staff discovered the distortion and called the new language "obviously a very far cry from the 1940 directive."[37] Nothing was done about it. Thereafter Hoover claimed that the Roosevelt memorandum authorized the FBI to tap in a wide variety of cases, though still with case-by-case approval by the Attorney General. State and local police were tapping happily in at least half the states. In most of these states wiretap evidence was admissible in state courts.

"The progress of science," as Brandeis had foreseen, was meanwhile improving the technology. The rise of the unwired microphone —the "bug"—gave the FBI a means of electronic surveillance they used without application to the Attorney General. In 1952, however, Attorney General Howard McGrath caught on and forbade the Bureau to install bugs involving trespass. But in 1954 Hoover procured a memorandum from Attorney General Herbert Brownell envisaging "the unrestricted use" of bugs "in the national interest" and omitting to require case-by-case authorization from the Attorney General.[38] Hoover took the Brownell memorandum as a general license for bugging, even with trespass. He could now switch back and forth, using bugs when he wanted to minimize an Attorney General's knowledge, taps when he wanted to maximize an Attorney General's complicity.

In 1961, as Kennedy became Attorney General, the situation was as follows: (1) the FBI could wiretap only on the written authorization of the Attorney General; (2) state and local police taps, often stimulated by the FBI, went freely along as state law permitted; (3) the FBI bugged ad lib at the director's discretion and without notice to Attorneys General; (4) the FBI indulged ad lib in surreptitious entry in order to install bugs or for other purposes, and did so without the knowledge of any Attorney General.*

III

The FBI leadership was pleased neither by John Kennedy's election nor by his brother's appointment. "We'll be stuck with the Kennedy clan," Clyde Tolson observed sourly, "till the year 2000."[39] But they were realists. The Kennedys were realists too. With so minuscule an advantage in the popular vote, the President-elect was not about to take liberties with a national icon. In any case, as Robert Kennedy said in 1964, "Father was a good friend" of Hoover's and his brother "didn't have anything against Hoover, and he thought it was well that Hoover stayed."[40] Immediately after the election Kennedy announced that he would keep Hoover on along with Allen W. Dulles of the CIA.

In the 1950s Robert had had more direct dealings than his brother with the director. His early impulse no doubt had been to place Hoover in the Great American Patriot niche along with Herbert Hoover and Douglas MacArthur. Then came his fight with the Bureau over the Annie Lee Moss case. Later, relations seemed to improve. "I saw [Hoover] on various occasions where he was very friendly and nice." Once in Justice, "I really deferred to him," Robert told Anthony Lewis in 1964.

---

* "There is no indication that any Attorney General was informed of FBI 'black bag' jobs, and a 'Do Not File' procedure was designed to preclude outside discovery of the FBI's use of the technique" (Church committee, *Final Report,* bk. II: 61; see n. 7).

I mean, I made a real effort because I recognized the fact that I was young and coming in there and all the rest of the business; and I was making so many changes, not only in organized crime but what we wanted to do in civil rights. . . . I made arrangements with my brother that he would call him every two or three months and then have him arrange to have J. Edgar Hoover, just by himself, for lunch. . . . It's what kept Hoover happy for three years because he had the idea that he had direct contact with the President, and he used to tell me that every month, I guess, Franklin Roosevelt used to have him over for lunch.[41]

Amenities were carefully observed between the Attorney General and the director. Katzenbach thought the relationship "very distant and formal. Bobby always felt embarrassed calling him Edgar."[42] Bobby himself believed that his effort, on the whole, had succeeded. On the surface, he said later, relations were "smooth. I knew that he didn't like me much. . . . But the relationship that we had was not difficult. I mean, it was not an impossible relationship."[43]

John Kennedy regarded Hoover with skepticism. "The three masters of public relations in the last half century," the President told me in October 1961, "have been Baruch, Hoover and Allen Dulles."[44] Once he summoned Theodore Sorensen and me to the residential part of the White House to discuss a speech. We arrived just as Hoover was leaving the lunch table. Kennedy conspicuously omitted to introduce us, remarking later that he had not wanted to upset Edgar too much.[45] One of his favorite lines, the last phrase of which he adapted to the occasion, went: "The three most overrated things in the world are the state of Texas, the FBI and" whatever was exasperating him most at the moment.[46] Still, getting on with Hoover seemed an elemental political necessity. As 1964 approached, Kennedy told Ben Bradlee of *Newsweek* "how FDR used to have Hoover over regularly [a thought Hoover constantly pressed in slightly exaggerated form on both Kennedy brothers], and said he felt it was wise for him to start doing the same thing, with rumors flying and every indication of a dirty campaign coming up. 'Boy, the dirt he has on those senators,' Kennedy said, shaking his head."[47] But Kennedy, as William Sullivan observed, "distrusted Hoover and wouldn't have dared to make a political request of him."[48]

Some Presidents, and Attorneys General, were beguiled by Hoover's gossip. "Edgar was not above relishing a story derogatory to an occupant of one of the seats of the mighty," Francis Biddle recalled of his own days as Attorney General. ". . . I confess that, within limits, I enjoyed hearing it."[49] "I didn't get the feeling that President Kennedy was that kind," observed Clark Clifford. "He wasn't a gossipy man. Some presidents . . . love to get little tidbits, particularly on their enemies and all. I didn't find that quality in the President."[50] According to Kenneth O'Donnell, the designated White House recipient of FBI reports about government officials, Kennedy "didn't like to hear about their sex life, he didn't want to hear whether they drank, he didn't want to hear anything personal about anybody." His reactions were certainly not always those that Hoover intended. Once the prim-prurient director sent over an FBI report describing a mettlesome American ambassador who, caught in a woman's bedroom, hastily departed through a window without his trousers. When the White House failed to react, Hoover queried O'Donnell. O'Donnell, who had had little use for Hoover since Rackets Committee days, said that, yes, the President had seen the report. Asked what he had said, O'Donnell replied: "He said that from now on he's going to hire faster ambassadors."[51]

Hoover, said Robert Kennedy, "was really of no particular importance to him." As O'Donnell put it, "We had a hell of a lot more problems than J. Edgar Hoover.... He was so far down the list. I don't think the President and Bobby even discussed it.... Bobby took care of his own problems pretty good. He never went crying to anybody."[52] Robert Kennedy later summed it up from his viewpoint: "It was important, as far as we were concerned, that [Hoover] remained happy and that he remain in his position because he was a symbol and the President had won by such a narrow margin and it was a hell of an investigative body and he got a lot of things done and it was much better for what we wanted to do in the south, what we wanted to do in organized crime, if we had him on our side."[53]

IV

For Hoover, the very existence of an Attorney General who was the brother of the President represented an unprecedented threat. It was not, of course, just the family tie. Brothership worked no political magic for Sam Johnson, for example, or Donald Nixon or Billy Carter. But Robert Kennedy was an aggressive executive in his own right. Moreover, if Roy Cohn can be believed, Hoover had cordially disliked him ever since the Annie Lee Moss incident.

Kennedy's informality certainly infuriated the director now. He was upset by Kennedy's excursions around the Department, and FBI memos of the period reflect a continuing surveillance by the Bureau of the Attorney General's movement. "This certainly proves the point we have been stressing," the director noted on the border of one, "—our employees should always be busy; engage in no horse play; and be properly attired. No one knows when & where A. G. may appear."[54] Once Hoover and Tolson came to the Attorney General's office. As the three men talked, Kennedy, to Hoover's repressed rage, idly tossed darts at a board on the wall. "In other words," explained a Tolson assistant, "he did not give the Director undivided attention." Hoover became even more upset when Kennedy missed the board, and darts lodged in the paneling. "It was pure desecration," the director said later. "Desecration of government property." Hoover and Tolson cut their visit short and later agreed, as the director told another subordinate, that it was "the most deplorably undignified conduct they had ever witnessed on the part of a Cabinet member."[55]

"I was in Bobby's office once when he summoned Hoover," William Hundley of the Organized Crime Section recalled. "I couldn't get over it." Hundley had been reporting on a political case where Hoover had been, as he saw it, dragging his feet. Kennedy asked whether Hundley wanted to hear Hoover's explanation. "That was too much, so I said 'Yes.' So he hit a goddam buzzer and within sixty seconds, the old man came in with a red face, and he and Bobby jawed at each other for about ten minutes. And Hoover kept looking at me."[56] "Nobody had ever buzzed for Hoover!" said Walter Sheridan, who as an ex-FBI agent observed the relationship with a certain relish. "And Hoover came. But I'm sure it griped him very much to come. And Bob would go in his office in his shirt-sleeves; nobody had ever done this before."[57] After one such call, Hoover, deeply disturbed, said to Assistant Director William Sullivan, "It is ridiculous to have the Attorney General walking around the building in his shirtsleeves. Suppose I had had a visitor waiting in my anteroom. How could I have introduced him?"[58]

Worst of all, the Attorney General did not sufficiently respect the Bureau's highly prized autonomy. Robert Kennedy's deference, which he evidently thought abundant, was from Hoover's viewpoint strictly limited. While the Attorney General was happy to appease the director with occasional White House luncheons, he insisted (with imperfect success) that FBI communications to the White House pass through his own office. No Attorney General had tried to do this since Biddle fifteen years before. He instructed the Bureau to send its press releases to Guthman's office instead of putting them out, as it had done for years, on its own letterhead. Instead of clearing Hoover's speeches and statements automatically, as his predecessors had done, Kennedy sometimes returned them with requests for revision "in the interest of accuracy or Administration policy."[59] He installed a direct line from his own office to the director's desk. Once when Hoover's secretary answered a Kennedy call, the Attorney General informed her curtly that hereafter he expected the director to pick up the phone himself.[60]

Hoover had always demanded that communications from the Attorney General to the FBI go through him to the agents. Kennedy did not hesitate to call FBI men working on cases without speaking to the director first.[61] Hoover was further irritated by Kennedy's habit of dropping in on regional FBI offices and asking questions about current cases. The Attorney General even persuaded FBI offices to place a photograph of John Kennedy next to the obligatory photograph of Hoover, though he affected to believe that it was always the same photograph, circulated by the Bureau to be put up ten minutes before his arrival.[62] In any case, he got around. As special agent William Barry, who often accompanied Kennedy, said later, "Hoover never visited the offices [Kennedy] visited." To Kennedy such visits were part of the Attorney General's responsibility. He wanted, as Barry said, to "let people know that the Attorney General did exist, that they were part of the Justice Department."[63] To Hoover the visits were an inexcusable intrusion.

Over the years the director had successfully withdrawn the Bureau from the oversight of the Department of Justice. The arrival at Justice of a President's brother, a brash young man determined to annex the Bureau to the Department, radically altered his position. It also fed his incipient paranoia. "For the first time in his career," as Ralph de Toledano described Hoover's view in his reverent biography, "Hoover was forced to deal with an Administration that was overtly hostile, that wanted him out."[64] The idea that the Kennedys were planning his dismissal seized possession of his mind. Byron White was occasionally mentioned as a possible successor. For a while Hoover got it into his head that Adam Yarmolinsky, a blameless and scholarly lawyer working for McNamara in Defense, was scheming to get his job. In his usual manner, he leaked items to the press designed to discredit Yarmolinsky.[65] Hoover was no more enthusiastic about the idea of a successor from inside the Bureau and harbored dark suspicions that one or another subordinate was aspiring to the directorship. "What the hell's wrong with wanting to be director?" said one of them (John P. Mohr). "Does the President get mad at every kid that wants to be President? . . . I never said that to Hoover, though."[66] To be in the line of succession was nearly as perilous in Hoover's FBI as in Mao Tse-tung's China.

From time to time—or so it seemed from the Attorney General's office—someone would organize a keep-Hoover campaign. Letters poured into Justice, many, Seigenthaler said later, "identical to other letters."[67] Actually Hoover had little to fear during Kennedy's first term. The political risks appeared too great. But on January 1, 1965, the director would have his seventieth birthday. Hundley was convinced "that the thing that finally destroyed their relationship was that Bobby mentioned to too many people who complained to him about Hoover that, 'Look, just wait,' and we all got the message that they were going to retire him after Jack got reelected and Hoover hit seventy. And it got back to him."*

Convinced that the Kennedys were out to get him, Hoover resorted to his traditional techniques of self-defense. He tried ingratiation. One finds in Robert Kennedy's papers the following letter from Hoover:

> After observing your car in the Department garage, I would like to thank you for coming to work on February 22nd, a national holiday. . . . The spirit you demonstrated—the spirit of Valley Forge and Monte Cassino—will, we hope, spread through the entire Department of Justice. Keep up the good work.[68]

What in the world was this? Flattery? Sarcasm? Kidding? In other moods he was more menacing. "Every month or so," Robert Kennedy said later,

> he'd send somebody up or a memo . . . to give information on somebody I knew or a member of my family or allegations in connection with myself, so that it would be clear whether it was right or wrong that he was on top of all of these things and received all of this information. He would do this also, I think, to find out what my reaction to it would be. . . . I remember on one occasion that somebody said that my brother and I had a group of girls on the 12th floor of the LaSalle Hotel and that, I think, the President used to go over there once a week and have the place surrounded by Secret Service people and then go up and have assignations. . . . A lot of it was so far fetched that even on the face of it it didn't make any sense. I mean, if you were going to do that kind of thing, you wouldn't go on over to the LaSalle Hotel with the Secret Service surrounding the place. But I think the idea was just so that you would know that they were continuously getting into this information.†

---

* Ovid Demaris, *The Director* (New York, 1975), 147; William Hundley, in interview by author, August 4, 1976. RFK in December 1964: "President Kennedy would have gotten a replacement before he left office" (RFK, in interview by Anthony Lewis, December 4, 1964, IV, 35, JFK Oral History Program).

† RFK, in Lewis interview, V, 2–3. Another example of Hoover's admonitory operation was provided by the disclosure in December 1977 of a memorandum from the FBI director to Robert Kennedy on June 5, 1963, containing assertions that Robert

In public, the Attorney General meticulously defended the director. One disaffected agent, having tried in vain to persuade Kennedy to act on his grievances, concluded: "In retrospect, it would seem that the Kennedys, having made a political decision to retain Hoover, temporarily felt that they had to put on a public face of supporting him."[69] Privately it was very different. If Robert Kennedy generally contained himself, his irrepressible wife could not. The director, who was perennially feuding with city police chiefs, particularly disliked Chief William H. Parker of Los Angeles. Once at a Department of Justice party Ethel Kennedy had some words with Hoover. "There was a little electricity between the two of them," said William Barry, who observed the scene. "On the way out she put in the FBI suggestion box [a note saying] 'Chief Parker in Los Angeles for Director.' "[70]

When a police system passes beyond the limit of dealing only with such conduct as is forbidden by the laws, Harlan Stone had said in 1924, "it is dangerous to the proper administration of justice and to human liberty." Forty years later Anthony Lewis asked Robert Kennedy whether he thought Hoover just a nasty person or truly dangerous. "No," Kennedy replied. "I think he's dangerous."[71] "He's rather a psycho," he told John Bartlow Martin, ". . . I think it's a very dangerous organization . . . and I think he's . . . become senile and rather . . . frightening."[72]

The word in the FBI, said William Sullivan, was that the two men in the world J. Edgar Hoover hated most were Martin Luther King second and Robert Kennedy first.*

Kennedy in 1960 had settled out of court a breach-of-promise suit, going back to 1951, for $500,000. The story was improbable on the face, for a decade-old breach-of-promise suit against a President-elect would have been generally discounted as publicity seeking. In any event, the woman named, Alicia Darr Purdom Clark, promptly denied that she and John Kennedy had been lovers or that she had ever received a cent from the Kennedys. She added not implausibly: "In fact Jack owed me money. . . . He used to borrow dollars from me for cab fares. He never paid them back" (see *New York Times*, December 15, 1977; *Washington Post*, December 16, 1977; *New York Post*, December 17, 1977; "Walter Scott's Personality Parade," *Parade*, April 2, 1978).

* Sullivan, in interview by author, July 26, 1976. Jack Anderson reported (*New York Post*, October 9, 1975) that Hoover told Herbert Jenkins, the Atlanta police chief and then president of the International Association of Police Chiefs, that the three enemies he hated most in the world were Kennedy, King and Quinn Tamm, a former FBI assistant director who had become executive director of the International Association.

(13)

The Pursuit of Justice: The Mob

THE ENCOUNTER between Robert Kennedy and J. Edgar Hoover was, within its peculiar limits, a fascinating case history in the politics of administration: the aggressive executive versus the supreme bureaucrat; the presidential brother versus the national hero. The limits were imposed on one side by the fact that even a presidential brother dared not provoke a national hero to resignation,[1] on the other by the fact that even a national hero dared not break with the President's brother. At stake in this first round was Robert Kennedy's determination to complete the unfinished business of the Rackets Committee and bring the men who ran the mob and the labor rackets to the bar of justice.

I

Hoover's obsession in 1961 remained the Communist movement. For years he had warned his fellow countrymen against the diabolic machinations of these godless masters of deceit. Despite the patriotic endeavor of the FBI, however, the threat, at least as measured by the director's rhetoric, apparently continued to grow. In an agitated memorandum a fortnight before John Kennedy's inauguration, Hoover informed the new Attorney General that the American Communist party presented "a greater menace to the internal security of our Nation today than it ever has since it was first founded in this country in 1919."[2]

Robert Kennedy was unmoved. Party membership had in fact drastically declined from its 1944 peak of 80,000. But Hoover needed the threat to preserve his mystique. "When the membership figures kept dropping lower and lower," William C. Sullivan reminded Hoover in 1971, "you instructed us not to give them out . . .

not even to the Justice Department."[3] The Attorney General, undeceived, saw communism as a danger *to* but hardly *in* the republic. "It is such nonsense to have to waste time prosecuting the Communist Party," he told Henry Brandon of the *London Sunday Times* in December 1961. "It couldn't be more feeble and less of a threat, and besides its membership consists largely of FBI agents."[4] "As far as having any real influence as a party in the United States," he observed in an interview with representatives of the Knight newspapers, "it's zero."[5] When I wrote a piece for the *Saturday Evening Post* in 1962 entitled "The Failure of World Communism," Hoover, who had described me in an internal FBI memorandum as "a stinker" as early as 1950 and had forbidden FBI agents to talk to me in 1954, minuted to an associate, "I understand better now the views of the A.G. since the latter is a great admirer of Schlesinger."[6] (As usual, the director exaggerated.)

The enemy within, in Kennedy's view, was something very different. The Rackets Committee had instructed him in the covert realities of power and corruption in American life. "Organized crime," he said succinctly in his first speech after becoming Attorney General, "has become big business."[7] What appalled him, as he told a congressional committee in 1963, was the "private government of organized crime, resting on a base of human suffering and moral corrosion," infiltrating business, labor, politics and government. The racketeer was no longer "someone dressed in a black shirt, white tie and diamond stickpin, whose activities affect only a remote underworld circle. He is more likely to be outfitted in a grey flannel suit and his influence is more likely to be as far-reaching as that of an important industrialist."[8]

In 1961 Jerry Wald, the Hollywood producer, proposed to Kennedy that *The Enemy Within* be made into a movie. Of the writers Wald mentioned, Kennedy promptly chose Budd Schulberg, whom he remembered as the author of *On the Waterfront,* the powerful Sam Spiegel–Elia Kazan film of 1954 about labor racketeers. Schulberg discussed *The Enemy Within* one night at Hickory Hill. What attracted him to the book, Schulberg said, was the theme that "something at the core of our society was beginning to rot." Responding, Schulberg recalled, "simply and modestly; in fact, diffidently," Kennedy said, "Good.... I wrote those last pages very carefully—I didn't want the book to seem to be aimed against a single man or a single union. It is the society that produces a Beck or a Hoffa or a Johnny Dio. I don't know how you are able to bring that out in a picture, but that seems to me the only real reason for making the picture." The next ten years, he told Schulberg, might mark a turning point in American history—either an America infected with corruption or the rebirth of the idealism with which the nation had begun.*

Kennedy was determined to stop the drain of power in America to obscure forces beyond moral and legal accountability. In insisting on the spreading threat of organized crime, he offended J. Edgar Hoover doubly—by dismissing the cherished Red menace and by raising a question the director had done his best for forty years to ignore.

Here one encountered another aspect of the gap between inside and public perceptions of the FBI. For the G-men had made their reputation as gangbusters. In 1934, after Roosevelt's anticrime legislation established federal jurisdiction over a variety of interstate felonies (including flight across state lines to avoid prosecution or even to avoid giving testimony in court), the FBI ended the careers of notorious outlaws like Dillinger. Nor had the Bureau let anyone forget these triumphs. They were not, however, triumphs over organized crime. The outlaws were petty entrepreneurs. Often, like Bonnie and Clyde, they were amateurs engaged in sporadic and desperate acts. They were leftovers from an individualist past, irrelevant to the new criminal world of the syndicates, the world characterized, as Daniel Patrick Moynihan wrote in 1961, by "a large, wealthy, and firmly entrenched criminal class."[9]

The much advertised lists of Public Enemies, Top Fugitives and Most Wanted Men kept up the illusion that the FBI was unrelenting in its war on criminals. In fact, of the hundreds of crooks thus honored, very few had any connection with organized crime.[10] While the Bureau had chased Bonnie and Clyde, it left Vito Genovese and Meyer Lansky of the syndicates to flourish in peace. In the meantime, Elmer Irey, chief of the Treasury Department's Intelligence Unit, quietly brought down Al Capone, Johnny Torrio, Waxie Gordon and Willie Bioff. Thomas E. Dewey in New York broke up the Lucky

* Budd Schulberg, "RFK—Harbinger of Hope," *Playboy*, January 1969. Kennedy liked Schulberg's script, but Wald, who, Schulberg said, "alone had the courage to produce it," died suddenly. A "labor tough" warned Twentieth Century-Fox that, if the picture were made, the Teamsters would refuse to deliver the print to the theaters. When Columbia, the distributor of *On the Waterfront*, showed a brief interest, William Bufalino, a Hoffa attorney, wrote a letter to the studio pointing out that Twentieth Century-Fox had wisely abandoned the project as soon as the possible consequences had been laid before it and that he felt confident Columbia would be intelligent enough to do likewise. (See Schulberg's introduction to Walter Sheridan, *The Fall and Rise of Jimmy Hoffa* [New York, 1972].) As for Kennedy, Schulberg wrote in *Playboy*, "I understood that it was not his role to ask any studio to produce his book."

The Pursuit of Justice: The Mob

Luciano ring. Harry Anslinger of the Bureau of Narcotics was spinning tales about the Mafia. Organized crime was not precisely a secret even in the 1930s, except evidently to J. Edgar Hoover. None of the mobsters above, save for a passing reference to Capone, was even mentioned in Don Whitehead's authorized history, *The FBI Story*, written with Hoover's cooperation in 1956.

Robert Kennedy had discovered Hoover's indifference to organized crime when he requested FBI dossiers on the Apalachin conferees in 1957. Apalachin shook the Bureau itself for a moment. William Sullivan of the Intelligence Division persuaded Hoover to assign the best FBI crime researcher, Charles Peck, to prepare a report on organized crime. The Bureau also started up some electronic surveillance. But, when Hoover read the Peck report, he denounced it as "baloney" and ordered it suppressed.[11] In 1959 the FBI New York office had over four hundred agents working on communism, four on organized crime.[12]

The shock to the Department of Justice lasted a little longer. Attorney General Rogers brought William Hundley over from the Internal Security Division to head up the Organized Crime Section of the Criminal Division. In Internal Security Hundley had found "cooperation from the FBI that was unbelievable."[13] In Organized Crime, Hundley found the FBI's noncooperation equally unbelievable. "It was like pulling teeth to get anything done in this field at all. . . . I had come out of Internal Security where you had agents coming out of your ears, and get over into Organized Crime and you couldn't find an agent."[14] Rogers also set up the Special Group on Organized Crime under Milton Wessell, a New York lawyer. When the group asked the FBI about Apalachin, "the G-men," said one of Wessell's assistants, "acted as if they had never heard of Apalachin."[15] Hoover denied FBI assistance to Wessell, who eventually retired, defeated, to New York. The director explained to the worshipful House Appropriations Subcommittee in 1961 that too many people were seeking "fantastic panaceas as to how to solve *local crimes.*" (Agent W. W. Turner noted that, while Hoover was turning down the Organized Crime Group, FBI agents were busy copying number plates of out-of-state cars parked in airports in the hope of finding a stolen car.)[16]

II

Why did Hoover veer away from organized crime? His own favorite explanation was legalistic. "The truth of the matter," he said in 1964 (and on many other occasions), "is the FBI had very little jurisdiction in the field of organized crime prior to September 1961."[17] This proposition was a transparent fraud. The 1934 legislation had given the FBI ample jurisdiction. Eminent gangsters were crossing state lines every day, for example, to avoid prosecution or the giving of testimony. When mobs put out contracts on their enemies, they tended as a matter of standard operating procedure to import gunmen from another state. Many federal statutes covered syndicate activities.* Hoover had carved out his spacious jurisdiction in internal security with virtually no statutory basis at all. As James V. Bennett, director of the Bureau of Prisons, put it, "If they want to do it, it's within the jurisdiction of the FBI. If they don't want to do something, they'll tell you it's outside the jurisdiction of the FBI."[18]

Why then? Former FBI agents laid great stress on Hoover's infatuation with statistics. He liked to regale Congress with box scores of crimes committed, subjects apprehended, crimes solved. Organized crime did not lend itself to statistical display. It required a heavy investment of agents in long, tedious investigations that might or might not produce convictions at the end. The statistical preoccupation steered Hoover toward the easy cases—bank robbers, car thieves, kidnappers and other one-shot offenses.†

The statistics race—each year had to be better than the year preceding—also increased the Bureau's dependence on local law enforcement. The FBI very often inflated its statistics by claiming credit for work performed by local police, as in the recovery of stolen cars.‡ This dependence argued further against the pursuit of organized

---

* "Among the statutes under the FBI's wing were acts relating to the kickback rackets, extortion, anti-racketeering, labor-management relations, unauthorized publication or use of communications, obstruction of justice, bankruptcy (the scam has long been a favorite Cosa Nostra fraud), the white slave traffic, perjury, misprision of felony, trust formation, interstate transportation of stolen property, interstate transportation of gambling devices, lottery tickets, and wagering data, hijacking, bribery, fraud by wire, and federal firearms control" (William W. Turner, *Hoover's FBI* [New York: Dell reprint, 1971], 162–163).

† William C. Sullivan, in interview by author, July 26, 1976; Turner, *Hoover's FBI*, 4, 16, 159, 246–253. Note William Hundley: "I concluded that the inability to build statistics in organized crime was a factor in the Bureau's reluctance to enter the area" (Pat Watters and Stephen Gillers, eds., *Investigating the FBI* [New York, 1973], 165).

‡ Warren Olney III, head of the Criminal Division in the years 1953–57, called Hoover's statistics "hogwash" and said of auto theft cases, "In at least half, and possibly more of these, the thieves are arrested and the cars returned by local officials" (*Newsweek*, December 7, 1964). Olney's cavalier attitude toward the Bureau doubtless explains Hoover's fierce opposition when Chief Justice Warren proposed Olney as chief counsel of the Warren Commission (see *Clandestine America*, January–February 1978).

crime. For the mobs often had their own arrangements with local police, politicians and businessmen. Hoover did not want to get into that. Even the admiring Toledano admitted that Hoover considered it "futile to take on the crime which is entangled with legitimate business or local politics until the community—national or otherwise—was ready for it."[19]

He also, according to Toledano, feared that "to make the attempt would expose the FBI to all the temptations of corruption and big money, returning it to its sorry state under the Wilson and Harding administrations"[20]—an unnecessary slur, it would seem, on the probity of his agents. Still there was little chance of their being bribed by the American Communist party. In addition, the great proponent of the Mafia thesis was Harry Anslinger, the director's ancient rival and a leading figure on his hate list. Beyond all this, one cannot omit the possibility that Hoover, who was among other things a right-wing ideologue, honestly believed that Communists were far more dangerous to the republic than organized criminals.

For whatever reason,* the director of the FBI had stayed out of a battle that the former counsel of the Rackets Committee considered crucial to the national future. After his experience with the Teamsters and the mobs, Robert Kennedy now found himself unexpectedly embroiled with a third secret organization, almost as impenetrable and self-hallucinated as the others, but this time operating under the color of law.

---

* More sinister reasons have been proposed and will only be noted here. I have no reason to believe that they are true—or false. According to *Time* (December 22, 1975): "Hoover was reluctant to move against organized crime. Some FBI agents think they know why. They tell stories of Hoover sometimes traveling to Manhattan to meet one of the Mafia's top figures, Frank Costello. The two would meet in Central Park. Costello apparently convinced Hoover that there was no organized Mafia—merely a loose collection of independent racketeers." The fact that Hoover met with Costello is confirmed by William Hundley and Edward Bennett Williams.

Hank Messick, author of several books on organized crime, points out ("The Schenley Chapter," *Nation*, April 5, 1971) that, according to the testimony of his fourth wife, Lewis S. Rosenstiel of Schenley Industries and a good friend of Hoover's was also a longtime friend of Meyer Lansky. Other testimony suggests that Rosenstiel and Lansky had been in business together during prohibition. Rosenstiel subsequently employed Louis B. Nichols, formerly an assistant director of the FBI, and in 1969 set up the J. Edgar Hoover Foundation. Messick raised the not uninteresting question: "How . . . can a man be a friend of J. Edgar Hoover on the one hand and a chum of Meyer Lansky on the other?"

III

The story is told of an early exchange between Kennedy and J. F. Malone, head of the FBI office in New York. "Mr. Malone," Kennedy said, "could you please bring me up to date on what's been happening with organized crime?" "To tell you the truth, Mr. Attorney General," Malone replied, "I'm sorry, but I can't, because we've been having a newspaper strike here."[21]

The national government had twenty-six investigative units at work on the domestic scene.[22] But none knew what the others had discovered about the underworld, and the FBI seemed to know least of all. This situation had led to Kennedy's call from the Rackets Committee for the pooling of intelligence through a national crime commission. Hoover hated to share FBI intelligence on the pretext that other agencies could not be trusted and that somewhere an informant would be betrayed. He hated even more to be caught without information to share. He therefore fought the national crime commission to the end.

Luther Huston, the departing information officer for Justice, described what may have been the climactic moment. Scheduled to pay his formal farewell to Hoover, Huston had to wait because the new Attorney General was already in the director's office. "He hadn't called or made an appointment. He had just barged in. You don't do that with Mr. Hoover. Then my turn came and I'll tell you the maddest man I ever talked to was J. Edgar Hoover. . . . Apparently Kennedy wanted to set up some kind of supplementary or overlapping group to take over some of the investigative work that the FBI had been doing. My surmise is that Mr. Hoover told Bobby, 'If you're going to do that, I can retire tomorrow. My pension is waiting.' "[23]

That evidently ended the national crime commission. Frustrated here, the Attorney General approached the problem circuitously. Two key agencies in the campaign against organized crime were the Internal Revenue Service and the Narcotics Bureau, both in the Treasury Department. Kennedy brought Secretary Dillon and Mortimer Caplin, who had been one of his law professors at Charlottesville and was now commissioner of internal revenue, together with Hoover and talked about the importance of sharing criminal intelligence.

> I said that this was something that I knew that President Kennedy was interested in (this was the advantage of being the President's brother), and it

was something that I was interested in. . . . I said, "This is what we're going to concentrate on, and this is what we're going to do. I want it done." . . . Then I got the Bureau of Narcotics. . . . There was no question that I could do it [only] because of my relationship. They wouldn't have paid any attention to me otherwise.[24]

Hoover, having prevailed on the national crime commission, had to go along on this more modest proposal. For the first time all the federal groups that knew anything about the underworld came together in the same room and exchanged information.

Kennedy gave the job of coordination not to the FBI but to the Department's Organized Crime Section. There researchers compiled a roster of leading racketeers, circulated the list among the investigative agencies and used the result as the basis for prosecutions. At the same time, Kennedy quadrupled the Organized Crime Section in size and encouraged its lawyers to conduct investigations and try cases. Recalling his problems on the Rackets Committee with Hundley, Kennedy replaced him by Edwyn Silberling, who had worked for District Attorney Frank Hogan in New York. In time he had problems with Silberling too. After two years he brought back Hundley, who had stayed on as one of his special assistants and had handled special assignments with dash and discretion.

Kennedy was resolved to force the FBI into action against the mob. If lack of jurisdiction was Hoover's alibi, then Kennedy would make FBI jurisdiction explicit; at least this would weaken the alibi. In April 1961 he submitted a legislative program. In September Congress enacted five of his eight proposals, the most important of which covered interstate travel in support of racketeering, interstate transportation of gambling equipment and interstate transmission of gambling information. Even with this enabling legislation, however, it remained a battle to get Hoover to acknowledge the existence of organized crime.

Then in 1962 Joseph Valachi, a member of the Genovese gang now in the Atlanta penitentiary, killed another prisoner whom he mistook for a fellow mobster commissioned to kill him. Faced with the death penalty, Valachi agreed to talk in exchange for life imprisonment. He knew a great deal, apparently had total recall and poured out voluble recollections. His account of Italian criminal "families" gave the disparate intelligence accumulating in Justice a unifying theory. "What he did," Hundley said, "is beyond measure. . . . In the past we've heard that so-and-so was a syndicate man, and that was about all. Frankly, I always thought a lot of it was hogwash. But Valachi named names. He revealed what the structure was and how it operates."[25]

Among the names Valachi provided was a new one for the phenomenon that Harry Anslinger had so long called the Mafia—La Cosa Nostra ("our thing"). Since Hoover had always scoffed at the idea of the Mafia, the new phrase allowed him to discover organized crime without appearing to admit that the detested Anslinger had been right. In early 1963 an article signed by Hoover and intended for the *Reader's Digest* reached Edwin Guthman's desk for clearance. Casually imbedded in the middle was a quick reference to the Cosa Nostra. The rest of the piece was routine. Hoover "just wanted," Guthman said later, "to get those two paragraphs printed so that he could say, 'The FBI knew all along.'"[26] Guthman demanded their deletion. Hoover withdrew the article.

This hardly seemed the way to make the most of Valachi's testimony. "We talked about it," recalled Robert Kennedy, "and said that if it was going to come out, it should come out in a more organized fashion."[27] This led to a piece by Peter Maas in the *Saturday Evening Post*. The McClellan committee then wanted Valachi to testify. Kennedy, Hundley said, was "really very reluctant"; Hoover even more so. Hundley warned that, if Justice did not cooperate, the committee would subpoena Valachi. After intricate negotiation, the FBI seemed to agree that Valachi's appearance would not compromise other underworld sources. "But we lost control," said Hundley. The committee, without consulting the Department, put the hearings on television. Valachi was unimpressive on the stand. Italian Americans raised a fuss, claiming a libel on their people.[28]

Hoover lost no time in expressing public displeasure. Valachi, he wrote, had only "corroborated and embellished the facts developed by the FBI as early as 1961." His public appearances, Hoover added, "magnify the enormous task which lies ahead."[29] All this implied that Kennedy was making his job harder. When newspapers thus construed Hoover, "he refused," said Kennedy, "to deny the story that he was upset about Valachi, which irritated me."[30] After all, the FBI had presumably agreed to this use of Valachi. "We didn't understand," Guthman observed later of this episode, "that they never really said what they were thinking."[31]

Hoover was engaged in a rearguard action. He had lost the battle. The importance of Valachi, Robert Kennedy said later, was that "for the first time the FBI changed their whole concept of crime in the United States."[32]

IV

Subversion was out. Organized crime was in. Hoover grudgingly went along. But he exacted his price. He got more money as well as more explicit and possibly wider jurisdiction, and he preserved the autonomy and secrecy of FBI operations.

Wiretapping remained the single FBI investigative technique requiring the specific approval, case by case, of the Attorney General. Kennedy, who had watched Jimmy Hoffa wilt before Frank Hogan's wiretaps in 1957, believed that tapping had a significant if restricted role to play in law enforcement. "My feeling," he said shortly after assuming office,

> is that the use of legal wiretaps should be limited to major crimes such as treason, kidnaping, and murder. In each instance it should only be done with the authority of a Federal judge. . . . At the same time, there is a great deal of indiscriminate wiretapping that now goes unpunished. Therefore, it is essential that the penalty for indiscriminate wiretapping be greatly stiffened. . . . Legalized wiretapping is a two-edged sword that requires the most scrupulous use. For that reason, I would not be in favor of its use under any circumstances—even with the court's permission—except in certain capital offenses.[33]

On a cold day in March 1961, he convened his advisers on the stone terrace at Hickory Hill to discuss the wiretap problem. Byron White and Herbert Miller were strongly for legislation. Archibald Cox and Burke Marshall thought a reasonable statute could be drafted. Ramsey Clark, Joseph Dolan and William Orrick demurred, Orrick most emphatically of all. Kennedy said to Orrick, "What if your child was kidnapped?" Orrick replied, "Well, Bob, hard cases make bad law." Kennedy, who could not imagine letting legal niceties halt the search for a kidnapped child, grew heated. "I wanted to get off that," Orrick said later. "He just stayed with it. He said, 'Well, I just don't understand your attitude.' I got a little irritated. I said, 'You asked us to come up with our own opinions and I did.' "[34]

Kennedy decided to go ahead. His goal was a comprehensive system by which all wiretapping, federal, state or local, would be made a federal crime, except when specifically authorized by a federal judge. In effect, he wished to move toward the British system, where tapping was forbidden without a warrant, though his proposal that the warrant be issued not by the executive (the Home Secretary) but by the judiciary improved on the British model. The FBI, however, demanded that the bill skip court orders for national security cases, a position he reluctantly accepted.[35] In the end, instead of seeking new legislation that year, Kennedy carelessly (and without White House clearance) decided to support a bill already introduced by Senator Kenneth Keating of New York.

The Keating bill, while purporting to limit federal wiretaps, would have permitted state and local cops to tap wires in any way authorized by state law. It was a poor bill. Civil libertarians attacked it, and Kennedy soon abandoned it. In 1962 Katzenbach drafted a bill[36] designed to clear up what Kennedy described as the "chaotic" situation. The new bill proposed to outlaw warrantless wiretapping, whether conducted federally or locally, publicly or privately, except in cases involving serious threats to national security. It defined cases where taps might be permitted under judicial supervision, limited the officials who could apply for court orders, required that each application state grounds in detail and provided for automatic termination of all judicial warrants.[37]

Some observers considered the 1962 bill a responsible effort to strike a balance between the competing claims of privacy and law enforcement. Francis Biddle, who had clerked for Holmes and defended civil liberties for a lifetime, testified for it. The bill "struck me at the time," said Alexander Bickel, "as by far the best solution to the wiretapping problem that had yet been put forward."[38] But the bill also roused a storm of criticism, led by the American Civil Liberties Union and by Kennedy's friend from Rackets Committee days Joseph Rauh.

The critics believed that a wiretap system was inherently uncontrollable and that the dangers to personal freedom far outweighed the gains to law enforcement. They denied the possibility of an American compromise along British lines. They found the categories of tappable crimes dangerously vague. Recalling the familiar phenomenon of "judge shopping," they questioned whether judicial warrants could provide effective control. In any case, where a search warrant authorized only a single search for specified objectives, a wiretap warrant was a dragnet. Nor did they believe that wiretap evidence made all that much difference. They quoted Justice Frankfurter: "My deepest feeling against giving legal sanction to such 'dirty business' . . . is that it makes for lazy and not alert law enforcement."[39] Where Kennedy sought to put an end to warrantless wiretapping, his critics demanded the flat prohibition of all forms of electronic surveillance.

The bill failed in Congress in 1962 and, despite expectation in

1963 that the Valachi testimony would help, it failed thereafter.[40] The chaotic situation continued. State and city cops went their own way. So did private tappers. Federal wiretaps remained under the control, not of the federal courts, but of the Attorney General.

Robert Kennedy authorized 140 wiretaps in 1961, 198 in 1962 and 244 in 1963 (as against 519 authorized in 1945, 214 in 1955 and 115 in 1960).[41] Nearly all were "national security" (as distinct from criminal) cases. Nearly all were directed against aliens. In three and a half years as Attorney General, Kennedy authorized taps on about sixteen American citizens involved in eight separate cases. (This figure omits an undisclosed number tapped in 1964 at the request of the Warren Commission.) Five of these cases had national security implications: defense leaks to newspapermen (Lloyd Norman of *Newsweek* and Hanson Baldwin and his secretary of the *New York Times*);* attempts by the Dominican government to influence sugar quota legislation (the clerk of the House Agriculture Committee; three officials of the Agriculture Department; an American national registered as a Dominican lobbyist; and, most inexcusably, the switchboard of a law office where one of the lawyers was working for the Dominicans); a high CIA official accused (wrongly) of having given classified information to a Yugoslav diplomat; and Dr. Martin Luther King, Jr., and two associates, tapped in order to test Hoover's assertion that King was involved with Communist agents. The three remaining taps on American citizens were urgently requested by the FBI without evident international pretext: on a former FBI agent whom Hoover claimed had revealed "confidential" Bureau information; on an Alabama Klan leader; and on Malcolm X, the black nationalist. In some cases—Baldwin and his secretary, Norman, the erring ex-FBI agent—the Bureau tapped first and got Kennedy's written approval later.†

In the main, Kennedy consented to Hoover's wiretap requests. Nor

---

* Baldwin had written a story about photographic surveillance of Soviet missiles by United States satellites. As a result of the publication of the story, the Soviet Union took steps to conceal their missiles, thereby causing great difficulties for American intelligence (see RFK, in interview by John Bartlow Martin, April 13, 1964, II, 9–10, JFK Oral History Program).

† Senate Select Committee to Study Governmental Operations with respect to Intelligence Activities, *Final Report*, bk. II, *Intelligence Activities and the Rights of Americans*, 94 Cong., 2 Sess. (1976), 63–65. This tabulation does not include wiretaps on foreign nationals. Such wiretaps sometimes caught Americans, including members of Congress—e.g., Senator Thomas J. Dodd, when the FBI tapped Michael Struelens, a Belgian who was operating in the United States as the agent for Moise Tshombe's secessionist regime in Katanga.

did he do much to tighten the controls he had inherited from his predecessors. Always the improviser rather than the planner, he handled wiretap authorizations with surprising casualness and inattention. "You never knew," Katzenbach said later, "whether [a tap] was disconnected or still going on, and you never knew what developed out of it, whether it was fruitful or not. So at no given time did any Attorney General know how many wiretaps there were and who they were on."[42] Kennedy could have done something administratively about that, as his successors, Katzenbach and Clark, tried to do thereafter.

But Kennedy did not promote wiretapping. For all his strong feelings about organized crime and Jimmy Hoffa, he authorized no wiretaps against racketeers or Teamsters. He continued to deplore the power given him as Attorney General to decide whose phone should be tapped; "there's no check on what I do whatsoever." In 1964 he condemned the continuing failure of Congress to transfer that power to the federal courts, where "you would . . . have to keep continuously making reports as to what you were doing."[43] He thought wiretapping a valuable tool in a very few very particular circumstances. He wished it, if used at all, to be hedged around by statutory safeguards. As Attorney General, he opposed its total abolition.

V

Kennedy evidently supposed that the power to authorize wiretaps was the power to contain the FBI's electronic surveillance. He could not have been more mistaken. The wild card was bugging. The war against organized crime had put Hoover on his mettle. The director was under exasperating pressure from the Attorney General. His reputation was on the line. He well knew how much ground the FBI had to make up. The quickest way was to do what he had long done in internal security: to bug the enemy and thereby draw in the information that would lay the groundwork for penetration.* He had already started bugging the mob in a small way after Apalachin. In 1961 he began to bug it in a big way. He did this, as he had always done, on his own. At no time did he seek bugging authorization from the Attorney General. In later years, however, when the public began to

* See Victor Navasky, *Kennedy Justice* (New York, 1971), 67. William Hundley said in 1975: "I think somewhere internally a decision was made that organized crime was heating up and they didn't have any informants so they'd better do something to catch up" (Ovid Demaris, *The Director* [New York, 1975], 144).

catch on to the extent of FBI bugging, he claimed vigorously that Kennedy had known what the FBI was doing—a claim that Kennedy with comparable vigor denied.

In December 1966 Hoover wrote to Congressman H. R. Gross of Iowa, "Your impression that the FBI engaged in the usage of wiretaps and microphones only upon the authority of the Attorney General of the United States is absolutely correct."[44] Hoover's suggestion that taps and bugs were on an equal basis was false. Courtney Evans, who had served as FBI liaison with Kennedy in Rackets Committee days, continued in that role in Justice. "It was my understanding at the time," Evans said in 1975, "that any tap required the written authorization of the Attorney General, but that no such authorization was required for the use of microphone surveillance."[45] Accordingly, when Evans briefed Kennedy in January 1961 on wiretap procedures, he said nothing about bugging.[46] "The Attorney General's personal approval was not sought [for bugging]," said Katzenbach, who succeeded White as deputy attorney general in April 1962 and Kennedy as Attorney General in September 1964, "nor was he even directly advised of any microphone surveillance despite their increased use through the late 1950's and early 1960's."[47]

Hoover nonetheless argued forcibly that Kennedy *knew*. When Harold Cooley, chairman of the House Agriculture Committee, met secretly with Dominican agents in a New York hotel room in 1961, Hoover, according to his own memorandum of a talk with Kennedy, told him "we are trying to cover" the meeting. Later he gave Kennedy a summary of what was said. Kennedy no doubt supposed that the meeting had been covered by an informant. Actually the FBI had bugged the room. An FBI review of the case in 1966 concluded, "Our files contain no clear indication that the Attorney General was specifically advised that a microphone surveillance was being utilized."[48]

Hoover claimed to Gross that Kennedy had "in different metropolitan areas . . . listened to the results of microphone surveillances."[49] The director had particularly in mind a session at the Chicago FBI office where FBI agents, obviously hoping to please the Attorney General, played a tape on which a Chicago hood complained to a crooked police captain that, after Kennedy had taken office, they couldn't fix cops any more.[50] In 1966 Hoover demanded that the Chicago agents prepare affidavits saying that in the light of the discussion Kennedy would have had to conclude that the Bureau was engaged in bugging. Some agents complied with Hoover's demand; others refused.[51] William Hundley, who was present, denied that Kennedy had any reason to believe it was an FBI tape.[52] Edwin Guthman, who was present, said, "The clear impression we received was that the FBI had obtained the recordings from local law enforcement sources."[53]

Hoover also produced two documents. One was a letter from Herbert Miller to Senator Ervin in 1961 reporting that the FBI had sixty-seven bugs in operation. Miller assumed, he said later, that the bugs had been legally installed—as, with the owner's consent, in a restaurant or apartment, or on an informant's person. "I had no knowledge then, and am firmly convinced that no one in the non-FBI section of the Department of Justice had knowledge that the FBI was in fact trespassing to place such devices. Had this been known to the Department, I am convinced that immediate steps would have been taken to stop the practice."[54]

Hoover's second document was an FBI request, initialed by Kennedy himself, for authority to lease a special telephone line in order to monitor microphone surveillance in New York City. Kennedy, observing that the request had to do with telephones, evidently thought that he was approving the leasing of a line to be used for wiretaps, and that the Bureau would come back to him for authorization in each specific case.[55] The FBI request was in any event disingenuous, since the leasing never took place. Navasky's conclusion is persuasive: "The FBI's purpose . . . was apparently not to lease a telephone line but to get the Attorney General's participation on the record. Whether or not Robert Kennedy realized the implications of what he was signing is something we will never know."[56]

Courtney Evans may have, with the best of motives, contributed to misunderstanding. He had been in the FBI for a quarter century and had great loyalty to the organization. He also had great respect for Kennedy. He saw his task as that of keeping the Attorney General and the director together. It was an impossible job. As William Hundley said, "Evans walked a very tight rope."[57] Still, "it worked very well for one basic reason," observed Katzenbach, "and that is Courtney would explain something to Bobby one way and explain something to Hoover another way. And I don't think anybody could have done the job in any other way."[58]

In July 1961 the Attorney General held a meeting on organized crime. According to Edwyn Silberling in 1966, Kennedy told Evans that he wanted the FBI to use more "technical equipment" against the syndicates.[59] G. Robert Blakey, a lawyer in the Organized Crime

The Pursuit of Justice: The Mob

Section, recalled "quite vividly" in 1966 "when you turned to Courtney Evans and told him more or less, 'Let's get some of this security equipment on the street. You tell me all the things it can do.' . . . You were telling the Bureau to stop making excuses for their failure to develop adequate information and to start using electronic equipment. . . . It now looks to an awful lot of good guys like myself that you are cutting out when the going is getting rough. . . . Your present posture indicates you are a liar or a fool. I know you to be neither."[60] After the meeting, Courtney Evans reported to Hoover:

> It was pointed out to the Attorney General that we had taken action with regard to microphone surveillance in these cases. . . . The Attorney General stated he recognized the reasons why telephone taps should be restricted to national-defense type cases and he was pleased we had been using microphone surveillances, where these objections do not apply, wherever possible in organized crime matters.[61]

On the other hand, Evans told the Church committee in 1975 that he had been "purposely vague" in talking about electronic surveillance because Hoover had instructed him not to discuss technical devices outside the Bureau—an admonition, Evans said, that applied even to the Attorney General.[62] And Evans had written Kennedy in February 1966, "I did not discuss the use of these devices with you . . . nor do I know of any written material that was sent to you at any time concerning procedure, or concerning the use, specific location, or other details as to installation of such devices."[63] "Judas Iscariot," Hoover said of Evans when he learned of this letter. "Judas Iscariot." ("Judas Iscariot?" exclaimed one agent. "Does the Director think he's Jesus, for Christ's sake?")[64]

VI

Who outside the Bureau knew about the bugging? "I knew for years that the FBI was making widespread use of electronic bugs in organized crime investigations," Hundley said later. "But the top brass of the Bureau would flat-out lie to me, denying it, whenever I officially asked about it. . . . I figured that this was obviously so delicate that it must be something that was just between the AG and the Director."[65] So he never discussed FBI bugging with Kennedy, any more than he had with Rogers before him; nor did he discuss it with Miller, his immediate superior, who in any case supposed it to be nontrespassory.[66]

Byron White did not know the FBI was bugging. In May 1961

Hoover had sent him one of his memoranda-for-the-record entitled "Technical and Microphone Surveillance." There is no evidence that White ever saw it, nor did Hoover release it in his 1966 barrage against Kennedy.* Katzenbach did not know, save for a single incident. Once an FBI report on Las Vegas casinos contained internal evidence of FBI bugging. Katzenbach brought the report to Kennedy. "We both thought," Katzenbach said later, "this is something that had just happened in Las Vegas and no place else.... In hindsight that was stupid on my part and on his. He said to me, 'Make sure this is stopped.' And I said to Courtney [Evans], 'Am I absolutely assured that this is stopped?' and Courtney said, 'Yes.' ... It was stopped in Las Vegas. That was exactly what we'd asked for and that's what we got."[67]

"You look back," said Henry Ruth of the Organized Crime Section, "and you feel stupid. We'd get furious because we'd propose an investigation and they'd say, 'There's absolutely nothing there!' *Now* I know what this meant—either they knew from bugging that there was nothing there, or they knew that whatever was there was tainted —it couldn't be used as evidence in court because it was the result of a bug."[68] "Until 1965," said Burke Marshall, "I did not know that the bureau engaged in unlawful electronic bugging without authorization or review by anyone outside the bureau."[69] "I believe," John Douglas wrote Kennedy in 1966, "that as Attorney General you did not know of any installation and use by the FBI of electronic listening devices in connection with investigations of organized crime."[70]

If the ignorance seemed singular, there were constraints against undue curiosity. "One thing you just don't do in the jungle of law enforcement," said Ramsey Clark, "particularly when you're in a staff meeting and here are twenty-five guys, is say 'Well, who was your informer?' or, 'Where did you get that information?'"[71] Dolan felt in addition that the electronic world was a mystery to the Attorney General. When Kennedy used phrases like technical equipment, "He didn't really know what he was talking about.... He had a very bad, poor, mechanical, technical, scientific background.... He couldn't tell a spark plug from a generator.... I was always surprised at his lack of knowledge of techniques."[72]

Certainly when the facts burst on him in 1966 Kennedy struck ev-

* Navasky, *Kennedy Justice*, 94–95, 448–449. Navasky surmises that Hoover did not use this memorandum in 1966 because it misrepresented the bugging authority Hoover claimed to have from the Brownell memorandum of 1954 and perhaps because White by this time was on the Supreme Court.

eryone as genuinely astonished. Hundley went to see him. "Unless he was the greatest actor in history," he said later, "he really got very upset. I liked Bobby Kennedy, but we weren't that close. What the hell, he fired me once. And he said, 'You knew about it? You knew and you didn't tell me?' . . . I came away convinced, and I'm convinced to this day, that he didn't know. . . . One thing he never was —he wasn't a liar." Hundley, thinking to himself, "I'd rather go down in history as a guy who might have moved around a little than as an idiot," told Kennedy that, even if he hadn't known, it would be better politics to say he had. Kennedy replied, "How can I? I didn't know."[73]

At the same time Hoover might have truly supposed, as a consequence of Courtney Evans's mediation, that Kennedy did know. "I think in part," Katzenbach said later, "the whole wiretap, bugging issue was really that. I really honestly think that Hoover thought that this had all been explained to Bobby by Courtney."[74] This, without malice toward Evans's "unfortunate human trait of trying to please everybody," appeared to be Kennedy's own conclusion.*

Robert Kennedy, in my judgment, had not understood that the FBI was bugging the mob, certainly not with trespass. Nor had he authorized wiretaps against the mob. Where then did he suppose that, beyond bugging by local cops, the increasingly voluminous FBI intelligence on organized crime was coming from? The answer was penetration. "They started to get informants," he told Anthony Lewis in 1964. "I asked them to go into it like they went into the Communist Party."[75] Hoover sustained this impression at every opportunity. "Infiltration, the same technique which had proven so successful in the FBI's drive against facism, communism, the Ku Klux Klan and other enemies of freedom," he said, "was brought to bear on the underworld."[76] "We have carried on a very intensive campaign against

---

* Frank Mankiewicz, in recorded interview by L. J. Hackman, September 9, 1969, 35, JFK Oral History Program. On the other hand, William Hundley recalled in 1971: "I was talking to Katzenbach one day, and Katzenbach told me that Hoover himself had told him, Katzenbach, that Bobby Kennedy did not know about the bugs. So rather cynically I said to Katzenbach, 'I hope you had a witness.' And he said, 'I had a witness. I had the best witness in the world.' He wouldn't tell me any more than that. Well, I found out later on from talking to Bobby. . . . This was during the Indiana campaign. I told him the story and he just laughed. He said, 'Well, the only mistake that Katzenbach made is when he told you that he had the best witness in the world. He really had the worst witness in the world.' I said, 'Who do you mean?' He said, 'The witness was President Johnson.' " (Hundley, in interview by J. A. Oesterle, February 22, 1971, 38, RFK Oral History Program.)

the Cosa Nostra. We have been able to penetrate it, and we know quite well what its activities are."[77]

The question remains: could Kennedy not have found out about the FBI's bugging? Here was a first-class administrator, an indefatigable question-asker, experienced in the war against crime, surrounded by clues. Granted the extenuating factors—the difficulties of dealing with Hoover, the Bureau's addiction to secrecy, the need to secure the Bureau's cooperation, the easy assumption that the Bureau was exploiting bugs laid down by local police forces, the equal ignorance of his deputies—still, why did it not occur to him to raise the bugging question with Miller or Silberling or Hundley—or Hoover?

In a later time he would readily agree that of course he should have done this. I imagine there were several reasons that he didn't. He was probably the busiest man in Washington, increasingly involved in affairs far outside the Department of Justice. And, though he was coming to understand the importance of the Bill of Rights, his sensitivity to civil liberties in these years was less than his concern about organized crime. So he did not pursue the question as he should have. Perhaps, like all his eminent predecessors, he did not want to know.

VII

Under Kennedy's pressure the national government took on organized crime as it had never done before. In New York, Robert Morgenthau, the federal attorney, successfully prosecuted one syndicate leader after another. The Patriarca gang in Rhode Island and the De Cavalcante gang in New Jersey were smashed. Convictions of racketeers by the Organized Crime Section and the Tax Division steadily increased—96 in 1961, 101 in 1962, 373 in 1963.[78] So long as John Kennedy sat in the White House, giving his Attorney General absolute backing, the underworld knew that the heat was on.

So did Jimmy Hoffa. After the Rackets Committee reports, Eisenhower's Department of Justice had decided in the summer of 1960 to indict Hoffa for mail frauds in connection with Sun Valley, a Florida real estate venture in which he had a personal financial interest. At the last minute, while James Dowd, the Justice Department lawyer, was making the case for indictment in a Florida grand jury room, the Department changed its mind and summoned Dowd back to Washington. Hoffa was supporting Nixon in the presidential campaign. Some thought this lay behind the cancellation of the indictment.

After the election, Attorney General Rogers went ahead with the case. Hoffa claimed he had been double-crossed. "I know for a fact," Allan Oakley Hunter, a former FBI man and California congressman, wrote Hoffa in an effort to divert his rage from Nixon, "that your side of the case was put before the Vice President and that he discussed the case with the Attorney General. . . . The Vice President has been sympathetic toward you and has felt that you were being subjected to undue harassment by certain parties. . . . Mr. Nixon having lost the election, I doubt that he has since been in a position to exercise any decisive degree of influence."[79]

Rogers, observed Paul Healy of the *New York Daily News,* has left the Kennedys "an inaugural present on their doorstep—the indictment—and is in effect saying: 'All right, let's see what you can do!' "[80] Robert Kennedy lost no time in responding to the challenge. He may well have put Herbert Miller in charge of the Criminal Division less because of Miller's criminal law experience, which was scant, than because of his experience as counsel for the anti-Hoffa members of the Teamster Board of Monitors. Kennedy then asked Walter Sheridan to set up a unit on labor rackets in the Organized Crime Section. It was an unconventional appointment. Sheridan was not even a lawyer. But he was a superb investigator, patient and careful; and he surrounded himself with crack lawyers, like James Neal and Nathan Lewin. J. Edgar Hoover took the Sheridan appointment as one more affront. He did not like competing investigative teams and he mistrusted agents who had left the Bureau. "Hoover hates my guts," Sheridan noted later.[81] But, though out of favor in the Washington headquarters, Sheridan, as an ex-agent, had many FBI friends and gained extensive cooperation in the field.

The Sheridan group became known popularly, though never in the Department, as the Get-Hoffa Squad. Hoffa quickly felt its impact. By October 1961 he was complaining to the press that twenty-nine grand juries had been convened to get him, that half the lawyers in the Department and half the agents in the Bureau were enlisted in the effort. "There were, in fact, at the time," Sheridan wrote later, "thirteen grand juries . . . sixteen attorneys . . . and perhaps thirty FBI agents."[82] Still this was not unimpressive. A number of Teamster leaders, including Anthony Provenzano and Barney Baker, were in due course convicted and sent to prison. But the essential objective was Hoffa himself.

Rogers's Sun Valley indictment was dismissed for technical reasons: the grand jury had not been properly empaneled. Kennedy moved for reindictment. Then an investigation of the Teamsters' Central States Pension Fund in Chicago disclosed a larger case. Soon a new indictment was in preparation, charging Hoffa with conspiring to defraud the trustees of the pension fund. Part of the charge included a misappropriation of more than $100,000 to rescue his Sun Valley investment. Since the new indictment covered Sun Valley, Kennedy decided to drop the Florida case and concentrate on the Chicago prosecution.[83]

In the meantime, a grand jury in Nashville indicted Hoffa on the charge of taking illegal payments from an employer in violation of the Taft-Hartley Act. This, like Sun Valley, was a case Kennedy had opened up in the Rackets Committee. In 1948 Hoffa had intervened to settle a damaging strike against a Detroit trucking firm in the company's favor. Shortly thereafter the Test Fleet Corporation, a truck-leasing company, was incorporated in Tennessee. One of the incorporators, signing only her maiden name, was Mrs. James Hoffa. The Detroit trucking firm became Test Fleet's main customer. Through the years this convenient arrangement had provided Hoffa with hundreds of thousands of dollars.

The Nashville trial began in October 1962. Soon thereafter E. G. Partin, a secretly dissident Teamster still in Hoffa's entourage, made contact with Sheridan. Sheridan was dubious. Partin had a criminal record. His stories were lurid. He reported that Hoffa had once asked him whether he knew anything about plastic bombs. "I've got to do something about that son of a bitch Bobby Kennedy," Partin recalled Hoffa as saying. "He's got to go." Kennedy had guts, Hoffa continued; he drove around by himself in a convertible, swam alone in his Hickory Hill pool and had no guards in the house. Sheridan questioned the story. Partin said he would take a lie detector test. Kennedy said wryly to Sheridan, "What do we do if that fellow passes the test?" For what it was worth, Partin did.[84]

Partin now functioned as a government informant in the Hoffa camp. The trial proceeded. The result was a hung jury. Hoffa was evidently still shooting fish in a barrel. The judge declared a mistrial and called for a grand jury investigation of jury tampering. Sheridan and James Neal, the Nashville prosecutor, were sure that, with Partin's testimony, they had quite enough evidence to indict Hoffa for conspiracy to fix the jury. In April 1963 Kennedy convened his top staff to consider what to do. Douglas, Marshall, Katzenbach, all felt they had a strong case. Cox said he would have no difficulty arguing the case before the Supreme Court. Two advisers were doubtful.

Shooting the rapids.

Skiing was a favorite sport of Ethel and Robert Kennedy's.

Robert Kennedy talks in his office at the Department of Justice with James Meredith, the first black man admitted to the University of Mississppi.

Chatting with employees at a Fuji Electric Company plant in Japan, 1962.

At a White House reception, the First Lady and President Kennedy greeting Ethel Kennedy and the Attorney General.

Robert, Jacqueline and Edward Kennedy lead the cortège following the coffin of John F. Kennedy to Arlington National Cemetery.

A distant handshake before Lyndon Johnson's first address as President to a joint session of Congress. Adlai Stevenson stands behind them.

The Attorney General with his wife and Averell Harriman at the Democratic convention in 1964, when Robert Kennedy announced that he would run for the Senate in New York.

The senatorial candidate speaking to a crowd in Watertown, New York.

The family lines up across the lawn at Hickory Hill: Robert, Ethel, Kathleen, Joseph, Robert, David, Courtney, Michael, Kerry, Christopher.

The crowd reaches out—California, 1968.

Thanking the crowd that gathered in Los Angeles to celebrate his victory in the California presidential primary, just before he left the room through an adjacent kitchen and was shot.

Senator Edward Kennedy delivers a tribute to his slain brother at St. Patrick's Cathedral in New York. Archbishop Terence Cooke is seated before the center of the main altar.

The grave at Arlington.

The Pursuit of Justice: The Mob

Hundley felt that it would come down to Hoffa's word against Partin. Ramsey Clark feared a Sixth Amendment problem—that is, that the claim would be made that Partin, an informer who had infiltrated the defense, had compromised Hoffa's constitutional right to counsel. Kennedy asked what the alternative was. "Should we have told Partin we didn't want to hear about jury tampering? And once we had heard about it, should we have done nothing about it?" It was decided to go ahead.[85]

In May 1963 Hoffa and five others were indicted for jury tampering. William Loeb of the *Manchester Union-Leader,* who had received a $500,000 loan from the Teamsters' pension fund five weeks before, wrote a flaming editorial denouncing the "persecution" of Hoffa. "The fight of James Hoffa against the Kennedys," Loeb said, "is becoming the fight of all Americans who want to stay free men and women."[86] Hoffa, as part of a series of delaying tactics, asked for a change of venue. The trial was scheduled for Chattanooga in January 1964. The Chicago trial was due later in the spring.

The pursuit of Hoffa was an aspect of the war against organized crime. The relations between the Teamsters and the syndicates continued to grow. An FBI electronic microphone, planted from 1961 to 1964 in the office of Anthony Giacalone, a Detroit hood, revealed Hoffa's deep if wary involvement with the local mob.[87] For national purposes a meeting place was the Rancho La Costa Country Club near San Clemente, California, built with $27 million in loans from the Teamsters' pension fund; its proprietor, Morris B. Dalitz, had emerged from the Detroit underworld to become a Las Vegas and Havana gambling figure.[88] Here the Teamsters and the mob golfed and drank together. Here they no doubt reflected that, as long as John Kennedy was President, Robert Kennedy would be unassailable. (And here Richard Nixon in October 1975 made one of his first sallies from his San Clemente fastness to play golf in the company of Frank Fitzsimmons, Hoffa's successor as head of the Teamsters, Anthony Provenzano, a leading suspect in Hoffa's murder, and the ex-convict Allen Dorfman.)[89]

VIII

He was tired, Robert Kennedy had said, of chasing people. Yet he was spending a conspicuous part of his life as Attorney General doing exactly that. All this engraved more deeply the public face he was trying to escape—the face of the implacable prosecutor.

His critics seized on the pursuit of Hoffa as a pretext for new criticism. Kennedy was represented as "single-minded" in that pursuit, as if chasing Hoffa consumed all his days and nights. In fact, Kennedy was one of the least single-minded men in Washington. No one except the President divided his mind among a greater variety of concerns and enterprises. When he thought about Hoffa, he thought hard about him; but thinking about Hoffa occupied a very small part of his time. I saw a great deal of him in these years and can hardly recall his mentioning Hoffa.

Thinking about Kennedy unquestionably occupied a greater part of Hoffa's time. "Between 1957 and 1964," report Ralph and Estelle James, who talked often to Hoffa in this period, "Hoffa's life was dominated by his fear of 'that little monster.' . . . Under Kennedy's direction, Hoffa believes, FBI agents followed him wherever he went, tapped his phone, opened his mail, and beamed electronic listening devices on him from half a mile away, aided by invisible powder they had rubbed onto his clothes."[90] Hoffa's paranoia gave rise to the myth that Kennedy had ordered the tapping and bugging of Hoffa. In 1969, under the Nixon administration—which was sympathetic to Hoffa, later granted him clemency and would have been delighted to dig up something on the Kennedys—the Justice Department was ordered by the Supreme Court to turn over all electronic overhearings related to the Hoffa cases, whether or not relevant to the indictments. After a thorough search, the Department found, as Sheridan summarized it, "that in the entire investigation in connection with the Hoffa cases there had not been one instance of wiretapping or bugging of Hoffa."[91]

The only bugs in the jury-tampering case were both legal. Neither was directed at Hoffa. One was authorized by the judge in order to record a Hoffa lawyer conspiring to fix a juror. The other was installed with Partin's permission in his car for a single ride (the tape turned out to be unintelligible).[92] In 1969 Sheridan learned that the FBI without telling anyone had bugged Moe Dalitz's office and recorded Dalitz's half of a phone conversation with Hoffa; had also monitored several Hoffa conversations in Teamster radio cars in Detroit. "I had not known about these overhearings," Sheridan said, "until long after I left the Department."[93] These tapes contributed nothing to the Hoffa prosecutions. Whether the FBI also opened Hoffa's mail, burgled his office or rubbed invisible powder on his clothes no one outside the FBI can say.

Still, though no illegal methods were used in the prosecutions of

The Pursuit of Justice: The Mob

Hoffa (a fact twice affirmed by the Warren Court, the most sensitive of all Supreme Courts to prosecutorial improprieties), Kennedy's pursuit of Hoffa raised troubling questions—questions well defined in a famous statement by Robert H. Jackson while still Attorney General:

> The most dangerous power of the prosecutor: that he will pick people that he thinks he should get, rather than pick cases that need to be prosecuted. With the law books filled with a great assortment of crimes, a prosecutor stands a fair chance of pinning at least a technical violation of some act on the part of almost anyone. . . . It is in this realm—in which the prosecutor picks some person he dislikes or desires to be embarrassed, or selects some group of unpopular persons and then looks for an offense, that the greatest danger of abuse of prosecuting power lies.[94]

This was the gravamen of the case against Robert Kennedy: that in singling out Hoffa, or Sam Giancana, or Joseph Aiuppe, the Chicago hood convicted under the Migratory Bird Act, or Louis Gallo, Crazy Joe's brother, convicted for false statements on a Veterans' Administration loan application for a home mortgage, he was abusing the prosecuting power. He was deciding that people were guilty and then looking for something they could be found guilty of. He was convicting them not for their real crimes but for slips that anyone might have made. Beginning with the criminal rather than with the crime led to selective justice. "Never in history," said Navasky about the Test Fleet case, "had the government devoted so much money, manpower and top level brainpower to a misdemeanor case."[95] Would it have done so, would it have bothered to bring the case at all, had the defendant not been Jimmy Hoffa? Hoffa was no doubt a menace to society, and the Get-Hoffa Squad might have a righteous purpose. But the precedents created might beget in other hands Get-NAM Squads, Get-ADA Squads, Get-Enemies-List Squads in any form.[96]

The question of discretionary justice bore with special weight on tax prosecutions. Kennedy and Mortimer Caplin had brought the Internal Revenue Service roaring into the battle against organized crime. After meeting with Kennedy, Caplin instructed the IRS investigators: "The Attorney General has requested the Service to give top priority to the investigation of the tax affairs of major racketeers. Such an undertaking . . . has my wholehearted endorsement." He added that racketeers would be "subjected to the 'saturation type' investigation. . . . Full use will be made of available electronic equipment and other technical aids." The IRS was soon bugging nearly as much as the FBI. In reviewing tax returns, Caplin gave priority to racketeers. In the end, 60 percent of all organized crime cases in these years were tax cases.[97]

This practice raised questions. Some lawyers believed that the purpose of the tax laws was to collect revenue, not criminals. Crooks should not be singled out. Their tax returns should be subject to the same random review as those of any other citizen. Kennedy thought the argument "specious."[98] So long as the same tax standards were applied to crooks as to other citizens, then it did not matter if their cases were moved to the top of the pile. Louis Oberdorfer, the highly scrupulous chief of the Tax Division, accepted a working compromise according to which the Criminal Division could make recommendations to the IRS for investigations (Oberdorfer was not then aware of the electronic methods used by the IRS), and the Tax Division would apply the same criteria to racketeers as to all other cases submitted by the IRS for possible action. "The whole time Kennedy was here," Oberdorfer said later, "never once did he try to push me to indict somebody or to push me not to indict somebody."[99]

The traditional criminal investigation, as G. Robert Blakey pointed out, moved "from the known crime to the unknown criminal." Someone committed a murder, a rape, a robbery, and the job of law enforcement was to find out who did it. The new world of the syndicates was characterized by the opposite problem—"known criminals but unknown crimes."[100] So you had to begin with the criminal. In addition, big shots rarely committed gross crimes themselves. That was what the "Enforcers" and "soldiers," like Joe Valachi, were for. Because top racketeers were remote from overt acts, they were vulnerable only on the margin, as in their tax returns. Nor were they forlorn individuals, outmatched by the massed power of the federal government. As Nathan Lewin said of Hoffa, "They had limitless funds and used them, and didn't play by the rules. . . . During the Nashville case Hoffa had six high-priced lawyers sitting in a hotel room to consult with the four other lawyers they had in the courtroom. That's more than the government had working on the trial. He probably spent as much money defending himself as the government spent bringing him to justice."[101]

Robert Kennedy was not the first government official to begin with the criminal rather than the crime. In March 1929 a group of Chicago citizens waited on President Herbert Hoover. They told him that their city was ruled by Al Capone. "At once," Hoover wrote later, "I directed that all the Federal agencies concentrate upon Mr. Capone. ... The Attorney General set up a special Deputy Attorney General and equipped him with the best men from every bureau of investigation in the government."[102] Later Hoover explained to Elmer Irey of the Treasury Department: "I always wanted to see something done about Capone"; after hearing the Chicago delegation, "I gave the order to put Capone in jail." Hoover and a group of cronies used to begin each day by tossing medicine balls at each other in the White House. "When the exercising starts," Secretary of the Treasury Andrew Mellon informed Irey, "Mr. Hoover says 'Have you got that fellow Capone, yet?' And when exercise is done and everybody is leaving, the last thing Mr. Hoover always says is 'Remember, now; I want that man Capone in jail.'"[103] Hoover's Get-Capone Squad did its job. Irey's T-men put Capone away for income tax evasion. Hoover was not condemned as Kennedy was in later years. Indeed, the conviction of Capone was regarded as one of the few accomplishments of his administration.

It was not as if Kennedy had decided to go after the mob and the Teamsters out of abstract prejudice. The Rackets Committee had dug up a mass of concrete information on lawbreaking. As Attorney General, he felt an obligation to pursue that information. The targets may have received disproportionate attention in the Department of Justice. But selectivity is inescapable in any situation of limited resources, and the suspects received due process in the courts. Was there still unfairness in concentrating on one set of lawbreakers rather than another? If there were, remedy lay in the larger constellation of forces outside the courtroom. The methods that sent Capone and Hoffa to prison achieved useful social results that might not have been achieved otherwise. When those methods are abused by unscrupulous prosecutors, other forces—the courts, the legislature, the press, public opinion—must act, and in the past have acted, to restore the balance. The criticism of his pursuit of Hoffa baffled and dismayed Robert Kennedy; but it was part of the process that kept that pursuit from creating precedents by which his successors could use less defensible methods against less deserving targets.

(14)

The Pursuit of Justice: Civil Rights

"I won't say I stayed awake nights worrying about civil rights before I became Attorney General," Robert Kennedy remarked in these years. He had always acted with impetuous decency when racial discrimination forced itself on his attention. But this was response to individual wrong, not to national shame. "My fundamental belief," he said soon after taking office, is "that all people are created equal. Logically, it follows that integration should take place today everywhere." But, he added, "other people have grown up with totally different backgrounds and mores, which we can't change overnight."[1] In the longer run, it would all work out; when his grandfather arrived in Boston, "the Irish were not wanted there. Now an Irish Catholic is President of the United States. There is no question about it. In the next forty years, a Negro can achieve the same position."[2] He saw civil rights in 1961 as an issue in the middle distance, morally invincible but filled for the moment with operational difficulty. He did not see racial injustice as *the* urgent American problem, as *the* contradiction, now at last intolerable, between the theory and the practice of the republic.

I

Nor did many white Americans. It is hard to recapture the myopia of another age. After the collapse of Reconstruction, the ex-slaves and their descendants had been consigned to legal and social inferiority, forgotten by the courts, by Congress, by Presidents. In the 1930s Franklin Roosevelt did more for black Americans than any President since Lincoln, thereby switching black political allegiance from the Republican to the Democratic party. But he did it initially by general aid to the dispossessed and by government appointments, White

House hospitality and other symbolic gestures for blacks. It was not until A. Philip Randolph, the leading black trade unionist, threatened a march on Washington that Roosevelt sponsored a direct if limited attack, through the Fair Employment Practices Committee, on the structure of segregation.

After the war, Congress rejected Truman's plea to continue the FEPC. With the legislative branch hostile and, after 1952, the executive indifferent, the civil rights movement turned to the courts. The National Association for the Advancement of Colored People challenged the constitutionality of segregation in a series of suits, many argued by Thurgood Marshall, a leading black lawyer. Under Chief Justice Earl Warren's leadership, the Supreme Court began to fill the void in the constitutional process.

The fifties were premonitory: in 1954 the Supreme Court decision ordering integration in public schools; in 1955–56 the bus boycott in Montgomery, the twenty-seven-year-old Baptist minister Martin Luther King, Jr., preaching the gospel of nonviolent resistance; in 1957 Governor Faubus of Arkansas defying the Supreme Court and Eisenhower's reluctant dispatch of federal troops to Little Rock to uphold the Constitution; the same year, the enactment of the first civil rights legislation since Reconstruction. The 1957 Civil Rights Act, strengthened by a second act in 1960, was intended to secure southern blacks the right to vote. But the laws were weak, and Eisenhower's Department of Justice applied them with all deliberate lethargy; nor, save for a few determined liberals in the Senate, did white Democratic politicians accord racial justice the highest priority. In the middle fifties Adlai Stevenson, the liberal hero, had actually contemplated an appeal to black leaders for a year's "moratorium" on agitation. No white leader seemed to understand what was going on in the consciousness of black America: the ebbing away of patience; the mounting bitterness; the spreading demand, all other roads blocked, for direct action. In 1958 King founded the Southern Christian Leadership Conference. In February 1960 the sit-ins began. The pace of protest was beginning to accelerate.

The Kennedys were abstractly in favor of equal opportunity. But it took presidential politics to involve them with the movement; and then the prospect of responsibility to make them think intensively about the problem. On an August morning in 1960 John Kennedy picked up Harris Wofford, his campaign man on civil rights, in his red convertible and said, as they drove downtown, "Now, in five minutes, tick off the ten things that a President ought to do to clean up this goddamn civil rights mess." Kennedy needed the black vote. He was also, in Wofford's view, appalled by the goddamn mess. "He considered it irrational. He was not knowledgeable about it. It was alien to most of his experience. He was ready to learn."[3] During the campaign Kennedy made much of the statistics of racial discrimination and promised vigorous presidential leadership in the cause of equal rights. "There is a good deal," he said, "that can be done by the executive branch without legislation. . . . Many things can be done by a stroke of the Presidential pen"—an executive order ending discrimination in housing, for example.[4]

The narrowness of Kennedy's victory strengthened the argument that the executive route offered the best immediate prospect of progress. Wofford doubted that Congress would pass civil rights legislation in the near future, and he was sure that the legislation already passed had not been fully used. "Although it is heresy in the civil rights camp to say this," he wrote the President-elect during the interregnum, the need now was for "a minimum of civil rights legislation and a maximum of executive action."[5] Nor was this view all that heretical. The liberal Southern Regional Council reminded the administration that the Presidency was "the center of American energy." John Hannah, chairman of the Civil Rights Commission, the independent government agency established under the Civil Rights Act of 1957, gave Kennedy a series of recommendations in February, all relying on executive authority.[6] "If we go into a long fight in Congress," Kennedy himself soon told Martin Luther King, "it will bottleneck everything else"—including measures of vital importance to black Americans, like the increased minimum wage and federal aid to education—"and still get no [civil rights] bill."[7]

With executive action the designated route, the Attorney General became the key actor. "I . . . kept [the President] advised," Robert Kennedy said later, "but I think it was just understood by us, which has always been understood, that I have my area of responsibility; and I'd do it. . . . If I had a problem about alternative steps, I'd call him. . . . But I wouldn't call him just to be gabby about what was going on in the south."[8] Of all his appointments, the assistant attorney general for civil rights was "the major one that I worried over. . . . The fellow that should naturally have been appointed was Harris Wofford. . . . I was reluctant to appoint him because he was so committed to civil rights emotionally and what I wanted was a tough lawyer who could look at things . . . objectively."[9] Byron White, who had decided during the campaign that Wofford was too

The Pursuit of Justice: Civil Rights

much a crusader, now proposed Burke Marshall, thirty-eight years old, a Yale Law School graduate and a member of the eminent Washington firm of Covington and Burling. Wofford, who had conducted a joint seminar with Marshall at Howard University, also generously recommended him (and himself became special assistant for civil rights in the White House).

Marshall arrived for an interview. He was "terribly nervous," John Seigenthaler recalled. ". . . He kept getting up and walking around."[10] At last he was ushered in to see the Attorney General. Marshall was as shy as Kennedy and as little adept at small talk. They faced each other gloomily and sat through intervals of painful silence. Marshall departed, convinced he had lost his chance. Kennedy wondered whether he would ever be able to communicate with Marshall.[11] But he gave him the job on White's say-so.

The next problem was getting him through the Senate Judiciary Committee. Kennedy went to Chairman Eastland's office and said, "I have Mr. Marshall outside who is going to be head of our Civil Rights Division. I thought you'd like to meet him. He's going to put the Negroes in your white schools in Mississippi." As Kennedy recorded the story in his journal, "Eastland snorted and said, 'I don't want to see him.' I said, 'Come on, see him for a minute.' So I brought Marshall in. They looked each other in the eye and exchanged some words. Afterwards Eastland said he wouldn't hold Marshall's appointment up but he wanted it understood that he was going to vote against him. As he put it, 'I'd vote against Jesus Christ if he was nominated for that position.' "[12]

Almost at once the Department of Justice confronted a crisis in New Orleans, where Judge Skelly Wright had ordered school integration and the Louisiana legislature was determined to forbid compliance by the New Orleans school board. Kennedy said, "We'll have to do whatever is necessary." "He was really mad," Marshall said later. ". . . It was the first time that either one of us had been involved directly . . . with the way that the segregation system worked in practice, and how difficult it was going to be. And they were so irrational about it down there."[13] Marshall instituted contempt proceedings. The state yielded.[14] The experience established a partnership. Kennedy was quickly impressed by the self-effacing Marshall's precise mind, incorruptible character, dry humor and intense moral conviction. There was no one on whose judgment he relied more during the rest of his life.

II

Robert Kennedy was not learned in the intricacies of civil rights—considerably less so than his brother, who had debated these questions in the Senate. Nicholas Katzenbach recalls taking the executive order establishing the President's Committee on Equal Employment Opportunity out to Hickory Hill one evening in February 1961. To his surprise he found John Kennedy there for dinner. Producing the order, he said to the Attorney General, "You've got to sign this and give it to the President." Robert Kennedy asked what the order meant. As Katzenbach started to explain, the President cut in with questions that Katzenbach could not have answered himself had he not been studying the problem for a week. Finally Robert said to his brother, "I don't know why the hell I sign this thing and give it to you. Why don't you sign it and give it to me?"[15]

Education began at once. When Kennedy and John Seigenthaler returned from an early tour of the Department, Kennedy said, "Did anything occur to you as strange in our visit around to these offices?" Seigenthaler said he was impressed that everyone was working so hard. Kennedy said, "Yes, but did you see any Negroes? . . . Get me a study of how many Negroes are working here."[16] Of the Department's 955 lawyers in Washington, it developed, only ten were black. At his first staff meeting in February, Kennedy, stressing the importance of example, called for "thorough integration" of all Justice's offices, north and south.[17] He wrote leading law schools asking for their best black graduates. In short order the Department had many more black lawyers than ever in history.

The same belief in the necessity of example led him to a private challenge of the Metropolitan Club, which refused to admit blacks even as guests for luncheon. That policy, he wrote the board of governors in April 1961, "does not seem to me logically tenable, humanly honest, or diplomatically sound." His protest unavailing, he wrote again in September, "It is inconceivable to me, in this day and age, that the privileges of this Club which holds such a unique and peculiar position in the Nation's Capital would be denied to anyone merely because of his race. . . . I cannot in good conscience remain a member and herewith submit my resignation."* (When I sent him

---

* When Arthur Krock, who had put Robert Kennedy up for the Metropolitan Club, later attacked John Kennedy for refusing a visa to Tshombe, the black secessionist leader in the Congo, the President proposed a deal: "I'll give Tshombe a visa

an editorial from the *Pilot,* the Boston diocesan weekly, commending his stand, he responded, "The *Pilot* put it very well. We Catholics are really coming along nicely, don't you think?")[18]

As he set to work on the problems of racial justice in the south, he soon concluded that the right to the vote was the heart of the matter. "From the vote, from participation in the elections, flow all other rights," he told Anthony Lewis in 1964. ". . . I thought it could make a major difference and be of far more help than anything else if they just . . . registered a hundred people a day. . . . That was the key to opening the door to all of what they wanted to accomplish in education, housing, jobs and public accommodation." This was, moreover, the area in which Congress had conferred a clear mandate and "in which we had the greatest authority." And "I felt nobody could really oppose voting."[19]

The Eisenhower administration, except for a few months at the end when Harold Tyler became chief of the Civil Rights Division, had enforced the voting rights act "with about the vigor and imagination," wrote Alexander Bickel, "displayed by William McKinley in enforcing the Sherman Antitrust Act."[20] Only six suits were brought, and none at all in Mississippi, where the exclusion of blacks from voting was most flagrant but also where the chairman of the Senate Judiciary Committee made his home. Kennedy and Marshall were determined to change all that.

III

A major problem in voting rights cases had been the difficulty in finding witnesses willing to testify against the system of exclusion and intimidation. "I understand from Tyler and others," Harris Wofford informed the Attorney General early in 1961, "that the FBI has been the bottleneck here. Apparently the FBI has given little or no priority to requests for investigation by the Civil Rights Division. Moreover, the FBI has, or uses, few if any Negro investigators. White FBI investigators, who often have a southern accent, run into great resistance from skeptical, fearful Negroes."[21]

J. Edgar Hoover had the racist instincts of a white man who had grown up in Washington when it was still a southern city. In 1946 he had complained to Attorney General Tom Clark that the Bureau was expending too much manpower "investigating murders, lynchings and

---

and Arthur can give him dinner at the Metropolitan Club" (Arthur M. Schlesinger, Jr., *A Thousand Days* [Boston, 1965], 577).

assaults, particularly in the Southern states." The result, he said, was only to enrage "vociferous minority groups" when the Bureau failed to produce immediate results.[22] In 1948 Joseph Rauh asked Clark to have the FBI look into the attempted murder of Walter Reuther. Clark, after conferring with the director, brought back the irrelevant but revealing reply: "Fellows, Edgar says no. He says he's not going to send the FBI in every time some nigger woman gets raped."[23]

In 1957, Hoover gave the Eisenhower cabinet a briefing on racial tensions. The south, the director said, was in a state of "explosive resentment over what they consider an unfair portrayal of their way of life, and what they consider as intermeddling." Southerners simply did not accept "mixed education" as the means "whereby the races can best be served. And behind this stalks the specter of racial intermarriages." The prosegregationist White Citizens Councils were nonviolent; their membership included "some of the leading citizens in the South." The Ku Klux Klan was "pretty much defunct." As for the "crusade for integration," its leaders were threatening violence, and its organizations were major targets for Communist infiltration.[24]

The tradition of cooperation with the local cops further set the Bureau against racial cases in the south. As Truman's Committee on Civil Rights had explained in 1948, it was "difficult for the FBI agent to break this relationship and to work without, or even against, the local police when a civil rights case comes along."[25] And, if local police should stop helping on stolen cars, FBI statistics would suffer. For reasons of policy as well as prejudice, Hoover succeeded in withdrawing the FBI almost completely from civil rights investigations.[26] Internally he preserved it as a lily-white agency.

It was easy enough to bring blacks into the rest of the Department. The FBI, however, was as resistant as the Metropolitan Club. When Kennedy asked Hoover about black agents, the director replied virtuously that the Bureau did not catalogue its employees by race, creed or color. Kennedy said that Hoover's answer was most commendable, but he still wanted to know how many black agents there were. Kennedy's insistence caused, as William Sullivan remembered it, an "uproar" in the Bureau. For there were no genuine black agents. Hoover had inherited a couple when he took over the Bureau in 1924. During the war he had made his chauffeur and office boy special agents in order to protect them from the draft. But none of the so-called black agents conducted real investigations or received, as white agents did, retraining in Washington; they mostly served as drivers. Hoover finally told Kennedy there were five black agents.

The Pursuit of Justice: Civil Rights

Professing great astonishment—five black agents out of five thousand—Kennedy instructed Hoover to begin hiring more at once.[27] This order infuriated the director. "He wanted me to lower our qualifications and to hire more Negro agents," Hoover told a reporter in 1970. ". . . I said, 'Bobby, that's not going to be done as long as I'm director of this bureau.' He said, 'I don't think you're being cooperative.' And I said, 'Why don't you get a new director?'"[28] In fact, Hoover gave ground, but even to call his recruitment tokenism—ten black agents by the end of 1962—would have been wild overstatement.*[29]

Kennedy's next move was to order the FBI to start gathering information about black voting patterns in the south.[30] But FBI agents, as John Doar, a Republican holdover whom Burke Marshall put in charge of voting litigation, quickly discovered, were not "geared up to their assignment in any way, shape or form." Many were southerners. All were accustomed to working with the friendly neighborhood sheriff. Doar began to supply them with elaborate questionnaires so that they would have no excuse for not coming back with the needed data. One 1962 memorandum, Doar recalled, "went on in the most minute detail for 174 pages, explaining, anticipating, cautioning and coaching the Bureau agents."[31] In time they learned.

And in time Hoover accepted inevitability on racial justice. "I don't think that he's got a great sympathy for this," Kennedy said in 1964. "I think that he also recognizes where the power is and what he has to do; and, once he reaches that decision, that is paramount. I think he reached the decision that we were going to do things in civil rights and that that's the way it was going to be. . . . So that either you'd have to do it or you'd have to get out. . . . When they did things, frequently they did them damned well."[32]

IV

The Rackets Committee had given Robert Kennedy a favorable reputation in the white south. He knew the welcome would not last. In March 1961 he sent over to Justice Hugo Black at the Supreme Court an editorial torn from an Alabama paper. The editorial lamented that, while his native state ought to salute "a great judge and great man," Black was "so unpopular that were he to visit Bir-

---

* By 1977 there were only 139 blacks among the Bureau's 8400 agents (*U.S. News & World Report*, August 29, 1977).

mingham hardly a corporal's guard of personal friends would greet him." Kennedy wrote Black, "My congratulations to you."[33]

Early in May, Kennedy determined to go south himself. The occasion was Law Day at the University of Georgia, where two black students had gained uneasy entry through federal court order. Griffin Bell, who had managed the Kennedy campaign in Georgia, made the advance preparations and accompanied Kennedy from the Atlanta airport to the university at Athens. It was Kennedy's first address as Attorney General. He declared his personal belief in the Supreme Court's decision on school desegregation. "But my belief does not matter—it is now the law." Those who defied judicial rulings challenged "the foundations of our society." "I say to you today that if the orders of the court are circumvented, the Department of Justice will act. We will not stand by and be aloof. We will move."[34] The audience, to his astonishment, gave him an ovation. "Never before, in all of its travail of by-gone years," wrote Ralph McGill, the liberal editor of the *Atlanta Constitution*, "has the South heard so honest and understandable a speech from any Cabinet member."[35]

In enforcing the law, Kennedy said in Georgia, he hoped "to achieve amicable, voluntary solutions without going to court." He was "very sensitive," Katzenbach remembered, "as to the explosive nature" of the situation.[36] Southerners had first to have a chance at self-correction; "you didn't solve all the South's problems for it."[37] Kennedy and Marshall, as Carl M. Brauer summarized it, believed that Negro rights had "failed to survive after the Civil War because they had been established by an alien federal force; when that force was removed, the Negroes' rights rapidly withered and died. They hoped to see civil rights take root this time and were therefore determined to make the absolute minimal use of federal force."[38] "I don't think," Kennedy told Peter Maas in March 1961, "we would ever come to the point of sending troops. . . . I cannot conceive of this administration's letting such a situation deteriorate to that level."[39]

There were no negotiators more patient than Marshall and Doar. Kennedy also used his two southern assistant attorneys general, Ramsey Clark of Texas and Louis Oberdorfer of Alabama, as well as his southern assistant, John Seigenthaler of Tennessee. Preparing for the new wave of school desegregation in the fall of 1961, these men traveled about conferring with local educational officials. "I'd go in," said Seigenthaler, "my southern accent dripping sorghum and molasses, and warm them up. Burke would tell them what the law was. . . . a

The Pursuit of Justice: Civil Rights

pretty effective team."[40] In September schools were desegregated without violence in New Orleans, Atlanta and Memphis.

V

"The hardest problems of all in law enforcement," Kennedy had told the University of Georgia, "are those involving a conflict of law and local custom."[41] The white south's customs were rooted in a bitter history. The Supreme Court's law came on them as a threat to tradition, womanhood and social order. Southern blacks, awakening after so many years to their constitutional rights, were growing as militant for federal law as whites were for local custom. The negotiating approach underestimated both the intractability of the old-school whites and the passion of the new-school blacks.

In December 1960 the Supreme Court had outlawed segregation in the terminals as well as in the trains and buses used in interstate transportation.[42] The white south largely ignored the decision. The following May, James Farmer of the Congress of Racial Equality (CORE), an organization inspired by Gandhi's principles of nonresistance, led a small party, black and white, on a journey to assert constitutional rights in southern bus stations. The Freedom Riders traveled through Virginia, the Carolinas and Georgia with an occasional fracas and arrest but without major trouble. Then, dividing into two groups, one Greyhound, one Trailways, they entered Alabama. In Anniston a screaming white mob burned one bus, boarded the second and beat up civil rights workers. In Birmingham, members of the Ku Klux Klan, promised fifteen minutes of immunity by the police, set on the Riders with baseball bats, lead pipes and bicycle chains. Gary Thomas Rowe, Jr., an FBI informant in the Klan, had alerted his superiors. The FBI neglected to pass on the warning to Kennedy.[43] "Everybody who got off the bus," Rowe wrote later, "was clubbed, kicked or beaten. . . . When people looked up, I couldn't see their faces for blood. . . . I observed several FBI men . . . taking movies of the beatings." No Klansman was arrested.[44] It was Mother's Day, Eugene (Bull) Connor, the Birmingham police commissioner, later explained, and he had let most of his force off to perform filial duties.

"I never knew they were traveling down there," Robert Kennedy said in 1964, ". . . before the bus was burned in Anniston."[45] The first Washington reaction was one of dismay mingled with a certain exasperation. When Peter Maas had asked Kennedy in March about the sit-ins, the Attorney General had replied, "My sympathy is with them morally."[46] But undue militancy threatened the strategy of suasion. In the White House, John Kennedy, preparing for meetings with de Gaulle and Khrushchev in Europe, thought the Riders an unnecessary burden. "Tell them to call it off," he said to Harris Wofford. "Stop them." "I don't think anybody's going to stop them right now," Wofford said.[47]

Plainly the Riders were within their constitutional rights. Plainly the federal government had an obligation to protect travel in interstate commerce. Robert Kennedy sent John Seigenthaler to Birmingham to see what could be done. Seigenthaler found the beleaguered group, heads bloody and bandaged, still in the bus terminal. Simeon Booker, the black newspaperman, told him, "I don't believe we'll ever get out of here." After long negotiations—the airlines had received bomb threats—Seigenthaler took them on a plane to New Orleans. As they disembarked, he ran into Barry Goldwater. "This is horrible," Goldwater said. "Just horrible. Never should have happened. I'm glad you're with them."[48]

With the first group *hors de combat,* more Riders descended on Birmingham to take their place. Acting on the principle of initial resort to local authority, Robert Kennedy asked for assurances of safe passage across the state. Seigenthaler met with Governor John Patterson. Patterson had been a strong Kennedy man in 1960. "He was," Robert Kennedy remembered in 1964, "our great pal in the south."[49] Times had changed. Patterson now launched into a tirade. He assured Seigenthaler that Alabama could keep the peace without the Kennedys. "By God," he said, "I'm telling you if federal marshals come into Alabama, there'll be blood in the streets." Floyd Mann, the state director of public safety and a man of courage, told Seigenthaler his troopers would protect the bus on the highways.[50]

But no one could be found to drive the Greyhound bus to Montgomery and on to Mississippi. Kennedy called the bus company:

GEORGE CRUIT (the Greyhound superintendent). Drivers refuse to drive.
KENNEDY. Do you know how to drive a bus?
CRUIT. No.
KENNEDY. Well, surely somebody in the damn bus company can drive a bus, can't they? . . . I think you should—had better be getting in touch with Mr. Greyhound or whoever Greyhound is and somebody better give us an answer to this question. I am—the Government—is going to be very much upset if this group does not get to continue their trip. . . . Under the law they are entitled to transportation provided by Greyhound. . . . Somebody better get in the damn bus and get it going and

get these people on their way. Mr. Cruit, I think that if some of your people would just sit down and think for a few minutes that somebody would be able to drive a bus 80 or 90 miles.*

Mr. Greyhound eventually solved the problem. Floyd Mann's state troopers escorted the group to the outskirts of Montgomery.

A menacing crowd, carrying chains and ax handles, surrounded the Montgomery terminal. "The passengers are coming off," John Doar reported to Kennedy over the telephone. Then: "Oh, there are fists, punching. A bunch of men led by a guy with a bleeding face are beating them. There are no cops. It's terrible. It's terrible. There's not a cop in sight. People are yelling 'Get 'em, get 'em.' It's awful."[51] Seigenthaler, who was circling the terminal in a car, saw a Freedom Rider, a white girl, struggling to escape. A fat woman was chasing her, beating her over the head with a pocketbook; in front a young skinny kid "was facing her and dancing backwards like a boxer and smacking her in the face." Seigenthaler got out of his car. The girl said, "Mister, get away. Leave me alone. . . . You're only going to get killed. This is not your fight." Seigenthaler tried to push her into the car. Suddenly he was clubbed from behind. He lay unconscious on the ground for half an hour. FBI agents on the scene took careful notes but raised not a finger.[52] Seigenthaler awakened much later in the hospital with a concussion. In Washington, Peter Maas saw Robert Kennedy immediately after he heard about Seigenthaler. He was, Maas recalled, "possessed by an enormous anger . . . as if he had been down in Montgomery himself and been hit."[53] Kennedy phoned Seigenthaler: "You did what was right." Seigenthaler said from his hospital bed, "Let me give you some advice. . . . Never run for Governor of Alabama. You couldn't get elected."[54]

Local authority had manifestly failed to preserve civil peace. On Sunday, May 21, Robert Kennedy sent in five hundred marshals with Byron White in command. Meanwhile Martin Luther King, Jr., was flying to Montgomery. Governor Patterson informed Kennedy that he and General Henry Graham of the Alabama National Guard could not guarantee King's safety. Kennedy said, "I don't believe that. Have General Graham call me. I want to hear a general of the United States Army say he can't protect Martin Luther King." But Kennedy took no chances. "Fifty marshals," Patterson later said disgustedly,

* Transcript of Kennedy-Cruit conversation, May 15, 1961, RFK Papers. The call was recorded by Cruit, not by Kennedy. One of Kennedy's statements—"We have gone to a lot of trouble to see that they get to this trip and I am most concerned to see that it is accomplished"—was later used in Alabama and elsewhere in an effort to show that Kennedy had put CORE up to the Freedom Rides.

"met King at the airport and escorted him through town . . . just like he was the president of the United States."[55]

Patterson told Byron White rather inconsistently that Alabama could handle the situation. According to Patterson, White thereupon advised Kennedy to pull out the federal force.* Certainly, White explained at a press conference, the marshals were there only to maintain order and would not intervene if the cops arrested the Freedom Riders; "I'm sure they would be represented by competent counsel."[56] But Kennedy rejected the recommendation and told White to stay on in Montgomery.

Fifteen hundred blacks gathered on Sunday evening to hear King at the First Baptist Church. An angry white mob burned an automobile in front of the church and evidently meant to burn the church too. King called Kennedy at the Department of Justice. Kennedy assured him that the marshals were on their way, adding that, so long as he was in church, "he might say a prayer for us." "He didn't think that was very humorous," Kennedy recalled in 1964. Even when the marshals arrived, it was a serious question whether they could hold the church. "At one point," said Burke Marshall, "it really looked as if the mob might overcome the marshals and get in there." Airborne troops were put on alert at Fort Benning nearby. Military intervention was the last thing the Kennedys wanted, except that defiance of federal law and racial war were even worse. But, reinforced by the valiant Floyd Mann and a squad of state troopers and finally by the National Guard, the marshals drove the mob back. The enraged whites did not disperse, however, and the blacks in the church dared not leave.

Through the long night Kennedy was on the phone with Patterson and with King. "Robert showed no knowledge whatsoever of the problem," Patterson complained later, "and he ran the whole affair from his command post in the Justice Department, and making telephone calls at two or three o'clock here in the morning, telling us we didn't have enough policemen on a certain corner. . . . He didn't understand who these people were. . . . They were known Communists, some of 'em."[57] At one point Patterson said that the affair would ruin them both politically. "Now, John, don't tell me that," Kennedy replied evenly. "It's more important that these people survive than for us to survive politically."[58]

* A telephone operator at Maxwell Field, where White made his call, was the wife of a state trooper and "monitored" White's calls for Patterson (Howell Raines, *My Soul Is Rested* [New York, 1977], 310).

The Pursuit of Justice: Civil Rights

Around four in the morning King berated Robert Kennedy for allowing the situation to continue. "Now, Reverend," Kennedy said, "don't tell me that. You know just as well as I do that if it hadn't been for the United States marshals you'd be as dead as Kelsey's nuts right now." There was a long silence. Finally King said, "All right. All right." Perhaps he was baffled by the reference. "Kelsey's nuts" was evidently an Irish expression of unknown provenance.[59] A militant young Rider, John Lewis, later called the battle of the First Baptist Church "a real testing moment . . . without the support of the federal government at that time and a commitment, I think it could have been real bad."[60]

Around five in the morning Byron White sent William Orrick, also down from Washington, to negotiate a truce with the National Guard commander. "I was treated," Orrick recalled, "like I might have been treated in Russia. . . . There wasn't a sign of the American flag . . . just the Confederate flags. I've been four and a half years in the Army, and I know GIs like the back of my hand. They were just outright hostile. . . . The general was a lily white Wasp. He was polishing his boots when I came in and talking to his staff about being clean." After an initial refusal the Confederate leader agreed to get the people in the church safely home. (Orrick was left behind in charge of the marshals and civic tranquility in Birmingham. He called Washington and said, "I don't know how to be a law enforcement officer. I'm a corporation lawyer from San Francisco." Kennedy said, "Yeah." Orrick said, "You remember my background. I'm in the Civil Division." Kennedy said, "Yeah. Can't you do it?" Orrick said, "Yes, yes." Kennedy said, "Well, don't bother me. . . . Do it." He did.)[61]

VI

Kennedy's plan was to move the Freedom Riders out of Alabama as quickly as possible. "I thought that people were going to be killed," he said in 1964, "and they had made their point. What was the purpose of continuing with it?"[62] He called for a "cooling-off" period. James Farmer told a reporter, "We had been cooling off for 100 years. If we got any cooler we'd be in a deep freeze."[63] Kennedy said that racial troubles would embarrass the President of the United States in his meeting with Khrushchev. Ralph Abernathy, King's number two man in the Southern Christian Leadership Conference, said, "Doesn't the Attorney General know that we've been embarrassed all our lives?"[64] The Freedom Riders determined to press on to Mississippi. "I don't think any of us thought that we were going to get to Jackson," said James Farmer. "Everyone on that bus," recalled another Rider, "was prepared to die."[65] Nor was this hysteria. James P. Coleman, the former governor of Mississippi, warned Burke Marshall that his successor, Ross Barnett, could not be trusted and that the Riders would be killed before they reached Jackson.[66]

Kennedy now turned to his friend Senator Eastland. "He always kept his word," Kennedy said later, "and he always was available, and he always told me exactly where he stood and what he could do and what he couldn't do. He also told me who I could trust and who I shouldn't trust in the state of Mississippi." Eastland promised there would be no violence. "I think Jim Eastland really took a responsibility for it," Kennedy said. Eastland added that the Riders would be arrested as soon as they arrived in Jackson. "I said to him that my primary interest was that they weren't beaten up. So I, in fact, I suppose, concurred [in] the fact that they were going to be arrested, though I didn't have any control over it."[67]

When Martin Luther King called him from Jackson on the night of the arrests, Kennedy's preoccupation was with getting the Freedom Riders—Farmer among them—out of jail. To his surprise, King said they would stay in.

KING. It's a matter of conscience and morality. They must use their lives and their bodies to right a wrong.
KENNEDY. That is not going to have the slightest effect on what the government is going to do in this field or any other. The fact that they stay in jail is not going to have the slightest effect on me.
KING. Perhaps it would help if students came down here by the hundreds —by the hundreds of thousands.
KENNEDY. The country belongs to you as much as to me. You can determine what's best just as well as I can, but don't make statements that sound like a threat. That's not the way to deal with us.
[A silence]
KING. It's difficult to understand the position of oppressed people. Ours is a way out—creative, moral and nonviolent. It is not tied to black supremacy or Communism but to the plight of the oppressed. It can save the soul of America. You must understand that we've made no gains without pressure and I hope that pressure will always be moral, legal and peaceful.
KENNEDY. But the problem won't be settled in Jackson, Mississippi, but by strong federal action.
KING. I'm deeply appreciative of what the administration is doing. I see a ray of hope, but I am different than my father. I feel the need of being free now!

The Pursuit of Justice: Civil Rights

KENNEDY. Well, it all depends on what you and the people in jail decide. If they want to get out, we can get them out.
KING. They'll stay.[68]

King also had his practical side. Even before the Freedom Ride, he had suggested that the Interstate Commerce Commission act against segregation in the terminals. Kennedy had responded that the ICC was an independent commission, not subject to presidential order and notoriously slow-moving on its own.[69] Now Katzenbach's Office of Legal Counsel proposed (a lawyer named Robert Saloschin had the idea) that the Attorney General formally petition the ICC. On May 29, nine days after the Montgomery mob had tried to burn down the First Baptist Church, Kennedy, in a quite novel administrative step, asked the ICC to issue regulations ending segregation in interstate bus terminals. On September 22, 1961, the order was issued. Kennedy's negotiators set to work again, persuading local officials to take down WHITE and NEGRO signs. Though mopping-up operations were required in McComb, Mississippi, and elsewhere, Jim Crow was soon banished from bus travel. The Department then turned to the railroads and airlines. By 1963, the Attorney General could say, "Systematic segregation of Negroes in interstate transportation has disappeared."[70]

VII

Education and transportation were important; but voting rights remained the primary target. Negotiation proved no more successful here, though, as Marshall observed, the effort was essential if only to expose the illusion that white southern communities had "the will and the power to correct wrongs themselves."[71] Mediation failing, the next step was the lawsuit. Voting rights cases had ordinarily been argued by local federal attorneys; but Marshall sent his own lawyers into the field and the courtroom. John Doar, a lanky, reticent man of great personal courage, led many of these expeditions into the south. He even invaded Mississippi. Kennedy may have thought that Eastland's wink licensed this violation of his sanctuary. At any rate, Kennedy said later, Eastland "never made any effort to stop us from doing anything in the state of Mississippi, or try to impede anything that we did in the state."[72]

In conducting interviews, Doar's lawyers concentrated on blacks, who were generally frightened by FBI agents, and the agents concentrated on whites, who were often frightened by Justice Department lawyers.[73] Each suit required thousands of pages of evidence. "The Division," Doar said later, "was not prepared to take the terrible risk of losing a single case because of lack of proof. We faced tough judges. We wanted the proof to be so overwhelming so as to lock up the trial judge . . . and to convince the country as well."[74] In the end, Kennedy's Department of Justice brought fifty-seven voting suits, including thirty in Mississippi and one in Jim Eastland's own Sunflower County.[75]

The voting rights thesis was not universally accepted. The Civil Rights Commission, though all for black enfranchisement, denied that it was a cure-all. Its 1961 report, Burke Marshall complained, "went out of its way" to point to counties in the deep south where blacks registered freely with no discernible effect on the caste system.[76] For that matter blacks voted without constraint in the north, but black inequality remained. The administration did not believe such points invalidated the strategy. "If it does not bring change by itself," Marshall said, "the vote is nonetheless the key to possible change."[77]

Black leaders suspected the administration's motives. "I felt that what they were trying to do," said Lonnie King of the Student Nonviolent Coordinating Committee (SNCC), "was to kill the Movement, but to kill it by rechanneling its energies."[78] Vincent Harding, the black historian, thought it an attempt " 'to get the niggers off the street.' [The Kennedys] probably recognized that the constant movement on the streets might well lead to the tearing and the breaking of the fabric. . . . That they were probably deathly afraid of." Harding believed the breaking "absolutely necessary for something real to take place."[79] The Kennedys were determined on peaceful change. In June 1961, meeting with representatives from King's Southern Christian Leadership Conference (SCLC), CORE and SNCC, Robert Kennedy argued that voter registration would be far more productive than demonstrations. "I said that it wasn't as dramatic; and that perhaps there wasn't going to be as much publicity. . . . But I thought that's where they should go and that's what they should do. I had some conversations with Martin Luther King along those lines. I think that they rather resented it."[80]

He was more persuasive than he supposed. Marshall and Wofford followed up in subsequent meetings. The Taconic, Field and Stern foundations offered financial support. The black leaders understood that the administration would provide protection. One SNCC activist recalled someone, perhaps Wofford, saying that, if it were necessary in the course of protecting people's right to vote, "the Kennedy Administration would fill every jail in the South."[81] In August, after heated debate between "direct action" and "voter registration" wings, SNCC decided to join the campaign.[82] James Forman, SNCC's revolutionary-minded director, saw registration work "as a tool by which consciousness might be aroused, politicized, and organized."[83] In September James Farmer brought in his comrades at CORE.[84] In November Martin Luther King, after noting that the civil rights movement was laboring on many fronts, declared with emphasis: *"The central front, however, we feel is that of suffrage."* The vote would "give us the concrete tool with which we ourselves, can correct injustice. . . . This is the pattern for changing the old South, and with it the nation as a whole."[85] In January 1962 the Voter Education Project came into existence—"Education" because contributions to an educational activity collecting information on registration problems were tax-exempt. (Kennedy said later, "I was able to work out with Mort Caplin for them to receive tax-free status.")[86] The VEP was supposed to last for two and a half years. It was still going strong fifteen years later with John Lewis, the Freedom Rider, as executive director.

Early results, outside the cities, were disappointing. In the rural south the drive bogged down in white intimidation, black fear and apathy. Roy Wilkins of the NAACP thought it futile to work the countryside. But Forman of SNCC, welcoming the hatred of the sheriff and the Klan, believed that violence "would create more exposure and thereby more consciousness."[87] The argument between voter registration and direct action was adjourned. Voter registration in a hostile setting *was* direct action. And it was action, as one CORE worker later put it, with widespread repercussions. "The fact that activity was brought to the smallest towns and rural areas instilled black residents there with enormous hope and pride. . . . [It] left these communities with a legacy of organizational skills, higher expectations, and, most importantly, the sense that they could take positive action to change their own lives."[88]

It also wore out Robert Kennedy's southern welcome. "The Freedom Riders do not seem to have hurt President Kennedy much," wrote Samuel Lubell, the expert political observer. ". . . It is 'brother Bobby' in the Attorney General's office, rather than President Jack, who has been blamed." Lubell asked a Mississippi housewife to name the biggest problem in the country. She replied: "Kennedy has too many brothers."[89]

VIII

At the same time, the invasion of the rural south exposed a grave weakness in the Kennedy strategy. The civil rights activists had interpreted the administration's assurance of cooperation as a promise of protection. They felt bitterly betrayed when white sheriffs, policemen and good old boys struck back with apparent impunity.

In Itta Bena, Mississippi, in the summer of 1963, fifty-seven blacks made a night march to the house of a deputy sheriff to ask police protection for voter registration. The next day all over fourteen years old were peremptorily tried, convicted, fined and sent to prison for months on charges of disturbing the peace. In Clinton, Louisiana, twelve blacks wrote respectful letters to the mayor and district attorney requesting the establishment of a biracial committee to combat racial tensions. They were arrested on charges of intimidating public officials. A black walking down the street in Clarksdale, Mississippi, wearing a T-shirt with CORE on the front and FREEDOM NOW on the back was arrested for parading without a permit.[90]

These were the milder cases. As activists went in increasing numbers into the deep south, as southern blacks asserted their rights with new vigor, local retaliation grew more atrocious. Beating became frequent; murders were not uncommon. The rage of those who believed they were defending the Constitution became harder to contain or to answer. Why did not the federal government use injunctive sanctions? Why did not FBI agents make on-the-spot arrests? Why not bring cases involving constitutional guarantees directly into the federal courts? Was national authority powerless to protect American citizens whose only offense was to use constitutional methods to claim constitutional rights? These questions came to torment the Department of Justice.

Under the federal system police power was reserved for local authorities. The national government could intervene only when, as Robert Kennedy said, there was a specific and clear "federal responsibility"—as when Alabama failed to protect interstate travel or when local authorities defied federal court orders.[91] Nor did existing legislation provide sure footing for more general intervention. Sections 332–334 of Title 10 of the United States Code permitted the President to send federal troops in case of a widespread breakdown of law and order. It was not a remedy for sporadic incidents of brutality by local police officials. Sections 241–242, Title 18, of the Code had been enacted during Reconstruction to prevent the deprivation of civil rights. But the first section required proof of conspiracy, the second of specific intent. The Supreme Court had long since narrowed their scope and attenuated their force.

Burke Marshall sought to make it easier to initiate criminal prosecutions when local cops or mobs interfered with persons exercising constitutional rights in the cause of racial justice. He got the FBI to make investigations of alleged police brutality and encouraged the filing of criminal informations to get around the reluctance of southern grand juries to return indictments.[92] The Department of Justice in March 1962 sent up a bill that would have made forms of police brutality a federal crime; no one pressed the bill in Congress, and there were no committee hearings.[93] Beyond the infirmities in the law, the southern system of justice remained the most formidable obstacle. In civil rights troubles, white police were more likely to arrest the victims than the leaders of mobs. White juries rarely convicted white men charged with violating the rights of blacks. White judges often imposed heavy bail or harsh sentences on civil rights workers while going easy on segregationists. The rules of federal-state comity discouraged federal interference in state criminal proceedings. With only forty attorneys, Marshall felt he could deploy limited manpower more profitably in voting than in protection cases.

"The point about protection," Marshall wrote to a civil rights advocate,

> is the most difficult and frustrating we have to live with under the federal system. I say over and over again—hundreds of times a year—that we do not have a national police force, and *cannot* provide protection in a physical sense for everyone who is disliked because of the exercise of his constitutional rights. The marshals we have used are taken from duty in the service of papers, and the like, in many states. At most, I can round up maybe 100, for short-term duty. They are not police officers. They are not hired for that, and we have no budget for it. Congress would never grant one. . . . There is no substitute under the federal system for the failure of local law enforcement responsibility. There is simply a vacuum, which can be filled only rarely, with extraordinary difficulty, at monumental expense, and in a totally unsatisfactory fashion.[94]

Lawyers understood Marshall's point. Asked privately in 1964 whether he thought the decision against a vast federal police presence in the absence of specific court orders was wise, Thurgood Marshall of the NAACP, victor in the school desegregation case and a dozen other civil rights cases, replied, "I certainly do. . . . The law is quite clear that the federal government is not the policing authority. Policing authority rests with the several states. That," he added, "... some of us can understand, but the average layman cannot understand it."[95] Certainly civil rights activists risking their lives in the war for the Constitution did not. "Careful explanations of the historic limitations on the federal government's police powers," as Robert Kennedy said the same year, "are not satisfactory to the parents of students who have vanished in Mississippi or to the widow of a Negro educator shot down without any reason by night riders in Georgia."[96] "If we are murdered in our attempts," cried one SNCC worker to the Kennedys, "our blood will be on your hands; you stand in the judgment of God and our people."[97]

IX

The anguishing dilemma led Burke Marshall in 1964 to write *Federalism and Civil Rights,* a small volume that, beneath lucid prose, was packed with perplexity and near-despair. Under the federal system, as Marshall later put it, "no matter how far reaching the equitable decrees of the federal courts may be, the states and local political institutions are going to retain operating control over all of the institutions involved in the granting or denial of equal rights. . . . There are many things the federal court can do to prevent misuse of state power, but it cannot replace the system of justice—of unfair police, biased juries, and locally elected judges applying a double standard in a segregated courtroom."[98] Or it could do so only by abandoning the federal balance, at least in connection with the police power.

This course seemed to Marshall full of hazard. It would require the creation of a national police force. Only a few years before, Justice Robert H. Jackson had warned somberly that "the establishment of the supremacy of the national over the local police authorities" could be a first step toward a totalitarian state.[99] Nor was there reason to believe that a national police force could easily overcome massive local opposition. "Nothing short of the pervasive presence of armed men will do," wrote Alexander Bickel. ". . . As a regular and more or less permanent device, it is something from which we recoil, deeming it destructive of the values of a free society."[100] There had been no alternative to sending the Army to Little Rock. But this could not become the routine way of enforcing federal law. The federal balance had historically been the means by which a far-flung, diverse and turbulent nation had preserved a measure of cohesion. It was not to be lightly discarded.

The Pursuit of Justice: Civil Rights

Thus Marshall's bleak choice: keeping the federal balance at the cost of terrible injustice to civil rights workers; or seeking justice for civil rights workers with unforeseeable consequences for the federal balance. Marshall in the end favored the preservation of the federal system. Yet he understood that this could have awful consequences too—above all, in cynicism about the power, or will, of law and government to achieve justice.[101] His pessimism was mitigated only by his conviction that new local perceptions and new federal statutes might give the executive branch new opportunities. "The final cure," he said, "can come only from the political process."[102]

The question remained whether this argument was not put too absolutely—whether, within the confines of federalism, limited federal intervention in critical times and places might not still have made a difference. As pressure rose, the Department of Justice found itself doing things each new year it had declined to do the year preceding. This confirmed Marshall's suggestion that the question was one of political as well as of constitutional possibility. "Notwithstanding all the elaborate answers which the Justice Department produced, most of them in the language of constitutional construction and executive propriety," wrote a pair of thoughtful critics, "the true answer was to be found in the remaining power of southern white supremacy in Washington."[103] Increase in intervention therefore had to await increase in opposition to white supremacy, and this had to await increase in crisis. In the meantime, as John Doar said, "you've just got to keep going back. . . . Laws and court decisions and speeches up in Washington mean nothing. You've got to come *here* [he was musing in Mississippi] and chip away. You'll lose some games and win others—you've got to expect that. You'll think it's taking forever—you've got to expect that too. But the only alternative would be police state methods. . . . So you do the only thing you can do."[104]

In 1964 Anthony Lewis asked Robert Kennedy whether he would alter the system that gave primary responsibility for law enforcement to the states and communities. Kennedy said:

> No . . . I still think it's wise. I think that for periods of time that it's very, very difficult. . . . I just wouldn't want that much more authority in the hands of either the FBI or the Department of Justice or the President of the United States. . . . You would have accomplished much more if you had had a dictatorship during the period of time that President Kennedy was President because you would have gotten . . . all kinds of domestic legislation. You would have been able to protect our open spaces . . . to do something about congestion in the cities and . . . about the slums. . . . We could have sent perhaps large numbers of people down to Mississippi

and be able then to protect that group down there. But I think that it comes back to haunt you at a later time. I think that these matters should be decided over a long range of history, not on a temporary basis or under the stress of a particular crisis. . . . I think it's [best] for the health of the country.[105]

A generation rendered sensitive by Watergate to the case for constitutional process finds this view more persuasive than did the men and women who went south in defense of elemental rights in the early 1960s. For a time Robert Kennedy became almost as unpopular among civil rights workers as he was among segregationists.

X

Federal judges, Burke Marshall wrote, were "a principal factor in efforts to make federal rights for Negroes a reality in the South."[106] Of all forms of federal presence around the country, the judicial presence was the most solemn. Nothing lay more clearly within the field of executive initiative than good judicial appointments. Yet nothing in Robert Kennedy's attorney generalship received more valid criticism than his early recommendations for the southern bench.

Every judicial nomination had to have the approval of the Senate Judiciary Committee. In the spirit of local patriotism Chairman Eastland wished Kennedy's first appointment to come from Mississippi; wished, in addition, the appointee to be his college roommate, William Howard Cox. With many more appointments coming up, the administration thought it essential to keep Eastland reasonably happy. The nomination of a "close friend" of Eastland's as district judge in Mississippi, Roy Wilkins wired John Kennedy, "is not a surprise in the light of the general situation." But Cox on the bench, he added, boded ill "for any litigation not keyed to the mores of 1861. For 986,000 Negro Mississippians Judge Cox will be another strand in their barbed wire fence, another cross over their weary shoulders and another rock in the road up which their young people must struggle."[107]

Wilkins could hardly have been more prescient. Still there was nothing specific against Cox. He had not been associated with the Klan or the White Citizens Council. He had no public record at all. The FBI found him blameless. The American Bar Association gave him its highest rating—"exceptionally well qualified." Robert Kennedy had Cox in. "We sat on my couch in my own office; and I talked to him. I said that the great reservation I had was the question of whether he'd enforce the law and whether he'd live up to . . . the interpretation of the Constitution by the Supreme Court. He assured me that he would. He was the only judge, I think, that I had that kind of conversation with. He was very gracious; and he said that there wouldn't be any problem. . . . I was convinced that he was honest with me, and he wasn't."[108]

Soon after Cox's nomination, the administration sent three black names to the Judiciary Committee—two, like Cox, for district judgeships, and Thurgood Marshall for the circuit court. This last nomination was exceptional. Up to that point only one Negro, William Hastie, had been appointed to the circuit court. The famous story of Eastland's remark to Robert Kennedy—"tell your brother that if he will give me Harold Cox I will give him the nigger"[109]—is perhaps apocryphal, but was true is some vaguer sense. Cox helped soften Eastland for Marshall. When Congress adjourned without acting on Marshall's nomination, John Kennedy gave him a recess appointment. In May 1962 a Judiciary subcommittee brooded over Marshall but rendered no report to the full committee. "Keating and Javits," Kennedy said later, "raised a fuss continuously and we didn't raise too much because I'd had a conversation with Jim Eastland [who said] before it was over he'd put it through. So that there wasn't any reason to get all excited about it and I told Thurgood Marshall that he'd be appointed. So he was relaxed."[110] On June 8, 1962, Kennedy's list of phone messages contained one from Eastland: "The matter you all discussed on the telephone this morning is all right with him and Senator Stennis." Kennedy noted in his crabbed script: "Don Wine [for federal attorney in Iowa] & Thurgood Marshall."[111] In September the Judiciary Committee approved Marshall. In the end the Kennedys appointed ten black judges. Eastland, said Robert Kennedy, held some up for a time but "never . . . caused us any trouble."[112] They were an odd couple.

Still Cox was a heavy price to pay. He no sooner got on the bench than he denied the Department of Justice the right, granted in the 1960 Civil Rights Act, to inspect public voting records in a Mississippi county where no black had registered for thirty years. No judge was reversed more regularly thereafter on civil rights cases.[113] Reversal no doubt increased Cox's fury. Early in 1963 he sent a letter to a Mississippi county registrar charging that the Attorney General typically preceded voting suits by "a political barrage of propaganda for voter consumption among negroes."[114] Cox was only warming up. In an October letter to John Doar, who had had the impertinence to ask for a trial date in a voting case: "I spend most of my time fooling with lousy cases brought before me by your department in the Civil Rights field and I do not intend to turn my docket over to your department for your political advancement." Cox went on to call Doar stupid, unless he was trying to impress his "boss man."[115] Kennedy frigidly wrote Cox that he was turning the letter over to the ABA's Standing Committee on Federal Judiciary.[116]

Robert W. Meserve, chairman of the ABA committee, conferred with Cox and thought matters were under control. Then in March 1964, when Doar was trying to expedite black registration in a Mississippi county, Cox roared against the applicants in open court as "a bunch of niggers . . . acting like a bunch of chipanzees."[117] Leon Jaworski of the ABA committee wrote Burke Marshall, "This latest outburst was very disappointing to Meserve. I have strongly recommended that Committee action be taken recording a strong disapproval of Judge Cox's conduct."[118] (In a few years, Doar and Jaworski joined in even more spectacular disapproval of official misconduct.)

Cox was only one of the sour Kennedy appointments to the district courts of the Fifth Circuit, covering the deep south from Florida to Texas. Judge E. Gordon West, named at the behest of Senator Russell Long of Louisiana, called the school desegregation case from the bench "one of the truly regrettable decisions of all time."[119] Judges Robert Elliott of Georgia and Clarence Allgood of Alabama were nearly as blatant. Their strategy was the ruthless use of judicial discretion and procedural manipulation to protract civil rights cases, turning every action, in Marshall's phrase, into "an endless chain of litigation."[120]

Why such appointments? Administration senators, according to firm tradition, proposed the judges for their own states, especially for the district bench. Southern senators were particularly in need of propitiation in 1961 because they held committee chairmanships vital to Kennedy's program—not only Judiciary itself, but Finance, Armed Services and Foreign Relations. Justice's information about the candidates was inadequate. FBI reports, said Burke Marshall, were "worthless."[121] The ABA generally went along with the legal establishment, hardly a sure guide in the south (or elsewhere). None of the judges appointed was a segregationist on the public record, except for Elliott; and Elliott was endorsed by the courageous liberal judge Elbert H. Tuttle as well as by black leaders in Georgia. (Nor was the public record necessarily an indicator. Alexander A. Lawrence of

Georgia, appointed in later years, was a segregationist in politics but an integrator on the bench.) One civil rights official attributed to Kennedy's Justice Department the romantic view that "every redneck who came down the pike was another Hugo Black."[122]

It was evident all too quickly that the administration had not done well. Robert Kennedy wrote Eleanor Roosevelt in May 1962 that, while they had made every effort to make sure the new judges would do their duty, "I must say that we have had some disappointments . . . as I have had in a lot of areas."[123] He learned, as usual. After early 1962, Navasky has written, "he nominated no more judicial disasters."[124] Indeed, the final Kennedy record of southern judicial appointments was, despite public impression to the contrary, comparable to that of the Eisenhower administration. It is well known that Eisenhower, who, as a Republican, had no southern senators he was required to propitiate, appointed to the southern bench wise and fearless men like Tuttle, John M. Wisdom and Frank Johnson (about whom Robert F. Kennedy, Jr., wrote his senior honors essay at Harvard in 1976). He also had his share of duds.* A careful analysis of judges named by Eisenhower and Kennedy in the Fifth Circuit showed that each was responsible for five segregationists, Eisenhower for eight moderates and Kennedy for three, Eisenhower for two integrationists and Kennedy for eight.[125] Still damage was done.

XI

The selection of southern judges was one point at which the practice of the executive-action strategy fell considerably below the theory. Another, for a painful twenty months, was the campaign promise of an order ending discrimination in housing "by a stroke of the Presidential pen." The President in 1961 found the problems involved—legal, political, administrative—more complex than the campaigner had anticipated in 1960.

He almost put out the housing order in the fall. Then, after he and Robert Kennedy walked the beach at Hyannis Port over Thanks-

---

* One of them, Ben C. Dawkins, Jr., the chief judge in the western district of Louisiana, advised Robert Kennedy that "forced association cannot and will not work" and that civil rights legislation would be as "unworkable" as the Eighteenth Amendment. "I don't believe the Supreme Court is unworkable," Kennedy replied. ". . . I hope that several years from now we both will agree that none of the problems were insurmountable and our country and all of its people are better off because of the work of the three branches of the Federal Government." (Ben C. Dawkins, Jr., to RFK, June 18, 1964; RFK to Dawkins, August 4, 1964, Burke Marshall Papers.)

giving pondering the question, he decided to try first for a department of urban affairs. He intended to appoint Robert C. Weaver, an eminent black economist, as secretary. Legislative leaders made it clear that Congress would not create the new department if he issued the housing order. He agreed to postpone the order. The House Rules Committee, hating the idea of the first black cabinet member in history, killed the reorganization bill anyway. This was the congressional mood—and explains why there appeared no alternative to the executive-action route.

Counterpressure mounted on the civil rights side. An "Ink for Jack" campaign began. Thousands of pens descended on the White House. The President, recalling that the fatal phrase came from Harris Wofford, suggested that they be piled on Wofford's desk. As the issue became a symbolic test of the executive-action strategy, civil rights groups wanted to extend the order beyond housing affected by federal loans and guarantees to cover housing financed by savings and loan associations and even banks. The 1962 elections were drawing near. Democratic congressmen, including northern liberals, were apprehensive about the impact the order might have on the campaign. "There's no question," Robert Kennedy said later, "that we waited until after the election because of the political implications."[126] The order, finally promulgated on Thanksgiving eve, was limited in its reach. It proved neither the calamity predicted by opponents nor the blessing anticipated by advocates.

The housing order raised an interesting question, little discussed at the time. The civil rights leaders, seeking every road to equality, had no fear of the Presidency. "The power inherent in Executive orders," Martin Luther King, Jr., said in early 1961, "has never been exploited; its use in recent years has been microscopic in scope and timid in conception."[127] Opponents disagreed. "An order of this nature," Senator Sam Ervin protested to John Kennedy, "would constitute an invasion of the legislative field. The Constitution vests the legislative powers of the Federal government in the Congress and none in the President."* Indeed Congress had regularly rejected antidiscrimination amendments to housing bills. But the constitutional objection was generally discounted in those years as a neo-Confederate pretext. Perceptions sharpened by the Imperial Presidency

---

* Sam Ervin to JFK, October 6, 1962, JFK Papers. In 1955 Justice Black had said that executive orders not based on legislative command looked like legislation to him and that "the Constitution does not confer lawmaking power on the President" (*Peters* vs. *Hobby*, 349 U.S. 331, 350 [1955]).

The Pursuit of Justice: Civil Rights

found it more impressive later. Archibald Cox, recalling in 1975 that the order was issued "at a time when Congress would have rejected such legislation," noted that, though the pressures had been great and the results commendable, "in retrospect one has doubts about the method."[128]

If there could be doubt whether, except in compelling circumstances, a President should through executive order take a quasi-legislative action that Congress would not take, there could be no doubt about presidential power to combat racial discrimination by contractors doing business with the federal government. In establishing the President's Committee on Equal Employment Opportunity, John Kennedy charged it "to permanently remove from Government employment and work performed for the Government every trace of discrimination."[129]

Nixon had headed a much weaker committee of this sort under Eisenhower. The Kennedy executive order not only forbade discrimination but imposed on government contractors the requirement of "affirmative action" to assure equality in employment. Kennedy, desperate, like all Presidents, to find things for his Vice President to do, asked Lyndon Johnson to serve as chairman of the new committee. Johnson, his intimate friend William S. White reported, "privately flinched" from the assignment, fearing that as a southerner he would be blamed if the committee were a bust.[130] Kennedy insisted. Finally, Johnson, whose civil rights record before 1957 had been deplorable but who was himself wholly lacking in racial bigotry and perhaps perceived political advantage in proving himself where he had previously been regarded with suspicion, accepted.

As chairman, Johnson was uneasy from the start. One of the public members was Robert Troutman, Jr., an amusing and energetic Georgian who had known young Joe Kennedy years before and had been a Kennedy lieutenant in 1960. Troutman's contribution was Plans for Progress, a campaign to sign up firms in voluntary agreements to employ blacks. Johnson resented Troutman's access to the Kennedys as well as his initiative on a committee of which the Vice President was nominal head.[131] Robert Kennedy lacked Troutman's faith in voluntary action, but respected his organizational drive and was impressed that a southerner, who still pronounced the word "Nigra," cared about equal rights. "As aware as he was of the inadequacies of Troutman's approach," said Seigenthaler, "he felt, 'At least we've got something going here.'"[132] Despite opposition from civil rights groups, Plans for Progress had a small success. In 1962, Troutman, discouraged by Johnson's attitude, retired to Atlanta.

After September 1962 the executive vice-chairman was Hobart Taylor, a black lawyer from Detroit, a Texan by birth and a long-time Johnson man. Though the executive order empowered the committee to conduct hearings, terminate contracts and recommend criminal penalties for companies furnishing false information, Johnson and Taylor favored conciliation and cajolery. It was not, Johnson said, "a persecuting or prosecuting committee."[133] No hearings were held, no contracts were canceled. Since the committee lacked statutory authorization, this caution was understandable. It was also unproductive. Robert Kennedy and the successive Secretaries of Labor, Arthur Goldberg and Willard Wirtz, came to feel that the committee was badly run and that it was Johnson's fault. "There wasn't any problem about making it an effective organization," Kennedy said later, ". . . just if the Vice President gave it some direction. It was mostly a public relations operation. I mean, it accomplished a good deal more than it had accomplished under Nixon. But a lot of it was public relations. Secondly, there wasn't any adequate follow-up. Thirdly, the head of the staff . . . Hobart Taylor, whom I have contempt for because I thought he was so ineffective."[134]

XII

"What do you see as the big problem ahead for you?" an interviewer asked Robert Kennedy in May 1962. "Is it Crime or Internal Security?" Kennedy answered, "Civil rights."[135] Yet, for all their good intentions, for all their sensitivity to racial injustice, for all their unpopularity with the segregationists, the Kennedys after a year and a half were proving something of a disappointment to civil rights leaders. The refusal to call for legislation, the failure to protect civil rights workers, the interminable litigation over voting rights, the southern judicial appointments, the prolonged postponement of the stroke of the pen, the leniency with government contractors—all these were beginning to convince the movement that good intentions were not solving many problems.

Within the government itself, the Civil Rights Commission became a strong voice of concern. The commission's authority was limited to investigation, including the holding of hearings, and recommendation. Under Eisenhower it had been a cautious and rather technical body, compiling information and proposing modest remedies. When the new Department of Justice preempted the practical ground, the commission saw itself increasingly as a source of fresh ideas, moving out ahead and educating a larger public.[136] This forward conception turned it into a critic of the Kennedy strategy.

The commission had thus questioned the administration's bet on voting litigation, arguing instead for an across-the-board attack on inequality through legislative as well as executive action. It campaigned vigorously for the housing order and for the attempt to broaden its coverage. And it hit very hard on the question of southern justice. Father Theodore Hesburgh, the president of Notre Dame, was an influential member. On his annual retreat in 1961, Hesburgh read documents on police brutality that "just made my blood run cold. . . . With these horrible things going on all over, somehow I felt a cry of anguish, or a real loud blast from my moral soul." He therefore wrote an addendum to the 1961 report demanding more protective intervention by the federal government.[137] This question much preoccupied the commission in subsequent years.

When the commission met with the President in 1961, an argument arose over the number of southern state universities that admitted blacks. Kennedy had one figure; the commission's expert another. "He was right and our staff fellow was wrong," Hesburgh said. ". . . That impressed our office quite a bit." Still, for all the knowledge and incisiveness of the Kennedy brothers, Hesburgh felt that "the civil rights issue really imposed itself upon them, rather than they imposing themselves on civil rights." He had begun, he said, "with great optimism," but after the first year "I felt rather pessimistic."[138]

As the Department of Justice saw it, the commission was always getting in the way. "They had a very unpleasant meeting with Bob Kennedy," Harris Wofford recalled, "which turned all of them against Bob Kennedy, who seemed to be treating them as if he could tell them what to do."[139] The commission did indeed annoy Kennedy. "I didn't have any great feeling that they were accomplishing anything of a positive nature," he said in 1964. "I thought it was almost like the House Un-American Activities Committee investigating communism. . . . They were not objective investigations. . . . So I had no confidence in them." Moreover, "they were investigating violations of civil rights in areas in which we were making investigations. I thought that they could do more in the north. I thought that there were . . . subjects that they could go into which perhaps would be helpful. But . . . they were going over old ground, and they were doing what we were really doing: voting."[140]

Kennedy was overreacting; essentially because as a strong executive he wished to hold as many elements as possible under his own control. Hesburgh, a strong executive himself, understood the Attorney General's exasperation: "I'm sure that there were many times," he said in 1966, "when they thought we were complicating their business because it's always easier if you have one organization attending to business rather than two." But the commission's value, Hesburgh argued, was "precisely in being a kind of national conscience, a kind of burr under the saddle of the administration."[141] He was right. Few agencies have had a better record of recommendations translated into statutes than the Civil Rights Commission. Still, Kennedy found criticism from within the family wounding.

XIII

As for the black leadership, it gave the Kennedys mixed reviews. "This administration," Martin Luther King said in early 1962, "has reached out more creatively than its predecessors to blaze some new trails," notably in voting rights and in government appointments. Its "vigorous young men" had launched "imaginative and bold forays" and displayed "a certain *élan* in the attention they give to civil-rights issues." Still the "melancholy fact" was that the administration was "aggressively driving toward the limited goal of token integration." King demanded much more and so, he asserted, did the American people. "The nation is ready and eager for bold leadership in civil rights."[142]

Even blacks within the administration were somewhat dispirited. The loyal Robert C. Weaver sensed an "overcautiousness" in the President.[143] Roger Wilkins, a young lawyer in the foreign aid program, Roy Wilkins's nephew, contended in a 1962 memorandum (set down for Ralph Dungan to pass on to the Kennedys) "that this Administration seems to be using appointments and the achievement of voting rights as an excuse for doing little or nothing else. . . . Presidential indifference is the unkindest cut of all."[144]

The activists risking their lives on southern back roads were bitter. "The young Negro militants," wrote Loren Miller, the black civil rights attorney, "'don't believe in liberals at all.'" Let liberals shut up, Miller concluded, until they were "ready to enlist as foot-soldiers and subordinates in a Negro-led, Negro-officered army under the banner of Freedom Now."[145] "Kennedy is the smartest politician we have had in a long time," said Bayard Rustin, a founder of CORE in the forties and a special assistant to King in the fifties. "He calls the Negro leaders together and says in effect: 'I want to help you get money so Negroes can vote.' That's when he is bowing toward us. Then he turns and bows to the Dixiecrats and gives them Southern racist judges who make certain that the money the Negro gets will not achieve its purpose."[146] In the summer of 1962 disillusioned CORE leaders even considered "aggressive nonviolent action" against the Kennedys.[147] Forman of SNCC regarded John Kennedy as "quick-talking, double-dealing" and his voter registration drive as preparation for his reelection in 1964.[148]

Those who dealt personally with the Kennedys could not share this bitterness. Something about them—their openness, interest, the alertness of their sympathy—redeemed the hesitancy of their policy and offered hope for the future. "He was always ready to listen," said Martin Luther King of John Kennedy.[149] "He doesn't act as if he knows everything," said Clarence Mitchell, the NAACP's Washington representative, of Robert Kennedy. "He is always willing to listen. . . . The whole Kennedy family seems to have . . . an attitude of decency which means a lot to people."[150] "They would listen very carefully," said Thurgood Marshall, "but they would always be frank and give their objections to what you were proposing, give their reasons for it. . . . I think their frankness was the important factor in dealing with organizations and individuals."[151]

And yet, and yet. "On the one hand," said Martin Luther King's friend Vincent Harding, King "really hoped that he could believe in people like Bobby; and on the other hand, a certain black wisdom told him that he had better not try to believe in them."[152] And they had one manifest disagreement. King was sure the nation was eager for bold leadership in civil rights. Discerning no such national eagerness, doubting whether presidential exhortations could create an emotional urgency the white majority was resolved not to feel, knowing the resistance they would encounter on Capitol Hill, the Kennedys felt they had to row to their destination with muffled oars. To ardent spirits they seemed friendly but somehow detached; uninvolved? After a talk with John Kennedy, King said to Harris Wofford, "I'm afraid that the fact is he's got the understanding and he's got the political skill . . . but the moral passion is missing."[153]

This is the way matters stood in the early autumn of 1962.

(15)

The Pursuit of Justice: Ross Barnett and George Wallace

THE KENNEDY CIVIL RIGHTS STRATEGY, however appropriate to the congressional mood of 1961, miscalculated the dynamism of a revolutionary movement. "Every civil rights victory," Loren Miller proudly said, "adds to the Negro's intransigence; he becomes ever more impatient and demanding."[1] "It is not always when things are going from bad to worse that revolutions break out," Tocqueville had said long before. ". . . Patiently endured so long as it seemed beyond redress, a grievance comes to appear intolerable once the possibility of removing it crosses men's minds."[2]

I

The possibility of removing grievances crossed many men's minds. So James Meredith, his spirit quickened by John Kennedy's inaugural address, applied on January 21, 1961, for admission to the all-white state university at Oxford, Mississippi. Had Nixon been elected, he said later, he might not have applied.[3] Meredith was a lonely, taciturn and quixotic man of courage and purpose. "Nobody handpicked me," he said later. "I believed, and I believe now, that I have a Divine Responsibility to break White Supremacy in Mississippi, and getting in Ole Miss was only the start."[4]

Everyone recalls the roll of events grimly unfolding: Meredith's rejection by Ole Miss; his suit against the university, filed with the encouragement of Medgar Evers, the state NAACP director; the "calculated campaign of delay, harassment and masterly inactivity" waged by Ole Miss—a campaign, the Fifth Circuit Court added, that would have done credit to Quintus Fabius Maximus; the court's ruling in June 1962 that Meredith must be admitted forthwith; more delay, more harassment; on September 10, the ruling handed down from the Supreme Court by Hugo Black, an Alabaman, commanding no further interference with the judicial order; on September 13, Ross Barnett, the governor of Mississippi, on statewide television: "We will not surrender to the evil and illegal forces of tyranny."[5]

The Justice Department had been in touch with Meredith from nearly the start and supported him as *amicus curiae* during the appeal before Justice Black. Hoping to avert trouble, Robert Kennedy now began a series of phone conversations with Barnett—twenty between September 15 and September 28. He also considered the advisability of a presidential statement. On September 17 he asked me to come to the Department. My journal:

> I went over . . . about six thirty and found the legal group in Bobby's garish office. Everyone was in shirtsleeves except Nick Katzenbach, who sat saturninely in the background and said softly that he saw no reason to issue a statement at that time. Guthman had drafted a statement, to which I added a quotation from the Mississippi Legislature in 1832 denouncing the interposition doctrine. Bobby pondered this and then engaged in quiet conversation with his people about the best mode of protecting the Negro student when he tried to register. The mixture of shirtsleeved casualness, soft voices and evident determination was impressive. In the end, Bob agreed with Nick about the statement, and it was deferred. Instead, he issued quiet orders and his troops dispersed. He told me, by the way, that he regarded Governor Barnett . . . as genuinely loony—that he had been hit on the head by an airplane propellor last summer and had never been the same since.[6]

The conversations continued. Barnett wobbled between bluster and placation. On September 25:

> BARNETT. That's what it's going to boil down to—whether Mississippi can run its institutions or the federal government is going to run things. . . .
> KENNEDY. I don't understand, Governor. Where do you think this is going to take your own state?
> BARNETT. A lot of states haven't had the guts to take a stand. We are going to fight this thing. . . . This is like a dictatorship. Forcing him physically into Ole Miss. General, that might bring on a lot of trouble. You don't want to do that. You don't want to physically force him in.
> KENNEDY. You don't want to physically keep him out. . . . Governor, you are a part of the United States.
> BARNETT. We have been a part of the United States but I don't know whether we are or not.
> KENNEDY. Are you getting out of the Union?
> BARNETT. It looks like we're being kicked around—like we don't belong to it. General, this thing is serious.
> KENNEDY. It's serious here.
> BARNETT. Must it be over one little boy—backed by communist front—backed by the NAACP which is a communist front? . . . I'm going to

treat you with every courtesy but I won't agree to let that boy to get to Ole Miss. I will never agree to that. I would rather spend the rest of my life in a penitentiary than do that.

KENNEDY. I have a responsibility to enforce the laws of the United States. . . . The orders of the court are going to be upheld. As I told you, you are a citizen not only of the State of Mississippi but also of the United States. Could I give you a ring?

BARNETT. You do that. . . . Good to hear from you.[7]

But Barnett's tone was more often plaintive than truculent. Though a doctrinaire segregationist, he really did not wish to take on the federal government, and he liked to be liked. Kennedy later abandoned the idea that he was loony. "An agreeable rogue, and weak," he called him in 1964. ". . . I suppose I thought he must have been sane. I thought that after we got into it a bit that it was in his interest. I'm influenced a lot by whether what a person does or says he's going to do is in their interest in doing it."[8]

The pace accelerated. Federal marshals escorted Meredith to the university. They were several times turned back. Once Barnett read a grandiloquent proclamation rejecting Meredith—and then gave him the embossed document as a souvenir. Eastland suggested that Kennedy might back down a little. Kennedy: "You don't really believe that, Senator. You've been in the Senate too long to believe that." Barnett proposed a show of force, federal marshals with their guns drawn, as a cover for his own retreat. Even Eastland thought this ridiculous, but Kennedy was willing to try anything. When the moment came, the crowd seemed too menacing for the drama. "A lot of people are going to be killed," Barnett told Kennedy. "It would be embarrassing to me." "I don't know if it would be embarrassing," said Kennedy, "—that would not be the feeling." Good old boys from the country were coming by truckload into Oxford. In Washington apprehension grew that federal marshals might not be enough.[9]

"Sending in troops is a hell of a thing for the country," Robert Kennedy said early on.[10] His consuming fear was a mini-civil war with GIs and Mississippians shooting each other down. "What I was trying to avoid, basically," Robert Kennedy said in 1964,

was having to send troops. . . . What [Barnett] was trying to accomplish was the avoidance of integration at the University of Mississippi, number one, and, if he couldn't do that, to be forced to do it by our heavy hand; and his preference was with troops. Because he wants to be an agreeable fellow, he continued to have these conversations with me, where he got [in] deeper and deeper, where he was trying to satisfy and please me and trying to talk me out of James Meredith coming to the University of Mississippi. While he was doing that, he ... got more and more involved himself. He had people pulling and pushing at him from so many different directions that I think he just got himself into a bigger and bigger box. He eventually pulled me in with him.[11]

II

On September 28, Robert Kennedy met with General Maxwell Taylor, chairman of the Joint Chiefs of Staff, and Cyrus Vance, who had become Secretary of the Army two months before. Maps of Mississippi were improbably unrolled in the Pentagon War Room. Later that day the Attorney General told me

> he understood better now how Hitler had taken over in Germany. "Everyone in Mississippi is accepting what this fellow is doing," he said. "There are no protests anywhere—from the bar or from professional men or from professors. [He forgot the valiant historian James Silver on the Ole Miss faculty.] I wouldn't have believed it." I asked him how his talks with Barnett had been. He said, "Some of them have been hard to believe. Today Barnett said to me, 'Why can't you persuade Meredith to go to another college? I could get some money together and we could give him a fellowship to any university he wanted outside the state. Wouldn't that be the best way to solve the problem?'" Bobby couldn't believe it.[12]

Up to this point the President had been held in reserve. The time had come to see whether his personal intervention could sway Barnett. Early Saturday afternoon, September 29, I was summoned to the Oval Office. The Attorney General, Burke Marshall and Kenneth O'Donnell were with the President. "Matters were approaching a climax, and the President was about to call Barnett. As the phone rang, the President, with the air of a master of ceremonies, announced, 'And now—Governor Ross Barnett.' Bobby said, mocking a prizefight manager, 'Go get him Johnny boy.' The President, rehearsing to himself, said, 'Governor, this is the President of the United States—not Bobby, not Teddy, not Princess Radziwill' [Jacqueline Kennedy's sister, then married to Prince Stanislaw Radziwill]. Then the call came through, and he got down to business."[13]

Kennedy was firm, patient and impersonal. "I don't know Mr. Meredith," he said, "and I didn't put him in the University, but on the other hand under the Constitution I have to carry out the orders of the Court. . . . I would like to get your help in doing it."[14] He made this point in one form or another for several minutes. After the conversation ended, the President said bemusedly, "You know what that fellow said? He said, 'I want to thank you for your help on the poultry problem.'" Turning to his brother, he said, "You've been fighting a sofa pillow all week." They called Barnett back in another hour. The President reported that Barnett had said, "Just tell 'em to cool off and you can sneak him in. I'll bring everyone up to Oxford—and then you can register him in Jackson." Robert Kennedy said: "What a rogue!"[15]

Early that Saturday evening Barnett proposed sneak registration again. This time the Kennedys reluctantly accepted it. Three hours later Barnett canceled it. At midnight Norbert Schlei of the Office of Legal Counsel came to the White House with a proclamation ordering persons obstructing justice in Mississippi to desist and disperse and an executive order federalizing the Mississippi National Guard. Kennedy took Schlei into a small study on an upper floor, sat down at a table, turned on a lamp and read the documents. After a moment he asked, "Is this pretty much what Ike signed in 1957 with the Little Rock thing?" Schlei pointed to a few refinements. Kennedy signed, snapped off the light and headed into the hall. Then he paused and rapped the table with his hand. "You know," he said, "that's General Grant's table." They said good night. As Schlei went down the stairs to tell waiting reporters what had happened, Kennedy suddenly sprinted to the top balustrade and called down to him: "Don't tell them about General Grant's table."[16]

Sunday morning Robert Kennedy and Barnett had a rough conversation:

KENNEDY. The President is going on TV tonight. He is going through with the statement [he] had with you last night. He will have to say why he called up the National Guard; that you had an agreement to permit Meredith to go to Jackson to register. . . .
BARNETT. That won't do at all.
KENNEDY. You broke your word to him. . . .
BARNETT. Don't say that. Please don't mention it. . . . Why don't you fly him in this afternoon; please let us treat what we say as confidential. . . . We will go on and do it any way. Let's agree to it now and forget it. I don't want the President saying I broke my word. . . . We will cooperate with you.

The theory of registration on Sunday was that few students would be around. "You won't mind," Barnett said, "if I raise cain about it?" Kennedy said, "I don't mind that; just say law and order will be maintained."[17] It seemed finally that Barnett had come aboard. When Robert Kennedy went over that Sunday night to the White House to hear the presidential telecast, "we thought," he said later, "that it had been accomplished."[18]

III

"Oh, God, I hope nothing happens to Meredith," Robert Kennedy had said earlier that day to Budd Schulberg. "I feel responsible for him. I promised we'd back him up all the way—and I'm worried for McShane and the others, too."[19] James McShane, who had been on the Rackets Committee staff, was now chief marshal, and Kennedy had designated him as Meredith's escort. John Doar was with McShane and Meredith at the Millington Naval Air Station near Memphis. There, too, were Louis Oberdorfer and Joseph Dolan, rehearsing the federal marshals.

It was a typical mixture of preparation and improvisation. On Sunday morning Kennedy had asked Katzenbach whether he had any plans for the afternoon. Katzenbach said no. Kennedy said, "Well, I'd like you to go down there and follow through on this plan and be in charge of things." Katzenbach picked up Edwin Guthman and Norbert Schlei. Kennedy added an old football friend, strong as a bull and faithful in a pinch, Dean Markham.[20] Harold Reis, an able lawyer in the Office of Legal Counsel, poked his head into the office. Kennedy said, "Harold, you can help. Can you go too?" It was not till they were halfway to the Andrews Air Force Base that Reis learned where he was going. (He said later, "The next time I'll ask, 'Go where?' ")[21] Burke Marshall and Ramsey Clark manned the Justice headquarters. Kennedy bade Katzenbach a characteristic farewell: "If things get rough, don't worry about yourself; the President needs a moral issue."*

In Oxford, Katzenbach found hundreds of people milling about the Lyceum, the university's administrative building. Soon Meredith arrived on campus flanked by McShane and Doar—"two of the bravest men I have ever known," Meredith called them later. "I never saw either of them weaken under any and all conditions of danger."[22] He was spirited into a dormitory, but the crowd supposed him in the

* Jean Stein and George Plimpton, *American Journey* (New York, 1970), 104. The humorless English editor Anthony Howard, reviewing *American Journey* in the *New Statesman* (June 18, 1971), seized upon this remark as proof of Robert Kennedy's callous determination to sacrifice everyone to the greater glory of the Kennedys. Katzenbach responded with admirable restraint that, while Howard had made "manifestly clear his dislike for humour in tense moments, he does not make explicit the fact that the statement was made in jest to cover up a deep concern and affection. Perhaps this fact will have some significance for those readers less familiar with the context than Mr. Howard, who may possibly have thought the remark serious" (*New Statesman*, July 2, 1971).

Lyceum around which federal marshals, in white helmets and bright orange vests, had stationed themselves. After a time the state police, despite Katzenbach's protestations, were withdrawn. Hard-faced men from the countryside, many armed, began to appear. The crowd, at first merely noisy and raucous, turned ugly. As it grew dark, people started to throw bricks and bottles. Five minutes before the President went on the air in Washington, Katzenbach told the marshals, some hurt and bleeding, to protect themselves by discharging tear gas.

Kennedy's speech was designed for a different occasion. It assumed that Meredith had arrived on campus in relative tranquility and appealed to white Mississippi's sense of honor, "won on the field of battle and on the gridiron." There was no reason, he concluded, "why the books on this case cannot now be quickly and quietly closed."[23] At Ole Miss the mob howled obscenities and surged forward toward the line of marshals. In a while the crash of bottles was punctuated by the crackle of bullets.

The President had no idea things were falling apart in Oxford. Now the reports from the front grew suddenly alarming. The Attorney General asked Guthman what it was like at the Lyceum. "Pretty rough," said Guthman. "It's getting like the Alamo." Robert Kennedy: "Well, you know what happened to those guys"—a famous response that, as Guthman wrote later (without irony), "raised our morale and helped us through the night."[24] With the marshals under siege—many injured, tear gas running low, gunfire increasing, reports of deaths—and under the President's personal order not to shoot except to protect Meredith's life,* Katzenbach made a bitter decision and asked Washington to send in the Army.

As usual, the Pentagon's plans were impressive. Cyrus Vance, looking at the military timetable, promised the President quick action. But in Memphis the troops had gone off alert after hearing the speech. When the summons arrived, the first group, according to the Army theory of riot control, was armed only with nightsticks. The situation in Oxford had long since passed this point. "So they stood out in the dark at Memphis," Katzenbach said later, "opening crates of guns and opening crates of gas . . . by flashlight."[25] After two hours Katzenbach asked the White House where the devil the Army was. John Kennedy, in between conversations with Barnett, called Vance and the Pentagon. Vance, consulting his schedule, assured him the troops were on their way.

* Compare with Kent State and Jackson State in 1970.

Robert Kennedy said later:

> That happened six, eight, ten times during the course of the evening. "They're leaving in twenty minutes." We'd call twenty minutes later, and they hadn't even arrived to get ready to leave. "They're ready to go now," and they hadn't been called out of their barracks to get into the helicopters yet. "They're in the helicopters now." They were just forming up. "The first helicopter's leaving and will be there in forty minutes." The first helicopter went in the air and then circled and waited for the rest of the helicopters. You know, all that kind of business. . . . They said they'd get there in two hours if I gave them the notice—and they didn't arrive for five hours. In the meantime, our marshals were being overwhelmed. . . . Two people were killed right at the beginning, so we had visions of the whole night—and then their getting in and killing Meredith. . . . It was so frustrating for the Army to continuously give false, wrong, inaccurate information.

As the hours dragged on, John Kennedy called Vance in the Pentagon, General Creighton Abrams in Memphis—"the worst and harshest conversations with Cy Vance and with the General that I think I've ever heard him [conduct]," Robert recalled.[26]

Even after the troops arrived in Oxford, there was inexplicable delay. At the Lyceum, the marshals had finally run out of tear gas. At the airport, half a mile away, the field commander, operating by the book, waited for his whole force to disembark and fall in before moving. Agonizing moments passed. John Kennedy sent the commander a coldly furious message: "People are dying in Oxford. This is the worst thing I've seen in forty-five years. I want the military police battalion to enter the action. I want General Billingslea to see that this is done."[27] In the end, it took the Army over an hour to make the last half mile.

"It was a nervous time for the President," Robert Kennedy reflected, "because he was torn between, perhaps, an Attorney General who had botched things up and the fact that the Attorney General was his brother."[28] Robert Kennedy felt a terrible responsibility. His brother had placed him in charge. Now everything was going wrong. The call for troops was itself a confession of failure. Still worse, the troops had not come. The President, wrote Theodore Sorensen, who was present, "cursed himself for ever believing Barnett and for not ordering the troops in sooner."[29] Robert Kennedy recalled: "We could just visualize another great disaster, like the Bay of Pigs, and a lot of marshals being killed or James Meredith being strung up."[30]

In retrospect, the Attorney General believed that it had been right to delay the order to the troops. Barnett had promised to keep things under control. Burke Marshall considered it "doubtful whether the President had any constitutional choice about refusing in advance to accept the word of the governor of a state."[31] In any event, it would have been hard to justify military intervention before trouble began. "If we had sent the troops in, and then they had a riot," said Robert Kennedy, "that would have been disastrous." But, once the shooting started, "the only way to deal with that kind of operation is to have overwhelming force. . . . The question of the evening would have been quite different if the troops had gotten there at the time that they were supposed to have gotten there." Still, "I was the Attorney General. The fact that I said that the troops would arrive and they didn't arrive was my fault."[32]

In Oxford they hung on through the wild night. The Army and daybreak brought a melancholy quiet to the embattled campus. Guthman turned wearily to Katzenbach and said, "What'll we do in the morning?" "Why," Katzenbach replied, "we're going to register Mr. Meredith at 8 o'clock."[33] So they did, and another wall crumbled. In the next months Meredith doggedly pursued his destiny in face of harassment by loutish classmates. He prevailed. "I am a graduate of the University of Mississippi," he was able to write Robert Kennedy in September 1963. "For this I am proud of my Country—the United States of America. The question always arises—was it worth the cost? . . . I believe that I echo the feeling of most Americans when I say that 'no price is too high to pay for freedom of person, equality of opportunity, and human dignity.'"[34]

Robert Kennedy had already replied to Meredith's question in a speech the Saturday night after the Battle of Ole Miss: "We live in a time when the individual's opportunity to meet his responsibilities appears circumscribed by impersonal powers beyond his responsibility. . . . But even today there is so much that a single person can do with faith and courage, and we have had a number of outstanding examples just this week. . . . James Meredith brought to a head and lent his name to another chapter in the mightiest internal struggle of our time."[35]

IV

The Oxford crisis, most of all the military intervention, shocked the white south. It also shocked the Kennedys. They had never thought it would come to this. Their assumption in 1961 was that unreasonable problems would yield to reason and law. Ole Miss showed them how stubborn, savage, deeply rooted the problems were. "We lacked," Guthman reflected, "a sense of Southern history."[36] They had been brought up to believe, for example, that Reconstruction was a matter of southern whites rescuing their states from ignorant and incompetent ex-slaves—the view reflected in *Profiles in Courage* where John Kennedy had described Thaddeus Stevens as "the crippled, fanatical personification of the extremes of the Radical Republican movement."[37] Now, after reading the Mississippi legislature's report on Oxford, he told Robert he could never take this view of Reconstruction again. "He said," his brother recalled, "that they can say these things about what the marshals did and what we were doing . . . and believe it. They must have been doing the same thing a hundred years ago."[38] The next year, when Medgar Evers, Meredith's friend and counselor, was murdered in front of his house in Jackson, the President said sadly to me, "I don't understand the South. I'm coming to believe that Thaddeus Stevens was right. I had always been taught to regard him as a man of vicious bias. But when I see this sort of thing, I begin to wonder how else you can treat them."*

After Oxford, the Kennedys began to understand how profoundly the republic had been trapped by its history. They were men endowed by a bitter ancestral history of their own with a conviction of the precariousness of social forms in face of the bloodiness of human existence. "Before my term has ended," John Kennedy had told Congress in his first annual message, "we shall have to test anew whether a nation organized and governed such as ours can endure. The outcome is by no means certain."[39] Nothing tested the nation more severely than the challenge of racial justice. If survival were the issue, far better to use force in support of law than to accept violence in defiance of law.

This was the way that most Americans, including many white southerners, perceived the Battle of Ole Miss. Thus a courageous Mississippi legislator, Karl Wiesenburg, argued that Barnett had followed "the road to riot" and that the bloodshed at Oxford was the "price of defiance."[40] "Tell [Wiesenburg] for me," Robert Kennedy wrote the federal attorney in Oxford, "that he is the one who deserves a Pulitzer Prize or more. It is all very well for we in the North to talk about these matters. That takes no courage at all. But people

---

* Author's journal, June 20, 1963. Alas, he had been thus taught by the Harvard history department.

such as you and Mr. Wiesenburg are the ones who really carry the banner."[41] The southern Vice President applauded the action. Lyndon Johnson had not in fact been consulted. "Rightly or wrongly," observed Guthman, "Bob felt his presence would complicate the discussions rather than further them."[42] Johnson had even been permitted to spend the climactic weekend on his Texas ranch and might well have been disaffected; but on his return to Washington he spoke to the southern Secretary of State, who passed his message along to the White House. "The situation in Mississippi," Dean Rusk reported Lyndon Johnson as saying, "had been handled better than he could ever have thought of handling it."[43]

Around the world the use of troops dramatized as nothing else could have done the commitment of the administration to the cause of racial justice. Howard P. Jones, the ambassador to Indonesia, wrote the Attorney General, "This was a battle which *had* to be won. . . . What might have been a severe set-back to our prestige in Asia and Africa was turned into a gain."[44] "For one small Negro to go to school," the representative of Upper Volta told the UN General Assembly, the American government "threatens governors and judges with prison. . . . It sends troops to occupy the University of Mississippi."[45]

Only American black leaders lacked enthusiasm for the Kennedy performance. Sitting with Martin Luther King and James Baldwin, the black novelist, in a Boston railway station shortly after Oxford, William Goldsmith, the political scientist, listened to their "despairing reactions. . . . It was not only the clumsiness and hesitancy with which the whole business was handled that depressed them, but the lack of moral conviction in the President's remarks as he spoke patronizingly of war heroes and football stars to the rioting students and yahoos in Oxford that awful Sunday night."[46] The behind-the-scenes dealing with Barnett, King felt, "made Negroes feel like pawns in a white man's political game."[47]

King was despondent. In March 1963 he described 1962 as "the year that civil rights was displaced as the dominant issue in domestic politics. . . . The issue no longer commanded the conscience of the nation." He ascribed this to the readiness to accept token victories— one man in the University of Mississippi—as evidence of serious change. "In fairness," King concluded, "this Administration has outstripped all previous ones in the breadth of its civil-rights activities. Yet the movement, instead of breaking out into the open plains of progress, remains constricted and confined. A sweeping revolutionary force is pressed into a narrow tunnel."[48]

V

On February 23, 1963, John Kennedy finally submitted a legislative program on civil rights. His message to Congress enumerated in ringing language the costs of racial discrimination. "Above all," he said, "it is wrong."[49] His recommendations included, as King agreed, "constructive measures," especially in the voting field.[50] But on the whole the proposals gravely disappointed the civil rights leadership—nothing serious about fair employment, school desegregation, public accommodations or federal protection for civil rights workers.

Burke Marshall was convinced that school desegregation legislation could not possibly pass and that "problems of law enforcement in some places, before the free exercise of the franchise, are almost insurmountable at present under the federal system."[51] So voting was still paramount. Could even voting reform pass? "We thought that it was very difficult," Robert Kennedy said in 1964, "but that it was such a basic right, that we had so much on our side, that we might be able to get it through." The bill, however, fell into a vacuum of apathy. "There wasn't any interest in it," said Kennedy. "There was no public demand for it. There was no demand by the newspapers or radio or television. There was no interest by people coming to watch the hearings. . . . Nobody came. Nobody paid any attention."[52]

In the meantime, King and the SCLC leadership held a two-day strategy review in Dorchester, Georgia. A tacit alliance, they decided, had developed between the administration and the movement. If the movement could create a public demand, the administration would respond. They decided also to make their next move in Birmingham, Alabama. If that brutal city, so raw in its emotion and so grim in its segregation, could be turned around, "the results," as Stanley Levison, King's close associate, put it, "would radiate across the South."[53] Early in April 1963 King launched a campaign to end discrimination in the department stores and lunch counters of downtown Birmingham, where the police commissioner Bull Connor had boasted a year earlier he could solve the racial problem with "two policemen and a dog."[54]

A moderate city administration was about to take over in Birmingham. Robert Kennedy urged King not to force the issue while the horrible Connor was still in power. King, who had agreed to an earlier postponement, declined this one. "For years now I have heard the word 'Wait,'" he soon wrote. ". . . This 'Wait' has almost always meant 'Never.'"⁵⁵ He wrote this from the jail where Bull Connor thrust him after he defied a local injunction and led a protest march on Good Friday. King was held incommunicado. His wife, unable to reach him, telephoned John Kennedy. She could not reach him either. Then Robert Kennedy returned her call: "The President wasn't able to talk to you because he's with my father who is quite ill. He wanted me . . . to find out what we can do for you." Coretta King expressed her fears for her husband. "We have a difficult problem with the local officials," the Attorney General replied. "Bull Connor is very hard to deal with. . . . But I promise you I will look into the situation." The FBI in Birmingham checked that night. The next day John Kennedy told Mrs. King that her husband was well and would ring her shortly. In fifteen minutes King was on the phone. She told him about her appeal to the Kennedys. King said, "So that's why everybody is suddenly being so polite."⁵⁶

King had put his time to good use composing his moving Letter from Birmingham Jail. Released on bond after eight days, he led the campaign into a new phase. On May 2 several thousand black children marched. Bull Connor's police arrested almost a thousand. King characteristically thought that participation in the protest would give the children pride in their race, belief in their capacity to influence events, a "sense of their own stake in freedom and justice."⁵⁷ Robert Kennedy characteristically thought the children might be hurt.⁵⁸ (Malcolm X objected too: "Real men don't put their children on the firing line.")⁵⁹ Another march took place on May 3. This time Connor's cops retaliated frightfully with nightsticks, pressure fire hoses and growling police dogs. On May 4 newspapers across the land (and around the world) ran appalling photographs of the dogs, teeth bared, lunging viciously at the marchers.

The Attorney General sent Burke Marshall and Joseph Dolan to Birmingham. They found a desperate situation. The white leaders would not talk to Martin King. "They wouldn't talk to anybody that *would* talk with him," Marshall said later. ". . . Somebody had to bridge that." The blacks had their own suspicions about Marshall. King subsequently acknowledged "initial misgivings," fearing that Marshall had been sent to urge a cooling-off period.⁶⁰ Marshall met around the clock with everybody, listening endlessly, talking quietly, forever seeking common ground. He tried to show the whites that King was not intending revolution; all he wanted was recognition of "what was right and what was unfair. And once he got that in a way that was public, then that was enough."[61] He tried to persuade the blacks to accept pledges of future action on desegregation and job discrimination: the important thing was to establish the principle.

A week of marathon negotiations produced an agreement on a measure of desegregation and black employment. Then Bull Connor arrested King again. The Reverend Fred Shuttlesworth, another black leader, prepared to lead the marchers back into the streets. A bloody clash loomed ahead. "Once again," wrote King's best biographer, "the Kennedy touch was needed."[62] Dolan phoned the Attorney General. "It was just a real tense situation," Andrew Young, King's top lieutenant, recalled. ". . . I never knew what [Kennedy] said to Fred Shuttlesworth. But when they got through talking, things, you know, were pretty much resolved. And I guess I began to get an appreciation for that kind of way of working with people, rather than with principles and laws. . . . He was very much the diplomat. And, you know, I began to like that."[63] The march was canceled, and Kennedy secured King's release. On May 10 the Birmingham settlement was announced.

That night segregationists bombed the house of King's brother and the motel where the civil rights leaders had their headquarters. In savage response angry blacks streamed down the streets, throwing rocks, breaking windows, burning shops and even attacking police officers. "Let the whole fucking city burn," some shouted. ". . . This'll show the white motherfuckers!"[64] Nothing like it had ever happened in the south. "The passivity and nonviolence of American Negroes could never again be taken for granted," two southern political scientists wrote later. ". . . The 'rules of the game' in race relations were permanently changed in Birmingham."[65]

Despite the renewal of violence then and in months to come, the Birmingham settlement held together. In that summer and that city it was a remarkable achievement. Marshall "did an invaluable job," King finally conceded.[66] "Bobby Kennedy, Burke Marshall and Joe Dolan . . . did some phenomenal things," Andrew Young said. ". . . You began to get a kind of unofficial, personal reconciliation with both whites and blacks, which was very new. . . . Birmingham was in such a state then that either the black or white community could have gotten out of hand any minute. . . . The country in 1963 could have gone either way."[67]

Not everyone was so pleased. Arthur Hanes, the retiring mayor, cursed out Robert Kennedy. "I hope that every drop of blood that's spilled he tastes in his throat," Hanes said, "and I hope he chokes to death."[68]

VI

On May 24, a few days after the Birmingham settlement, Robert Kennedy met with a group of black writers and artists brought together by the novelist James Baldwin. The meeting came about in the following manner.

Birmingham convinced Kennedy that the next great battlefield for racial justice lay in the cities. James Baldwin was born in Harlem. His extraordinary *New Yorker* piece of November 1962, "Letter from a Region in My Mind," had exposed in searing words the humiliation, despair and rage of Negro Americans. Baldwin and Kennedy had met the year before at the White House dinner for Nobel Prize laureates. They had agreed then that they wanted to talk some more. Now Kennedy invited Baldwin to breakfast at Hickory Hill.

Baldwin was a brilliant, passionate, sensitive, dramatic man imbued with a conviction of utter hopelessness about the black fate in white society. "The Negro's experience of the white world," he had written in the *New Yorker,* "cannot possibly create in him any respect for the standards in which the white world claims to live."[69] His belief, one felt, was that all whites by definition hated all blacks and that white liberals were worst of all because they pretended to deny their innermost feelings. Nonetheless he caught an early plane to Washington. "We had a very nice meeting," Kennedy said later.[70] "I was really quite impressed by him," said Baldwin. ". . . He seemed honest and earnest and truthful."[71] Burke Marshall, who was present, said, "He and Bob Kennedy had a rather good conversation about the cities."[72] Baldwin's plane had been late, however, and Kennedy had to leave for another engagement. He therefore proposed that Baldwin assemble a group with thoughts about the northern ghetto.

This led to the meeting in the Kennedy family apartment at 24 Central Park South in New York. Baldwin, acting on short notice, made an effort to enlist experts on the northern city, like Kenneth B. Clark, the social psychologist, Edwin C. Berry of the Chicago Urban League and Clarence B. Jones, an attorney for Martin Luther King. But what Baldwin called "this sociology and economics jazz" was not his métier.* He also invited the playwright Lorraine Hansberry and

---

* Harold Cruse, *The Crisis of the Negro Intellectual* (New York, 1967), 193–194. Cruse adds: "This failure to discuss the racial conflicts either in terms of possible

the singers Lena Horne and Harry Belafonte—artists concerned, like Baldwin himself, less with solutions than with the anguish of the problem. Then he brought along Jerome Smith, a young civil rights worker, who began as a Gandhian pacifist, became a Freedom Rider and a CORE field worker and, according to the historians of CORE, "had probably spent more months in jail and been beaten more often than any other CORE member."[73] He was now in New York for medical treatment.*

Robert Kennedy and Burke Marshall had spent an unpleasant morning urging owners of chain stores to desegregate their lunch counters in the south. The white executives seemed to feel, Kennedy recalled, that "the Devil Incarnate had arrived in New York, and they were asked to meet with him."[74] They turned out not to be the only people in New York that day who regarded the Attorney General as the devil incarnate.

Clark and Berry arrived armed with statistics and proposals. They never had a chance. Jerome Smith, as Baldwin put it later, "set the tone of the meeting because he stammers when he's upset and he stammered when he talked to Bobby and said that he was nauseated by the necessity of being in that room. I knew what he meant. It was not personal at all. . . . Bobby took it personally." This was perhaps understandable. To say, as the Attorney General heard it, that being in the same room with Robert Kennedy made him feel like throwing up seemed a rough way to begin. "Bobby took it personally," Baldwin continued, "and turned away from him. That was a mistake because he turned toward us. We were the reasonable, responsible, mature representatives of the black community. Lorraine Hansberry said, 'You've got a great many very, very accomplished people in this room, Mr. Attorney General. But the only man who should be listened to is that man over there.' "[75]

Smith talked on with vehement emotion. He told what he had been through in the south. He said he was not sure how much longer he could stay nonviolent. He said, "When I pull the trigger, kiss it good-

---

practical solutions, or in terms of American economic and sociological realities, made Baldwin's assault on white liberals a futile rhetorical exercise; it was further weakened by the intellectual inconsistencies, incoherence and emotionalism of his line of argument."

* Also present were Edward False, James Baldwin's secretary, Baldwin's brother David and Thais Aubrey, a friend of David Baldwin's; and three white men: Rip Torn, the actor, Robert P. Mills and Henry Morgenthau III, a television producer who was to tape an interview of Baldwin by Kenneth Clark later in the afternoon (R. P. Mills to Burke Marshall, June 7, 1963, Marshall Papers).

bye." Baldwin asked him whether he would fight for his country. He said, "Never! Never! Never!"[76] This shocked Kennedy, for whom patriotism was an absolute. "We were shocked that he was shocked," said Kenneth Clark. ". . . Bobby got redder and redder and redder, and in a sense accused Jerome of treason, you know, or something of that sort. Well, that made everybody move in to protect Jerome and to confirm his feelings. And it became really an attack!"[77]

"This boy," Lena Horne said afterward, "just put it like it was. He communicated the plain, basic suffering of being a Negro. The primeval memory of everyone in that room went to work after that. . . . He took us back to the common dirt of our existence and rubbed our noses in it. . . . You could not encompass his anger, his fury, in a set of statistics, nor could Mr. Belafonte and Dr. Clark and Miss Horne, the fortunate Negroes, keep up the pretense of being the mature, responsible spokesmen for the race."[78] Lorraine Hansberry said to Kennedy, "Look, if *you* can't understand what this young man is saying, then we are without any hope at all because you and your brother are representatives of the best that a white America can offer; and if *you* are insensitive to this, then there's no alternative except our going in the streets . . . and chaos."[79] The whites, she said, were castrating the Negroes. She talked wildly about giving guns to Negroes in the street so that they could start killing white people.[80]

Kennedy said, as he had before, that his grandparents had encountered discrimination and now, two generations later, his brother was President; a Negro would be President within forty years. Baldwin replied furiously, "Your family has been here for three generations. My family has been here far longer than that. Why is your brother at the top while we are still so far away? That's the heart of the problem."[81] Kennedy tried to turn the conversation to statistics and legislation. "In that moment, with the situation in Birmingham the way it was," said Lena Horne, "none of us wanted to hear figures and percentages and all that stuff. Nobody even cared about expressions of good will."[82]

Kennedy said he had come in search of ideas. Baldwin suggested that John Kennedy personally escort two black students whom Governor George Wallace was loudly threatening to bar from the University of Alabama. Robert Kennedy thought this theatrical posturing. (Asked about this proposal two days later, James Meredith said, "I don't think this would be the proper thing for a President of the United States to do.")[83] They denounced the FBI. Kennedy, who privately agreed, passed the question to Burke Marshall, who said that "special men"—that is, lawyers from the Civil Rights Division—went into areas where the Bureau seemed delinquent. This answer, said Clark, "produced almost hysterical laughter."[84] Birmingham came up. When Kennedy explained how closely he had worked with Dr. King, they jeered and cried, "That's not true."[85]

Kenneth Clark: "It became really one of the most violent, emotional verbal assaults . . . that I had ever witnessed before or since." Baldwin: "Bobby didn't understand what we were trying to tell him . . . didn't understand our urgency." Kennedy: "They seemed possessed. They reacted as a unit. It was impossible to make contact with any of them." Clark: "Bobby became more silent and tense, and he sat immobile in the chair. He no longer continued to defend himself. He just sat, and you could see the tension and the pressure building in him."

It went on for three hours; then suddenly stopped, out of sheer exhaustion. Two incidents as the meeting broke up increased Kennedy's shock. Clarence Jones, King's lawyer, drew Kennedy aside and said, "I just want to say that Dr. King deeply appreciates the way you handled the Birmingham affair." Kennedy said, "You watched these people attack me over Birmingham for forty minutes, and you didn't say a word. There is no point in your saying this to me now." Harry Belafonte had tried to smooth things over earlier by mentioning to the group the hospitality he had enjoyed at Hickory Hill; after a time, he had fallen into uncomfortable silence. Now he said to Kennedy, "Of course you have done more for civil rights than any one else." Kennedy said, "Why do you say this to me? Why didn't you say this to the others?" Belafonte said, "I couldn't say this to the others. It would affect my position with these people, and I have a chance to influence them along a reasonable way. . . . If I sided with you on these matters then I would become suspect."[86]

The meeting shattered them all. Clark and Baldwin talked it over that night. "Our considered judgment," Clark said, "was that the whole thing was hopeless; that there was no chance that Bobby heard anything that we said. . . . Kennedy was not unimpressive. He didn't minimize or condescend. But he just didn't seem to get it."*

---

* Kenneth Clark, in recorded interview by Jean Stein, January 30, 1970, 5, Stein Papers; Clark, in interview by author, September 9, 1976. Clarence Jones on June 7 sent a letter to the *New York Times*, in which he said: "The Attorney General and Mr. Burke Marshall have been more vigorous in their prosecution of actions in behalf of civil rights than any previous Administration. . . . [But] when the chief legal officer of the United States displays a certain shock over the sentiments expressed by the participants at that meeting, that fact . . . is indicative of how the Administration

Clark told James Wechsler in a day or two, "The fact that Bobby Kennedy sat through such an ordeal for three hours proves that he is among the best the white power structure has to offer. . . . There were no villains in that room—only the past of our society."[87] That is what made it all seem so hopeless.

Kennedy said to me on his return to Washington, his voice filled with despair: "They don't know what the laws are—they don't know what the facts are—they don't know what we've been doing or what we're trying to do. You can't talk to them the way you can talk to Martin Luther King or Roy Wilkins. They didn't want to talk that way. It was all emotion, hysteria—they stood up and orated—they cursed—some of them wept and left the room." I worried (as I noted) "that his final reaction would be a sense of the futility rather than of the urgency of trying to bridge the gap. He may have felt himself that I might have had this fear, because he called me later in the evening on another matter and seemed thoroughly calm."[88]

In subsequent months he tried to explain to himself why there had been this outburst against him. Of course the meeting was misconceived. He was interested in policy, the blacks, Clark and Berry apart, in witness. What Clark called the "excruciating sense of impasse"[89] seemed inevitable. Guilt, Kennedy thought, was also a factor. "There was a complex about the fact that they had not been involved personally themselves, they were not suffering like Negroes were suffering. . . . You've seen it with white people . . . children of wealthy parents . . . who've got some social problem about where they stand in life . . . and therefore become extreme and difficult emotionally."[90]

But none of this could quite explain away the violent jolt he received that spring afternoon. He began, I believe, to grasp as from the inside the nature of black anguish. He resented the experience, but it pierced him all the same. His tormentors made no sense; but in a way they made all sense. It was another stage in education. Thirteen years later it remained for Kenneth Clark "the most intense, traumatic meeting in which I've ever taken part . . . the most unrestrained interchange among adults, head-to-head, no holds barred . . . *the* most dramatic experience I have ever had."[91]

---

underestimates the explosive ingredients inherent in the continued existence of racial discrimination." He sent a copy to Robert Kennedy, who sent it along, on June 12, to Marshall with the wry note: "He is a nice fellow & you have swell friends."

VII

But education came in the main from the rush of events. Racial justice was no longer an issue in the middle distance. Robert Kennedy now saw it face to face, and he was on fire. To complete the Birmingham settlement, he had to get King's demonstrators out of jail. He called on his old UAW friends, Walter Reuther, Jack Conway and Joseph Rauh, and $160,000 in bail money was rapidly on its way. He began to prod the federal government across the board. For two years he had heard from Lyndon Johnson's Committee on Equal Employment Opportunity bland reassurances about the steady increase of blacks in government jobs. But, when the committee met on May 29—its first meeting since the previous November—he discovered that, aside from the Post Office and a Veterans' Administration hospital, only 15 of the 2000 federal employees in Birmingham were black—less than 1 percent in a city that was 37 percent black.[92] He was furious.

He remained furious. At the committee's next meeting, twenty days later, the Attorney General was on the warpath. Jack Conway was there representing the federal housing agency. "Within a matter of three or four minutes," Conway recalled, "the Vice President found himself on the defense because Bob just tore in . . . and asked for facts and statistics." Kennedy turned on James Webb, head of the National Aeronautics and Space Administration, an amiable and competent executive and a Johnson protégé. NASA had contracts of $3.5 billion and, Kennedy discovered, only one and a half men in Washington working on equal employment. A stinging colloquy followed:

KENNEDY. I asked how many people you have got in your program and you said one and a half men.
WEBB. I am not sure. I can furnish you that, but with nine centers throughout the country we are putting a great deal of effort on it. . . .
KENNEDY. What is the experience and background of the people you have selected for these jobs? . . . Do they have other responsibilities?
WEBB. Oh, yes. They have the responsibility, if they are in the Personnel Department, of operating a total personnel system of which this is a part. . . .
KENNEDY. Mr. Webb, I just raised a question of whether you can do this job and run a center and administer its $3.9 billion worth of contracts and make sure that Negroes and non-whites have jobs. . . . I think that unless we can get down into the specifics, Mr. Webb, unless you get down to the specifics and the particular individuals and find out what

they are doing and have them understand that . . . this Committee and the President of the United States are interested in this program, I don't see that the job will be done. . . .
WEBB. I would like to have you take enough time to see precisely what we do.
KENNEDY. I am trying to ask some questions. I don't think I am able to get the answers, to tell you the truth.

Johnson, obviously angry, slumped grimly in his chair, his eyes half closed. "It was," said Conway, "a pretty brutal performance, very sharp. It brought tensions between Johnson and Kennedy right out on the table and very hard. Everybody was sweating under the armpits. . . . And then finally, after completely humiliating Webb and making the Vice President look like a fraud and shutting Hobart Taylor up completely, he got up. He walked around the table . . . shook my hand . . . and then he went on out."[93]

Subsequently Willard Wirtz, the Secretary of Labor, charged that, in spite of the committee's self-congratulatory publicity, two thirds of the companies holding government contracts still did not employ blacks. Kennedy backed Wirtz vigorously. It was not enough, Kennedy told the committee, to make "generalized statements." "Why hasn't somebody followed it up, what companies have you actually gotten in touch with, is anybody going to see any of the companies? . . . You have to go out and look for these people. I thought that that should be the policy and that we should push it."[94] In July, Robert Kennedy told his brother that they

> were having a difficult time with Johnson and the committee because of his oversensitivity of any outside criticism. One of the great problems has been the fact that this committee has not really accomplished what . . . the press releases would indicate that it had, the result being a stepped up effort which Burke, Bill Wirtz and I have had to take with a great deal of care. Johnson was so furious several weeks ago with Bill Wirtz and for a while it appeared that he would never talk to him. This was all because Bill Wirtz had given some statistics on the number of government contractors who had no Negro employees.[95]

These were, Kennedy recalled, "the sharpest disputes I had with Vice President Johnson." When he took Wirtz's statistics over to his brother, the President "almost had a fit. . . . He said, 'That man can't run this Committee. Can you think of anything more deplorable than him trying to run the United States? That's why he can't ever be President.' "[96] This was the autumn of 1963.

VIII

A new crisis was building in Alabama. An ambitious and cocky politician named George Wallace had been elected governor. During his campaign he had promised to place himself in the doorway of any schoolhouse under court order to admit blacks. On his inauguration in January 1963 he noted that he was standing where Jefferson Davis had stood when he became president of the Confederate States of America; and now, "from this Cradle of the Confederacy, this very heart of the great Anglo-Saxon Southland, . . . I draw the line in the dust and toss the gauntlet before the feet of tyranny. And I say, Segregation now! Segregation tomorrow! Segregation forever!"[97] Martin Luther King considered Wallace "perhaps the most dangerous racist in America today. . . . I am not sure that he believes all the poison he preaches, but he is artful enough to convince others that he does."[98]

King was right. Privately Wallace was less intransigent than his rhetoric. Aware that black students were applying to the University of Alabama at Tuscaloosa, he had asked Senator John Sparkman to say to the White House, "Please give Alabama as much breathing time as possible," adding that he was under no misapprehension about his ability to stop anything.[99] "Perhaps if we put this off until next September," John Kennedy had told his brother in November 1962, Ole Miss etched in both their minds, "we might . . . get a favorable solution."[100] But delay was impossible. On May 21 the federal district court ruled that the university must admit the black applicant to its summer session.

The Attorney General had already begun preparations to prevent Tuscaloosa from becoming another Oxford. The university's president and board of trustees were ready to comply with the court order. The administration now sought to rally Alabama business leaders in a campaign to dissuade Wallace from defiance. "We wrote down into a book," Robert Kennedy recalled, "the names of every company with more than one hundred employees, I think, in the whole state of Alabama. All those names were distributed at a cabinet meeting. . . . A cabinet member . . . called, I guess, every one of them."[101] He tried to talk to Wallace himself. The governor refused his calls—when asked his opinion of Robert Kennedy, his reply, according to an observer, was "too revoltingly obscene" for repetition[102]—but finally consented to a meeting.

On April 25, Kennedy, accompanied by Marshall and Guthman, arrived at the state capitol. State troopers, their steel helmets painted with Confederate flags, surrounded the building. "The point," recalled Kennedy, "was to try to show that my life was in danger in coming to Alabama because the people hated me so much." Actually, "they were all very friendly, the people. I shook hands with everybody." But Wallace "had the biggest State Troopers you ever saw all guarding the way in, and they all had big sticks. . . . One of them took his stick and put it into my stomach . . . and belted me with the stick. . . . Not for laughs at all. They were most unfriendly."[103]

Wallace began by asking Kennedy whether he had any objection to his taping their conversation. "Whatever you like, Governor," Kennedy replied, realizing at once that Wallace planned to use the meeting for political effect. After desultory chat, Kennedy said, "I didn't know whether we might discuss the problem we are perhaps facing here in the state." "I don't hear good," said Wallace. Kennedy said, "I don't think that the Union or the country means anything unless the orders of the land are enforced." He continued:

> KENNEDY. Do you think it is so horrifying to have a Negro attend the University of Alabama?
> WALLACE. I think it is horrifying for the federal courts and the central government to rewrite all the law and force upon people that which they don't want. . . . For a hundred years we operated under what the Supreme Court said was legal . . . and spent millions and millions of dollars building a beautiful educational system. . . . I will never submit myself voluntarily to any integration in a school system in Alabama. . . . There is no time in my judgment when we would be ready for it in my lifetime.

They continued talking across each other, Kennedy reiterating his duty to uphold the Constitution, Wallace reiterating his determination not to submit to federal tyranny and hoping as he went to trap Kennedy into damaging admission. After a time Wallace said it looked as if the matter would wind up in court. "As long as it winds up in Court," Kennedy said, "I will be happy, Governor. That is all I ask. . . . I just don't want it to get in the streets. I don't want to have another Oxford, Mississippi." This gave Wallace his opening: "You folks are the ones that will control that matter, because you have control of the troops."

> KENNEDY. We have a responsibility, Governor, to insure that the integrity of the courts is maintained . . . and all of the force behind the Federal Government will be used to that end.

WALLACE. . . . That is what you are telling me today, if it is necessary you are going to bring troops into Alabama.
KENNEDY. No, I didn't say that, Governor.
WALLACE. Well, you said all the force of the Federal Government.
KENNEDY. To make sure that the orders of the court are obeyed.
WALLACE. I know, but all the force includes the troops, doesn't it?
KENNEDY. Well, I would hope . . . that we would be able to litigate a settlement.
WALLACE. But it does involve troops if the law is disobeyed.
KENNEDY. Well, I am planning and hoping that the law will be obeyed. . . . Maybe somebody wants us to use troops, but we are not anxious to.

Wallace caught the personal thrust of Kennedy's last remark and fell into a trap himself. "I can assure you this," he said, "that I do not want you to use troops, and I can assure you that there is not any effort on my part to make a show of resistance and to be overcome." Kennedy said dryly, "I am glad to hear that." As they talked on, Kennedy appeared increasingly incredulous, speaking, wrote Marshall Frady, "with a curious low, dull uncertainty, as if not quite sure that he was actually engaging with the governor of Alabama about the kind of question he seemed to be engaged in." Toward the end Wallace tried to retrieve his point about the troops. "According to you all's attitude," he said, "you in the background say we may have to send troops and jail you as a governor of a state." "We never said that, Governor," Kennedy said sharply. In a moment, Wallace: "Let us get it straight. You would not use—" Kennedy replied that he expected the court order would be obeyed. "I have no plans to use troops. You seem to want me to use troops." Wallace: "Well, then we could say you are not going to use troops." Kennedy objected, rallied, evaded Wallace's snare and returned the conversation to the question of the supremacy of law. They circled around each other for a few more moments.[104] Then Kennedy departed in a state of bemusement.

Three weeks later John Kennedy himself went south. He spoke first in Tennessee. "For one man to defy a law or court order he does not like," the President said, "is to invite others to defy those which they do not like, leading to a breakdown of all justice and all order." He added that any citizen who sought "to subject other human beings to acts that are less than human, degrades his heritage."[105] He went on to Alabama, where Wallace accompanied him on the helicopter from Muscle Shoals to Huntsville. They talked about Birmingham. Kennedy observed that the very people who objected to Negroes working in downtown stores had Negroes serving their tables at home. Wallace said that the problem in Birmingham was that "faker" Martin Luther King. King and Fred Shuttlesworth, Wallace elegantly continued, vied with each other to see "who could go to bed with the most nigger women, and white and red women too."[106]

IX

The Kennedys could not make out what Wallace was going to do. It looked, Burke Marshall told the cabinet on May 21, as if he meant "personally to prevent the entry of a Negro student into the University. He has intended to require his own arrest or removal by force, and to require the federal government to use troops to enforce the court order."[107] Bulletins from the president of the university and from anti-Wallace trustees were not illuminating. "They'd report," Robert Kennedy recalled, "that he was acting like a raving maniac. So the result was that when you're trying to make plans . . . should you make plans on the basis of what a reasonable man would do? . . . You couldn't do that. The great question for us was not having to arrest the Governor, not having to charge him with contempt, and not having to send troops into the state of Alabama—and yet getting the students into the University."[108]

Did Wallace really want to be arrested? "We changed our minds a number of times about that," Kennedy recalled.

> I don't think that he wanted to go to jail, and there were some tough federal judges in Alabama who might have sent him to jail. . . . The other major question for us, if he was going to stand in the door, how many troops did we need? We didn't want to go through the same thing that we went through at the University of Mississippi. If you start having violence and you only have 300 troops and the police weren't going to help, how many troops did you need? . . . Dr. [Frank] Rose [the university president] made it quite clear that [Wallace] wouldn't step aside . . . for marshals. We had to have troops to get him to step aside. . . . So the final plans for the University of Alabama were really not made until that morning.[109]

June 11 was the day the black students planned to register. The federal judge warned Wallace's lawyers that, if Wallace violated the court order in a substantial way, he would receive a substantial sentence. The Attorney General also contemplated the immediate federalization of the Alabama National Guard. "That was before the first confrontation, so the first step would have been taken by us rather than by them. The President said, 'Let's wait,' . . . and that was the correct thing, as it turned out."[110]

"It is June 11th," Robert Kennedy wrote a Virginia friend, "and I am in the midst of trying to register two of your fellow countrymen at the University of Alabama and for one reason or another am having some difficulty."[111] Someone had proposed bringing the students onto the campus with troops. Katzenbach, who was in charge in Tuscaloosa, disagreed: "I think we should let Wallace have his show." In the early morning, Kennedy and Katzenbach worked out a final plan over the telephone. Katzenbach would escort the students to the university ("Dress as if you were going to church," John Doar told them), leave them in his automobile and, if Wallace blocked the doorway to registration, simply declare them registered and take them to dormitories to which they had already been assigned. This would permit Wallace to have his show. It would also permit the Justice Department to avoid arresting him for contempt because the students would not be physically present. "Dismiss George Wallace as a sort of second-rate figure," Robert Kennedy told Katzenbach, "wasting your time, wasting the students' time, causing a great fuss down there." If Wallace persisted in obstruction, then federalize the Guard; but leave the onus for that on Wallace. (And have the regular army on the ready at Fort Benning across the border in Georgia, troops sitting in helicopters; the Attorney General was not about to repeat the dismal Oxford experience with a dilatory army.)[112]

Shortly before 11 A.M. Katzenbach arrived and began the long walk under the broiling Alabama sun to the registration building. Inside the building a highly nervous Wallace repeatedly asked a state detective, "Ben, do you think they'll actually arrest me?" He sent word to Katzenbach through the National Guard commander that there would be no problem; he just wanted a chance to say something.[113] Now, standing incongruously behind a lectern, a microphone draped around his neck, he awaited Katzenbach. White semicircles painted in the doorway indicated where Wallace should stand in order to look his best on television; this irritated Katzenbach, who felt the situation was sufficiently theatrical already. Katzenbach began by saying he had a presidential proclamation commanding Wallace to cease and desist from unlawful obstructions. Wallace, holding up his hand like a traffic cop, stopped Katzenbach and read a proclamation of his own denouncing the "Central Government." They stood together, the rangy Katzenbach towering over the bantam governor, "exchanging vaguely irritable and exasperated phrases," as Frady saw it from a distance, "like a short, idle, haphazard argument on some street corner; Katzenbach with arms folded tightly and a faint expression of pained sufferance, beginning to glisten a little with sweat." Katzenbach again asked Wallace to step aside: "If you do not, I'm going to assure you that the orders . . . will be enforced. From the outset, Governor, all of us have known that the final chapter of this history will be the admission of these students." "I stand according to my statement," said Wallace. Katzenbach went back to the car. Wallace retired inside the auditorium.[114]

The President federalized the National Guard. Katzenbach took the students to their dormitories. No one stood in the doorway there. When the students appeared again for registration in the afternoon, Wallace stepped aside. Nor did he block the enrollment two days later of a third black student at the university's branch in Huntsville.

Wallace had lost—essentially, Robert Kennedy thought later, because of the appeal to respectable opinion in the state. "He was getting fifteen to twenty calls every day from business people," said Burke Marshall. "He'd have to guarantee them that there wouldn't be any repeat of the Oxford incident, that there wouldn't be any violence." Kennedy said: "Wallace really didn't know what he was going to do, I'm convinced, up until at least a couple of days before and, maybe, a few hours before. . . . If he had received great popular support in the state . . . standing in the door, continuing to stand in the door, I think that's what he would have done. But he was trying to get off the hook."[115]

Wallace explained his defeat: "I can't fight bayonets with my bare hands." Skeptics noted that there had been no bayonets to fight.[116] Still, as Robert F. Kennedy, Jr., wrote perceptively in 1978, Wallace "did not fear defeat as a political pitfall." "A good fight and a noble defeat" were never disqualifications in the south. "In the past, defeat had been imposed upon Alabama, and in a way it had a redemptive quality."[117] The tableau remained: the defiant Wallace standing in the schoolhouse door; the sweating Katzenbach making the lonely walk back to the limousine.

The encounter did not extinguish Wallace. But black students were now in the University of Alabama. At the end of the long day, Robert Kennedy scrawled notes to his children. To David: "Shortly after you left my office the two negroes attempted to register. . . . They were opposed by Governor Wallace but then Jack called up the National Guard and tonight at 6:00 they are registered and preparing to attend classes tomorrow." To Michael: "I hope when you are Attorney General these kind[s] of things will not go on."[118]

(16)

The Pursuit of Justice: Martin Luther King

ON THE NIGHT of Wallace's capitulation John Kennedy delivered a television address to the nation. It was a response not alone to Birmingham and Tuscaloosa but to an entire springtime of gathering outrage and atrocity—the white postman from Baltimore murdered on a "freedom walk" in Alabama; black demonstrators in Mississippi slugged, stomped on and then arrested for disturbing the peace; protests, riots; hardening resolve, hardening resistance. The President, deeply disturbed, decided the time had come to assert leadership and appeal to the nation. His advisers disagreed. O'Donnell and O'Brien did not think he should get personally involved. Sorensen was dubious. Burke Marshall later recalled to Robert Kennedy that, at the White House strategy meeting, "you were the only one who urged him to do it." "He just decided that day," Robert himself said. ". . . He called me up on the phone and said that he was going to go on that night."[1]

I

It was a busy week for John Kennedy. On Monday he had given a notable speech on foreign policy at American University. For most of the next day he and Robert were on the telephone discussing developments in Tuscaloosa. They could not know until late Tuesday afternoon whether the President might not have to go on television, as his brother later put it, to announce "the occupation of Tuscaloosa or the arrest of the Governor." At last the good news from the campus: "a pleasant moment," said Robert, "after working so hard."

An hour before the telecast the Attorney General and Burke Marshall met the President and Sorensen in the cabinet room. The President, Robert said later, "thought that he was going to have to do it extemporaneously, so that the two of us talked about what he'd say

... outlining and organizing" while JFK made notes "on the back of an envelope or something." Sorensen made notes too; then left the room. John Kennedy's casualness stunned Marshall: "I remember him sitting there, putting down these notes, without any speech, when he was about to go on television, on what I thought was [an issue] of momentous importance." Five minutes before the President went on the air Sorensen returned with most of a draft; no peroration, however. John Kennedy, his brother recalled, "went over it quickly, decided it said what he wanted to say. . . . Then the President used a little of the off-the-cuff stuff at the end. . . . The speech was good. I think that it, . . . if he had given it extemporaneously, would have been as good or better."[2]

It was, in fact, a great speech, its power deriving from a passionate declaration on racial justice never before uttered by an American President: "We are confronted primarily with a moral issue . . . as old as the scriptures and . . . as clear as the American Constitution." Its power came too from its unusual sense of identification with the victims of segregation. Let the white American, Kennedy said, contemplate the plight of his black fellow citizen. "Who among us would be content to have the color of his skin changed and stand in his place? Who among us would be content with the counsels of patience and delay?" The time had come, he said, "for this Nation to fulfill its promise" of freedom.[3]

That night the white killer shot down Medgar Evers in front of his house in Mississippi. A few days later, Roy Wilkins spoke at the funeral in Jackson. One man pulled the trigger, Wilkins said, but "the Southern political system put him behind the rifle." A great crowd gathered behind the cortège, chanting, "We want the killer! We want the killer! . . . We want equality! We want freedom!" Some headed toward the business district. Policemen with growling dogs massed to block them off. The mourners began to throw rocks and Coke bottles. Cops took out their riot guns. Then John Doar in shirtsleeves stepped between the groups. He said to the blacks, "I'm your friend. You can't win this way. . . . Don't throw bottles, that's what they want you to do." James Meredith, who was there, said Doar "restored order in an act of bravery and judgment seldom matched in human history."[4]

Medgar Evers, a war veteran, was buried in the Arlington Cemetery in Washington. Charles Evers, Medgar's brother: "Bobby sat with me all during the funeral, and he consoled me. President Kennedy carried Mrs. Medgar and I and the children back to the White

House. We stayed there for the rest of the day."[5] Robert Kennedy gave Charles Evers his personal phone numbers. "He said I could call him any time, day or night, if Negroes were being harassed and intimidated. . . . Whenever I had the need to call him, I never found it too late or too early."[6]

It was a stormy time. There was trouble in Cambridge, Maryland, where a black protest movement and the local authorities were in bloody collision. Kennedy called a meeting in his office. "I'll never forget it," said John Lewis of SNCC. ". . . Somehow he was able to bring the people together. . . . He asked questions and he also did a great deal of explaining, trying to convince some of the officials of Cambridge—some of them were very stubborn. . . . Before the meeting was over, people were talking to one another in fellowship, and we were getting pictures made together."[7]

In Prince Edward County in Virginia, there had been no public education at all since 1959, the local board of supervisors preferring to close schools rather than to integrate them. White parents had set up "private" schools for their children. Seventeen hundred black children had no place to go. In 1961 the Department of Justice had sought a judicial order requiring the county to reopen the schools; but the case had progressed glacially in the courts. In February 1963 John Kennedy told his brother that some way must be found in the meantime to educate the black children. Kennedy called in a bright and resourceful New York lawyer, William J. vanden Heuvel. Vanden Heuvel worked out a plan for a private operation called the Prince Edward Free School Association. "We would raise the money privately; we would lease the public schools from the County and teach these children in the most effective way until the courts reopened the schools. . . . Although Bobby was fully aware that there were many pitfalls . . . he never hesitated once in giving the go-ahead." With highly qualified teachers coming in from outside, the Free Schools even attracted a handful of white children. In May 1964 the Supreme Court ordered Prince Edward County to reopen its public schools.[8]

Such activity was mostly behind the scenes. The militants of racial justice continued to condemn the Attorney General for not doing enough. A few days after the murder of Medgar Evers, Kennedy spoke to an angry demonstration in front of the Department of Justice. Jack Newfield, a radical reporter from the *Village Voice* of New York, was in the crowd. "I had, by then, been jailed twice in civil rights demonstrations," he wrote later, "and with pure fury stared at Kennedy's crew-cut face. It was, I remember, a hard Irish face; alert, but without much character, a little like the faces that used to follow me home from Hebrew school, taunting, 'Christ killer.'" Someone shouted that they hadn't seen many Negroes come out of the building. "Kennedy tensed up even more. His skin seemed to draw even tighter around his sharp features, and the hostility radiating from his blue eyes became even more intense." He shouted back, "Individuals will be hired according to their ability, not their color." Newfield thought it "exactly the sort of impersonal, legalistic response, blind to the larger moral implications of our protest, that we felt made Kennedy such an inadequate Attorney General."[9]

On September 15, fifteen sticks of dynamite blasted the Sixteenth Street Baptist Church in Birmingham, killing four small girls who were changing into choir robes in the basement. Robert Kennedy said the next year:

> The responsibility for the bombing might have been those two Klansmen. But in the last analysis . . . it's Governor Barnett and Jim Eastland and John Stennis and the business community. . . . It's George Wallace and political and business leaders and newspapers. They can all deplore it . . . [but] they're the ones that created the climate that made those kinds of action possible. . . . With all the smiles and all the graciousness of Dick Russell and Herman Talmadge and Jim Eastland and George Smathers and [Spessard] Holland . . . none of them really made any effort to counter this. And they're the ones, really, who have the major responsibility, rather than these stupid figures who think that they become national heroes by taking on these tasks.[10]

II

"I shall ask the Congress," John Kennedy had said in his speech on the night of Tuscaloosa, ". . . to make a commitment it has not fully made in this century to the proposition that race has no place in American life or law."[11]

Kennedy's minimal February program had died before an indifferent nation. James Baldwin had not even been aware of its existence. Now Bull Connor and George Wallace had at last made civil rights a legislative possibility. The blacks were in the streets, moreover, and the President felt he would lose control over an increasingly dangerous situation unless he exerted leadership. He also was sensitive to the verdict of posterity. "There comes a time," he told Luther Hodges, his Secretary of Commerce, "when a man has to take a stand and history will record that he has to meet these tough situations and ultimately make a decision."[12]

Hodges, a southerner, was predictably doubtful. But O'Donnell and O'Brien also opposed civil rights legislation, fearing it would wreck the rest of the administration's program. "Every single person who spoke about it in the White House," Burke Marshall said later, "—every single one of them—was against President Kennedy's sending up that bill." Only Robert Kennedy wanted it. "He urged it, he felt it, he understood it. And he prevailed. I don't think there was anybody in the Cabinet—except the President himself—who felt that way on these issues, and the President got it from his brother."[13]

Robert Kennedy was much irritated in later years by the theory that his brother "only realized there was a civil rights crisis after Birmingham in 1963; or otherwise he would have tried to obtain . . . legislation in 1961 or 1962. . . . That was just a lot of hogwash. There wasn't anything he could do then. . . . Nobody was ready." Birmingham had not only created the mood but demonstrated the need. The discrimination in department stores and lunch counters, against which Martin Luther King had launched his protest, violated no federal statute. The moment had arrived, the Kennedys felt, to make equal access to places of public accommodation a matter of law. "For the first time," Robert Kennedy said, "people were enough concerned about it, and there was enough demand about it that we could get to the heart of the problem and have some chance of success."[14]

The administration bill also revived the voting rights proposals fruitlessly submitted to Congress in February. As for education, the drafters considered and ultimately abandoned the idea of deadlines for total school integration and settled instead on a provision authorizing the Attorney General to sue for school desegregation. As for federal funds used in discriminatory state or local activities, they originally supposed that withholding would be too much for Congress. Finding to their surprise general support for such a provision, they added it to the bill. The question of employment gave great difficulty. John Kennedy thought Truman had made a mistake fifteen years earlier "by prematurely throwing FEPC at the Congress." To include it now, he feared, might jeopardize the bill as a whole. The civil rights leadership and the labor movement protested. Hubert Humphrey carried their protest to the White House. Kennedy finally decided to endorse fair-employment-practices legislation in his message, but not put it in the bill.[15]

Doubts remained within the administration. The Vice President was a particular puzzle. Unable to decipher his warily delphic utterances in meetings, John Kennedy sent Burke Marshall to see him. Johnson at first filibustered, reminiscing at length about the way he had found jobs for Negroes when he worked for the National Youth Administration in Texas during the depression. Jobs, he said, were what mattered. Civil rights legislation "wouldn't get passed and was impossible and would cause a lot of trouble and was the wrong thing to do."[16] Robert Kennedy sent Norbert Schlei, who was in charge of drafting the bill, on a similar mission. Johnson, a little disgruntled, said he had asked for fifteen minutes alone with the President on the bill. Schlei was obviously an unsatisfactory substitute. The bill, Johnson said, "would be disastrous for the President's program and would not be enacted if submitted now." He said this, he explained, not because he opposed civil rights legislation—no one in the country wanted to do more for the Negroes—but because so little had been done to prepare the country for it.[17] In a few days Bobby Baker, the secretary of the Senate, took a poll that, as he reported to Mike Mansfield, the majority leader, "shows conclusively that it is virtually impossible to secure 51 Senators who will vote for the President's Bill."[18] Even the faithful Mansfield thought the bill had no chance.[19]

John Kennedy himself somewhat shared this pessimism, but saw no alternative except to go ahead. "We always felt that maybe this was going to be his political swansong," Robert Kennedy recalled the next year. ". . . He would ask me every four days, 'Do you think we did the right thing by sending the legislation up? Look at the trouble it's got us in.' But always in a semi-jocular way. It always seemed to me quite clear that was what we needed to do."[20] The President agreed. The reason, Robert said, was

> not only the passage of legislation, but what in my judgment was even more important, to obtain the confidence of the Negro population in their government and in the white majority. I thought there was a great danger in losing that unless we took a very significant step such as the passage of legislation. . . . There's obviously a revolution within a revolution in the Negro leadership. We could see the direction of Martin Luther King going away from him to some of these younger people, who had no belief or confidence in the system of government . . . and thought . . . that the way to deal with the problem is to start arming the young Negroes and sending them into the streets, which I didn't think was a very satisfactory solution because, as I explained to them, there are more white people than Negroes and although it might be bloody, I thought that the white people would do better.[21]

III

The bill went to Congress on June 19, 1963. "In the way he had of getting everything organized at once," said Burke Marshall, Robert Kennedy took command.[22] Together he and Marshall talked to all the members of Congress they could find. He proposed that the President invite influential groups to the White House—lawyers, educators, clergymen, businessmen, labor leaders, hotel, restaurant and theater owners. Some in the White House continued to think John Kennedy should not get so personally identified with the fight. The Attorney General disagreed. (So did his brother.) The whole point, Robert Kennedy said later, was to display "the active involvement of the President" as well as to show local leaders "why it was in their interest to do something rather than to wait until violence occurred."[23] Robert planned the effort, "saw that the meetings took place, did the groundwork for them, did the follow-up on them" (Burke Marshall).[24] The two Kennedys and Johnson addressed group after group in their contrasting styles—the President crisp and businesslike, the Vice President emotional and evangelical, the Attorney General blunt and passionate. Vincent Harding recalled Robert Kennedy at one meeting: "He said something about how *he* felt he would respond if he were a black person at this particular time; on a certain level, I had the feeling that he was serious in trying to say how he would feel as a black person, even though I thought that at certain levels it was really impossible for him to do more than *want* to feel that."[25]

The civil rights leaders thought that the bill, in Joseph Rauh's words, "contained the Administration's best estimates of what could be enacted, rather than what was needed."[26] Still, as Rauh told them, "It is the most comprehensive civil rights bill ever to receive serious consideration from the Congress of the United States."[27] Their major disagreement with the administration now came over tactics.

In the previous December, Bayard Rustin, the talented black organizer, had called on A. Philip Randolph, the revered president of the Brotherhood of Sleeping Car Porters. Recalling Randolph's 1941 victory in threatening a march on Washington and getting the wartime FEPC in exchange, Rustin proposed a new march.[28] The Kennedys were about as enthusiastic over a march on Washington as Roosevelt had been twenty-two years before. "We want success in Congress," the President told the black leaders in the cabinet room on June 22, "not just a big show at the Capitol. Some of these people are looking for an excuse to be against us; and I don't want to give any of them a chance to say, 'Yes, I'm for the bill, but I am damned if I will vote for it at the point of a gun.' It seemed to me a great mistake to announce a march on Washington before the bill was even in committee. The only effect is to create an atmosphere of intimidation —and this may give some members of Congress an out."[29]

Speaking with dignity and force, A. Philip Randolph, James Farmer and Martin Luther King defended the march.[30] The blacks were already in the streets; better that they march under nonviolent leadership; if the march were called off, they might turn to new and desperate leaders. "It may seem ill-timed," King said. "Frankly, I have never engaged in any direct action movement which did not seem ill-timed. Some people thought Birmingham ill-timed." The President said, "Including the Attorney General."

"This is a very serious fight," John Kennedy said. "The Vice President and I know what it will mean if we fail. . . . A good many programs I care about may go down the drain as a result of this—so we are putting a lot on the line. What is important is that we preserve confidence in the good faith of each other. I have my problems with Congress; you have yours with your own groups. We will undoubtedly disagree from time to time on tactics. But the important thing is to keep in touch."[31]

The civil rights leaders came away impressed by the President's commitment. "Joe," Kennedy had said to Rauh, "this is going to be a long, tough fight, but we have to do it."[32] "I liked the way he talked about what *we* are getting," said King. "It wasn't something that he was getting for you Negroes. You knew you had an ally."[33]

IV

If the march could not be headed off, the Kennedys decided that it would have to be made a success. John Kennedy talked to Walter Reuther, who shared the concern that an all-black march might lose votes on the Hill. Reuther proceeded to bring in white leaders, the churches and the labor movement. Jack Conway, now back with the UAW, served as his representative in the planning sessions.[34] Within Justice, Robert Kennedy, following his principle that a good man could do anything, gave the charge to John Douglas, the newly appointed assistant attorney general for the Civil Division. For the next five weeks Douglas worked full-time on the march. "Good administration," he told his assistant Alan Raywid, "presumes what can go wrong will go wrong," and he directed Raywid to draw up a list of everything that might conceivably go wrong with a march. The list, extending finally to nearly seventy-five items, covered everything from route and timetable, the sound system and security forces, to food, soft drinks (in paper cups, so there would be no bottles to throw) and toilet facilities.

The Douglas group, meeting twice a day in Justice, kept its hand as invisible as possible. Working through Conway, they persuaded the planners in New York to forgo the idea of a demonstration on Capitol Hill in favor of a march from the Washington Monument to the Lincoln Memorial. Remembering Birmingham, they forbade the District police to include police-dog units in their riot-control precautions. They brought in Jerry Bruno, the king of advance men, to work out the platform arrangements. In every way they sought to carry out the Attorney General's instruction that, as Douglas put it later, "the government not give the impression that they were worried about violence . . . [but rather] an impression of organization and confidence."[35]

By August 15, President Kennedy was concerned that the march might not be large enough. If less than 100,000 came out, he told me, it might persuade legislators that the demand for civil rights legislation was exaggerated.[36] He need not have worried. A quarter of a million came to Washington on August 28, 1963, to hear Martin Luther King's dream: "Free at last! Free at last! Thank God Almighty, we are free at last!"

Others wished to seize the occasion for more drastic statement. John Lewis of SNCC forced the issue by preparing a tough speech. "We cannot support the Administration's civil rights bill," he planned to say. "There's not one thing in the bill that will protect our people from police brutality. . . . I want to know—which side is the federal government on?" The next time, Lewis's text concluded, "we won't march on Washington, but we will march through the South, through the Heart of Dixie, the way Sherman did."[37] All this upset the religious leaders, especially Archbishop Patrick O'Boyle, who said he would withdraw unless Lewis moderated his views. Burke Marshall spoke to Reuther, and there were tense last-minute negotiations in the small office behind Lincoln's statue in the Memorial. "I looked up at Abe," Reuther recalled, "and I said, 'Abe, I need your blessing and your help.' "[38] Even James Forman of SNCC was sufficiently carried away by the mood to aid in the revision of Lewis's speech, though he repented later.[39]

Had the Kennedys, in the language of the time, co-opted the March? What they did effectuated rather than betrayed the intentions of the planners—of Randolph, Rustin and King, of Roy Wilkins and Whitney Young. The revolutionaries of course wanted to go further than the respectables. "Behind our backs," Forman said afterward, "they and the Kennedy administration developed plans of their own as to how the March on Washington could be used to advance their own respective interests."[40] "There wasn't a single logistics aspect uncontrolled," wrote Malcom X. ". . . Who ever heard of angry revolutionists swinging their bare feet together with their oppressor in lilypad park pools, with gospels and guitars and 'I Have a Dream' speeches?" He called it the "Farce on Washington."[41] As King gave his famous oration, some in the crowd, joining hands, swaying back and forth, cried almost ecstatically, "Dream some more." But one black man shouted furiously: "Fuck that dream, Martin. Now, goddamit, NOW!"[42]

It remained a beautiful day—a day that we saw then as the beginning of a new era but that came to seem in retrospect the end of an old one. No demonstration, Bayard Rustin wrote ten years after, "has influenced the course of social legislation and determined the shape of institutional reform to the degree that the March did."[43] Perhaps so; certainly that afternoon in August had a purity that no one present can ever forget. Yet it also marked the effective, and no doubt inevitable, end of white and black collaboration in the mass movement for racial justice. Thereafter the movement took its own course under black leadership, assumed new forms and passions, suffered vicissitudes and disenchantments, but bravely persevered in the necessary fight.

V

Among those who viewed the March on Washington with particular loathing was J. Edgar Hoover. Though the FBI under Robert Kennedy's pressure had finally entered the struggle for racial justice, Hoover's personal feelings about blacks had not abated. As if in compensation for the ground he had been forced to give on civil rights, he redoubled his determination to discredit the movement—discredit the Kennedy administration too, if it persisted in its alliance with Martin Luther King. In so doing, the director fell back on the cry that had never failed him in the past: the ineluctable threat, evidently undiminished despite all his effort, of Communist infiltration into American institutions.

He first had to extirpate heresy in his own ranks. Before the march, William C. Sullivan, the assistant director in charge of the FBI's Domestic Intelligence Division, sent Hoover a memorandum asserting that the Communist party had failed "dismally" in its forty-year effort to influence the American Negro. A subsequent memorandum pointed out that less than two hundred Communists were planning to take part in the march. These memoranda infuriated the director. They suggested, he noted sarcastically, that Communists were having an "infinitesimal" effect on the blacks. They reminded him "vividly," he wrote Sullivan, "of those I received when Castro took over Cuba. You contended then that Castro and his cohorts were not Communists. . . . Time alone proved you wrong."[44]

The assistant director was in trouble. Hoover stopped speaking to him, and, luckily for the historical record, the two men confined themselves to written exchanges for several weeks. Sullivan had no doubt he must provide the director the words he wanted to hear. He said later: "We had to engage in a lot of nonsense which we ourselves really did not believe in. We either had to do that or we would be finished."[45] Certainly Sullivan, who hoped to succeed Hoover, would have been finished. Sounding for all the world like a Communist caught in some wretched deviation, Sullivan confessed error and affirmed his leader's infallibility. "The Director is correct. We were completely wrong. . . . It may be unrealistic to limit ourselves as we have been doing to legalistic proof or definitely conclusive evidence that would stand up in testimony in court or before Congressional committees [a little dangerous irony here?]. . . . It is obvious to us now that we did not put the proper interpretation upon the facts which we gave to the Director." And, on Martin Luther King: "We must mark him now, if we have not done so before, as the most dangerous Negro of the future in this Nation from the standpoint of communism, the Negro and national security."[46]

These last were above all the words that Hoover wanted to hear. He had long since made up his mind about the iniquity of Dr. King. In May 1961, reading in an FBI memorandum that King had not been investigated, Hoover wrote on the border, "Why not?" In January 1962 he told the Attorney General that a leading King adviser was a Communist.[47] In February he scribbled on an FBI memorandum: "King is no good." In May he put King on the list of people to be rounded up in event of a national emergency. In October the FBI opened a formal investigation of King and the SCLC. In November, after King told the *Atlanta Constitution* that FBI agents were often southern-born and pals of the local police, an enraged Hoover directed Cartha (Deke) DeLoach, head of the Crime Records Division, to call King and set him straight. When King neglected to return DeLoach's call, DeLoach described him as "a vicious liar" who "constantly associates with and takes instructions from [a] . . . member of the Communist Party."[48]

In the meantime Hoover bombarded Robert Kennedy with baleful memoranda about King's allegedly sinister associations. The following, of April 1962, is typical:

> This Bureau has recently received additional information showing the influence of Stanley David Levison, a secret member of the Communist Party, upon Martin Luther King, Jr. You will recall that I have furnished you during the past few months substantial information concerning the close relationship between King and Levison.
>
> A confidential source who has furnished reliable information in the past advised on April 16, 1962, that he had learned that Levison is forming in King's name an organization to be known as the Ghandi [sic] Society for Human Rights. Levison contemplates sending invitations signed by King to approximately twenty prominent people to attend a luncheon on May 17, 1962, in Washington. . . . You as well as the President, Senator Clifford Case, Senator Eugene McCarthy and former Attorney General William P. Rogers are among those being considered to be invited. . . . The informant said that he is under the impression that Theodore Kheel . . . Harry Belafonte . . . and A. Philip Randolph are involved in the formation of the organization.

A handwritten note on the document put the Attorney General on notice that he was not to file and forget: "This is a very sensitive source. I assume the White House knows about Levison."[49]

If it was hard to regard inviting William P. Rogers and Clifford Case to a Gandhi Society luncheon as a major threat to the republic, Stanley Levison did present the Attorney General a more difficult problem. A few days later, the Senate Internal Security Subcommittee, no doubt tipped off by Hoover, subpoenaed Levison and interrogated him in executive session. "To dispose of a question causing current apprehension," Levison told the committee, "I am a loyal American and I am not now and never have been a member of the Communist Party." He went on, however, with the leftist attorney William Kunstler at his side, to challenge the committee's right to inquire into political beliefs and thereafter took the Fifth Amendment. He did so, he later explained, because he feared the session would turn into an attack on King.[50] Actually no one brought up King. Instead Eastland, who sounded as if he had been briefed by the Bureau, asked such questions as: "Isn't it true that you are a spy for the Communist apparatus in this country? . . . Isn't it true that you have gotten funds from the Soviet Union and given them to the Communist Party of the United States?" Levison declined to answer. Finally, after much exasperated quizzing and effective stonewalling, McClellan terminated the hearing, calling it "one of the shabbiest performances I have ever heard before a Senate Committee by any witness."[51]

Levison was a New York lawyer of independent means and benevolent disposition who, with introductions from A. Philip Randolph and Bayard Rustin (both resolutely anti-Communist), had met King in Montgomery in 1956. King was not skilled in organizational matters. SCLC affairs were in chronic disorder. Tactful and self-effacing, Levison helped supply King's administrative deficiencies. Soon he was donating much of his time to the SCLC, raising money, trying to straighten out the internal finances, writing King's formal addresses, contributing legal passages to his articles and books, providing King professional counsel and personal understanding.[52] King came to rely heavily on him. Coretta Scott King described him as one of her husband's "most devoted and trusted friends."[53]

VI

Stanley Levison, Hoover informed Robert Kennedy, was a secret member of the CPUSA national committee charged with controlling King. The Bureau came up with a second supposed Communist around King. This was one of his executive assistants, a young black named Hunter Pitts (Jack) O'Dell, whom Hoover also declared to be a member of the national committee. In October 1962 the Bureau leaked incriminating material about O'Dell to southern newspapers. Soon King placed him on temporary leave.[54] No incriminating material was leaked on Levison, except the general allegations to the Internal Security Subcommittee. Probably there was none to leak.

The allegations greatly troubled Kennedy and Marshall. They simply took Hoover's word that Levison was a secret party muckamuck. However hopeless the Bureau was in organized crime and civil rights, internal subversion was its undisputed field of expertise. The CPUSA was swarming with FBI informants. Levison's appearance before the

Senate committee was hardly reassuring. At Hoover's request, Kennedy authorized a national-security wiretap on Levison's office telephone in March 1962 and on his home telephone in November. The Bureau also planted a microphone in Levison's office, though as usual without telling the Attorney General.[55] The wiretaps on Levison's phones produced no evidence of Communist deviltry; but this only showed, the Bureau replied, what a truly secret muckamuck he was.[56]

Kennedy and Marshall admired King's courage and leadership. They thought it essential that his gospel of nonviolence prevail. Accordingly they decided that he must be warned for his own protection and for the protection of the movement. Nothing would play more effectively into the hands of white supremacists than proof that Martin Luther King was under Communist control.

The warning process began early. Kennedy asked Harry Belafonte about Levison. Belafonte, supposing that Levison was under consideration for a government appointment, gave a warm endorsement. Kennedy shook his head and said, "No. Martin ought to get rid of him."[57] Harris Wofford, King's old friend, was asked to speak directly to King about Levison. King was incredulous.[58] John Seigenthaler spoke to him. King said he did not like to accuse people who volunteered to help the cause; in any case, his associates could change neither his will nor the movement's policies.[59] Burke Marshall spoke to him. Robert Kennedy spoke to him. King remained incredulous.

Once the Kennedys decided to go all-out for civil rights legislation, Levison was no longer just a King problem. If word of his role reached the Hill, "not only would it damage [King]," Kennedy observed, "but it would also damage all of our efforts and damage any possible chance of the passage of legislation."[60] The Kennedys had committed themselves to King. "The basic identity of constitutional and political interest," wrote Katzenbach, ". . . is the necessary predicate of all subsequent events. Anything which discredited Dr. King, or his movement, would have been a disaster to the Kennedy administration. . . . More importantly, it would have been a disaster to the country."[61] Kennedy directed Burke Marshall to find out what the hard evidence against Levison was.

Levison had indeed known Communists in New York. He had worked with them in the Henry Wallace and anti-McCarthy campaigns. He was, in fact, a goodhearted and undiscriminating liberal of the type for whom there was no enemy to the left. His twin brother,

Roy Bennett, the New York correspondent for Aneurin Bevan's paper, the *Tribune* of London, was a democratic socialist and an outspoken anti-Stalinist. Levison had fallen under the suspicion of the Bureau because, he eventually came to believe, a business acquaintance under FBI investigation had tried to ingratiate himself with the Bureau by denouncing Levison.[62] Nor did the Bureau ever offer any proof of party membership. Early in 1963, it had even reported that Levison had criticized the CPUSA on the ground of Communist neglect of civil rights.[63] In 1964 the New York FBI office told Hoover: "Mr. Levison is not now under CP discipline in the civil rights field. There has been no indication, however, that Mr. Levison has not continued his ideological adherence to communism."[64] William C. Sullivan told me in 1976 that he had never seen any evidence that Levison was a party member.[65] Andrew Young considered him "a conservative influence . . . very cautious about becoming involved with [i.e., against] the war in Vietnam, for example."[66]

When Marshall now applied to the FBI for the hard evidence, he was told that Levison was something far more baleful than a secret member of the CPUSA. The Bureau advised him in the most formal and emphatic manner and for the first time (though Hoover must have muttered something of the sort to Eastland, judging by Eastland's questions before the Senate committee) that Levison was in fact a key figure in the Soviet intelligence apparatus in the United States. Marshall was further advised that disclosure of this information to King would endanger an FBI agent in place inside the KGB.[67]

It is hard to know what to make of this. It would have been an act of gross bureaucratic imperialism for the FBI to invade CIA territory and run an agent in Moscow. Possibly Hoover meant a New York agent known as Fedora, "officially a Soviet diplomat with the United Nations," Edward Jay Epstein has written, who began in March 1962 to supply the Bureau with information about Soviet espionage.[68] Hoover's first warnings about King's Communist adviser had been pre-Fedora; but perhaps Hoover checked Levison with his new hot source, and Fedora obligingly confirmed the director's suspicions. The Levison wiretap was placed in the same month that Fedora started talking to the FBI. CIA counterintelligence later came to regard Fedora as a double agent under KGB control. If this were so, then the KGB may have collaborated with the FBI in setting up Levison, both agencies wishing to discredit King and destroy his alliance with Kennedy, the KGB receiving the added benefit of heightened racial bitterness in America.

Or perhaps Hoover had simply got it into his head that Levison was a Communist, as he had got it into his head that the Communists dominated the civil rights movement, and was prepared to say anything to make others accept what he so urgently believed the truth. Certainly the story the Bureau told Marshall was difficult to reconcile with Hoover's earlier portrait of Levison as a top party functionary. When people entered the Soviet intelligence service, they ordinarily abandoned all connection with the CPUSA (note Whittaker Chambers). But Marshall, whose specialty was civil rights, not Communist espionage, understandably believed the FBI story.

In June 1963 all anyone had was the certification by the high priest of national security that Stanley Levison, Martin Luther King's intimate adviser, was a top Soviet intelligence operative—and this at a time when the Kennedy administration was staking its future on the integrity of the civil rights movement.

The Attorney General's next move was to bring in the President. On June 22, after his meeting with the civil rights leaders, John Kennedy invited King to stroll in the Rose Garden outside the Oval Office. Kennedy began (so King later told Andrew Young) by saying that Eastland and others were denouncing the March on Washington as a Communist trick. The FBI, Kennedy said, was greatly concerned; "I assume you know you're under very close surveillance." He warned King against discussing significant matters over the phone with Levison, whom Hoover regarded, Kennedy said, as "a conscious agent of the Soviet conspiracy."* (King, noting that Kennedy had walked him out into the garden, reflected, "The President is afraid of Hoover himself. . . . I guess Hoover must be buggin' him too.")[69]

Then Kennedy said (so King later told Levison), "You've read about Profumo in the papers?" The fall of the British Secretary of State for War had dominated the spring headlines. Kennedy: "That was an example of friendship and loyalty carried too far. Macmillan is likely to lose his government because he has been loyal to a friend. You must take care not to lose your cause for the same reason." He named Levison and O'Dell. "They're Communists. You've got to get rid of them. . . . If they [the opponents of civil rights] shoot *you* down, they'll shoot *us* down too—so we're asking you to be careful." King finally said, "I know Stanley and I can't believe this. You will

---

* Kennedy's wiretapping reference was obviously to Levison's phone. King's phone was not tapped for another four months.

have to prove it." Kennedy said that Burke Marshall would show the proof to Andrew Young.[70]

King wrote O'Dell in ten days making his temporary resignation permanent. He reminded O'Dell of the attacks on the movement as Communist-inspired; "in these critical times we cannot afford to risk any such impressions."* In O'Dell's case there was indication of at least past Communist connections. As for Levison, King awaited the Marshall-Young meeting.

They met at the federal courthouse in New Orleans, where Marshall was discussing a civil rights case. Marshall walked Young around the corridors and told him that the FBI considered Levison a Soviet spy. "Burke never said anything about any evidence he had," recalled Young; "he always quoted what the Bureau said it had. I didn't feel this was conclusive. They were all scared to death of the Bureau; they really were." Young reported back to King. King was still reluctant to break with Levison. "I induced him to break," Levison told me. "I said it would not be in the interests of the movement to hold on to me if the Kennedys had doubts. I said I was sure it would not last long."[71]

VII

It did not last long. In the meantime, however, the Kennedys went bail for the movement. The President in his July 17 press conference said there was "no evidence" to show that any civil rights leaders were Communists or that the demonstrations were Communist inspired. "I think it is a convenient scapegoat to suggest that all the difficulties are Communist and if the Communist movement would only disappear that we would end this."[72] "Based on all available information from the FBI," Robert Kennedy wrote senators, ". . . we have no evidence that any of the top leaders . . . are Communists, or Communist controlled. This is true as to Dr. Martin Luther King, Jr., about whom particular accusations were made, as well as other leaders."[73]

Could they be sure? There was one way to find out, the Bureau said. That was to tap King's telephone. This possibility had been on Hoover's agenda for some time. He had directed Sullivan to push the

---

* King wrote O'Dell that, after a "thorough inquiry," the SCLC was "unable to discover any present connections with the Communist party on your part" (Martin Luther King, Jr., to H. P. [Jack] O'Dell, July 3, 1963; in Victor Navasky, *Kennedy Justice* [New York, 1971], 143–144; emphasis added).

Attorney General's office on wiretaps for King, and Sullivan had been faithfully pushing.[74] Kennedy himself could hardly escape the question. If Levison was indeed a top Soviet agent, then, as Marshall put it later, "it would not be responsible for . . . the Attorney General to refuse a tap" on the American leader with whom Levison had established so intimate a relationship.[75] They were all "scared to death" of the FBI, Andrew Young had said. They were not scared without reason. The still sacrosanct Hoover had vast power to do damage to King, to the civil rights bill, to the Kennedys. In the short run, Hoover had only to leak to the Hill and the right-wing press. In the longer run, he could do to John Kennedy what he had done to Truman ten years before over the case of Harry Dexter White; he could tell a congressional committee that a President had deliberately ignored his solemn warnings and had thereby endangered the republic. If Robert Kennedy refused a tap on King and anything went wrong, Hoover would have a field day. On the other hand, a tap might end the matter by demonstrating King's entire innocence, even to the satisfaction of the FBI.

Such considerations undoubtedly led Kennedy to raise with Courtney Evans on July 16, 1963, the possibility of "technical coverage" on King. This was the meeting that Hoover cited half a dozen years later to support his claim that Kennedy was pressing the idea on a reluctant FBI. Asked whether Kennedy had in fact originated the idea, Evans testified in 1975, "No, this is not clear in my mind at all. . . . There were pressures . . . from both sides, the Bureau wanted to get more specific information, and the Department wanted resolved the rather indefinite information that had been received."[76] Asked where the idea came from, Sullivan said, "Not from Bobby. It came from Hoover. . . . The whole impetus came from us."[77] "To say or imply that this tap was the original conception of Robert Kennedy—that he was the moving force in this situation—or that he had any doubt whatsoever about Dr. King's integrity or loyalty is false," said Katzenbach.[78]

In any case, on July 23 Hoover made a formal request for wiretap authorization. On July 24 Kennedy rejected the request. The Bureau kept up its pressure. It put out a report on King's "Affiliations with the Communist Movement." Kennedy commented acidly that, if that report reached the Hill, he would be impeached.[79] Then, though King and Levison did not meet for another year or so, King decided that his promise to drop Levison had been a mistake,[80] and they resumed telephonic communication—a fact Hoover joyously passed on to Kennedy. Kennedy had a natural desire to find out whether this renewal of association would hurt the common cause. The civil rights bill was in trouble on the Hill. On October 7 Hoover again requested authorization for taps on King's home telephone and on the New York SCLC office. Kennedy was worried but agreed to go ahead "on a trial basis, and to continue it if productive results were forthcoming." A few days later Hoover requested a tap on the Atlanta SCLC office. "The Attorney General is apparently still vacillating in his position as to technical coverage," Evans reported back. Kennedy finally consented, stipulating that all the King taps be evaluated "at the end of thirty days" and that the question of continuing the surveillance be decided then. Thirty days from October 21, 1963, was November 20, 1963 . . . On its own, the FBI maintained taps on King's home phone till mid-1965, on the SCLC phones for even longer, on Levison and at least one other King associate, not to speak of at least twenty-one microphone installations in King's hotel and motel rooms.*

The Kennedys authorized the taps on King for defensive purposes —in order to protect King, to protect the civil rights bill, to protect themselves. "Bobby Kennedy resisted, resisted, and resisted tapping King," said Sullivan. "Finally we twisted the arm of the Attorney General to the point where he had to go. I guess he feared we would let that stuff go in the press if he said no."[81] Installing the taps shifted responsibility for King to Hoover; and the Kennedys were confident that King was clean and that the taps would yield nothing of interest. What was less excusable, if understandable for a period after November 22, 1963, was the failure of the Attorney General to terminate the taps.

Though outsiders have condemned the taps as indefensible in any context, neither King nor, for that matter, Levison held the taps against the Kennedys in this particular context. The SCLC people did not feel all that threatened by wiretapping. After all, John Kennedy had personally warned King about FBI surveillance. "We knew," Andrew Young said in 1976, "they were . . . bugging our phones; but that was never really a problem for us. It's hard to remember back then, but when you were anxious about your life, civil liberties

* Sixteen reported in Church committee, *Final Report*, bk. III, 81, 103, 115–116 (see n. 44); five more in Department of Justice, "Report of Task Force to Review King," 127–128 (see n. 46). One of these was installed by the New York field office without Hoover's authorization and remained despite instructions from Clyde Tolson that it be removed "at once."

seemed a tertiary consideration. In our conduct of a nonviolent movement there was nothing that we did not want them to know anyway."[82] Beyond this, they specifically and sympathetically recognized the dilemma in which Hoover had placed the Kennedys and therefore were not alienated by the decision to take protective action. King had declined to endorse John Kennedy in 1960 and remained opposed in principle to the idea of endorsing presidential candidates. In 1964—after the tapping had begun—he wrote in *Why We Can't Wait,* "And yet, had President Kennedy lived, I would probably have endorsed him in the forthcoming election."[83] What is even more fascinating is that these lines were actually written for King by Stanley Levison.[84]

In 1976, Levison said: "I was neither an international agent nor even a domestic party member, but at that time Hoover's credibility was unchallenged: it would have diverted the movement at a critical stage to take on so difficult a civil liberties battle." As for Robert Kennedy: "I really understand his position. You have to recall the time. We weren't too far away from the McCarthy period. They were so committed to our movement, they couldn't possibly risk what could have been a terrible political scandal. When I realized how hard Hoover was pressing them and how simultaneously they were giving Martin such essential support, I didn't feel any enmity about their attitude toward me."[85]

VIII

The wiretap authorization did not content Hoover. The Bureau had expanded its dissertation on King, and in October Hoover directed that the resulting top-secret "monograph" be sent around the government. One of his assistant directors warned him that it could be taken "as a personal attack on Martin Luther King. . . . This memorandum may startle the Attorney General, particularly in view of his past association with King, and the fact that we are disseminating this outside the Department. He may resent this." Hoover on the border: "We must do our duty."[86] The Attorney General was more than startled. "Bobby got furious," said Katzenbach,[87] and demanded that the Bureau retrieve all copies at once. Hoover, sensing Kennedy's rage, quickly agreed that the document be recalled. Afterward he complained bitterly to his associates;[88] then reissued the monograph a year later in an amplified edition with authorization from a new

White House (granted by Bill Moyers of all people) to distribute to "responsible officials in the Executive Branch."[89]

Kennedy had been furious because the document was one-sided and "very, very unfair." It expatiated on King's tie with Levison but contained none of the abundant "offsetting material . . . which indicated that he didn't want to have anything to do with the Communists."[90] An added reason for his outrage was that the monograph was indeed a highly personal attack, including an indictment, in Burke Marshall's words, of "the moral character and person of Dr. Martin Luther King."[91]

King was not only a great and honorable citizen and a noble leader: he was also, like other distinguished leaders, a passionate man. This was well known to close associates and did not disturb them. Some white friends explained it in psychological terms as an unconscious attempt to prove himself as virile as his father. Black friends stressed the importance of machismo, the affirmation of masculinity, among subjugated peoples; they recalled the historic obligations of evangelical preachers in the south to the women of the congregations. In any case, as one told me, "Martin really believed in the gospel of love." Those who worked with King accepted this as an expression of both a cultural tradition and a demonstrative temperament.

After the exertions and triumphs of the March on Washington, King had relaxed in his suite at the Willard Hotel with friends of both sexes. Further developments were recorded on a hidden microphone. It is not clear who bugged the room. Kennedy, Marshall and Katzenbach, when they heard about it later, assumed it had been done by the Washington Police Department, with the tape then passed on to the FBI. The FBI was quite capable of planting the bug itself, but this has not been proved.* In any event, the results of the August séance accounted for the zeal with which the Bureau bugged King's hotel rooms in the future.

Robert Kennedy was genuinely shocked by the revelations but did not feel that King's private life had anything to do with his probity as a public leader. Hoover abominated sex in general and regarded interracial sex in particular as evidence of moral degeneracy. King, it appeared, was not only subversive but depraved, a more frightening menace than ever. Within the Bureau, Sullivan, still

---

* The first FBI bug on King established by the Church committee was planted on January 5, 1964, also at the Willard (Church committee, *Final Report,* bk. III, 120 [see n. 44]).

trying to redeem himself, called a meeting on the King problem. A nine-hour session on December 23, 1963, resulted in a plan, as the penitent Sullivan explained in a memorandum to the front office, to reveal King to the country "as being what he actually is—a fraud, demagogue and scoundrel"—and thereby "to take him off his pedestal and to reduce him completely in influence." Hoover noted on the memorandum: "I am glad to see that 'light' has finally, though dismally delayed, come to the Domestic Int. Div. I struggled for months to get over the fact that the communists were taking over the racial movement but our experts here couldn't or wouldn't see it."[92]

There followed a weird crusade. The Bureau on Hoover's orders stalked Martin Luther King much as allied psychological warfare had stalked Nazi *Gauleiter* during the Second World War, calling on all the resources of deception, counterespionage and black propaganda to "neutralize," as a Hoover memorandum put it in April 1964, "or completely discredit the effectiveness of Martin Luther King, Jr. as a Negro leader."[93] If supposed Communist influence on King was Hoover's real concern, his effort would obviously have been to neutralize and discredit Stanley Levison. But it was King himself whom Hoover unfathomably hated. When *Time* made King Man of the Year in 1963, Hoover scribbled on the press release, "They had to dig deep in the garbage to come up with this."[94] When King received the Nobel Peace Prize in 1964, Hoover said he was the "last one in the world" who should have got it.[95]

The Bureau expended much of its energy, it must be said, on singularly inane objectives—trying to stop King's honorary degrees, the publication of his articles, his meetings with British leaders after he collected his Nobel Prize. The vendetta reached its climax on November 18, 1964, when the director, in a rare press conference, denounced King as "the most notorious liar in the country." King responded that Hoover must be "faltering" under his burdens. On November 24, in a speech in Chicago, Hoover carried on wildly about "zealots of pressure groups" who indulged in "carping, lying and exaggerating" and were "spearheaded by Communists and moral degenerates."[96]

The hotel tapes had given Hoover a weapon against King, but not an easy one to use. Goaded by King's defiance, Hoover ordered Sullivan to prepare a composite tape, culling high spots from Washington, San Francisco and Los Angeles, and to mail it to Mrs. King. If the marriage broke up, Hoover reasoned, this would diminish King's stature. The package also contained a brutal letter: "King, there is only one thing left for you to do. You know what it is. You have just 34 days. . . . You better take it before your filthy fraudulent self is bared to the nation."[97]

By the time the Kings got around to opening the package, the deadline had long passed. Since her husband often spoke extemporaneously, Mrs. King had asked for tapes of his speeches; and the FBI tape had been added to the pile. They listened to the tape. It was, said Andrew Young, "basically just a bunch of preachers that were relaxin' after a meeting. . . . Toward the end there was a recording of somebody moanin' and groanin' as though they were in the act of sexual intercourse, but it didn't sound like anybody I knew, and certainly not Martin."[98] When they saw the letter, "we began to realize that this was the most serious kind of intimidation we had so far experienced." They had no doubt that the tape and letter came from Hoover. King said, "What does he think I am?"[99]

Hoover, who seems to have taken leave of his senses that November, also dispatched DeLoach to offer newspapermen the dossier on King's private life. When Ben Bradlee of *Newsweek* reported this to Katzenbach, now Acting Attorney General, "I was shocked," Katzenbach testified, ". . . and felt that the President should be advised immediately." Katzenbach and Marshall thereupon flew to President Johnson's Texas ranch on November 28. "I told the President," Katzenbach said, "my view that it should be stopped immediately and that he should personally contact Mr. Hoover. I received the impression that President Johnson took the matter very seriously and that he would do as I recommended."[100] Johnson, according to Hugh Sidey, a conscientious reporter, had enjoyed listening to the tapes, even to the noise of the bedsprings;[101] and what in fact he did, so far as the record shows, was to instruct Bill Moyers to warn the Bureau that Bradlee was an enemy.[102]

The refusal of newspapers to touch the King tapes attests to the standards of decency the press observed in those forgotten days. Legislators were equally scrupulous. In the midst of the civil rights debate Senator Richard Russell of Georgia asked the Justice Department what the rumors were all about. When Katzenbach briefed him, he "just wasn't interested; wondered why I was wasting his time. He's a pretty good fellow on hitting below the belt. He said to me, 'You and I are a mile apart on civil rights, but I'll tell you, I'm a hundred miles away from George Wallace.'"[103]

The tapes presented a dilemma, however, to King himself. Summoning a group of advisers to New York, he outlined alternatives: either he could extend the hand of peace and conciliation to Hoover, or he could dare Hoover to do his damnedest. Kenneth Clark and

Clarence Jones urged the second course: "Let Hoover reveal his damned tapes"; it would hurt Hoover more than it would King. Others felt that disclosure would destroy King's "image," especially among his white supporters. At the end, King said, "I'm going to extend the hand of peace." Clark said angrily, "Damn it, you may be Christ-like, but you're not Christ." The others laughed, but Clark felt the time had come when love and conciliation were not enough.[104]

The summit meeting took place on December 1, 1964. Contrary to mythology, Hoover did not bring up King's private life. Most of the meeting consisted of a monologue by Hoover on the Bureau's marvelous record in the south. DeLoach, who was present, described it as "more or less of a love feast." Andrew Young, who was also present, thought it more like "a mutual admiration society."[105] The session quieted the public feud but altered no private feelings. King told someone over the phone later, "The old man talks too damned much." The FBI excised this sentiment before they passed the transcript on to Hoover, fearing his rage.[106] Six years later, Hoover, in an otherwise fictitious account of the meeting, said of King, "I held him in complete contempt."[107] This was a sentiment that King certainly reciprocated.

IX

"The United States," Robert Kennedy told the Senate Commerce Committee on July 1, 1963, "is dominated by white people, politically and economically. The question is whether we, in this position of dominance, are going to have not the charity but the wisdom to stop penalizing our fellow citizens whose only fault or sin is that they were born. That, Mr. Chairman, is why Congress should enact this bill, and should do it in this session."[108]

The House of Representatives proved more receptive than the administration had anticipated. The Judiciary Committee added a fair-employment-practices provision and strengthened the bill in other particulars; and, on the day of the March on Washington, John McCormack, now Speaker after Rayburn's death, predicted that an FEPC could pass the House. Katzenbach and O'Brien regarded this thought as "a disaster," Katzenbach said later, "but, if you were to interview Speaker McCormack, he would say this was probably the key to achieving the civil rights bill as it finally came out, and he might be right. . . . I'm delighted that he did it, although at the time I could have shot him."[109]

Determined to bring out of the House a bill the Senate could accept without amendment, Robert Kennedy resisted the strengthening process. The Kennedys thought they faced a hard choice: either to accept the liberal Democratic bill, lose the vote and gain an issue; or to seek Republican support for a modified version of the administration bill. John Kennedy doubted whether Republicans would go along with any bill that contained what he wanted. But he decided to make the try. He had a crucial ally in William McCulloch of Ohio, a man of principle and ranking Republican on the House Judiciary Committee.

In mid-October the President called the House leaders to the White House. He was never more persuasive. To his astonishment, not only McCulloch but Charles Halleck, the conservative Republican leader, agreed to support a bill acceptable to the civil rights leadership, even with the FEPC. The Attorney General thought that the President's eloquence had swept Halleck along, "that finally he nodded his head in assent, and he had given his word, so he didn't want to go back on his word. But the President could never understand."[110] Robert Kennedy now saluted the House bill as superior to the original administration draft.

The battle promised to be more difficult in the Senate. "States' rights, as our forefathers conceived it," Kennedy said in his opening statement to Eastland's Judiciary Committee, "was a protection of the right of the individual citizen. Those who preach most frequently about states' rights today are not seeking the protection of the individual citizen, but his exploitation. . . . The time is long past—if indeed it ever existed—when we should permit the noble concept of States' Rights to be betrayed and corrupted into a slogan to hide the bald denial of American rights, of civil rights, and of human rights."[111] But the Judiciary Committee had never brought a civil rights bill to the floor and was not ready to break this tradition. (The administration planned to evade this by routing the bill also through the more cooperative Commerce Committee.) The Judiciary Committee's constitutional sage was the charming and formidable Sam Ervin—an authentic expert, save that his Constitution stopped with the ten amendments adopted in 1789; he appeared to regard the rest, especially the Fourteenth and Fifteenth, as apocrypha. A stack of law books piled on his desk, Ervin called the bill "as drastic and indefensible a proposal as has ever been submitted to this Congress."

For nine days between July and September, the Attorney General was the administration witness. A courteous but implacable duel took place. It was an exhausting business. One day Ethel Kennedy, encountering Ervin at a White House dinner, said, "What have you been doing to Bobby? He came home and went straight to bed." On the last day, Kennedy made a personal appeal to Ervin, telling him that, if he came out against discrimination and in support of the bill, he could make "a major difference in ending these kinds of practices, as well as bringing the country through a very difficult period of transition."

>ERVIN. The only thing you have a right to ask of me is that I stand and fight for the Constitution, and that is what I am doing now. You are not correct in saying that I have never spoken out against discrimination. . . . As a citizen, lawyer and judge in North Carolina, I have always stood for the right of all men to stand equal before the law. . . .
>
>KENNEDY. I asked you whether, in your judgment, any discrimination existed in the State of Mississippi against Negroes. You said to your knowledge it did not. I don't see how you can . . .
>
>ERVIN. I told you the truth, Mr. Attorney General. I have never been in the State of Mississippi in my life, except on one occasion when I was asleep in a Pullman on a train which passed through the northern portion of Mississippi on the way to Memphis. I said I could not corroborate by personal knowledge any conditions in Mississippi. . . .
>
>KENNEDY. I would say, Senator, I have a lawyer here who could take you down into some of these places and maybe your eyes would be opened.
>
>ERVIN. I have got to stay here and fight the destruction of Constitutional government which this bill contemplates, and haven't time in this session of Congress. . . .

Kennedy made a final try. "Senator," he said, "it would only take forty-eight hours. Would you be willing to do that?" Ervin said, "I do not have even forty-eight hours to spare from my fight to preserve Constitutional principles and the individual freedoms of all citizens of the United States."[112]

Ervin sought always to bring the colloquy around to abstract principles; Kennedy, to concrete conditions. For the Attorney General, life had taken racial justice out of the middle distance. Civil rights had displaced organized crime as the issue of law enforcement closest to his heart. "The more he saw," Burke Marshall said, ". . . the more he understood. The more you learned about how Negroes were treated in the South, . . . the madder you became. You know he always talked about the hypocrisy. That's what got him. By the end of a year he was so mad about that kind of thing it overrode everything else." When Victor Navasky asked Marshall to measure the rise in Kennedy's civil rights consciousness, Marshall shot his right arm up toward the sky.[113]

(17)

The Politics of Justice

"I AM GETTING OUT of all political activities as fast as I can," Robert Kennedy said in his first interview as Attorney General. "Partisan politics played no role when I was chief counsel for the McClellan Labor-Rackets Committee. They will play no part now."[1] He told the assistant attorneys general at his first staff meeting: "No politics—period. You don't attend political functions, you don't speak on political matters, you don't get involved in any way."* He was, Ramsey Clark said later, "incredibly sensitive about excluding political influence from legal decisions."[2] To keep politics out of prosecutions, he put a Republican, Herbert J. Miller, Jr., in charge of the Criminal Division and soon gave William Hundley back the job he had held in the Eisenhower administration as chief of the Organized Crime Section.†

I

Still the campaign manager of 1960 could hardly expect to take the veil altogether in 1961, especially when his brother was President. Though he shielded his department from partisan politics, Robert

---

* As recalled by Ramsey Clark, in Richard Harris, "The Department of Justice," *New Yorker*, November 15, 1969. Note Clark's testimony before the Senate Judiciary Committee, Subcommittee on Separation of Powers, March 28, 1974, 6 (mimeographed): "Presidential appointees and their personal assistants in the Department of Justice should be prohibited from giving, receiving or soliciting political contributions, from managing or advising a political party or campaign while in office . . . from attending political meetings, public or private; from political speeches and endorsements. Robert F. Kennedy asked this of his assistants when he became Attorney General."

† It is a comment on both the caliber and the nonpartisanship of the Kennedy Department of Justice that the Watergate crowd turned to so many of its members in their time of trouble—Nixon and Richard Kleindienst to Miller, John Mitchell to Hundley, John Dean to Charles Shaffer, Howard Hunt to William Bittmann.

Kennedy himself kept a vigilant eye on party affairs. He installed Paul Corbin in the Democratic National Committee. This inevitably caused wide offense. It offended J. Edgar Hoover, who assured the press and the House Un-American Activities Committee that Corbin had been a Communist. The Attorney General, Courtney Evans told the Bureau, "seems to have gone completely overboard in trying to defend Corbin. He has suppressed any and all references to our report detailing Corbin's communist activity."[3] It offended Hubert Humphrey. "Who is this fellow Corbin?" Humphrey wrote irritably to John Bailey, the national chairman. ". . . This man has no place at the DNC unless we are trying to make enemies and lose friends. . . . To say the least, I am shocked and to be frank about it, I am damned good and mad."[4] It doubtless offended the long-suffering Bailey. It certainly was not popular in the White House. John Kennedy could never understand why his brother valued Corbin, and Kenneth O'Donnell detested him. But Corbin, as ever, had his uses. He sniffed truculently around, smelled graft, some fancied, much real, and eventually uncovered highly dubious goings-on lower down in the national committee itself, thereby confirming Robert Kennedy's regard for him and producing a schism in the Irish Mafia.

The Attorney General also took a lively interest in patronage. "He passed on applicants for the top, appointive positions," J. Edward Day observed of the Post Office Department. ". . . He telephoned in person or sent word through his staff about certain appointments of postmasters and rural letter carriers. One afternoon I talked to him three times by telephone about a single rural letter carrier who was to be appointed in a small town in Mississippi in which Bobby was intensely interested."* I don't know whether this last was an example; but Robert Kennedy particularly wanted to increase the number of blacks in government service. Among those whom he nagged relentlessly was Adlai Stevenson, not one of his favorites at best. After a time, Stevenson finally offered a job to Frank Montero, a well-qualified Negro but a Bronx Reform Democrat and for that reason objectionable to the ancient Bronx boss, Charlie Buckley, whom the Kennedys remembered with gratitude as their original supporter in New York. A member of Lawrence O'Brien's staff called me (I

---

* J. Edward Day, *My Appointed Round: 929 Days as Postmaster General* (New York, 1965), 9. This does not imply a great upheaval. Day wrote: "During my first year in office only 70 of 35,000 postmasters were removed. As many of them were Democrats as Republicans and the charges against each were of an extremely serious nature" (ibid., 13).

served as liaison between the President and Stevenson) and said the Montero appointment had to be stopped. I disagreed but consented to look into the matter. To my delight, I discovered the UN mission was hiring Montero on the insistent and repeated request of Robert Kennedy.[5]

On another occasion the White House politicos opposed an appointment for James MacGregor Burns, the Williams political scientist, on the ground of his seditious activities as an antiorganization Democrat in Massachusetts. My notes at the time:

> I brooded about this for a while and finally sent a memorandum to the President, with a copy to Bobby, asking whether he knew there was a White House veto on Burns. The President instantly took the matter up, called in Kenny [O'Donnell] and said he could see no reason why Burns should not receive an appointment. Ken said that Jim had been fighting the organization. The President said that this did not matter; Jim was a good fellow, he liked him, and the State Committee was terrible anyway.... The same day I received a memo from Bobby saying that there was no tenable objection to Jim's appointment.[6]

Robert Kennedy followed New York politics with particular interest. He had been outraged by the cavalier treatment given to Herbert Lehman and Eleanor Roosevelt, in the 1960 campaign, by Carmine de Sapio, the Tammany leader, and his protégé Mike Pendergast, the state chairman. "I understand," he wrote John Bailey early in 1961, "the recommendations of Mike Pendergast in New York are being accepted. This seems to me most inadvisable if true. I would appreciate a report on it."[7] For all their personal loyalty to men of the past like Charlie Buckley, the Kennedys wanted to put a new face on the party in what was still the nation's most populous state.

Thus early in 1962 John Kennedy astonished Edward R. Murrow, whom he had brought into the administration as head of the United States Information Agency, by suggesting that he run for the senate in New York. "It was one of the few times," observed Donald Wilson, Murrow's deputy, "I've seen Ed totally at a loss for words. He didn't really say anything so the matter was dropped. I was informally asked by Bob Kennedy a few days later whether I thought Murrow would be interested or not and I said . . . he had told me very frankly that he didn't have any interest in it, and that was the end of it."[8]

In the same spirit Robert Kennedy sought a fresh candidate for governor. In 1961 he had, over Buckley's opposition, named Robert Morgenthau federal attorney in New York City. No doubt he took dynastic satisfaction in appointing the son of the man who had reintroduced Joseph Kennedy to Franklin D. Roosevelt thirty years before. In 1962 he thought that Morgenthau, who had rapidly proved himself a first-class public servant, might be a good candidate for governor.[9] When the embattled Democrats gathered in Syracuse, Kennedy persuaded Buckley to switch from Frank O'Connor, the candidate of the old school, to Morgenthau. O'Donnell told me dryly the day after Morgenthau's nomination, "Charlie Buckley says this morning that, when he put over [Frank] Hogan in Buffalo in 1958 [as the nominee for senator], he was a boss, but now, when he puts over Morgenthau in Syracuse, he becomes a statesman."[10] Morgenthau proved a colorless candidate, however, and Nelson Rockefeller won reelection.

The major family political enterprise in 1962 was the election of Edward Kennedy to the Senate from Massachusetts. "The person who was primarily interested in having him run was my father," Robert Kennedy told John Bartlow Martin in 1964, ". . . just as I would never have been Attorney General if it hadn't been for him. . . . He just felt that Teddy had worked all this time during the campaign and sacrificed himself for the older brother and we had our positions and so that he should have the right to run, that it was a mistake to run for any position lower than that. . . . If it was left up to [Teddy] he probably would have run for Attorney General," an elective office in Massachusetts. Robert added: "I think that some of the people at the White House mumbled about the fact that . . . it would hurt the President but as far as the President and I were concerned, I was pleased that he was running and I think the President was pleased that he was."[11]

The Attorney General went up to Hyannis Port in August to help prepare Ted for a debate with his opponent in the Democratic primary, Edward McCormack, the Speaker's nephew. "Have no feah, we are heah," Robert announced on arrival. The two brothers discussed the debate as they tossed a football on the lawn. Ted wondered how best to explain why he should be in the Senate. Robert answered, "If you get that question, tell them about public service. Tell them why you don't want to be sitting on your ass in some office in New York." He suggested that Ted ask McCormack what he thought about the situation in West Irian; "he'll think it's West Iran and he'll talk about the Middle East and he'll look like a fool."[12] Edward did well in the debate, without benefit of West Irian.

It was an angry primary. Ancient resentment of the Kennedys

among Irish pols mingled with wrath at Edward's presumption in the intellectual community. The admirable Mark DeWolfe Howe of the Harvard Law School spoke of the candidacy as "reckless" and "childishly irresponsible." This was wounding. "What bothered [Ted] most," said Gerald Doherty, who helped Stephen Smith run the campaign, "was the almost total boycott by the liberal establishment."* But the voters gave him the nomination by a wide margin. My journal on primary night: "I received two phone calls. . . . The first was from Bobby in Hyannis Port to say that, in view of Eddie McCormack's performance in the primaries, he wished that I would persuade Mark Howe to endorse George Lodge [the Republican candidate] in similar terms for November. No sooner had he hung up than a call came [in the same vein] from Ethel in McLean."[13]

Though Robert Kennedy was by now taking strong liberal positions on most issues, he continued to suspect the liberal establishment. He thought that "professional liberals" had a "sort of death wish, really wanting to go down in flames. . . . Action or success make them suspicious; and they almost lose interest. I think that's why so many of them think that Adlai Stevenson is the second coming. But he never quite arrives there; he never quite accomplishes anything. . . . They like it much better to have a cause than to have a course of action that's been successful."[14] John Kennedy, it must be said, sometimes felt the same way. "The only one [of them] I care about," the President once remarked to Ben Bradlee, "is Joe Rauh. He's great."[15] Robert wasn't always too sure about Rauh.

He did in fact make exceptions. One was George McGovern, who, after an effective interlude as Food for Peace director, was thinking of trying again for the Senate. He consulted with Robert Kennedy. "His question to me was . . . can you win? You know, he didn't believe . . . in these long-range hopeless efforts." When McGovern came down with hepatitis in the midst of his campaign, Robert sent Ethel out to South Dakota. "I was very ill then," McGovern recalled. "I could hardly hold my head up. . . . The publicity was fantastic. We had maximum coverage on television, radio and the press, and she was gay and hopeful. . . . I never knew until later that she was four or five months pregnant at that time. She has held a special place in my heart ever since. Indeed, I probably could not have made it to the Senate without her."[16]

* Burton Hersh, *The Education of Edward Kennedy* (New York, 1972), 160, 175. Mark Howe, before his untimely death, became a friend and supporter of Edward Kennedy.

II

In May 1961 Congress passed a bill creating seventy-one new judgeships. This, along with normal attrition among older judges, meant that the Kennedys made 128 judicial nominations by mid-October 1962. For a year they were sending names to the Hill at the rate of nearly ten a month.*

The Attorney General traditionally recommended judicial nominations to the President. Robert Kennedy took his responsibility conscientiously but had one small problem. He really could not understand why anyone wished to be a judge. Going on the bench took people out of the fight; "it's so boring, isn't it?" "Anybody he really liked, he didn't want to make a judge," noted Joseph Dolan, who handled the initial explorations in Justice.[17]

Still people inexplicably yearned for the bench. Appointments had to be made, a crossfire of pressures endured. The party organization had little influence in the process. "We never cleared, we never checked, we never called the Democratic National Committee about judicial appointments," Dolan said.[18] In New York, Buckley and De Sapio forwarded lists of names. "None of these recommendations was accepted," Robert Morgenthau recalled in 1971.[19] The White House politicos, O'Donnell especially, argued tenaciously for deserving Democrats. "The President was more understanding," recalled Robert Kennedy. ". . . We appointed some [Republicans], and that didn't go over well [with O'Donnell], and then some of the time I'd turn [Democrats] down because I didn't think they were qualified."†

---

* Harold W. Chase, *Federal Judges: The Appointing Process* (Minneapolis, Minn., 1972), 49. Professor Chase wanted to make a study of the way judges were appointed and asked Katzenbach, a college classmate, whether he could observe the Kennedy process firsthand. "Before we could go ahead, we needed the approval of Robert Kennedy. His reaction was typical for him. Judicial selection was the people's business as well as his. He was willing for me to do the study and call the shots as I saw them but he wanted to be reassured (by Katzenbach) that I would do a responsible job" (ibid., x). Chase was set up in a conference room between the offices of Katzenbach and Joseph Dolan, who did the preliminary screening of judicial possibilities. His book is interesting and illuminating. See also Victor Navasky, *Kennedy Justice* (New York, 1971), 259.

† RFK, in recorded interview by John Bartlow Martin, April 13, 1964, I, 41–42, JFK Oral History Program. Of Kennedy's 130 judicial appointments, 11—8.5 percent—were Republicans; Eisenhower's proportion of Democrats, 15 out of 201 judges, had been even smaller—7.5 percent. Kennedy and Eisenhower were both following precedent. The only President in more than half a century to appoint less than 90 percent of his judges from his own party was Hoover (82.7 percent). J. C. Goulden,

The Politics of Justice

The American Bar Association's Standing Committee on the Federal Judiciary spoke for the legal establishment. Justice regarded the ABA imprimatur as desirable but not essential. "I would be very surprised," Katzenbach told the ABA House of Delegates in 1962, "if this committee were omniscient and infallible. . . . At least some of the judges found by this committee to be qualified will . . . prove to have been bad appointments."[20] After all, the ABA had given the egregious Judge W. Harold Cox its highest rating. Nor did the ABA, having insinuated itself into the appointing process during the Eisenhower administration, want to risk its position now by giving too much offense. "The Kennedy people weren't the corporate types," one member of the committee said; "in a lot of areas we just didn't synchronize. I had the idea that if we turned down too many judges, Bob Kennedy and Katzenbach would have told us to go to hell." In the end, 6.3 percent of Kennedy's judges, as against 5.7 percent of Eisenhower's, failed the ABA test.[21]

By far the strongest pressure on the process was the Senate. "Basically," Robert Kennedy said in 1964, "it's grown up as a senatorial appointment with the advice and consent of the President." Sometimes senators had interests contrary to the administration's interests; "and this is where the struggle takes place. The President of the United States is attempting to obtain the passage of important legislation in many, many fields; and the appointment of a judge recommended by the chairman of a committee or a key figure on a committee can make the whole difference on his legislative program."[22]

Robert Kerr of Oklahoma was the second ranking Democrat on the Senate Finance Committee. Since the doughtily reactionary Harry Byrd of Virginia was chairman, Kerr was essential to the success of the administration's tax proposals. He was an imperious figure, generally accounted, after the departure of Lyndon Johnson, the most powerful and ruthless man in the Senate. Now he demanded that Luther L. Bohanon, an Oklahoma friend, be named district judge. Both Justice and the ABA found Bohanon unqualified. Byron White and William Geoghegan so informed Kerr. "Young men," said Kerr, "I was here a long time before you came. I'm going to be here a long time after you go. I stand by my recommendation."[23] Meanwhile tax legislation stalled. The President asked the secretary to the Senate, Bobby Baker, to find out from Kerr what the problem was. "Tell

---

The Benchwarmers: The Private World of the Powerful Federal Judges (New York: Ballantine reprint, 1976), 66; Chase, *Federal Judges*, 72, 77.

him," the senator said, "to get his dumb fuckin' brother to quit opposing my friend."[24] Robert Kennedy was determined not to yield; "I struggled and fought about that." John Kennedy had other concerns. "He just [felt] we weren't going to get any legislation through that committee unless we had Bob Kerr." It was the only judicial appointment, Robert said later, in which "we really . . . were on opposite sides."[25]

The dilemma was genuine enough. "It was the judge that I felt strongest about, and [Kerr] was really so blatant about it that I really disliked him. I might say that President Kennedy rather liked him. . . . He was so effective—I mean, the way he operated." In the end the Attorney General capitulated. "You really have to balance off. It sounds terrible. . . . [But] you stand fast on principle, and Kerr doesn't get his judge, and you don't get any tax legislation. They play it as tough and as mean as that. . . . He liked the President; and through his efforts we were able to obtain the passage of a good number of bills that would have never gotten by. . . . He knew his stuff, and he was the only person who could handle Byrd." So Bohanon became a judge—and turned out, to general surprise, not too bad, at least on civil rights.[26]

One ABA plank was opposition to the appointment of persons over sixty. (They also opposed judges who had not had at least fifteen years of practice, including "a substantial amount of trial experience"—a standard that did not excite the Attorney General.)[27] A united front of Texans, from Vice President Johnson to Senator Ralph Yarborough, were calling for the appointment to the federal bench of Sarah T. Hughes, a respected state judge who became sixty-five in 1961. The Attorney General mentioned the ABA objection. "Sonny," Sam Rayburn told him, "in your eyes everybody seems too old." Kennedy asked Ramsey Clark, another Hughes backer, to explain in three minutes why she should be nominated. Clark replied: "There are three reasons. First, we need women judges. She has served twenty-six years on the bench and has been a good judge. Second, women live longer than men, so if you want to be scientific about it, give her the benefit of the doubt. Third, a gentleman never asks a lady her age." "Bob was standing there," Clark recalled, "and he just whirled around and said something like, 'Let's do it.' . . . Bob was a joyous person in so many ways."[28] Judge Hughes retired in 1975 after fourteen years of distinguished service on the federal bench.

Robert Kennedy was also determined to appoint a Mexican American; "there had never been one," he told Clark, "and it was way past due." The ABA disapproved three names submitted by the Department. After a talk with Kennedy, the committee agreed to give Reynaldo B. Garza a "qualified" rating. The Vice President later exhorted Garza: "Reynaldo, I want you to be such a great judge that when you walk down the streets of Brownsville, all the little Mexican-American boys will think you're the second coming of the Lord."[29]

John Kennedy, I noted in my journal in July 1961, "was quite funny on the problem of appointing judges—there were so many appointments to be made, he said, that every senator thought he had a God-given right to have his own bum appointed. 'Even I have mine,' he said."[30] His bum was Francis X. Morrissey of Boston, Joseph Kennedy's loyal retainer across the years and head of John Kennedy's Boston office in his congressional period. The ambassador hated to harass his sons to find out what they were up to; instead, he had come to rely on reports from Morrissey. A cheerful, round-faced little man, Morrissey was not without his subtleties and decencies; but the sons had come to see him almost as their father's spy, nor did they suppose for a moment that his appointment would elevate the federal judiciary.

A few days later (my journal again): "The President complained of the press concentration on the allegedly prospective appointment of Frank Morrissey . . . and the simultaneous neglect of the excellent judicial appointments under way in the rest of the country." McGeorge Bundy, who was present, remarked that this was one more sign Morrissey's appointment would cause unnecessary trouble. The President said, "Look: my father has come to me and said that he has never asked me for anything, that he wants to ask me only this one thing—to make Frank Morrissey a federal judge. What can I do?" Bundy answered forthrightly that his father knew he shouldn't ask this, that the President knew he should reject the request, and that his father would know that he was right to reject the request. "The President looked gloomy and said that Morrissey couldn't have worked for him for eleven years without picking up something in the way of a sense of public service and that in any case he would be greatly superior to his predecessor Windy Bill McCarthy."[31] (This conversation should be noted, among other reasons, for the candor John Kennedy invited from his staff.)

The ABA had meanwhile rendered a devastating report on Morrissey. Anthony Lewis of the *New York Times* asked the Attorney General whether he meant to appoint him. "He really was furious," Lewis recalled, "and could be extremely gruff and angry. He said, escorting me to the door, 'We are going to appoint Frank Morrissey just to show that the *New York Times* isn't making the judicial appointments around here.' "[32] But they didn't appoint Morrissey (though they did leave the judgeship vacant).

III

Except for the disastrous southern judges, the Kennedy-Kennedy record in the circuit and district courts was in the main excellent. The Supreme Court, of course, mattered most of all. These were, said Katzenbach, speaking of John Kennedy, "almost the only judicial appointments he took seriously. . . . The others he was perfectly satisfied to leave to other people's judgment, and he would ask only occasional questions about them. The Supreme Court [appointments] he did feel were personal."[33] His first opportunity came with the resignation of Justice Charles E. Whittaker in the spring of 1962.

"I had originally been for putting a Negro on," Robert Kennedy said in 1964. ". . . My first recommendation was [Judge William H.] Hastie." Hastie, a Harvard Law School graduate, appointed by Truman in 1949 as the first black circuit court judge, had proved himself steady, able and hard working. The Attorney General was dismayed by the resistance he encountered. "I went up and saw [Chief Justice Earl] Warren about Hastie. He was violently opposed to having Hastie on the Court. . . . He said, 'He's not a liberal, and he'd be opposed to all the measures that we are interested in, and he would just be completely unsatisfactory.' " Robert's old friend Justice Douglas agreed with Warren. Hastie, he told Kennedy, would be "just one more vote for Frankfurter."[34]

"A lot of people in the White House," Robert Kennedy recalled, "were opposed to having a Negro"—not on racial grounds, but because it seemed too political, "too obvious." The President called in Clark Clifford, who after observing that the judiciary had been Truman's great failure, exhorted Kennedy to make only distinguished appointments. When Kennedy mentioned Hastie, "I said I thought it would be a mistake for him to reach out just to put a Negro on the bench" for the sake of having a Negro; Hastie's record was "reasonably good" but not great. Robert Kennedy argued back that obviousness was no reason for rejection, that Hastie "was a good judge, and that it was an appropriate time. . . . If you were going to consider the five or six best judges of the Circuit Court, you'd put him there. So that was the basis of it. . . . I didn't know when another vacancy would come, and I thought that it would mean so much overseas." Finally Katzenbach, after an analysis of Hastie's opinions, assessed them as "competent and pedestrian. . . . When [I said] I thought his opinions were rather pedestrian, this just killed him with President Kennedy."[35]

Clifford was high on Paul Freund of Harvard. So was Katzenbach, though he asked the President whether there would be a problem if he named a second Jew with Frankfurter still on the Court. "He blew up at that and . . . said, 'Why the hell shouldn't I?'" Naming a Harvard professor was more difficult. "We've taken so many Harvard men," Robert Kennedy said to me, "that it's damn hard to appoint another."[36] Warren and Douglas were cool on Freund, no doubt supposing he too would be one more vote for Frankfurter.[37] Other names were considered: two eminent state judges, Roger Traynor of California and Walter Schaefer of Illinois; the president of the University of Chicago, Edward Levi; the Texas lawyer Leon Jaworski; Arthur Goldberg, the Secretary of Labor (the President crossed Goldberg off the list, saying that would come later; he was needed in the cabinet now).[38]

Senator Russell soon threatened to bring a delegation over to ask the President for a conservative. The President, wishing to forestall the request, now proposed appointing Byron White at once. O'Donnell objected, reminding him of the hard time his brother had given them "whenever we tried to reward a nice young man, who had helped us politically, with a Federal judgeship." White, O'Donnell said, "doesn't have any of that Oliver Wendell Holmes background that the Justice Department is always demanding when we try to give somebody a judge's job."[39] The Attorney General himself was dubious—not on the merits but because he could not conceive why White, whom he saw as a man of action, would want to go on the bench, and because he felt he needed him in the Department. Katzenbach dealt with the second point by remarking that, since Kennedy had just lost John Seigenthaler, who had left to become editor of the *Nashville Tennessean,* it would be hard on him to lose White too; "you ought to consider it before recommending Byron." Kennedy, bridling, said, "I'm not going to stand in Byron's way. I can handle the Justice Department without Byron."[40]

On March 30, 1962, I was with the President when the White House telephone operators tracked down White somewhere in the west. "Well, Byron," Kennedy said, "we've decided to go ahead on you." There was a moment's silence, and the President said, "We want to get the announcement out in twenty minutes, so we need an answer right away." Another silence, and the President said, "All right, we'll go ahead." Turning to me: "Could you write a statement right away explaining why I am choosing White." He gave some reasons, and I called Bobby, who gave some more. Make the point, the Attorney General characteristically said, that White was no mere professor or scholar but had actually seen 'life'—in the Navy, in private practice, in politics, even on the football field. So White left Justice, with Katzenbach taking his place as deputy attorney general. As for the Court, the President said to me, "I figure that I will have several more appointments before I am through, and I mean to appoint Freund, Arthur Goldberg and Bill Hastie."[41]

Frankfurter, now seventy-nine years old, was beginning to show the infirmities of age. John Kennedy at one point sympathetically asked Max Freedman of the *Manchester Guardian,* Frankfurter's designated biographer, whether the Justice would be willing to resign if he and the President could agree on a successor. I later asked Kennedy what Frankfurter had replied. Kennedy said, "I guess he decided that he was indispensable to the court."[42] Over the summer, however, Frankfurter recognized he could not continue.

"The President called me in the middle of the week," Robert Kennedy wrote in a memorandum in early September 1962,

> and said that he had heard from Warren that Frankfurter was not going to return to the Court. We discussed who might replace him and he thought about putting Paul Freund on. I made the point that Archie Cox had come to work for the Administration and had done a fine job while Paul Freund had refused the position of Solicitor General. Therefore, I thought that Archie Cox deserved the appointment more than Paul Freund.
> We talked about the necessity of putting a Jew on. I said I thought if a Jew was placed on the Court it should be Arthur Goldberg although I thought it was very difficult to part with him. We discussed it a couple of times again and the only reservation about Arthur Goldberg was the fact that he was so valuable to the Administration and could handle labor and management in a way that could hardly be equalled by anyone else.
> Finally, however, the President called and said he had talked to Arthur Goldberg and that Goldberg was anxious to get the appointment. . . . Certainly a major factor in giving up the services of Arthur Goldberg was the necessity of replacing Frankfurter with a Jew. The President said that Mike Feldman [of the White House staff] indicated clearly that the various Jewish organizations would be upset if this appointment did not go to a person of the Jewish faith.[43]

Frankfurter must have regretted his refusal of Kennedy's earlier proposal. As Dorothy Goldberg later put it, "Arthur and Justice Frankfurter were at opposite poles in their thinking."[44] Nor was the Justice a great admirer of the Attorney General. "What does Bobby understand about the Supreme Court?" he told an interviewer in 1964. "He understands it about as much as you understand about the undiscovered 76th star in the galaxy."[45]

The Attorney General was kinder about Frankfurter. I will never forget one of the Justice's last public appearances. It was at the swearing-in of Carl McGowan as judge of the District of Columbia Court of Appeals. Frankfurter had asked to say a few words.

> He sat in his wheelchair and spoke fluently and coherently, though not very relevantly, for about twenty minutes. Since everyone expected a short tribute to McGowan, and since the Justice did not mention McGowan and showed every sign of being able to go on for hours, a restiveness crept over the courtroom. People passed notes, and finally Joe Rauh, who had accompanied the Justice, leaned over and suggested that perhaps he had talked long enough. The Justice said cheerfully—and loudly—"I may be Joe Rauh's judge, but he is not my lawyer"—and continued. Finally something happened to his microphone and, though he went on talking, no one could hear him. Judge [David] Bazelon said, "Mr. Justice, Mr. Justice, your power has gone"—a terrifying metaphor, given the occasion. Finally the Justice stopped, and Joe wheeled him out. . . . There were mixed reactions afterward. Tony Lewis considered it a great tragedy for the Justice to expose himself in his rambling and garrulous old age. Bobby Kennedy, however, with whom I rode away, said, "If that experience gave the old man half an hour of pleasure, no one in the room had such pressing business that he couldn't stay for a few extra minutes."[46]

After the Goldberg appointment, John Kennedy mused about Cox and Freund. "Bobby thinks it would be impossible to appoint them both," he said, "but I don't see why. After Archie has been down here a little while, he will seem more Washington than Cambridge. I think we'll have appointments enough for everybody."[47]

IV

"I shall withhold from neither the Congress nor the people," John F. Kennedy said in his first annual message, "any fact or report, past, present, or future, which is necessary for an informed judgment of our conduct and hazards."[48] Imperfect as the execution of this pledge later was in foreign affairs, Kennedy's statement was a deliberate repudiation of the theory devised by the Eisenhower administration of an absolute presidential right to deny information to

Congress. This supposed right, born in response to the irresponsible requisitions of Joe McCarthy, received in 1957 the name of 'executive privilege' and thereafter acquired with mysterious rapidity the status of ancient and hallowed constitutional doctrine.

Toward the end of the Eisenhower years Congressman Porter Hardy, chairman of a House Subcommittee on Foreign Operations and Monetary Affairs, tried to get records relating to the foreign aid program in Peru. Eisenhower promptly ordered that the documents be withheld. When Kennedy came in, the State Department renewed the Eisenhower directive.[49] On March 10, 1961, the frustrated Hardy dropped a letter of complaint at the White House. Before he reached home, the new President had called him. Three days later Secretary of State Rusk promised delivery of the documents. At the next hearing, however, State Department witnesses showed up with a letter from Rusk forbidding them to testify. Hardy complained again to Kennedy. The Department's legal adviser hastily withdrew the Rusk letter, asking Hardy to "treat it as though it had not been sent," and transmitted the documents.[50]

"You seem more willing than previous Presidents and Administrations," James Reston of the *New York Times* said to Robert Kennedy on *Meet the Press* in September 1961, "to give information sought by Congress." The Attorney General replied:

> I was associated with a Congressional committee for five or six years and had battles with the Executive Branch of the government regarding obtaining information. I think it is terribly important [in order] to insure that the Executive Branch of the government is not corrupt and that they are efficient, that the Legislative Branch of the government has this ability to check on what we are doing in the Executive Branch of the government.
>
> So in every instance that has been brought to our attention in the Department of Justice so far by various departments of the Executive Branch where this question has been raised, we have suggested and recommended that they make the information available to Congress. We will continue to do that.
>
> I don't say that there might not be an instance where Executive privilege might have to be used, but I think it is terribly important, with the Executive Branch of the government as powerful and strong as it is, that there be some check and balance on it. And in the last analysis the group that can best check and insure that it is handling its affairs properly is the Congress of the United States. So we will lean over backwards to make sure that they get the information they request.[51]

There were cases where withholding had a serious point; but these, Robert Kennedy felt, were the rarest exceptions. John Kennedy invoked executive privilege only once. In February 1962 a Senate committee, on an expedition of harassment, demanded to know by name which Pentagon officials had deleted warlike passages from speeches by fire-eating generals and admirals. Byron White, as Acting Attorney General, sent the President a cautionary memorandum, which, he said, "accurately reflects the views of the Attorney General." No doubt executive privilege had to be asserted in this particular case, White wrote, but Justice was concerned about "internal pressure in State and Defense, particularly the former, to use this invocation as precedent for future situations." The President had to make clear "whether or not this Administration is adopting the Eisenhower principle and will apply it automatically as was done in the past Administration."

The memorandum acknowledged the "great appeal" of the Eisenhower principle for the executive branch.

> [But] it is not enough to assert "managerial responsibility" without at the same time weighing the needs of Congress for the information withheld. From the viewpoint of Congress, automatic application of this principle would make meaningful investigation almost impossible in many situations. . . . The Executive branch has some tendency to hide its errors and many Congressional investigations have disclosed errors which would not otherwise have come to the attention of an agency head. . . . Furthermore, I am inclined to believe that the internal advice rule, however honestly designed to protect subordinate officials from Congressional criticism, as often as not has the effect of protecting those whom we claim to be responsible, for frequently the information withheld would show that an agency head got good advice and ignored it.

Justice therefore recommended an explicit presidential declaration that the use of the privilege in this single case "is *not* to be regarded as precedent for its invocation in other circumstances where Congressional questioning of subordinate officials has more justification in bringing out relevant information. Each case will be looked at on its own merits."[52]

The President followed this recommendation. That he really believed in an executive responsibility to supply information to Congress was shown in a few weeks when Porter Hardy again sought foreign-aid documents, this time about Angola, and the State Department again withheld them. Within an hour after the question was raised in a press conference, Hardy received the records.[53] Later, John Kennedy wrote Hardy that, because he was convinced "your investigation will be both constructive and careful and of real help to both the Congress and the Executive Branch," he was directing the State Department to give the committee everything pertinent except personnel files; even these would be turned over "for your eyes only as Chairman."[54]

Where Kennedy's pledge of full disclosure failed was in areas, like Cuba and Vietnam, about which Congress made no requests for information. Where Congress requested, Kennedy, in the words of Raoul Berger, "sharply limited resort to executive privilege."[55] Congressman John Moss observed of executive privilege in 1963, "The powerful genie . . . momentarily is confined." He added prophetically: "but can be uncorked by future Presidents."[56]

V

In the field of law enforcement, Robert Kennedy confounded those who had predicted he would play politics with justice. "The top political animals in the Kennedy administration," recalled Ronald Goldfarb of the Criminal Division, "helplessly watched Robert Kennedy's organized crime drive knock off politician after politician around the country." At one meeting, lawyers reported on recent indictments. The Attorney General asked questions, including inevitably, "Was he Republican or Democrat?" After several answered "Democrat," Kennedy observed with a smile, "If you guys keep this up my brother is going to have to take me out of here and send me to the Supreme Court."[57] His Department of Justice indicted two Democratic congressmen, three Democratic judges, five Democratic mayors, divers smaller fry.

Bringing some of these cases was difficult. There was the case of Judge J. Vincent Keogh of the New York State Supreme Court. The Kennedys owed nothing to Judge Keogh, but they owed a great deal to his brother Congressman Eugene Keogh, a distinguished Irishman of the old school, a long-time friend of Joseph Kennedy's, influential both in Congress and in New York politics and, in Robert Kennedy's judgment, one of the "five people who were most helpful to the President in the election."[58] But Gene Keogh's brother, it began to appear, had taken a bribe to induce a colleague on the bench to go easy in sentencing a man convicted of bankruptcy fraud. The matter arose in Robert Kennedy's first year. The evidence against Keogh was persuasive but not conclusive. Department of Justice lawyers watched to see what the Attorney General would do.

The White House was watching too. One day the President asked Seigenthaler whether his brother planned to indict Vincent Keogh. Seigenthaler said there were problems. John Kennedy said, "My

God, I hope that he doesn't. Gene Keogh was my friend, and, if there's any way I can honestly help him, I'd want to help him."[59] O'Donnell suggested that they drop the case and let Judge Keogh resign. Perhaps to make it clear that politics would not affect his decision, Robert Kennedy put the Eisenhower holdover, William Hundley, in charge. "It was not an open-and-shut case," Hundley recalled. ". . . I don't have any doubt that Kennedy was hoping that the grand jury investigation would show that Keogh didn't do it." But the investigation convinced Hundley that the government's evidence was credible and that Keogh had in fact taken the money.[60] "You've *got* to prosecute this," Byron White said to Robert Kennedy. The Attorney General buried his face in his hands and said, "Goddam it, I told my brother I didn't want this job."[61] Then he said, "If the evidence is there, as difficult as it would be for the President of the United States to hurt his friend, and as difficult as it would be for me, we'll proceed."[62] "He didn't just sit back and say, 'I disqualify myself,'" Hundley recalled. "That's the easy way out: 'I disqualify myself.' Then he could go running back to Gene Keogh and say, 'Well, it was that son-of-a-bitch Hundley.' . . . He never did that. It was his decision. . . . He took the heat personally."[63]

When Hundley said he thought they just had to go ahead, Kennedy said, "Remember, if we lose this case, you and I are going to look like a couple of real shits." "That," Hundley observed later, "was his way of saying, 'Make damn sure you win.'"[64] Vincent Keogh was convicted and sentenced to two years in prison. "It was a very painful case for Bob Kennedy," said Hundley. ". . . But we were closer after that than we had ever been before."[65] Someone at the Democratic National Committee later said to Walter Sheridan, "I can't believe that you couldn't have fixed that case." Sheridan said, "Of course we could have, but that's the difference [between] you and us."[66]

Another painful case involved George Chacharis, the mayor of Gary, Indiana. It appeared that Chacharis had received over $200,000 in payoffs and failed to report them in his tax returns. There was no evidence that Chacharis had used the money for himself; he had faithfully plowed it back into his political organization and evidently did not suppose he had done anything wrong. Congressman Ray Madden of Gary, a powerful figure in the House, brought Chacharis to see the Attorney General. Madden reminded Kennedy that Chacharis, a Greek immigrant who had come up the hard way, had been the driving force for John Kennedy in Indiana when Kennedy needed help. As the conversation proceeded, Chacharis, an emotional man who had actually been proposed as ambassador to Greece, broke down and cried. His attorney was the Democratic National Committeeman from Indiana. The prosecutor was aggressive, theatrical and, in the view of some in Justice, a grabber of headlines. But the pressure of evidence overcame the pressure of politics. Chacharis was indicted, convicted and sent to prison.[67]

Another case involved Matthew H. McCloskey of Philadelphia, a veteran Democratic fund raiser and Kennedy supporter whom John Kennedy named ambassador to Ireland in 1962. The McCloskey Construction Company had built—very badly—a Veterans' Administration hospital in Massachusetts. The Civil Division proposed a suit against the McCloskey firm for faulty construction and breach of contract. "We made that recommendation to the Attorney General," said John Douglas, "and he didn't bat an eyelid; he just said, 'Go ahead.'"[68]

A couple of cases complicated the Attorney General's prickly relations with the Vice President. Fred Korth, a Johnson protégé, had succeeded John Connally as Secretary of the Navy. Korth, it was discovered in 1963, was using department stationery, the Navy yacht *Sequoia* and other official facilities on behalf of his bank back in Fort Worth. Robert Kennedy, over Johnson's protest, recommended Korth's dismissal. The President agreed. "Clark Clifford," Kennedy reminded Johnson in 1964, "was also for retaining Korth but after reviewing the material (and also, incidentally, arguing with us at the Department of Justice) he came to the conclusion that Korth should be relieved."[69]

Then there was the case of Bobby Baker, so long Johnson's *homme de confiance*. "I have two daughters," Johnson used to say. "If I had a son, this would be the boy."[70] Congressional investigations began to turn up evidence that eventually led to Baker's conviction for tax evasion and fraud. The Vice President was sure Robert Kennedy was pursuing Baker in order to force Johnson off the ticket in 1964. Actually both Kennedy and Johnson were, in different ways, on the spot. The Attorney General, Katzenbach said later, "never got into much of the details of the case. . . . I don't really think he wanted to know a great deal about it. . . . He was sure that Johnson would believe that somehow he was behind this, and [that] it was designed to embarrass Lyndon Johnson, which is the way President Johnson often thought."*

* Nicholas Katzenbach, in recorded interview by L. J. Hackman, October 8, 1969, 9, RFK Oral History Program. When Kennedy and Johnson discussed Bobby Baker

The Politics of Justice

Ironically, as it was in some sense easier to prosecute Kennedy loyalists than Johnson loyalists, so, in at least one major case, it was easier to prosecute Democrats than Republicans. Soon after he became Attorney General, Kennedy was faced with the problem of the relationship between the Boston textile manufacturer Bernard Goldfine and Sherman Adams, a governor of New Hampshire and subsequently President Eisenhower's chief of staff. The disclosure that he had accepted favors from Goldfine had forced Adams to resign in 1958. The favors, it now appeared, went far beyond hotel rooms and the famous vicuña coat. By 1961 Goldfine, old and sick, was ready to talk. His lawyer was Robert Kennedy's one-time friend and later antagonist Edward Bennett Williams. Goldfine claimed, Robert Kennedy noted in February 1961, that Adams had received "more than $150,000 in cash over the period of about five years." Goldfine also implicated a former Democratic governor of Massachusetts and a couple of Republican senators, among them Styles Bridges of New Hampshire. "Jack called me the other day and said that he understood Styles Bridges had cancer and, obviously, we did not want to develop this information about him as he was dying."[71]

One problem was that Goldfine himself was so ill with arteriosclerosis that he could not always remember things coherently. "Sunday of last week," Kennedy wrote, "[he] burst into tears and said he couldn't go on because his mind was so befuddled." A trail of cashier's checks Adams had given his Washington landlady seemed to corroborate Goldfine's allegations in general; but Goldfine himself would obviously not be a strong witness. "I am not optimistic," said Kennedy; "however, I think there is probably a fifty-fifty chance. He's got everything to gain and nothing to lose."[72]

Kennedy turned the case over to the indispensable Hundley. Hund-

---

in 1964, Johnson emphasized "that Bobby Baker got into all this difficulty after he, Lyndon, had left the Senate. He said Bobby Baker wanted to go to Puerto Rico on one occasion when he was Vice President, when he, Johnson, was going down to the inauguration of Bosch. [He meant the Dominican Republic.] He said for some reason Bobby's request concerned him and he didn't take him. Later on, he said, he found out he went anyway. But he said he could have gotten into so much difficulty if he had taken him as part of his official party. Secondly, he said God must have been watching over him because he did not have financial dealings with Bobby. He could very well have done so because if Bobby asked him to loan him $10,000 for the purchase of some stock he certainly would have done so. He said the only business deal he had with Bobby Baker was in connection with the purchase of some insurance. The insurance company then placed $1500 (I think that was the figure) worth of advertising with his television station. He said this really didn't mean anything because the competitor company was willing to place twice as much" (RFK, memorandum, August 4, 1964, 3–4, RFK Papers).

ley interviewed Adams, who seemed extremely nervous—as if he were ready to jump out the window, Hundley thought—and, confronted by the cashier's checks, admitted receiving money from unremembered donors, but not, he insisted, from Goldfine. In the end, gaps remained in the evidence. Obviously the Kennedys could not afford to bring a case against Adams and lose it. This would look like a bungled attempt at political vengeance. Because it would not be hard to confect a defense—people might always arise to swear they had given the money to Adams out of disinterested patriotism—Louis Oberdorfer, as head of the Tax Division, recommended against prosecution.*

It is said, though I have been unable to verify the story, that John Kennedy sent the incriminating data on Adams over to Eisenhower at Gettysburg.[73] The new President was keenly aware of his predecessor's continuing popularity and might have thought it useful to put the old general under obligation. The relations between the two men were cool. On inauguration day, as they rode together to the Capitol, Kennedy had asked what Eisenhower thought of Cornelius Ryan's vivid account of D-day, *The Longest Day*. The new President "was rather fascinated," Robert Kennedy recalled in 1964,

> that Eisenhower never read the book and in fact hadn't seemed to have read anything. He thought he had a rather fascinating personality, could understand talking to him why he was President of the United States . . . [but] just felt that he . . . hadn't done any homework, didn't know a great deal about areas that he should know. I think he always felt that Eisenhower was unhappy with him—that he was so young and that he was elected President and so he always, feeling that Eisenhower was important and his election was so close, . . . went out of his way to make sure that Eisenhower was brought in on more matters and that Eisenhower couldn't hurt the Administration by going off on a tangent and that's why he made such an effort over Eisenhower, not that Eisenhower ever gave him any advice that was very helpful.[74]

According to the story, Eisenhower, after looking at the Adams dossier, sent back a message to Kennedy expressing fervent hope that Adams be spared further humiliation. This was not the reason the Department of Justice failed to indict Adams; but Eisenhower pre-

---

* William Hundley, in recorded interview by J. A. Oesterle, December 9, 1970, 21, RFK Oral History Program; Hundley, in interview by author, August 4, 1976; Louis Oberdorfer, in interview by author, December 29, 1976. The Department of Justice had recently lost a case where J. Truman Bidwell, chairman of the board of governors of the New York Stock Exchange, escaped conviction by persuading a jury that he had come upon money in other ways than those charged in the indictment.

The Politics of Justice

sumably did not know this, and the apparent favor may well have, for a period, restrained his criticism of his successor.*

VI

The most painful cases of all involved friends of the family. Igor Cassini—Cholly Knickerbocker, the gossip columnist of Hearst's *New York Journal-American*—was no friend of Robert Kennedy's. But his brother Oleg made dresses for Jacqueline Kennedy and attended White House parties. And Igor—Ghighi to his intimates—was an acquaintance of Joseph P. Kennedy's in Florida. He was also a friend of the Dominican dictator Trujillo, with whose bloody regime the United States had recently broken relations; and he claimed one Palm Beach evening that Trujillo would reform if the United States restored recognition; adding darkly that, if Washington did not alter its policy, the Dominican Republic would fall to communism.[75] The old ambassador was sufficiently impressed to tell the President. In April 1961 the State Department sent the veteran diplomat Robert Murphy to take a look. Cassini was at Murphy's right hand.

After their return Robert Kennedy heard rumors that Cassini's interest in Trujillo was more than academic. He thereupon instructed the FBI to investigate reports that Cassini, who had not registered as a foreign agent, was taking money from the Dominican tyrant. Cassini protested. "I've performed this function with Murphy," he told the Attorney General, "and then I come back, and somebody starts a rumor, and you start an investigation." He swore to God that he was clean. The investigation, he pleaded, was hurting him with his newspapers; "the Department of Justice is just finishing me." The FBI, after several weeks, came up with nothing. Impressed by Cassini's vehemence and by his invocation of the Almighty, Kennedy told the Bureau to discontinue; it was, he said later, "the only investigation I

---

* Another version of what may be the Sherman Adams story appears in Bobby Baker with Larry King, *Wheeling and Dealing: Confessions of a Capitol Hill Operator* (New York, 1978), 82–84. According to this account, a federal grand jury was on the verge of indicting Eisenhower's "former aide, 'Mr. Jones'" for income tax evasion. Mrs. Eisenhower feared that "Jones might commit suicide." The former President asked Senator Dirksen to ask President Kennedy "as a personal favor to me, to put the Jones indictment in the deep freeze. . . . He'll have a blank check in my bank if he will grant me this favor." According to Dirksen, as rendered by Baker, Robert Kennedy strongly opposed dropping the indictment, and the President told his brother, "If you can't comply with my request then your resignation will be accepted." JFK later cashed in his blank check by insisting that Eisenhower and Dirksen publicly endorse the test ban treaty of 1963.

called off since I've been Attorney General." Back in New York, Cassini airily informed an interviewer that his Dominican visit had been "well known to the White House. . . . But Trujillo has such a reputation for having paid off everybody that anybody who ever went there was supposedly paid off. . . . I was not among the lucky ones."[76]

He was lying through his teeth. At an early point the Dominican consul general in New York reported to El Supremo that Cassini "entertains the idea of arranging a meeting for you with Mr. Joseph P. Kennedy, father of the President, or with the President himself, both of whom, according to Cassini, are his intimate friends and with whom he maintains close and frequent relations." Cassini assertedly shared in payments of nearly $200,000 stashed away in a Geneva bank account.*

For a time the matter lay dormant. Then Trujillo was killed. A new democratic regime opened the Trujillo files to newspapermen and congressional investigators. The journalist Peter Maas got onto the story. Maas remarked to someone in this period how much he liked Robert Kennedy. He was told, "Forget it if you run the Cassini story, because the lead . . . involves Bobby's father; 'ruthless' Bobby'll get you for that." Maas said to himself, "If that's the way it is and Bobby is going to get me, the hell with it. I'm not giving up on the story." His wife thought that at least he was obligated, as a friend, to tell Kennedy what he had discovered.

Maas went to see the Attorney General. Kennedy asked him what it was all about. Maas: "I've just been doing a long piece on Ghighi Cassini." Kennedy, almost half-rising out of his chair: "No. No. We've looked through all that. . . . There's nothing to it." Maas: "There is a lot to it." Maas told Kennedy in detail what he had found. "He sat there," Maas said later, "and didn't say anything at all. He sat there kind of hunched over in that big chair in that big room with his chin on his fingers. . . . I finished. All he said was, 'Thank you very much,' and I left."[77]

Kennedy sent the FBI back to uncover what it had missed. More pleas from Cassini and his friends: "There was an awful lot of pressure . . . not to prosecute," Kennedy said later.[78] Cassini's wife wrote the President expressing shock at "Bobby's harsh and punitive attitude." Her husband, she said, could not understand "why the son

* Brock Brower, *Other Loyalties* (New York, 1968), 101. For another view of the case, see the account by Cassini's lawyer, Louis Nizer, in the chapter "Foreign Agent," in *Reflections without Mirrors* (Garden City, N.Y., 1978).

The Politics of Justice

of a man whom he considered one of his closest friends for 17 years . . . should now be determined to bring him down to total ruin."[79] The President, according to Ben Bradlee, was "obviously upset, and wondered out loud about the virtue of prosecuting Cassini."[80] The Attorney General went ahead. Cassini pleaded nolo contendere, paid a $10,000 fine. "If there was one thing that turned me completely pro-Bobby," said Maas, it was the Cassini case. ". . . I was so used to fixes in covering politics that this was such an extraordinary thing. There were fifteen different ways his people could have fouled up the investigation or done something to have it thrown out of court. But it obviously never entered his mind."[81] Robert Kennedy told Maas, "God knows this was the last case in the world I was looking to prosecute, but what's right is right."[82]

The saddest case involved someone far closer to the Kennedy family than Igor Cassini. James M. Landis had been a faithful friend of Joseph Kennedy and all his children for nearly thirty years. He had performed legal work, written articles, helped the father on his memoirs, drafted legislation and speeches for the sons. He was a singular and in some ways eccentric man. Gruff taciturnity concealed a certain inner perversity. He never, for example, despite protestations from Joseph Kennedy and from his own law partners, sent Kennedy bills for his legal services. He was terribly negligent about his own affairs. In 1956, under business pressures, he had delayed filing an income tax return, applied for one extension, forgot to apply for another, put the whole thing out of his mind. The next year he filled out his tax form but could not figure out how to answer the question whether he had filed a return the year before; so he deposited the amount owed the government in a separate bank account and put the return in a drawer. He did the same thing for the next three years.

After the 1960 election, John Kennedy asked Landis, who, among other things, was an expert on the administrative process, to prepare a report on the regulatory agencies. This assignment led to a routine security check and in turn to the discovery that the Internal Revenue Service had no recent tax returns from Landis. With the help of Joseph Kennedy's accountant, new tax forms were filled out; and, with the help of a loan from Joseph Kennedy (the money Landis had set aside covered taxes and interest but not penalties), he filed delinquent returns, paying $48,000 in 1961 and another $46,000 in 1962. The critical issue now was whether the late filing was voluntary. If deemed voluntary, the IRS would not recommend prosecution. When the IRS asked Landis why he decided to file, Landis, in his way, said shortly, "Because Joe Kennedy told me I'd damn well better."[83] Was it voluntary when the father of a President directed a citizen to pay his back taxes?

Had Landis not been a friend of the Kennedys, his setting aside the money would have been taken as evidence of good faith; his inability to file would have been laid to not uncommon psychological blocks (Landis had in fact been seeing a psychiatrist); his late returns would have been accepted, and the case closed. But, with a friend of the President involved, no one was willing to declare the action voluntary. Commissioner Mortimer Caplin of the IRS passed the buck to the Justice Department. On Katzenbach's insistence, and for self-evident reasons, Robert Kennedy disqualified himself. "Bobby had nothing to do with it," said Katzenbach later. "I wouldn't let him. I said, 'You cannot make a decision not to prosecute Landis. If you can't make that decision, don't make any.' "[84] Louis Oberdorfer, the head of the Tax Division, disqualified himself on the ground of possible conflict of interest; he had consulted Landis before his confirmation hearing, Landis had never billed him, therefore he might be thought to owe something to Landis. This left the case to Katzenbach, who made the decision to prosecute. No doubt he felt that otherwise the Republicans would say that Robert Kennedy had fixed the case to protect his father's friend.

Landis was not a well man. He was undergoing neurological treatment at the Columbia Presbyterian Hospital. He pled guilty. Everyone supposed, in view of the circumstances, that, like the far worse malefactor Igor Cassini, he would receive a fine and a suspended sentence. He came, however, before a self-righteous judge who, after a lecture, sentenced him to thirty days in prison. Robert Morgenthau, the prosecutor, was furious. This was not a fraud case; a sentence so harsh for a man so ailing made no sense in terms of rehabilitation, deterrence or anything else. Justin Feldman, Landis's partner, said to Morgenthau: "He emotionally can't survive it. What can we do?" "There's only one thing we can do," Morgenthau replied. "The Attorney General has the right to determine that he should serve the sentence in a hospital, and not in a jail."[85]

Robert Kennedy at once certified that Landis should serve his sentence in a hospital. The unyielding judge, rejecting the plea of Landis's physician that he needed the facilities at Columbia's Neurological Institute, sent him to the Public Health Service Center on Staten Island, where he was flung into a ward largely populated by screaming psychotics. Feldman went to Washington to ask for

Landis's transfer to a hospital. Katzenbach agreed that the Attorney General had the authority to make the transfer but opposed his doing it: "There'll be a whole series of stories, and we're back where we started from—cronyism and favors to friends." Then Feldman saw Kennedy:

KENNEDY. What does Nick say?
FELDMAN. Nick says that you shouldn't do it.
KENNEDY. Does he say I shouldn't do it, or I can't do it?
FELDMAN. He says you shouldn't do it.
KENNEDY. Oh, I can't believe that.... [punching the intercom to Katzenbach] Is Justin's legal opinion correct that I can do it? ... You know, Nick, I don't understand you sometimes.... Sure we have to worry about the reaction of people in the press, and so forth, but if any goddam reporter wants to say that the Kennedy Administration, having prosecuted one of the best friends they've ever had—somebody who's been practically a father to me, who helped me get through my law school exams, and who's been close to Ted and close to the whole family and close to my father, and has done us so many favors—if they want to say that, having prosecuted him, having exposed him to the public through this, that we are now soft on criminals by having him serve that stupid thirty days in some degree of comfort, they can go to hell![86]

That settled that. It was an unhappy business. Reading a sympathetic piece by David Lawrence in *U.S. News & World Report,* Robert Kennedy scribbled a note to Lawrence: "I just wanted to let you know how understanding and kind I thought your article was on Jim Landis. He has suffered terribly, as a sensitive proud person would. Your piece will help him to stay alive mentally and physically."[87]

Reflecting about the parade of cases—Landis, Chacharis, Keogh and the rest—Kennedy said in 1964, "It's one of the reasons I was rather reluctant to become Attorney General because I knew I'd get into these kinds of cases as well as somebody that wanted to be a judge and all that other business. That's why I think it's ... got some dangers to it for a person involved in politics to be Attorney General.... It is a position that should really be removed from politics or as completely as it can be."[88]

(18)

Justice and Poverty

HE WAS TIRED, Robert Kennedy had said, of chasing people. The Rackets Committee had persuaded him that the American malaise was a problem not just of crooked individuals but of a corrupt system. The Department of Justice now gave the problem a larger context. He increasingly perceived a nation stained with inequities—in the distribution of power, in the dispensation of justice, in access to opportunity. The "essential" trouble, he wrote in 1964, was "poverty —poverty of goods and poverty of understanding."[1] The New York World's Fair might salute a shining future; "but less than an hour away in Harlem, people live in squalor and despair more closely resembling the nineteenth century. A few hundred miles away, in the remote hovels of Appalachia, the life of the people is, if anything, worse than it was a hundred years ago."[2] Such disparities were unacceptable. "Government belongs where evil needs an adversary and there are people in distress who cannot help themselves." It was his ambition, he said, to make the department over which he presided "more than a Department of Prosecution and . . . in fact, the Department of *Justice*."[3]

I

"The law, especially in criminal cases," he said in his first interview as Attorney General, "favors the rich man over the poor in such matters as bail, the cost of defense counsel, the cost of appeals, and so on."[4] In his first press conference he announced a committee to explore the plight of the poor in federal courts. Early in 1963 the committee, headed by Professor Francis Allen of the University of Chicago Law School, submitted a searing report, "Poverty and the Administration of Federal Criminal Justice." The findings documented the conviction Kennedy had taken from the Rackets Committee that the United States had in fact two systems of criminal law. Most guarantees of due process—the rights to counsel, to present evidence and call witnesses, to trial by jury, indeed to the very presumption of innocence itself—were effective only for those who could pay for them. The poor lost out at every point along the line.

The Allen committee devoted particular attention to bail, the most visible example of the power of money in the system of justice. Every year thousands of poor people remained behind bars for months after arrest. "They are not proven guilty," Kennedy said. "They may be innocent. They may be no more likely to flee than you or I. But they must stay in jail because, bluntly, they cannot afford to pay for the freedom."[5] In March 1963 Kennedy instructed federal attorneys to release defendants in specified categories without bail. (In the first year the default rate, 2.5 percent, turned out to be slightly less than that for those released on bail, and a thousand man-years of liberty were saved.)[6] In the spring of 1964 he convened the National Conference on Bail and Criminal Justice. In due course Congress passed the federal Bail Reform Act.

He took up the problem of counsel for indigent defendants. "Any person haled into court, who is too poor to hire a lawyer," Justice Black wrote for a unanimous court in the 1963 case of *Gideon* v. *Wainwright*, "cannot be assured a fair trial unless counsel is provided for him." *Gideon* applied to state courts. But within ten days of the decision the Department of Justice drafted the bill that, as the Criminal Justice Act of 1964, extended guarantees of competent defense to every stage of federal judicial proceedings.[7] Kennedy then established the Office of Criminal Justice to deal with social issues affecting the criminal process from arrest to rehabilitation.

He gave strong support to James V. Bennett, the notably humane director of the Bureau of Prisons. "Let us reject the spirit of retribution," he said in one speech, "and attempt coolly to balance the needs of deterrence and detention with the possibilities of rehabilitation." J. Edgar Hoover noted on the border, "Sounds like some of Bennett's philosophy," and thereafter fretted about Kennedy's "soft treatment approach to criminals."[8] But, over Hoover's opposition, Kennedy and Bennett closed down the gloomy dungeons of Alcatraz.[9] They set up halfway houses to help ease the return of convicts to civilian life. Kennedy worried especially about youthful offenders, too often incarcerated with, and thereafter indoctrinated by, their hardened seniors.

In 1963 they began planning youth centers for persons under twenty convicted of federal crimes.*

He was much concerned, as were Bennett and the President, with inequality in sentencing. "On pardons and commutations," Robert Kennedy said later, "we made a real major effort and really major breakthrough. President Eisenhower didn't believe in them because he thought it was interfering with judicial prerogatives."[10] John Kennedy, Bennett wrote in his memoirs, "whose compassion exceeded that of most men, struck out against the injustices that he perceived in our sentencing procedures," reducing the sentences of more than one hundred prisoners and granting unconditional pardons to five hundred more who had demonstrated good citizenship after release. "Without exception," said Bennett, "Kennedy approved my recommendations for executive clemency, and he invariably reminded me to let him know when I came across a glaring example of excessive sentencing."

Robert Kennedy's "contribution to even-handed justice," Bennett added, "was also immense." Bennett instanced the case of a destitute young man who robbed a bank in quest of money to support his family and then, overcome with remorse, turned himself in to the FBI. He got forty years in the penitentiary. The Attorney General had it reduced to fifteen years, the more customary sentence for bank robbers.[11] (Kennedy was fond of Jim Bennett. At the surprise party marking the director's twenty-fifth anniversary as head of the prison system, the Attorney General gave him a cake with a file baked inside.)[12]

The case of Junius Scales aroused particular attention. Scales had been the only Communist sent to prison under the membership clause of the Smith Act. There was no suggestion of espionage or other criminal deeds. He had received a longer sentence than top Communists convicted under other sections of the act. After the Red Army invaded Hungary in 1956, he had broken with the party and was thus serving his sentence as an ex-Communist. In 1962 anti-Communists of the left, led by Norman Thomas and Joseph Rauh, urged his release. But Scales, even as an ex-Communist, flatly refused on

---

* Dr. Robert Coles attended the dedication in 1968 of the Robert F. Kennedy Youth Center in Morgantown, West Virginia. An old miner said to him, "I'm sure they'll take a lot better care of those boys than they did with us when we went into the mines. I was 15, like they must be, going into that Center, and there was no Robert Kennedy looking over us, no sir, there wasn't—just a lot of greedy coal operators that didn't care if we lived or died" (Robert Coles, "Youthful Offenders," *New Republic*, October 4, 1969).

grounds of principle to identify people he had known in the party. This infuriated J. Edgar Hoover. The release of Scales, he told the Attorney General, would make it impossible for the FBI to insist that Communists or ex-Communists name names in the future. Byron White and Nicholas Katzenbach successively recommended against commutation of Scales's sentence.[13]

"There was some fuss about it," Kennedy told John Bartlow Martin in 1964,

> and I guess Norman Thomas and a lot of other people came to see me at various times or wrote me letters and I said that . . . I would take a look at it but I wasn't going to take any look at it if they picketed or made it appear that it was going to be because of political reasons. . . . I just asked them if nobody would get in touch with me for a period of time that I would take a look at it and if I thought it should be done that I'd do it. And nobody did do anything and I never heard for a period of time and I looked at it. . . . I just thought that . . . based on the penalties for others, the amount of time of his sentence and . . . the problems he had at home [a sick wife] that . . . I had his sentence commuted.
> I never discussed it with the President.[14]

Anthony Lewis recalls the Attorney General mumbling late in 1962, "We're going to let your friend Scales out." He said it, Lewis continued, "embarrassedly, almost grumpily; he did not like to look soft."[15]

Scales was back with his family on Christmas Eve. Rauh summed up the significance of Kennedy's decision: "The act of granting clemency to Scales without his 'cooperation' by 'naming names' is a repudiation of the loyalty test long used by the FBI. . . . For the first time since the rise of McCarthyism an Attorney General has refused to treat a man's unwillingness to inform on others as a ground for withholding favorable government action in his case."[16]

John Stewart Service, the old China hand, who had been dismissed from the State Department on security grounds in Eisenhower days and subsequently won reinstatement in the courts, sued State for his back pay. John Douglas of the Civil Division believed that Service's suit had merit and that Justice should settle but warned the Attorney General there would be objection on the Hill. Word promptly came back to go ahead.[17] A well-known scholar on Sino-Soviet affairs applied for the validation of his passport to permit travel to mainland China. The CIA and the FBI scented espionage, because the scholar, who had once worked for the research side of CIA, had, in violation of regulations, taken copies of his own studies with him when he moved on to the RAND Corporation. Might he not have taken other documents and be planning to defect to Peking? Kennedy told Abba

Schwartz, head of the Bureau of Security and Consular Affairs at State, he was sure any violation was technical; but the FBI was pressing for criminal action. It would be a tragedy to ruin a man on flimsy evidence. Would Schwartz look into the matter? After talking to the scholar, Schwartz agreed with Kennedy. Together they persuaded the security agencies that the scholar was at most subject to administrative reprimand. "The decent instinct of RFK," Schwartz said later, "saved an individual and an important career."[18]

There were other such cases. "I should have been happy, looking back," his most distinguished living predecessor wrote him early in 1962, "to think that I had done as much for civil liberties when I was Attorney General as you have done in your first year." "Such praise, from you especially," Kennedy replied to Francis Biddle, "is tremendously appreciated."[19]

II

Argument before the Supreme Court was the responsibility of the solicitor general. Few solicitors general had discharged this duty with more style than Archibald Cox. He knew the law, and he knew the Court; and, like all the best solicitors general, he entered so intimately into decisions as to become, at times, a sort of tenth justice. The Attorney General had not known Cox well before 1961. Their most extended contact had come in 1958–59 when Cox was working with John Kennedy on labor legislation and Robert Kennedy had argued for more stringent provisions than Cox, or John Kennedy, thought wise.[20] But the two men quickly established relations of mutual confidence.

It had become a custom for Attorneys General to argue one case in person at the summit. Even had there been no such custom, Kennedy would have wished to appear before the Court. He wanted, as Burke Marshall said, "to show to himself and everybody else that he could do it."[21] The obvious field was civil rights. But "I had done so much in civil rights," Kennedy recalled. "I was up to my ears in civil rights . . . so I selected an apportionment case."[22]

In a number of states the overrepresentation of rural areas, whether in state legislatures or in party primaries, had given the countryside disproportionate power against cities and suburbs. "The yokels hang on," as H. L. Mencken had written in 1928, "because old apportionments give them unfair advantages. The vote of a malarious peasant on the lower Eastern Shore counts as much as the

Justice and Poverty

votes of 12 Baltimoreans."[23] By 1962, despite large population shifts, apportionment lines in more than half the states had not been redrawn for over a quarter century.[24] City mayors found the situation intolerable. So did political scientists. Malapportionment was held the cause of a host of troubles—especially the neglect by state government of the cities and the urban poor, the consequent encroachment of the national government and the enfeeblement of federalism. Still there were, as Marshall observed later, "lots of reasons" for Robert Kennedy not to get into it. Situations of malapportionment had historic sanction. Reform threatened vested political interests, especially in the south, where the Attorney General was sufficiently unpopular anyway. Nevertheless Kennedy insisted. He saw apportionment as an issue of deep concern and wide consequence. The case he chose at the end of 1962 involved the county-unit system in Georgia.

Earlier in the year the Court had changed its mind about its power to deal with inequality in voting. In 1946 it had pronounced unequal representation a political question, beyond judicial remedy. "Courts," Justice Frankfurter warned in *Colegrove* v. *Green*, "ought not to enter this political thicket."* But did citizens really have no recourse when unequal representation paralyzed the very processes of political self-correction? With the increase in urban and suburban population in the fifties, protest rose against the impasse created by judicial restraint. In 1958 Senator John Kennedy, adapting Lincoln Steffens's phrase, called discrimination against city dwellers in the apportionment of state legislatures "the shame of the states."[25] In the same year, Anthony Lewis, Robert Kennedy's Harvard classmate and after 1961 his increasingly close friend, made a tightly reasoned argument for judicial intervention in the *Harvard Law Review*.[26]

Tennessee presented a case in point. A law passed in 1901 still determined the composition of the state assembly. Legislators showed no inclination to change the law against their own interest. Local remedies were exhausted. As the Kennedy administration took over, a Tennessee lawsuit—*Baker* v. *Carr*—was making a slow ascent toward the Supreme Court.[27] Robert Kennedy's Tennessee pals—Seigenthaler, John Jay Hooker, Jr., E. William Henry—asked that the Department of Justice enter the case as *amicus curiae*. The solicitor general's intervention in fact rescued the case. Accepting Cox's prop-

---

* *Colegrove* v. *Green*, 328 U.S. 549, 556 (1946). Though Frankfurter wrote the opinion of the Court, actually only two other justices agreed with him that representation was a political question and not justiciable. Justice Rutledge concurred in the result on other grounds and was responsible for the 4–3 decision.

osition that gross and unreasonable malapportionment was in conflict with the equal protection clause of the Fourteenth Amendment, the Court held in *Baker* v. *Carr* in March 1962 that apportionment was a justiciable issue and that courts could provide relief. Though it declined to reach the question of substantive standards, it reversed its 1946 decision in effect if not in form. Robert Kennedy promptly saluted the decision as "a landmark in the development of representative government."[28]

"The right to fair representation and to have each vote count equally," President Kennedy said in his next press conference, "is, it seems to me, basic to the successful operation of a democracy."[29] Senator Richard Russell, Georgia on his mind, observed grimly that the Court had "set out to destroy . . . the system of checks and balances."[30]

III

The Georgia county-unit system had survived four earlier challenges before the Supreme Court.[31] The issue it presented was not, strictly, apportionment but suffrage. The system heavily weighted the Democratic primaries in favor of low-population rural counties. One vote in Echols County counted as much as 99 in Fulton County. The issue was whether or not 16 percent of the electorate had the right to decide statewide nominations (indeed, elections; for Georgia was then a one-party state).

This, Cox said in a memorandum to Kennedy, was an "easier" question than legislative apportionment. "The distribution of seats in the legislature almost inevitably requires some choice between different theories of representation. There is no reason not to give everyone an equal vote in a statewide election." However, he warned the Attorney General against adopting the position "that all votes must be given equal weight. In my opinion, we should not argue for this dogmatic interpretation even in the case of statewide elections, for although Justices Black and Douglas might buy it, the argument is very unlikely to command the assent of a majority. Furthermore, we do not need to go so far in the present case." Cox recommended the narrower argument that any departure from equality of voting power had to have "rational foundation in terms of a permissible State policy." Kennedy's problem of advocacy, Cox said, was to knock down all conceivable justifications for discriminating in favor of the country voter. "The best argument for you to make will be whatever you, yourself, find most persuasive. . . . The burden of convincing the Court that it is just wrong-*wrong*-WRONG will come in oral argument, for the point is just as much emotional as rational."[32]

Kennedy retired over the Christmas holiday in 1962 with Cox's memorandum, a lengthy brief from the solicitor general's office and a yellow legal-sized pad, on which he scratched page after page of notes.[33] On January 17, 1963, improbably clad in morning coat and striped trousers, looking, said one reporter, "like a nervous and uncomfortable bridegroom,"[34] Kennedy confronted the Court in the case of *Gray* v. *Sanders*. It was his first, and last, appearance as a lawyer in a courtroom. His mother, his wife, two sisters, his brother Edward, his sister-in-law Jacqueline and four of his children were in the audience. The Kennedys, it was observed, outnumbered the justices.

The Attorney General spoke without notes. His argument partook of Cox's constitutional caution. Kennedy thus asked the Court only to determine the validity of the existing Georgia system, not "of some other county-unit system which has not yet been enacted." The "ideal" was "to have one's vote . . . given equal weight with the votes of other citizens," but he was not, he said, "arguing that in all cases all votes must be identical in value." Still any deviation from the ideal must be for "a full, good and complete reason." Ultimately at stake, he concluded, was the capacity of state government to deal with the problems of an increasingly urban and suburban nation.[35] Overcoming his early unease, he finished with a flourish by quoting "that old Massachusetts saying, 'Vote early and vote often,'" and concluding: "With Georgia's county-unit system, all you have to do is vote early."[36] He handled questions from the bench with dispatch and was adjudged to have performed his task in style. (Success did not go to his head. A few days later, a group of students came in to see him. "Do you know what they asked me?" he said to Joseph Dolan, and he quoted a question about reapportionment. Looking at Dolan "with that look he has," Kennedy said, "They got a lot of nerve asking the Attorney General of the United States questions like that. They should ask a lawyer.")[37]

On March 18 the Court, speaking through Justice Douglas, struck down the county-unit system. Douglas distinguished the issue of suffrage from that of legislative representation. Then, sweeping beyond Kennedy's argument, he proposed a conclusion applicable to both issues: "The conception of political equality from the Declaration of Independence, to Lincoln's Gettysburg Address, to the Fifteenth, Seventeenth, and Nineteenth Amendments can mean only one thing—one person, one vote."[38]

This was Robert Kennedy's destination too. He was all for the courts plunging into the political thicket. "He wanted, instinctively," said Marshall, "to see the democratic process work right. It was the same instinctive reaction he had about the Negro vote. If you set up a political structure dependent on the vote and rig it so that the vote doesn't count, that's no good."[39] Cox wished the same result but by a different route. A strong liberal in objectives, he was conservative about the role courts should play in attaining them. "In a state constitutional convention," he wrote the Attorney General, "my vote would go to apportion both houses of a bicameral legislature in accordance with population, but I cannot agree that the Supreme Court should be advised to impose that rule upon all 50 states by judicial decree. . . . The court's ability to make the system work depends upon exercising enough self-restraint not to get too far ahead of the country on too many fronts."[40]

A flood of apportionment cases was now rising toward the Court. The problem of substantive standards, avoided in *Baker* v. *Carr,* could no longer be escaped. In August 1963 Cox recommended that representation on the basis of population be required in one house of every state legislature but that deviations—substantial but not extreme—be permitted in the other house. "We should not argue that both houses must be apportioned on the basis of the principle—one man, one vote."[41] Kennedy wanted to go faster and farther. But he deferred to Cox's knowledge of the Constitution and the Court. And, as Anthony Lewis, whose expertise on the issue gave him a lively role behind the scenes, said later, "Bobby was not in a position to order Archie to say something he did not believe; to have a fight with his Solicitor General, moreover, would not help the case because the court . . . might see any brief filed over Archie's head as a political, not a legal, document."[42]

Still Kennedy kept pushing Cox in the gentlest way, suggesting, directly and through intermediaries, that the solicitor general's briefs, if they did not affirm the one-man, one-vote standard, must at least not discourage plaintiffs who wished to move toward it. A Colorado case, where malapportionment had been sustained by a popular referendum, gave Cox particular difficulties. As Cox and Marshall were taking an elevator to Kennedy's office to discuss the case, Marshall said, "Look: Bob won't order you to file a brief you really think you shouldn't file. He won't file any brief without your name. But you

Justice and Poverty

must recognize his problem. At your urging we have supported the plaintiffs in all these cases. Suddenly to turn around and oppose the Colorado plaintiffs puts him in an impossible position." Cox said, "I'll work out something."[43]

Cox still believed that the Court would not buy one-man, one-vote; nor did he think it would be good for the Court if it did. But, recognizing the problem, he drafted language in the Colorado case, that, as Kennedy said, "would satisfy his own conscience and would cover what I thought should be the position of the United States Government."[44] Cox, as he freely confessed thereafter, was wrong in his forecast. In June 1964 Chief Justice Warren, speaking for a nearly unanimous Court, ruled that both houses of a state legislature had to be apportioned on the basis of population. When the Court was first asked to treat malapportionment as a justiciable issue, Cox said a decade later, "the counsel of caution was ardently advocated [but] the Court overrode the objections, entered the political thicket, and emerged stronger than ever before."[45]

On retirement, Warren called the reapportionment cases the most important decisions of his Court. This seems an overstatement. The reapportionment revolution did not have the results predicted in the reinvigoration of representative government, the salvation of the cities or the strengthening of federalism.[46] Evidently malapportionment was not the root of all evil. Nonetheless, by outlawing manifest distortions and irrationalities, the reapportionment decisions increased the chance of finding solutions within the political process.

As for Kennedy, Cox remembered two salient qualities. One was his willingness to listen. "He often had strong immediate reactions; but, if you said, 'Now, wait, Bob . . .' and outlined other considerations, he would wait, listen, reconsider." The other was his legal intuition. "He did not know a great deal about case law. But he had the quality Hugo Black had so strongly. I would present a technical problem to him in technical terms—very often a problem remote from his training or experience—and he could put his finger at once on the gut issue."[47]

IV

Robert Kennedy's main connection with businessmen was through the Anti-Trust Division. He had long embraced its guiding principle. "Too much power scares me," he said in his first interview, "whether we find it in a trade union or in a corporation."[48] But, as he told Lee

Loevinger, the assistant attorney general in charge, antitrust was "a strange field of law" for him.[49]

Loevinger, a fluent Minnesotan, spent too much time for the Attorney General's comfort making speeches around the country and too little taking hold of his organization. "He was not an administrator," said Seigenthaler, "and he never really got that division going."[50] On his part Loevinger evidently felt inhibited by the administration's desire not to hurt business confidence at a time of nascent economic recovery. "It is probably true," he told a reporter, "that we are affected by business uncertainties to the point where we are holding up cases with a novel or uncertain legal approach. We are sticking pretty much to the predictable, to the established lines."[51]

In 1962 Kennedy asked Ramsey Clark and Joseph Dolan to survey the Anti-Trust Division. Their report confirmed Kennedy's feeling that, as Clark put it, most antitrust cases arose from the complaints of competitors; there were "no priorities or purpose; you just sat there and whatever happened, happened."[52] The next year Kennedy moved a reluctant Loevinger over to the Federal Communications Commission. William Orrick took his place.

In antitrust, as elsewhere in Justice, the Attorney General was determined to keep politics out. "The Anti-Trust Division during the period I was there," Loevinger said later, "was run on a strictly merit basis, and I never had one hint from either Bob Kennedy or Byron White or anyone else that it should be run any other way. . . . There was simply no pressure from either of the Kennedys."[53] Orrick said: "He would sign the complaint, and he'd ask, 'Is it right? Must you always sue our largest contributors?' And he laughed, but then he'd sign it. There was no question with him about ducking."[54]

In spite of his nondescript antitrust record, Robert Kennedy was regarded with gloomy mistrust by businessmen. In November 1961 he spoke to the Economic Club of New York. Joseph Kennedy dropped by his suite at the Waldorf while his son was changing into a dinner jacket. "I see you're living it up, really in the tall cotton, aren't you?" said the ambassador. "My father's a millionaire," said the Attorney General. The title of his speech—"Vigorous Anti-Trust Enforcement Assists Business"—was evidently thought up by someone who supposed that businessmen really believed in free competition. Kennedy began with a trail of jokes, all of which fell flat, and went downhill from there. He had hoped to repeat the success of his Georgia speech where he candidly told a southern audience he intended to enforce civil rights decisions. Candor about enforcing the antitrust law had less success. When he finished, the applause, reported Edwin Guthman, was "scarcely perfunctory."[55]

Then came the great steel battle of 1962. This episode had its origin in the administration's effort to hold down prices and wages in the bellwether automotive and steel industries and thereby to break, in Walt Rostow's phrase, "the institutional basis for creeping inflation."[56] This policy, fully understood by the union leadership, was, as Roger Blough, U.S. Steel's executive officer, mystifyingly said a dozen years later, "simply not comprehended by those negotiating the steel contract on the company side." He added that this belated illumination might "help explain President Kennedy's reaction to the steel price increase and make his reaction more understandable."[57] Indeed it might.

The administration had thought its wage-price guideposts secure when it induced the Auto Workers and then the Steelworkers to accept noninflationary contracts. A few days after the steel wage agreement, on a Tuesday afternoon in April, Blough made his celebrated call on the President to announce U.S. Steel's decision to raise prices six dollars a ton. Five other companies promptly followed suit. Blough later justified his *démarche* by condemning the idea of a President setting out "to substitute his own action for the action of the marketplace by trying to set prices for any competitive product."[58] Kennedy agreed that, if Blough's challenge succeeded, it meant the end of the government's stabilization effort. He felt, moreover, that Blough, who had said nothing to him, to Secretary of Labor Goldberg or to David McDonald of the Steelworkers about raising prices, had personally double-crossed them all. "You kept silent," Goldberg rebuked Blough, "and silence is consent. One thing you owe a President is candor."[59] Kennedy, coldly furious, called McDonald: "Dave, you've been screwed and I've been screwed."[60]

The details of the battle for price stability are amply recorded elsewhere; but Robert Kennedy's participation is relevant here. "The President called me in my office around 6:00 P.M.," he noted in a memorandum dictated a few days later, ". . . to tell me that Blough had been in to see him. . . . Obviously he was outraged." The next day Sorensen read the Attorney General the statement the President planned to make in his press conference. Robert Kennedy:

> I thought the statement was (1) too personal; and (2) that the President's statement should be one of sorrow for the country and the betrayal of the steel executives rather than on any personal feeling. I suggested, therefore, that he bring in about the Sergeants in Vietnam, the reservists who had

been called up, the unions that had kept their wage demands down, and the other sacrifices that were being made. . . . It was agreed that Sorensen would write it up and the President will give it along those lines."[61]

So far, so good. But the President had also told his brother on the first day that "he was particularly anxious that we should check on the newspaper report of the interview of the President of Bethlehem Steel." Bethlehem was the second largest steel company; and the press had quoted Edmund F. Martin, its president, as saying in a stockholders' meeting shortly before, "There shouldn't be any price rise. We shouldn't do anything to increase our costs if we are to survive."[62] When Bethlehem imitated U.S. Steel and put up its prices, the question arose of price fixing in violation of the antitrust laws. The Attorney General accordingly asked the FBI to check Martin's exact words with the reporters who wrote the stories. Preliminary investigation in antitrust cases was a routine mission for the Bureau. This one was executed with unbecoming alacrity.

Katzenbach instructed Courtney Evans to have the agents interview the steel executives at their offices. He gave no specific directions about interviewing the newspapermen.[63] With its knack for the strict construction of orders, the Bureau evidently felt free to question the reporters at any place or time. FBI agents thereupon visited them at their homes in Philadelphia and Wilmington before dawn the next morning. This caused great excitement in the newspapers, with much scholarly reference to police-state tactics, the Gestapo and the dreaded "knock on the door."

The Attorney General, as usual, took full responsibility for the Bureau. In actuality, beyond his general request that the FBI find out what Martin had said, he had nothing to do with the midnight calls. "That was a decision the FBI made," he said privately, ". . . nor did they discuss it with me, nor did I even know who they were interviewing."[64] "We were the ones," said William Sullivan of the FBI, "who made the decision to interview [them] at night, not Kennedy."[65] The Attorney General often wondered about the bizarre timing. "He was sometimes suspicious," observed Douglas Dillon, "that things like this might have been done on purpose by Edgar Hoover to embarrass him. I can't have any judgment on that, but I know that that was his feeling."[66]

V

If Robert Kennedy must be acquitted on the Gestapo charge, there can be no question that he was prepared to play against U.S. Steel, as he himself said later, with a "hard ball." He convened a grand jury to see whether the steel companies had violated criminal law. "Then we looked over all of them as individuals. . . . We were going to go for broke—their expense accounts and where they'd been and what they were doing. I picked up all their records. . . . I told the FBI to interview them all—march into their offices the next day. . . . We weren't going to go slowly. . . . So all of them were hit with meetings the next morning by agents. All of them were subpoenaed for their personal records and . . . their company records."[67]

At the same time, there was strong public reaction against the companies. The price increase, said William Scranton, Republican candidate for governor in Pennsylvania, was "wrong for Pennsylvania, wrong for America, wrong for the free world."[68] The combination of national indignation and hard ball had its effect. On Friday morning Clark Clifford, who had been brought in to help Goldberg in negotiations with Blough, reported that U.S. Steel was ready to roll back halfway; what would the President say? "Not a damn thing," said Kennedy. "It's the whole way."[69] Late Friday afternoon Blough surrendered. It had been an intense seventy-two hours.

"Jack was very anxious to make peace with industry," Robert wrote a few days later. "His political strength rested with staying in the middle of the road. That was why it was so difficult to attack him, he felt. Therefore, it was important to make up to business so that they would not consider him or the Administration anti-business." Clifford and Charles Bartlett, who had also been active behind the scenes in arranging talks with steel executives, "were anxious that the Grand Jury be delayed or forgotten. I was very anxious that I continue although in low key." Clifford "expressed himself as very anxious that we do not take any action against the companies. . . . I had a strong exchange with him that caused Jack to say later to Charlie Bartlett, joking I think: 'What we need in this Administration is a good Attorney General that can be fixed.'"[70] One likes that "joking I think."

The Attorney General finally accepted the line. On Monday night, according to Blough, he assured the general counsel of U.S. Steel that the administration was not vindictive and there would be no further problems with subpoenas and grand juries.[71] The Attorney General was talking, however, about inquiries related to the recent price rise. The Anti-Trust Division had been preparing other indictments against the steel industry before Blough exploded his bomb. "Those were subsequently delayed slightly," said Loevinger, "in order to avoid any impression that they were the result of the steel pricing matter."[72] In these matters the steel companies eventually pleaded nolo contendere.

The President's quest for peace was not helped when word got around that, like his father, he thought that all steelmen were sons-of-bitches. Robert Kennedy, reflecting later on his brother's attitude toward businessmen, said, "Well, he never liked them. I mean, he just always felt . . . that you couldn't do anything with them and there's no way to influence them. I suppose the fact [was] we were brought up thinking that [way]. . . . My father thought businessmen didn't have any public responsibility and we just found out that they were antagonistic."[73] Robert Kennedy concluded for himself the January after the steel episode: "The business community always has a greater mistrust of any Democratic Administration than of a Republican Administration. It is an ideological reflex—obsolete, in my opinion—but that's one of the facts of life. I don't know that businessmen, the big ones, anyway, no matter what we do, will ever be in love with us."[74]

The Kennedys kept on hoping, however, and ended in the worst of both worlds. The steel battle was something of a shock for the President as well as for Blough. Kennedy did not like to use that much power and realized it could not be easily used again; and he did not like to excite that much enmity. His policy toward business thereafter was one of mild appeasement. Archibald Cox, who had been through earlier struggles as chairman of Truman's Wage Stabilization Board, suggested in June that the President might be given authority to delay vital price or wage increases until a public commission rendered a report on economic impact. Kennedy was disturbed, not, as he told me, at the content of Cox's speech but at the timing.[75] The timing was indeed unlucky. The bottom fell out of the stock market the same day, and the White House hastily disclaimed responsibility for Cox's ruminations. (Cox, a little wounded, spoke to Robert Kennedy about the White House reaction. The Attorney General said: "That is an outrage. I read your speech in advance and approved it. You're not supposed to have any political sense. If anyone is to blame for that speech, it's me"—whereupon he called for his car and went over to the White House to set everybody straight.[76]

John Kennedy, Cox said in retrospect, "thought of power as a bank account. You could only draw out so much. He didn't understand sufficiently that power can also be a snowball, gathering momentum as it rolls."[77] In any event, antitrust policy remained in the doldrums, nor did the administration support with much enthusiasm the valiant efforts of Estes Kefauver and his antimonopoly committee on the Hill. Appeasement was in vain. Most businessmen, perceiving that the Kennedys did not like them, responded to their attitudes rather than to their actions and credited them with antibusiness designs they did not have.

The question remained whether the steel crisis had led, as was charged then and later, to a gross misuse of executive authority, especially by Robert Kennedy. "After this display of naked power," wrote Erwin D. Canham in the *Christian Science Monitor,* "whatever its provocation or justification, how free will the American economy be?"[78] "The Government set the price," cried the *Wall Street Journal.* "And it did this by the pressure of fear—by naked power, by threats, by agents of the state security police."[79] In the *New Republic,* Professor Charles Reich of the Yale Law School, noting that the government had demobilized as soon as the price increase was rescinded, asked: "Can acts or conditions that are criminal on Tuesday become less criminal by the following Monday? Are crimes by steel and other industries permitted so long as the criminals 'co-operate' with the administration?" Reich concluded, "It was dangerously wrong for an angry President to loose his terrible arsenal of power for the purposes of intimidation and coercing private companies. . . . Congress has given the President no power to fix the price of steel."[80]

It could be responded that Congress had not given U.S. Steel power to fix the cost of living. Weighty national interests were involved. When Blough made clear his determination to wreck the stabilization effort, Kennedy had to choose between stopping him or letting him get away with it. American Presidents had tried to defend the general welfare against private corporations since the age of Jackson, and Kennedy was in a respectable tradition. Once he had decided to stop Blough, he could no more risk losing than Andrew Jackson could have risked losing to Nicholas Biddle. "Supposing we had tried and made a speech about it, and then failed," John Kennedy said later. "I would have thought that would have been an awful setback. . . . There is no sense in putting the office of the Presidency on the line on an issue, and then being defeated."[81]

So they played with a hard ball, and won. There was no transgression of law or the Constitution. There was, however, selective deployment of executive power. When asked in 1964 whether the possession of so much discretionary authority was not alarming, Robert Kennedy replied, "Yes, it is, and rather scary, there's no question about that; and it can be abused and misused." Still the alternative, he thought, "would have been bad for the country . . . and it would have been bad all around the world because it would have indicated that the country was run by a few manufacturers, and I don't think we would ever have reestablished ourselves. . . . I agree it was a tough way to operate but under the circumstances we couldn't afford to lose it."[82]

As Professor William Goldsmith observed in his magistral study of presidential power, executive aggression sometimes reflects "significant dislocations in the political process itself, which have created conditions and circumstances where it becomes clear that nothing short of an overwhelming mustering of presidential power and influence can correct the balance of public and private interests." In the steel case Goldsmith concluded that "the administration did not overstep the limits of executive power . . . and acted quite properly to protect the common good."[83] The guideposts were preserved. Inflation was contained. Under Kennedy the rate of increase in consumer prices was what another decade would regard as unimaginably small: 1.2 percent in 1962; 1.6 percent in 1963.

Nor did the Kennedys emerge intoxicated with their use of power. Success did not even embolden them to seek improvements in the stabilization policy beyond the guideposts. They simply did not want another major fight with business. In view of this aftermath, it was not perhaps such a famous victory as it seemed at the time. As the circumstances faded from the public mind, what lingered, especially in the business community, was the fantasy of the Attorney General ordering FBI agents to pound on doors in the dead of night. The story quickly expanded to include businessmen as well as reporters; in a few years Lyndon Johnson was reminiscing about "the FBI interviewing Barry Goldwater at dawn."[84] The incident, suitably embellished, consolidated the image of Robert Kennedy as ruthless prosecutor riding roughshod over individual rights, any means to an end.

VI

The Kennedys were more resolute in fighting for the poor and dispossessed than they were in fighting against the rich and powerful. Justice for the Negro was only the most dramatic commitment. There were the Spanish-speaking Americans—half of whom, Robert Kennedy pointed out in August 1963, earned less than the average per capita income, far too many "still the victims of poverty and of social and economic discrimination." When he named a delegation of jurists to represent the United States at the Inter-American Congress of Attorneys General, a majority "for the first time in history" were Spanish-speaking Americans.[85]

Then there were the American Indians. Ramsey Clark's office in Justice, the Lands Division, disposed of more money than any other in the Department; but the Attorney General was not deeply moved by land titles and condemnations. "He thought it was a great bore," Joseph Dolan recalled. ". . . One day he made a great discovery: Ramsey had Indians. And then the friendship began to blossom."[86] Ramsey had Indians because his division dealt with Indian land claims. The division's traditional role had been to oppose Indian claims. Clark and Kennedy now perceived the opportunity to try the novel policy of settling the claims. This approach was not altogether popular. Professional Indian lawyers and witnesses, who had been living off the litigation, did not like to see the cases resolved. Indians themselves, with exalted ideas about the value of their land, were often disappointed by the results. Still Clark, with Kennedy's backing, persisted.[87]

Congress, which had to pass appropriations in each particular case, was especially resistant to big payoffs to Indians. But political pressure on Indian issues, Clark recalled, "would never come directly to me. Bob would never pass it on, just never." When the Oklahoma delegation, led by the redoubtable Robert Kerr, objected to the size of a proposed settlement with the Cherokee Nation, the Attorney General intervened personally. Clark: "Bob didn't have much patience with that because his primary instincts were not legal but humanitarian. . . . 'For God's sake we owe it to the Cherokees, and don't worry about these niceties.' . . . He felt we pushed them around and said so."[88] He said so in speeches too, describing the red man as "the victim of racial discrimination in his own land," pointing out that "the infant mortality rate among Indians is nearly twice that of any other racial group in the country; and their overall life expectancy is twenty years less."[89]

Clark used to wonder why Kennedy cared so much. "He may have had some specific experience with Indians that I don't know about," Clark said, but finally decided that "he just had this burning passion to help people who had been denied justice."[90]

VII

The settlement of land claims and the enforcement of civil rights statutes could go only so far in the redress of grievances. If government belonged where evil needed an adversary and people in distress could not help themselves, then government must devise new forms of action.

It all began mildly enough when Robert Kennedy in his first press conference spoke about the "alarming increase" in juvenile delinquency. The predicament of the young always concerned him; in part, no doubt, because of the contrast between his own economically secure childhood and the scramble for survival among kids in the slums. So much depended on where one began. Jack Newfield once asked him what he might have become if he had not been born a Kennedy. He replied, "Perhaps a juvenile delinquent or a revolutionary."[91] Widespread delinquency seemed to him a self-evident symptom of derangement in the social order.

This had not been the prevalent view in his Department. In the January 1961 issue of the FBI's *Law Enforcement Bulletin*, J. Edgar Hoover laid about at those "muddle-headed sentimentalists who would wrap teenage brigands in the protective cocoon of the term 'juvenile delinquency.'" The very phrase, he said, should be "banished forever from our language." He continued this barrage throughout Kennedy's attorney generalship, fulminating periodically against all who would "coddle" those "beastly punks."[92] The Attorney General, undeterred, insisted that juvenile delinquency must receive "priority attention." He named as his special assistant charged with coordinating the federal effort his intimate friend of so many years David Hackett.[93]

Hackett knew nothing about juvenile delinquency. But he was an intelligent man with organizational drive. "Though hardly an idea man himself," said one historian, "the square-jawed former hockey star excelled at recruiting original thinkers, persuading them to join the administration, and then sitting around a table to knock heads. . . . He batted around ideas as he had once shot hockey pucks, never holding onto them for detached or deep speculation, but outpacing many other Kennedy aides in shrewdness, dexterity and guts."[94]

Ignorance may well have been an advantage in a field beset by competing diagnoses. "Everyone I talked to," Hackett said later, "had a conflicting area, and I just listened."[95] The traditional social work approach had seen juvenile delinquency as an expression of individual maladjustment, rooted in the disordered slum family and requiring educational or psychiatric remedy. But some sociologists had long doubted whether case treatment was in fact the answer to delinquency. Hackett encountered the ideas set forth by two professors at the Columbia School of Social Work, Lloyd Ohlin and Richard A. Cloward, in their 1960 book *Delinquency and Opportunity*. Ohlin and Cloward argued that delinquency was more a product of social than of individual pathology. It was what happened when a culture excited middle-class aspirations and then maintained barriers —of status, income, education, race—that made these aspirations unattainable for the poor by legitimate means. The disparity between ideals and opportunities left the poor with the choice of accepting inferior status, thereby emasculating themselves, or of asserting identity through defiance and lawlessness.

Delinquency was thus not the function of individuals nor of groups but of "the social systems in which these individuals and groups are enmeshed." Its cure, Ohlin and Cloward suggested, lay not in changing the client but in changing the structure of opportunity. "The major effort of those who wish to eliminate delinquency should be directed to the reorganization of slum communities."[96] Not everyone accepted the "opportunity theory." Those who traced delinquency to the disturbances of early childhood, for example, considered it excessively optimistic in its intimations of rapid social improvement.[97] Yet its very optimism made it attractive to activists who wanted to *do* something.

While Hackett was pursuing ideas in New York, he was also promoting organization in Washington. The Children's Bureau in the Department of Labor hoped to dominate any federal antidelinquency effort. Hackett, who was greatly impressed by the opportunity theorists, feared that the Children's Bureau was more interested in treatment than in prevention. Robert Kennedy thought the antidelinquency program needed visibility. In May 1961 John Kennedy established the President's Committee on Juvenile Delinquency and Youth Crime, with Robert Kennedy as chairman and Hackett as executive director. A poor title: as it worked out, it might better have been named the Attorney General's Committee on Poverty and Urban Reorganization.[98] Congress passed the Juvenile Delinquency Act in September.

Hackett and Ohlin, who became head of the Office of Juvenile Delinquency, enlisted a number of ardent spirits. In time they were called "Hackett's guerrillas" and lived, as one said, "off the countryside of the government and foundations."[99] The deeper they got into the subject, the more they saw delinquency as a cover word for poverty. "We made no distinction between the two," Hackett said later.[100] Soon they began to see it also as a cover word for racial discrimination. The attack on delinquency required, they believed, comprehensive planning to coordinate federal effort at the local level, where services were actually delivered. Instead of working through a collection of uncoordinated agencies, they wished to create "new local structures through which public and private agencies cooperate."[101]

The Committee on Juvenile Delinquency thus joined the National Institute of Mental Health and New York City in funding a program on New York's Lower East Side called Mobilization for Youth. Mobilization for Youth experimented with a diversity of new approaches —preschool education, vocational training and placement, employment of people from the neighborhood, decentralization in welfare departments, day care and community service centers, legal services for the poor. In 1962 planning began for Harlem Youth Opportunities Unlimited (HARYOU), which had come into being under the direction of Dr. Kenneth Clark when Harlem residents protested the city's decision to import an out-of-neighborhood agency to work with black youth. The Juvenile Delinquency Committee, Clark said later, gave HARYOU "its basic financial and psychological support"; David Hackett's "involvement was such that it could be accurately described as that of an adjunct member of the HARYOU staff."[102]

Hackett meanwhile sent out advance men to stimulate other communities to prepare their own plans. As the committee staff roamed the country seeking promising sites for projects, "we were dismayed," Ohlin said later, "by the absence of demonstrated indigenous leadership in the slum communities."[103] This argued for a planning period to permit the development of local institutions capable of handling outside grants. By the end of 1963, with its initial appropriation coming to an end, the committee had made seventeen grants for demonstration projects in sixteen cities. Along with their insistence on comprehensive planning (followed by careful evaluation of results), the guerrillas had reached certain political conclusions: that the orthodox welfare bureaucracies had a vested interest in regarding delinquency as a problem distinct from poverty and race; that the poor themselves offered a basis from which to challenge the established social service

Justice and Poverty

agencies; that involving the poor in their own salvation through "community action" would enhance their confidence and mobilize them as a constituency. The watchword was "institutional change."[104]

VIII

"Bob Kennedy gave me complete responsibility for it," said Hackett, "and we only asked him to do things that we needed his help on. He gave us in essence no direction." But, Hackett continued, he was eager to be involved. He interrogated the experts, visited projects, chatted with youth gangs in the streets of East Harlem,[105] talked up the program in speeches.

He helped particularly in dealing with Congress, first getting the legislation through and then keeping Edith Green happy thereafter. Mrs. Green, a comely and strong-minded woman who had led the Kennedy forces in Oregon before Los Angeles, was chairwoman of the House subcommittee handling the program. Her ties were with the Children's Bureau. The Juvenile Delinquency Act meant one thing to Hackett's guerrillas, something quite different to Edith Green. She had expected a scattering of small pilot projects flung into operation as fast as possible and administered by agencies already in the field. She profoundly disliked Hackett's conception of a long planning period followed by comprehensive efforts, as she put it, "to bring about any social reforms either city-wide or nation-wide." Mobilization for Youth was her bête noire, dismissed with contempt as that "two million dollar Cloward-Ohlin experimentation program." She finally summoned Hackett to her office for an accounting. The discussion was heated. Thereafter it seemed better for Hackett to stay out of Mrs. Green's way.

Finally Robert Kennedy, of whom Mrs. Green was fond, came himself. Wesley Barthelmes, her administrative assistant, accustomed to seeing legislators call on cabinet members, was surprised by Kennedy's readiness to go to the Hill and spend time on what was, compared to civil rights and organized crime, a relatively small program. The Attorney General contended quietly that projects like Mobilization for Youth were not inconsistent with the aims of the legislation. Phone calls followed: "Well, Mrs. Green, is it going to your satisfaction? I hope we can reach an agreement. It's a very important program." Mrs. Green, only a bit mollified, did not relent in her determination to keep the guerrillas from running wild. Her attitude toward the Attorney General, recalled Barthelmes, was that "of a sorrowful mother for an errant son, which is an attitude Mrs. Green had toward a good number of things. . . . [But] it wasn't sorrowing mother toward an errant son in respect to Dave Hackett."[106]

The Attorney General made another congressional intervention in 1963 at the behest of his sister Eunice. Fifteen years before, Eunice had served in the Department of Justice as executive secretary to the National Conference on Juvenile Delinquency. After marrying Sargent Shriver she had worked with teenage delinquents in Chicago. Her consuming interest now was in a domestic peace corps modeled on Franklin Roosevelt's Civilian Conservation Corps as well as on the undertaking her husband was running with such élan overseas. She worried the President about it until he finally said he had heard enough: "Why don't you call Bobby? See if Bobby could get it going. It's not a bad idea."[107]

She called Bobby, who put Hackett on it. Hackett suggested a cabinet-level committee with the Attorney General as chairman and Richard Boone of the Ford Foundation as staff director. Boone, who had begun as a community organizer in Chicago, has recorded his impressions of the period: "The most important thing about Robert Kennedy then and later was his ability as a listener. He did not pontificate. . . . The thing I remember most was his anxiousness to learn, his ability to put proper questions so everyone could learn, his conservatism in that he did not believe the federal government could do all things for all people, his belief that . . . one of the principal functions of the federal government was to support citizen participation at the local level and to build wherever possible from the bottom up rather than from the top down."[108]

Boone organized a feasibility study, the Attorney General brought his cabinet colleagues together for three Saturday-morning meetings, and in February 1963 the President recommended the establishment of a national service corps designed to apply the Peace Corps principle to the domestic scene. "We visited a state hospital for the mentally retarded on a bright April day when you would have expected all the children to be playing outside," Robert Kennedy said as he portrayed the need to a House committee.

> The children were inside, standing in a room which was bare but for a few benches. The floor was covered with urine. Severely retarded patients were left naked in cubicles, which suggested kennels. . . . Patients were washed by a device resembling a car wash. . . . The only toilets for the approximately seventy patients in a large ward were located in the middle of the

room, permitting no privacy. The hospital's hard-working but inadequate staff could provide at best only custodial care.

There is not even custodial care for great numbers of migratory farm workers, who live in almost unbelievable squalor. . . . One family had been living in their car for three months. . . . The mother was seriously ill. The children were suffering from malnutrition, and were unbelievably dirty because of the lack of sanitary facilities. . . . They had no money and virtually no hope; they did not know where to turn for help.

The Attorney General mentioned other national shames: the Indians, the Alaskans, the illiterates. As thousands of Americans had already volunteered to serve in far corners of the world, so "we are convinced that Americans are equally willing to take on the toughest jobs in this country, whether in a city slum, an Indian reservation or a mining town. . . . Every sixth citizen in the United States needs our help; there are five of us who should help him." The program, he concluded, asked Americans "to invest a year of their lives, at no salary and under Spartan conditions, to help millions of their fellow citizens who, through no fault of their own, are denied the essentials of a decent life. I am proud to admit that this concept is idealistic."[109] The legislation passed the Senate in 1963 but failed in the House. The idea survived.

Kennedy meanwhile took the District of Columbia as his personal responsibility. In 1962 he began paying visits, without publicity and often without notice, to Washington public schools. He organized an annual benefit—Ella Fitzgerald performing one year, Sammy Davis, Jr., the next—to raise a fund to prevent teenage blacks from having to drop out of school for economic reasons. He also arranged for playgrounds, recreation centers, sports programs, summer job programs. He knew these were no more than palliatives, but they "were at least intended," as he later explained to his brother's successor, "to show the children and juveniles that their government cared about their problems."[110]

Typically, he asked his assistant on transportation matters, Barrett Prettyman, Jr., an able young lawyer who had clerked for three Supreme Court justices, to take on juvenile delinquency in Washington. The second precinct led all the rest in juvenile crime. Kennedy discovered that the Dunbar High swimming pool had been closed for eight years for want of $30,000 to make necessary repairs. "He couldn't believe it," Prettyman said. They raised the money in the next two weeks.[111] Patrick Anderson, the information officer for the Committee on Juvenile Delinquency, accompanied the Attorney General on an inspection of the pool, an occasion, Anderson said later, when "I saw him, within the space of ten minutes, at his very best and very worst." An official from the city recreation department, perhaps hoping for commendation, approached him. The Attorney General pointed out curtly that the shallow end of the pool was too deep for small children and asked him what he was going to do about it. "Grant that the man was a bumbler," Anderson wrote later. "A Southern politician would have thrown his arms around his shoulders, listened to his problems—and in five minutes had his promise. . . . But Kennedy had no time for this." Then, moments later, as he began to leave the area, hundreds of black children ran after him, calling his name. "Kennedy moved among them slowly, smiling, rubbing their heads, squeezing their hands, reaching out to the smaller ones who could not get near him. This was not done for show —there were no reporters or photographers along—but because he loved those slum children, loved them as much as he disdained the fool of a bureaucrat who could not give him the answers he wanted."[112]

IX

"That the Kennedys were serious in this approach to juvenile delinquency," wrote Kenneth Clark, "was reflected in the tremendous amount of time and energy which Robert Kennedy devoted to this responsibility."[113] Those involved in the poverty wars often speculated about the reasons for this intense personal concern.

Richard Cloward and Frances Fox Pliven suggested that one motive was political—the desire "to strengthen the allegiance of urban blacks" to the Democratic party.* Certainly, because the Juvenile Delinquency Committee had a three years' supply of funds and kept the lowest of profiles, it provided a means of getting money to blacks in the inner city without provoking further strife with Confederates on Capitol Hill. But this had more to do with preserving urban peace

* Frances Fox Pliven, "The Great Society as Political Strategy," *Columbia Forum*, Summer 1970; Frances Fox Pliven and Richard A. Cloward, *Regulating the Poor: The Functions of Public Welfare* (New York: Random House, Vintage reprint, 1971), ch. 9. David Hackett could recall later only two grants made for political reasons (and both met the committee's criteria). One, made to appease the ravenous appetite of Congressman Adam Clayton Powell in Harlem, involved a grant for his own welfare organization, set up as a rival of HARYOU, an action followed later by Powell's capture of HARYOU and expulsion of the stubbornly independent Kenneth Clark; the other was a program requested by Congressman Albert Thomas of Houston. (David C. Hackett, in interview by author, January 27, 1975.)

than with attracting urban votes. By 1963 the civil rights struggle in the south assured the overwhelming popularity of the Kennedys in the ghettos, even if they had done nothing about juvenile delinquency. Many blacks, in addition, did not vote; and helping the black underclass carried with it the backlash risk of estranging the white working class.

The committee's problem was the opposite: not that of responding to an impassioned constituency but that of creating one. The President could never understand why the poor were not angrier. "In England," he remarked to me one spring day in 1963, "the unemployment rate goes to two per cent, and they march on Parliament. Here it moves up toward six, and no one seems to mind."[114] Hackett's guerrillas were in fact far out in front of both those their programs were designed to benefit and the Democratic National Committee. "The war on poverty," Moynihan accurately observed, "was not declared at the behest of the poor."* He could have added: nor at the behest of the politicians.

Robert Kennedy was of course determined to secure his brother's reelection; but the Committee on Juvenile Delinquency was not an important factor in his calculations for 1964, except as the failure to redeem implied promises might cause trouble. His concern about poverty had deeper sources. Richard Boone attributed it to his compulsive exploration of social reality. "Bobby best understood things by feeling and touching them," he said. "He did feel and he did touch and he came to believe and to understand."[115] Dr. Leonard Duhl of the National Institute of Mental Health, one of Hackett's guerrillas, thought the clue lay in Robert Kennedy's personal history—in his "notion of what an extended family is, and how a family works, and the mutual relationships between a family. When Dave Hackett started to take him around . . . to visit the ghettos," he responded both because he felt so keenly the misfortune of children denied the nourishment of family and because his extended family embraced all children in distress.[116]

All this was true enough. But the question was never a mystery to David Hackett. This was simply the Robert Kennedy who twenty years before at Milton rushed to the side of the underdog and never

---

* D. P. Moynihan, *Maximum Feasible Misunderstanding: Community Action in the War on Poverty* (New York, 1969), 25. Even Cloward and Pliven concede that the programs were "thrust upon a Congress and a public that were at the outset virtually indifferent to the specifics of the legislation" (Pliven and Cloward, *Regulating the Poor*, 266).

worried about embarrassing his friends. Life had only enlarged his knowledge of underdogs—first the Rackets Committee, then the civil rights movement, then the poverty wars. His convictions about participation, his readiness to bypass established bureaucracies, his impulse to experiment with new institutional forms, above all, his instinct for sympathy: these were the key to his growing identification with the minorities of the republic—and theirs with him.

(19)

The Kennedys and the Cold War

THE LAST SEVEN CHAPTERS record an unusually preoccupied life. Few Attorneys General had ever been so busy in so many diverse directions. Yet the Justice Department occupied only a portion of Robert Kennedy's days. In foreign affairs, his brother was navigating tricky waters with a crew of strangers. When storms blew up, there was all the more reason to summon a shipmate of longer standing. On that awful evening in April 1961, as the bad news began to trickle in from the Cuban beaches, the President said to Kenneth O'Donnell, "I should have had Bobby in on this from the start."[1] After the Bay of Pigs he took care to have Bobby in on the critical international decisions.

I

A son of the Cold War, John Kennedy saw it not as a religious but as a power conflict. He did not believe in holy wars. In 1958 he had rejected the proposition that "we should enter every military conflict as a moral crusade requiring the unconditional surrender of the enemy."[2] He was an incisive and persevering critic of John Foster Dulles. He opposed Dulles's idea of responding to local aggression by massive nuclear retaliation at times and places of American choosing. He opposed Dulles's excommunication of the neutralist states of the Third World. He opposed Dulles's insistence on regarding the islands of Quemoy and Matsu off the Chinese coast as casus belli. He worked for closer economic ties with Poland and Yugoslavia, for increased assistance to India and other underdeveloped countries, for the independence of Algeria and of Indochina. He described Castro as "part of the legacy of Bolívar" and his revolution as the result "of the frustration of that earlier revolution which won its war against Spain but left largely untouched the indigenous feudal order." "The world-wide struggle against imperialism, the sweep of nationalism," he wrote, "is the most potent factor in foreign affairs today."[3] When Chester Bowles prepared an article for *Foreign Affairs* advocating the admission of Communist China to the United Nations under a two-China policy, "I showed it to Jack Kennedy, and he enthusiastically endorsed it."[4] Within the Democratic Advisory Council Kennedy sympathized with Harriman, Bowles and Stevenson as against the imperious Dean Acheson and the dedicated Cold Warriors.

Kennedy believed in coexistence because he knew what war was like. "The romanticist point of view of war," said his intimate friend Charles Spalding, "was just stupid as far as he was concerned. He had a high regard for courage and what you inescapably have to do, but he was no romantic about war."[5] His father, moreover, continued to view the Cold War as hopeless folly. "America comes with dollars and talks of economics," the ambassador wrote in 1956, "while the communists come with ideas and talk of justice." If communism were expanding, it was because of the "vacuum of the spirit created by our own pre-occupation with economic and military problems alone." America's pretension of world leadership was full of dangers for the United States: above all, Joseph Kennedy pointed to "an imperialism of the mind, the attempt to make every state into a copy of America."[6] Though the son supported the containment policy, the paternal doubts could not have been entirely without impact.

Kennedy's interest in negotiation with the Soviet Union went back at least to 1953.* His concern grew as the decade wore on. "For over two years," he said publicly in 1960, "I have been urging that we should negotiate with the Russians at the summit or anywhere else. . . . It is far better that we meet at the summit than at the brink." Negotiation would not be easy. But the superpowers had "certain basic interests" in common, and progress in areas of shared concern "might well end the current phase—the frozen, belligerent, brink-of-war phase—of the long Cold War."[7]

One such area was arms control. In 1959 Kennedy argued against the resumption of nuclear testing (as recommended by Governor Nelson Rockefeller), and called for a test-ban agreement.[8] Here Kennedy's old friend from his father's ambassadorial days in London,

---

* That year he sent me for comment a memorandum by Marshall Shulman of Columbia entitled "Starting Point for a Discussion of Possibilities for Negotiation with Soviet Union under Present Circumstances," October 19, 1953; Evelyn Lincoln to author, November 5, 1953, Schlesinger Papers.

David Ormsby-Gore, British delegate to the nuclear-weapons talks at Geneva and the United Nations, played an important role. Robert Kennedy later called him "the motivating force to have the President make this a major area of interest." Ormsby-Gore actually provided the statistics John Kennedy used so effectively in campaign speeches describing how few people in the American government were working on disarmament.[9]

Another area might be central Europe. When George Kennan's heretical disengagement proposals in his BBC lectures of 1958 brought the foreign policy establishment, led by Acheson, down on his head, Kennan, brooding in his Oxford study, was astonished to receive a letter from John Kennedy about his lectures:

> I should like to convey to you my respect for their brilliance and stimulation and to commend you for the service you have performed by delivering them. . . . Needless to say, there is nothing in these lectures or in your career of public service which justifies the personal criticisms that have been made. I myself take a differing attitude toward several of the matters which you raised in these lectures—especially as regards the underdeveloped world [Kennan had expressed skepticism about economic aid to poor countries]—but it is most satisfying that there is at least one member of the "opposition" who is not only performing his critical duty but also providing a carefully formulated, comprehensive and brilliantly written set of alternative proposals and perspectives.[10]

After Kennan defended his disengagement proposal in a subsequent article, Kennedy wrote: "You have disposed of the extreme rigidity of Mr. Acheson's position with great effectiveness and without the kind of *ad hominem* irrelevancies in which Mr. Acheson unfortunately indulged last year."[11]

In 1960 Kennedy took a restrained line over the collapse of the Paris summit meeting after the shooting down of the American U-2 spy plane over the Soviet Union. Adlai Stevenson told me he thought Kennedy's postsummit remarks had been "perfect."[12] Kennedy himself was privately critical of a statement put out by the Democratic Advisory Council. He told me "he could not go along with the passage condemning Eisenhower for having gone to the summit without assurance (as a result of preliminary low-level negotiations) that there would be positive results."[13] He took his negotiating credo from Liddell Hart, whose book *Deterrent or Defense* he reviewed that year: "Keep strong, if possible. In any case, keep cool. Have unlimited patience. Never corner an opponent, and always assist him to save his face. Put yourself in his shoes—so as to see things through his eyes. Avoid self-righteousness like the devil—nothing is so self-blinding."[14]

"We should be ready to take risks," he wrote in 1960, "to bring about a thaw in the Cold War."[15]

II

Kennedy joined his call for negotiation with growing concern that an apparent decline in the relative American position might turn the terms of negotiation against the United States. He charged in the campaign that the United States was in trouble—that the Soviet Union had been far more successful in identifying itself with nationalism in the Third World; that the massive-retaliation strategy left the United States helpless in face of aggression too limited or local to justify the use of nuclear weapons; even that Russia was well on its way to nuclear superiority.

The first two points in the indictment were not much disputed. Nor, for the most part, was the third. Legend has it that in 1960 Kennedy and the Democrats knowingly foisted on the American voter the false notion of a "missile gap." In fact, far from being a cynical Democratic fabrication, the idea had been first put forward in 1957 by the so-called Gaither committee, appointed by Eisenhower to examine the American defense position and including in its panels such experts as Jerome Wiesner of the Massachusetts Institute of Technology, soon to become Kennedy's science adviser, William C. Foster, soon to become head of the Arms Control and Disarmament Administration, I. I. Rabi of Columbia and James Killian of MIT. This was not a gang of ideological Cold Warriors. "The USSR," the Gaither report said, "will probably achieve a significant ICBM delivery capability with megaton warheads by 1959. . . . U.S. will probably not have achieved such a capability. . . . This appears to be a very critical period for the U.S."[16]

Eisenhower's Secretary of Defense subsequently confirmed the theory of the gap.[17] The *New York Times* and the *Washington Post* issued grave warnings about it. Retired generals—James M. Gavin in *War and Peace in the Space Age,* Maxwell Taylor in *The Uncertain Trumpet*—enthusiastically expounded it. "Fifteen more years of a deterioration of our [military] position," Henry Kissinger wrote in *The Necessity for Choice* in 1960, ". . . would find us reduced to Fortress America in a world in which we had become largely irrelevant."[18] It is hardly surprising that the Democrats accepted it in good faith in their campaign.

Even critics of the hard line perceived ominous changes in the power balance. In August 1960 George Kennan sent Kennedy a stern letter. "We may, by January," he concluded, "be faced with an extremely disturbing if not calamitous situation. It will in any case be an unfavorable one and in urgent need of improvement." Kennan called for "a strengthening of our defense posture, particularly in the conventional weapons." He urged Kennedy to avoid commitments about summit meetings but hoped that some alleviation might come through reciprocal concessions worked out in private discussions with Moscow. Kennedy replied that he was "very much in accord with the main thrust of your argument, and with most of your particular recommendations."[19]

After the election, Adlai Stevenson, whom Kennedy had named head of a task force on foreign policy, warned the President-elect: "This revolutionary age confronts us with a potential shift in the world power balance of a magnitude hitherto unknown."[20] At the end of December, asked for his thoughts about Kennedy's inaugural address, Stevenson recommended first of all "a frank acknowledgment of the changing equilibrium in the world and the grave dangers and difficulties which the West faces for the first time."[21]

III

In the view from Moscow any capitalist election was, as Khrushchev said, "a circus wrestling match." Still marginal distinctions were worth noting. When the Eisenhower administration in the heat of the canvass asked the Russians to release two American fliers shot down over the Arctic Circle, Khrushchev put it to the Politburo that this would help Nixon. "We thought," he later recalled, "we would have more hope of improving Soviet-American relations if John Kennedy were in the White House." The release of the fliers was deferred.[22]

Khrushchev's remark was not necessarily a compliment. It may have meant simply that he supposed Kennedy would be easier to hornswoggle. In any case amiable signals flashed from Moscow after the election to Harriman, Bowles and the President-elect's brother. On December 12, 1960, Mikhail Menshikov, the Soviet ambassador, invited Robert Kennedy to luncheon. "Khrushchev," Menshikov said, "admired Senator Kennedy's intelligence and vigor and believed that it was now possible to have clear and friendly understanding between the USSR and the US." The ambassador blamed past trouble on middle-level American officials who had distorted the Soviet position on major issues. "He said," Robert Kennedy reported to Dean Rusk, "that he foresaw no barrier to resolving the difficulties between the two countries; that the Soviet Union had no objection to Berlin remaining free under the United Nations, and that he felt that this was another case in which the position of the Soviet Union had been distorted."[23]

The Soviet ambassador continued to hustle members of the incoming administration till John Kennedy, wanting to end the indirect approaches, asked David Bruce to find out specifically what Menshikov had in mind. Menshikov handed Bruce a formal document. Kennan, to whom Kennedy showed the paper, found it "considerably stiffer and more offensive" than Menshikov's own remarks and believed it had been drafted in the Kremlin. He advised Kennedy that "these people had no right whatsoever to rush him in this way. . . . In any case, it was difficult to see how an American President could conceivably meet with people who were putting their signatures to the sort of anti-American propaganda which had recently been emanating from Moscow and Peking."[24]

As the incoming administration struggled to decide from conflicting evidence whether Moscow intended to cooperate or to make trouble, Khrushchev himself appeared to answer the riddle. In a pugnacious speech on January 6, 1961, the Soviet leader proclaimed the irresistible triumph of communism. This would take place neither through world war, he said, because nuclear war would destroy civilization, nor through local war, which could so easily grow into nuclear war. It would come, he explained, through "national liberation wars" in the Third World—the "only one way of bringing imperialism to heel." Citing Vietnam, Algeria and Cuba as promising examples, Khrushchev called Asia, Africa and Latin America "the most important centers of revolutionary struggle against imperialism" and pledged full Soviet support to the insurgencies. "Communists are revolutionaries," he concluded, "and it would be a bad thing if they did not take advantage of new opportunities."[25]

In retrospect it is possible to surmise that Khrushchev's belligerence was intended less as a challenge to the United States than as part of a complex maneuver involving Communist China. In reaffirming his rejection of nuclear war and his belief in "peaceful coexistence," he insisted on positions that Peking found abhorrent. By imbedding them in an otherwise truculent context, Khrushchev may have been trying to prove to the world Communist movement that nuclear coexistence was not incompatible with revolutionary militancy. Perhaps he thought that his bellicosity would bemuse the Chinese while his softer words would gratify the west. Inevitably Peking and Washington heard only the passages written for the other.

Certainly no one in Washington then recognized the extent of Russian-Chinese differences. Much of the State Department continued for three or four more years to go on about "the Sino-Soviet bloc" as if it had been a marriage made in heaven. Nor, recalling Khrushchev as the man who had banged his shoe on a United Nations desk a few months before, did many conceive him as notably subtle. So Washington missed his subtleties, if indeed they were there, and heard only boasts and threats. The State Department so read the Moscow mood in a report to the next President: "There is confidence that the bloc's growing economic and military power will enable it to operate increasingly from a position of strength in dealing with the West. . . . This self-confident posture indicates that vigorous Soviet actions on the international scene are to be expected."[26] The Khrushchev speech appeared to substantiate Hans Morgenthau's proposition: "While Stalin conducted a Cold War of position, Khrushchev was the champion of a Cold War of movement."[27]

The speech, Robert Kennedy said later, was "a major factor. . . . The President made everybody on the National Security Council read the speech and he also made the military people all read the speech."[28] John Kennedy himself took it not only as the authoritative exposition of Soviet policy, especially in its emphasis on national liberation wars, but as a calculated personal test. He responded by devoting his inaugural address a fortnight later almost exclusively to foreign affairs.

This was, he hyperbolically announced, an "hour of maximum danger. . . . Let every nation know, whether it wishes us well or ill," he added with a flourish, "that we shall pay any price, bear any burden, meet any hardship, support any friend, oppose any foe, in order to assure the survival and the success of liberty." But, like Khrushchev, Kennedy mingled hard with soft. He condemned the arms race, asked to "bring the absolute power to destroy other nations under the absolute control of all nations," observed that "civility is not a sign of weakness" and declared: "Let us never negotiate out of fear. But let us never fear to negotiate."[29]

Latter-day critics have concentrated on Kennedy's grandiloquent response—paying any price, bearing any burden, etc.—to what he saw as Khrushchev's flung gauntlet. That passage attracted no attention at the time. It was the cant of the age. The fresh note struck that day was very different. Surveying reactions to the address, the *New York*

Times reported as widely "singled out . . . for special mention" the sentence about never fearing to negotiate.[30] This was appropriate. The passage on negotiation reflected Kennedy's deeper purpose. He did not intend the inaugural as a trumpet blast summoning Americans to war, nor was it so read in 1961. "I wanted to tell you," Eleanor Roosevelt said in a handwritten letter to the young President, "how I felt about your Inaugural address. I think 'gratitude' best describes the kind of liberation and lift to the listener which you gave. I have re-read your words several times and I am filled with thankfulness. May we all respond to your leadership and make your task easier."[31]

IV

For all the inaugural rodomontade, Kennedy had no illusions about a pax Americana. He felt that previous Presidents, especially Eisenhower through his network of pacts, had overcommitted the United States, as in Southeast Asia. He made no new security commitments during his own Presidency. His essential view, declared in a speech nine months after the inauguration, was "that the United States is neither omnipotent nor omniscient—that we are only 6 percent of the world's population—that we cannot impose our will upon the other 94 percent of mankind—that we cannot right every wrong or reverse each adversity—and that therefore there cannot be an American solution to every world problem."[32]

He looked ahead to what he called in 1962 "a world of diversity" —a world of nations, various in institutions and ideologies, "where, within a framework of international cooperation, every country can solve its own problems according to its own traditions and ideals." The "revolution of national independence," as he saw it, was the source and guarantee of the world of diversity. Communism was one element in this pluralistic world. But diversity, he argued, was ultimately incompatible with the Communist dogma that all societies passed through the same stages and all roads had a single destination. "The great currents of history," he said, "are carrying the world away from the monolithic and toward the pluralist idea—away from communism and toward national independence and freedom."[33] In his American University speech of June 1963, he summed up his policy in a deliberate revision of Wilson's famous line: "If we cannot now end our differences, at least we can help make the world safe for diversity."[34]

This was his abiding objective. But, if he did not think there could be an American solution to every world problem, he did not think there could be a Soviet solution either. That was the immediate issue. Khrushchev's speech left no doubt in Washington that the Cold War of movement was on full blast. Lest this drive the world toward the ultimate war, Kennedy considered it imperative to restore the military balance now tilting so alarmingly (it was believed) in the Soviet favor. This meant both overcoming the alleged gap in nuclear missiles and creating a new capacity to fight nonnuclear war.

Eisenhower had stubbornly declined to do these things.[35] As a general, he was far less impressed by the Joint Chiefs of Staff, about whose business he knew everything, than he was by the Secretary of the Treasury, about whose business he knew nothing. He did not think the Russians crazy enough to start a war. He discerned a self-serving budgetary design behind the wailing at the Pentagon wall. He believed that an increase in defense spending could wreck the sacred free-enterprise system and turn America into a garrison state. So he was damned if he would move. In a not unusual irony, Eisenhower was right for the wrong reasons; Kennedy, who did move, was wrong for the right reasons.

Kennedy moved on two fronts, increasing both nuclear and conventional force. After becoming President, he discovered that the CIA questioned the missile gap.[36] McNamara shared this skepticism. But the professional military remained obdurate. No one could be quite sure where the truth lay. Kennedy, in addition, was reluctant to get into a fight with the Joint Chiefs at a time when McNamara was struggling to gain control of the military establishment. General Curtis LeMay, who spoke for the Air Force in the JCS, thought there should be at least 2400 Minutemen missiles; General Thomas Powers, head of the Strategic Air Command, talked to Kennedy of 10,000.[37] When Kennedy and McNamara imposed a limit of 1000, it almost provoked, Under Secretary of Defense Roswell Gilpatric recalled, "a major cleavage with the Chiefs."[38]

The decision to build only 1000 was itself an overreaction, as some in the administration felt at the time and most felt eventually. By autumn 1961 the new reconnaissance satellite persuaded even the Pentagon that the Russians had produced only a tiny proportion of the missiles claimed by the gap-mongers. "If we had had more accurate information about planned Soviet strategic forces," McNamara said later, "we simply would not have needed to build as large a nuclear arsenal as we have today."[39] The build-up had unhappy consequences. It sent the wrong message to Moscow. It ended any hope of freezing the rival strategic forces at lower levels. It compelled Khrushchev to start worrying about the Soviet missile gap.

At the same time, Kennedy called for an increase in conventional force. "We must regain the ability," he had said in June 1960, "to intervene effectively and swiftly in any limited war anywhere in the world."[40] This policy was less controversial at the time. It caused even more trouble in the end. For a dozen years men of good will had sought ways of saving the world from nuclear suicide. The best way to make sure nuclear weapons would never be used, it appeared, was to abandon the Eisenhower-Dulles strategy of predominant reliance on the bomb. "Flexible response," through the multiplication of "options"—a pet word of the day—would make the punishment fit the crime and thereby, it was supposed, more effectively discourage criminality. The nuclear arsenal should be only the shield against a Soviet first strike. Limited-war forces should become the active element in American military strategy. The purpose of all this was precisely to insure against nuclear catastrophe. This view had been elaborated by theorists at MIT, Harvard, Princeton and RAND. It was urged with persuasive force by Maxwell Taylor in *The Uncertain Trumpet*. Kennedy and McNamara embraced it wholeheartedly. It was supported by most of the scientists, economists, political scientists and historians in the Democratic party.*

"Flexible response" was adopted for NATO reasons. It was designed to enable the west to respond to Soviet aggression in Europe

---

* The major dissent in the party's intellectual ranks came from Thomas K. Finletter and Stuart Symington—both of whom served as Secretary of the Air Force under Truman—and Roswell Gilpatric, who had served as under secretary. Their protest was unwisely discounted as the view of otherwise intelligent men who had spent too much time with the air marshals. Gilpatric summed up the opposition case in a prescient letter to the *New York Times* in 1954. The survival of communism in North Korea, North Vietnam and China, Gilpatric said, suggested that "regardless of the amount of United States or United Nations force committed to a local war in the Far East, the odds are against the free world's winning it by conventional arms. A foreign policy based on a willingness and ability on the part of the United States to engage in local wars does not make much sense. . . . There is less likelihood of a 'brush fire' war becoming a major conflict if United States forces are not brought into the combat theatre. . . . Direct intervention by military means should be minimized or wholly avoided. In the Far East the chances of heading off local wars or sealing them off once started hinge largely on non-military measures. . . . By no longer trying to block Communist China's admission to the United Nations the United States might be able to bring about a reduction of tension in southeast Asia that would lessen the chances of further Communist 'nibbling' or 'brush-fire' type of aggression" (*New York Times*, December 29, 1954; see also Thomas K. Finletter, *Power and Policy* [New York, 1954]).

without immediate resort to nuclear weapons. But a fateful side effect was to create forces that could be thrown into local conflicts in the Third World. Taylor's *Uncertain Trumpet* had forecast this possibility in an ominous comment on Dulles's appeal for American intervention to save Dien Bien Phu in 1954: "Unfortunately, such [conventional] forces did not then exist in sufficient strength . . . to offer any hope of success."[41] Not only would the creation of capabilities now make such intervention feasible; the escalation process, imperceptibly raising the level, step by small step, could make commitment irreversible. "One effective way of keeping out of trouble," Bernard Brodie, a penetrating critic of flexible response, later wrote, "is to lack the means of getting into it."[42]

We missed these fatal implications at the time. The diversification of the American defense posture, along with new initiatives in foreign aid, seemed the best way to stabilize that changing power equilibrium about which even men like Kennan and Stevenson had warned Kennedy and about which Kennedy, through a long campaign, had warned the nation. We all saw it as a prelude not to war but to negotiation. Kennedy never tired of quoting Winston Churchill: "We arm to parley."

v

In June 1961 Kennedy met Khrushchev in Vienna. The President's hope was to make a standstill agreement with the Soviet Union. Each superpower, he proposed, should abstain from doing things that, by upsetting the rough balance into which the postwar world had settled, might invite miscalculation and compel reaction by the other. As everyone knows, Khrushchev brusquely rejected Kennedy's general idea (apart from Laos) and threatened specifically to conclude a treaty with East Germany that would extinguish western rights in West Berlin. Kennedy replied that so drastic an alteration in the global balance was unacceptable. Khrushchev himself, he observed, would not submit to a comparable shift in favor of the west. Khrushchev rejoined that, if America wanted war over Berlin, there was nothing the Soviet Union could do about it; he was going to sign the treaty by December 31.*

---

* The legend has arisen that Khrushchev browbeat and bullied Kennedy at Vienna. A reading of the record dispels that impression. Each man made his points lucidly and vigorously. Each held his own. Neither yielded ground. Kennedy, said Khrushchev, "impressed me as a better statesman than Eisenhower. . . . He felt perfectly confident to answer questions and make points on his own. This was to his credit,

Earlier in the year Kennedy had asked Dean Acheson to undertake special studies of the problems of NATO and Germany. Probably he did this in order to hear the "worst case." The result was to define the issue of Berlin in the bleakest terms. In Acheson's view the way to answer Khrushchev was to make the most conspicuous preparations for a military showdown, including the proclamation of a national emergency. The west, he argued, could only lose by negotiation. Merely to propose negotiations would be an admission of weakness. After Acheson alarmed Harold Macmillan by expounding this line during the British Prime Minister's visit to Washington in early April, Averell Harriman said to me, "How long is our policy to be dominated by that frustrated and rigid man? He is leading us down the road to war."[43]

The President listened to Acheson but, as Presidents do, kept his own counsel. "I was never quite sure," Acheson said later, "whether Jack Kennedy was completely sold on the conclusions."[44] His doubts were justified. Meditating on the two influential columnists of the day, the Achesonian Joseph Alsop and the anti-Achesonian Walter Lippmann, Kennedy observed to Bundy and me in May 1961, "I like them both, but I agree more with Lippmann than I do with Alsop." (Bundy said, "That's exactly what Joe is afraid of.")[45] Asked later what the President thought of Acheson, Robert Kennedy said in 1965: "He respected him, and found him helpful, found him irritating; and he thought his advice was worth listening to, although not accepted. On many occasions, his advice was worthless."[46]

In fact, John Kennedy had long advocated talking with the Russians about Berlin. "I do think it may be possible for us to reach a *modus vivendi* with them," he had said in December 1959, "particularly if they feel that any real attack on our position in Berlin would bring war."[47] His policy after Vienna was clear enough: to increase military readiness in order to lay the basis for negotiation. In July the President requested more defense appropriations, called out 150,000 reservists and announced a program, which he soon regretted, of fallout shelters for protection against nuclear attack. At the same time, he rejected Acheson's idea of a national emergency, rejected also the notion of dramatizing the crisis by a tax increase and, explicitly ac-

---

and he rose in my estimation at once. . . . He was my partner whom I treated with great respect. It was my judgment that . . . he wouldn't make any hasty decisions which might lead to military conflict. . . . I think that Kennedy was more intelligent than any of the Presidents before him" (N. S. Khrushchev, *Khrushchev Remembers* [Boston, 1970], 458, *Khrushchev Remembers. The Last Testament* [Boston, 1974], 497–500).

knowledging Russia's security interests in central Europe, declared in a speech on Berlin, "We believe arrangements can be worked out to meet those concerns."[48]

Robert Kennedy disagreed in minor detail. The "great battle" for five days before his brother's speech, he noted,

> was whether we should ask for a tax increase. I was the one who fought for that policy and was supported by all of the Cabinet with the possible exception of Dillon, plus Edward R. Murrow. On the other side was Sorensen and Walt[er] Heller and the financial people [the Council of Economic Advisers]. They felt it would not do any good financially and, in fact, might harm the economy of the country. I felt first that it would be helpful psychologically. It would give everybody the sense of participation which they were lacking at the present time.
>
> The day before the speech we heard some rumblings that Congress might cut down on the foreign aid program if we asked for the tax increase. I think it was this more than anything else that finally determined Jack not to go for it. The following weekend he asked me if I didn't think he was right. I said, "Why don't you admit that you were wrong about it?"[49]

The Attorney General also opposed the fallout-shelter program. "I was a minority of one," he said later. ". . . I thought during that period of time that really you're never going to get it going very well and if we got too far out on a limb on it it was just going to collapse eventually."[50] He was appalled by the horrid emotions the program unleashed. In September, Father L. C. McHugh, a former professor of ethics at Georgetown, argued in *America,* the Jesuit magazine, that shelter owners had the moral right to kill unsheltered neighbors clamoring for admission.[51] Over Thanksgiving, in a Hyannis Port conclave, I presented at the President's direction a critical review of the shelter program. When I discoursed before assembled potentates on the divisive results of the *sauve-qui-peut* ethic, the Attorney General interjected sourly, "There's no problem here. We can just station Father McHugh with a machine gun at every shelter."[52]

In Moscow, meanwhile, Khrushchev directed a group of nuclear scientists, among them Andrei Sakharov, the father of the Soviet hydrogen bomb, to prepare a new series of nuclear tests in order, Khrushchev explained, to bolster the Soviet policy on Berlin. "To resume tests after a three-year moratorium," Sakharov protested, "would undermine the talks on banning tests and on disarmament, and would lead to a new round in the armaments race." Later, at dinner, Khrushchev held forth in characteristic fashion: "Sakharov is a good scientist. But leave it to us, who are specialists in this tricky business, to make foreign policy. Only force [counts]—only the disorientation of the enemy. We can't say aloud that we are carrying out our policy from a position of strength, but that's the way it must be. I would be a slob, and not chairman of the Council of Ministers, if I listened to the likes of Sakharov."[53]

The announcement of the Soviet decision to resume testing produced, Robert Kennedy recorded,

> the most gloomy meeting at the White House . . . since early in the Berlin crisis. I had talked to Jack previously and he was at a loss to explain Khrushchev's decision to resume testing. It was obviously done to try to intimidate the West and the neutrals. . . . I offered the explanation that we were as puzzled about this as Khrushchev must have been puzzled about our invasion of Cuba [the Bay of Pigs]. As we discussed at the time, he must have thought there was something sinister and complicated behind it all or otherwise, we would not have done anything quite as stupid.

The meeting considered steps to be taken if the Soviet Union tried to shoot down allied planes flying to West Berlin. "The major point of contention raised by Jack was if anti-aircraft guns fired on our planes whether we should fire back in that case. General [Lyman] Lemnitzer and General [Maxwell] Taylor felt very strongly that we should fire back. Jack raised the question as to whether we should not have some control over that action. . . . McNamara finally came out for not firing back at land targets without permission."[54]

The atmosphere was grim. "It is obvious," Robert Kennedy continued,

> that as we get closer to D-day the situation becomes more difficult. The people are less and less anxious to stand firm. It is my feeling that the Russians feel this, feel strongly that if they can break our will in Berlin that we will never be able to be good for anything else and they will have won the battle in 1961. They speak with one voice—they do not have to worry about opposition or what other countries think. Their plan is obviously not to be the most popular but to be the most fearsome and to terrorize the world into submission.
>
> My feeling is they do not want war but they will carry us to the brink. . . . I remember Chip Bohlen said in the beginning of the year that 1961 was going to be a fatal one on decision. This was the year the Russians were going to come the closest to nuclear war. I don't think there is any question but that that is true.
>
> After the meeting Jack asked me what I thought. I said I wanted to get off. He said, "Get off what?" and I said, "Get off the planet." I said to all of them that it was much more cheerful at the Department of Justice and that I was not going to come into that room again or have anything to do with them. . . . I told him I wasn't going to take Paul Corbin's advice and run against him in 1964—I didn't want the job.[55]

VI

"I want to take a stronger lead on Berlin negotiations," the President informed Rusk on August 21.[56] "All wars start from stupidity," he said to Kenneth O'Donnell. "God knows I'm not an isolationist, but it seems particularly stupid to risk killing a million Americans over an argument about access rights on an Autobahn."[57] "I am almost a 'peace-at-any-price' President," he told his friend the painter William Walton.[58]

He grew increasingly frustrated in his dealings with the State Department. Those who supported negotiation, like Harriman, Bohlen and Stevenson, were excluded from the Berlin discussions. The pro-negotiation cables from Ambassador Llewellyn Thompson in Moscow were discounted. The head of the Berlin working group, Foy Kohler, was an all-out Achesonian. "If we make it a choice between the status quo and atomic war," Harriman said to me somberly at the end of August, "we will get atomic war."[59] Since the Berlin crisis of 1958–59, the Department had not come up with a fresh thought on Berlin. "The only person who had had any innovations or any ideas or even questions," Robert Kennedy observed, "was Jack himself."[60]

In a White House meeting on September 4, 1961, the President laid out a Berlin negotiating program: the submission of the legal dispute to the World Court; the transfer of the United Nations to West Berlin; the internationalization, under UN control, of the autobahn to Berlin; a UN plebiscite in Berlin; a nonaggression pact between the NATO and Warsaw Pact powers. Perhaps, he said, he should offer these points in the speech he was about to give to the UN General Assembly. Stevenson said they were all excellent points, except the one about moving the UN to Berlin. Kennedy said, "I don't think enough of the UN not to be prepared to trade it for a nuclear war."[61]

The prospect of negotiation encountered wrathful opposition in the country. "Kennedy," said James L. Buckley, "has chosen to identify himself with that segment of American society which is either unwilling or unable to regard Communism as more than a childish bugaboo."[62] Barry Goldwater, already a contender for the next Republican nomination, inveighed against Kennedy's "no-win policy" and asked, in the title of his popular book, *Why Not Victory?* "Our objective," Goldwater wrote, "must be the destruction of the enemy as an ideological force possessing the means of power.... Our effort calls for a basic commitment in the name of victory which says we will never reconcile ourselves to the Communists' possession of power of any kind in any part of the world."[63]

The frenetic atmosphere put the very idea of negotiation in jeopardy. James Wechsler of the *New York Post*, interviewing Kennedy in September, found him "disturbed by the frustrated fury of many of his countrymen who believe our national manhood can be affirmed only by some act of bloody bluster." On the other hand, Kennedy was not prepared to accept humiliation. If the west were pushed out of Berlin, he believed, it would transform the whole European balance and make peace impossible. "Caught in the crossfire of Russian intransigence and domestic Know-nothingism," Wechsler wrote, "he is both keeping his head and sustaining his nerve."[64]

If Professor Robert Slusser's detailed reconstruction of the debate within the Kremlin is correct, the situation may have been even more dangerous than Washington supposed.[65] Khrushchev probably had to contend with his own "why not victory?" crowd. Then Kennedy's military preparations, including even the egregious shelter program, made it clear that the Soviet Union could not win Berlin by psychological warfare. This very likely strengthened Khrushchev against Frol R. Kozlov and the hard-liners. The erection of the Wall in August meanwhile stopped the flight of refugees, thereby reducing the East German pressure for a separate treaty. In October, Khrushchev postponed the treaty deadline. The Berlin crisis, for a moment so frightening to the world, subsided, and was rather quickly forgotten.

Kennedy's desire for a peaceful solution was manifest throughout. "Several attempts have recently been made," Professor Slusser wrote later,

> to depict John F. Kennedy as a dogmatic anti-Communist, a Cold Warmonger whose actions helped create the very crises with which his administration tried to cope. . . . The evidence of Kennedy's patient search for negotiations with the Soviets over Berlin is part of the historical record, and it is only by ignoring the plain facts that the authors in question have managed to construct their image of Kennedy as a Cold Warrior.[66]

Khrushchev clearly agreed. A notable by-product of the Berlin crisis was the extraordinary personal correspondence between the two leaders, initiated by the Russian in order, as he wrote Kennedy, to bypass the foreign office bureaucracies and to eliminate the propaganda obligatory in formal communications.[67]

At home Kennedy went on a speaking tour to vindicate the idea of negotiation against those Americans, like Acheson, who considered it stupidity or, like Goldwater, treason. As long as we understood our

The Kennedys and the Cold War

vital interests, Kennedy declared in November 1961, "we have nothing to fear from negotiations at the appropriate time, and nothing to gain by refusing to take part in them." He condemned "those who urge upon us what I regard to be the pathway to war: equating negotiations with appeasement, and substituting rigidity for firmness." He concluded with deep feeling: "If their view had prevailed, we would be at war today, and in more than one place."[68]

VII

The Berlin episode confirmed John Kennedy's misgivings about the State Department. The next President, he had said in 1960, "will face a world of revolution and turmoil armed with policies which seek only to freeze the status quo and turn back the inevitable tides of change."[69] Kennedy genuinely sought to move beyond the status quo with policies responsive to a world of revolution. His State Department seemed a stuck record, spinning endlessly in the grooves of the past.

The Kennedy skepticism was of long standing. The boys had doubtless learned it at their father's knee. Their own travels in the early 1950s had verified the ambassador's discontents. In 1960 (as recalled by Peter Lisagor) John and Robert Kennedy discussed their plans to regenerate the Department. Their father listened patiently. Finally he said, "Sons, I want to tell you that I once went to see Franklin D. Roosevelt, who made much the same kind of talk that you're making now. He lamented the State Department. He talked about razing the whole thing and starting from scratch. He didn't do a damn thing about it, and neither are you."[70]

They tried. The first problem was to gain control of the national security machinery. Robert Kennedy later summarized his impressions of his brother's impressions of the crucial appointments:

> McNamara he thought the most highly [of]. . . . Rusk speaks very well, [was] awfully loyal and a very nice man. . . . But as far as focussing attention on what should be done himself and sticking with his guns . . . he didn't have that. . . . He didn't have any strong point of view. . . . The President and I discussed on a number of occasions [the possibility] after the [1964] election of moving Rusk out perhaps to the UN and appointing Bob McNamara Secretary of State.* . . . McNamara, under President Kennedy, would have been a good Secretary of State . . . because President Kennedy knew so much about it that he could make the major deci-

---

* Rusk, on accepting the appointment, had told Kennedy that for financial reasons he could remain for only four years.

sions. . . . Under Lyndon Johnson I'm not so certain he would be a good Secretary of State. . . .

[Adlai Stevenson] was always complaining [but] he was the best ambassador we could have had there. . . . Averell Harriman, of course, performed the kinds of functions he performed tremendously well and, of course, the President was very pleased with what he did in Laos and the test ban. . . . He thought [George Ball] was able enough but didn't have any rapport with him particularly. . . . Tommy [Llewellyn] Thompson he thought was outstanding. . . . He liked Ed Murrow very, very much. . . . [But] he really felt at the end that the ten or twelve people in the White House who worked under his direction with Mac Bundy . . . performed all the functions of the State Department.[71]

Kennedy to an exceptional degree became his own Secretary of State—more so than FDR, thought Harriman, who had served them both. "Roosevelt selected the things that he wanted to deal with himself and then left to Sumner Welles the handling of the [other] things. . . . Kennedy dealt with every aspect of foreign policy. . . . He knew about everything that was going on."[72] Still, even if the President might try to know everything, he could not do everything. After the Bay of Pigs, Robert became his brother's eyes and ears around the national security establishment. "If you wanted to get a dissenting idea into the White House," Michael Forrestal told David Halberstam, ". . . the best channel—almost the only channel—was Bobby Kennedy."[73] Kennedy ambassadors, frustrated by State Department orthodoxies, made the Attorney General's office a port of call on home leave. "Where I had need to bring pressure on the State Department," said John Kenneth Galbraith (India), ". . . I found a very good ally in Bob."[74] He was, said William Attwood (Guinea, later Kenya), "the most attentive listener in town."[75] The national security community soon recognized him as a major countervailing force on international decisions. "He seemed to have a damn good intelligence collection apparatus," said Roswell Gilpatric of Defense, "that kept him very well informed of what was brewing."[76] "Kennedy, a student of guerrilla warfare," observed Patrick Anderson, "was applying its techniques to intergovernmental relations."[77]

VIII

The Attorney General's dissatisfaction with the State Department was acute. He nagged the Secretary about the Department's dilatoriness in hiring blacks. Sending Rusk, for example, a *Washington Afro-American* editorial entitled "Anti-Colored U.S. State Department," Kennedy wrote, "Confidentially, there is a great deal of feeling that the fellow who is handling the matter over there is an Uncle Tom and is just not getting the job done."[78]

The Kennedys were also exasperated by State's philosophic attitude toward the travel restrictions that mocked America's pretense of being a truly open society. The Immigration and Nationality Act of 1952 excluded from the United States past and present members of proscribed organizations, such as the Communist party and Communist-front organizations, and advocates of proscribed doctrines, such as communism. However, it also empowered the Attorney General, when State so recommended, to grant waivers for reasons of compassion or of the national interest. The Eisenhower administration administered the proscriptive sections of the act with enthusiasm. Dulles selected Scott McLeod, a Joe McCarthy protégé, as head of the Bureau of Security and Consular Affairs. In the Dulles atmosphere, consuls abroad automatically denied visas to all remotely suspicious persons.

The Kennedys thought it all ridiculous. Exchange agreements with Communist countries permitted the entry of party members from behind the Iron Curtain; but artists, writers and scientists from western Europe or Latin America whom someone had charged with committing an offense against American ideas of political propriety were regularly turned away. Their admission, the President and the Attorney General believed, was unlikely to destroy the Republic. Exposure to the United States might even have a salutary effect. In 1962 President Kennedy appointed Abba Schwartz administrator of the bureau. No greater contrast with McLeod could have been imagined. Schwartz, a liberal, a law partner of James Landis's, a close friend of Eleanor Roosevelt's, had long experience in refugee and immigration problems. He had served as liaison between Mrs. Roosevelt and the Kennedys in the 1960 campaign. "We've lost a good deal of time," the President told Schwartz,

> and I'm fed up with the image we have as a police state. I keep seeing reports about excluding visitors because of their political views. We act like a closed society. I want you to change that. . . . You will be my personal appointee. I expect you to assert your authority and act for me. You know what I want—an Open Society—with the freest possible movement in and out of the country. And a new immigration law. Keep in touch with the Attorney General. I don't know what you'll find in the State Department but you'll just have to work that out.[79]

What Schwartz found in the Department, he wrote later, was

total unawareness of "the President's conception of what the Bureau should and should not do." The Secretary appeared indifferent; indeed Kennedy had never mentioned Rusk in his talks with Schwartz. The Passport and Visa offices contained what Schwartz described as "the hard-core remnants of the McCarthy era."[80] But, as directed, Schwartz kept in touch with the Attorney General. Together they vigorously used Justice's waiver authority to reopen the United States to those formerly excluded.

When, for example, Professor Kaoru Yasui, a Japanese winner of the Lenin Peace Prize, was invited to the United States in the autumn of 1963, his visa application was at first turned down. Schwartz got on the case, discussed it with the Kennedys, the Attorney General issued the waiver and Yasui made his visit. The republic survived, though in a few months Schwartz had to justify the action before seven closed sessions of the House Un-American Activities Committee.[81] Carlos Fuentes, the Mexican novelist, had been refused a visa in 1962 before Schwartz came to the Department. He applied again in 1964. Angie Novello sent a note to Harold Reis of Justice: "It seems he got into a fight with Ambassador [Thomas] Mann who called him a Communist which Fuentes has denied. Would you check with Abba Schwartz about this? The Attorney General is interested in this and thinks he should be granted a visa."[82] Schwartz at once recommended to Rusk that State request a waiver from Justice. Mann continued to object. Rusk stalled. Finally George Ball, Acting Secretary on a day when Rusk was out of town, sent the request over to Justice. Kennedy promptly gave Fuentes his visa.[83]

He favored admitting foreigners to the United States—and permitting them to stay when it was dangerous for them to return home. Once the Iranian ambassador told Rusk that the Shah wanted twenty Iranian students in American colleges sent back to Iran. The Secretary explained to the Attorney General that they were Communists, and the United States had better get rid of them. Kennedy consulted his old friend William O. Douglas in the justice's capacity as an expert on Iran. "I told him," said Douglas, "that that meant the Shah was making up lists for the firing squad"; the students should not be sent home "unless there was a real interest of the national security of this country because these students were lawfully here." "Don't do it," he said to Kennedy, "unless the FBI can prove conclusively that they actually are Communists." In a few weeks Kennedy called back: "The FBI report is in, and not a bloody one of these kids is a Communist, so I just told Rusk to go chase himself."[84]

The freedom of Americans to travel abroad had also suffered attrition under the Cold War. In the forties and fifties the Department grew accustomed to refusing passports to politically suspect citizens. In 1958 the Supreme Court outlawed this practice in the absence of statutory authority.[85] Eisenhower asked Congress to grant the authority. Senator Kenneth Keating of New York introduced a bill giving the Secretary of State power to withhold passports. Nothing happened. The Kennedy administration declined to support the Keating bill. In 1961, however, the Court, by upholding the constitutionality of the Internal Security Act of 1950, brought into play provisions in that law forbidding passports to members of organizations required to register under the act. Robert Kennedy promptly construed the statute as entitling a spurned applicant "to be confronted with the precise information against him and to be apprised of the source of such information."[86] This interpretation outraged Frances Knight, the director of the Passport Office, and she refused to accept it. (Later, the security-obsessed Keating signed a senatorial démarche to the Department designed to entrench Knight in her job.) Robert Kennedy initiated a test case, which resulted in a Court decision in 1964 to invalidate the passport provision in the Internal Security Act.[87]

The most irksome constraint on travel came from the practice of placing the presumably more offensive Communist countries—China, North Vietnam, North Korea, Albania, Cuba—off limits. The President, Schwartz said, "abhorred" travel control. "Everyone should be able to go to China, or any other place, if they can get in," John Kennedy said. "We know too little about China. The bans should be removed."[88] Backed by Robert Kennedy, Ball, Harriman and Edward R. Murrow, Schwartz repeatedly recommended to the Secretary of State that the restrictions be lifted. Rusk, fearing an outcry on the Hill, declined to act. Schwartz concluded that the President, facing so many difficulties with State, "must have decided that others than himself should deal with the Secretary on this problem rather than for him to direct that the restrictions be removed over the Secretary's spoken or silent objections."* His brother's activity in this field, otherwise laudable, was not calculated to endear the Attorney General to the Department.

* Abba Schwartz, *The Open Society* (New York, 1968), ch. 5. Restrictions on travel to Cuba, Vietnam, North Korea and Cambodia were finally removed fourteen years later by President Jimmy Carter, in March 1977.

IX

The essential Kennedy problem with State was how to annex the Department to the New Frontier. It was difficult to do anything about Rusk; so the presidential eye moved on to the under secretary. Ironically, Chester Bowles was the most devoted New Frontiersman in the Department. The President liked him and shared most of his outlook on the world. But, save for his first-class ambassadorial selections, Bowles had had small impact on the entrenched bureaucracy. One "trouble" with that generous-hearted, intelligent, imaginative man, as his friend Galbraith conceded from New Delhi, was the "uncontrollable instinct for persuasion which he brings to bear on the persuaded, the unpersuaded and the totally irredeemable alike."[89]

At Kennedy's suggestion Rusk asked Bowles in July 1961 whether he would not like to become a roving ambassador. A disturbed Bowles called the President, who promptly invited him to luncheon. "This is a luncheon which I shall never forget," Bowles wrote Stevenson (in a thirteen-page, single-spaced letter).

> ... I have never heard the President talk as thoughtfully and passionately on foreign affairs. He said precisely the things you and I have been advocating for years, and he said them well.
>
> He then expressed his deep disappointment at the failure of the State Department effectively to translate his views into action. He went on to say that changes must be made, and since it was generally assumed that the Under Secretary was in charge of administration, I was the logical one to change.[90]

An affectionate Bowles lobby swung into action and saved him for a moment. Three weeks later Robert Kennedy sent his brother a glowing account by Ambassador Philip Kaiser of Bowles's performance at a conference of American diplomats in Lagos. "This is the kind of thing Bowles should be doing all the time," the Attorney General wrote.

> I am sure conferences such as these will be going on around the world continuously and he could be our best and most forceful emissary. I would think that working out something like this with Bowles and putting George Ball or Roswell Gilpatric as Under Secretary would be the answer. I know it is difficult but there is no question that with Rusk and Bowles in the two top positions things are going to continue to flounder at the State Department. Rusk is no detail man and with both of them in those top jobs things are going to get steadily worse.[91]

George Ball, who succeeded Bowles in November 1961, brought a refreshing crispness to the job. But Ball's interest lay in policy, not in management. The administrative responsibility fell to George McGhee, under secretary for political affairs and Rusk's best friend in the Department. Nothing improved. "In every conversation you had with [McGhee]," Robert Kennedy said later, "you couldn't possibly understand what he was saying. I was involved with him a good deal in 1962, and it was just impossible." Finally the President told his brother, "If you feel so strongly . . . why don't you go see Dean Rusk and ask him to get rid of him." Accompanied by the monstrous Brumus, the Attorney General called on the Secretary of State one Saturday morning "and said I thought it was discouraging and gave him some examples of the fact that George McGhee didn't know what he was doing." Rusk asked whether this was something personal. Kennedy said no, it wasn't personal. Rusk said wearily he would take it under consideration.[92]

McGhee was soon shipped off as ambassador to Bonn, and the seventy-year-old Harriman took his place. Harriman had the signal advantages of wisdom, confidence and the knowledge of how to deal with Presidents. Presidents, Harriman said, always look around the room to see who agrees with a proposed decision and who does not. "I've learned . . . that you have a split second. . . . You can't wait." Harriman seized those split seconds and, when he disagreed, explained why in a few blunt sentences—a talent that won him the White House nickname of "the crocodile." "Mouth open, and I bite, you know," said Harriman.[93] He also had a singular capacity to get things done within the Department.

But even Harriman could not take care of everything. In an effort to tighten the internal workings, Robert Kennedy sent William Orrick over from Justice in late 1962 to become deputy under secretary for administration. Orrick later recorded his marching orders from the President. Two things in particular bothered John Kennedy: "Number one, he could not understand the Foreign Service. He wanted me, if I could, to interpret . . . the Foreign Service to him by whatever means I could. And, secondly, it just annoyed him beyond measure that he couldn't get answers out of the Department."[94] State regarded Orrick with suspicion as the agent of the Attorney General. When Orrick overcame that, he discovered both that the problems were deep and that the Kennedys to some extent misconceived them. With relief he seized the chance to come back to Justice in 1963 as chief of antitrust. "After the Orrick experience," John Seigenthaler said later, "there just was the feeling that what the hell can you do about it?"[95]

All this activity insured the Attorney General's unpopularity with the professionals—and theirs with him. "They all had problems with Bob," said Orrick. ". . . When I'd say something nice about them, Bob would say, 'Well, you don't really know them.' "[96] They saw him, said Donald Wilson of the United States Information Agency— who, like Orrick, admired the Attorney General—"as a headstrong, unreliable upstart in the field of foreign affairs. . . . He was regarded as quite a menace by most of the people in the State Department. . . . He'd be pretty outrageous sometimes in some of the things he'd talk about or get excited about. You weren't ever sure whether he was just speaking for himself or for the President. Actually, I think in most cases he was speaking for himself, and if he thought what he elicited . . . was of significance, he would pass it on to the President. If he thought it wasn't, then he wouldn't."[97]

X

Robert Kennedy summed up his own views in a memorandum to his brother in April 1962 proposing themes for a presidential speech to the Foreign Service Association (views rendered by the President soon after in less provocative language). "Innovations, imagination," he wanted his brother to tell the diplomats, "yes, even revolutionary concepts are essential. . . . *It is your responsibility not just to carry out policies that have been established but to suggest and come forth with new ones.*" Foreign policy, the Attorney General thought the President should point out, was no longer a matter of transactions among chancelleries. "More and more the people themselves are determining their country's future and policies. Therefore, greater attention has to be given than has been true in the past to these new and sometimes revolutionary elements"—labor leaders, intellectuals, students.

> A major effort must be made to meet with representatives of all kinds of groups. . . . For those discussions our Foreign Service must know what we are doing here in this country; understand internal problems that we are facing—unemployment and racial difficulties—and know also what remedial steps we are taking. They must understand what this government has accomplished for its people in a social way such as social security, minimum wage, housing, and what we are trying to do in the future. They must know our history and our culture so that they can discuss these matters freely and with candor.[98]

The Kennedys had a romantic view of the possibilities of diplomacy. They wanted to replace protocol-minded, striped-pants officials by reform-minded missionaries of democracy who mixed with the people, spoke the native dialects, ate the food, and involved themselves in local struggles against ignorance and want. This view had its most genial expression in the Peace Corps, its most corrupt in the mystique of counterinsurgency. The gospel of activism became the New Frontier's challenge to the cautious, painstaking, spectatorial methods of the old diplomacy. Of all the New Frontiersmen, no one was a greater enthusiast for action diplomacy than Robert Kennedy.

What was sometimes later described as Kennedy activism was in fact its opposite. So in Italy the White House after long and painful argument induced the Department to remove the veto imposed by the Eisenhower administration on a center-left government in Rome. This withdrawal of American intervention in Italian politics was peculiarly criticized by State Department people as itself an act of intervention.[99] And in special circumstances activism was useful—especially so in places where the United States in the preceding decade had intervened *against* social change. In India, Africa and Latin America activist ambassadors gave valuable counsel to governments struggling against massive difficulties. But action diplomacy was easier to advocate than to execute. John Paton Davies, Jr., the old China hand, inspected the scene with dismay. "Bold new ideas and quick decisions," he wrote, "were asked of men who had learned from long, disillusioning experience that there were few or no new ideas, bold or otherwise, that would solidly produce the dramatic changes then sought." Davies was not surprised that the Foreign Service did not win the confidence of the New Frontier. "Crusading activism touched with naiveté seldom welcomes warnings of pitfalls and entanglements."[100]

The issues were ably canvassed in a letter from Philip Bonsal, one of the best and most liberal-minded of the old school, to Robert Kennedy's friend the journalist John Bartlow Martin, who served with distinction as ambassador to the Dominican Republic. Acknowledging Martin's achievements, Bonsal observed that they "involved your direct and forceful participation in many of the top level decisions with which these [Dominican] governments were confronted. . . . You functioned much as would the authoritative coach of a rather backward football team." Still Bonsal could not help wondering

> whether if we had let the Dominicans stew in their own juice politically while assisting them economically they might not have cooked up a stew better adapted to their palates and digestions than what was in the event served up to them. . . . A process involving the constant participation of

the American Ambassador, no matter how high his motives or how great his political skill, in the domestic affairs of the country to which he is accredited cannot produce constructive results.[101]

Perhaps there was more to be said for the old diplomacy than Robert Kennedy, at least, realized in 1961. Philip Graham of the *Washington Post* made the case after the President spoke to him late in 1962 about superseding Rusk by McNamara. "Defense," Graham wrote John Kennedy, "needs action, movement, and above all a competence and courage to take decision after decision after decision. . . . In State, energy and dynamism can be specious qualities." Apologizing for the "effrontery" of his letter, Graham concluded: "It is just that I—who have a ghastly weakness for action, movement, and go—have painfully learned the value of wisdom, slowness and the kind of calm sense owned by a handful of men such as David Bruce."[102]

The New Frontier style suffered too often from this ghastly weakness—as the State Department style suffered from passivity, complacency, careless identification with the possessing classes and the traumas of the Dulles-McCarthy years. The Kennedys, observed Orrick, "held no brief for the time-honored traditions of diplomacy," according to which "you must be patient and listen and do anything but get involved. . . . They wanted to get involved every place. . . . For a few underdeveloped countries that might be desirable. But mostly it isn't. It just isn't. And they never understood that."[103]

Action diplomacy, carried too far, entangled the United States in the fortunes of nations beyond the area of American interest or understanding. It encouraged the illusion that an internal crisis in a remote land might affect the peace of the world. It led American diplomats to try to do things in foreign countries that the people of the country ought to have done for themselves. It nourished the faith that American "know-how" (odious word) could master anything; the "when in doubt, do something" approach to an intractable world; the officious solicitude that degenerated into cynical manipulation and finally into bloody slaughter.

The professionals were right to question New Frontier activism in the execution of policy. They were equally wrong to resist, as so many did, all departures in the substance of policy from the hallowed doctrine as revealed to Acheson and Dulles years before. Dulles had purged the Department of independent-minded Foreign Service officers and converted it into a mighty temple of Cold War orthodoxy. Rusk was no heretic. The failure of State to contribute to the

The Kennedys and the Cold War

President's drive for Berlin negotiations showed the grip of Cold War dogmas. "There would never be any initiative that would come from the State Department," Robert Kennedy said later with only minor exaggeration. ". . . I would think 60 per cent of this sort of new concepts or new ideas or plans really came from the President—oh, no, maybe 80 per cent came from the President and the White House, of which probably 60 of the 80 per cent came from the President himself."[104]

Much of John Kennedy's initiative was devoted to moving beyond the Acheson-Dulles theory of the Cold War. In subsequent years critics sought oddly to portray the President himself as a rigid and zealous Cold Warrior. An English historian spoke of "that most dangerous and megalomaniac of Administrations—the late John Kennedy's."[105] "He prosecuted the Cold War more vigorously, and thus more dangerously," wrote an American author, "than did Eisenhower and Dulles."[106] Khrushchev, perhaps a better authority, disagreed. "I had no cause for regret once Kennedy became President," the Soviet leader wrote in his memoirs. "It quickly became clear he understood better than Eisenhower that an improvement in relations was the only rational course. . . . He seemed to have a better grasp of the idea of peaceful coexistence than Eisenhower had. . . . From the beginning, he tried to establish closer contacts with the Soviet Union with an eye to reaching an agreement on disarmament and to avoiding any incidents which might set off a military conflict."[107]

(20)

The CIA and Counterinsurgency

THE STATE DEPARTMENT reminded the citadel of caution, professionalism and entrenched Cold War ways. But diplomats were no longer in control of foreign policy. The Pentagon and the CIA had grown far more than State at the pap of the Cold War. Almost at once the Kennedys were forced to confront the power of the military-intelligence complex. The occasion was the invasion of Cuba in April 1961 by the so-called Cuban Brigade, a band of twelve hundred anti-Castro exiles, recruited, trained and launched by the CIA on a plan approved by the Joint Chiefs of Staff.

I

"This will just be some thoughts on Cuba and the effect it has had on the Administration and the President," said Robert Kennedy in a memorandum dictated on June 1, six weeks after the disaster.

> I was brought in on the Cuban situation about four or five days prior to the actual event—I think about the twelfth of April. Dick Bissell [the CIA's deputy director of plans] at Jack's instructions came over to the Department of Justice and briefed me. He told me at that time that the chances of success were about two out of three and that failure was almost impossible because . . . even if the force was not successful in its initial objective of establishing a beachhead, the men could become guerrillas and, therefore, couldn't be wiped out and would be a major force and thorn in the side of Castro. This, as it later turned out, was completely incorrect. I think that the President might very well not have approved of the operation if he had known that the chances of these men becoming guerrillas was practically nil.
>
> Subsequently, I attended some meetings at the White House. Afterwards I said to Jack that I thought that . . . based on the information that had been given to him by Dick Bissell, Allen Dulles, the Joint Chiefs of Staff, Mac Bundy and the others . . . there really wasn't any alternative to ac-

cepting it. These men had to be gotten out of Guatemala and Nicaragua; and if we brought them back to the United States and turned them loose, it could be a tremendous problem both here in this country and abroad. The chances of success as outlined by the CIA and outlined by the Joint Chiefs of Staff were extremely good.[1]

In 1964 he gave John Bartlow Martin additional reasons for his brother's decision. The advocates of the operation—Dulles, Bissell, General Lyman Lemnitzer, chairman of the Joint Chiefs of Staff—had, the new President supposed, been "trusted by his predecessor; so he thought that he could trust them and when they said it was much more apt to succeed than Guatemala [where the CIA had overthrown a leftist regime in 1954], when the military looked it over and said it was a good plan, then he went ahead." President Kennedy also had to reckon the political repercussions if he were to disband his predecessor's Cuban liberation corps in the face of expert assurance that the project would prevail. "If he hadn't gone ahead with it, everybody would have said it showed he had no courage because . . . it was Eisenhower's plan, Eisenhower's people all said it would succeed, and you turned it down."* In the last days before the landing, Robert Kennedy added, a highly decorated Marine colonel brought in an ecstatic report on the Brigade's military prowess. This, Robert Kennedy thought, "was the most instrumental paper in convincing the President to go ahead."†

Back to Robert's June 1 memorandum:

> Jack on the first day realized there was going to be difficulty. He called me down in Williamsburg where I was speaking and said we had run into some trouble. He asked me to come to the White House. When I arrived

---

* RFK, in recorded interview by John Bartlow Martin, March 1, 1964, II, 17, JFK Oral History Program. When Eisenhower and Kennedy met the day before the inauguration, "President Eisenhower said with reference to the guerrilla forces which are opposed to Castro," as Clark Clifford, who accompanied Kennedy, recorded his words, "that it was the policy of this government to help such forces *to the utmost*. At the present time we are helping train anti-Castro forces in Guatemala. It was his recommendation that this effort be continued and accelerated" (Clifford to JFK, January 24, 1961, attaching "Memorandum on Conference between President Eisenhower and President-elect Kennedy and their Chief Advisers on January 19, 1961," JFK Papers; emphasis added).

† RFK, in Martin interview, II, 4–5. Kennedy added (6–7): "The one person who was strongly against it was Arthur Schlesinger. And Arthur Schlesinger came to my house . . . and I remember having a conversation with him in which he said that he was opposed to it and I said I thought that everybody had made up their mind and that I thought he was performing a disservice to bring it back to the President. . . . I remember at the house telling him that once the President had made up his mind, once it seemed to have gone this far, that we should make all efforts to support him, and he should remain quiet. Which he did." For an extended account of the Bay of Pigs, see Arthur M. Schlesinger, Jr., *A Thousand Days* (Boston, 1965), chs. 10–11.

there there was a meeting going on and the situation already looked dark.

He agreed to permit the Navy to come in closer to shore and ended the meeting by saying he wanted to be kept closely advised, that he'd rather be called an aggressor than a bum. In other words we didn't want to have this thing planned and the United States support [it] and have it go wrong.

That afternoon Dick Bissell called me at the Department of Justice and said that troops had been able to capture the air fields and the situation looked better. We had continuous conferences and conversations that day. The situation didn't seem to improve. There was also reports of shortages of ammunition.

Jack told them to bring in the [ammunition] ships and gave his permission. It then turned out that the ship the CIA had in mind was the ship that was supposed to arrive there two or three days later and they couldn't get it there any earlier and they took no cognizance of the ammunition ships that had run out on the action. It was complete lack of communication. Nobody was able to determine what was going on really there. At D plus one the information was again very gloomy. There was talk of trying to evacuate the men. We kept asking when the uprisings were going to take place. Dick Bissell said it was going to take place during the night. Of course, no uprisings did take place.

A critical time was on D plus one when the CIA asked for air cover. Jack was in favor of giving it. However, Dean Rusk was strongly against it. He said that we had made a commitment that no American forces would be used and that the President shouldn't appear in the light of being a liar. It was pointed out of course that the alternative was possibly destruction. I took the position that we didn't really have enough information to know whether the air cover would make any difference or not. If the air cover should save the operation, perhaps we should take that step. On the other hand if it just meant the delay of a few hours before absolute and ultimate collapse, there wasn't any sense in it. It was, therefore, decided that the Navy would make a reconnaissance over the beach and try to determine where the fighting was taking place and whether there was any possibility or chance of these men holding out. Admiral [Arleigh] Burke was given that assignment. He explained that it would take six or seven hours to get a reply and that meant that there couldn't be any air cover that day because we didn't get the request until about noon or one o'clock. Anyway we went ahead with that and they came back about seven o'clock that night and said they couldn't see any fighting going on and it would appear that the beach[head] was extended to about ten miles.

The next report came about 11:45 the following morning which was that the beach[head] was about to collapse. . . . The President for the previous three hours was battling hard to make arrangements to evacuate. By the time we received this information, however, the men were in the water. It was too late to send the destroyers in because they could be destroyed by artillery fire. He ordered them, however, to run up and down the beaches as close as they could and try to pick up any survivors. Over a period of the next six or seven days they picked up 25 or 30 men. Once again lack of communications had caused incalculable harm. Ultimately from the dispatches that I read and studied the CIA should have known that this was in bad shape and that we should take action to evacuate these men at a much earlier time than we did.

I think it was incompetency and lack of communications and nervousness. Dick Bissell always twists his hands and he was twisting them even more by the time this was over and for the following week. Allen Dulles for the next six or seven days looked like living death. He had the gout and had trouble walking and he was always putting his head in his hands. It even had a great physical effect on Jack. I noticed him particularly a week from the following Saturday when we had a talk for a half hour before the meeting began and even during the meeting he kept shaking his head, rubbing his hands over his eyes. [Robert Kennedy later told Martin, "We'd been through a lot of things together, and he was more upset this time than he was any other."]

He felt very strongly that the Cuba operation had materially affected the standing—his standing as President and the standing of the United States in public opinion throughout the world. We were going to have a much harder role in providing leadership. The United States couldn't be trusted. The United States had blundered. During the midst of this conversation about the difficulty in re-establishing a position and the fact that he felt that he had been badly undermined, Mrs. Lincoln [his secretary] walked in, heard him say this, and said, "Oh, no, everybody thinks you are doing wonderfully."[2]

II

During the long gray hours of the Bay of Pigs, John Kennedy decided he had better find out why, after all the expert assurance, the operation had ended as that rarity, an immaculate failure. He therefore summoned General Maxwell Taylor out of retirement to perform an autopsy. Robert Kennedy, Allen Dulles and Admiral Arleigh Burke joined Taylor on a board of inquiry. The Cuba Study Group met for six weeks in April and May and interrogated some fifty witnesses. The Attorney General told his associates to report during this period to Byron White, observing dryly: "It will be terrible if the Department improves while I'm gone."[3] May 1961—the month of the Freedom Rides—was not an easy month in which to go. After spending the day on the Bay of Pigs, Kennedy generally worked in his office on racial justice and other matters till late at night.

The transcript shows that the Attorney General took the lead in examining the witnesses. His unsparing questions disclosed how pathetically ill considered the adventure was. His June 1 memorandum recorded some of the things he learned:

> What comes out of this whole Cuban matter is that a good deal of thought has to go into whether you are going to accept the ideas, advice and even

the facts that are presented by your subordinates. Before you can rely on an individual you have to know him pretty well. . . . Does he exaggerate? does he push his project too much because he is interested in it? does he therefore alter or inflate the facts that are involved because he wants to sell the idea? If you work with a person for a long period of time, you take that into consideration when you are considering his ideas. But here the President didn't have a chance to work with these people. He was taking them at face value and when they told him that this was guerrilla country, that chances of success were good, that there would be uprisings, that the people would support this project, he accepted it. And that is going to be the difference between the President before Cuba and after Cuba. . . .

The fact that we have gone through this experience in Cuba has made the President a different man regarding his advisers, and the Joint Chiefs of Staff are well aware of this. They realize far better now what their responsibilities and obligations are in this field. This evidently they did not realize before. Their study of the Cuba matter was disgraceful. The President was looking to them for their military evaluation and they really didn't give it the attention that was necessary and study that was essential and didn't analyze the facts. For instance they didn't make any study whether this country was proper guerrilla country. It was guerrilla country, but it was guerrilla country between 1890 and 1900. Now, with helicopters, it is no longer guerrilla country and there was no way these men fighting in here in this swampy area could possibly supply themselves. This should have been realized by the military.

The military had realized all too little. Their assessment of an earlier version of the invasion plan, Robert Kennedy scribbled in private notes on the Study Group meetings, showed "what really bad work the Joint Chiefs of Staff did on this whole matter. The plan as they approved it would have been even more catastrophic than the one that finally went into effect." The Chiefs were supposed to pass on military feasibility. "There is considerable evidence that initially at least they did not give the plan adequate study and attention and that at no time did they individually or as a body properly examine all of the military ramifications." There was "no explanation as to how C.E.F. [Cuban Expeditionary Force] could possibly hold this beachhead for a long period of time. How would they get all the ammunition ashore by daybreak. How would they keep their airport from being knocked out. How would they keep soldiers from coming through the swamp after them."[4] One reason, Admiral Burke explained to his colleagues on the board, was that the military review had to be done "on a personal study basis by the Chiefs themselves. The emphasis on utmost secrecy did not permit the usual staffing."[5] This plea that they should be excused because they had had to do the work themselves no doubt struck the Attorney General as further proof of their incompetence.

The board of inquiry was oddly constituted. Dulles and Burke were in effect investigating themselves. Their real function was to preserve the CIA and JCS from feelings of persecution.* The Attorney General was guarding the presidential interest. Taylor, as chairman and draftsman, concentrated on securing a unanimous report. "I was far more critical . . . of the military," Robert Kennedy said later, "than perhaps Maxwell Taylor wanted to be."[6] For his part, Taylor, caught in a crossfire, had, he said later, "more difficulty with the Chiefs than with the others."[7]

The Eisenhower administration, the report concluded, ought to have recognized by November 1960 the impossibility of keeping the American hand secret and should thereupon have assigned the project to Defense as an overt American operation. "Failing such a reorientation, the project should have been abandoned." If the national interest required that it go ahead, "restrictions designed to protect its covert character should have been accepted only if they did not impair the chance of success."[8] Taylor did not think, however, that President Kennedy's much criticized cancellation of a D-day air strike "materially" affected the outcome.[9] Actually Castro had dispersed his planes and, he told John Nolan of the Justice Department in 1963, had moved fifty antiaircraft guns to the area shortly after the invasion began. As Nolan reported: "It was for this reason that he said that air cover for the Brigade would not have been decisive; his antiaircraft was so strong that it would have been able to knock out even much stronger air support."† Even if, against these precautions, the strike had been tactically successful, it would still have left 1200 CIA Cubans on the beachhead, surrounded by an avid enemy force two hundred times its size.

The board of inquiry gave Robert Kennedy a new friend. Maxwell Taylor was fifty-nine years old, articulate, dashing, urbane, both a consummate Army politician and an authentic war hero. "I was terribly impressed with him," the Attorney General said later, "—his intellectual ability, his judgment, his ideas."[10] For his part, Taylor was

* According to the egregious Howard Hunt, Colonel J. C. King of the CIA was the board's "general factotum," and Hunt himself was assigned to Dulles's office to provide "documentary and other answers to questions—or rather charges—made by the . . . inquisitors" (E. Howard Hunt, *Give Us This Day* [New York: Popular Library reprint, 1973], 213).

† Nolan was in Cuba with James B. Donovan to negotiate the exchange of Bay of Pigs prisoners (Nolan to RFK, n.d. [April 1963], RFK Papers).

greatly taken by young Kennedy; he told him—it was Taylor's highest praise—that the Attorney General could have made his old 101st Airborne Division; "you're the kind of guy we wanted around to take a hill or hold a trench."[11] He was impressed by Kennedy as an interrogator, "always on the lookout for a 'snow job,' impatient with evasion and imprecision, and relentless in his determination to get at the truth." He was impressed too by Kennedy's attitude toward his brother—"a reversal of the normal fraternal relationship of a big brother looking after a younger one. In this case, Bobby, the younger brother, seemed to take a protective view of the President."[12] And he welcomed Robert Kennedy's instinct for organization—something Taylor found conspicuously wanting in the President. "You'll have to remember my brother doesn't think the way you do," the Attorney General would say. "He thinks about issues and people," not about structure.[13] A warm friendship, solidified on the tennis court, survived subsequent policy disagreements and lasted to the end of Robert Kennedy's life.

III

The collapse of the "missile gap" had given the Kennedys an early skepticism about the Joint Chiefs. The President would sometimes look up and down the cabinet table during military discussions and ask sardonically, "Who ever believed in the missile gap?" (Only Maxwell Taylor would raise his hand.)[14] After the Bay of Pigs, the Kennedys began to question the Chiefs' professional competence. They also resented their public relations tactics. The new President was not one for men in uniform with pointers reading aloud sentences off flip charts he could read much faster for himself. In the spring of 1961 Kennedy received the Net Evaluation, an annual doomsday briefing analyzing the chances of nuclear war. An Air Force general presented it, said Roswell Gilpatric, the deputy secretary of defense, "as though it were for a kindergarten class. . . . Finally Kennedy got up and walked right out in the middle of it, and that was the end of it. And we never had another one."[15] Nor was the President any fonder of the public displays so dear to the armed forces. "John Kennedy," wrote Jerry Bruno—who, as advance man, had to deal with these matters—"hated military pageants—with a passion. And his brother Robert hated them even more."[16] In 1962 the Battle of Ole Miss completed their disenchantment. "The Army had botched it up," Robert Kennedy said, adding, "but we didn't have an exercise with the Army in which they didn't screw it up."[17]

Of the inherited Joint Chiefs, they liked best David Shoup, the commandant of the Marine Corps, who believed that the job of the Marines was "to teach fighting, but not hate."[18] They liked least Curtis LeMay of the Air Force. Every time the President had to see LeMay, said Gilpatric, "he ended up in a sort of fit. I mean he would just be frantic at the end of a session with LeMay because, you know, LeMay couldn't listen or wouldn't take in, and he would make what Kennedy considered . . . outrageous proposals that bore no relation to the state of affairs in the 1960s." But LeMay's popularity in the ranks and on the Hill gave him immunity. "We would have had a major revolt on our hands," said Gilpatric, "if we hadn't promoted LeMay."[19]

Except for Shoup, the military leaders were Cold War zealots. They had sedulously cultivated relations with powerful conservative legislators—John Stennis, Mendel Rivers, Strom Thurmond, Barry Goldwater. They hunted and fished with right-wing politicians, supplied them aircraft for trips home and showed up at their receptions. The alliance between the military and the right disturbed the Kennedys. This was why the President backed McNamara so vigorously in the effort to stop warmongering speeches by generals and admirals.

Direct military excursions into politics were still more disturbing. Radicals of the right were conducting an impassioned crusade not only against negotiation with the Soviet Union but also against social measures at home (the fluoridation of water was deemed a particular threat) and against the Warren Court. The John Birch Society was flourishing. The Minutemen were training their members in guerrilla warfare. Major General Edwin A. Walker, the right-wing demagogue who had made a menacing appearance at Ole Miss during the Meredith affair, was in a sense the heir of Major General George Van Horn Moseley, who had gone, in the thirties, from high Army commands to the domestic fascist movement. When the popular thriller *Seven Days in May* depicted a Pentagon attempt to take over the government, the President remarked, "It's possible. It could happen in this country, but the conditions would have to be just right. If, for example, the country had a young President, and he had a Bay of Pigs, there would be a certain uneasiness." If there were a second Bay of Pigs, the military would begin to feel it their patriotic obligation to preserve the nation. "Then, if there were a third Bay of Pigs, it could happen. . . . But it won't happen on my watch."[20] Still, he took no chances and, to the dismay of the Pentagon, encouraged John Frankenheimer to film the novel as a warning to the republic.*

In November 1961 the President assailed the extremists in a series of speeches on the west coast. "They call for 'a man on horseback,'" Kennedy said. ". . . They find treason in our churches, in our highest court, in our treatment of water. . . . They object quite rightly to politics intruding on the military—but they are very anxious for the military to engage in their kind of politics."[21] On the President's return, Walter Reuther, a cherished target of the right himself, congratulated Kennedy on the speeches. Kennedy asked Reuther what he thought the federal government could do, within the First Amendment, to curb right-wing extremism. Reuther, who never liked to be at a loss for a program, said he would make some recommendations. Kennedy said, "Fine. Give them to Bobby. He's greatly concerned, and I've asked him to work on it."[22]

Reuther handed the assignment to his brother Victor and Joseph Rauh. In December 1961 they gave the Attorney General a memorandum addressed particularly to the problem of the radical right and the armed services, and recommending, among other things, withdrawal of tax exemptions from right-wing foundations and reexamination of free radio and television time for radical-right commentators.[23] The memorandum, which received fairly wide distribution around the government, soon leaked, producing an aggrieved counterattack on the Attorney General.[24] For this and other reasons, the administration moved cautiously on the Reuther recommendations.

But the Kennedys continued to worry about the problem. The President tried to interest Senator John Pastore of Rhode Island, chairman of the Senate Communications Subcommittee, in doing something about right-wing harangues on the airwaves. Eventually, as Charles Daly of the White House congressional staff put it, "he abandoned the idea of pushing Pastore because they agreed it would look too much like a purge."[25] Instead, in October 1963, Kenneth O'Donnell asked Wayne Phillips, a former reporter now in the administration, to see whether the "fairness doctrine"—the rule that a radio or television licensee must afford a reasonable opportunity for contrasting viewpoints on controversial issues—could be used to

* Frankenheimer: "Those were the days of General Walker and so on. . . . President Kennedy wanted *Seven Days in May* made. Pierre Salinger conveyed this to us. The Pentagon didn't want it done. Kennedy said that when we wanted to shoot at the White House he would conveniently go to Hyannis Port that weekend" (Charles Higham and Joel Greenberg, *The Celluloid Muse: Hollywood Directors Speak* [New York: New American Library, Signet reprint, 1972], 92).

counter extremist commentary. Phillips moved to the Democratic National Committee and encouraged persons and organizations attacked on the air to demand reply time. The effort resulted in over five hundred replies in the next few months and doubtless had an inhibiting effect on right-wing broadcasts.[26]

In the meantime, the President counted on Robert McNamara to contain the military. Robert Kennedy shared his brother's admiration of and affection for the Secretary of Defense. He became another new friend, closer even than Maxwell Taylor. The Kennedys also thought highly of Gilpatric, Cyrus Vance and the other civilian officials. Still, as civilians, the McNamara people remained outsiders; so, after the Cuba board of inquiry finished its work, Kennedy kept Taylor on as military representative in the White House and a year later, when Lyman Lemnitzer's term expired, made him chairman of the Joint Chiefs of Staff. With Taylor reinforcing McNamara, Kennedy believed that the Joint Chiefs of Staff, in the absence of further Bays of Pigs, were under control.

IV

But the Joint Chiefs of Staff had only approved the Bay of Pigs. The CIA had invented it. "I made a mistake," the President said to me while the Cubans were still fighting on the beachhead, "in putting Bobby in the Justice Department. He is wasted there. Byron White could do that job perfectly well. Bobby should be in CIA. . . . It's a hell of a way to learn things, but I have learned one thing from this business—that is, that we will have to deal with CIA. McNamara has dealt with Defense; Rusk had done a lot with State; but no one has dealt with CIA."[27]

Dealing with CIA was more of a problem than any of us imagined. The Bay of Pigs raised acute questions about the Agency's responsiveness to higher authority. "We found out later," Robert Kennedy said in 1964, "that, despite the President's orders that no American forces would be used, the first two people who landed on the Bay of Pigs were Americans—CIA sent them in." Haynes Johnson's excellent book *The Bay of Pigs* reported CIA operatives telling the Cuban Brigade that, if the President tried to call off the invasion, they should "arrest" the operatives and go ahead anyway—"virtually treason," Robert Kennedy thought.[28]

Dulles and Bissell, it was evident, had misled the White House about vital features of the plan—especially the uprising behind the

lines that, they had given the White House to understand, would follow the landings. "It was believed," as Rusk told the board of inquiry, "that the uprising was utterly essential to success." So too Bundy: "Success in this operation was always understood to be dependent upon an internal Cuban reaction."* It turned out that Dulles and Bissell had no reason to expect an uprising. A CIA Special National Intelligence Estimate in December 1960 foresaw no development "likely to bring about a critical shift of popular opinion away from Castro" and predicted that any disaffection would be "offset by the growing effectiveness of the state's instrumentalities of control."†
The White House had been misled too about Castro's army. The Attorney General, in his personal jottings, observed that we "never would have tried this operation if [we] knew that Cuba forces were as good as they were and would fight." And the CIA had given a totally false impression about the ease with which the invaders could slip away from the beachhead to become guerrillas in the back country.[29]

In addition to misinformation, one surmises that there were equally vital thoughts withheld. It is hard to believe that Dulles and Bissell assumed the operation would succeed within the limits imposed. They may well have assumed that, if it faltered, the President, having gone so far, would have no choice but to follow the road to the end and send in American troops. CIA operatives actually assured the Brigade leaders American military assistance would be there if they needed it.[30] Howard Hunt, the original chief of political action for the project, had no doubt about this. When Kennedy publicly excluded the use of American troops before the invasion, "I did not take him seriously. The statement was, we thought, a superb effort in misdirection."[31]

Better "an aggressor than a bum" may have been Kennedy's first reaction. But, despite great pressure, he held the line. The CIA plan-

* In the May 4 meeting of the Cuba Study Group. Lemnitzer on May 18: "The ultimate effect centered upon the uprisings that would be generated throughout the island and the reinforcements which would be gravitating toward this particular beachhead. . . . I remember Dick Bissell, evaluating this for the President, indicated there was sabotage, bombings, and there were also various groups . . . asking or begging for arms." Robert Kennedy noted after the April 26 meeting: "Evidently no probability of uprisings written up and put in memo form. No formal statement of opinion was given or asked for (RFK Papers)."

† CIA Special National Intelligence Estimate, December 8, 1960. Richard Goodwin asked Bissell for CIA's evidence on the extent of disaffection in Cuba. Bissell said to General Cabell, Dulles's deputy, "Don't we have an NIE on it?" Cabell: "Yes." The NIE, for obvious reasons, was not shown to the White House (Goodwin, in interview by author, June 11, 1977).

ners did not reckon with his inherent prudence and his ability to refuse escalation. Reflecting, that summer at Hyannis Port, on those who had wanted to go in with full force, Kennedy said, "We're not going to plunge into an irresponsible action just because a fanatical fringe . . . puts so-called national pride above national reason. Do you think I'm going to carry on my conscience the responsibility for the wanton maiming and killing of children like our children we saw here this evening?"[32] In 1965, Dulles reminisced with Tom Wicker of the *New York Times* about the Bay of Pigs. Kennedy, he said, obviously had not liked the idea. In order to get him to go along, Dulles had to suggest repeatedly, without ever saying so explicitly, that, if Kennedy canceled the project, he would appear less zealous than Eisenhower against communism in the hemisphere. "This was a mistake," Dulles said. "I should have realized that, if he had no enthusiasm about the idea in the first place, he would drop it at the first opportunity rather than do the things necessary to make it succeed."[33]

The second withheld thought was a plan to assassinate Castro. That plan made no sense in isolation. The elimination of Castro in a vacuum would only have led to a more violent Cuban regime under Fidel's radical younger brother Raul or under the Argentine revolutionist Che Guevara. In the context of invasion, however, the murder of Castro might produce enough shock and disorganization to put the regime in jeopardy. As early as December 1959, Colonel J. C. King, chief of CIA's Western Hemisphere Division, recommended that "thorough consideration be given to the elimination of Fidel Castro" in order to "accelerate the fall" of his government.* Dulles and Bissell approved King's inquiry.[34] In May 1960, Howard Hunt, offering his recommendations to Bissell, listed first: "Assassinate Castro *before* or coincident with the invasion. . . . Without Castro to inspire them the Rebel Army and *milicia* would collapse in leaderless confusion."[35] Though Dulles and Bissell said not a word about it at the Bay of Pigs meetings or thereafter to the board of inquiry, the CIA had pursued, if with spectacular ineptitude, its plan to murder Castro before or during the invasion.

* Actually the American ambassador to Cuba, Arthur Gardner, had proposed to Batista in 1957 that the CIA or FBI murder Castro. Batista said, "No, no, we couldn't do that: we're Cubans" (as told by Gardner to Hugh Thomas, *Cuba or the Pursuit of Freedom* [London, 1971], 947).

V

Intelligence agencies, sealed off by walls of secrecy from the rest of the community, tend to form societies of their own. Prolonged immersion in the self-contained, self-justifying, ultimately hallucinatory world of clandestinity and deception erodes the reality principle. So intelligence operatives, in the CIA as well as the FBI, had begun to see themselves as the appointed guardians of the Republic, infinitely more devoted and knowledgeable than transient elected officials, morally authorized to do on their own whatever they believed the nation's security demanded. Let others interfere at their peril. J. D. Esterline, the CIA's supervisor of planning for the Bay of Pigs, bitterly told the board of inquiry, "As long as decisions by professionals can be set aside by people who know not whereof they speak, you won't succeed."[36]

The CIA had struck out on its own years before. Congress had liberated it from normal budgetary restraints in 1949. Through most of the 1950s the fact that the Secretary of State and the director of Central Intelligence were brothers gave the Agency unusual freedom. "A word from one to the other," wrote Howard Hunt, "substituted for weeks of inter- and intra-agency debate."[37] Eisenhower, reluctant to commit conventional armed force, used the CIA as the routine instrument of American intervention abroad. Covert-action operators, working on relatively small budgets, helped overthrow governments deemed pro-Communist in Iran (1953) and Guatemala (1954), failed to do so in Indonesia (1958), helped install supposedly pro-western governments in Egypt (1954) and Laos (1959) and planned the overthrow and murder of Castro in 1960.

Congress and the press looked on these activities, insofar as they knew about them, with complacency. Only one group had grave misgivings and informed criticism; expressed, however, in the deepest secrecy. This, improbably, was the President's Board of Consultants on Foreign Intelligence Activities, created by Eisenhower in 1956 and composed of unimpeachably respectable private citizens.

Almost at once the board had appointed a panel, led by Robert Lovett and David Bruce, to take a look at CIA's covert operations. "Bruce was very much disturbed," Lovett told the Cuba board of inquiry in 1961. "He approached it from the standpoint of 'what right have we to go barging around into other countries buying newspapers and handing money to opposition parties or supporting a candidate for this, that or the other office?' He felt this was an outrageous interference with friendly countries. . . . He got me alarmed, so instead of completing the report in thirty days we took two months or more."³⁸

The 1956 report, written in Bruce's spirited style, condemned

> the increased mingling in the internal affairs of other nations of bright, highly graded young men who must be doing something all the time to justify their reason for being. . . . Busy, moneyed and privileged, [the CIA] likes its "King Making" responsibility (the intrigue is fascinating—considerable self-satisfaction, sometimes with applause, derives from "successes"—no charge is made for "failures"—and the whole business is very much simpler than collecting covert intelligence on the USSR through the usual CIA methods!).

Bruce and Lovett could discover no reliable system of control. "There are always, of course, on record the twin, well-born purposes of 'frustrating the Soviets' and keeping others 'pro-western' oriented. Under these almost any [covert] action can be and is being justified. . . . Once having been conceived, the final approval given to any project (at informal lunch meetings of the OCB [Operations Coordinating Board] inner group) can, at best, be described as pro forma." One consequence was that "no one, other than those in the CIA immediately concerned with their day to day operation, has any detailed knowledge of what is going on." With "a horde of CIA representatives" swarming around the planet, CIA covert action was exerting "significant, almost unilateral influences . . . on the actual formulation of our foreign policies . . . sometimes completely unknown" to the local American ambassador. "We are sure," the report added, "that the supporters of the 1948 decision to launch this government on a positive [covert] program could not possibly have foreseen the ramifications of the operations which have resulted from it." Bruce and Lovett concluded with an exasperated plea:

> Should not someone, somewhere in an authoritative position in our government, on a continuing basis, be . . . calculating . . . the long-range wisdom of activities which have entailed our virtual abandonment of the international "golden rule," and which, if successful to the degree claimed for them, are responsible in a great measure for stirring up the turmoil and raising the doubts about us that exist in many countries of the world today? . . . Where will we be tomorrow?³⁹

In December 1956 the full board passed on to Eisenhower its concern about "the extremely informal and somewhat exclusive methods" used in the handling of clandestine projects.⁴⁰ (Among those signing this statement was another board member, Joseph P. Kennedy. "I know that outfit," the ambassador said after the Bay of Pigs, "and I wouldn't pay them a hundred bucks a week. It's a lucky thing they were found out early.")[41] In February 1957 the board pointed out to the White House that clandestine operations absorbed more than 80 percent of the CIA budget and that few of the projects received the formal approval of the so-called 5412 Special Group, the National Security Council's review mechanism. The CIA's Directorate of Plans (i.e., covert action), the board said, "is operating for the most part on an autonomous and free-wheeling basis in highly critical areas." All too often the State Department knew "little or nothing" of what the CIA was doing. "In some quarters this leads to situations which are almost unbelievable because the operations being carried out by the Deputy Director of Plans are sometimes in direct conflict with the normal operations being carried out by the Department of State."[42]

When this happened, State did not always prevail. Indeed, State was often itself a CIA target. In 1957 the CIA station in Indonesia decided that the United States should back a military revolt against Sukarno. "We began to feed the State and Defense departments intelligence," one CIA man said later. ". . . When they read enough alarming reports, we planned to spring the suggestion that we should support the colonels." The spooks moved on many fronts, even fabricating a Sukarno mask for an actor to wear in a pornographic film to be ground out in the blue movie mills of Los Angeles and used thereafter to discredit the Indonesian leader. John Allison, the ambassador in Djakarta, opposed the idea of overthrowing the regime. "We handled this problem by getting Allen Dulles to have his brother relieve Allison of his post within a year of his arrival in Indonesia."[43]

The Indonesian adventure—a far more exact model for the Bay of Pigs than Guatemala—was a total failure. The colonels rebelled in February 1958 after Allison's departure. Though Allen Dulles had personally promised to keep the new ambassador, Howard P. Jones, apprised of CIA activity in Indonesia, Jones was not informed that CIA was giving military assistance to the rebels.[44] Eisenhower, fully aware of the CIA role, piously described American policy as one of "not to be taking sides where it is none of our business." As the rebellion collapsed in May, a CIA pilot, Allen L. Pope, was shot down and captured.[45] "There was no proper estimate of the situation," the board told Eisenhower in a meeting in December 1958, "nor proper prior planning on the part of anyone, and in its active phases the operation was directed, not by the Director of Central Intelligence, but personally by the Secretary of State, who, ten thousand miles away from the scene of operation, undertook to make practically all decisions down to and including even the tactical military decisions." The chief result, the board said, had been to strengthen the Communists in Indonesia. There were "no present provisions," it added, "for any regular external review of Clandestine Cold War programs and no formal accounting of them." It begged Eisenhower once more to reconsider these "programs which find us involved covertly in the internal affairs of practically every country to which we have access."[46]

The board pressed its campaign in 1959 and 1960. Allen Dulles made minor organizational changes. In 1959 the 5412 Special Group began for the first time to meet regularly.[47] The board was not satisfied, then or later. When Dulles, Bissell and J. D. Esterline briefed the board late in 1960 on the Cuban project, its members, Lovett particularly, registered dismay, especially over the manner in which the planning was being administered.[48] In its last written report to Eisenhower, in January 1961, the board said grimly: "We have been unable to conclude that, on balance, all of the covert action programs undertaken by CIA up to this time have been worth the risk or the great expenditure of manpower, money and other resources involved. In addition, we believe that CIA's concentration on political, psychological and related covert action activities have tended to detract substantially from the execution of its primary intelligence-gathering mission. We suggest, accordingly, that there should be a total reassessment of our covert action policies."[49] "I have never felt," Lovett told the Cuba board of inquiry, "that the Congress of the United States ever intended to give the United States Intelligence Agency authority to conduct operations all over the earth."[50]

The Board of Consultants had no visible impact. Allen Dulles ignored its recommendations. Eisenhower gave it no support. But its testimony demolishes the myth that the CIA was a punctilious and docile organization, acting only in response to express instruction from higher authority. Like the FBI, it was a runaway agency, in this case endowed with men professionally trained in deception, a wide choice of weapons, reckless purposes, a global charter, maximum funds and minimum accountability.

VI

The Bay of Pigs dramatically verified the board's forebodings. The President called in Lovett. Lovett told him that CIA was badly organized, dangerously amateurish and excessively costly. It ought to be run, he said, in a hard-boiled fashion. This, he said, had not been possible with Dulles as director and Eisenhower as President.[51]

Determined to deal with CIA, Kennedy began by reviving the Board of Consultants. He called it the President's Foreign Intelligence Advisory Board and named James R. Killian, Jr., of MIT as chairman and Clark Clifford as a member. "I've made a terrible mistake," Kennedy told Clifford. A second Bay of Pigs would destroy his administration. "I have to have the best possible intelligence," he said. ". . . This has come early. I would hope that I could live it down, but it's going to be difficult."[52] Between May and November 1961, the Foreign Intelligence Advisory Board met twenty-five times —more than in its previous five years of existence.[53] Because the board enjoyed greater presidential support under Kennedy than before (or since), most of its recommendations were adopted. Clifford became chairman in 1963. But the board was an imperfect watchdog. It was not organized to find out things an agency adept at concealment wished to conceal. "I was not conscious," Clifford said later, "of any activity in the Kennedy administration in which the CIA was being used improperly."[54]

As for CIA itself, Kennedy began by redefining its mandate. In National Security Action memoranda 55 and 57 he transferred paramilitary operations from CIA to Defense and sought to restrict the size of the covert operations remaining to CIA. Obviously the Agency had to have new leadership. "Allen Dulles handled himself awfully well, with a great deal of dignity," Robert Kennedy said of the period after the Bay of Pigs, "and never tried to shift the blame. The President was very fond of him, as I was." Still, all recognized he had to go. "The President spoke to me about becoming head of CIA, and I said I didn't want to become head of the CIA and I thought it was a bad idea to be head of CIA, in addition, because I was a Democrat, and brother."[55] In time they settled upon John McCone, neither a brother nor a Democrat but a properly hard-boiled Republican industrialist with government experience. Bissell was replaced as chief of the clandestine services by Richard Helms, an OSS-CIA veteran whose background lay in secret intelligence rather than in dirty tricks. The 5412 Special Group was reconstituted with new authority over CIA covert action and with Maxwell Taylor as chairman.

In the months after the Bay of Pigs Kennedy thought he had put together a foolproof combination to keep CIA under control: tough McCone, the hard-driving executive, as director; experienced Helms, the perfect professional, as deputy director for plans; tough Taylor as chairman of the new Special Group; tough Clifford on the Foreign Intelligence Advisory Board. To complete the chain the President quietly gave Robert Kennedy an informal watching brief over the intelligence community.

VII

Taylor wanted to go much farther. His Cuba report concluded with a proposal for an extraordinary reorganization of the entire government in order to fight the Cold War. "We are in a life and death struggle," the report said, asking the President to consider the proclamation of a national emergency, to review treaties restraining "the full use of our resources in the Cold War" and to reexamine the adequacy of his "emergency powers." Cold War strategy, Taylor recommended, should be decided by an interdepartmental strategic resources group in charge of all situations around the planet certified as "critical" by a Cold War indications center.[56]

Kennedy rejected nearly all of this. He had uses for Taylor but not for his organizational fantasies. Rusk understandably saw the scheme as Taylor's takeover bid for control of foreign policy. Robert Kennedy, filled with inchoate urgencies after the Bay of Pigs and also beguiled by Taylor, had endorsed the grandiose plan but does not appear to have objected to its disregard thereafter. The President did, however, pluck from the exercise not only Taylor himself, whom he saw as a handy instrument for managing a benighted JCS, but also fragments of Taylor's bureaucratic dream. The Cold War indications center thus emerged briefly as the Crisis Center in the State Department (where Robert Kennedy installed his brother-in-law Stephen Smith, who intelligently concluded it was a waste of time and soon departed).

One aspect of the Taylor approach—the idea of concerted action in critical countries—appealed to a President who had believed ever since his visit to Vietnam in 1951 that the characteristic mode of Communist military pressure was not direct confrontation but indirect aggression and especially guerrilla warfare. Subsequent guerrilla successes in Cuba and Laos, accompanied now by rising guerrilla threats in Latin America and Africa, provided the background from which the famous Khrushchev speech derived its plausibility and menace. With nuclear war inconceivable and limited war improbable, guerrilla war had evidently become the chosen Soviet weapon. If

Kennedy was deceived about the efficacy of this threat, so no doubt was Khrushchev. In any event Kennedy in 1961 saw counterguerrilla action as the way to plug the great gaping hole in the fabric of peace.

The impetus behind counterinsurgency did not come from the military.[57] Taylor had advocated conventional force for limited war, not special forces for guerrilla war, though he was delighted to add counterinsurgency to the menu of "options" available in the name of flexible response. The impetus came rather from Kennedy himself and from social scientists he brought to Washington, notably the economic historian Walt Rostow (in the White House in 1961 and thereafter in the State Department) and the political scientist Roger Hilsman (director of the Bureau of Intelligence and Research in State; a veteran of guerrilla fighting in Burma during the Second World War).

The theorists did not see counterinsurgency as any permanent solution to the turmoil of the Third World. In a speech to the Special Forces at Fort Bragg in June 1961, Rostow argued that communism could best be understood "as a disease of the transition to modernization." Guerrilla warfare was the means by which "scavengers of the modernization process" sought to exploit emergent revolutionary aspirations.[58] Counterguerrilla action was the shield that would protect the development process from Communist disruption until the nation gained the social strength to control the situation itself. If counterinsurgency meanwhile persuaded Moscow to drop the weapon of national-liberation wars, the world could look forward to an era of tranquility.

At his first National Security Council meeting, on February 1, 1961, the President directed McNamara to instruct the Pentagon to place more emphasis on counterinsurgency.[59] In March, Kennedy told Congress that guerrilla warfare had been since 1945 "the most active and constant threat to Free World security."[60] Following a study by a committee under Bissell of the CIA, Kennedy created in January 1962 a new NSC committee designated Special Group (Counterinsurgency). Where the Special Group was intended to control CIA covert action, Special Group (CI) was supposed to coordinate overt American efforts to help foreign governments threatened by guerrilla insurrection. Maxwell Taylor was named chairman. Robert Kennedy was an ardent member.

The model of successful counterinsurgency lay at hand in Ramón Magsaysay's victory over the Hukbalahaps in the Philippines in the early 1950s. "All out friendship or all out force" had been Magsaysay's theory: military action combined with land reform, honest elections and generous amnesty, the counterguerrilla forces acting as "brothers of the people."⁶¹ And the Magsaysay formula had an indefatigable American proponent in Brigadier General Edward G. Lansdale, already legendary in 1961 at the age of fifty-three. After working with Magsaysay, the attractive and fervent Lansdale had moved on to Saigon as CIA station chief. Graham Greene portrayed him in *The Quiet American* (1956) as Alden Pyle, the CIA agent who, "with his gangly legs and his crew cut and his wide campus gaze . . . seemed incapable of harm." Pyle's dream was to establish a Third Force in Vietnam, opposed equally to the colonialist French and the Communist Viet Minh. The result, as rendered by Greene, showed the horrible consequences of ignorant good intentions. "He comes blundering in, and people have to die for his mistakes. . . . God save us always from the innocent and the good."* (Asked about *The Quiet American* in later years, Lansdale said innocently, "Well, Graham Greene calls his books entertainments. I found it very entertaining.")⁶² His next literary incarnation was in William J. Lederer's and Eugene Burdick's *The Ugly American* (1958) as Colonel Edwin B. Hillendale, the officer recommended by Magsaysay to the American ambassador in Sarkhan (Vietnam) because of his ability "to go off into the countryside and show the idea of America to the people." "Every person and every nation," opined Colonel Hillendale, "has a key which will open their hearts. If you use the right key, you can maneuver any person or any nation any way you want."†

There was something to both portraits. "I took my American beliefs with me into these Asian struggles," Lansdale wrote later, "as Tom Paine would have done." He combined confident ideological naiveté and a disregard of consequences with genuine affection for alien lands and a certain political realism. As a student of Sun Tzu and Mao Tse-tung, he seized upon a basic point about "people's war"—that any struggle between a government and Communist insur-

---

* Graham Greene, *The Quiet American* (New York: Bantam reprint, 1957), 10, 12, 186. The plot turns on Pyle's support of General Trinh Minh Thé, the dissident chief of staff who was fighting both the French and the Viet Minh. The Greene character tells Pyle: "General Thé's only a bandit with a few thousand men; he's not a national democracy. . . . You can't trust men like Thé. They aren't going to save the East from communism" (151). For Lansdale's account of his relations with Thé, see his *In the Midst of Wars* (New York, 1972), esp. 189 ff., 308 ff.

† William J. Lederer and Eugene Burdick, *The Ugly American* (New York: Fawcett reprint, 1960), 153, 233. Hillendale was *not* the Ugly American (nor was that term used invidiously; it was applied to Homer Atkins, who was physically ugly but devoted himself to building dams and roads in backward countries).

gency is "over which side will have the allegiance of the people." This meant that "social injustice, bullying by military or police, and corruption must be seen as grave weaknesses in the defense of a country." Washington policy makers, he believed, were too infatuated with "the brute usages of our physical and material means" to understand that government "of the people, by the people, for the people" was "the strongest defense any country could have against the Communists." He had his own equivalent of the sayings of Chairman Mao: "The harder a Communist attack on a weak point in the social fabric, the more honest we must become in strengthening it. . . . The poorest view of an insurgency is from an office desk."[63] The lesson of the Philippines, he wrote, "was that there must be a heartfelt *cause* to which the legitimate government is pledged, a cause which makes a stronger appeal to the people than the Communist cause. . . . When the right cause is identified and used correctly, the *anti*-Communist fight becomes a *pro*-people fight."[64]

His trouble was that he identified the "right cause" in terms of American beliefs brought to Asian struggles. In the end, innocence was not enough. Still, his emphasis on the political character of people's war—on preempting the revolution and thereby taking the human base away from the guerrillas—was at the heart of the Kennedy theory of counterinsurgency.

VIII

The mission of Special Group (CI) was less the waging of guerrilla war than its prevention. It was essentially an ad hoc, trouble-shooting, expediting body, established, not to create policy, but to make a slow-moving bureaucracy act quickly. It spent the most time on Latin America, then on Southeast Asia—Cambodia, Laos, Siam; not very much, however, on Vietnam.[65]

Counterinsurgency was not intended as a gospel of counterrevolution. "The United States does not wish to assume a stance against revolution, per se, as an historical means of change," the CI Group said in a 1962 policy statement. "The right of peoples to change their governments, economic systems and social structures by revolution is recognized in international law. Moreover, the use of force to overthrow certain types of government is not always contrary to U.S. interests. A change brought about through force by non-communist elements may be preferable . . . to a continuation of a situation where increasing discontent and repression interact."[66]

Nor was counterinsurgency conceived in military terms. Robert Kennedy defined it as a political strategy. "A military answer," he wrote,

> is the failure of counterinsurgency. . . . Insurgency aims not at the conquest of territory but at the allegiance of man. . . . That allegiance can be won only by positive programs: by land reform, by schools, by honest administration, by roads and clinics and labor unions and even-handed justice, and a share for all men in the decisions that shape their lives. *Counterinsurgency might best be described as social reform under pressure.*
>
> Any effort that disregards the base of social reform, and becomes preoccupied with gadgets and techniques and force, is doomed to failure and should not be supported by the United States.[67]

"It wasn't just a case of getting out and shooting guerrillas, by any manner or means," Taylor said later. "For the first time, I, at least, sensed the tremendous political and social aspects to this problem." Even the Joint Chiefs of Staff got religion, at least on paper, proclaiming improbably that the United States must "align itself, whenever possible, with the dynamic forces of social and economic progress."[68] The official doctrine placed great store on "civic action." The Special Forces were instructed in harvesting crops, digging wells, curing diseases, delivering babies and other benign undertakings.[69] The goal was "winning the hearts and minds" of the people.

The CI Group was more effective, however, in other areas—especially in training Latin Americans to cope with insurgencies. Academies in Washington and Panama instructed police officers in riot control, a practice much criticized later. But, as John Bartlow Martin observed in the Dominican Republic, "the police, trained under Trujillo, knew nothing but to shoot to kill. Teaching them how to control riots with means short of deadly force seemed humanitarian."[70] Latins also learned wider arts of counterinsurgency. Nor were they fighting phantoms. "Of course we engage in subversion, the training of guerrillas, propaganda! Why not?" Castro told Herbert Matthews of the *New York Times* in 1963. "This is exactly what you are doing to us."[71] Actually Castro had begun his covert action program against Latin America in the spring and summer of 1959, some months before the United States went into the business against him.[72]

By 1963 the progressive democratic regime led by the dauntless Romulo Betancourt in Venezuela was Castro's main target. Castro plainly saw Betancourt as a greater threat than, say, Perez Jimenez, the Venezuelan dictator in the fifties, would ever have been. "If the Communists have been so hostile to my regime," as Betancourt said in 1963, "it is . . . because we are carrying out the type of social action that strips the Communists of support and followers."[73] The protection of Venezuelan democracy became a primary American concern. Latin America, we thought in the early sixties, might be facing an ultimate choice between the Castro way and the Betancourt way. "You represent," John Kennedy told Betancourt when he visited the White House, "all that we admire in a political leader." Betancourt's fight for democracy, Kennedy continued, had made him "a symbol of what we wish for our own country and for our sister republics. And the same reasons have made you the great enemy of the Communists in this hemisphere. . . . You and your country have been marked number one in their efforts to eliminate you and what you stand for."[74]

The Havana radio beamed a steady barrage in support of the Communist-controlled insurgency. "When the people of Venezuela are victorious," cried Blas Roca, the veteran Cuban Communist, in January 1963, ". . . then all America will take fire."[75] In November 1963 the Cuban government staged a "Week of Solidarity with the Venezuelan Revolution" to cheer on the disruption of the presidential election scheduled for December. Later in the month the Venezuelans discovered four tons of arms shipped by Castro to a cache on their northwest coast.[76] Castro's campaign was a flop. Despite the threat that voters would be picked off by revolutionary snipers, 90 percent went to the polls. United States technical assistance to the Venezuelan police unquestionably helped the Betancourt government to put down the guerrillas, though no amount of police efficiency would have availed had not Betancourt's social policy won hearts and minds. For the first time in Venezuelan history one elected president peacefully succeeded another. The insurgency faded away.

Police training had its risks. There is no evidence that the American schools ever offered courses in torture. Still the instruction was much concerned with the psychology of interrogation; and too many of the students added torture when they got home. The Costa-Gavras film *State of Siege* was much exaggerated but had its point. There was also the danger that police training might be used for the repression of progressive democrats seeking constitutional change as well as of terrorists sent in from abroad. This was much on Robert Kennedy's mind. He kept stressing, Gilpatric recalled, the importance of distinguishing "subversion from outside the country" from "revolutionary situations developing within the country."[77]

CIA and Counterinsurgency

IX

For a season in 1961–62 counterinsurgency was the rage in Washington. The President took a highly publicized personal interest, enlarging the Special Forces, sending to Fort Bragg for their literature on guerrilla war, putting them in green berets as a mark of distinction.[78] By June 1963 the Special Forces numbered nearly 12,000 men. Counterinsurgency training had been given to 114,000 American officers and nearly 7000 from foreign countries.[79] Foreign Service officers, even ambassadors, had to attend counterinsurgency seminars before assignment to the Third World.

The Counterinsurgency Group met regularly. Robert Kennedy was its goad. The activity and the era put him in an inordinately gung-ho mood. After the Bay of Pigs and the Berlin Wall, he did not feel his brother could afford another setback. "The great events of our nation's past," he had written in *The Enemy Within*, "were forged by men of toughness."[80] The guerrilla, brave and hardy, fighting in the shadows, evoked memories of a more heroic America—Francis Marion, the Swamp Fox; Mosby's Raiders; Merrill's Marauders. The Attorney General cross-examined those called before the CI Group as caustically as, in the same period—before the Committee on Equal Employment Opportunity—he cross-examined officials whose agencies had not hired enough blacks. "If the man knew what he was after," said Averell Harriman, who became chairman of the CI Group in 1963, "he got very sympathetic questioning from Bobby. If Bobby got the idea he did not know, . . . he treated him as if he was a witness on the stand. . . . It was not a very pleasant experience."[81] After a notably harsh session, a man from the State Department told a reporter, "If one of you guys writes one more time about his looking like a choirboy, I'll kill you. A choirboy is sweet, soft, cherubic. Take a look at that bony little face, those hard opaque eyes, and then listen to him bawl somebody out. Some choirboy!"[82] Such pressure was valuable when the question was minority employment. In foreign affairs, it could lead to ill-judged activism.

Fortunately, however, the new gospel had inherent limits. Despite the President's benediction and the Attorney General's zeal, counterinsurgency retained strong opponents within the government. The Army was institutionally hostile to freewheeling officers like Lansdale and irregular formations like the Green Berets. Guerrilla action was simply beyond the conception of an opulent military establishment dedicated to high-technology war. The State Department, except for Harriman, who thought counterinsurgency had its uses in Latin America, was even less enthusiastic. "The amount of effort and theology with which that whole business was invested," George Ball said later, "was totally incommensurate with anything we ever got out of it. I think it led us into messing into a lot of situations where we would have done much better to have stayed out."[83]

Counterinsurgency faced still deeper problems. The theory the Kennedys had taken from Lansdale—winning the people by "social reform under pressure"—had a superficial plausibility. But it was not carefully thought through. Very few governments under guerrilla attack cared much about their own dispossessed. That was precisely why they were vulnerable. Magsaysay and Betancourt were the exception, not the rule. The regimes most severely challenged were those most suicidally determined to hold on to despotic power and privilege. Modernization and reform might well undermine whatever stability the regime had without eliciting the active loyalty of a long-suffering populace. And since the American ambassador was by definition debarred from using the ultimate sanction—withdrawal of American support—he lacked leverage to force apprehensive oligarchs to take measures they believed threatening to their own survival.

This was the fatal fallacy in the liberal theory of counterinsurgency.[84] With the United States so often obliged to work through repressive local leadership, the reform component dwindled into ineffectual exhortation. The professional military, American and native, lacked ability or desire to make social revolutions. Armies inevitably did what came naturally. "While the policy purports to cover the full spectrum of counter-insurgency," wrote Charles Maechling, Jr., the CI Group's staff director, "it in fact only fully addresses itself to the equipment and training aspects."[85] "It is simply much easier," Robert Komer of the White House reported to McGeorge Bundy, "to get people moving on active problems like Laos, Vietnam, or Thailand than to get them to focus on the preventive medicine (e.g. civic action or police programs) needed to forestall such problems arising elsewhere."[86]

In military hands, counterinsurgency shifted from winning the hearts and minds of the people to controlling their behavior, if necessary by brutal coercion. "When the going gets tough," as Knute Rockne had said, "the tough get going." "People tend to be motivated," wrote Morton H. Halperin, a counterinsurgency theorist of the new school, "not by abstract appeals, but rather by their perception of the course of action that is most likely to lead to their own personal security."[87] Or, as it was formulated by the Green Berets, "When you've got 'em by the balls, their hearts and minds will follow." The Special Forces themselves tended by a self-selecting process to attract, with notable exceptions, men whose taste was less for good works than for violence. The "dirty dozen" complex compounded trouble. As Peter De Vries rewrote Rockne, "When the tough get going, the going gets tough."[88]

Despite the original intent, counterinsurgency moved irresistibly toward counterrevolution. Robert Kennedy watched this development with dismay. "He was, in all fairness to him," said Michael Forrestal, who sat in on the meetings, "as worried about dictatorships of the right as he was about dictatorships of the left."[89] To John Bartlow Martin, Kennedy spoke in 1964 about the "conflict" within the American government. The idea that "it doesn't matter what kind of system you have so long as it's anti-Communist . . . was against the philosophy of the President and against mine."[90] "As time went on," Maxwell Taylor recalled, "the business diminished and his interest also diminished."[91] Ralph Dungan of the White House wrote the Attorney General in January 1963 urging the CI Group's dissolution.[92] It was decided to let it linger, but its heyday had passed. As a weapon, counterinsurgency was turning cruelly in the hand of the user. In the end it was a ghastly illusion. Its primary consequence was to keep alive the American belief in the capacity and right to intervene in foreign lands. God save us always from the innocent and the good. The failure of counterinsurgency was another phase in the education of Robert Kennedy.

(21)

The Cuban Connection: I

THERE REMAINED, after the Bay of Pigs, the exasperations of Cuba itself: of an exultant Castro, more galling and dangerous than before; of an elated Kremlin with ever closer ties to Havana; of eager guerrillas dispatched by Cuba against democratic Latin governments; of right-wing clamor in the United States over that putatively terrible threat ninety miles from Key West; of brave Cuban exiles, sent to the beaches by American folly and now herded miserably into Castro's prisons.

I

The night the Bay of Pigs collapsed, Maxwell Taylor was struck by John Kennedy's already "deep remorse" about the Cubans captured by Castro.[1] "During the months after the invasion," Kenneth O'Donnell wrote later of the President, "he thought of those prisoners constantly. . . . Within the privacy of his office, he made no effort to hide the distress and the guilt that he felt." He had had trouble sleeping, he told O'Donnell one morning; "I was thinking about those poor guys in prison down in Cuba. I'm willing to make any kind of a deal with Castro to get them out."[2] As Robert Kennedy said in 1964: "The one thing that really hung over from the Bay of Pigs was the fact that 1150 or so prisoners remained in jail and that they were going to die and not only did we have the responsibility for carrying out the Bay of Pigs in an ineffective way but also cost people's lives. . . . So we wanted to do whatever was necessary, whatever we could, to get them out. I felt strongly about it. The President felt strongly about it."[3]

Consequently when, a month after the invasion, Castro offered to exchange the prisoners for an indemnity of five hundred bulldozers, the President asked Mrs. Roosevelt, the always reliable Walter Reuther and two Republicans—Milton Eisenhower, president of Johns Hopkins University, and George Romney, president of American Motors—to head a fund-raising committee. Eisenhower accepted, though with "an odd sense of foreboding."[4] Romney declined. Most Republican leaders promptly denounced the proposal. Barry Goldwater fulminated against "surrender to blackmail." "Human lives," said Richard Nixon in one of his communiqués on public morality, "are not something to be bartered."

There were other problems. From start to finish Castro spoke with rare consistency of an "indemnity" of five hundred bulldozers. The committee gagged at the implications of indemnity, preferring to talk of an "exchange." Castro gagged at that. Moreover, the machines Castro specified—D-8 Super Caterpillar bulldozers—seemed better suited for the construction of airfields and missile bases than for agricultural work. The committee offered farm tractors. Castro finally said he would settle for the dollar value of the bulldozers, which he estimated at $28 million. By now Republican criticism was reaching a crescendo. Eisenhower wrote bitterly to Kennedy and threatened to resign. The committee expired at the end of June 1961 in a burst of recriminatory statements to and from Castro. "Well, boys," Castro told a committee of the prisoners, "the Americans are not going to give you those tractors." Offering them drinks, he explained that Mrs. Roosevelt was a *"vieja chocha,"* a silly old lady, and Reuther, a "labor baron." In Key West, exiles formed the Cuban Families Committee for the Liberation of the Prisoners of War.

Nine months later, at the end of March 1962, the prisoners were brought to trial. Roberto San Román, whose brother Pepe was in the dock but who had himself escaped from the beachhead, flew from Florida to Washington. Brushed off by the State Department, he went to the Attorney General. "This man was completely different," San Román said later. "This was like talking to a Brigade man. He was very worried about the Brigade." Finally the Attorney General said, "All right, Roberto, . . . I give you my word we will do everything possible to keep them from being shot." He invited San Román to telephone "ten times a day" and sent him to see Richard Goodwin at the White House, who, among other things, got President João Goulart of Brazil to ask Castro to spare the prisoners.[5]

Robert Kennedy now proposed an exchange of $28 million worth of agricultural products for the prisoners. This was peculiarly his initiative. On the evening of April 5, I noted in my journal, "the President called me at 7 o'clock to find out what the Food-for-Prisoners deal is all about. This is an operation which had been approved by the Special Group and is strongly backed by Bobby. . . . We had all assumed that the President knew about it, but apparently no one had told him. This morning Adlai Stevenson had mentioned it to him, and JFK had not known what he had been talking about. The President asked me to check into the matter and let him know how far things had gone. I called Bobby, who seemed a little surprised and chagrined that his brother did not know about it, and agreed to call him and bring him up to date. JFK's mood over this lapse was less one of indignation than of wistfulness."[6]

On April 8 the Revolutionary Tribunal gave the prisoners thirty years at hard labor—or, it added, Washington, if it cared so much, could buy their freedom by paying fines of $62 million. Two days later, representatives of the Cuban Families Committee, led by Alvaro Sanchez, Jr., arrived in Havana with pledges of $28 million in agricultural products. Castro stuck to his new figure. To prove good faith, however, he said he would release sixty sick and wounded prisoners to the United States. For this first installment he expected an interim payment of $2.9 million.[7]

The sixty men arrived in Miami exactly one year after they had left Nicaragua for the Bay of Pigs. Sanchez called the Attorney General. "I saw you on TV," Kennedy said. "I watched everything." Explaining that the government could not pay the ransom, he advised the exiles to form a fund-raising committee. But the idea of ransom drew a bad press. Most Americans wanted to forget the Bay of Pigs. Public relations sages advised the Cubans to sign up an eminent chairman for a sponsoring committee. Kennedy said to forget about a chairman; "what you need is a man who knows how to deal with Castro."[8] He recommended James B. Donovan, who had been general counsel of OSS during the war and who, the preceding February, after meticulous negotiation, had effected the exchange of the Soviet spy Colonel Rudolf Abel for Francis Gary Powers, the U-2 pilot.[9]

Donovan took the case without knowledge of the Attorney General's interest[10] (the two men had never met) and without fee. Reports from the prisons gave an alarming picture of hunger, sickness and degradation. At the end of August, Donovan went to Cuba. Castro asked about the $2.9 million due for the prisoners released in April. Donovan assured him it would be taken care of. After discussion they agreed, in effect, that Castro could call the ransom indemnification and in return would take it in medicine and food.

There were new complications. Soviet arms shipments to Cuba were frightening some Americans. In September, Robert Kennedy noted that it seemed "virtually impossible for us to send $60 million worth of equipment to Cuba with part of our population and a number of political leaders calling for an invasion of Cuba"; $25 million perhaps, but not $60 million.[11] Donovan became the Democratic senatorial candidate against Jacob Javits (Robert Kennedy thought he should retire from the race; other Democrats thought he should spend more time campaigning). In early October, though suffering from acute bursitis, Donovan flew again to see Castro. On October 20 he received Castro's shopping list. Two days later John Kennedy announced the discovery of nuclear missile bases in Cuba.

II

Redeeming the prisoners was only part of the unfinished business with Castro. There was also the regime itself, now by Castro's own statement a Marxist-Leninist outpost in the western hemisphere. On April 19, 1961, as resistance was ending on the beaches, Robert Kennedy added a prescient final sentence to a memorandum: "If we don't want Russia to set up missile bases in Cuba," he wrote the President, "we had better decide now what we are willing to do to stop it."

He identified three possible courses: (1) sending American troops into Cuba—which "you have rejected . . . for good and sufficient reasons (although this might have to be reconsidered)"; (2) placing a strict blockade around Cuba—which as an act of war "has the same inherent problems as Number (1)" and as "a drawn-out affair . . . would lead to a good deal of world-wide bitterness"; or (3) calling on the Organization of American States to prohibit the shipment to Cuba of arms from any outside source, including both the Soviet Union and the United States. "At the same time they would guarantee the territorial integrity of Cuba so that the Cuban government could not say they would be at the mercy of the United States." Perhaps the OAS might be persuaded to do this, he ruminated, "if it was reported that one or two of Castro's MIGS attacked Guantanamo and the United States made noises . . . that we might very well have to take armed action ourselves. . . . Maybe this is not the way to carry it out but something forceful and determined must be done. . . . The time has come for a showdown for in a year or two years the situation will be vastly worse."[12]

On the same day—D-day plus two—there was a meeting at the

White House. Robert Kennedy recalled it in his memorandum of June 1, 1961:

> It was a very gloomy meeting. Lemnitzer, Burke, Rusk, Mac Bundy, Bissell, Allen Dulles, several others present. Everybody really seemed to fall apart. I said in rather strong terms that I thought we should pick ourselves up and figure what we were going to do that would be best for the country and the President over the period of the next six months or a year. . . . Jack and I then left the meeting and took a walk and they worked for another three or four hours. I came back and visited them around three o'clock. There was discussion about whether we should send American troops into Cuba. Chip Bohlen was strongly in favor of doing something like this. Dean Rusk advised against it. There was other discussion about establishing a blockade. Ultimately, it ended up in not doing a great deal.[13]

Chester Bowles also remembered this meeting. The "consensus," he said later, "was to get tough with Castro. Some of the people at the meeting were very outspoken and took an attitude of 'He can't do this to us. We've got to teach him a lesson.' If the President had at that point . . . decided to send in troops or drop bombs or whatever, I think he would have had the affirmative votes of at least 90 percent of the people."[14] "We were hysterical about Castro at the time of the Bay of Pigs and thereafter," Robert McNamara said later.[15]

Bowles stoutly opposed the prevailing militancy. His own thoughts were deemed insufficiently militant. "Later on," Robert Kennedy said in his June 1 memorandum:

> a plan came in from a task force that was studying Cuba which was just God awful. It was presented by Chester Bowles at the next National Security meeting. I said that I thought it was a disgrace; and a new task force was formed which came in with some suggestions and ideas which made far more sense. . . .
>
> Chester Bowles hasn't contributed a great deal. He talks in such general language. It is very difficult to pin him down as to specific action. He started complaining after one of the meetings on D plus two that he was against Cuba. I told him that he might have been against it before but that he was for it from then on. However, ultimately it got in *Time* magazine that he was complaining around town that he was against the project and his position has been badly undermined with the President. . . . The other great question is getting an Assistant Secretary of State for Latin America. I thought John Connally would do the job. Not an expert in the field but at least he is a man of action. . . .
>
> I had a slight flare-up with Lyndon Johnson at one of these meetings. At D plus two we started to go around the table to try to find out who was in favor of the project. We had the impression he was just trying to get off it himself. I had a talk with Dean Rusk after D plus two and I believe with McNamara to make sure that everybody in their Departments understood

that the important matter was to stand firm and to not try and pass the blame off to somebody else. This could lead only to bitter recriminations and even more disaster. They all accepted that and I think we had very little difficulty along those lines.[16]

I had gone to Europe shortly after the Bay of Pigs. When I returned early in May, I attended meetings of the Cuban task force on postdebacle policy. "There was complete agreement," I noted, "against any thought of direct intervention. There was general opposition, the Pentagon and CIA dissenting, to the idea of enlisting a Cuban Freedom Brigade in the United States Army." At the National Security Council meeting the next day, McNamara expressed Department of Defense opposition to this idea too. "He also said that both the Army and the Navy rejected an Air Force plan for an assault against the Castro regime."[17] Ah, the Air Force!

"The Cuba matter is being allowed to slide," Robert Kennedy said on June 1. "Mostly because nobody really has the answer to Castro. Not many are really prepared to send American troops in there at the present time but maybe that is the answer. Only time will tell."[18] The Attorney General was unquestionably right on one point: nobody had the answer to Castro.

John Kennedy politely asked Richard Nixon, "What would you do now in Cuba?" "I would find a proper legal cover," Nixon replied (by his own account), "and I would go in."[19] In mid-June the Cuba Study Group chimed in. "There can be no long-term living with Castro as a neighbor," Maxwell Taylor, Robert Kennedy and their associates solemnly concluded. The group saw two possible policies: either to hope that time and internal discontent would eventually end the threat, "or to take active measures to force its removal. . . . Neither alternative is attractive. . . . While inclining personally to a positive course of action against Castro without delay, we recognize the danger of dealing with the Cuban problem outside the context of the world Cold War situation."*

Senator Mike Mansfield, who was regularly wiser on questions of foreign policy than most members of the National Security Council, offered the best answer. "If we yield to the temptation to give vent to our anger at our own failure," he wrote the President, "we will, ironically, strengthen Castro's position." Mansfield sensibly recommended "gradual disengagement of the U.S. government from anti-

* Cuba Study Group, "Conclusions," Recommendation 6, June 13, 1961, Schlesinger Papers. The context makes it entirely clear that "Castro" was used throughout the document as shorthand for "the Castro regime." "Removal," for example, meant overthrow of the regime, not the assassination of Castro.

Castro revolutionary groups, . . . a taciturn resistance to the political blandishments or provocations from those at home who would urge that we act directly in Cuba, . . . a cessation of violent verbal attacks on Castro by officials of the government" and full steam ahead on the Alliance for Progress because without economic progress *"Castroism is likely to spread elsewhere in Latin America whether or not Castro remains in power in Cuba."*[20] Robert Kennedy agreed over the long run. "If the Alliance for Progress goes into operation fully," he said in 1963, "if reforms, social, economic and political, are put into effect, then Communism and Castroism will collapse in Latin America."*

III

But neither the Alliance for Progress nor the diplomatic and economic isolation of Cuba promised immediate results. With his brother under Communist harassment in Berlin and Southeast Asia and under Republican harassment in the United States, with Castro's operatives plotting against democratic regimes in Latin America, Robert Kennedy was determined to find quicker ways of striking back. In the interstices of his other battles of 1962—with the segregationists and with the mob, with Jimmy Hoffa and with Edgar Hoover—he now began to expend much time and concern on the overthrow of the Castro regime. He vividly felt, as Maxwell Taylor said later, "that the United States had suffered a great humiliation in Cuba, as we had, and hoped it would be possible to reverse that in some way by utilizing the Cuban exile resources, assisting as we could on the American side."[21]

He turned to the CIA, which, as the Justice Department's Office of Legal Counsel extravagantly contended in January 1962, had through the Presidency "the constitutional power . . . *by any means necessary* to combat the measures taken by the Communist bloc" and to do so "without express statutory authorization."[22] The Attorney General had had a hand in John McCone's appointment, and, despite nearly a quarter century's difference in age, the two men became good friends—a friendship sadly consolidated when Ethel Kennedy provided daily solace during the fatal sickness of McCone's wife. McCone proved, as expected, an able executive and, as not expected

---

* He added: "If effort is not made and reforms are not forthcoming, we will have problems in South America even if there is no Cuba or Castro" ("Robert Kennedy Speaks His Mind," *U.S. News & World Report*, January 28, 1963).

by some of us, a detached analyst of intelligence, even when the intelligence might clash with his own robustly conservative views. Robert Kennedy used to kid him about his conservatism and try to nudge the Agency to the left. Thus he wrote McCone early in 1962 suggesting he "talk to Jack Conway, Arthur Goldberg and perhaps Walter Reuther. . . . You might pick up some good ideas from these people. . . . Arthur is a good judge on who is effective in the labor movement. Jack Conway is a bright articulate fellow, who feels very strongly but makes a good deal of sense."[23] (The Attorney General said to me more than once that Jack Conway was exactly the sort of man who might be able to make some sense out of CIA.)

With sure bureaucratic instinct, the Agency seized on the Cuban problem as the way of making its comeback from the Bay of Pigs. "We wanted to earn our spurs with the President," as Richard Helms said.[24] But as usual it thought it alone knew how to do the job. The CIA wished to organize Castro's overthrow itself from *outside* Cuba, as against those in the White House, the Attorney General's office and State who wished to support an anti-Castro movement *inside* Cuba. The CIA's idea was to fight a war; the others hoped to promote a revolution. Any successful anti-Castro movement inside Cuba would have to draw on disenchanted Castroites and aim to rescue the revolution from the Communists. This approach, stigmatized as *Fidelismo sin Fidel,* was opposed by businessmen, both Cuban and American, who dreamed of the restoration of nationalized properties. But the CIA alternative was probably dictated less by business interests than by the Agency's preference for operations it could completely control—especially strong in this case because of the Cuban reputation for total inability to keep anything secret.

As I wrote in July 1961 to Richard Goodwin, the White House liaison for Cuba, the CIA's Cuban Covert Plan contemplated "a *CIA* underground formed on criteria of operational convenience rather than a *Cuban* underground formed on citeria of building political strength sufficient to overthrow Castro." The CIA specifications favored those Cubans "most willing to accept CIA identification and control" and discriminated against Cubans who insisted on running their own show. I had in mind the anti-Castro radical Manuel Ray, who was believed to have the most effective network on the island. "The practical effect," I concluded, "is to invest our resources in the people least capable of generating broad support within Cuba."[25]

These disagreements were temporarily papered over at the end of August 1961 when the Cuba Task Force—which included George

Ball and some Latin Americanists from State, Goodwin from the White House and a CIA delegation led by Richard Bissell—came up with a formula. They all agreed, as Goodwin reported to the President, on a campaign directed "toward the destruction of targets important to the economy, e.g., refineries, plants using U.S. equipment, etc." This was the CIA plank; but Goodwin also won nominal CIA acceptance of "the principle that para-military activities ought to be carried out through Cuban revolutionary groups which have a potential for establishing an effective political opposition to Castro within Cuba."[26]

But the Goodwin plank was against the CIA's operational code. The Agency could not bring itself to trust those it could not control. In the early fall Bissell was told, perhaps in a meeting with the President and the Attorney General, to "get off your ass about Cuba."[27] After a meeting with Bissell, Esterline and other Agency people on October 23, I noted: "At bottom, there is a conflict between operational interests and diplomatic interests. CIA wants to subordinate everything else to tidy and manageable operations; hence it prefers compliant people, like [Joaquin] Sanjenis [head of Operation 40, a right-wing clandestine group funded by the CIA] to proud and independent people, like Miro [Cardona, the head of the Cuban Revolutionary Council and Castro's first prime minister]."* Hoping to bring the CIA into line, Goodwin proposed to the President in early November that Robert Kennedy "would be the most effective commander of the anti-Castro campaign."[28] At just this point, the famed General Lansdale returned from a trip to Saigon. Robert Kennedy, remembering Lansdale's doctrine of preempting the revolution and aware that the Army did not want him in Vietnam, thought that the savior of Magsaysay might have the answer to Castro.

On November 4, 1961, Cuba was the subject of a White House meeting. Present, according to Robert Kennedy's handwritten notes, were

> McNamara, Dick Bissell, Alexis Johnson [the deputy under secretary of state for political affairs], Paul Nitze, Ed Lansdale (the Ugly American). McN said he would make latter available for me—I assigned him to make survey of situation in Cuba—the problems & our assets.
> My idea is to stir things up on island with espionage, sabotage, general

---

* Author's journal, October 23, 1961. The next day Miro told me, "I can fight against Castro—against the corruption of the past, against Prio [Socarras, a right-wing Cuban politician who was trying to launch a new exile movement]—against Batista—but, if I have to fight the CIA on top of all this, I declare myself vanquished" (ibid., October 24, 1961).

The Cuban Connection: I

disorder, run & operated by Cubans themselves with every group but Batistaites & Communists. Do not know if we will be successful in overthrowing Castro but we have nothing to lose in my estimate.[29]

Lansdale made his survey. He recommended "a very different course" from the CIA "harassment" operations of the summer, conceived and led as they were by Americans. Instead, the United States, Lansdale argued, should seek out Cubans who had opposed Batista and then had become disillusioned with Castro. His theory was to work within Cuba, taking care not to "arouse premature actions, not to bring great reprisals on the people there." The objective was to depose Castro in the same way Castro had deposed Batista—to have "the people themselves overthrow the Castro regime rather than U.S. engineered efforts from outside Cuba."[30]

The President decided in favor of the Goodwin-Lansdale thesis and against the CIA. At the end of November he put out a top secret instruction "to use our available assets . . . to help Cuba overthrow the Communist regime."[31] Lansdale was appointed chief of operations, reporting to a new review committee known as the Special Group (Augmented).* Operation Mongoose was born.

IV

Mongoose, like the baby in the old story, was attended at the cradle by good fairies with divergent wishes. The President's wish was that, as Taylor described it, "all actions should be kept in a low key." Since "anything big was going to be charged to the United States," Mongoose had to be kept small, functioning at what was known in intelligence circles as a low noise level.[32] The American hand was to be concealed. Nor did the President wish undue activity to jeopardize the lives of the Bay of Pigs prisoners.

The Attorney General had a separate wish, as rendered in CIA notes of a meeting at Justice with Mongoose planners in January 1962: that "no time, money, effort—or manpower . . . be spared." Mongoose was "top priority."[33] But he was never clear how the time, money, etc., were to be used.

Lansdale's wish was activity—a lot of it—leading to internal revolu-

* The regular Special Group—Taylor, McGeorge Bundy, Alexis Johnson, Gilpatric, Lemnitzer and McCone—would meet at two o'clock every Thursday afternoon. When its business was finished, Robert Kennedy would arrive, and it would expand into the Special Group (CI). At the end of the day, Cuba would become the subject, and the group, with most of the same people, would metamorphose into Special Group (Augmented).

tion. He had a multitude of ideas: nonlethal chemicals to incapacitate sugar workers; "gangster elements" to attack police officials; defections "from the top echelon of the Communist gang"; even (at least according to one witness before the Church committee; Lansdale later disclaimed the project) spreading word that Castro was anti-Christ and that the Second Coming was imminent—an event to be verified by star shells sent up from an American submarine off the Cuban coast ("elimination by illumination," a waspish critic called it). In February, Lansdale presented a six-phase plan designed to culminate the next October in an "open revolt and overthrow of the Communist regime."[34] All this was a little rich for the Special Group (Augmented), which directed him instead to make the collection of intelligence the "immediate priority objective of U.S. efforts in the coming months." While the group was willing to condone a little concurrent sabotage, the acts "must be inconspicuous," it told Lansdale, and on a scale "short of those reasonably calculated to inspire a revolt." It further insisted that all "sensitive" operations, "sabotage, for example, will have to be presented in more detail on a case by case basis."[35]

The Augmented Group could prescribe policy to Lansdale. It was harder for Lansdale to prescribe operations, which remained in the hands of CIA. Task Force W, the CIA unit for Mongoose, soon had four hundred American employees in Washington and Miami, over fifty proprietary fronts, its own navy of fast boats, a rudimentary air force and two thousand Cuban agents. The Miami headquarters became for a season the largest CIA station in the world. All this cost over $50 million a year.[36] The CIA had its special wish for Mongoose too. Whereas the Special Group (Augmented) had accepted the presidential decision that "the one thing that was off limits was military invasion," the Agency persisted in seeing the objective as the creation of "internal dissension and resistance leading to eventual U.S. intervention" (October 1962).[37] The Agency, in short, was more bent than ever on fighting a war. It proved this by the men to whom it offered command of Task Force W.

Bissell's first choice, if Howard Hunt can be believed, was Hunt himself, an operative notorious in the Cuban community for his division of the exiles into (as one anti-Castro exile put it) the "good guys," who did his bidding, and the "bad guys," who "refused to be coerced into accepting his standard operating procedures."[38] Hunt, however, declined the job on the ground that "it was obvious there was no serious interest in overthrowing Castro, and I was reluctant to

The Cuban Connection: I

conduct operations for their own sake, to give the appearance of activity."[39]

The next CIA candidate was no more amenable to the Lansdale-Goodwin political strategy. William King Harvey had begun as an FBI counterespionage agent, renowned for having turned the Nazi spy William Sebold into a double agent during the Second World War. Fired by Hoover for drunkenness in 1947, he caught on with the CIA and became one of its celebrated operators. His great coup, the "Berlin tunnel," had enabled the CIA for many months in 1955–56 to intercept communications between East Berlin and Moscow. He was a histrionic fellow who always packed a gun, even in CIA headquarters in Langley. "If you ever know as many secrets as I do," he would say mysteriously, "then you'll know why I carry a gun."[40] Far from wanting the independent Cuban movement envisaged by Lansdale, Harvey was determined to reduce his Cuban operatives to abject dependence. "Your CO [case officer] was like your priest," one of Harvey's Cubans said later. ". . . You learned to tell him everything, your complete life."*

Lansdale found Harvey intensely secretive, almost paranoid. Lansdale finally said to him, "I'm not the enemy. You can talk to me." But the momentum of the overblown Miami establishment generated its own excesses. "Mostly the things we needed were not the things they wanted to do," Lansdale said later. "Still, if the equipment exists, the temptation to use it becomes irresistible." Lansdale would ask what they expected random hit-and-run raids to accomplish. They had no good answer. A bridge would be blown up. "Why did you do it?" Lansdale would say. "What communications were you trying to destroy?" Harvey would reply, "You never told us not to blow up the bridge." Lansdale made his directives increasingly precise in the hope of stopping aimless sabotage and saving courageous Cubans from pointless death.[41]

Harvey protested to McCone about the "tight controls exercised by the Special Group" and the "excruciating detail" he was expected to provide.[42] The controls must have had some effect. "They never let us fight as much as we wanted to," lamented Ramón Orozco, a Cuban commando, "and most of the operations were infiltrations and

---

* Taylor Branch and George Crile III, "The Kennedy Vendetta," *Harper's*, August 1975. The speaker was Eugenio Rolando Martinez, who learned the lesson of obedience so completely that, when Howard Hunt asked him a decade later to break into the Watergate, Martinez, still on a CIA retainer and supposing this to be a CIA operation, obliged without second thought.

weapons drops."[43] In October 1962 Robert Kennedy pointed out that, after almost a year of Mongoose, "there had been no acts of sabotage and that even the one which had been attempted [against the Matahambre copper mines] had failed twice."[44] CIA itself complained that same month, "Policymakers not only shied away from the military intervention aspect but were generally apprehensive of sabotage proposals."[45]

Still Harvey's Cubans evidently did more than Washington imagined. "The difficulties of control were so great," Taylor Branch and George Crile have written, "that the Agency [itself] often didn't know which missions were leaving in which directions." Harvey's people included soldiers of fortune like William (Rip) Robertson, a flamboyant figure who, in defiance of presidential orders, had landed on the beach at the Bay of Pigs. "When we didn't go [on missions]," said Orozco, "Rip would feel sick and get very mad." Once Robertson told Orozco, "I'll give you $50 if you bring me back an ear." Orozco brought him two, and "he laughed and said, 'You're crazy,' but he paid me $100, and he took us to his house for a turkey dinner."[46] They all sounded crazy. It was the "dirty dozen" spirit, action for action's sake, without concern for the safety of the Cubans involved or for the reprisal effect or for political follow-up.

Lansdale, Robert Kennedy said in 1964, "came to cross purposes with CIA and they didn't like his interferences."[47] "Revolutions have to be indigenous," Lansdale said in retrospect. ". . . We have a tendency as a people to want to see things done right—and, if they aren't, we step in and try to do them ourselves. That is fatal to a revolution." Harvey, however, had the decisive advantage of operational control. The political strategy fell by the wayside.[48] As for Robert Kennedy, he found Harvey and his meaningless melodrama detestable. "Too much 'Gunsmoke stance' for the Attorney General," said Howard Hunt.[49] "Why lose lives," Kennedy used to say to Taylor and to Lansdale, "if the return isn't clearly, clearly worth it?"[50] As for Harvey, he "hated Bobby Kennedy's guts," said a CIA colleague, "with a purple passion."[51]

The Attorney General was always dissatisfied with Mongoose. He wanted it to do more, the terrors of the earth, but what they were he knew not. He was wildly busy in 1962—a trip around the world in February, the steel fight in April, civil rights always, Ole Miss in September, organized crime, Hoffa, apportionment, fighting with Lyndon Johnson about minority employment, fighting with Edgar Hoover about everything. Castro was high on his list of emotions, much lower

The Cuban Connection: I

on his list of informed concerns. When he was able to come to meetings of Special Group (Augmented), as he did his best to do, he made up in pressure for what he lacked in knowledge. His style there, as everywhere, was to needle the bureaucracy. If there was a problem, there had to be a solution. He conveyed acute impatience and urgency. With the intelligence-collection phase ending in August 1962, the Mongoose group meditated a "stepped up Course B Plus" intended to inspire open revolt. Kennedy, who was away on the west coast, endorsed B Plus in a message to Taylor. "I do not feel," he said, "that we know yet what reaction would be created in Cuba of an intensified program. Therefore, I am in favor of pushing ahead rather than taking any step backward."[52]

In October he urged the Augmented Group, in the name of the President, to give more priority to sabotage. The group responded by calling for "new and imaginative approaches with the possibility of getting rid of the Castro regime."[53] The State Department recommended the use of Manuel Ray, the anti-Castro radical. "I do believe," Lansdale wrote Robert Kennedy on October 15, "we should make a real hard try at this—since helping Cubans to help themselves was the original concept of Mongoose and still has validity." But CIA had always rejected Ray as too independent. Lansdale added: "I believe you will have to hit CIA over the head personally. I can then follow through, to get the action desired."[54] . . . On the same day, CIA experts were poring over photographs just taken by a U-2 plane over western Cuba.

v

The CIA had yet another program against Castro, the one initiated in 1960 and dedicated to his death. The Agency had considered assassination within its purview since the early Eisenhower years when it gave a special unit responsibility for, among other things, kidnapping and murder. The Church committee found no evidence that this special unit tried to kill any foreign leaders.[55] There are indications, however, that CIA operatives abroad tried, or at least wished, to kill Chou En-lai in 1955.* But the fever seems not to have struck in full

---

* An Air India plane on which Chou En-lai had booked passage in Bandung, Indonesia, for the Afro-Asian Conference in April 1955 blew up in midair. Chou En-lai, who at the last minute flew instead to Rangoon to meet Nasser, was not on board. A detonating mechanism was recovered from the wreckage. The Hong Kong police described the incident as "carefully planned mass murder." On November 21, 1967, an alleged American defector named John Discoe Smith claimed in *Literturnaya Gazeta*

force until the last Eisenhower year. In August 1960 the CIA decided to kill Patrice Lumumba, the pro-Soviet Premier of the newly independent Congo, and delivered a bag of poison to Leopoldville for that purpose. (Lumumba's actual murder the following January was, however, the work of his fellow countrymen and not of the CIA.) In August also, the CIA set in motion the plot to kill Castro.

The early planning was evidently confided to a team of humorists. One idea was to dust Castro's shoes, if he chanced to leave them outside his hotel room, with thallium salts in the expectation that this would cause his beard to fall out and destroy his charisma. Another was to lace a box of cigars with a chemical that produced temporary disorientation and get Castro to smoke one before delivering a speech. Since Castro's speeches often gave an impression of disorientation anyway, it is not clear how much difference the toxic cigar would have made. By August 1960 the Agency had progressed to the project of impregnating cigars with botulinum, a poison so deadly that a man would die after putting one in his mouth. The cigars were ready in October and were delivered to an unidentified person the following February.[56]

The Agency also may have recruited Marie Lorenz, a pretty German girl whom Castro had taken as a mistress in 1959 and later cast off. She fell in with Frank Fiorini, an adventurer who had fought beside Castro, but turned against him and went to work for CIA; under the name of Frank Sturgis, Fiorini figured in the Bay of Pigs and later in Watergate. The CIA, Lorenz claimed in 1976, appealed to

---

(Moscow) that he had delivered the explosive mechanism on behalf of CIA to a Chinese Nationalist in Hong Kong (see Brian Urquhart, *Hammarskjold* [New York, 1972], 121; and *New York Times*, November 22, 1967). The deputy chief of the special unit told the Church committee that the recommendation to murder Chou was disapproved in Washington and the CIA station was "strongly censured" (Church committee, *Final Report*, bk. IV, 133; see n. 55). According to W. R. Corson's intermittently well-informed but too often undocumented book, Allen Dulles canceled the assassination of Chou lest General Lucian Truscott, whom Eisenhower had inserted into CIA as guardian of the presidential interest, inform the White House (W. R. Corson, *The Armies of Ignorance* [New York, 1977], 365–366). Despite all this, though, someone apparently blew up a plane on which Chou would have traveled except for his last-minute change of plan.

The year before, according to documents made public in 1978 under the Freedom of Information Act, the CIA designed a mind control experiment under the code name Artichoke to assess this "hypothetical" problem: "Can an individual of [deleted] descent be made to perform an act of attempted assassination involuntarily under the influence of Artichoke?" Sheffield Edwards, Artichoke's security officer, was the man who in 1960 proposed bringing in the mob to murder Castro. (See Nicholas M. Horrock, "C.I.A. Documents Tell of 1954 Project to Create Involuntary Assassins," *New York Times*, February 9, 1978.)

The Cuban Connection: I

her patriotism, promised her money for her old age and asked her to kill Castro. Sturgis gave her two poison capsules, which she secreted in a jar of cold cream. When she arrived in Havana, Castro greeted her warmly, took his phone off the hook, ordered food and coffee and then fell asleep on the bed with a cigar, evidently not a CIA model, in his mouth. Lorenz went to the bathroom and opened the cold cream. "I couldn't find the capsules," she said in 1976. "They had melted. It was like an omen. . . . I thought, 'To hell with it. Let history take its course.' "[57]

The Agency decided to turn to experts. When Castro's revolution swept into Havana at the end of 1958, it swept out not only Batista but the dictator's partners in the North American mob. Batista and the criminal entrepreneur Meyer Lansky fled on the same day. The closing of the casinos, the bordellos and the drug traffic cost the mob perhaps $100 million a year. Back in God's country, Lansky was reputed to have persuaded his associates to join in a pledge of a million dollars for Castro's head. Frank Sturgis claimed in 1975 that the mob had offered him $100,000 in 1959 to kill Castro. The masterminds of CIA now decided the syndicate possessed uniquely both the motives and skills required to rid the world of the Cuban revolutionary. Since the mob had its own grudge against Castro, a gangland hit would be less likely to lead back to the American government.[58]

The CIA commissioned Robert Maheu—a former FBI agent, later a private eye involved for a time with Hoffa's friend Eddie Cheyfitz and now working for Howard Hughes—to put out the contract. Maheu subsequently said that assassination was presented to him as "a necessary ingredient . . . of the overall invasion plan."[59] Maheu brought in John Rosselli, a minor crook-about-town he had known in Las Vegas. Rosselli, who had no illusions about his middling rank in the underworld, brought in the Chicago big shot Sam Giancana, who was a don and could make the right connections. Giancana's vital connection for this purpose was Santos Trafficante, Jr., the boss of organized crime in Florida; not so long before, in Havana.

CIA case officers made their contact with the underworld notables before they informed their own chief, Allen Dulles.[60] One would have supposed that an alliance between the CIA and the mob might have required prior approval at least by the CIA director, if not by the Special Group. That this was not the case suggests the liberties casually taken even by lesser CIA officials in the Agency's golden age.

In the fall of 1960, CIA installed Giancana and Rosselli in a Miami Beach hotel. The Agency stuck staunchly by Giancana even after J. Edgar Hoover sent Bissell in October a report that, "during recent conversations with several friends, Giancana stated that Fidel Castro was to be done away with shortly." For his part Giancana, plotting away in Miami and jealously apprehensive that his girl, the singer Phyllis McGuire, might have her own plots in Las Vegas, asked the CIA to arrange an illegal wiretap in the room of his putative rival, the comedian Dan Rowan. The Agency obliged: anything to keep Giancana happy. When the tap was discovered, the Agency did its best to stop prosecution.[61]

As for Trafficante, he was a leader in his field. He had been a prime suspect in the barbershop murder of Albert Anastasia in 1957. Later that year he had been picked up at the Apalachin seminar. Havana was his base, and he was the only syndicate boss to stay on after the revolution. Castro imprisoned him in 1959. For an enemy of the people, Trafficante lived behind bars in surprising comfort. Chums from the mainland visited him, among them the Dallas hood Jack Ruby.[62] On release in September 1959, Trafficante went to Tampa. With his Cuban business presumably destroyed, but with part of the gang still in Havana, Trafficante had both motives and men for the CIA job.

It may have been more complicated than that. Why, after all, had Castro let Trafficante go? A Federal Narcotics Bureau document in July 1961 reported rumors in the exile community that Castro had "kept Santo [sic] Trafficante, Jr., in jail to make it appear that he had a personal dislike for Trafficante, when in fact Trafficante is an agent of Castro. Trafficante is allegedly Castro's outlet for illegal contraband in the country."[63] While banning drugs at home, Castro might have wished to earn foreign exchange by permitting them to flow through Cuba to the United States, as they had done so lucratively under Batista. He might also have hoped to promote drug addiction in the United States—even as Chou En-lai organized the export of Chinese opium in order to demoralize American troops in Vietnam.* If Trafficante was indeed a double agent, one can see why Castro survived so comfortably the ministrations of the CIA.

With Giancana shot seven times in the throat and mouth as he was frying sausages in his Chicago kitchen in June 1975, with Rosselli hacked up, stuffed into an oil drum and dumped into the sea near

* Or so, according to the Egyptian editor Mohammed Heikal, Nasser's great confidant, Chou told Nasser in 1965, adding, "The effect this demoralization is going to have on the United States will be far greater than anyone realizes" (see Heikal, *The Cairo Documents* [Garden City, N.Y., 1973], 306–307).

Miami in July 1976, it is impossible to know how they viewed their CIA mission. Rosselli, according to some accounts, was in his way a patriot, persuaded he was serving his nation. But he had also entered the country illegally and may have looked on patriotic duty as insurance against deportation (as it turned out to be).* The cynical Giancana, a draft dodger during the Second World War, very likely entered his country's service now exclusively in the expectation that he would thereafter be immune to prosecution. For the rest, he evidently did not take it all too seriously. He told one friend that Maheu was "conning the hell out of the CIA." According to Rosselli, when Giancana heard that local police had discovered the CIA wiretap in Las Vegas, he almost swallowed his cigar "laughing about it."[64] One has the strong impression that the hoods, if they did not regard the whole thing as a big joke, at most only went through the motions of carrying out their assignment.

Their first idea was to slip some pills into Castro's drink shortly before the Bay of Pigs. After one batch of CIA pills failed to dissolve, a more soluble batch killed some innocent monkeys and was deemed suitable. The obliging Trafficante produced a Cuban who, he said, had access to one of Castro's favorite restaurants. Maheu gave the Cuban the pills and $10,000. Castro survived. A second attempt was made in April immediately before the Bay of Pigs. Castro survived.[65]

After the Bay of Pigs, the Castro project was, in the CIA patois, "stood down"—i.e., suspended. In the meantime William K. Harvey had entered the picture. In January 1961, before Kennedy's inauguration, Bissell discussed with Harvey, and soon directed him to establish, an "executive action capability" for the disabling of foreign leaders, including assassination as a "last resort." No one has been able to discover that the executive-action crowd did much apart from Cuba.[66] In April 1962, Richard Helms, who had now succeeded Bissell, ordered Harvey to reactivate the Castro project. Whatever else Harvey was, he was a professional, and he found the six-link operation—CIA to Maheu to Rosselli to Giancana to a Cuban exile to a Cuban assassin—intolerably loose. He thereupon instructed Rosselli to cut out Maheu and Giancana. Now it all started again: poison pills in April 1962; a three-man assassination team in June; talk of a new team in September; Castro always in perfect health. Harvey began to

* In 1971 the CIA intervened with the Immigration and Naturalization Service to discourage Rosselli's deportation (Church committee, *Interim Report*, 85; see n. 15).

doubt whether the operation was going anyplace. He finally terminated it in February 1963.[67] The mob's conning of CIA came to an end.

CIA's stalking of Castro did not. Some genius proposed that James Donovan, during his negotiations for the Bay of Pigs prisoners, give Castro a scuba diving suit contaminated by a tubercle bacillus and dusted inside with a fungus designed to produce skin disease. Donovan, who knew nothing of this, innocently foiled the Agency by giving Castro a clean diving suit on his own. Then Desmond FitzGerald, who replaced Harvey as head of Task Force W in January 1963, suggested depositing a rare seashell, rigged to explode, in a place where Castro might skin-dive and pick it up. This inspiration proved beyond the Agency's technical capacity.[68]

VI

Who authorized the CIA to try to murder foreign leaders? The answer remains obscure. In the Lumumba case, Eisenhower said something in a meeting of the National Security Council that at least one person present understood as an assassination order. A week later Gordon Gray, Eisenhower's special assistant for national security affairs, passed on to the Special Group the President's "extremely strong feelings on the necessity for very straightforward action"; not intending, however, to imply assassination. The next day Allen Dulles sent the assassination order to the CIA station in Leopoldville.[69]

One doubts whether this is really what Eisenhower had in mind. Assassination seems out of character for him. It was contrary, moreover, to what John Eisenhower described as his father's philosophy that "no man is indispensable."[70] But a mist of ambiguity envelops such situations. Intelligence people might fear to say too much on the ground that Presidents do not, or should not, want to know too much. Certainly words like "removal" and "elimination" caused trouble, then and later. To most people around a table, they meant removal from political office. To specialists in dirty tricks, they could mean removal from life.

The Castro authorization is even less documented. Richard Bissell assumed that Allen Dulles had cleared the idea with Eisenhower, using a "circumlocutious approach" in order to maintain "plausible deniability." But, according to Thomas Parrott, the CIA officer who served as secretary of the Special Group, Dulles's practice was to in-

The Cuban Connection: I

sist on specific orders rather than "tacit approval." Parrott found the theory of the "circumlocutious" approach "hard to believe." As for the Special Group, while it approved the plan to train Cuban exiles for an invasion of their homeland, it never approved—and probably, though the evidence is murky, never considered—any plot to kill Castro.[71]

Yet that plot was an integral part of the invasion plan. And it is hard to suppose that even the runaway agency mordantly portrayed in the reports of the President's Board of Consultants would have decided entirely on its own to kill the chief of a neighboring state. Dulles must have glimpsed a green light somewhere in 1960. Could it have been flashed by the Vice President of the United States? "I had been," Richard Nixon said in 1964 of the invasion project, "the strongest and most persistent advocate for setting up and supporting such a program."[72] Philip Bonsal, American ambassador to Cuba in 1959–60, called Nixon "the father of the operation."[73] Brigadier General Robert Cushman, Nixon's military aide and later his deputy director of the CIA, described him to Howard Hunt in 1960 as "the project's action officer in the White House."[74] On the other hand, Gordon Gray told the Church committee that such descriptions greatly exaggerated Nixon's role.

Nixon's apprehensive allusions to the Bay of Pigs in the privacy of his own Presidency remain enigmatic. On September 18, 1971, according to John D. Ehrlichman's notes, Nixon instructed him to tell CIA to turn over "the *full* file [on the Bay of Pigs] *or else.* . . . π [Ehrlichman's shorthand for the President] was involved in Bay of Pigs. π must have the file—deeply involved."[75] On July 23, 1972—six days after Hunt, Martinez and the Cubans were arrested in the Watergate building—Nixon brooded to H. R. Haldeman:

> Of course, this Hunt, that will uncover a lot of things. You open that scab, there's a hell of a lot of things, and we just feel that it would be very detrimental to have this thing go any further. . . . [Tell people] "Look, the problem is that this will open the whole, the whole Bay of Pigs thing, and the President just feels that ah, without going into the details"—don't, don't lie to them to the extent to say there is no involvement, but just say ". . . the President believes that it is going to open the whole Bay of Pigs thing up again."

And later that same day, again to Haldeman:

> If it gets out that this is all involved, the Cuba thing, it would be a fiasco. . . . It is likely to blow the whole Bay of Pigs thing, which we think would be very unfortunate—both for the CIA, and for the country.

The same day, later still, this time Haldeman speaking:

> The problem is it tracks back to the Bay of Pigs . . . The leads run out to people who had no involvement in this, except by contracts and connection, but it gets into areas that are likely to be raised.*

Whether or not it had been so commanded by someone in the White House, the CIA in the Eisenhower years had confidently taken unto itself the authority to kill foreign leaders.

VII

What of the Kennedy years? Did John and Robert Kennedy authorize the CIA to continue its attempts to murder Castro in 1961–63?

---

* Staff of the *New York Times*, *The End of a Presidency* (New York, 1974), 330, 335–336, 347–349.

In a notarized statement received by the Church committee on March 9, 1976, Nixon, while asserting that there were "circumstances in which presidents may lawfully authorize actions in the interests of the security of this country, which if undertaken by other persons, or even by the president himself under different circumstances, would be illegal," claimed (for what it is worth) that "assassination of a foreign leader" was "an act I never had cause to consider and which under most circumstances would be abhorrent to any president" (Church committee, *Final Report*, bk. IV, 157–158; see n. 55). The committee did not submit specific interrogatories about the Bay of Pigs.

In August 1976, Congressman Thomas Downing of Virginia released affidavits from Robert D. Morrow, who said he was a CIA contract agent in 1960, and Mario Kohly, Jr., the son of a right-wing Cuban exile, now deceased. The affidavits claimed that the elder Kohly had told them of an agreement between himself and Nixon (in the words of Morrow's affidavit) "for the elimination of Miro Cardona and all the leftist Cuban Revolutionary Front leaders in order that Kohly could immediately take over the reins of power in Cuba, once a successful invasion of exiles being trained by the CIA had been accomplished. . . . [Manuel] Artime [commander of the Cuban Brigade] and his followers were to be assassinated by [Kohly's] force once a successful landing had been accomplished."

In October 1963, Robert Morgenthau procured the indictment of the elder Kohly on charges of conspiracy to counterfeit Cuban pesos. Kohly was convicted and sentenced to a year in prison. On March 9, 1965, Nixon wrote Judge Edward Weinfeld asking for a suspension or reduction of Kohly's sentence on the ground that "the patriotism, courage and energy of the exiles in attempting to mount a counterrevolution have been in the past, and may in the future again be regarded as advantageous to the interests of the United States." (See *Richmond Times-Dispatch*, August 1, 3, 1976; *Newport News* [Virginia] *Daily Press*, August 1, 1976. I am indebted to Eston Melton of the *Times-Dispatch* for assembling the documents on this interesting but inconclusive matter.)

In a weird book entitled *Betrayal* (New York: Warner reprint, 1976), Morrow claimed that he had discovered nuclear missile sites in Cuba in 1961 and that the Kennedys deliberately suppressed the evidence. He described the CIA leadership as bitterly antagonistic toward the Kennedys. Robert Kennedy was depicted as the nemesis of Kohly and his anti-Castro counterfeiting scheme. The book's accuracy may be judged by its account of Owen Brewster, who had retired in 1952, as sitting senator from Maine in 1962 (ibid., 95).

The Cuban Connection: I

Though the assassination plan was confided to Robert Maheu, though it became a staple of Sam Giancana's table talk and a joke among the mob, there is *no* evidence that any Agency official ever mentioned it to any President—Eisenhower in 1960, Kennedy after 1960, Johnson after 1963—except (in Johnson's case) for operations already terminated. The practice of "plausible denial" had, as Colonel William R. Corson, a veteran intelligence officer, put it, "degenerated to the point where the cover stories of presidential ignorance really are fact, not fiction."[76]

Nor was the Castro murder plan submitted to the Special Group, the supposed control mechanism for covert action, either in 1960 or thereafter; nor to the Special Group (Augmented), sitting on top of Mongoose. Nor was it disclosed after the Bay of Pigs to Maxwell Taylor and his review board.[77] Rusk, McNamara, Bundy, Taylor, Gilpatric, Goodwin, Rostow, all testified under oath that they had never heard of it (nor had Kenneth O'Donnell,[78] nor, for that matter, had I). On every occasion in the Kennedy years when CIA officials might naturally have brought it up—Bissell's briefings of his old Yale friend Mac Bundy after the inauguration, the Bay of Pigs meetings, the Taylor board, the missile crisis—they studiously refrained from saying a word.

The argument that the Kennedys knew and approved of the assassination plan comes down, in the end, to the argument that they *must* have known—an argument that, of course, applies with equal force to Eisenhower and Johnson. The CIA, it is said, would never have undertaken so fearful a task without presidential authorization.

In John Kennedy's case, Bissell and Helms offered contradictory theories about the nature of that authorization. Bissell assumed the project had been cleared with Kennedy, as with Eisenhower, in ways that were tacit, "circumlocutious," camouflaged, leaving no record. Helms thought CIA's authority was derived, not from supposed "circumlocutious" talks, but from the "intense" pressure the Kennedys radiated against Castro. The CIA operators were undoubtedly misled by the urgency with which the Kennedys, especially Robert, pursued Mongoose. "We cannot overemphasize the extent," the CIA inspector general said in 1967, "to which responsible Agency officers felt themselves subject to the Kennedy Administration's severe pressure to do something about Castro and his regime." "It was the policy at the time to get rid of Castro," said Helms, "and if killing him was one of the things that was to be done in this connection, that was within what was expected." Having been asked "to get rid of Castro," Helms added, ". . . there were no limitations put on the means, and we felt we were acting well within the guidelines." No member of the administration told Helms to kill Castro, but no one had ever specifically ruled it out, so the Agency, he believed, could work for Castro's overthrow as it deemed best. Moreover, as Helms said, "Nobody wants to embarrass a President . . . by discussing the assassination of foreign leaders in his presence."[79]

Still it seems singular that, even if the CIA people believed they had an original authorization of some yet undiscovered sort from Eisenhower, they never inquired of Kennedy whether he wished these risky and disagreeable adventures to continue. The project after all had begun as part of the Cuban invasion plan. In this context the murder of Castro had an arguably rational, if wholly repellent, function. After the Bay of Pigs and the abandonment of invasion fantasies, the radical change in context ought surely to have compelled reconsideration both of the project itself and of the alleged authorization. The Mongoose committee was demanding at this time that all "sensitive" operations be presented in "excruciating" detail, case by case. But the Agency, without consulting superior authority, resuscitated the assassination project on its own, the murder of Castro now becoming, without the invasion, an end in itself—a quite pointless end, too, in the unconsulted judgment of the CIA's Intelligence Branch. In October 1961 the Special Group asked for a contingency plan in the event Castro died from whatever cause. The CIA Board of Estimates responded that Castro's death "by assassination or by natural causes . . . would almost certainly not prove fatal to the regime." Its main effect would probably be to strengthen the Communist position in Cuba.[80] Unfortunately the Intelligence Branch and the Clandestine Services were hardly on speaking terms.

It appears that the CIA regarded whatever authorization it thought it had acquired in 1960 as permanent, not requiring review and reconfirmation by new Presidents or, even more astonishingly, by new CIA directors. For neither Bissell nor Helms even told John McCone what his own Agency was up to. Harvey, after supplying Rosselli with a new batch of poison pills in 1962, briefed Helms and, according to the 1967 report by the CIA inspector general, "obtained Helms' approval not to brief the Director." "For a variety of reasons which were tossed back and forth," Harvey said later, "we agreed that it was not necessary or advisable to brief him." One reason was that the project had "arisen with full authority insofar as either of us

The Cuban Connection: I

knew long before I knew anything about it, and before the then-Director became Director." Harvey also knew that McCone, a devout Catholic, would fiercely disapprove. When assassination arose in another connection, McCone told Harvey, "If I got myself involved in something like this, I might end up getting myself excommunicated." Much later, in August 1963, McCone read in the *Chicago Sun-Times* that Giancana had a relationship with CIA. He asked at once for an explanation. Helms gave him a memorandum that described the operation as having been closed out before McCone took over. "Well," said McCone, "this did not happen during my tenure," unaware of what was still happening during his tenure.*

VIII

There is evidence, in other connections, of John Kennedy's attitude toward assassination. Lumumba had not been killed during his tenure; but Nasser of Egypt wrote the new President soon afterward reproaching the American government for the part he was sure it had had in Lumumba's murder. "Political assassination," Kennedy replied, while his own CIA was hustling the mob to poison Castro, ". . . should be . . . vigorously investigated and condemned."81

Then, on May 30, 1961, a group of Dominican patriots gunned down Rafael Trujillo, the most sadistic and squalid of Latin American tyrants. To its credit, the Eisenhower administration had established contact with anti-Trujillo Dominicans, and in December 1960 the Special Group approved a program of covert support for the dissidents. Henry Dearborn, the able American consul in the Dominican Republic, was in charge of the operation. The dissidents believed—and Dearborn agreed—that successful action against the regime required the assassination of Trujillo. On January 12, 1961, eight days before Kennedy took over, the Special Group approved the transfer of three revolvers and three carbines to the conspirators. Since the leading conspirators were generals, they had sufficient access to arms of their own; their point was evidently to obtain symbolic support from the United States. The Kennedy White House

---

* Church committee, *Interim Report*, 99–108; see n. 15. According to Corson, McCone was "fired for not knowing what was going on in the CIA with respect to the Castro 'hit'" (Corson, *Armies of Ignorance*, 35). This seems improbable. McCone left in April 1965. Johnson apparently first learned of the CIA assassination plots from a column by Drew Pearson in the spring of 1967. Johnson's demand for an investigation then led to the Inspector General's Report of May 23, 1967 (Church committee, *Interim Report*, 179).

knew in a general way about the contacts, and approved. It did not know about the transfer of arms.

In May rumors began to circulate that Trujillo might be assassinated. "I looked into the matter," Robert Kennedy said in notes dictated two days after Trujillo's death, "after I had a discussion with Allen Dulles over at the Pentagon. I called the President. He had known nothing about it and it was decided at that time that we'd put a task force on the problem and try to work out some kind of an alternative course of action in case this event did occur. Dick Goodwin from the White House worked on it."[82] Goodwin promptly got from CIA the details of its covert program in the Dominican Republic. When he read that the dissidents had received weapons "attendant to their project efforts to neutralize TRUJILLO," he circled the paragraph, underlined "neutralize" and took the document in to Kennedy.[83]

This was the first the White House knew about weapons. Kennedy reacted at once. "If Trujillo goes, he goes," he said, "but why are we pushing that?" In fact, Kennedy did not want Trujillo's overthrow until he knew what would come thereafter. He detested Trujillo and favored the OAS sanctions against him, but for international reasons, preferred the Trujillo regime to a Communist takeover.[84] He told Goodwin to advise Dearborn that the United States was not going to get involved in assassination and that we were not going to give any more weapons to anyone. Dearborn replied that, after a year of dealing with the conspirators, it was "too late to consider whether United States will initiate overthrow of Trujillo." Goodwin drafted a rejoinder intended to preserve friendly relations with the rebels while avoiding American implication in their plot. Kennedy personally strengthened the draft by adding: "US as a matter of general policy cannot condone assassination. This last principle is overriding."[85] The cable was sent on May 29. The Dominicans who killed Trujillo the next day did so for Dominican reasons and with Dominican weapons.

Neither Eisenhower nor the Kennedys nor the CIA ordered Trujillo's assassination. At most, they were sympathetic to Dominicans who saw no other way to liberate their country. When Trujillo was killed, the President was in Paris, where Pierre Salinger, running ahead of hard information, told reporters that Trujillo was dead, a statement that some thought indicated American foreknowledge. In Washington, however, there was only confusion. "When Allen Dulles

The Cuban Connection: I

called me yesterday morning," Robert Kennedy said in his June 1 notes, "the reports still had not been verified. A half hour later he called me back and said that it looked like it was probably 99 chances out of 100 that Trujillo had in fact been assassinated." Kennedy's observations indicated a degree of ignorance among top government officials incompatible with an authorized CIA operation:

> We had been in contact with some of the generals who were anti-Trujillo. They had been asking for some arms and it had been decided in the last week or so that we wouldn't furnish them. I was quite surprised that the extent of their requests were for sub-machine guns. It didn't seem to me very extensive. . . .
>
> We still don't know how much popular support this anti-Trujillo group has. We don't know who is involved in it; we have at the present time no contact of any kind with them; we haven't received a report from the consul indicating that he has any contact with them. . . . The great problem now is that we don't know what to do because we don't know what the situation is.[86]

IX

As for Castro: in November 1961, after recommending Tad Szulc, the Latin American correspondent of the *New York Times*, for a job in the administration, Goodwin brought him in to see John Kennedy. According to notes Szulc made immediately after the talk, the President asked what the United States might do about Cuba, "either [in] a hostile way or in establishing some kind of dialogue." Then Kennedy said, "What would you think if I ordered Castro to be assassinated?" Szulc said the murder of Castro would not necessarily change things and it was not anything the United States should be doing. Szulc's notes: "JFK then said he was testing me, that he felt the same way . . . because indeed U.S. morally must not be part[y] to assassinations. JFK said he raised question because he was under terrific pressure from advisers (think he said intelligence people, but not positive) to okay a Castro murder." Szulc remembered Kennedy going on "for a few minutes to make the point how strongly he and his brother felt that the United States for moral reasons should never be in a situation of having recourse to assassination."[87] If Kennedy had ever planned to give such an order, he would hardly have begun by telling the *New York Times* about it. A day or two later, Goodwin, out of curiosity, raised the question with Kennedy, observing that it sounded like a crazy idea to him. "If we get into that kind of thing," Kennedy said, "we'll all be targets."[88] That same month Kennedy said in a speech, "We cannot, as a free nation, compete with our adversaries in tactics of terror [and] assassination."[89]

Kennedy's reference to pressure from the intelligence people is puzzling, since the relevant CIA officials still alive in 1975 (Dulles died in 1969) all denied ever having discussed assassination with him. But there was evidently something in the air. Kennedy's old friend Senator George Smathers of Florida used to press him in those days to take a tougher stand against Castro. "My feeling," Smathers said in 1964, "was that he was not sufficiently aware as to the importance of Cuba, and I used to talk with him rather insistently about it. . . . He always identified me with pushing, pushing, pushing." On one occasion they speculated about Castro's assassination. Kennedy, Smathers recalled, was certain it could be done but doubted whether it would accomplish what he wanted. Smathers thought Kennedy "horrified" at the idea. Smathers continued to push. At last, one summer evening in the White House, "I remember that he took his fork and just hit his plate and it cracked and he said, 'Now, dammit, I wish you wouldn't do that. Let's quit talking about this subject. . . . Do me a favor. . . . I don't want you to talk to me any more about Cuba.' . . . And I never did."[90]

The only evidence that any Kennedy was told about the CIA operations came in the spring of 1962. CIA officials, anxious to protect Sam Giancana from the legal consequences of the wiretap he had demanded on Dan Rowan's Las Vegas telephone, brought insistent pressure on the Justice Department to refrain from prosecution. At first they spoke vaguely to Justice about Giancana's part in "CIA's clandestine efforts against the Castro government." This meant, they explained, that CIA was utilizing underworld sources in Havana for intelligence purposes. Robert Kennedy, unimpressed, scribbled on the FBI report of the CIA representations: "Courtney I hope this will be followed up vigorously." It was. The Agency continued to object, saying in April 1962 that prosecution "would lead to exposure of most sensitive information relating to the abortive Cuban invasion in April 1961." This was still not enough.[91]

Finally, on May 7, 1962, Lawrence Houston, the CIA's general counsel, explained why the case was so momentous. The CIA, he told Robert Kennedy, had recruited Giancana to murder Castro; therefore the Las Vegas prosecution involved national security. It was Houston's understanding, as he later testified, that "the assassination plan aimed at Castro had been terminated completely," and he so informed the Attorney General. He did not know that it had been resurrected and that Harvey had already passed on a new vial of CIA poison pills to Rosselli. Houston recalled that Kennedy was "upset" by CIA's use of Giancana. "If you have seen Mr. Kennedy's eyes get steely and his voice get low and precise, you get a definite feeling of unhappiness." Kennedy told Houston in sarcastic understatement, "I trust that if you ever try to do business with organized crime again— with gangsters—you will let the Attorney General know." Kennedy subsequently told J. Edgar Hoover about the CIA plot against Castro in terms that led Hoover to describe it as a situation "which had considerably disturbed him."[92] Plainly Kennedy had known nothing about assassination plots.

Houston did not recall that Kennedy expressed himself on the principle of assassinating Castro. Kennedy thought he had. In 1965, pressed by a group of Peruvian intellectuals—one person insisting, "Castro! Castro! What have you done about Castro?"—Kennedy said to his interpreter, "Tell them that I saved his life."[93] In 1967 Jack Anderson, breaking the story about the CIA and the mob, wrote that "Bobby, eager to avenge the Bay of Pigs fiasco, played a key role in the planning."[94] Kennedy, outraged, said to his assistants Peter Edelman and Adam Walinsky, "I didn't start it. I stopped it. . . . I found out that some people were going to try an attempt on Castro's life and I turned it off."*

X

Had the Attorney General approved the assassination of Castro, he would have been more appreciative of Giancana's patriotic zeal. Moreover, the gangster no doubt thought he had another, and equally esoteric, hold on the Kennedys. For, through his friend Frank Sinatra, Giancana had met in March 1960 a pretty girl named Judith Campbell whom Sinatra had introduced to John Kennedy the month before. If Campbell can be believed, she devotedly cultivated her relations with both men, the don and the President, over the next two years.[95]

White House logs show that Campbell telephoned some seventy times after January 1961 in pursuit of her friendship with John Ken-

* Seymour M. Hersh, "Aides Say Robert Kennedy Told of CIA Castro Plot," *New York Times,* March 10, 1975. See also the testimony of another Kennedy senatorial assistant, Frank Mankiewicz: "He told me that there was some crazy CIA plan at one time for sending some Cubans in to get Castro which he called off" (Mankiewicz, in recorded interview by L. J. Hackman, October 20, 1969, 70, RFK Oral History Program).

nedy.[96] One cannot conclude whether she was doing it out of a weakness for Presidents or whether she was put up to it by Giancana so that the underworld might get something on Kennedy. It seems improbable that she had a more complicated role. "I couldn't imagine her being privy to any kind of secret information," said William Campbell, her ex-husband. "She wouldn't understand it anyway. I mean . . . they weren't dealing with some kind of Phi Beta Kappa."* In any case, Hoover, in February 1962, informed the Attorney General about Judith Campbell's associations with Giancana. On March 22, Hoover brought a memorandum about her to one of his luncheons with the President. The Campbell calls ceased.[97]

Between CIA protection and the blackmail potentiality, Giancana expected immunity from federal prosecution. He was badly disappointed. The Attorney General remembered him well as the powerful Chicago racketeer who had giggled before the Rackets Committee. "Robert Kennedy was always out to get him," William Hundley said later. "He would raise hell about him. . . ." "Bobby pushed to get Giancana at any cost."[98] "They can't do this to me," Giancana said to Edward Bennett Williams, whom he tried to hire as his lawyer. "I'm working for the government."† But they did. He was put under heavy surveillance. FBI cars clogged the street near his house. FBI agents followed him everywhere—to the Armory Lounge, his favorite bar; to church; to the golf course, where four agents played the hole behind him. When he missed a putt, they would all boo (or so he claimed). Giancana sent a message to the Attorney General: "If Bobby Kennedy wants to talk to me, I'll be glad to talk to him, and he knows who to go through." Lest this allusion be unclear, the intermediary explained how close Giancana was to Sinatra.[99] Such a message was not calculated to impress Kennedy. Receiving no response, Giancana then sued in federal court for relief. The judge obligingly instructed the FBI agents to play golf at least two foursomes back. For unknown reasons—perhaps the CIA again—the federal attorney declined cross-examination. Later Giancana, given immunity from prosecution by a grand jury, refused to testify, was held in contempt and went to prison for the first time since 1942.[100] On his release, after a year, he went into gilded exile in Cuernavaca.

* *New York Post*, December 22, 1975. Campbell herself thought it "possible that I was used almost from the beginning" (Judith Exner, *My Story* [New York, 1977], 142).

† Williams repeated this statement to Hundley, who said it was ludicrous. Then Williams asked Maheu, an old schoolmate. Maheu verified Giancana's claim (Edward Bennett Williams, in interview by author, January 23, 1976).

The Cuban Connection: I

The Sinatra connection raised problems. Sinatra had been an enthusiastic Kennedy fund raiser in the campaign. He had sung at the inaugural gala. Peter and Patricia Lawford were in his intimate circle. But "it seemed he almost took a pleasure," Peter Lawford said later, "in flaunting his friendship with Giancana. . . . Giancana often stayed at Frank's home in Palm Springs."[101] Sinatra was financially involved, moreover, in dubious casinos and racetracks. A report of August 13, 1962, prepared by the Organized Crime Section at Robert Kennedy's request, set forth in detail Sinatra's associations with the mob.[102] Six months earlier, the Kennedys had already decided to draw away. Sinatra, expecting to entertain Kennedy in his Palm Springs house, had put in a helicopter pad and made other preparations. Shortly before a California trip in the spring of 1962, Kennedy called Peter Lawford. "I can't stay there," he said. "You know as much as I like Frank I can't go there, not while Bobby is handling this [Giancana] investigation."[103] Kennedy then compounded the humiliation by staying at the Palm Desert house of Bing Crosby, not only the rival troubadour of the day but a Republican. The President's action deeply wounded Sinatra. The lovely actress Angie Dickinson told me the next year that she had heard Sinatra say, "If he would only pick up the telephone and call me and say that it was politically difficult to have me around, I would understand. I don't want to hurt him. But he has never called me." I asked Angie about Lawford and Sinatra. She said, "Well, the President excluded Frank, so Frank excluded Peter."[104]

John Kennedy appreciated Sinatra's services in 1960 and liked him personally; no one, when the mood was on him, could be more charming than Sinatra. I think the President may have felt a little badly about it. For a moment in late 1963 Sinatra was on the guest list for a White House state dinner; at the last minute, on a pretext, the invitation was withdrawn. It was subsequently said that Robert Kennedy shared this regret and ignored recommendations from the Organized Crime Section for an investigation of Sinatra.[105] According to Hundley, however, his people investigated Sinatra with care and found nothing incriminating beyond associations.[106] Sinatra himself said in 1976: "I read the report about how Bobby Kennedy protected me from investigation by Government agents and now realize that after five grand-jury subpoenas, two [Internal Revenue Service] investigations (which probably utilized about 30 men) and a couple of subpoenas to Congressional committees, if you have a close friend in high office, you don't need any enemies."[107]

XI

The record shows that the only assassination plot disclosed to Robert Kennedy involved Sam Giancana—and that Kennedy did his best thereafter to put Giancana behind bars. As the CIA's inspector general put it in the 1967 report, "The Attorney General was not told that the gambling syndicate operation had already been reactivated, nor, as far as we know, was he ever told that CIA had a continuing involvement with U.S. gangster elements."[108] Nor did any of these arresting facts emerge in the course of Operation Mongoose. Helms testified that he never told Robert Kennedy about any assassination activity and never received any assassination order from him. Harvey testified that he never informed the Special Group (Augmented) or any of its members of the ongoing plots. Lansdale testified that Harvey had never told him about any such activities and that he had never discussed assassination with Robert Kennedy.[109]

The subject of assassination came up at one of the Augmented Group's meetings, on August 10, 1962. Robert Kennedy was not present. McNamara raised the question—one can only assume, in view of his ready dismissal of the idea a few days later, either in an academic survey of options or in a moment of acute frustration. McCone and Murrow took sharp exception. The "consensus," Lansdale said, "was . . . hell no on this and there was a very violent reaction." Nevertheless Lansdale inexplicably produced a memorandum three days later that, among other things, asked Harvey to look into the question of "liquidation of leaders." (No one knew that Harvey had been looking into this question for some time.) On reading the memorandum, McCone blew up, called McNamara and demanded that it be withdrawn. "I agreed with Mr. McCone," McNamara said, "that no such planning should be undertaken." When McCone's stern disapproval of assassination was later communicated to Helms and Harvey, neither thought it necessary to tell their boss about Rosselli.[110]

Nor is it correct to say that John Kennedy did not communicate his own disapproval of assassination. He took care to send CIA his statement of May 29, 1961, that the United States could not as a matter of general policy condone assassination. It was a statement he never thereafter withdrew, qualified or amended. No doubt the CIA people took it as another of those superb efforts in misdirection to which they were addicted in their own daily work. Perhaps the failure

The Cuban Connection: I

of the Kennedys, McCone and others at the top specifically to forbid the assassination of Castro may have reinforced the CIA's delusion that killing foreign leaders was permissible. On the other hand, since none of them, including McCone, knew that Castro's assassination remained so heavily on CIA's mind, they would probably have regarded such an order as superfluous.

Several circumstantial points strengthen the conclusion that the Kennedys knew nothing about the continuing assassination policy. There is the McCone problem. If the Kennedys had been informed, the informer would have had to stipulate that they not mention the plots to McCone, who was deliberately not informed. Given John Kennedy's reliance on McCone to bring the Agency under control and Robert Kennedy's close personal friendship with McCone, it strains credulity to suppose that either would have accepted such a stipulation from some subordinate CIA official. In any case, both Bissell and Helms denied ever talking about assassinations with either Kennedy.

Then there is the problem of the Bay of Pigs prisoners. If the Kennedys had any obsessive feeling about Cuba, it was to save the lives of the prisoners. Nothing would more surely have doomed the prisoners than the assassination of Castro, whether attributed to anti-Castro Cubans or to the CIA.

Some have written that the Kennedys had got their Irish up and were determined to get even with Castro at any cost.[111] This overlooks the fact that the CIA had organized the plots well before the Irish moved into the White House. The Kennedys no doubt felt a personal animus toward Castro; but, if they were consumed by a vendetta, they would have had the perfect pretext when the Soviet Union sent nuclear missiles to Cuba in October 1962. Many advisers urged them then to seize the opportunity, invade Cuba and smash Castro forever. Robert Kennedy led the fight against this course. John Kennedy made the decision against it.

Then there is the fact that Allen Dulles withheld from the Warren Commission all information regarding the assassination plots. One obvious reason might have been his fear that, if Robert Kennedy now learned about the extent of the plots, he might hold the CIA responsible for his brother's death.

The available evidence clearly leads to the conclusion that the Kennedys did not know about the Castro assassination plots before the Bay of Pigs or about the pursuit of those plots by the CIA after the Bay of Pigs. There is a final consideration. No one who knew

John and Robert Kennedy well believed they would conceivably countenance a program of assassination. Like McCone, they were Catholics. Robert, at least, was quite as devout as McCone. Theodore Sorensen's statement about John Kennedy applied to them both: assassination "was totally foreign to his character and conscience, foreign to his fundamental reverence for human life and his respect for his adversaries, foreign to his insistence upon a moral dimension in U.S. foreign policy and his concern for this country's reputation abroad and foreign to his pragmatic recognition that so horrendous but inevitably counterproductive a precedent committed by a country whose own chief of state was inevitably vulnerable could only provoke reprisals." "I find," said McGeorge Bundy, "the notion that they separately, privately encouraged, ordered, or arranged efforts at assassination totally inconsistent with what I knew of both of them, . . . their character, their purposes, and their nature and the way they confronted international affairs." McNamara said it would have been "totally inconsistent with everything I knew about the two men."[112] I too find the idea incredible that these two men, so filled with love of life and so conscious of the ironies of history, could thus deny all the values and purposes that animated their existence.

(22)

Robert Kennedy and the Missile Crisis

EARLY IN 1961 Robert Kennedy had become acquainted with a Soviet official named Georgi Bolshakov. Nominally the embassy press attaché, Bolshakov conveyed the impression that he was in fact Khrushchev's personal representative in Washington. That may well have been the case. Certainly the CIA considered him a top KGB agent.[1] "If so," said Ben Bradlee, "he was a gregarious spy, could drink up a storm, and liked to hand wrestle."[2] "He was Georgi to everyone," recalled James Symington, who succeeded Seigenthaler as the Attorney General's assistant, "and he seemed to find satisfaction in being kidded. With self-deprecating nods, smiles, and circus English, he enjoyed Bob's predilection for harmless buffoons, and had almost unlimited access to the inner sanctum."[3]

I

Bolshakov was full of chaff and badinage. In November 1961 Kennedy noted, "Russian told me K[hrushchev] is Kennedyizing USSR Gov.—bringing in young people with new vitality, new ideas—I told this to Jack who laughed & said we should be Khrushchevizing the Am. Gov."[4] After the FBI men woke up the reporters during the steel imbroglio, Bolshakov observed to the Attorney General that "he saw in the papers that we were learning a few things from the Russians i.e., sending the police around in the middle of the night."[5] Later: "Georgi said that what had happened in the steel dispute had made a big impression in the Soviet Union but that Khrushchev still honestly believes the country is run by the Rockefellers, the Morgans and the big financiers on Wall Street. He said Khrushchev had his eyes opened tremendously on his visit to the United States but still many of those who report to him report the old fashioned ideas and thoughts and do not realize what the United States is like today."[6]

They talked every fortnight or so. "I met with him about all kinds of things," Robert Kennedy said in 1964. ". . . Most of the major matters dealing with the Soviet Union and the United States were discussed. Arrangements were made really between Georgi Bolshakov and myself. . . . Unfortunately—stupidly—I didn't write many of the things down. I just delivered the messages verbally to my brother and he'd act on them and I think sometimes he'd tell the State Department and sometimes perhaps he didn't."[7]

They reviewed the preparations for the Vienna meeting. They went through the Berlin crisis of 1961 together. "I kept telling Georgi Bolshakov we would fight. He said he kept reporting it."[8] In the last days of the crisis there was a frightening confrontation of American and Soviet tanks at the Brandenburg Gate. "I got in touch with Bolshakov and said the President would like them to take their tanks out of there in twenty-four hours. He said he'd speak to Khrushchev, and they took their tanks out in twenty-four hours. So he delivered effectively when it was a matter of importance."[9]

In the spring of 1962, when the Kennedy administration was laboring to establish a neutralist Laos under Prince Souvanna Phouma, the Communist Pathet Lao resumed the military offensive and derailed the negotiations. Robert Kennedy, summoning Bolshakov, said that his brother had relied on Soviet assurances there would be no new hostilities and "felt now he had been double-crossed." This, the Attorney General emphasized, was a personal message to Khrushchev. Several days passed before Bolshakov returned with an answer.

> He said this was personal from Khrushchev to the President. He said there would not be any further armed action in Laos but they were anxious that the whole matter be resolved peacefully. . . . Georgi came back to see me the following day and I told him that the President was pleased with the message and again, that we were going to do all that we could with Souvanna Phouma but Khrushchev also had to work on his people on the other side.[10]

Khrushchev was "very pleased with the settlement in Laos," Bolshakov soon reported, but worried about American troops in Thailand. "Georgi said," Robert wrote his brother, "that Khrushchev understood that the reason the troops were sent in was because of the possibility of an outbreak in Laos. Therefore, now that the agreement had been made in Laos . . . Mr. Khrushchev hoped that it was possible for the United States to withdraw its troops from Thailand."[11] The President told Robert to reply that withdrawal would begin in ten days.[12] "Khrushchev sent back a message that it meant a great deal. So some of these crises which were building up and which perhaps [were] due to misunderstanding were discussed and an effort made to resolve them through these kinds of discussions."[13]

The Attorney General was not the only unconventional channel. On September 30, 1961, Bolshakov delivered to Pierre Salinger the first in the extraordinary exchange of letters initiated by Khrushchev as the Berlin crisis was subsiding. Thereafter the letters were passed along in cloak-and-dagger fashion, Salinger meeting Bolshakov at Washington street corners or bars, receiving documents enclosed in folded newspapers or placed surreptitiously in the pocket of his trench coat. On one rainy night, Bolshakov, the transaction completed, clapped Salinger on the back and said, jovially, "Every man has his Russian, and I'm yours."[14]

He was above all Robert Kennedy's Russian. An authentic friendship grew. Officially Robert Kennedy remained on Moscow's enemies list. *Za Rubezhom,* the weekly political journal, described him in June 1962 as an enemy of the working class, defender of monopolies, organizer of guerrilla warfare against Cuba, champion of preventive war.[15] But Bolshakov, on behalf of the Kremlin, invited him to visit the Soviet Union. The President thought not, feeling a visit by his brother would "ruffle a lot of feathers over in State."[16] Then the Russians indicated they would welcome the Attorney General as successor to Llewellyn Thompson, now about to leave Moscow after five years as ambassador. "The President spoke to me once about sending me," Robert Kennedy recalled. ". . . In the first place I couldn't possibly learn Russian. I spent ten years learning French. And secondly . . . for the first couple of months I might have done something but, after that, I don't think . . . the amount of good it would have done would have remained."[17] President Kennedy finally decided, as he told Thompson, that Bobby "was too greatly needed in Washington."[18]

In the meantime, the Foreign Service was "strongly" urging the appointment of Foy Kohler, a rigid Cold Warrior. "I had been involved in a lot of conferences with Foy Kohler," Robert Kennedy said later. ". . . I wasn't impressed with him at all. He gave me rather the creeps and I don't think he'd be the kind of a person who could really get anything done with the Russians. . . . Finally, my brother said well, . . . if I could come up with a decent candidate he'd send him. . . . [I] was not able to offer any alternative so he was finally appointed."[19]

The Georgi-Bobby exchanges and the Khrushchev-Kennedy correspondence provide the counterpoint against which the public declarations of the period must be read. Behind the obligatory Cold War rhetoric, the two leaders were trying to forestall conflict and to seek accommodation. All this built in the course of 1962 a measure of mutual understanding, even of mutual confidence.

II

Having established a measure of confidence, Khrushchev proceeded to abuse it. He had begun to ship military equipment in growing amounts to Castro. The administration was disturbed. It would have been far more disturbed had it known that Khrushchev was sending nuclear missiles too. But in early September, Anatoly Dobrynin, the new ambassador, gave Robert Kennedy a reassuring message from Khrushchev for his brother: not to worry, no offensive weapons, no dirty tricks to embarrass the administration during the impending congressional election. Shortly afterward Bolshakov returned from Moscow with further reassurance. He had met with Khrushchev and Anastas Mikoyan, the first deputy chairman. This was the time to lower tensions, Khrushchev had said; Castro was getting only defensive weapons. Here Mikoyan had interjected: short-range, surface-to-air missiles for use against planes; in no circumstances would long-range, surface-to-surface missiles go to Cuba.*

Of course they were lying. But had the American secret war against Castro left the Russians no alternative but to send nuclear missiles secretly to Cuba? Certainly Castro had the best grounds for feeling under siege. Even if double agents had not told him the CIA was trying to kill him, the Mongoose campaign left little doubt that the American government was trying to overthrow him. It

* Bolshakov read the notes of his Moscow talk to Charles Bartlett on October 24. The Russian, Bartlett reported to Robert Kennedy, was "clearly puzzled and disturbed" but insisted "he could not believe there were long-range missiles on the island. . . . He agreed with me that if things were as they appeared, he was in the position of having been deceived by his own officials" (Bartlett to RFK, October 26, 1962, RFK Papers; see also Robert F. Kennedy, *Thirteen Days: A Memoir of the Cuban Missile Crisis* [New York, 1971 ed., with afterword by Richard E. Neustadt and Graham T. Allison], 5). Bolshakov's reaction contradicts the claim of some revisionist historians that Khrushchev was innocent of deception, that the Americans just misunderstood his messages.

would hardly have been unreasonable for him to request Soviet protection. But did he request nuclear missiles?

The best evidence is that he did not. Castro's aim was to deter American aggression by convincing Washington that an attack on Cuba would be the same as an attack on the Soviet Union. This did not require nuclear missiles. "We thought," he told Jean Daniel of *L'Express* in November 1963, "of a proclamation, an alliance, conventional military aid." It was Khrushchev who thought of nuclear missiles. "The initial idea," Castro said, "originated with the Russians and with them alone." Khrushchev's proposal, Castro said to Daniel with emphasis, *"surprised us at first and gave us great pause."* No doubt he worried (rightly) that the Soviet missile bases in Cuba would be an intolerable provocation to Washington. So he resisted the missiles. "When Castro and I talked about the problem," Khrushchev recalled, "we argued and argued. Our argument was very heated. But, in the end, Fidel agreed with me." "We felt that we could not get out of it," Castro told Claude Julien of *Le Monde* the next March. "This is why we accepted them. It was not in order to ensure our own defense, but primarily to strengthen socialism on the international plane." "We finally went along," Castro told Daniel, "because on the one hand the Russians convinced us that the United States would not let itself be intimidated by conventional weapons and secondly because it was impossible for us not to share the risks which the Soviet Union was taking to save us. . . . It was, in the final analysis, a question of honor."*[20]

Why did Khrushchev wish to force nuclear weapons on Castro? In his memoirs he alleged the protection of Cuba as his primary motive. The thought, he wrote, was "hammering away at my brain; what will happen if we lose Cuba?"—much as in American brains the thought was starting to hammer away about the dire consequences if Washington "lost" Vietnam. Losing Cuba, Khrushchev believed, would be a "terrible" blow, gravely diminishing Soviet influence throughout the

---

* In other moods Castro told other stories. Thus he insisted to Herbert Matthews of the *New York Times* in October 1963 that the missile idea was his alone, "not the Russians," and reiterated this after Matthews read the Daniel interview (Herbert L. Matthews, *Return to Cuba* [Palo Alto, Calif., 1964], 16). Possibly he wanted to reassure the romantic Matthews that Cuba was its own master. In 1967, he gave Matthews substantially the same account he had given to Julien and Daniel in 1963 (Matthews, *Fidel Castro* [New York, 1969], 225). In later years he told K. S. Karol and Frank Mankiewicz that the missile idea had come from Khrushchev (see K. S. Karol, *Guerrillas in Power: The Course of the Cuban Revolution* [New York, 1970], 261–262; Frank Mankiewicz and Kirby Jones, *With Fidel: A Portrait of Castro and Cuba* [Chicago, 1975], 174).

Third World, especially in Latin America[21]—the domino theory, I expect. It would also, though Khrushchev did not say this, expose the Soviet Union to devastating ideological attack by Peking.

Still, if the protection of Cuba had been the only point, this could have been done far more simply, as Castro had proposed, through a proclamation or an alliance or the stationing of Soviet troops on the island. If nuclear weapons were to be used, tactical weapons would have been easier to install, harder to detect and less likely to provoke. As Graham Allison later wrote in his careful study of the crisis: "It is difficult to conceive of a Soviet deployment of weapons less suited to the purpose of Cuban defense than the one the Soviets made."[22] Long-range nuclear missiles, in short, served Russian, not Cuban, purposes. Khrushchev, as Castro told Herbert Matthews in 1967, "was acting solely in Russian interests and not in Cuban interests."[23] The secret war against Castro was therefore *not* the cause of the Soviet attempt to make Cuba a nuclear missile base.

By 1962 Khrushchev was in a state of acute frustration—blocked in Berlin, at odds with Peking, stalled in the Third World, left badly behind by the inordinate American missile build-up. Inside the Soviet Union industrial growth was slowing down; agriculture was in its usual trouble; generals were demanding a larger share of limited resources for the military budget; old-line Stalinists were grumbling against internal liberalization. Khrushchev was desperate for a change of fortune.

The emplacement of nuclear missiles in Cuba would prove the Soviet ability to act with impunity in the very heart of the American zone of vital interest—a victory of high significance for the Kremlin, which saw the world in terms of spheres of influence and always inflexibly guarded its own. It would go far to close the Soviet Union's own missile gap, increasing by half again Soviet first-strike capacity against American targets.* It would do so without the long wait and awful budgetary strain attendant on an intensified missile production program. Secrecy would conceal the missiles until they were deployed. Once they were operational, Kennedy, as a rational man, would not go to nuclear war in order to expel them. If they were discovered prematurely, the congressional elections, not to speak of Kennedy's past irresolution on Cuban matters, would delay the American response. With one roll of the nuclear dice, Khrushchev

---

* According to Herbert Dinerstein, it would have advanced "the Soviet attainment of nuclear parity by almost a decade" (H. S. Dinerstein, *The Making of a Missile Crisis* [Baltimore, Md., 1976], 156).

might redress the strategic imbalance, humiliate the Americans, rescue the Cubans, silence the Stalinists and the generals, confound the Chinese and acquire a potent bargaining counter when he chose to replay Berlin. The risks seemed medium; the rewards colossal.

A plunger, he plunged. He sent 42 medium-range (1100-mile) nuclear missiles, 24 intermediate-range (2200-mile) missiles (which never arrived), 42 IL-28 nuclear bombers, 24 antiaircraft missile sites (SAMs) and 22,000 Soviet troops and technicians. This was something, he bragged to Castro, Stalin would never have done.[24] He explained his objective in his memoirs: "Our missiles would have equalized . . . 'the balance of power.' "[25] As Mikoyan put it in a secret meeting with Communist diplomats in Washington on November 30, 1962, the purpose of the deployment was to achieve "a definite shift in the power relationship between the socialist and the capitalist worlds."*

III

Of Khrushchev's dream the Americans knew nothing. But Cuba remained a problem; and, for a diversity of reasons—Mongoose, the inertia at Foggy Bottom, the Republican exploitation of the Castro issue in the fall campaign—Robert Kennedy had seized the lead in Cuban policy. Early in September he privately recorded his concern that "Cuba obtaining [nuclear] missiles from the Soviet Union would create a major political problem here." The defensive surface-to-air missiles identified by American overflights, he feared, were only the first step. "We would have to anticipate there would be surface to surface missiles established in Cuba. What was going to be our reaction then?"[26]

He had already directed Norbert Schlei, a new assistant attorney general, to see what the United States could do under international law to forestall missile bases in Cuba. Schlei produced a brief that justified intervention on the principle of self-defense, ideally with the sanction of the Organization of American States. Missile shipments,

* According to the testimony of Janos Radvanyi, then the Hungarian chargé in Washington (see Chalmers Roberts, *First Rough Draft* [New York, 1973], 205). It should be added that this too was the conclusion of Michel Tatu, *Le Monde*'s Moscow correspondent from 1957 to 1964, writing from Soviet sources in his book *Power in the Kremlin: From Khrushchev to Kosygin* (New York, 1969). He called Khrushchev's adventure "a truly dynamic move . . . undertaken in order to alter the world balance of power in their favour . . . an inexpensive means of altering the strategic balance" (229, 231).

he concluded, might be countered by "total blockade" or by "'visit and search' procedures."* The Schlei memorandum led to a White House meeting on September 4. The Attorney General urgently recommended a presidential statement warning the Russians that long-range missiles would raise the gravest issues. "My point is that I think it is much more difficult for them to take steps like that after you have made that statement." Rusk demurred, saying that the problem with the Soviet Union was worldwide, not just in Cuba.[27] The President accepted his brother's proposal. With Katzenbach and Schlei, Robert Kennedy drafted a statement issued, with modifications, the same day.

Despite such precautions, however, almost no one in the administration believed Khrushchev mad enough to do what in fact he was doing. Though the Attorney General had apprehensions, his attention was soon diverted by James Meredith and the Battle of Ole Miss. Though John McCone had presentiments, he never communicated them to the Kennedys† and went off to Europe on a honeymoon. But the Republicans, led by Keating of New York and Capehart of Indiana, jeered at the administration view that Russia was only sending defensive weapons. At the end of September, a House Republican caucus called Cuba "the biggest Republican asset" in the approaching election. On October 5, Clare Boothe Luce wrote in *Life:* "What is now at stake in the decision for intervention or nonintervention in Cuba is the question not only of American prestige but of American survival." On October 10, Keating claimed "100 percent reliable" evidence from exiles that nuclear missile bases were under construction. In the *New Yorker,* Richard Rovere reported a war party in Washington as active as the party that had produced the war over Cuba in 1898.[28]

On October 15, a U-2 camera discovered the sites. Studying the

---

* When Schlei suggested that the Monroe Doctrine gave the United States special rights in the hemisphere, John Kennedy snapped: "The Monroe Doctrine. What the hell is that?"—meaning: what the hell standing did it have in international law? The answer was, of course, none; and Kennedy, who knew how much Latin Americans resented unilateral declarations from Washington, never mentioned the doctrine throughout the subsequent crisis. (The Schlei memorandum, completed about August 29, 1962, is reprinted in appendix 1 of Abram Chayes, *The Cuban Missile Crisis: International Crises and the Role of Law* [New York, 1974], 108–132. See also Schlei to Chayes, May 22, 1968, in the same book, 132–134; and Schlei, in recorded interview by John Stewart, February 20–21, 1968, 6–12, JFK Oral History Program.)

† Robert Kennedy said in 1965, "I never even heard about it, and I used to see him all the time. . . . It was certainly never communicated to the President" (RFK, in recorded interview by author, February 27, 1965, 22, JFK Oral History Program).

blown-up photographs, Robert Kennedy, as he wrote in his excellent posthumous book *Thirteen Days,* saw only what seemed the clearing of a field, as for a farm or the basement of a house.[29] The CIA photo-interpreter traced out the missile sites for him. Reverting to his preoccupations of a few days before, Kennedy asked, "Can they hit Oxford, Mississippi?"[30] John Kennedy was both infuriated by the Soviet deception and alarmed by the Soviet design. He saw the project precisely as Khrushchev saw it. It was, Kennedy said, "an effort to materially change the balance of power," "a deliberately provocative and unjustified change in the status quo"[31]—just what he had counseled Khrushchev against in Vienna. The consequences of so swift an alteration in the power equilibrium might be incalculable. If the United States accepted it, where might the plunger, dizzy with success, plunge next? How long could a fragile peace survive such shocks? Therefore, the President decided, the missiles had to be removed.

But how? The catchwords *hawk* and *dove* made their debut in the missile crisis.* Within the closed meetings of the so-called Executive Committee of the National Security Council, Robert Kennedy was a dove from the start. If you bomb the missile sites and the airports, he said on the first day, "you are covering most of Cuba. You are going to kill an awful lot of people and take an awful lot of heat on it." If the Americans said they were bombing because of the missiles, "it would be almost [incumbent] upon the Russians to say that we are going to send them in again and, if you do it again, we are going to do the same thing in Turkey."[32] Listening to the war cries of the hawks, he sent his famous note to Sorensen: "I now know how Tojo felt when he was planning Pearl Harbor."[33] His steadfast allies were McNamara, Gilpatric, Ball, Llewellyn Thompson, Sorensen, Stevenson and Lovett.

The most formidable of the hawks was Dean Acheson, backed by Maxwell Taylor ("a twofold hawk from start to finish," he later described himself),[34] the Joint Chiefs (save for Shoup), McCloy, Nitze, and, initially, Dillon and McCone. Others shifted their views as the debate progressed. Bundy, Kennedy wrote at the time, "did some strange flipflops. First he was for a strike, then a blockade, then for doing nothing because it would upset the situation in Berlin, and

---

* I do not recall their use at the time; but Stewart Alsop and Charles Bartlett thrust them into circulation soon thereafter in their article "In Time of Crisis" (*Saturday Evening Post,* December 8, 1962). Of course Jefferson had invented the term "war hawk" in 1798.

then, finally, he led the group which was in favor of a strike—and a strike without prior notification, along the lines of Pearl Harbor."³⁵ Rusk was equally perplexing. At first he was for a strike; later he was silent or absent. He had, Robert Kennedy wrote laconically in *Thirteen Days,* "other duties during this period of time and frequently could not attend our meetings."* Privately, Kennedy was less circumspect. Rusk, he thought in 1965, "had a virtually complete breakdown mentally and physically."³⁶ After the crisis, Rusk explained that his function, as he saw it, was to keep the group from moving too far or too fast. "He said," Kennedy noted, "he had been playing the role of the 'dumb dodo' for this reason. I thought it was a strange way of putting it."³⁷

While the deliberations went on, the deliberators maintained the fiction of business as usual. During the week of secrecy an unknowing Joseph Dolan brought the Attorney General a paper to sign. Robert Kennedy seemed more than usually preoccupied. "The room looked different," Dolan recalled, "and I was just trying to remind him that he had a human being in the room. I says, 'Something looks different here,' and he just looks at me, and he says, 'I'm older.' And so I stuck the thing in front of him, and he signed it without a word."³⁸

IV

"I could not accept the idea," Robert Kennedy wrote later, "that the United States would rain bombs on Cuba, killing thousands and thousands of civilians in a surprise attack."³⁹ The moral issue was paramount in his mind. "We spent more time on this moral question during the first five days," he said, "than on any single matter."⁴⁰

For a while he listened more than he talked, exerting what Gilpatric called a "disciplinary presence"⁴¹ on the Executive Committee, seeking to raise hard questions, to elicit alternatives, to force his colleagues to consider the implications of possible decisions. But he could not conceal moral anguish. Acheson detested moral anguish. He thought Robert Kennedy "moved by emotional or intuitive responses more than by the trained lawyer's analysis." In particular, he could not abide Robert Kennedy's talk about a "Pearl Harbor in reverse." On Thursday, October 18, the imperious old man had a pri-

---

* RFK, *Thirteen Days,* 24. Acheson commented: "One wonders what those 'other duties and responsibilities' were, to have been half so important as those they displaced" (Acheson, "Dean Acheson's Version of Robert Kennedy's Version of the Cuban Missile Affair," *Esquire,* February 1969).

vate talk with the President. When John Kennedy brought up Pearl Harbor, Acheson decided that the President was simply repeating "his brother's clichés." He told the President—or so he later claimed—that this was a "silly" way to analyze the problem: "It is unworthy of you to talk that way."[42] Subsequently he denounced Pearl-Harbor-in-reverse as "a thoroughly false and pejorative analogy."[43]

Later that Thursday afternoon, however, the Executive Committee, without Acheson, substantially agreed—Taylor and the Chiefs dissenting—on a visit-and-search blockade, the idea broached by Schlei weeks before, arrived at independently and advocated persuasively by McNamara and Gilpatric and soon to be rechristened "quarantine," in memory of Franklin Roosevelt. They so reported to the President. But the next day Bundy reopened the issue of the strike. Acheson was present. John Kennedy was away campaigning. He had spoken with the President that morning, Bundy said, and, now speaking for himself, he favored "decisive action with its advantages of surprise and confronting the world with a *fait accompli*."[44] Sorensen intervened (I am quoting the record made at the time by Leonard C. Meeker, the State Department's deputy legal adviser), saying it was not fair to the President to reconsider a matter on which they had all reached a decision the day before. Robert Kennedy, according to his own notes dictated twelve days later: "I said I thought this was such a vital and important matter that obviously no solution was going to be completely correct and that people should still express themselves and voice and discuss their ideas."

Acheson then spoke, Kennedy said, "eloquently and at some length."[45] According to Meeker:

> Mr. Acheson said that Khrushchev had presented the United States with a direct challenge, we were involved in a test of wills, and the sooner we got to a showdown the better. He favored cleaning the missile bases out decisively with an air strike. . . .
> Secretary Dillon said he agreed there should be a quick air strike. Mr. McCone was of the same opinion. General Taylor said . . . it was now or never for an air strike. He favored a strike. If it were to take place Sunday morning, a decision would have to be made at once. . . . For a Monday morning strike, a decision would have to be reached tomorrow. Forty-eight hours' notice was required. Secretary McNamara said he would give orders for the necessary military dispositions. . . . He did not, however, advocate an air strike.[46]

When he had heard Acheson lay down the militant case during the Berlin crisis, Robert Kennedy thought that he "would never wish to be on the other side of an argument with him."[47] But with the blockade decision on the brink of reversal, he was not to be intimidated. Meeker summarizing his remarks:

> The Attorney General said with a grin that he too had had a talk with the President, indeed very recently this morning. There seemed to be three main possibilities . . . one was do nothing, and that was unthinkable; another was an air strike; the third was a blockade. He thought it would be very, very difficult indeed for the President if the decision were to be for an air strike, with all the memory of Pearl Harbor and with all the implications this would have for us in whatever world there would be afterward. For 175 years we had not been that kind of country. A sneak attack was not in our traditions. Thousands of Cubans would be killed without warning, and a lot of Russians too. He favored *action,* to make known unmistakably the seriousness of United States determination to get the missiles out of Cuba, but he thought the action should allow the Soviets some room for maneuver to pull back from their over-extended position in Cuba.[48]

As Kennedy himself recalled a dozen days later: "I said I just did not believe the President of the United States could order such a military operation. I said we were fighting for something more than just survival and that all our heritage and our ideals would be repugnant to such a sneak military attack."[49]

He talked, said Douglas Dillon, "with an intense but quiet passion. As he spoke, I felt that I was at a real turning point in history. . . . The way Bob Kennedy spoke was totally convincing to me. I knew then that we should not undertake a strike without warning. . . . With only one or two possible exceptions, all the members of the Excom were convinced by Bob's argument."[50] Said Alexis Johnson of the State Department: "Bobby Kennedy's good sense and his moral character were perhaps decisive."[51]

It was a compelling moment. Everyone in the room remembered it for a long time. But the record suggests that its impact was not instantaneous. On Saturday afternoon the group met with the President. McNamara made a forceful case for blockade as "the only military course of action compatible with our position as a leader of the free world." The air strike planned by the Joint Chiefs of Staff, he said, would involve eight hundred sorties. "Such a strike would result in several thousand Russians being killed." McNamara doubted that Moscow would take it "without resorting to a very major response. In such an event, the U.S. would lose control of the situation which could escalate to general war."

Maxwell Taylor made the opposing case, Acheson having disgustedly retired to his country seat. "Now was the time to act," Taylor said, "because this would be the last chance we would have to destroy these missiles. If we did not act now, the missiles would be camouflaged in such a way as to make it impossible for us to find them." Taylor scouted McNamara's "fear that if we used nuclear weapons in Cuba, nuclear weapons would be used against us"—a mysterious remark, for there is no other reference to an American nuclear attack on Cuba. The "Air Strike Scenario" prepared for the meeting specified that the missiles and sites were to be destroyed "by conventional means." Probably Taylor was seeking to counter McNamara's point about the risk of escalation to general war, and the rapporteur became confused.

The Attorney General informed the President that the air strike was supported by Taylor, the Chiefs, Bundy and, with minor variations, by Dillon and McCone (the last two, however, disclaimed this support before the meeting was over; Robert Kennedy had been more persuasive the day before than he knew). As for himself, he believed it essential to begin with a blockade. If the Russians did not stop work on the missile bases, it would always be possible to move on to the strike.[52] For a moment there was silence. Then Gilpatric said: "Essentially, Mr. President, this is a choice between limited action and unlimited action; and most of us here think that it's better to start with limited action."[53]

John Kennedy said that the IL-28 bombers Moscow had given Castro did not bother him. "In his view the existence of fifty planes in Cuba did not affect the balance of power, but the missiles already in Cuba were an entirely different matter." He gave orders to begin with the blockade; also to make contingent preparations for an air strike and invasion. "The President acknowledged that the domestic political heat following his television appearance [to announce the crisis] would be terrific. He said he had opposed an invasion of Cuba but that now we were confronted with the possibility that by December there would be fifty strategic missiles deployed there. In explanation as to why we have not acted sooner . . . he pointed out that only now do we have the kind of evidence which we can make available to our allies in order to convince them of the necessity of acting."[54]

McNamara later thought that Robert Kennedy's arguments "did much to sway the President" to the quarantine.[55] Robert Kennedy gave the credit to McNamara. No one knows when John Kennedy reached his decision. "Most of those who attended the meeting on Saturday afternoon," Robert Kennedy wrote a month later, "felt he had made up his mind then. I think it is true that he had pretty much decided but he . . . held out his interest in a quick strike at the missile bases until Sunday morning." Then the head of the Tactical Air Command told him that even a very considerable strike might leave missiles capable of being fired back at the United States.[56]

Perhaps John Kennedy did not really make up his mind till Saturday or Sunday; or perhaps, having made his mind up earlier, he had simply, in the presidential manner, reserved his views. The advisers he trusted most—his brother, Sorensen, McNamara—had all advocated quarantine since at least Wednesday. He had provisionally endorsed it himself on Thursday. The hawks never considered him an ally. "It had been apparent after the first day or two," wrote Taylor, "that President Kennedy was inclining strongly to the side of the quarantine."[57] Acheson decided on Thursday that the President had been subverted by Robert's clichés. One imagines that the President's insistence on further military consultation expressed, not indecision, but a desire to establish a record. Well aware of the Chiefs' capacity for political reprisal, he may well have concluded he had better make a show of canvassing the military alternative to the end. He evidently found this exercise more than a little nerve-racking. Gilpatric saw Kennedy after LeMay had boomed forth on the beauties of an air attack. "He was just choleric. He was just beside himself, as close as he ever got."[58] To Kenneth O'Donnell, Kennedy said savagely, "These brass hats have one great advantage in their favor. If we . . . do what they want us to do, none of us will be alive later to tell them that they were wrong."[59]

V

Critics have called it a needless crisis. Kennedy's conduct, according to R. J. Walton, was "irresponsible and reckless to a supreme degree." Driven by "the *machismo* quality" in his character,[60] by rage over deception, by egotistical concern over personal prestige, by fear of setbacks in the elections, by a spurious notion of international credibility, Kennedy exaggerated the danger, rejected a diplomatic resolution and instead insisted on a public showdown. His purpose was the conspicuous humiliation of Khrushchev—eyeball to eyeball. Pursuing so insensate a course, he risked the incineration of the world in order to satisfy his own psychic and political needs.[61]

If Kennedy's idea had been to seek a showdown with Khrushchev, he went about it in a strange way. Instead of making a big issue of

Soviet military aid to Castro during the summer of 1962, he minimized and, in the increasingly agitated Republican view, excused this aid. As late as the day before the missiles were discovered, Bundy said on national television that there was "no present evidence" and in his judgment "no present likelihood" of a "major offensive capability" in Cuba.[62] Indeed, according to some of the same critics, Kennedy's warnings about the arms shipments were so weak that the Soviet Union honestly misinterpreted them as a green light for nuclear missiles[63]—a view obviously incompatible with their theory he was on the prowl for confrontation.

Most critics have left the impression that, once the nuclear missiles were in Cuba, Kennedy should have done nothing at all. But suppose he had not forced the missiles out. Khrushchev by his own statement had sent the missiles in order to alter the balance of world power. American acquiescence would have been a stunning vindication of the Soviet 'Cold War of movement.' In a secret message via Bolshakov in June, Khrushchev had already warned the Kennedys of his intention to begin again in Berlin.* Had the missiles remained, the sixties would have been the most dangerous of decades. And acquiescence would have produced a shattering reaction in the United States. "If you hadn't acted," Robert Kennedy told his brother, "you would have been impeached." The President said, "That's what I think—I would have been impeached."[64]

R. J. Walton was an exception among the revisionists in conceding that, "given the political realities, Kennedy had to get the missiles removed."[65] But he and others have asserted that, instead of negotiating them out, Kennedy manufactured a public crisis. Even if he had not sought a showdown in August, he definitely sought one in October: both for personal reasons—obsession with his image, Irish temper, machismo, etc.—and for political reasons—the November election. He should, say, have discussed the missiles when Andrei Gromyko, the Soviet foreign minister, called on him at the White House three days after their discovery. If the Executive Committee had not yet figured out what to do, why did he not call Gromyko back as soon as the decision was made and before instituting the quarantine? Why did he not yield to Khrushchev at once the things

---

* On June 18, 1962, Bolshakov gave Robert Kennedy a message from Khrushchev. Khrushchev said that, if the United States continued to insist on occupation rights in West Berlin, "the Soviet Union will face the necessity of signing a peace treaty with the GDR [German Democratic Republic] and the question of liquidation of war remnants will be solved and on this basis the situation in West Berlin—a free demilitarized city—would be normalized" (RFK Papers).

that would enable the Soviet leader to remove the missiles with dignity: a no-invasion guarantee for Cuba and the removal of American Jupiter missiles from Turkey?

Charles Bohlen, that brilliant aficionado of Soviet policy, attended the meetings on the first two days. Departing on the third day, to take up new duties as ambassador to France, he left Kennedy a valedictory memorandum. The missiles, Bohlen agreed, had to be eliminated; and "no one can guarantee that this can be achieved by diplomatic action—but it seems to me essential that this channel should be tested out before military action is employed."[66] On the same day, Sorensen, summing up the discussion thus far, defined a choice between what he called "the Rusk or the Bohlen approaches." Rusk, he said, favored a limited strike without prior warning. Bohlen and "all blockade advocates" favored a "prompt letter to Khrushchev, deciding after the response whether we use air strike or blockade. . . . If you accept the Bohlen plan, we can then consider the nature of the letter to K[hrushchev]."[67]

Critics claim that Kennedy rejected the "Bohlen plan." In fact Kennedy did his best to pursue the plan. For two days, at his direction, Sorensen and others worked on letters to the Kremlin. On October 20, Sorensen reported to the President: "No one has been able to devise a satisfactory message to Khrushchev to which his reply could not outmaneuver us"[68]—by, for example, demanding submission of the dispute to the UN or to a summit meeting, thereby plunging the whole affair into a protracted diplomatic wrangle and making other forms of American reaction difficult while the missile bases were rushed to completion. The not unreasonable decision was therefore to announce the quarantine *before* beginning talks with the Russians.

After the announcement, the President began to lay the foundation for a peaceful resolution. On Tuesday, October 23, he sent his brother to make clear to Dobrynin the implications of Khrushchev's course. Robert Kennedy's memorandum of the meeting contains details omitted from *Thirteen Days*. The Attorney General reminded the ambassador that his brother, on the basis of Soviet assurances, had taken a "far less belligerent position [on the arms shipments] than people like Senators Keating and Capehart, and he had assured the American people that there was nothing to be concerned about. I pointed out, in addition, that the President felt he had a very helpful personal relationship with Mr. Khrushchev. Obviously, they did not agree on many issues, but he did feel that there was a mutual trust and confidence between them on which he could rely." The Attorney

General noted that the American President had met Khrushchev's request for the withdrawal of American troops from Thailand. Sneaking nuclear missiles into Cuba now, he said, displayed the Soviet leaders as "hypocritical, misleading and false." So far as he knew, Dobrynin stoutly replied, there were no nuclear missiles in Cuba. "Dobrynin seemed extremely concerned."[69]

Everyone was extremely concerned. Plans were circulated for the evacuation of top officials to underground installations outside Washington. "I'm not going," Robert Kennedy told Edwin Guthman. "If it comes to that, there'll be sixty million Americans killed and as many Russians or more. I'll be at Hickory Hill."[70]

VI

"I sat across from the President," Robert Kennedy scribbled on a pad. It was Wednesday night, October 24. Two Soviet ships had approached to a few miles of the quarantine line.

> This was the moment we had prepared for, which we hoped would never come. The danger and concern that we all felt hung like a cloud over us all. . . . These few minutes were the time of greatest worry by the President. His hand went up to his face & covered his mouth and he closed his fist. His eyes were tense, almost gray, and we just stared at each other across the table. Was the world on the brink of a holocaust and had we done something wrong? Isn't there some way we can avoid having our first exchange be with a Russian submarine—almost anything but that, he said. . . . We had come to the edge of final decision—& the President agreed. I felt we were on the edge of a precipice and it was as if there were no way off.[71]

Robert thought inexplicably of Joe's death, of Jack's brushes with death. Then word came that the Russian ships had stopped in the water.[72] So far so good; but the quarantine met only part of the problem. It could stop the delivery of additional missiles to Cuba. It could neither remove those already there nor prevent the completion of the bases. From the start, the Kennedys and their chief advisers had known that this was the task of negotiation, and they were prepared to negotiate. When they were trying to execute the Bohlen plan, one of Sorensen's trial drafts to Khrushchev had the President say that, if the missiles were removed under effective surveillance, "I would be glad to meet with you . . . and to discuss other problems on our agenda, including, if you wish, the NATO bases in Turkey and Italy."[73] On Friday, October 19, according to the Meeker record,

"More than once during the afternoon Secretary McNamara voiced the opinion that the US would have to pay a price to get the Soviet missiles out of Cuba. He thought we would at least have to give up our missile bases in Italy and Turkey and would probably have to pay more besides."[74] The next day McNamara again said, "We would have to be prepared to accept the withdrawal of US strategic missiles from Turkey and Italy and possibly agreement to limit our use of Guantanamo to a specified limited time. He added that we could obtain the removal of the missiles . . . only if we were prepared to offer something in return."[75]

It was at this Saturday meeting that Adlai Stevenson, arriving late from the UN in New York, proposed that the quarantine, which he supported, be accompanied by an immediate statement of the American negotiating position. He specifically suggested, according to the NSC minutes, "a settlement involving the withdrawal of our missiles from Turkey and our evacuation of Guantanamo." Most present felt that to begin with concessions would legitimize Khrushchev's action and give him an easy triumph. It was Stevenson's timing and his Guantanamo proposal, Robert Kennedy said later, not his Turkish thoughts, that created his reputation as the supreme dove.[76] In the general frustration and fatigue, everyone jumped on Stevenson.

The President emphatically disagreed that the initial presentation to the UN should include our notion of an eventual political settlement. He also "sharply rejected the thought of surrendering our [Cuban] base. . . . He felt that such action would convey to the world that we had been frightened into abandoning our position." However, "he agreed that at an appropriate time we would have to acknowledge that we were willing to take strategic missiles out of Turkey and Italy if this issue was raised by the Russians. . . . But he was firm in saying we should only make such a proposal in the future."[77] Stevenson, in what O'Donnell, who was present, called "an impressive show of lonely courage,"[78] held his ground. He reiterated "his belief that we must be more forthcoming . . . that the present situation required that we offer to give up such bases in order to induce the Russians to remove the strategic missiles."[79]

The President said afterward to O'Donnell, "I admire [Stevenson] for saying what he did."[80] Robert Kennedy, not a Stevenson fan at best, did not like it. "We had a rather strong argument with him," he wrote in his contemporaneous notes. ". . . I suggested [privately to the President] that we get someone else up at the United Nations to replace Stevenson as he was such a weak man in these kinds of negotiations."[81] In the end, John McCloy was summoned to sit at Steven-

Robert Kennedy and the Missile Crisis

son's right hand. The President sent me to New York also to help on the UN presentation. (After reading my draft speech for Stevenson, the President called for the deletion of the more truculent passages, especially the threat of an American strike if the build-up persisted.) The Attorney General took me aside as I was rushing for the plane. "We're counting on you to watch things in New York," he said. "That fellow is ready to give everything away. We will have to make a deal in the end; but we must stand firm now. Our concessions must come at the end of negotiation, not at the start."[82] In *Thirteen Days* he made an *amende honorable*:

> Stevenson has since been criticized publicly for the position he took. . . . I think it should be emphasized that he was presenting a different perspective than the others, one which was therefore important for the President to consider. Although I disagreed strongly with his recommendations, I thought he was courageous to make them, and I might add they made as much sense as some others considered during that period of time.[83]

The last line was pure Robert Kennedy. And the disagreement, it should be emphasized, was not over the necessity for but the timing of negotiations.

In short, the advocates of quarantine assumed from the start that their course implied diplomacy somewhere down the road. The questions were when the trading should begin, how long it should take and what was to be put on the block. Critics later accused Kennedy of waiting too long, imposing too peremptory a deadline and refusing the most obvious deal—Cuban missiles for Turkish missiles.

VII

"I would sum it up, Prime Minister," John Kennedy told Harold Macmillan on October 25, two days after the Soviet ships turned back, "by saying that by tomorrow . . . we should be in a position to know whether there is some political proposal that we could agree to"—perhaps, he had explained earlier, withdrawing the missiles in exchange for an international guarantee of Cuba—"and whether the Russians are interested in it or not. . . . On the other hand, if at the end of 48 hours we are getting no place and the missile sites continue to be constructed then we are going to be faced with some hard decisions."[84]

Critics have detected ulterior motives behind the forty-eight-hour deadline. Unless Kennedy forced Khrushchev to retreat before the election on November 6, the journalist I. F. Stone argued in 1966, "the nuclear menace from Cuba would certainly have cost the Democrats control of the House of Representatives. . . . If Kennedy was so concerned [about peace] he might have sacrificed his chances in the election to try and negotiate. . . . Kennedy could not wait. But the country and the world could."[85] The argument lacked Stone's customary cogency. What chance would negotiations have had if the administration were trounced by a Republican party shouting for the invasion of Cuba? Repudiation of a dovish President by a hawkish electorate would have doomed any hope of a peaceful resolution. And in the meantime some of the nuclear bases would have become operational.

If negotiations were protracted, in short, their success required a strong Kennedy showing in the election. This perception only complicated Kennedy's problem. He thought the missiles an unmitigated political disaster. "We've just elected Capehart in Indiana," he said when he handed the U-2 photographs to O'Donnell, "and Ken Keating will probably be the next President."[86] If he had wished, as charged, to exploit the crisis for political advantage, the one course that would infallibly have insured a Democratic triumph in 1962 was the air strike. Ironically, this was in the main advocated by Republicans and opposed by Democrats on the Executive Committee—which suggests how little party politics mattered during the thirteen days.

The problem remains of the validity of the administration's claim that the bases were about to become operational. Critics have challenged this argument on diverging grounds. Ronald Steel has contended, correctly, that the long-range missile sites would not have been operational until mid-November; therefore Kennedy had plenty of time for negotiation, and the deadline must have derived from the election. Steel, however, overlooked the medium-range missile sites, four out of six of which, Barton J. Bernstein has argued, citing a CIA estimate, were already operational by Tuesday, October 23. Therefore, according to Bernstein, the deadline had already passed, and Kennedy must have had some base motive for pretending otherwise.[87]

The CIA estimate did indeed list four medium-range missile "sites" as "fully operational." But it added, "We are unable to confirm the presence of nuclear warheads."* "Fully operational," in short, had an exceedingly narrow significance. Obviously the presence of nuclear warheads, not the technical operability of the sites, determined the deadline. No one could be sure when the warheads

---

* CIA, Office of Current Intelligence, "Readiness Status of Soviet Missiles in Cuba," October 23, 1962, JFK Papers. Needless to say, Bernstein, in the manner of revisionist scholarship, suppressed the passage about nuclear warheads.

would arrive. McCone thought that the missiles would be operational by the end of the week.[88] "The last 24 hours' film," Kennedy told Macmillan on October 24, "show that they are continuing to build those rockets."[89] "What was clear," scrawled Robert Kennedy in his notes on that evening, "was that the work in Cuba was proceeding and several of the launching pads would within a few days be ready for use."[90]

The reason for the negotiating deadline was simply the conviction that, once nuclear warheads were in place and pointed at the United States, the terms of trade would undergo drastic change. "It is obvious," wrote Michel Tatu of *Le Monde,* "that if this work could be completed under cover of diplomatic negotiations over broader issues . . . Khrushchev would have won all he wanted: not only strategic reinforcement as a result of his newly built Cuban base, but also the diplomatic initiative resulting from his greater strength."[91]

Forty-eight hours remained. Was there a "political proposal" on which both sides could agree? On Thursday, October 25, Kennedy had cabled Khrushchev his hope that the Soviet Union would "permit a restoration of the earlier situation." Khrushchev's famous reply, arriving Friday evening, was a rather marvelous letter in the annals of correspondence among statesmen. While rearguing the Soviet case with due vehemence, Khrushchev set forth in highly personal language his fears about the slide toward catastrophe, ending with his knot-of-war image ("the more the two of us pull, the tighter that knot will be tied"). He concluded with a proposal: if the United States gave Cuba a no-invasion pledge, "this would immediately change everything"—no more arms sent to Cuba, no further need for Soviet military specialists in Cuba.[92]

Kennedy had no problem about what he had already described to Macmillan as a "trade of these missiles for some guarantee for Cuba."[93] He had never wanted an American invasion of Cuba, during the Bay of Pigs or thereafter. On Friday night the Executive Committee went to bed happy for the first time in eleven days. Relief was premature. On Saturday a second letter, signed by Khrushchev but having the ring of a declaration by the Presidium, added the Turkish missiles to the list of Soviet conditions. We do not know what had gone on in Moscow. Khrushchev well understood that the Turkish missiles—Jupiters of an ancient vintage—were obsolete. Nonetheless their renunciation, he later claimed and may have thought at the time, would have "symbolic" value.[94] It would be something to show the Stalinists and the Chinese, and it might cause difficulties for the United States in NATO. On the other hand, Khrushchev may have temporarily lost control of the Presidium. There were hawks in the Kremlin too.

The Executive Committee, Robert Kennedy wrote, decided that the change in tone "indicated confusion within the Soviet Union." He dryly added: "but there was confusion among us as well."[95] For the Turkish missiles raised problems. It was not that anyone except General LeMay supposed them of much use. The President had ordered the forever dilatory State Department to get them out of Turkey months before and was incensed to find them still there. When McNamara and Stevenson had argued in the first week that Turkish missiles were a reasonable trade for Cuban missiles, Kennedy had agreed. Still, for the United States by unilateral decision to sacrifice the defense of a NATO ally would understandably affront the Turks, whose objections had delayed the missile withdrawal, and might well upset NATO.

Dubious as Harold Macmillan had been at the start about the American reaction, and fearful as he remained throughout of the dangers of escalation, the Prime Minister never wavered in his resistance to the bargaining away of NATO assets. "He may *never* get rid of Cuban rockets except by trading them for Turkish, Italian or other bases," he mused on the day of Kennedy's television speech. "Thus Khrushchev will have won his point." Toward the end of the crisis: "Anything like this deal would do great injury to NATO." Ten years later: "To make an exchange would have been fatal. If the President had done that, all credibility in the American protection of Europe would have gone."[96] Henry Kissinger, later no mean bargainer himself, took the same line outside the government.[97] Llewellyn Thompson, whose opinion carried particular weight because of his knowledge of the Soviet leadership, warned that a Turkish deal would be seen in Moscow as "proof of weakness" in Washington.[98] Nevertheless, as Robert Kennedy said soon after, "it was a rather reasonable offer," and "we would have difficulty explaining [refusal] if discussions were prolonged."[99] On the climactic Saturday the President therefore instructed Gilpatric to draw up a scenario for the early removal of the Turkish missiles—this regarded still as an item for subsequent negotiations rather than an immediate response to the second Khrushchev letter.[100]

Then word arrived that a U-2 plane had been shot down over Cuba, its pilot killed. Four days before, the Executive Committee had recommended, in such an eventuality, "immediate retaliation upon the most likely SAM site involved."[101] Washington's reaction now was very macho—"almost unanimous agreement," in Robert Kennedy's words, "that we had to attack early the next morning . . . and destroy the SAM sites." The Joint Chiefs joyfully reminded the President "that they had always felt the blockade to be far too weak a course and that military steps were the only ones the Soviet Union would understand." "There was the feeling," said Robert Kennedy, "that the noose was tightening on all of us." The President pulled everyone back. "It isn't the first step that concerns me," he said, "but both sides escalating to the fourth and fifth step—and we don't go for a sixth because there is no one around to do so."[102] According to Graham Allison, Kennedy's order to call off the Air Force reprisal was "received with disbelief" in the Pentagon. Soon he increased the dismay of the hawks by ordering the defusing of the Turkish missiles. Allison: "For some members of the group, this was the darkest moment."[103]

VIII

In the early afternoon the State Department submitted a draft reply to Khrushchev flatly rejecting the Turkish deal. "I disagreed with the content and tenor of the letter," Robert Kennedy said later.[104] Everyone remembers his own inspired suggestion that the President forget the second Khrushchev letter and answer the first. "There were sharp disagreements," Robert Kennedy recalled. The hawks, dreaming of a Monday morning war, rallied behind the hard line. The Attorney General persisted in his criticism of the State Department letter. The President asked him to try a draft himself. In forty-five minutes Robert Kennedy and Sorensen produced a new letter offering a no-invasion guarantee in exchange for the removal of all offensive weapons systems from Cuba, all this to be accompanied by termination of the quarantine and UN inspection. The President dispatched it without delay.[105]

The deftness with which this letter elided the Turkish problem has obscured the dénouement. For, soon after the letter went off, the President instructed his brother to talk once more to Dobrynin. The two men met half an hour later at the Department of Justice. There are two accounts of this Saturday night meeting: one written three days afterward by Robert Kennedy, and one written in 1971 on the basis of Dobrynin's dispatches by Anatoly Gromyko, a Soviet historian and son of the foreign minister.[106] Kennedy began the conversation by emphasizing the gravity of the situation. If Cubans were shooting down American planes, he said, Americans were going to shoot back. "We had to have a commitment by at least tomorrow that those bases would be removed. This was not an ultimatum, I said, but just a statement of fact." Dobrynin recalled Kennedy as very blunt and very tough.[107] According to the Gromyko account, Kennedy said that, "should war break out, millions of Americans would die. The U.S. government, he said, was trying to avoid this. Later he gave his opinion that he was sure that the Soviet Union adhered to the same view. Any delay in finding ways out of the crisis was fraught with great danger."

Kennedy went on to say, according to the Soviet version, that "the Pentagon was exerting strong pressure on his brother" in connection with the shooting down of the U-2. "Kennedy noted that, in the United States, among the highly placed generals there were many stupid heads who were always eager for a fight. He did not exclude the possibility that the situation could get out of control and lead to irreparable consequences." These remarks reflected the Attorney General's opinion, but did not appear in his own memorandum of the conversation. Later Khrushchev, dictating his memoirs, recalled Dobrynin's sketch of an exhausted Robert Kennedy—"one could see from his eyes that he had not slept for days"—saying: "Even though the President himself is very much against starting a war over Cuba, an irreversible chain of events could occur against his will. That is why the President is appealing directly to Chairman Khrushchev for his help in liquidating this conflict. If the situation continues much longer, the President is not sure that the military will not overthrow him and seize power. The American army could get out of control."[108] The escalation from the Dobrynin-Gromyko version of the *situation* getting out of control to the Khrushchev version of the *U.S. Army* getting out of control attests to Khrushchev's melodramatic temperament, spirited memory and desire to portray himself as the savior of American democracy from a military coup. While the Kennedys did not altogether dismiss *Seven Days in May,* it is unlikely that Robert Kennedy would have confided such forebodings to the Soviet ambassador.*

* Elie Abel has suggested that Khrushchev may have confused the Kennedy-Dobrynin meeting with the postcrisis negotiations over the removal of IL-28 bombers. The Russians, he wrote, "had been given reason to believe that if a fire-fight started the Washington 'hawks' might overpower the 'doves,' invade Cuba and get rid of Castro. . . . 'We were happy to leave them believing that could happen,' one of the American negotiators recalled." (Abel, *The Missile Crisis* [New York: Bantam reprint, 1966], 191. See also Abel, "The Khrushchev Version of the Cuban Missile Crisis," *Washington Post,* January 4, 1971.)

Dobrynin then asked what the Americans proposed. Once the Russians agreed to remove the missiles and dismantle the bases, Kennedy said, "in return, if Cuba and Castro and the Communists ended their subversive activities in other Central and Latin American countries, we would agree to keep peace in the Caribbean and not permit an invasion from American soil." Both accounts say that Dobrynin was the first to mention the Turkish missiles. "I replied," Kennedy reported to Rusk, "that there could be no quid pro quo—no deal of this kind could be made. . . . It was up to NATO to make the decision. I said it was completely impossible for NATO to take such a step under the present threatening position of the Soviet Union. If some time elapsed—and per your instructions, I mentioned four to five months—I said I was sure that these matters could be resolved satisfactorily." This understanding, the Attorney General added, would be canceled at once if the Soviet government tried to claim public credit for it. They parted. Robert Kennedy's last words, Dobrynin cabled Moscow, were: "Time will not wait, we must not let it slip away."

So concluded a singular exercise in secret diplomacy—secret not only in process, as most diplomacy must be, but in result, which is generally inadmissible. Macmillan and NATO were told nothing, nor was the American Congress, nor even the Executive Committee. "They were very private," Douglas Dillon said of the Kennedy-Dobrynin talks, "and were not always necessarily reported in great detail, even to those of us on the ExComm. . . . All of us felt that we just couldn't take [the Turkish missiles] out as part of the deal, even though we knew that they were coming out anyway."[109] Probably no one except the Kennedys, McNamara, Rusk, Ball and Bundy knew what Robert Kennedy had told Dobrynin. The American people certainly did not know until Robert Kennedy himself described the meeting in *Thirteen Days,* a half dozen years later—and then his account was so muted that Harold Macmillan believed to the end of the day that no such bargain was ever struck, and critics continued to portray John Kennedy as recklessly preferring confrontation to negotiation.*

* See, e.g., FitzSimons: "In face of this admittedly reasonable proposal, President Kennedy persisted in refusing to negotiate, preferring to force the Soviet retreat at the risk of war rather than even discuss a 'not unreasonable' proposal" (Louise FitzSimons, *The Kennedy Doctrine* [New York, 1972], 167). Also Bernstein: "Why, on Saturday, the 27th, when the only issue blocking settlement was American withdrawal of our missiles from Turkey, did the administration reject this condition and risk . . . moving toward nuclear war?" (Barton J. Bernstein, "'Courage and Commitment': The Missiles of October," *Foreign Service Journal,* December 1975). Also Horowitz: "Khrushchev's offer . . . to exchange the missile bases in Turkey for the bases in

The Russians made one attempt to put the deal on the record. Two days after their decisive conversation, Dobrynin brought Robert Kennedy an unsigned letter from Khrushchev to the President spelling everything out. After brooding over the letter, the Attorney General called the Soviet ambassador to his office. Robert Kennedy's scribbled notes for the interview define the American position:

> Read letter—Studied it over night.
> No quid pro quo as I told you.
> The letter makes it appear that there was.
> You asked me about missile bases in Turkey. I told you we would be out of them—4–5 months. That still holds. . . . You have my word on this & that is sufficient.
> Take back your letter—Reconsider it & if you feel it is necessary to write letters then we will also write one which you cannot enjoy.
> Also if you should publish any document indicating a deal then it is off & also if done afterward will further affect the relationship.*

Dobrynin withdrew the letter. Nothing was heard of it thereafter.†

In short, the Kennedys made a personal, but not official, pledge that the Turkish missiles would go. On October 29, the day after the settlement, John McNaughton, the general counsel of the Defense Department, told an interdepartmental task force: "Those missiles are going to be out of there by April 1 if we have to shoot them out."[110] With NATO assent, they went. On April 25, 1963, almost exactly five months after Robert Kennedy's talk with Dobrynin, McNamara sent John Kennedy a handwritten note: "The last Jupiter missiles in Turkey came down yesterday. The last Jupiter warhead will be flown out of Turkey on Saturday."[111]

Cuba was turned down" (David Horowitz, *The Free World Colossus* [New York, 1965], 386).

* RFK, handwritten notes, n.d. [October 30, 1962], RFK Papers. At one point Dobrynin said that of course the Soviet government would not publish the correspondence. Kennedy said, "Speaking quite frankly, you also told me your government never intended to put missiles in Cuba" (RFK to Dean Rusk, reporting on the interview, October 30, 1962, RFK Papers).

† Later the bargain was mentioned by Khrushchev and Anatoly Gromyko in their accounts of the crisis, though Gromyko, faithful to the agreement, based his account on *Thirteen Days* rather than on Dobrynin's cables. (See Khrushchev, *Khrushchev Remembers: Last Testament* [Boston, 1974], 512; Gromyko, "Diplomatic Efforts of the USSR to Liquidate the Crisis," *Voprosy Istorii*, August 1971.) The Russians evidently briefed Castro but swore him to silence too. He told Lee Lockwood in December 1966, "One day perhaps it will be known that the United States made some other concessions in relation to the October Crisis besides those which are made public" (Lockwood, *Castro's Cuba, Cuba's Fidel* [New York, 1967], 204). Castro told Herbert Matthews in October 1967: "Kennedy was willing to give up the Turkish and Greek [sic] bases" (Matthews, *Fidel Castro*, 225).

Was this secret diplomacy justified?—a testing question for those who think that no President should ever make a secret commitment. It is extremely doubtful that any Turkish agreement could have been made publicly in the forty-eight hours before the bases acquired nuclear warheads. If the deal appalled Harold Macmillan, it would have been even more appalling to NATO governments less determined to get along with Washington. At home the deal would have caused an uproar in Congress, in the Pentagon, among the voters; very likely within the Executive Committee itself. "I did not accept the explanation that the [Turkish] missiles had become obsolete," said General LeMay afterward, ". . . nor did any other military man I know."[112] Only secret diplomacy could have assured Khrushchev the Turkish withdrawal that, along with the Cuban no-invasion guarantee, covered his retreat before his opponents on the Presidium. More important, the willingness to make this additional concession doubtless helped persuade the Russians that the American government was truly bent on peace (and accounts for the indulgent treatment the Kennedys later received in Soviet accounts of the crisis). Perhaps there may be a place for secret diplomacy, at least when nuclear war is involved and when no vital interests of a nation or ally are bartered away.

As the world knows, on that golden Sunday morning, the day after Robert Kennedy and Dobrynin had their chat about the Turkish missiles, Khrushchev announced his nuclear retreat from Cuba. In Havana, Castro—who had not been consulted—cursed, kicked the wall in a rage and broke a mirror.[113] "The possibility that the Soviet Union would withdraw [the missiles]," he said later, "was an alternative that had never entered our minds."[114] Having begun his misbegotten adventure by lying to Kennedy, Khrushchev ended by lying to Castro.[115]

In Washington most of us felt a sense of limitless relief. Not all the Chiefs, however: "Admiral [George] Anderson's reaction to the news," Robert Kennedy noted, "was, 'We have been had.' General LeMay said, 'Why don't we go in and make a strike on Monday anyway.'" "The military are mad," the President told me the next morning. "They wanted to do this. It's lucky for us that we have McNamara over there."[116] "The first advice I'm going to give my successor," he said two weeks later, "is to watch the generals and to avoid feeling that just because they were military men their opinions on military matters were worth a damn."[117] Still, for the moment, even the original hawk, Dean Acheson, was confounded. On October

29, he congratulated Kennedy on his "leadership, firmness and judgment," adding that the dénouement "amply shows the wisdom of the course you chose—and stuck to."*

Contrary to the latter-day supposition, the President did not think the resolution would help him in the election. It was too bad, he said to me, that this had happened in the midst of the campaign. The Republicans would now feel compelled to denounce the settlement. They will say, he said, "that we had a chance to get rid of Castro and, instead of doing so, ended up by guaranteeing him."[118]

On Sunday he had said to his brother that this was the night he should go to the theater, like Lincoln. Robert Kennedy:

> I said if he was going to the theater, I would go too, having witnessed the inability of [Vice President] Johnson to make any contribution of any kind during all the conversations. Frequently, after the meetings were finished, he would circulate and whine and complain about our being weak but he never made . . . any suggestions or recommendations. On Saturday night he started to move around saying he heard that the people felt we were backing down. When I asked him for specifics he had none.†

"He was against our policy on Cuba," Robert Kennedy said the next year. ". . . I never quite knew what he was for but he was against it. . . . He was shaking his head, mad."[119]

"The 10 or 12 people who had participated in all these discussions," Robert Kennedy wrote that November, "were bright and energetic people. We had perhaps amongst the most able in the country and if any one of half a dozen of them were President the world would have been very likely plunged in a catastrophic war."[120]

IX

Loose ends remained. Castro in his rage refused to permit UN verification of the missile removal. He also refused to yield the IL-28 bombers. These, unlike the missiles, could be reasonably claimed as Cuban property. Khrushchev sent Mikoyan to Havana. Castro kept him waiting so long that Adlai Stevenson said it might be necessary

---

* A month later he wrote again, praising Kennedy's policy as "wisely conceived and vigorously executed" (Dean Acheson to JFK, October 29 and November 30, 1962, JFK Papers).

† RFK, memorandum, November 15, 1962, RFK Papers. Robert Kennedy told me in 1965: "[Johnson] was displeased with what we were doing. . . . He said that he had the feeling that we were being too weak . . . and that we should be stronger. We discussed it afterwards and the President knew it was because he was talking to perhaps some of his congressional friends" (RFK, in interview by author, February 27, 1965, 24, also 38, JFK Oral History Program).

to send James Donovan down to get him out.[121] Llewellyn Thompson advised Kennedy to insist on the IL-28s; Khrushchev, having swallowed a camel, would not strain at a gnat.[122] "Wondering at times," Sorensen said, "whether his stand was necessary," the President insisted.[123]

Castro was obdurate. Stevenson and McCloy, conducting the negotiations in New York, were prepared to drop UN inspection, give the Russians time to deal with the Cubans over the bombers, make the no-invasion pledge anyway and lift the quarantine. Robert Kennedy, as usual, thought Stevenson excessively weak. His own platform was no inspection, no pledge. He was, however, prepared to lift the quarantine at once if the Russians would withdraw the bombers in thirty days. Thompson supported an offer along these lines, deeming it important that "Khrushchev have something to show to his colleagues in the Kremlin."[124]

The Attorney General carried this proposal to Dobrynin on an evening when the Soviet ambassador was entertaining the Bolshoi Ballet. After the two men talked in private, Dobrynin introduced the President's brother to the dancers. The prima ballerina, the enchanting Maya Plisetskaya, said, "You and I were born on the same day and same year." "We gave each other a little kiss," Kennedy wrote in his journal. "I asked her where she would be on November 20th and she said, 'In Boston.' I said I would send her a present." Then he said a few words to the troupe, telling them that "I felt a little awkward speaking to them as I had trouble doing the two-step; that although I had read in the papers that there were some differences between their country and mine (to which they laughed) that all of us in both countries recognized excellence and that it was a great honor to have this group visit the United States."[125]

But the Russians rejected his proposal. Three days after the Bolshoi evening, Robert Kennedy held "the most unpleasant conversation I have had with Dobrynin. It made it seem that perhaps I had seen him too frequently. I said this to the President the next day. I said I thought it was good that I could do this but certainly not in every day exchanges nor developing a familiarity which made statements by me at critical times less effective."[126] Debate continued within the administration. "President reluctant to send in low level flights," Robert Kennedy noted (on the back of an envelope) regarding a meeting on Monday, November 19. ". . . How far can we push K[hrushchev]."[127] That afternoon the Attorney General warned Georgi Bolshakov that low-level reconnaissance, with all its attendant dangers, would start again unless the Russians promised to remove the bombers. He needed an answer, Kennedy said, before the President's press conference the next day.[128]

The next day—November 20—was Robert Kennedy's thirty-seventh birthday. Dobrynin came to his office in the morning. Smiling broadly, he said, "I have a birthday present for you," and handed him a letter from Khrushchev agreeing to remove the IL-28s in thirty days. "Reading the letter I noticed a number of rather humorous references"; also "that the letter was rather disorganized. Dobrynin said these letters were dictated by Khrushchev himself . . . walking around the room, never looking at the girl, . . . [who] just wrote as he talked." That afternoon John Kennedy announced the agreement. Bolshakov was in the Attorney General's office. "We had a drink together and listened to the President's news conference. He pronounced it very good. I then had him sing 'Happy Birthday' in Russian to Maya Plisetskaya who was in Boston. I don't know how he reported that back to the Kremlin."[129]

This was Bolshakov's farewell performance. The State Department had never liked his special relationship with the Attorney General; nor presumably had Dobrynin, who had by now established a special relationship of his own with the Attorney General. After Joseph Alsop exposed Bolshakov's role in a column, the Kremlin decided that his usefulness in Washington was over and recalled him. In March 1963, Robert Kennedy sent him a handwritten note in Moscow:

> There is still peace even though you have been gone from the United States for more than two months. I would not have thought that possible.
> Anyway we all miss you. I hope you are telling all your Communist friends what nice people we are over here—and that they believe you. . . . Give my best wishes to my friend Maya. Why don't you two jump into one of those brand new luxurious jet liners and fly over and see us? She could dance, I could sing and you could make a speech.
> Best wishes from your friend,
> Robert F. Kennedy[130]

X

Why had Khrushchev given up? "This is a mystery," Castro said bitterly the next March. "Maybe historians will be able to clarify this twenty or thirty years hence. I don't know."[131] The assurances about the Cuban guarantee and the Turkish missiles undoubtedly helped sweeten his retreat.* But the political concessions were face savers. The real reason Khrushchev pulled out was his hopeless military situation. In his explanation to the Supreme Soviet in December 1962, he emphasized that Cuba was to be attacked in two or three days. An American invasion of Cuba would have been a disaster for Khrushchev personally and for the Soviet claim to world revolutionary leadership—especially when Khrushchev's own recklessness had handed America the pretext. What Communist state would trust Soviet promises thereafter? And, if Kennedy were serious about invasion, Khrushchev could do nothing about it, short of nuclear war against a stronger nuclear power. He was not suicidal. "It would have been preposterous," Khrushchev said later, "for us to unleash a war against the United States from Cuba. Cuba was 11,000 kilometers from the Soviet Union. Our sea and air communications were so precarious that an attack against the US was unthinkable."† Lacking conventional superiority in the Caribbean, he could neither break the blockade nor protect Cuba against invasion. Lacking strategic superiority, Khrushchev could not safely retaliate elsewhere in the world.

"What would have happened," Barton J. Bernstein later asked for the critics, "if Khrushchev . . . had refused to back down, and had chosen war instead of humiliation?"[132] But Khrushchev had never for a moment considered choosing war; and Kennedy was prepared to help him escape humiliation. The missile crisis was a triumph, perhaps the only triumph, of flexible response. Had conventional

---

* On October 30, U Thant told Castro in Havana that the United States had proposed a UN inspection team "composed of persons whose nationalities would be acceptable to the Cuban government. . . . The United States told me [U Thant continued] that as soon as this system is set up they would make a public declaration, and if necessary in the Security Council, that they would relinquish any aggressive intentions against the Cuban government and would guarantee the territorial integrity of the nation. They asked me to tell you this." As Maurice Halperin well says, this offer "might have appeared to anyone except Fidel, as a real turning point in revolutionary Cuba's uncertain and extremely costly struggle for survival" (Maurice Halperin, *The Rise and Decline of Fidel Castro* [Berkeley, 1972], 196). However, since Castro chose to resist inspection to the end, the guarantee never went into formal effect. In his November 20 statement on the IL-28s, John Kennedy said only: "For our part, if all offensive weapons are removed from Cuba and kept out of the hemisphere in the future, under adequate verification and safeguards, and if Cuba is not used for the export of aggressive Communist purposes, there will be peace in the Caribbean" (*Public Papers . . . 1962* [Washington, 1963], 831). In practice, aerial reconnaissance took the place of inspection, and the United States without formal commitment refrained from invasion (which it had never intended in any case).

† Khrushchev, *Last Testament*, 511. According to Hervé Alphand, the French ambassador to Washington, "De Gaulle said there was really no risk. Because he was sure of what the Russian reaction would be. It was a sure decision" (interview in *W*, October 28–November 4, 1977).

strength remained at January 1961 levels, McNamara later informed Kennedy, "we would not have had enough forces to meet the minimum requirements stated by the Joint Chiefs of Staff to carry out a successful invasion of Cuba . . . even if we had put every available combat-ready unit not committed to an overseas theatre into the operation, leaving no reserve for other contingencies."[133] When Kennedy mobilized, Khrushchev had no choice but to cash in his chips and get out of the game. Kennedy's genius lay in making sure he had chips to cash in.

As for Kennedy, he had thought the odds on war, according to Sorensen, "between one out of three and even."[134] McNamara, recalling the magnificent sunset over the Potomac on Saturday evening, October 27, said later he had wondered how many more sunsets he was destined to see.[135] Did these highly intelligent men really believe we were on the edge of catastrophe? Recalling one's own tumult of emotion, and subtracting a certain relish in crisis not unknown on the New Frontier (not much shared, however, by the rather prudent Kennedys or by the analytical McNamara), I would say: one lobe of the brain had to recognize the ghastly possibility; another found it quite inconceivable. The President "believed from the start," his brother said, "that the Soviet Chairman was a rational, intelligent man who, if given sufficient time and shown our determination, would alter his position."[136] The two men had taken each other's measure in Vienna. A year's secret correspondence had enlarged each one's sense of the other. Kennedy's grim odds were based on fear, not of Khrushchev's intention, but of human error, of something going terribly wrong down the line. This is why he took such care to maintain tight control over American reactions.

In retrospect, I am bound to say that the risk of war in October 1962 seems to me to have been exaggerated—pardonably at the time and less pardonably in historical recapitulation. Still Khrushchev, no less than Kennedy, might have been betrayed down the line—and perhaps he was more at the mercy of his military than Kennedy was of the Pentagon.* Even with the justified assumption of reciprocal rationality a terrible risk remained. Robert Kennedy had hoped to in-

---

* Khrushchev told Norman Cousins in 1963, "When I asked the military advisers if they could assure me that holding fast would not result in the death of five hundred million human beings, they looked at me as though I was out of my mind or, what was worse, a traitor. The biggest tragedy, as they saw it, was not that our country might be devastated and everything lost, but that the Chinese or the Albanians would accuse us of appeasement or weakness" (Cousins, "The Cuban Missile Crisis: An anniversary," *Saturday Review*. October 15, 1977).

clude in *Thirteen Days* a discussion of the ultimate ethical question: "What, if any, circumstance or justification gives . . . any government the moral right to bring its people and possibly all people under the shadow of nuclear destruction?"[137] How many statesmen would raise such a question? How many philosophers answer it?

Had the Americans, as Soviet theology supposed, been looking for an excuse to smash Castro or, for that matter, the Soviet Union, they could hardly have found a better one than the Soviet attempt to make Cuba a nuclear outpost. Kennedy's restraint now persuaded Khrushchev of the point the Soviet leader had rejected in Vienna—that neither side dare tamper carelessly with the explosive international equilibrium. The Kremlin fell silent about Berlin and for some years thereafter showed a certain respect for existing world frontiers. On the other hand, the Russians, determined never to be caught again in a position of gross nuclear inferiority, stepped up their production of missiles. Within a decade they came close to parity with the United States. Khrushchev meanwhile disappeared from the scene, in part a casualty of Cuba. In dismissing him in October 1964, the Presidium spoke harshly of his "harebrained scheming, hasty conclusions, rash decisions and actions based on wishful thinking."[138] His downfall moderated the Cold War of movement. It also ended the de-Stalinization campaign, the loosening in the joints of a despotic society, the gusts of fresh air that this rollicking, erratic, passionate, indelibly human, curiously attractive figure brought to the nation he loved so much.

Once Khrushchev accepted the Vienna principle, it was possible to move toward détente. If nuclear missiles had remained in Cuba, there would have been no American University speech, no test ban treaty, no 'hot line' between the White House and the Kremlin, no relief from the intolerable pressures of the Cold War. After Cuba, relief was not only thought to be possible but felt to be imperative. During the crisis, talking with Ormsby-Gore, his friend of so many years, the President had suddenly burst out: "You know, it really is an *intolerable* state of affairs when nations can threaten each other with nuclear weapons. This is just so totally irrational. A world in which there are large quantities of nuclear weapons is an impossible world to handle. We really must try to get on with disarmament if we get through this crisis . . . because this is just too much."[139] This was Khrushchev's feeling too, the theme of his impassioned letter; and the crisis deepened both their urgencies. "If thou gaze too long into the abyss," said Nietzsche, "the abyss will gaze into thee."

XI

The record demands the revision of the conventional portraits of Kennedy during the crisis: both the popular view, at the time, of the unflinching leader fearlessly staring down the Russians until they blinked; and the later left-wing view of a man driven by psychic and political compulsions to demand unconditional surrender at whatever risk to mankind.[140] Far from rejecting diplomacy in favor of confrontation, Kennedy in fact took the diplomatic path after arranging the military setting that would make diplomacy effective.

The hard-liners thought him fatally soft. Dean Acheson in another year: "So long as we had the thumbscrew on Khrushchev, we should have given it another turn every day. We were too eager to make an agreement with the Russians."[141] Richard Nixon inevitably thought that Kennedy's doves had "enabled the United States to pull defeat out of the jaws of victory."[142] Or Daniel Patrick Moynihan in 1977: "The Cuban Missile Crisis was actually a *defeat*. . . . When anybody puts missiles into a situation like that, he should expect to have a lot of trouble with the United States, and real trouble—and all that happened was the agreement: 'O.K., you can have your man down there permanently.' "[143]

The revisionists, on the other hand, portrayed Kennedy as reckless and irresponsible. This was not the view of those in the best position to judge—neither of Khrushchev nor, in the end, of Castro himself. In a time of "serious confrontation," Khrushchev said, ". . . one must have an intelligent, sober-minded counterpart with whom to deal. . . . I believe [Kennedy] was a man who understood the situation correctly and who genuinely did not want war. . . . Kennedy was also someone we could trust. . . . He showed great flexibility and, together, we avoided disaster. . . . He didn't let himself become frightened, nor did he become reckless. . . . He showed real wisdom and statesmanship."[144] In 1967 Castro told Herbert Matthews that he thought Kennedy had "acted as he did partly to save Khrushchev, out of fear that any successor would be tougher."[145] And in 1975 Castro told George McGovern: "I would have taken a harder line than Khrushchev. I was furious when he compromised. But Khrushchev was older and wiser. I realize in retrospect that he reached the proper settlement with Kennedy. If my position had prevailed, there might have been a terrible war. I was wrong."[146]

In all this, Robert Kennedy was the indispensable partner. Without him, John Kennedy would have found it far more difficult to overcome the demand for military action. Even Senator Fulbright, in Kennedy's meeting with congressional leaders before his television speech, had advocated the invasion of Cuba as a "wiser course" than the quarantine.* It was Robert Kennedy who oversaw the Executive Committee, stopped the air-strike madness in its tracks, wrote the reply to the Khrushchev letter, conducted the secret negotiations with Dobrynin. "Throughout the entire period of the crisis," McNamara said in 1968, "a period of the most intense strain I have ever operated under, he remained calm and cool, firm but restrained, never nettled and never rattled."[147] "For this happy outcome to such long and agonizing negotiations," Adlai Stevenson wrote him, "I think you are entitled to our gratitude."[148] Khrushchev, recalling the discussions during the crisis, said the Americans "had, on the whole, been open and candid with us, especially Robert Kennedy."[149] "Looking back on it," said Harold Macmillan, "the way that Bobby and his brother played this hand was absolutely masterly. . . . What they did that week convinced me that they were both great men."[150]

John Kennedy himself, in the cruelest hour of the crisis, on the black Saturday before the golden Sunday, said fervently, "Thank God for Bobby."[151] As for Robert Kennedy, he sent a letter, "in that strange, little cramped handwriting," to Robert Lovett thanking him for his counsel and especially for a quotation Lovett had produced during the ordeal.

The quotation was: "Good judgment is usually the result of experience. And experience is frequently the result of bad judgment."[152]

---

* Fulbright's point was that a quarantine, by involving a direct confrontation with Soviet ships, would be more likely to provoke a nuclear war than an invasion that would pit Americans against Cubans. He evidently forgot about the 22,000 Russian soldiers in Cuba. He said later, "We had not gone through the days of considering various alternatives, advantages and disadvantages. . . . Had I been able to formulate my views on the basis of facts since made public rather than on a guess as to the nature of the situation, I might have made a different recommendation" (*Congressional Record*, December 10, 1973, S22289; see also interview with R. W. Howe and Sarah Trott, *Saturday Review*, January 11, 1975).